Armies, Wars and their Food

D. Vijaya Rao

FOUNDATION®
BOOKS

Delhi • Bengaluru • Mumbai • Kolkata • Chennai • Hyderabad • Pune

Published by
Cambridge University Press India Pvt. Ltd.
under the imprint of Foundation Books
Cambridge House, 4381/4 Ansari Road, Daryaganj, **New Delhi** 110 002

Cambridge University Press India Pvt. Ltd.
C-22, C-Block, Brigade M.M., K.R. Road, Jayanagar, **Bengaluru** 560 070
Plot No. 80, Service Industries, Shirvane, Sector-1, Nerul, **Navi Mumbai** 400 706
10 Raja Subodh Mullick Square, 2nd Floor, **Kolkata** 700 013
21/1 (New No. 49), 1st Floor, Model School Road, Thousand Lights, **Chennai** 600 006
House No. 3-5-874/6/4, (Near Apollo Hospital), Hyderguda, **Hyderabad** 500 029
Agarwal Pride, 'A' Wing, 1308 Kasba Peth, Near Surya Hospital, **Pune** 411 011

First published 2012

ISBN 978-81-7596-918-6

Published by Manas Saikia for Cambridge University Press India Pvt. Ltd. and printed at Sanat Printers, Kundli - 131 028.

The work on this book was catalysed and supported by
the Department of Science & Technology, Ministry of Science & Technology,
Government of India under its utilisation of Scientific Expertise of Retired Scientists Scheme.

Contents

Foreword

It is a common belief that armies move on their belly. One of the wars in the 'Hundred Years War' that took place in Europe is known as 'Kartoffel Kreig' i.e., Potato war. This is because the two fighting armies had nothing to eat when the potato crop failed due to infestation with late blight. Consequently, the war ended without a victor or vanquished. In all famous wars, the strategy of the winning side has been to cut off essential supplies. Once the supply route, particularly for food, is disrupted, the enemy's army is left with no choice but to withdraw. During World War II, all supply routes to the city of Leningrad (now known as St Petersburg), were cut off by the Germans. However, the brave Russians did not surrender and the battle of Leningrad became one of the most famous events of the German–Russian war front. Incidentally, Leningrad had a large gene bank containing a wide range at varieties of wheat, barley, potato and other crops collected by the famous Russian geneticist, N.I. Vavilov. Although the inhabitants of Leningrad were hungry, they did not raid the gene bank. When a young boy was asked as to why the gene bank was saved without anyone taking away the seeds for their meal, he replied, "Man is mortal, but genes are immortal". This is a profound statement that indicates the extent of the understanding of the value for posterity of the gene bank in ensuring sustainable food security.

Dr Vijaya Rao, one of our most eminent food scientists, has made a great effort to write *Armies, Wars and their Food,* both in historical and contemporary contexts. She has dealt with the epic wars of the past in considerable detail. Her coverage extends from early man to present day. She has brought out the importance of food in several great battles. Her analysis of our culinary history is fascinating. She has also dealt with the nutritional aspect of food and has underlined the need for safeguarding food security and our culinary capability. The food needs of armed forces under varying ecological conditions, such as desert areas and high altitude zones have been described in great detail.

The work on taking the benefits of modern food science and technology to the Defence Forces, which is currently in progress has also been described in great detail in the book. Thus, this book will be highly useful for all interested in the nutrition security of our armed forces, whether they are fighting in the ocean or in the air or on land.

The author's comprehensive understanding of the food needs of Defence Services both during peace and war periods is truly remarkable. Her wide experience of working as a scientist at the Defence Food Research Laboratory at Mysore and in the Joint Indo-Soviet Manned Space Mission, has given her the capacity to write this authentic book. Her style is simple and has the stamp of her authority and mastery in this field.

We owe a deep debt of gratitude to Dr Vijaya Rao for this contribution of great historical and contemporary value not only to Defence Services but also to all concerned with human food security and well being. I hope it will be read widely by scholars and scientists, and also by the leaders of our armed forces and by all those connected with ensuring adequate food of the right quality and variety, at the right time, to those shouldering the responsibility for our national security.

M.S. Swaminathan
Chairman
M.S. Swaminathan Scientific Research Foundation, Chennai
and Member of the Rajya Sabha

Preface

In the history of mankind, armies have always existed and been made to fight for one reason or another, but mostly at the behest of, and for the glory of, the individual ruler or government; to conquer and expand their territories, to add to their wealth and worth, and power and influence. In due course, war crafts were devised and perfected; bows and arrows gave way to cannons and gunfire, war logistics were developed, overt or subtle diplomacy was used in ways to gain the upper hand, failing which, the opponents went to war. In modern times wars have been fought for the same reasons as before but with more technical advancement and sophistication. However, their food remained much the same as ever for a very long time. Eventually due to individual effort, bold experiments, and increasing general awareness, improvements came. Lately, science and technology has played a crucial role in bringing the army foods and nourishment to the expected level of modernity, commensurate with advancements in other features of the war craft.

The common reader with interest in ancient knowledge and military history, wars, science, food, etc. faces a daunting task of finding suitable reading material presented in a concise manner. The main objective of writing this book originated in the felt need to provide a ready source of historical perspective on the armies of the past as well as contemporary times. This book contains well-researched scientific information on the foods and rations of armies as well as the role of science and technology in instituting significant improvements in their foods and provisioning both in times of war and peace.

The information presented in this book has been gathered mostly from scientific journals and books, reports and symposia proceedings, ancient Indian knowledge texts, books on European history, war books and memoirs of individuals and war veterans, unpublished text within research and military establishments, and the memories and experiences of the author, former colleagues and current leaders of research projects. An attempt has been made to bridge science and history for the benefit of the general reader.

I hope the book will help students and researchers in science and technology to become more aware of the needs of soldiers, sailors, airmen, officers, paramilitary personnel and others in the field, and evoke cutting edge scientific research to ensure that their food away from home is made as safe and nutritious as possible.

I hope the book will encourage military personnel to look at the Research and Development effort being carried out on their behalf by highly trained, skilled and knowledgeable scientists. Hopefully, they will be more proactive in supplying information about their special requirements.

I also hope that the food businesses will come to look at technologies available at research institutions before choosing to import under the generous government policies of today, and build the food industry to provide the necessary types and quantities of convenience foods and delivery systems to the Armed Forces.

The principal theme of the book is the historical development and status of armies, the evolution of their peace time and combat foods, known as army rations; and the supply and delivery systems prevalent at different periods of time.

The ancient knowledge texts of India have been used to derive ancient practices in armies in the provision of rations. It is the first time that the arts of war from three civilisations, namely India, China and the Roman Empire have been highlighted together (in Chapters 1–7). Chapters

8–13 illustrate ancient food thoughts, modern rations, combat packs and the role of science and technology in their development. The supply mechanism in the Indian Armed Forces has been especially described in detail to highlight the role of diverse active elements and participants to show that it is a concerted action of many that is required to support a huge force such as ours (detailed in Chapter 12). A great amount of effort, time and energy was necessary to bring out the facts, figures and photos presented in this chapter and most of the information and illustrations described in a comprehensive manner have become available for the first time. Such a variety of information is not available to students and researchers let alone to general readers in one source. Chapter 12 contains the never-before-seen inside workings of the food supply chain, unique photos of Training in Logistics, Quality Assurance and Catering in the Army and Navy. The functioning of the store rooms and galleys of a ship and a submarine are viewed from the inside.

It has taken a great amount of effort, time and perseverance to get permissions from the concerned departments to meet senior officers for discussions, to visit the various establishments, interact with officers and Other Ranks and to be allowed to take photographs. An even greater effort went in to get 'no objection certificates' for the completed text, figures and photos. However, all views expressed are my own and have no official endorsement. I have also taken it upon myself to visit distant places like Leh and Natu La in Sikkim to obtain first-hand experience of what high altitudes mean and how the people there live and how our Army personnel cope. To send supplies on a regular basis to these places admittedly requires a very well orchestrated system.

Chapter 13 on the science and technology component is unique in that it traces the state of Indian food industry from before the time of the East India Company to the present and shows the research carried out by Defence Research and Development Organisation (DRDO) laboratories in developing food for the Indian Armed Forces.

This book was not intended to be a work on the bare scientific issues about food and its properties. Some historically well-documented and significant examples of wars and their supplies have been chosen that marked the progression of time from the medieval to the present. Those readers who did not have occasion or opportunity to learn about certain important wars in Europe and America, as well as the two World Wars, the wars which followed in the next 60 years and the border wars in India would find brief descriptions about the causes which led to the outbreak of these wars. In such contexts are woven the food and supply situations that were managed by the respective rulers and governments. Chapter 14 deals at some length with these issues.

Though millennia have gone by, human nature and human wants remain much the same as ever. It is the human face of the war machine of the past and present that is brought out in this book.

I dedicate this book to the *Amar Jawans* of all times and places and lands, and to the memory of my parents who lived in Assam through the World War II and its aftermath, and through the India–China war. They knew first-hand the effect of wars on soldiers and civilians. They would have been happy that I had decided to join the scientific force in the service of the Armed Forces.

D. Vijaya Rao

Acknowledgements

This work was made possible with the award of a two-year book writing grant No. HU/UR/29/2002 by the Department of Science & Technology (DST), Ministry of Science and Technology, Government of India, under their scheme USERS.

I would like to express my gratitude and grateful thanks for this grant to the DST. It enabled me to travel and explore many avenues in the course of gathering research material. And more importantly, the grant of the project endowed my quest for unpublished or generally unavailable information with a semblance of official approval without which I would have been denied access and many doors would have remained closed. I particularly wish to acknowledge the help extended by Dr J.B.V. Reddy of the DST. While approving the proposal it was stated that I was required to also look for ancient literature where food related to the armies may be found. There is no one single work that would have told me about this aspect, no prior publication was found on this aspect in any of the military works which I could find and therefore, the search had to be wide and extended beyond what was originally intended.

I place on record my deep sense of gratitude and appreciation to the University of Mysore, Manasagangotri, Mysore for allowing me to present the proposal through the Department of Studies in Applied Botany, Seed Pathology and Biotechnology which wholeheartedly welcomed me, processed the paper work, and gave an affiliation and an official address from where to conduct my research. I am particularly thankful to the former Chairpersons and HOD, Prof. Shekhar Shetty, and Prof. H.S. Prakash who encouraged me to put up the project and who have been most encouraging and totally supportive throughout. Thanks are also due to Prof. R. Bharati Salimath, the immediate former Chairperson of the Department and to the current Chairperson Professor Niranjan for all the help and unstinted support, and to many staff members of the Department who helped at one time or another in different ways.

There are some among friends and former colleagues and co workers who are ever enthusiastic about new ideas and new efforts and one feels very confident that they will unhesitatingly provide bright inputs and constructive suggestions and mentoring when necessary. At the very outset I would like to thank Prof. Dr Ashok Sarbhoy (Late), Emeritus Scientist, Indian Agricultural Research Institute, New Delhi – who first drew my attention to the existence of a scheme in the DST under which I could submit a book writing proposal. Without his very active help in providing me the application format and scheme details I would have remained in ignorance. I remain ever grateful to him.

I consider myself extremely fortunate to have been able to discuss with Dr K.T. Achaya (deceased since then) an eminent food scientist and author of many scientific papers and books, Dr V. Prakash, immediate previous Director, Central Food Technological Research Institute (CSIR), Mysore, Dr T.R. Sharma (Late), former Director, Defence Food Research Laboratory, Mysore and former Advisor Life Sciences, DRDO, New Delhi, with the seed of the idea and the early drafts of the proposal and who meticulously read through, made suggestions and gave advice before submission to the DST. Their help in this regard was invaluable.

I am ever thankful and grateful to the following scientists as well for all that they have done in true and friendly scientific spirit. In the Defence Research and Development Organisation, I owe many thanks to Dr W. Selvamurthy, Chief Controller, Research and Development (DRDO) and

Chief Advisor, Life Sciences Group whose kind help enabled me to navigate the official channels and who also gave personal inputs during discussions and explained many futuristic trends in Defence Life Sciences. The support from his HQ has been invaluable for facilitating interaction with officers in the Army Head Quarters- Quarter Master General Branch, Directorate of Supplies and Transport, Remount Veterinary Service Corps, Office of Naval Logistics, Army Service Corps, South, Bangalore and other Defence Establishments under the DRDO. In various ways, I have received help in the form of technical literature and information and access to libraries from the following in the DRDO: Dr B.S. Bawa, Director, Defence Food Research Laboratory (DFRL), Dr S. Radhakrishna, Senior Scientist and many of my former colleagues of DFRL, Mysore and especially Sri A.N. Srivatsa formerly of the Packaging and Food Engineering Department; Dr P.S. Raju, Head of Fruits and Vegetable Technology, Col. Dr D.P. Attrey (Remount Veterinary Service) formerly Director, Field Research Laboratory, Leh and later as Director in Defence Institute of Physiology and Allied Sciences (DIPAS), New Delhi, Dr Narendra Kumar, Director, Life Sciences Group. I especially wish to express my gratitude and thanks to Dr Alka Chatterjee, Joint Director, Life Sciences Group, who took particular pains to smooth the rocky road encountered many a time. I thank Dr Zakhwan Ahmed, former Director and officers of the Field Research Laboratory, Leh. and Dr Mohinder Singh, Director, Defence Scientific Information and Documentation Centre (DESIDOC), Metcalf House, New Delhi.

A lot of factual information about rations and ration scales in the Indian Armed Forces, about the food procurement, supply and transport systems, about logistics, about catering and food service in peace and war, in the plains, in deserts, at high attitudes and in the ships and submarines, about the animals in war and their ration requirements could not have been obtained or comprehended without the so very helpful dialogues and informal discussions with senior officers of the following Armed Forces establishments: in the Army Head Quarters – the Quarter Master General's Branch, and particularly Col A.N. Datta; who at that time was Q-1(B) Assistant Quarter Master General (AQMG); the Deputy Director General Operational Logistics (DDGOL), the Directorate General of Supplies and Transport (DGST) and particularly the Commanding Officer and senior officers of ST-7/8 Laboratories in Old Delhi; the Commanding Officer of the Remount and Veterinary Services (RVS), and Col Rajpal (RVS) of the same office; the Commanding Officer Army Service Corps (ASC) Centre South, Bangalore, Col. P.D. Kulkarni, VSM Commander Junior Wing, ASC Centre South and other officers of the Army Catering College, ASC, Bangalore who provided substantial inputs from their long experience and active service, and for the tour of the premises.

Special thanks are also owed to the Principal Director of the Directorate of Clothing and Victualing, Integrated Head Quarters (Navy) for permission to visit Naval units in Mumbai, the Commanding Officer Commodore H.S. Chopra, and other officers of *INS Hamla,* Southern Naval Command for a tour of the premises and meaningful interaction, the Logistics Command Officer, Western Command for arranging tours of the Base Victualing Yard Mumbai and the Base Victualing Officer (BVO) and Commandant Cdr. Himanshu Dhuliya and his officers; the Destroyer *INS Mumbai* (in dry dock) and the submarine *INS Shankul* docked in Mumbai and the Logistics and Executive Officers of these two vessels and to friends for a personal and friendly non-official visit to *INS Trishul* which gave the feel of a busy, functioning and thriving ship. I wish to place on record my sincere thanks and appreciation to all the officers and staff of *INS Hamla* and of the ships and the submarine visited for generously giving their time, offering hospitality and even more importantly entering into lively discussions with great enthusiasm and interest in my project. Portions and excerpts from Indian Navy Book of Reference (INBR), the ASC Manual and Compendium of Ration Scales in the Armed Forces were generously provided by *INS Hamla* and the ASC Centre South respectively. An invaluable contribution to the history of ASC edited by Col P. D. Kulkarni VSM and published by the DGST and given to me by Col. Kulkarni is an acquisition that I would cherish. He spent a great amount of time explaining to me patiently how the supply system and ration transportation function and operate and what the supply system is all about and who take part in it. The Commandant and officers of the Institute of Aerospace Medicine, Indian Air Force, Bangalore were very helpful in giving a tour of the premises and explaining the pilot's needs in long duration flights and some technical points about aircrafts in general. I record my gratitude to them.

I owe special thanks of gratitude to former officers of the Indian Army, Gen. Y. N. Sharma (Retd) PVSM AVSM SM, of the 2nd Battalion of Grenadiers and General officer in Command, Central Command and a veteran of 1971 war, now in Hyderabad and Maj. General (Retd). S. G Vombatkere of the EMS, (now in Mysore) for agreeing to speak with me, explain the concept of 'Echelons' and provide an insight into the field delivery systems based on their own experiences. I am very thankful to them. I also wish to express my deep appreciation to Col. Par Chowdry, a World War II veteran belonging to the Outram Rifles who facilitated the meeting with Gen. Sharma in Hyderabad.

To Col. S. S. Rajpal, Director Technical, RVS, who most graciously walked me through the entire nutrition and feeding concepts as they pertained to the animals in military service at the present time and Col. Dr D. P. Atrey, also formerly of RVS for providing more technical inputs about the rearing, care of the animals and nutrition, I extend my heartfelt thanks to both of them.

I wish to extend my sincere thanks to scientists in CFTRI: Dr B. R. Lokesh, Head, Lipid Technology, Dr Appu Rao, Head Protein Technology, and Dr Lalitha Gowda, of the same department and to former scientist Dr M. K. Krishnakumari for having given generously of their time and sharing their knowledge whenever I needed technical information and clarifications. Dialogue and discussions on current nutritional developments happened with Dr Jamuna Prakash and Dr Shashikala of the Department of Studies in Food and Nutrition, Manasa Gangotri, University of Mysore. Their generosity and help in this respect are gratefully acknowledged.

The ancient and historical aspects of the subject as well as scientific information brought out in the book could only be obtained through intensive library searches and only to a limited extent from browsing the net. I record here my grateful thanks to the Directors of various organizations and custodians of libraries who made it possible for me to access the literature.

The foremost among those with the latest books, journals and reports in the field of Food Science and Technology and allied subjects is the library of the Central Food Technological Research Institute (CSIR), Mysore which is considered to be among the finest and the best stocked in Asia; one never comes away disappointed from this library. The Library of the University of Mysore, the Oriental Research Institute Library, Mysore; the Academy for Sanskrit Research, Melkote and its former Director Prof. M. A. Lakshmi Tatachar; the National Archives Museum and Library, New Delhi, the United Services Institute, New Delhi, the Institute of Defence Studies and Analysis (DSA), New Delhi, the City Central Library of Mysore State Libraries in Bangalore and Hyderabad, the Connemara Central Library, Chennai, and the Library of the Asiatic Society, Mumbai; Defence Services Staff College and Library, Wellington, Tamil Nadu, the Edmonton Public Library, Edmonton,. Alberta, Canada, the Brooklyn Public Library, New York and New York Public Library, New York

City. I cannot forget to offer my sincere thanks to Dr Jyotsana Bassu, a Penn State University student at the time who located relevant publications in the University library on request and sent me the extracted material.

There have been those enthusiastic and long suffering individuals who provided technical assistance in the course of my researches, in typing up the manuscript written in long hand and in maintaining the project related files and paper work required by the Mysore University whose help was invaluable: these are individuals within the University Department and outside. I extend my grateful and sincere thanks. I would like to make a special mention of Sri Madhusudan, Research Student, and Sri Ravishankar, Office Assistant, DOS in Applied Botany and Ms. Latha Raghu for their patience and effort. I would like to extend special thanks to friends like Dr Ramakrishna Gowda, formerly HOD of the Department of Studies in Physics, Mysore University who was ever ready with a helping hand to sort out the unintelligible and frustrating glitches encountered with the computer.

And most of all I would like to place on record my deep sense of special gratitude to my husband Dr D. Rajagopal Rao, my children and many family members who were ever enthusiastic about the whole project and who supported and encouraged me in a myriad ways that cannot be enumerated. They made it possible for me to spend long hours in libraries, in travel, work at home and glued in front of the computer. To all, I offer heartfelt thanks.

I would also like to thank the following organisations for their kind support to make this project a success.

Acknowledgements to the Ministry of Defence Establishments, Government of India

1. Directorate of Life Sciences, Defence R&D Organisation, MOD
   Ref: DLS/86/50186/Combat Foods-DVR, dt 24 Sep, 2008 – General Approval for chapters 9, 10, 11 and portions relevant to Indian Armed Forces. The material was researched from within the establishments and in house and public domain publications.
2. Principal Director of Victualing and Clothing, Integrated HQ, MOD (Navy)
   Ref: VG/2402/1; dt 08 May 2009 – For text and images pertaining to the Navy in chapter 12.
3. Directorate General of Military Intelligence, MI (through the Director General, Supplies and Transport) Integrated HQ, MOD (Army); dt 29 June, 2009 – For text and images pertaining to the Army in Chapter 12.

Note 1: As per the letter of MI Department the author posts a disclaimer that it is “Certified that the views expressed in the article are made by the author in personal capacity and do not have any official endorsement”.

Note 2: Under editorial advice certain text portions and images included in the first manuscript submitted to the MI have been removed in the final form without affecting the sum and substance of the matter in the chapter.

Acknowledgements to Various Museums

1. ‘Old Palm leaf Texts’ ancient manuscripts (Figure 2.1) reproduced with permission from the National Centre for History of Science, Oriental Research Institute, University of Mysore.

2. 'Ramayan Shield' by Ganga Baksh (Figure 4.1) reproduced with permission of Karyalay Nideshak Puratatva and Sangrahalay Vibhag, Albert Hall Museum, Jaipur, Rajasthan Government.
3. 'The Unicorn is found' (Figure 8.1), a wall tapestry reproduced with permission from The Metropolitan Museum of Art, Gift of John D. Rockefeller Jr., 1937 (30.80.2) image. For inside editorial use.
4. 'Veer Durgadas Rathore and King Ajit Singh in combat' by A.H. Mooler (Figure 11.1) reproduced with permission of the Mehrangarh Museum Trust, Mehrangarh Fort Jodhpur, Rajasthan.
5. 'Animal ambulances of the 1850s' artists not known (Figures 12.21 and 12.22). Reproduced with permission of National Archives of India, Government of India, New Delhi.

Guide to Refer to Ancient Literature and Notations in the Text

Almost all the text translations consulted herein are out of print books, not to be found easily. Other reference materials were compilations and translations that abstracted pages from different publications and books but did not include details regarding their sources. Certain texts and encyclopedias, glossaries, etc. were not available for general consultation.

In most ancient texts, each verse, sentence or a small paragraph is numbered serially. Sometimes the paragraphs run without a number. Grouped according to main topic and sub topic, the matter is arranged in book, chapter and verse format or Part and Section format or a Chapter and Section format or a Book and *sloka* format or *Kānda* and *Varga* format. Wherever quoted, the original formats have been utilised. Translators sometimes make no mention of the actual verses by their serial numbers but provide commentary for which the page number(s) in that book has been cited.

Since all the works referred to here were English translations from the original Sanskrit or edited versions of the translations, there could be an element of confusion regarding the authorship, translator/editor and dates of publication. Wherever possible, the full details have been provided.

1. **Ṛig Veda:** The English translation by Satya Prakash and Vidyalankar Satyakam (1980), exists in many volumes, each being again divided into books. The stanzas or *slokas* in each book are called the *Richas*. The reference to *Ṛg* Vol. 6 Book 75, Richa 14 would be read as Ṛg 6.75.14. Another example is Ṛg 10.101.2.

2. **Atharva Veda:** The text referred to was by T.H. Ralph Griffith, 1896. He translated and provided a detailed commentary on the *Atharva Veda* (AV). There are several books in the *Atharva Veda* which were consulted. These are numbered in Roman numerals – I, or XIX or XL, followed by *slokas* in Arabic numerals.

For example, AV I, 19 would refer to Book I, *sloka* 19 or simply put, it could also be shown as AV XIX 13, 28; AV XVI 7–8 and so on.

3. **ArthaŚāstra:** For the *ArthaŚāstra*, there were two important sources, one by the original translator R. Shamsastry and another by R. Kangle, 1972. Shamsastry's original version, in three separate publications which appeared between 1906 and 1910 is more easily referred to by page numbers than by chapter and verse. One therefore must look at the original to trace the relevant statement. It was also not easily available for reference as it was usually kept under lock and key. But Kangle's book, based on Shamsastry, provided the chapter and verse as well as profuse commentary and explanatory notes for the verses and was therefore, easier to follow. In Kangle, the reference to the book, chapter and verse are made very clear and unambiguous whereas in Shamsastry one has to go by the page number of the volume concerned. Therefore, Kangle rather than Shamsastry has been quoted more liberally depending on which explanation suited the discussion best.

ArthaŚāstra or AS is referred to by book, chapter and verse. For example, a statement referring to AS 2.19, 11–17 would indicate that it has reference to *ArthaŚāstra*, book 2 chapter 19, verses 11 to 17, and is sometimes followed or preceded by the source of the statement or explanation by Kangle, 1972 or Shamsastry, 1906, 1908 or 1910 or just 1906–1910 and the page number.

4. **Śukranīti:** The version consulted was written by Binoy Kumar Sarkar, 1914; The *Śukranīti* – The Sacred Book of the Hindus (English Commentary and English Translation by Gustav Oppert, 1882).

Śukra is referred to in the following order: chapter, section, and *sloka*(s) as in *Śukra* 4.3, 65–67. Sometimes the author's name (Sarkar, 1914) is given in parenthesis if there was an explanation or only a page number referring to the statement.

5. **Vishnupurānam:** The version consulted was written by Manmath Nath Dutt, 1894. In the *Vishnupurānam* or *DharmaŚāstra*, the order of reference is by part and section and sometimes by the page number. Vishnu 3.1 refers to statement or verse or *sloka* in Part 3, Section 1.

6. **Narasimhapurānam**: Only one book on the subject by Siddheswar Jena, 1987 was consulted. The *slokas* are taken from one chapter LII.

7. **Kāmandakīya Nītisāra:** The commentator was said to be Sankarārya (date unknown) according to Bhandarkar. The version consulted was a translation of an edition of an original Sanskrit version by Rajeshwar Sastri, 1886. Its English translation could have been written by anybody but only the editor Ganapati Sastri's (1912) name figures in the old, frail and withering text. Hence in place of anonymous author, the editor's name has been mentioned. This *Nītisāra* is referred by Book followed by *sloka* number as in Kā. 4.51 or Kā. 5.59–61.

8. **Nītiprakāsika:** *Nītiprakāsika* is said to be a bigger text attributed to the sage Vaisampāyana which has been copiously quoted in Gustav Oppert's original version of *Weapons, Army Organization and Political Maxims of the Ancient Hindus* (with special reference to gunpowder and fire arms) first published in 1880, a newer version or print came out in 1967. Reference is made to *Nītiprakāsika* by book and verse. Book 7, verses 6–8 are given as *Nītiprakāsika* 7.6–8.

9. **Amarakosha:** *Amarakosha of Amara Simha*, fourth edition by Lewis Rice, 1988 is a dictionary, thesaurus and a source for a variety of material. It is divided into *Kāndas* and *Vargas* or divisions.

Reference to the text is made by *Kānda*, *Varga* and verse/page number as in *Amarkosha* 1, *Kala* Varga, 130–134 or *Amarkosha* 2, *Vaishya Varga* followed by a number(s) indicating the verse(s) under discussion.

10. **Vymānika Śāstra:** *Vymanika Śāstra*, Aeronautics of Bharadwaja, 1973 G.R. Josyer, is said to be the author of this Sanskrit version. The commentator of this *Śāstra* is believed to be Bodhananda and the material appears as serially numbered *Sutras*. It is told that Honourable Subbarayappa Sastri had propounded the Bharadwaja's *Vymānika Śāstra* (part of *Yantra Śāstra*) as it is now known. The science of aeronautics in this ancient text is quite detailed in nature according to a scholar who is an aeronautics expert. Portions relevant to the topic of this book have been used here. The Sanskrit to English translations were made available to this author by the then Director Sri M.A. Lakshmi Tatachar, Academy of Sanskrit Research Melkote, Karnataka.

11. **Melkote documents:** Anon. Food Preservation in Ancient India, compilation of translated documents at the Academy of Sanskrit Research, Melkote, received 2004. It contains abstracted reference text on the subject of foods in ancient India. While doing this compilation, no proper record of the source was kept at the Academy and thus bits and pieces from various published texts were put together. After receiving this document it was not possible to trace the original source hence

it has been collectively labelled the 'Melkote Document' and used in reference as such. There are many references to the Ṛg Veda and one author named Dange. Ṛg Vedic statements can be easily confirmed because the *Richas* used in discussion are numbered as per standard practice.

12. **Babur Nama:** *Babur Nama, 'A Journal of Emperor Babur'*. Abridged, edited version of original translation by Annette Susannah Beveridge was recently written by Hiro, Dilip, 2006. This edition serially lists all the statements recorded in Babur's journal, referred here as *Babur*, 270, and so on.

13. **Ain-I-Akbari:** It is a detailed account of the times of Emperor Akbar, given by Sallami Abu-l-Fazl Gallami, originally in Persian. Its English translation by unknown individual(s) was brought out by the Royal Asiatic Society of Bengal, Calcutta, in 1939. A rare find for today, this book was nearly falling apart, with several pages torn beyond redemption or missing, and was found accidentally in a dusty, forgotten, never visited corner of a library. Statements from here are referred to as Ain.1, Ain.23 and so on.

14. **Sun Tzu:** There were two translations that were used, one by Samuel B. Griffith, 1963: *Sun Tzu, The Art of War* (translated) Oxford University Press and the more recent one by Lionel Giles 1999: *Sun Tzu. On the Art of War* (translated from Chinese, with note).

Sun Tzu's Art of War exists in 13 chapters and his maxims are identified by the chapter and verse and in the current book it is used along with the author's name. Giles systematically provided the chapter and verse reference while the contents in Griffith's translation are identified more by the page number. Reference to his maxims can be found as Giles: *SunTzu* chapter 1, verses 3–4.
Giles, Chapter 7.11 or simply *Sun Tzu*, 13.1
Griffith's comments are referred as, Griffith, 1963, page 31–33 and so on.

15. **Niccolo Machiavelli:** *Machiavelli: 'The Chief works and others'* by Allan Gilbert, 1965.
'*Prince*' was the chief work of Machiavelli. The Art of War is contained in Volume 2. There are several books within. The content is in the nature of running matter identified only with the page numbers. Reference to Machiavelli would be made as Machiavelli, Book 1, p. 576.

16. **Rāmāyana:** *Yoga Vashistha Rāmāyana* of Vālmiki by Viharilal Mitra, 1891 and *Vālmiki Rāmāyana* (condensed) in Poet's own words by P.P.S Sastri, 1935.

Rāmāyana is narrated in six major chronologically progressing sections known as *kāndas* viz. *Bālakānda, Ayodhya kānda, Aranya kānda, Kishkindhā kānda, Sundara kānda* and *Yuddha kānda*. There are references to other *kandas* as well. With every statement from Rāmāyana or Rām, the relevant *kānda* is mentioned as in *Rām Bālakānda*. But certain authors like Mitra use a chapter name like in Chap. 8, *Utpathi kānda*.

17. **Mahābhārata:** The source was a secondary one and the statements were quoted from other authors. But it does not take away from the material content of the reference. There are many divisions called *Parva* like *Bhisma Parva*, *Shanti Parva*, etc. followed by chapters. Statements from *Mahābhārata* are referred as Mhb. *Udyoga Parva* chapters 151 and 152 and so on.

Transliteration chart

The phonetic sounds with vowels *a, e, i, o, u* and certain consonants S, C, R, are different for the Sanskrit and Hindi words used in the text.

Ā, ā = aah; Ē, ē = a; ī = ee, ū = you, O = oa, Ć, ć = ch; Ṛ = rr, Ś = sh

ā - as in f*a*ther, Rāmāyana, Mahābhārata, Samhitā
a - as in but
ē - as in w*ay*, *Vēda or Veda*
e - as in b*e*d
ī - as in N*ea*t, Nīti
i - as in *it*
o- as in Ohm or Om
ū - as in b*oo*t, Kūta, Vyūha
u - as in p*u*ll, Upanishad
Ć, ć - as in *ch*art, Ćakra, Ćaraka, ćurna
Ṛ - as in *R*ig, Ṛ*g Vēda*
Ś, ś - as in *sh*ut, Śāstra

Section – I

Growth of Communities and Knowledge, Armies and Wars in the Ancient Period

1

In the Beginning

'To be ignorant of what occurred before you were born is to remain always a child. For what is the worth of human life unless it moves into the life of our own ancestors by the records of life history.'

Cicero

Advent of the Genus *Homo*

Archaeological finds of skeletal remains, skulls and pieces, teeth and jaw bones, stones and shaped or crafted tools, carbon dating, geological data, etc. provide information about each stage of human evolution as well as reveal the climatic conditions that prevailed at the time. They yield ample data to help in a reconstruction of the happenings that led to that particular stage of evolution and then their cataclysmic or quiet extinction. Exquisite anatomical details can be worked out with just a few pieces of bone by employing anthropometric techniques. Predicting size, height, stance and gait of the skeleton's owner gives an idea of how the species stood and moved. Experts can even add flesh, sculpt a near life-like face and build a body to go with it all. The size of the skull indicates the size of the brain within; the larger the brain box, the more evolved was the species in terms of its skill development, its ability to acquire and assess information and knowledge from the surroundings, process and use it for survival and so on. The shape, size and formation of teeth, the size of the jaw bone, etc. provides information on the kind of food the species may have subsisted on. The stones and tools found nearby or from a contemporary geological age would indicate how capable the various species were in making use of the available resources of food.

The saga of human evolution began in Africa. Our ancestor, the primate, principally vegetarian in eating habit, belongs to the super order placental mammal *Euarchontoglires* (Gore, 2003). After a separation from the quadruped to biped stage 7.5 million years ago (Chen, 1999), a succession of hominid species followed. Prominent among these were *Australopithecus robustus* or *Paranthropus robustus* meaning 'beside man' and 'strongly built' (Keyser, 2000), and a short 40–60 inch tall female *A. afarensis* christened 'Lucy' resembling part human (torso) and part chimpanzee (above neck (Oppenheimer, 2003, p. 6)) and then *Kenyanthropus platyops*, the flat faced Kenya man from 3.5 million years ago (Leaky, 2001). All were the progenitors of the human race. Both Lucy and Kenya man disappeared before the genus *Homo* came along 2.5 million years ago.

The wet and warm climate of the Pliocene changed into the Pleistocene's cold and dry ice age. Food got scarce. While the genus *Paranthropus* had developed large jaws to chew tough vegetable matter, the genus *Homo* resorted to using stones and making stone tools and developed larger brains (Oppenheimer, 2003, p. 7). The ice age caused green forests to wither and dry, leaving only tough vegetable matter as wild animals diminished. In the thaw following this, herbivores multiplied and the hominid species moved in search of better pastures. Climatic changes and food were the two driving forces that shaped this evolutionary process. Climate determined the type of food and its availability, and the food in turn exerted pressure on the species to adapt anatomically so that it could be eaten.

The Genus *Homo* in Search of Food

To possess larger brains, which is an energy expensive organ, must have bestowed some evolutionary advantages, speculates Oppenheimer, because in subsequent glaciations, brains kept getting bigger. This was also accompanied by the acquisition of greater skills. *Homo habilis* made its appearance two million years ago with larger brains and the ability to use stones and shape them into tools, heralding the hunter gatherer lifestyle. *Homo ergaster* is deemed to have been the first to do so 1.95 million years ago to become the Asian *Homo erectus,* the Java man (Oppenheimer, 2003, p. 14). This species was smaller than us and spread rapidly to the Middle East, Russia, India, the Far East and Southeast Asia. The African *Homo erectus*, also known as the Dmanisi hominids came less than two million years ago, learnt to butcher meat and dominated as a species for 1.5 million years. They looked a lot like modern humans from the neck down, were more powerfully built and were better endowed to hunt for food in the disappearing forests. The early species *H. habilis*, *H. rudolphensis* and *H. ergaster* which co-existed for a while probably lived a scavenger's life rather than that of a true hunter. *Homo erectus* gave way to another specialized group *H. rhodesiensis*. This species crafted a more sophisticated stone tool – large flat stones shaped on both sides like pointed tear drops and also sharp hand axes. This lot went to Europe. Around 350,000 to 300,000 years ago and another ice age later, a new large brained *Homo* was produced in Africa, known as the archaic *Homo sapiens* or *Homo helmei*. In the thaw that followed, this species spread to Eurasia 250,000 years ago. It may have given rise to the Neanderthals in Europe and Asia while giving some relatives to India and China as well (Oppenheimer, 2003, p. 10–16).

During every post glacial period in the Sahara, brief though it was (a few thousand years), there would be green coverage when the new human species would try to venture forth and step out of Africa in migratory attempts. The archaic Neanderthals, *Homo neanderthalus* also trekked far in their early migrations. There is fresh evidence from the Max Planck Institute of Evolutionary Anthropology gathered by Svante Paabo's team that determined the remains of bones found in Uzbekistan and Siberia were of Neanderthals. Until now the evidence had suggested that this archaic species had gone from Spain to Uzbekistan. However this new study places this species further East and proves that it did move out and colonise most of the Russian plains during a warming period. They analysed one million base pairs of Neanderthal DNA and found that modern and Neanderthal DNA sequences diverged 500,000 years ago (Green *et al.,* 2006). They inhabited these lands and co-existed with the other species but for some environmental or genetic reasons the Neanderthals disappeared about 28,000 years ago leaving the field open for *Homo sapiens*. Paabo, a noted researcher in evolutionary genetics and anthropology has plans to sequence the complete genome of Neanderthal material; more shall be known then.

Homo, the modern human genus, was born some 170,000 years ago in Africa (Oppenheimer, 2003, p. 98). Between 170,000 and 130,000 years ago there was severe glaciation and big game disappeared. The population, for its survival, had to innovate and adapt once again and this it did by learning to beach comb – for fish and shellfish. This practice may have begun as early as 125,000 years ago or even earlier. The existing tribe had practiced this manner of group hunting for seafood – left on the beaches by the receding tide lines. Evidence of beachcombing by way of fossilised split shells have been found in Africa, America and Australia which were peopled at different times once the exodus began in earnest (Oppenheimer, 2003, p. 76–80, 124–127, 163–164, 324, 338). By force of circumstances and by the evolutionary process, the vegetable eating early hominids became omnivore scavengers and then carnivores i.e. meat and fish eaters.

They first ventured out 120,000 years ago and went to the Levant but the ice age erased them. By the time the modern *H. sapiens* finally left Africa 70,000–80,000 years ago and made it to different places, there were other species living in Eurasia. The world was colonised in different places by the emerging genus *Homo*, it was *H. erectus* that led to *H. sapiens* from whom modern humans arose (based on genetic evidence).

Nasreen and Manju Clans

Modern humans originated as a single genetic line in Africa within the last 200,000 years and from there modern Africans, Europeans, Asians and Australoids emerged. Scientists believe that all non-African people have descended from the tribe that left Africa and went eastwards into Southeast Asia and China. The evidence has been based on the genetic work of Cann and co-workers (1987) on the mitochondrial DNA inherited solely from the maternal line. This original 'eve' labeled L301S daughter clans are for some quaint reason named Nasreen and Manju. The Nasreen clan became the only mother for Europeans, and Manju founded family in India. All non-African people can trace their ancestry back to that single 'eve' which branched off into several maternal clans. (Oppenheimer, 2003, p. 45, 48; Cann, Stoneking and Wilson, 1987). The early 'eves' who went to Yemen were isolated and dwindled away after some generations and there remained just one who gave rise to these two daughters and their clans. Multiple migrations radiating out after the first step out of Africa by one successful group characterise the divergence of the human race (Oppenheimer, 2003, p. 83–85). It is now found that there is greater genetic variation within Africa than there is among the peoples of the world. Underneath the skin colour, size and shape, brought on by mutations as adaptations to climate and temperature, we are all the same in our basic origins and our eating habits.

Road to Food and War

Early man walked long distances foraging for food everyday. If we believe that eating to appease hunger is a primal instinct, then fighting over for food is no less primal and comes naturally in the animal kingdom and with our animal ancestors. Someone, somewhere, at sometime becomes greedier and more assertive and more aggressive. Territories able to produce or provide food are made a cause for fighting. Land where food could be grown or found and where cattle could graze becomes coveted and a prized possession. If plenty of grass and grain grew in a region to sustain the people, the coveting and the desire to acquire nature's bounty led to wars and destruction.

The armies in rising civilizations, primarily the river valley and maritime ones, undertook long expeditions in exploration or to capture extra land and thereby wealth. Empires rose and fell, battles were fought, lost and won for land, expansion, greed, wealth accumulation and to propagate and impose ideologies.

There was a road to finding food and a road leading to wars for finding more food and land. Wars and food became irrevocably intertwined. There was also a road to gathering, learning and imparting knowledge. All these went on simultaneously in some cultures but as it so happened one segment became endowed with greater inputs and became more prominent than the others in many places. Learning and cultivation of knowledge, and development of skills, crafts and art came to be considered important for a refined way of life even as fighting was deemed to be necessary for consolidating and protecting territories. It was also resorted to for the accumulation of wealth to support the luxurious lifestyles of a few. The task of fighting fell to those who heard the call to fight and answered.

Equalitarian Society in the Beginning

From all evidence, the life of Stone Age man uneventfully revolved around hunting and food gathering. Vestiges of a placid life pattern are still seen in the hamlets and villages at the heart of Tamil country and elsewhere in the Indian subcontinent (and the Andamans), untouched by the developments at the post-agricultural revolution era (Aiyangar, 1995, p. 4). These hunters and food gatherers lived in an 'Equalitarian Society' called 'Primitive Communism'. They worked at their hardest to obtain enough food and other requirements to survive. Living was a serious business and every single able-bodied person participated (Lilley, 1965, p. 12–13), there was no scope for internal rivalries, observes Lilley, because it meant devoting time and effort away from activities necessary to provide food for survival and especially because there were no food surpluses, no storing and no hoarding. If they fought there would be no time to hunt for food.

Though they lived a savage life, wars were non-existent before the coming of agriculture in 10,000 BC. Each man walked long hours and far distances to gather food for the commune and tribe and his family. We will see later that the energy and protein content of the food which primitive people managed to gather was adequate, and nature endowed and blessed them with the necessary physical fitness for such daily work. As opposed to this, the people from a few thousand years post–agriculture and a couple of centuries post-industrial revolution experience various nutritional deficits and are beset with 'lifestyle diseases'.

In the new Stone Age, there evolved various skills and crafts such as weaving, bamboo working, herding, farming and fishing etc. (Aiyangar, 1995, p. 4). When the nomadic hunter/gatherers at last put down roots at the dawn of agriculture, it is believed that savagery gave way to barbarism, weakening the bases of primitive communism. Things changed with agriculture – one could till the field for oneself and one's family unit. Early in this transition, the society still remained 'equalitarian' as the land was communally owned and cultivable fields redistributed to different families from one year to the next. However, it was possible for a skillful family unit to innovate and produce enough grain and other food and achieve far better results than some other family units. These families advanced more rapidly, accrued greater dividends and began to feel superior to others who did not.

The Early People of India

This discussion pertains to the Indian subcontinent more than to any other geographic region and as such the people who inhabited this land and created civilizations in this part of the world are of primary interest. Anthropologists and geneticists are coming together to delve deep into the mysteries of the evolution of the diverse people of the world. Recent studies on the question of the 'peopling of South Asia' from a group of scientists at Tirupati Venkateswara University and North Bengal University along with scientists of the Yunan University, China, in the Laboratory for Conservation and Utilization of Bio-resources, have generated DNA analysis data from complete sequences of DNA and thrown light on the possibilities of the phylogeny of North Indians (Palnichamy et al., 2004; www.pubmedcentral.nih.gov). Another group of scientists based at the Max Planck Institute of Evolutionary Biology, Leipzig, including one from the Anthropological Survey of India, using mitochondrial DNA analysis data revealed the histories and linkages of various tribal populations of India (Cordaux et al., 2003; www.nature.com/ejhg/journal). There are many tribal groups and the Indians of today are likely to have descended from a common but complex heritage.

Herodotus of Halicarnassus, believed to have been the first historian, was a contemporary of Thucydides and both of them gave historical accounts of remote events as facts or myths. In Herodotus' *History* (Green, 1987), we find amidst a great amount of information, the story of Egypt, its culture, habits and traditions, about the Persian campaign and about India. According to his narratives, among the people who spoke Eastern languages, some lived in swamps and around rivers and ate raw fish (Herodotus 3.98). He found the Indians living to the east of these to be nomads who ate raw meat and were known as 'Padaei'. Of the cannibalistic customs of these nomads, Herodotus said that no man or woman, young or old who was unwell or sick, was allowed to live, wasting away the good flesh! He or she was at once killed by those closest to the person and eaten. The aging or the sick were killed and their flesh eaten in a festive banquet (Herodotus 3.99). However, not all the people behaved in this way.

There were tribes who would not kill any living thing – and in truly nomadic fashion they neither possessed houses nor sowed a crop. They only gathered a millet type of grain that grew on its own and this grain was boiled whole and eaten as such, husk and all. In this tribe too there was the custom that a sick person would just wander away into the desert, lie down and no one from the tribe would trouble him further (Herodotus 3.100). Presumably he died there but what became of him or his flesh is not told. Whereas these Indians were not subjects of Darius, and were black like the Ethiopians (Herodotus 3.101); other Indian neighbours of the city of Caspatyrus and the Pactyic country north of the rest of India were much like the Bactrians. In describing them Herodotus said they were the most war-like of the Indians and they went in quest of gold from the sand (Herodotus 3.102).

There were Pre-Aryans, numerous and well-settled as farmers, and who bred animal stock on their lands, in villages on the banks of the Indus. There were brown and black indigenous populations, Pygmies who were early arrivals from Africa and the proto-Mediterraneans who came later from the region of Mesopotamia and whose characteristics can still be seen among the Dravidians of the South. There were people from Central Asia with Mongoloid features whose descendents may be seen in the East and Northeast.

The Aryans coming into India were descendents of the people who invaded Iran and Asia Minor countries in Europe. Basham (1967) is of the view that there was an Aryan invasion around 4000–3000 years ago or about 1800 BC. These were semi-nomadic barbarians, possessing pale skin and light coloured hair and drove chariots and tamed horses. They came storming into India and the Indus valley civilisation. These invaders were related to the Hellenes, the Italiots, the Celts, the Germanic and the Slav people. Their physical appearance and bearing starkly contrasted with the indigenous people of this land. They came from the direction of Turkestan, conquered the Northwest and intermarried with the locals and spread to the central Indus and the Gangetic plains.

The original meaning of the word Arya, as intended in the Vedas conveys the sense of a people who followed and worshipped the fire cult – the fire god or lightning: the sacred fire – one fire or *Ekāgni* and triple fire or *Tretāgni.* These domestic fire rites were still performed in the houses of Brahmans and 'gorgeous sacrifices' were conducted by the *rajas* – kings in ancient India until the time of the Kurukshetra war.

They belonged in the regions north of the Vindhyas as opposed to Dāsyu people who followed the fireless cult and who belonged to regions south of the Vindhyas. From Vedic sources it is learnt that there was intimate commercial interaction between the South and the North from the age of the *Rishis* or sages, whose language was Sanskrit and thus it was inevitable that these two peoples, Aryans and Dāsyus, though violently opposed in cult, influenced each other heavily. They seemed to have developed in a parallel fashion and reached the same level of attainment in general and particularly in matters of culture. They lived their lives similarly, ate the same kind of food, wore the same type of clothes, observed similar customs and manners and followed similar amusements and methods of making love and war, their dissimilarity confined to matters of religion and literature.

The Aryans coming into India at first inhabited Eastern Afghanistan and Punjab, before their migration eastwards. To the easternmost direction was Bramhavarta, or their holy land, which lay, according to Manu, between the rivers Sarasvati (modern Sarsuti) and Drishadvati in the countryside near Thanesar (Bhandarkar, 1985, p. 3). It is here, says Bhandarkar that the system of castes and orders and the sacrificial religion arose. They spread east and south between the Himalayas and the Vindhyas, the latter forming their Southern boundary. Aryavarta was this region occupied by the Aryas. The furthest of the oldest Aryan province in the South was probably the Vidharbas or the Berars. Southern India was unknown in Pānini's time (seventh century BC) who had extensive knowledge of geography and mentioned various geographic places in his grammatical sutras (Bhandarkar, 1994, p. 6) with no specific mention of Southern India. Patanjali, also a grammarian is credited with the ultimate knowledge of Southern India. Mention is found in both Ramayana and Mahabharata of the inhabited country of Vidharba. Scholars are invariably of the opinion that placing any reliance on the Epics for chronological confirmation could be misleading. In the epic Ramayana, scouts and followers of Sugriva in search of the kidnapped Sita and her kidnapper Ravana passed through southern countries crossing the Vidharbas, Richikas and Mahishakas as well as Dandakāranya (modern Maharashtra) and the river Godavari, the latter being still densely forested. The Maharashtra area came under complete subjugation of the Aryans and was the last region in their southward migration for a time. They drove the native aborigines to the mountains, imposed their Northern Sanskrit language and interposed it into the local tongue which later evolved into different dialects. According to Bhandarkar, commenting on the history of the Dekkan (Bhandarkar, 1985, p. 9), evidence from etymological study and from various literary sources points to the fact that the Aryans penetrated to the Dekkan after the beginning of the seventh century BC and by 350 BC they had become fully familiar with the entire country down to Tanjore and Madura.

In the life lived by the Aryan invaders who brought along the Vedas, the Sanskrit language and the fire cult, there was borrowing and intermingling of words from the existing languages, culture and ways of life. They created class differentiation of people according to the assigned roles of work and service, and also based on the kind of food permissible which differed between them and the indigenous people (Braudel, 1995).

Subsequent civilisations emerged in several phases while overlapping each other. Those were the Indo-Aryans of the Vedic civilisation from 1400 BC to the AD seventh century, a medieval Hindu civilisation which lasted until the thirteenth century including the Kashmir kings whose saga was written by Kalhāna in his Rājatarangini (Stein, 1961). They were ousted by an Islamic-Hindu civilisation imposed by conquering Muslim invaders between the thirteenth and eighteenth centuries AD (Elliot & Dawson, 1877), who were in turned dislodged by yet another colonising power, the British.

Aryans and Dāsyus – Classification, Wealth, Worship and Wars

According to the ancient Tamil people (Aiyangar, 1995, p. 19), the Earth where nomads inhabited is divisible in five natural regions: Pālai (sandy desert land), Kurinji (mountainous country where the hunter tribes were established), Mullai (forests where the pastoral stage of organisation developed), Mārudam (the lower river/valley where the agricultural stage came on) and Neydal (the littoral region) where the fishing and sailing stage of development occurred, each stage existing and developing in its own region in parallel. It was several millennia before modern scientists recognised that in each region grew a race characterised by their profession fitting to that particular geographic region. There was of course a second and further vertical and horizontal division into classes based on the social standing of people, such as higher classes, working classes and personal servants, each being known by a different name (Melor, Vinaivalar and Adiyor respectively). Into this organization came Brāhmanas carrying the Arya cult in the first millennium before the Christian era and imposed another division forming four groups or *varnās*:

- *Brāhmana varnā* – who were believed to be experts in religio-magical ceremonies and thus enjoined to memorise and recite the immense Vedic and other literature such as Sruti and Smriti, and trained to correctly perform various Arya rites.
- *Kshatriya varnā* – kings (of several grades) and their blood relatives whose duty it was to protect the people along with the performing of various ceremonies and *yagnas* such as the great fire rites – known as *Rājasuya, Abhishēka, Vāgapēya, Aśvamēdha.*
- *Vaisyas* – who formed the majority of the people following ordinary pursuits and who also benefited from the minor fire rites conducted by the Brahmanas.
- *Sudras* or the serving classes – For reasons of social democracy which existed at that particular period among the Tamils in Southern India, and the secular nature of life there for millennia before the Aryans and their fire rites came, the efforts of the Brāhmanas to introduce this unnatural division of people into four categories did not succeed (Aiyangar, 1995 p. 20).

The Dāsyus and Aryans differed in various other ways too – wealth and lifestyle, beliefs, gods of worship and gods of war, ways of war, etc.

According to certain Ṛg Vedic mantras for performing Arya rites, it was the Dāsyus who lived in the cities under kings and who were wealthy; they owned property in the form of land, ornaments and jewellery, and as cows, horses and chariots though Dāsyu demons and the Arya gods both lived in opulent style (in castles of gold, silver, iron). The first sign of a conflict between the two may be found in Ṛg Veda's narration of mantras saying that Indra seized Dāsyu property and gave it away to his worshippers – the Aryas. And what can only be considered as further aggravation by the Arya worshippers, Arya gods (Indra) captured hundreds of Dāsyu castles built of stones. Agni, another god, tore and burnt the cities of Dāsyus who did not engage in the fire-cult. Brahaspati is said to have released the cattle of the Aryas from the confines of a prison in Dāsya land. The Ṛg Veda also mentions that both Dāsyus and Aryas owned similar types of chariots and weapons and used them in war (Aiyangar, 1995, p. 11–12)

Indra the 'cloud-compelling' lord of the atmosphere and the recipient of Vedic and fire sacrifices had the pride of place among the gods whom the Brāhmanas worshipped in Aryan India, but this was so mainly in the North (Aiyangar, 1995, p. 27).

On the other hand, in South India, quite independent of the Indra of the Aryans, it was Indiran who was the only god of all the people irrespective of caste, creed and gender in the Mārudam region and who was worshipped without fire rites. The festival invoking Indiran, who was considered the god of the plough, was one of merry making and love and was celebrated at harvest times and thus came to be associated with the modern 'Pongal' or 'bogi pandigai' where *bogi* was another name for Indiran. Celebration of Indiran then became extinct in the Mārudam region after the advent of the worship of Siva and Vishnu from the sixth century AD onwards. In the hilly regions of Kurinji, the Kuravar worshipped Murugan, the god of the hills, the abode of serpents. He represented the visage of an ever youthful and romantic boy-lover, his worship was accompanied with ritual dancing, the priest carrying a spear – a weapon of the hunters of the hill region. The spearhead was of stone in the Stone Age and made of iron in the Iron Age. It is believed that Murugan was the Tamil war-god and was assimilated by northerners with the non-vedic god Subramanian (Shanmukha, Kārtikeya) who is said to have invented the different forms of military formation (Aiyangar, 1995, p. 24, 39).

The Origin of Kingly Power and Influence

Aiyangar, deriving evidence from etymological sources describes at some considerable length the evolution of the notion of a king/patriarch from being a cowherd with many cattle to a man wealthy with cattle which needed large tracts of pastureland for sustenance. It was thus necessary to hold and control the wealth of pasture lands undivided into small bits, unlike arable land which could be cut up by families to farm as they desired. Thus, a joint family system evolved to retain pasture lands and it is believed that the patriarch of a tribe would thus wield great influence and power and become a king.

Love and war were the chief royal occupations or rather amusements, both subjects of ancient poetry. Wars were a means of developing martial powers, of achieving supremacy over others and for the privilege of wearing a triple crown as a liege lord of the Tamil country. Wars as such were not undertaken for the occupation of land, as evidenced by the intactness of the boundaries of the Serā, Sola and Pāndya kingdoms throughout the ages, or for causing bloodshed. It was a favourite amusement. It is said that in the battlefields the soldiers of these three dynasties wore decorative leaves and/or flowers distinct from each other. This hardly seems a war-like attire and conveys the impression that for the Tamil soldiers, war was truly merriment.

They announced their intent to initiate war by first lifting the enemy's cattle or keeping them penned. Forts were built in the lower river valley primarily to store the accumulated agricultural wealth as well as precious metal. The season for fighting began after harvest and before the next sowing. Wars were not fought on cultivable land but took place on wasteland. Therefore, they did not ruin the lands on which they were fought.

That some form of art of war existed at that time can only be surmised from the names of army's division into 'front ranks' and 'back ranks'. It is not clear as to when the army's divisions began to be made into chariot warriors, elephant warriors, horse warriors and foot soldiers. This is similar to the descriptions in the ancient Indian Art of War where chariots, elephants and horses played their battle roles along with the foot (Aiyangar, 1995, p. 32–39). In the beginning of the Old Stone Age, the Aryans of the North exerted their influence with subtle and slow infiltration into the life of Tamils. This slow penetration is believed to have begun in the third millennium BC when Parasuram and a few of his followers settled south of the Vindhyas. According to Aitreya Brāhmana (Aiyangar, 1995, p. 84–85), many sons of the sage Viśwāmitra also migrated southwards. According to Aiyangar, the epic *Rāmāyana* can be placed somewhere in the beginning of the second millennium BC. Rāma is said to have crossed the river Godavari during a period when the non Aryan Rākshasas predominated in the South, even as the most southern Arya 'colony' was that of the sage Agastya on the banks of the river. The same author states that Tamil soldiers took part in the age of *Mahābhārata*. There were no Rishis of any kind in the Tamil land though religious ideas, texts and Sanskrit language spread to the region.

It is now widely taken as fact that the Aryans brought the Vedas into India and many other literary works are dated after that. These have become the sacred texts of the Hindus and are the fount of knowledge of our past, the bed rock of our beliefs, the basis of moral guidelines for everyday living and conduct. They are the repository of wisdom laid down for kings and commoners, priests and soldiers, traders and farmers, students and toilers, the young and the old, the poor and the rich, neighbours, friends and enemies, males and females, and in war and peace.

Thus, the essence of all knowledge in Hindu India is said to lie in these works written in the Sanskrit language.

The search for literary material concerning the armies, wars and foods of the past will have to begin with a scrutiny of at least some of these texts. It is therefore thought appropriate that some exploration is in order at this point to understand the origin and essence of these knowledge texts, what they mean, what they contain and what kind of information may be obtained from them.

References

Aiyangar, P.T. Srinivasa, *Pre Aryan Tamil Culture*. Asian Educational Services, New Delhi, Madras, 1995, p. 4–89.

Basham, A.L., *The Wonder that was India*. Revised edition, Rupa & Co., New Delhi, 1967.

Bhandarkar, D.R., *Lectures on the Ancient History of India on the period 650–325 BC*. Asian Educational Services, New Delhi, 1994, First Published, 1919.

Bhandarkar, R.G., *Early History of the Dekkan Down to Mohammedan Conquest 2nd.*Asia Educational Services, New Delhi, 1985 (First Published 1895, First Reprint,1979).

Braudel, Fernand, *A History of Civilization* (translated from French by Richard Mayne) Penguin Books, 1995.

Cann, R.L., Mark Stoneking and Allan C. Wilson, 1987. 'Mitochondrial DNA and Human evolution'. *Nature*, 325: 31–36.

Chen, J.D. 1999. 'Evolutionary aspects of Exercise'. In Simopoulos, A.P. (ed) *Evolutionary Aspects of Nutrition, Health: Diet, Exercise and Genetics and Chronic disease*. World Rev. Nutr. Diet. Basel, Karger, 84: 106–117.

Cordaux, Richard, Nilmani Saha, Gillian R. Bentley, Robert Aunger, S.M. Sirajuddin, Mark Stoneking, 2003. 'Mitochondrial DNA Analysis Reveals diverse histories of Tribal Populations from India'. *European J.Hum. Genet*, 11(3): 253–264.

Elliot, Sir H.M., *History of India As Told By Its Own Historians*.Vol II &Vol III. Edited by John Dawson (Volumes 1–8) Allahabad, Kitab Mahal, 1877.

Gore, Rick, 2002. 'Dmanisi Finds'. *National Geographic*, Aug 202 (2).

Gore, Rick, 2003. 'The rise of the mammals'. *National Geographic*, April 203 (4): 2–37.

Green, Richard, Johannes Krause, Susan E. Ptak, Andrew W. Briggs, Michael T. Ronan, Jan F. Simons, Lei Du, Michael Egholm, Jonathan M. Rothberg, Maja Paunovic and Svante Paabo. 2006. 'Analysis of one million base pairs of Neanderthal DNA'. *Nature,* 444: 330–336.

Herodotus, *The History*. Translated by David Greene, The University of Chicago Press, Chicago, London, 1987.

Keyser, Andre W. 2000. 'New Finds in South Africa'. *National Geographic,* May 197(5): 76–83.

Leaky, Meave, 2001. 'Meet Kenya Man'. *National Geographic,* Oct 200(4): 84–89.

Lilley, S., 1965. Men, *Machines and History: The Story of Tools and Machines in Relation to Social Progress*. International Publishers, New York.

Oppenheimer, Stephen, 2003. *The Real Eve: Modern Man's Journey Out of Africa*. Carroll and Graf Publishers, New York, p. 6–338.

Palanichamy, Malliya Gounder, Chang Sun, Suraksha Agrawal Bandelt, Qing-Peng Kong, Faisal Khan, Cheng-Ye Wang, Tapan Chaudhuri, Venkatramana Palla, and Ya-Ping Zhang. 2004. 'Phylogeny of Mitochondrial DNA Macrohaplogroup N in India Based on Complete Sequencing: Implications for the South Asia'. *Am. J. Hum Genet*. 75(6): 966–978.

Stein, M.A., 1961. Kalhāna's Rājatarangini. *A Chronicle of the Kings of Kasmir*. Translation, introduction, commentary, appendices, Motilal Banarasi Das, Delhi, A. Constable, London.

2

The Knowledge Literature in Sanskrit

Knowledge Texts

Rituals and prayers, knowledge of the sciences and arts, religious dictats and cannons, and the wisdom of thought and action which have come to be commonly accepted in India are embodied in the ancient Indian texts. These contain observations and details starting from the creation of the universe to how life is to be lived on the Earth in a just, correct, appropriate, ethical and worshipful manner. The role of the kings and armies, the state's administration and foreign policy, education, social behaviour and responsibilities of people are all described in these texts which exist in the form of Sanskrit literature as the religious *Vedas*, the narrative *Purānas*, the poetic renderings of *Itihāsa* (Rāmāyana and Mahābhārata Kāvyas) and many authoritative works providing a vast kaleidoscope of knowledge. The chronology of the Vedic period is conjecture and is guessed from the subject context, language, style of narration or writing and astronomical observations which have been made in the text. The Vedas are part of Śruti – that which has been heard and thus not a work of man (Minor, 1982, Krishnamachariar, 1937).

The four Vedas – *Ṛg Veda*, *Yajur Veda*, *Sāma Veda* and *Atharva Veda* are the principle sources of knowledge and are believed to have originated in the form of a primitive Veda from *Brahma* himself. In *Vishnupuranam* (Dutt, 1894), the word *Brahma* is said to be derived from the root *Vriha* (Fig. 2.1), which means to increase, because it is infinite and is the cause by which the Vedas developed. The great tree of Veda has 1000 branches emanating from the root Vriha giving out the four Vedas from where all others emerged (Vishnu 3.3; Krishnamachariar, 1937, p. 178).

All the Vedas are in the form of hymns, prayers, directions of functions of the Brahmanas and of the performance of various ceremonies and sacrifices by the kings. The *Ṛg Veda* contains all the hymns of all the Vedas. From these four Vedas, arose the six Vēdāngas – *Siksa* – rules and

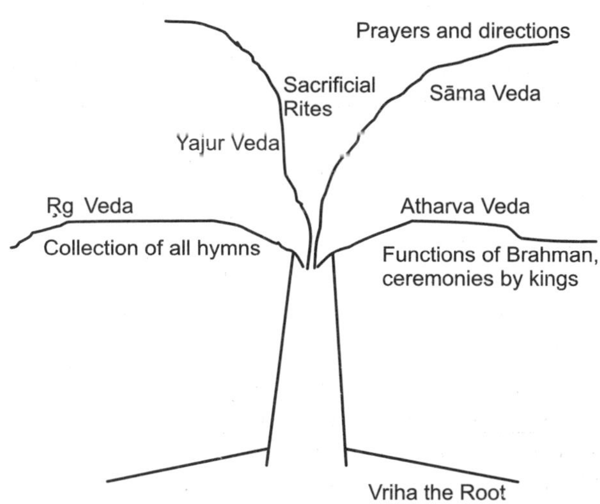

Fig. 2.1: Tree of Vedas of Knowledge (Vishnupurānam 3.3)

pronunciation, *Vyākarna* – grammar, *Kalpa* – rituals, *Nirukta* – etymology or glossary, *Jyotish* – astronomy and *Chhandas* – prosody or metre (Vishnu *3.6*) and the four Upavedas known as *Āyus*, *Dhanus*, *Gandharva* and *Tantra* as per Śukra, 4.3, 51–52 (Sarkar, 1914).

The Vedas have *Samhitās, Brāhmanas, Sutras, Upanishads* and *Aranyakas* produced by various disciples of the four main authors and their disciples in turn. The growth of knowledge is similar to a forest of trees. Brahmanas and Aranyakas are books of prayer designed to relate the ritual to the sacred texts while the Upanishads are philosophical writings attached to the Vedas. At the end of each Brahmana is placed the Aranyaka or forest of books to explain the symbolism of the sacrifices. These works also belong to the time of Yajur, Sāma and Atharva Vedas (~1500 BC to 800 BC).

Table 2.1: Principle sources of knowledge in the ancient Hindu literature: the Vedas and their offshoots

I	The Four Vedas	: Ṛg, Yajur, Sāma and Atharva Vedas
	The six Angas or Vēdāngas	: Siksa (rules), Kalpa (ritual), Vyākarna (grammar), Nirukta (glossary), Chhandas (metre) and Jyotish (astronomy)
II	Mimāmsa	: Theology
	Nyāya	: Logic
	Dharma	: Law
	Purānas	: Descriptions of the Universe, generations, genealogical dynasties
III	The four Upavedas	: Āyur Veda, Dhanur Veda, Gandharva Veda and Tantra
IV	The Eighteen Purānas	: Brahma, Padma, Vaishnava, Saiva, Bhagavata, Narady, Mārkandeya, Agney, Bhavishyat, Brahma vaivartta, Lainga, Varaha, Skanda, Vāmana, Kaurmma, Matsya, Garura and Brahmānda
V	The Epics	: Rāmāyana and Mahābhārata

Sutras or Vēdāngas are links and are actually manuals of instructions in the six sciences, though astrology is also included along with astronomy in another version. These sutras are said to have been propounded somewhere between 800 BC and 350 BC.

In addition, there are eighteen Purānas and Itihāsa, according to the sage Parāsara as narrated in Vishnupurāna (Dutt, 1894, pp. 185–186).

The Four Vedas

The origin and division of the Vedas, known as the trees of the forest of knowledge, has been diagrammatically represented in greater detail in Figure A-1 of Annexure 1. The *Ṛg Veda*, dated by some between 1700 BC and 1500 BC but placed at 1500 BC (Bose, 1971) is a collection of 1017 hymns plus 11 others; in all there are 1028 *suktas* in 8 *ashtakas* or octaves of *khandas* or sections and *adhyāyas* or chapters. It has 2006 *vargās* or classes, 10,417 *riks* or verses and 153,826 *pādas* or words. By another classification, there are 10 *mandalas* or circles or classes and 8 *anuvkas* or sections. *Mandalas* 2–7 are attributed to a single family and are probably the oldest. Scholars speculate that *Mandala* 9 containing some hymns could have been introduced later.

The same source explains that *Yajur Veda* is a prayer book of *mantras* or chants for the priests as is *Sāma Veda* and is also a songbook of 1,547 stanzas. All except 75 stanzas also occur in the *Ṛg Veda*. *Atharva Veda* contains hymns of charms and spells against maladies and the effective use of herbs, dietary instructions attributed to the first physician *Dhanawantari*. All these books are dated between 1500 BC and 800 BC (Melkote Documents). *Atharva Veda* given to Sumanta exists in two *Samhitas*. In the 20 books containing 731 hymns, many of the hymns are drawn from the *Ṛg Veda*.

The *Yajurvedic* mantras are read in any order without verse or music, but the service of an Ādhwarya or priest is required for conducting sacrifice and the mantras are to be read thrice (Śukra *4.3*, 65–67). There are two texts – the black and the white. The white one is attributed to Yajnavalkya Vyāsaneya and is said to consist of 40 chapters. Out of 40, fifteen chapters are said to have been added at a later date. In a similar way, Jaimini divided the *Sāma Veda*. *Āyurveda*, an upaveda of Ṛg Veda is that knowledge by which one acquires health from a study of physique and medicines (Śukra *4.3*, 71–72). *Dhanurveda*, an upaveda of *Yajur Veda* is the science of Archery by the study and mastering of which one can become proficient, in fighting, in the use of arms and weapons and in the formation of battle arrays. It thus comprises the entire concept of military science and craft and not just that of the bows and arrows. Martial arts employing arms and legs, dueling, hand to hand fighting, throwing of arms and implements such as spears and javelins at a fixed point, formation of battle arrays or *Vyuhas* according to the signals given by musical instruments, arrangement of the chariots, elephants, cavalry and the foot all find their place in *Dhanurveda* (Śukra *4.3*, 73–74).

Mimāmsa or *Nyāya* is that science by which the expressions of the Vedas are explained and interpreted according to the ceremonies of the Brāhmanas (Śukra *4.3,* 92–93).

Gandharva Veda is said to be the science of music by which one can understand various voices, e.g. *Udatta* and *Anudatta*, produced by the instruments and throat together with the beats of times (Śukra *4.3*, 75–76). It depicts seven art forms – dance, music, decoration of men (perhaps women too), mimicry, gambling, magic and entertainment.

Yoga Śāstra and *ArthaŚāstra* are the wise sciences (Śukra *4.3*, 100–101, 110–111).

Tantra is the Upaveda of Atharva Veda in which six uses of *mantras* to the adored beings are described along with various means of counteracting the effects of *mantras*, as well as *mantras* for ceremonies.

Distinction between Arts and Sciences

It is easily noticeable to the reader that statements like 'this is science' and 'that is art' have been made above. It is important here to explain who made this distinction and what kinds of knowledge are assigned to the two categories. By tradition and custom, we have come to believe and accept that Śukrāchārya, the son of Brighu, preceptor of the *Daityas* (Demons) was an outstanding expert in the science of war (Sen Sarma, 1975, p. 161–178). The arts and sciences are infinite, according to Śukrāchārya and thus cannot be enumerated. But it was possible to classify some principle ones and he proceeded to do just that. He identified and categorised 32 primary *vidyās* or sciences and 64 *kalas* or arts. *Vidya* or science is described as that which can be 'said or uttered' and *kala* or art is that which can be 'done'. But why should such a distinction have been made?

The early tradition of passing down knowledge by oral means *Śruti* required both speech and hearing and probably the dumb (who would most likely be deaf too) could not acquire knowledge in this way. Creative arts and crafts would not pose any hurdles to those who were speech and/or hearing challenged. The remaining three senses plus the use of hands and legs would be sufficient. No one said such a person could not be taught.

Since some of the important sources of relevant information on the practice of war craft in ancient times are most likely to be found in these two categories of knowledge books, it was thought to be appropriate to list the sciences and some of the arts. There are 32 sciences which include the *Vedas* (4), their *Upavedas* (4) and *Vēdāngas* (6), *Itihāsa* (1) and several other works such as *ArthaŚāstra* (Śukra *4.3*, 55–59). Of the 64 arts or *kalas,* 23 arts are themselves derived from the *Vedas* through *Upavedas*. These 23 arts emanate from *Gandharva* (7), *Āyurveda* (10), *Dhanurveda* (5) and *Tantra* (1). The other forms of arts are listed in Table 2.2. It is evident by the names that outside of scholarship and academics, it is these art forms which built and gave life to the civilization, its cities and forts and sustained the people and the kingdom. The distillation of wine and liquor and the cooking of food are described as arts. Every kind of human activity is shown as an art form.

Table 2.2: Arts of various kinds

- Melting, powdering of stones, metals preparation of salts
- Employment and use of arms and legs
- Dueling, hand to hand fighting in combat
- Throwing of arms and implements
- Battle arrays, formation
- Arrangement of horses, elephants, chariots in war (Part of Dhanurveda science)
- Propitiation of gods by various seats and posture
- Act of driving horses and elephants
- Earthen, wooden, stone and metal vessel –
  Their cleaning
  Their polishing
  Their dyeing
  Picture drawing
- Construction of tanks, palaces, squares
- Construction of clocks, watches, musical instruments, dyeing with colours
- Act of putting down the actions of water, air, fire
- Preparation of boats and conveyances
- Preparation of threads and ropes
- Testing of gems whether good or bad
- Testing of gold, other metals
- Preparation of artificial gold and gems and ornament making
- Softening of leather
- Flaying of skins from the bodies of animals
- Milking
- Churning
- Swimming
- Cleaning of domestic utensils
- Cleaning of clothes
- Shaving
- Extraction of oil from seeds and flesh (fats), drawing of ploughs and climbing trees
- Knowledge of working to please
- Making bamboo straw vessels (cane work, basket work)
- Pumping and withdrawing water
- Making glass vessels
- Preparation of tools and implements form iron
- Preparation of saddles for horses, elephants, bulls, camels
- Maintenance, entertainment and nursing of children
- Punishment of offenders by whipping
- Writing of characters in various languages
- Making and preservation of betel (betel nut, or *supari* in Hindi)
- Speed in taking but delay in giving

Source: Śukra 4.3, 150–200

The Age of the Purānas

The *Purānas* are the store house of ancient history and provide a special dimension to the material information found in narrative form about history of kingdoms and wars and the dynasties that existed and vanished long before any written records could be found. The *Purānas* appeared around the same time as the *Sutras* (600–200 BC) although work on these texts must have been initiated at the very beginning of the Aryan culture, since Vyāsa, while choosing his four disciples to arrange the four principle *Vedas*, also chose Suta to document and arrange *Itihāsa* and the *Purānas*. Vyāsa's disciple Suta had six disciples. Three of them compiled three principle *samhitas* while Lomaharsha or Romaharsha (Suta) himself compiled a fourth one which is named after him. The sum and substance of the four *samhitas* or *Purānas* created by Vyāsa's disciples are embodied in the *Vishnupurānam*, as Parāsara explains to Maitreya while discussing the origin and branching of the Vedas. According to this, Brahma is the first of all Purānas. As may be discerned from the names shown in Table 2.1, the Purānas exalt the three members of the Divine Triumvirate or *Tri-murti* – Brahma, Vishnu and Siva, called respectively *Rajasa*, *Sāttvic* and *Tamas Purānas*. There are also 18 Upa-purānas (Krishnamachariar, 1937). In *Brahma Purāna*, the Creator of the universe and successive generations, the genealogies of patriarchs and kings, the Manawantaras as well as the royal dynasties are described.

The *Vishnupurānam* is a comprehensive source of knowledge about all matters pertaining to the universe and the Earth and provides us an insight not just into the dynastic continuation but also into the origin and understanding of all sources of knowledge. The purānic narrations often sound both celestially mythical and real in human terms.

There were other very important works that came about at the same time as the *Sūtras* or *Purānas*. *Pāninyam* (grammar of Pānini) and the Buddhist canons written in Pali language, the *Dhammapadas* – some 423 verses expounding Buddhist ethics as well as the 500 Jātaka tales describing the precious births of the Buddha and the social customs of the time (Melkote Documents) were written in this period.

The Age of Mahābhārata and Rāmāyana

The chronological positioning of *Mahābhārata* and *Rāmāyana* remains a topic of scholarly conjecture and somewhat of a mystery. Vālmiki's *Rāmāyana* and Vyasa's *Mahābhārata* both are original tales of valour, honour and the triumph of good. In both *Rāmāyana* and *Mahābhārata*, the two *avatārs* (incarnations) of the god Vishnu were personified and brought to this Earth in human and kingly form (Sri Rāma and Sri Krishna respectively) to fight battles and triumph over evil in a time of such antiquity that the origin of those epics can but be speculated at.

Their antiquity is guessed from the events and personages described, the culture and habits enumerated as intrinsic part of the narrations, the class divisions in the society, the knowledge texts referred to in the story, the kingly pursuits followed, the nature of education provided to the fighting classes and the princes, language used to write and searching for cross reference of the epics in other literature that could be dated.

From all these accounts they seem to be far apart in time and space. *Rāmāyana* is an Aryan dynastic tale of *Kshatriya* kings clearly placed in Aryan times. The pre-Vedic Harappan culture is dated between 2200 BC and 1500 BC (Rahman, 1984) while *Vedas* are believed to have appeared around 1700 BC. Rāma was said to be born in the *Treta Yuga* (a period covering 1,296,000 years!).

Their kingdom maintained a huge standing army of conventional *Akshauni* as in the post Vedic times and fought conventional wars with their enemies (the hideous demons) at one time but the next time round they had to resort to Brahman supernatural powers granted by the sages Viswamitra and Vashista and employed magical acts to destroy the demons. It is difficult to reconcile all these facts logically to correctly position *Rāmāyana*. Some scholars believe that it was written in 400 BC during the Mauryan period (*ArthaŚāstra* and *Manusmriti* are also from the same period 320–200 BC (Jha, 1921) but suffered many accretions over the following centuries.

Mahābhārata is a tale of kings and valour and of a *Mahāyudh* (Great War) fought to settle land disputes. The epic is all about battle fields, royal courts and the general life of the soldier of the *Kshatriya* class, not about sacrifices and prayerful chants. Many scholars place it around the fifth century BC to the third century AD the same period as the Roman Republic. These scholars were also emphatic that this glorious tale did not belong to any one period but that it was like a museum where relics of different ages have been stored in an hopelessly ill assorted and confused manner. Chakravarty (1972) was of the opinion that all social customs and religious beliefs of the times are reflected in *Mahābhārata*, but neither Mahaveera nor Buddha (fifth century BC) made any mention or reference to the existence of these texts. Gita whose author is unknown though believed to be Vyasa (Minor, 1982) always referred to in the context of *Mahābhārata* was never considered a part of the *Sruti* like the *Vedas*, but a part of *Smriti*. The variety of content and the vast, wide and deep knowledge – every line of science and arts found in *Mahābhārata* depict rapid progress in intellectualism and more thought in action. Compared to *Rāmāyana*, *Mahābhārata* comes across with a more human face, more secular and more popular in character, less mythical and with a greater historical probability (Krishnamachariar, 1937).

Rāma and certain holy places of the *Rāmāyana* find frequent references in *Mahābhārata*, but neither one hero, nor one event of *Mahābhārata* is to be found in the *Rāmāyana*. This is further evidence of its existence anterior to *Mahābhārata*.

Both *Mahābhārata* and *Rāmāyana* bear tales of wars, hence these could not have belonged to the pre-Vedic period. By tradition, the *Vedas* are believed to belong to a very remote and distant past millions of years ago on the completion of the *Yugas* the concept of which in terms of human years (as shown in Annexure 2, Tables A-2.1 to A-2.3) does permit such time frames encompassing millions of years. And even if many believe that these two tales were written around the same period, scholars conclude that *Rāmāyana* is anterior to *Mahābhārata* (Krishnamachariar, 1937, p. 64–71).

It stretches ones credibility to imagine, much less believe that at the same time as the Roman Republic and Mauryan kingdom and the writing of *ArthaŚāstra* and *Manu Smriti*, Rāmā was engaged in fighting demons of supernatural strength with his own special celestial powers. Another anachronism is that the highly evolved, intelligent *Homo sapiens* appeared much later (Oppenheimer, 2003), endowed with the intelligent capacity to develop language skills and the art of communication, than the times estimated in the *Yugas*. Who were the advanced and intelligent human characters with celestial powers in the two Epics appearing as Rāmā and Krishna? We are again left with the mystery of the dates of the Epics unresolved.

Indian Treatises on the Art of War

ArthaŚāstra: The science of polity or the art of governance known as ArthaŚāstra is claimed not by two, or three but seven authors in different time periods after it was handed down by Brahma (Bhandarkar, 1994, p. 96). In this list are included Manu, Bharadwāja and Gaurasiras who have been for some reason passed up because they were mere mortals and not gods or demi-gods. There have been several abridgements of *ArthaŚāstra*. The text attributed to Kautilya (also called Chānakya) from 320 BC admittedly is the most famous and the best known work and is deemed to have been written in the court of Chandragupta Maurya.

ArthaŚāstra was written by Chānakya in 15 books containing altogether 180 sections. It was discovered by chance in Kerala by Shamsastry, the chief librarian of the Oriental Research Library at Mysore and translated into English by him. It was published for the first time during 1906–1910 (Shamasastry, 1906–1908 a,b; 1910). It is essentially a socio-political and socio-economic treatise of the Hindus. Another work of translation and commentary written by Kangle (1972) in two volumes provides substantial explanations with footnotes on almost all the verses.

Observations, suggestions, recommendations and maxims pertaining to the administration of the state, the king's armies and troops, their strength and care and their entitlements in rewards can be found interspersed here. Books 9 and 10 and again 13 and 14 are devoted to the marches, war, means of taking a fort and secret practices in war. It is necessary to scroll through the entire treatise to glean material relevant to food in general. Information can be found in the form of definite recommendations on the rations for horses, elephants, camels, bullocks and mules. One learns from this about food (as grain) given towards one meal of an Aryan male, of a child, of females and men of lower classes. Importance had been given to the art of moving armies.

Śukranīti: Śukracharya's *Śukranīti* precedes Kautilya's *ArthaŚāstra* and is also considered to be one among the sacred books of the Hindus (Sarkar, 1914). It consists of descriptions and guidelines of the duties of princes, the functions of the crown prince and other state officials, general rules of morality and conduct as well as a very detailed treatment of the character of people and friends, king's functions and state craft and what can be taken to mean the 'art of war' of that time. In the subject topics discussed, both *Śukranīti* and *ArthaŚāstra* are very similar.

Śukracharya's *Śukranīti*, purported to be written in 22,000 *slokas* is an ancient work of civil, social and military codes of conduct and maxims that describe how to classify knowledge as arts and sciences, social customs and creeds, means of gaining and keeping treasure, the responsibilities and the duties of kings and princes. On war and the army, it describes particularly fortresses, kinds of armies, their loyalties and importance to the king, recommendations on their organization, strength and deployment as well as salaries. It emphasises the moral and physical characteristics that make a good soldier and warrior.

The only reference to anything concerning food of the soldier are found as injunctions on the size of vessel (measuring one *prastha* or more) to cook food for one or several people that must be carried as personal baggage along with food and water (Sarkar, 1914). Śukra is believed to have followed on the traditions of Manu because it closely follows *Manusmriti* in sentiment and language according to Gustav Oppert, who originally edited the text, and Sarkar (1914), who wrote another commentary on it.

Kāmandakīya Nītisāra: The similarities between *Śukranīti* and *ArthaŚāstra* extend to a later treatise known as *Kāmandakīya Nītisāra* written by Kāmandaka (Ganapati Sastri, 1912) who was said to be a disciple of Kautilya (whether a contemporary figure or not is not stated). His writings were the most popular work of all Sanskrit books on the island of Bali since the fourth century AD.[1]

Kāmandakīya, some scholars hold, is based on the Hitopadesha model; others believe it predates the latter and say that certain maxims found in *Mahābhārata*, rather the very words, are similar to those in *Kāmandakīya*. *Mahābhārata* certainly existed before both *Hitopadesha* and *Kāmandaka*. Even casual comparison of sections on diplomacy, etc. shows that *Kamandakiya* is very similar to Kautilya's works whose influence is very persistent throughout the treatise. The *Kāmandakīya* maxims are found in 19 chapters and cover almost all subjects under polity. The maxims on modes of war and other matters of warfare may be found principally in chapters 10 and 15 to 19. Its commentator is said to have been Śankararya (Bhandarkar, 1994, p. 97).

Kāmandaka, a Buddhist by faith was believed to have been a disciple of Chānakya and much influenced by him, but wrote his *Nītisāra* in a style quite different from the style of previous scholars. There is, according to its English translator (possibly Gustav Oppert) who worked on Rajeswar Shastri's Sanskrit version, 1886, which was edited by Ganapati Sastri (1912), an earnest and moral advocacy of truth, justice, and honesty in sections on diplomacy even though he said all that Chānakya believed and advocated. Among other things, he also said that taking recourse to forgery, perjury and even poisoning to put down opposition was a way of war.

Alluding to army and warfare there are brief and terse statements made on the strength of the army, military expeditions, system of encamping, the various modes of warfare and movements of generals, surprise, and the arrangement of troops including the functions of elephants and horses. It was recognised by him too that a garrison in a fort should have an abundant supply of provisions and drinking water in preparation for a long siege. The situation where troops were well fed, when the inmates of the camp were cheerful, and when the elephants were sufficiently 'mad' without imbibing intoxicating liquors would indicate that every effort had been made to prepare for war so that no famine should undermine their will to hold out. It was also customary before a battle that the elephants be fed intoxicants to make them more spirited and take part in the fight.

The legends associated with ArthaŚāstra and Śukranīti: The origin of *ArthaŚāstra* is obscure and steeped in ancient lores and claims of god's beneficence to mankind. Kangle, introducing the treatise to readers (1972, p. 56), says its origin is to be found in *Śantiparva* of *Mahābhārata*. In the legend it says that at the beginning of creation in the *Krita Yuga*, men conducted themselves properly, and without rulers and without any fear or form of punishment. They acted according to some established form of *dharma* or rules and codes of conduct. But inevitably their earthly pursuits led to anarchy and put the gods in a quandary and a state of apprehension. They ran to Brahma, the Creator, for help. Assuring them of suitable action to stem this wildness among the people, Brahma composed a treatise to provide guidance to people for orderly and peaceful existence on the Earth. It contained the *trivarga* of *Dharma*, *Vrtta* and *Kama*, and other lores. This *Nītisāra* contained *Danda Nīti* or punishment, a means by which man can be prevented from deviating from the righteous and Aryan path. It is believed also through ancient custom and tradition (Ganapati Sastri, 1912, introduction to *Kāmandakīya*) that the science of polity was written in 10 million chapters. The first abridgement was made by Lord Shiva to a more reasonable size of 10,000 chapters. This is known as *Vaishalakshya Śastra*. It was still too big for the comprehension of mere mortals and so was reduced to 5,000 chapters into a treatise called *Bahudantaka Śastra*. This reduction was attributed to Indra. Vrihaspati further condensed it to 3,000 chapters. It was however the sage Śukracharya or Bhārgava who prepared it into 1,000 chapters with 22,000 *slokas* (Śukra: verse 851) which is known as *Śukranīti*. We see how over the ages the original contents came to be abridged in successive stages by the sages or *Rishis* to facilitate the proper acquisition and understanding of the knowledge contained within by the people in their short life span. All the abridgements were concerned with Nīti or Danda Nīti.

A comparison of the text with *ArthaŚāstra* shows that there is no hint or any reference any where to the existence of the *ArthaŚāstra*. Does it signify that Śukrā's treatise came long before Kautilya's? It seems to be so since Śukra goes on to say (Śukra, verses 855–856) 'In the three worlds there is no other Nīti like that of the poet Śukra, and this is the sole **N**īti for politicians, and all others are worthless as political codes' and also that 'Śukranīti is the genuine or real Nītisāra or science of morals, others are pseudo sciences'.

Kautilya himself lends credence to this premise. It was he (Kautilya) who first reformed this science at the end of the age of *Rishīs*. The very first line of Kautilya's *ArthaŚāstra* opens in Book 1 Chapter 1 with, '*Ohm*, Salutation to Śukra and Brahaspati,' and goes on to declare that, 'this single treatise on the science of politics has been prepared mostly by bringing together (the techniques of) as many treatises on the science of politics as have been composed by ancient teachers for the acquisition and protection of the Earth' (Kangle, 1972, AS 1.1.1). It was not meant for the ruling of the Earth or even for the conquest of the whole world and certainly did not suggest anything beyond the borders of India. The descriptions pertained only to the territories lying between the Himalayas and the sea. The establishment of a social order was more important based on the *Varna* and *Asrama* system. The concept of *ArthaŚastra* appears to predate *Mahābhārata* in that Arjuna, the hero of *Mahābhārata* was described as an expert in *ArthaSāstra* and that the best of kings followed this Śastra (Kangle, 1972, p. 3). While scholars debate the origin and precedence of the early treatises of the Sastra, all of which are now non-existent, Kautilya's *ArthaŚastra* is the earliest work now available on the institutions of the kings and *purohita* (priests and Brahmans), on the percepts of administrative matters, and state policy framed by *purohitas* to guide the kings in everything from personal conduct, state craft and foreign policy to the matters concerning war and peace. The priests held sway over kings and the populace alike. They advised, guided and thus in a way controlled the decision-making process of the kings and nobles, the rich and the powerful. One finds a remarkable similarity of purpose between the Aryan Brahmanas and the priests in ancient Egypt.

The ArthaŚāstra Manuscript: Believed to have been lost, this palm leaf manuscript (at least one version) was discovered in Kerala, and lovingly and painstakingly read and translated from Sanskrit to English and then published in parts in the Mysore Reviews by the Chief Librarian of the Oriental Research Institute, R. Shamasastry, between 1906 and 1908. Other sections were published in 1910. The manuscript preserved in the Oriental Research Institute Library at Mysore is around 18 inches long and about 2–2.5 inches wide; it contains 100 wafer thin palm leaves, very brown and fragile, containing about 5–6 lines of engraved writing per page with approximately 100 words to a line. This version is most beautifully engraved in a closely written text in a script that looks like Telugu-Kannada mixed alphabets. The leaves are of course piled one over another and placed between 2 sturdy flat planks/strips of wood, all joined by two strong strings running through one or two punched holes in the book like a binder. The entire contraption is bound over and over with a strong cotton string.

The text is arranged in 15 books which have 180 sections (Kangle's English translation) and amazingly there is not just one book or designated section to study about war, its polity and its conduct or even about the army. The subject is spread all over and recurs in different books and sections. There are many such ancient manuscripts waiting to be studied by scholars. A likeness of this ancient text in a typical ancient Palm leaf manuscript is shown in Fig. 2.2. A manuscript strung between two thin wooden planks and bound by a thin string can be seen. There are racks full of manuscripts in various stages of preservation and scholarly study. During one special exhibition of ancient literature, the *ArthaŚāstra* was kept for public display in the Oriental Research Institute Library but is not generally available for viewing except on special request.

Fig. 2.2: Stacks of ancient palm leaf manuscripts in the Oriental Research Institute Library, Mysore. Palm leaf writing material, other than carving on stone and copper plate writing, was the medium to write on in ancient India before the advent of paper. The pen is a thick needle with a sharp point with which the script is engraved on the parched pale coloured palm leaf. Kohl black is smeared on the engravings to make them visible. The technique is prevalent and much practiced by artists in rural Orissa to carve what are called *patachitra* using themes from Krishna's life and the Rāmāyana on long scrolls.

Source: Oriental Research Institute Library, Mysore.

Vymānika Śāstra

Resurgent interest in things and practices of ancient India are not restricted to archaeological excavations but also extend to disseminating knowledge available in literature and freshly gathered information via technical seminars and symposia. Two such events in the recent past were on the subject of Advances in Powered Flight and Aerospace Sciences in 2003 organised by the Aeronautical Society of India, Bangalore and the First National Convention on Science of Tradition of Food: India's Heritage of 5000 years in 2004 jointly organised by the Central Food Technological Research Institute, Mysore and Academy of Sanskrit Research, Melkote, India. Ancient Indian knowledge about aeroplanes or *Vimāna* and the food prescribed for the pilots is contained in a text known as *Vymānika Śāstra*. The antiquity of *Vimāna* and hence that of the *Vymānika Śāstra* is explained in reference to other momentous events. The one time that the use of a *Pushpak* or *Vimāna* occurred in the context of earthly war was in *Vālmiki Rāmāyana* (Sastri, 1935). According to the legend Sri Rāma and his entire entourage were seen to take off in the *pushpak*, which belonged to the vanquished Lanka king

Rāvana and head towards Ayodhya. Rao, an officer of the Indian Air Force (Rao, 2003, p. I L80) has found some definitions for the *Vimāna* during his researches on the subject and described his findings in a paper presented at the International Seminar on Aerospace. '*Vi* means bird and '*māna*' means 'like' or similar to, thus a craft flying like a bird. Rao also states that he found in Kautilya's *ArthaŚāstra* and the epics *Bhāgavata* and *Mahābhārata*, statements and references to warriors in the sky, in terms such as *saubhika* and *ākāshayodha* (sky-warrior). That there definitely existed the science, skill and the craft of aviation in ancient times is vouchsafed by the existence of a *Vymānika* or *Vymānika Śāstra* believed to have been written by the sage Bharadwaja. For a detailed analysis of the craft related text, Rao's paper is revealing. Like every other literature text of the ancients, this treatise also cannot be easily dated. Sage Bhāradwaja belonged to the Vedic period and was considered to be one of the seven Rishis according to Manwantara as given in *Vishnupurānam* (Dutt, 1894). Other Sanskrit scholars researching the ancient text (Hanumantarao and Anand, 2004, p. 57, 58) find that the author Bharadwaja was also the *Sutrakarta* Bharadwaja and hence must be the same individual who was the *Suktadrashtara* of the sixth *mandala* of Ṛg Samhita. Bharadwaja is also the son of Bharata in the Puranas and claimed to belong to the Angirasa lineage. He has mentioned the *Pushpaka Vimāna* in the *Vymānika Śāstra* as being one of the 25 types of aircrafts found in *Treta Yuga*. Since another 55 types of such crafts were mentioned in *Dwāpara Yuga*, these authors conclude that Bhāradwaja straddled both the *Treta* and *Dwāpara Yugas*. The commentary on this Śāstra is provided by Bodhananda and appears as *Sutras*.

The antiquity of the text is subject to conjecture since the contents are said to have been revealed in their entirety to a scholar, the venerable Sri Subbarayappa, and were translated from Sanskrit by G.R. Josyer (1973) according to the transcript and information obtained from the Sanskrit scholar M.A. Lakshmi Thatachar, Director, International Academy of Sanskrit Research, Melkote, Karnataka. Thus, it could not have been written up until sometime in the nineteenth century. What is discussed here emanated from the English translations that were provided by the Academy.

Uncannily, the sastra is quite detailed in its knowledge content, particularly the descriptions and directions pertaining to the construction of planes. There were *Shakuna*, *Sundara*, *Rukma* and *Tripura Vimāna* among the several types. Not just that, metal alloys were employed in aircraft construction and therefore, there were people of the time who possessed detailed knowledge about smelting and alloying of various metals for use in aviation and such other intricate scientific details (Josyer, 1973). *Shakuna Vimāna* – the bird like and propeller driven craft had internal combustion and was made of *rajaloha*. *Sundara Vimāna* was a jet propulsion system, made of *rajaloha*. Rukma Vimāna was like a hovercraft, had a golden appearance but was made of *rajaloha* and harnessed solar energy. Tripura Vimana, which was a multiuse vehicle for travelling under water, on land and in space, was made of *Trinetra Loha*, which made it extremely light (Rao, 2003). There was no description of *Pushpaka Vimāna*.

And there were so many devices, controls and capabilities in these and other vehicles that one wonders when and where and how these extraordinary modernistic concepts were lost to generations and millennia of the Indian people, leaving them today to buy or re-invent such technologies. Therefore, it is no wonder that food for pilots would have been an elaborate exercise as well in those ancient times. There definitely were pilots to steer these crafts or pilot cum air warriors as suggested by the term *Ākāsh yoddha*.

The Art and Science of Weights and Measures

Standardisation of weights and measures is essential for carrying on trade in both domestic and international commerce. And it is also necessary for ensuring proper trade practices so that one gets the exact quantity by weight, volume and number of goods one paid for at the prevailing market prices. In ancient India, weights and measurements had been standardised by the time of Kautilya and were much in everyday use. These were necessary in everyday transactions such as for paying state salaries and for apportioning grain rations for men and animals. Further, various measurements were required for building roads, houses, digging wells and erecting walls and forts, constructing carts and chariots and aerial vehicles, for measuring ropes and cloth, in determining the height and stature of animals for war and farm work, as well as for estimating distances to travel and the speed of chariots when the kings went on expeditions.

One of the important reforms instituted by the first Emperor of China when he unified the country was to standardise weights and measures. The Indian system of weights used in historical times is of Harappan origin. Kautilya's *ArthaŚāstra* (320 BC) while codifying every aspect of polity and governance, also described concisely the various terms used for weights and volumes for grains, wood, liquids, silver, gold and copper (AS 2.19) under the activity heading 'Standardisation of weights and measures'. In the Roman Republic too (200 BC–AD 600), matters were just as orderly and meticulous in regard to quantities and measures as they were in other facets of the Roman government.

The ancient Indian nomenclature for weights and measures has been commented upon and interpreted by a succession of Sanskrit authors and scholars over a period of time. Translation into other languages, English included, has produced a bewildering array of terms and their equivalents. Therefore it is desirable to address the question of weights and measures here to appreciate how and in what measures the food stuffs and other essential goods were doled out, and in what currency they were paid for. The value of money in terms of metal weights, was a very important aspect of the smithy – iron, gold, silver and copper not only swelled the royal treasury, but enhanced the king's power and influence. Grains and money featured as part of the salaries and stipends paid to government employees, which included the various types of troops, arms establishments and their chiefs and maintenance staff, and all others connected with the royal and state establishment.

The terminologies have metamorphosed considerably since they were first described. The main sources for the information discussed in these pages are Kautilya's *ArthaŚāstra* and its commentaries (Kangle, 1972), *Amarakosha of Amara Simha* (Rice, 1988), the Epigraphical Glossary (Sircar, 1966), the Sanskrit-English dictionary (Monier-Williams, 1899) and Achaya's treatment of the History of Indian Food (Achaya, 1998 and 2000), a truly comprehensive exposition of origins and history of Indian foods and food habits.

Grains and Seeds as Weights

Natural grains and seeds at first served as weights in the barter system. Masabeans, *gunja* berries, barley corn, rice grains, pepper and mustard seeds and *ratti* (*rati*) seeds or *rattis* (Fig. 2.3) served the purpose. Naturally occurring, these seeds were produced in farms and forests, which when parched in the sun and allowed to dry in the open slowly lost their moisture and attained a constant weight and remained so under normal storage.

Fig. 2.3: The brilliant red *Abrus precatorius seeds – Ratti*, just bursting out of the pods which fall from the tree. The pods split along the centre seam from the tip downwards and twist and curl back to expose the seeds. The seeds fall easily and scatter while some stay attached to the pod.

It is to be assumed that people discovered this property of the seeds by trial and error and observation over many seasons, and being the handiest and the most easily accessible articles, put them to good use as weights and counter weights. In one such equivalence, Achaya (1998, p.195) reported a comparison of seed weights (Table 2.3). It shows diligence on the part of early traders.

Table 2.3: Natural grains and seeds as weights

1 pepper seed (*likya*)	= 1 black mustard seed
3 black mustard seeds	= 1 white mustard seed
6 white mustard seeds	= 1 midsize barley corn
3 barley corns	= 1 *krsnala* or *rati* or *ratti*

Source: Achaya, 1998

Terminologies: Not only for revenue and trade purposes but for levy and tax collection from the farmers, grain was the chief form of payment. This practice has existed from the time of the Indus civilisation where taxes from farms and towns were collected as grains which were then stored in large granaries constructed for the purpose. Large granaries have been excavated from the Harappa-Mohenjodaro sites. The larger measures for grain were *Adhaka, Drona, Khari* and *Vaha* while the smaller measures were known as *Prastha, Kuduva, Prasrta, Pala* and *Palardha* (AS 2.19, 30–33). Very elaborate but precise instructions (AS 2.19, 11–17) are given for the construction of balances or *Samavrtta* to weigh grains in different capacities. Balances consisted of two metal pans on a beam or a single pan at the end. The bigger sized balance was called the *Parimani.*

The grain weights and the modern equivalents in kilograms are shown in Table 2.4 where the weight equivalents have been calculated using the value of 1 *adhaka* = 3–4 lbs, (here it has been taken to be 4 lb) as shown by Kangle's commentary on ArthaŚāstra.

Table 2.4: Grain measures–ancient terms and their modern equivalents

Larger measures of grains
1 adhaka = 4 lbs = 1.814 kg
1 drona = 4 adhakas = 7.2 kg
1 khari = 5 dronas = 36.0 kg
1 vaha = 20 kharis = 720.0 kg
Smaller measures
1 adhaka = 4 prastha *or*
1 prastha = ¼ adhaka = 0.4525 kg or 450g = 4 kuduvas
1 kuduva = ¼ prastha = 0.1131kg or 100g
1 prasrta = 0.0565kg
1 prasrta = 2 palas
1 pala = ½ prasrta = 0.02825 kg = 28g
½ pala = 1 palardha = 0.0141 kg or 14g
Other small volumes/approximate measures
1 nikunchaka = a small pailful
1 kuduva = 4 nikunchaka (12 handfuls)

Source: Kangle, 1972: ArthaŚāstra part III, p. 208

(More details on grain weights, coinage and currency values and measurements of size and length, time and space have been provided in Annexure 3.)

Endnote

1. Kāmandaka's works were discovered in Bali among Hindu sacred books. Recorded history says Hindu inhabitants (expatriates from India) retired to Java, taking their sacred books. In the fourth century AD after Java became predominantly Buddhist, they fled to Bali with all their household gods and sacred books.

   After their exile there was no further interaction with India. Thus the Kāmandakīya Nītisāra could only have been imported from India at a date quite anterior to the fourth century, which fact Bali itself has acknowledged according to the researches of Sir Stamford Raffles in his introduction to Kāmandakīya (Kā. p. ii).

References

Achaya, K.T., *Indian Food: A Historical Companion*. Oxford University Press, Delhi, 1998.

Achaya, K.T., *The Story of Our Food*. Universities Press, Hyderabad, 2000.

Bhandarkar, D.R., *Lectures on the Ancient History of India on the period from BC 650 to 325*. Asian Educational Services, New Delhi, 1994, p. 96–97.

Bose, D.M. (Chief Ed), *A Concise History of Sciences in India*, S.N. Sen and B.V. Subbarayappa (eds) Indian National Science Academy, New Delhi, 1971.

Dutt, Manmath Nath, *Vishnupurānam* or *Dharmasāstra*. Elysum Press, H.C. Das, Calcutta, 1894, p. 171–186 and Part 3 Sections 1, 3, 6 and Part 4 Sections 3 and 5.

Ganapati Sastri, T. (Ed), *Kāmandakīya Nītisāra*. Commentator Sankararya. (English translatior – Anon). (Original Sanskrit version by Rajeshwar Sastri: 1886). Trivandrum Sanskrit Series number 14. Trivandrum, 1912.

Hanumantarao, H. S. and Anand, Padmashree. Studies of Ancient Indian Food Science & Technology with particular reference to Pilot Food mentioned in Bhāradwāja's Vymānika Śāstra. In '*First National Convention on Science & Tradition of Food-India's Heritage of 5000 years*'. July 25–27, 2004. CFTRI, Mysore and Academy of Sanskrit Research Melkote. Souvenir, p. 57–60.

Jha, Gangadhar, *Manusmriti – The Ancient Laws of Manu with the Bhasya of Medatithi*. University of Calcutta, 1921.

Josyer, G.R., *Vymānika Śāstra. Aeronautics of Bharadwaja*. Coronation Press, Mysore. 1973.

Kangle, R.P., *The Kautilya ArthaŚāstra* Second Edition. Bombay University, Motilal Banarasi Das, 1972. p. 56–208; AS Book 1 Chapter 1; Book 2 Chapter19; Book 3.

Krishnamachariar, M., *History of Classical Sanskrit Literature.* Tirumalai Tirupati Devasthanam Press, Madras, 1937, p. I–Cx, 60–75, 178–180.

Melkote documents: Food Preservation in Ancient India. Compilation of translated documents (Anon). Academy of Sanskrit Research, Melkote; received 2004.

Minor, Robert N., *Bhagavad-Gita*. Heritage Publishers, 1982.

Monier-Williams, Sir M., *Sanskrit-English Dictionary*, Clarendon Press Oxford, 1899.

Oppenheimer, Stephen, *The Real Eve: Modern Man's Journey Out of Africa*. Carroll & Graf Publishers, New York, 2003.

Rahman, A. (ed), *Science and Technology in Indian Culture*. National Institute of Science &Technology and Development Studies, 1984.

Rao, M.P. Aviation Science in Ancient India. In Symposium on '100 Years since First Powered Flight &Advances in Aerospace Sciences. Aeronautical Society of India. Proceedings R. Balasubramanian (ed) Bangalore. 2003. p. IL74-83.

Sarkar, Benoy Kumar, *The Śukranīti – The Sacred Book of the Hindus*. (English Commentary and English Translation by Gustav Oppert, 1882; The Panini Office, Bhuvaneswari Asram, Allahabad, 1914. Sukra: Chapter 4, Section 3, verses 55–59, 71–111, 150–200 and 851–856.

Sastri, P.P.S., *Vālmiki Rāmāyana Condensed.* In Poet's own words. G.A. Natesan & Co. Madras, 1935.

Sen Sarma, P. (Maj. Retd)., *Kurukshetra War: A military Study*. Dhiren Roy Darbari Udjog, Ganganagar, 24 Parganas. 1975, p.161–178.

Shamasastry, R., *Chānakya's ArthasŚāstra – The Science of Politics,* Chapter XXX, Mysore Review, Mysore 1906–1908*a.*

Shamasastry, R., *The ArthasŚāstra of Chānakya*. Books I–IV, Mysore Review, Mysore. 1906–1908*b*

Shamasastry, R., *The ArthasŚāstra of Chānakya* (English Translation). Books V–XV. British India press, Bombay, 1910.

3

Ancient Arts of War

"Without the Army there is neither kingdom nor wealth nor power".

Śukra 4.7.78

Indian Art of War

There is not one single Indian work that may be called the book of the 'Art of War'. The details about state craft, the rules of governance, the art of diplomacy and the codes and maxims to wage wars lie scattered in many ancient texts. The ruling classes and those aspiring to or designated to rule and the noblemen (usually all belonging to the Kshatriya class who would be generals and commanders) were meant to be educated from childhood, trained from a young age in Śastras and martial arts and to be thoroughly acquainted with the relevant subjects. The military writers of ancient India such as Śukrāchārya, Kautilya, and Kāmandaka have each laid down, in their time, the doctrines, instructions and codes of behaviour and conduct for kings, rules of governance, the constitution of an army, organizing marches and encampment, heraldry and battle arrays, the use of logistics in siege and even sharing and distribution of the spoils from conquered territories. These three texts are part of our ancient knowledge literature which were discussed briefly in Chapter 2. The specific food *per se* for the men engaged in war (actual description of foods, quantity, meal portions) was not a subject which apparently engaged any of the authors. It would probably be more correct to say that arrangements for food in general were thought of and planned for. When food was available, the men ate what others in their social class and stature were accustomed to eat in that period.

The need for a king and an army was felt long ago. From references in the Vedas and the Epics we learn that an army wing always existed and there were air warriors too but the existence of a navy is not easy to ascertain. Referring to Aitreya Brāhmana, Dikshitar (1944) explained that in the war between *Asuras* and *Devas*, the latter were defeated due to lack of a leader and an organized way, and therefore a leader or a king was elected from among them. Further, if *Devas* and *Asuras* were to be identified with Aryans and Dravidians respectively, there is historical evidence to believe that Dravidian political institutions were a model to be copied and adopted by the Aryans. There were 'stringent laws and conventions to bind' society together and for maintaining social harmony and peace in the kingdom. Observances of customs introduced into the country and of rules of caste/race were to be maintained in the same condition. *Śukranīti* (Sarkar, 1914) also describes the functions of a king. Family life, marriage, property and the duties of different classes were all conducted as per the religio-social dictats and there was strict enforcement (Śukra 4.5, 92–93). The king could punish those who infringed on the laws and customs and the police and the army were the instruments of enforcement.

The king and protection of his kingdom became the focus of life in the land and the king's responsibilities included the well being of his subjects. A mutual dependence ensued – the people contributing to the growth of the wealth and the king raising an army for territorial and wealth protection as well as for purposes of expansion and foreign expeditions. *ArthaŚāstra* has stentorially decreed rules and dictats for the king to abide by, for the outcome of a successful kingship based on religious beliefs and the prevailing social order. These constituted the administrative policy for governance and foreign affairs, the responsibilities of the martial class (*Kshatriyas*) as a whole in the defense of territory and protection of its subjects, the methods of conducting war and rules of engagement, and the art of negotiation and peacemaking. A more direct description of kingly requirements to become a successful monarch is provided in the *Amarakosha* (Rice, 1988). There were seven requisites of a regal administration as per this early literature:

- *A monarch*: He is the most important *hereditary* administrator, at once capable and sensible, brave but wise, smart but crafty. Well-versed in the *Kshatriya dharma* and yet respectful towards the Brāhman priestdom.
- *A Prime Minister*: He is one whom the king needs for administering the kingdom according to his own (king's) perceptions, his whims and fancies, his wisdom or capriciousness and his kindness or brutality. A Prime Minister is ably assisted by counsellors.
- *An ally or allies*: These are 'a must' for the safety and protection of the king's own kingdom and to call upon in times of war.
- *Treasure*: Without ample treasure, neither king nor kingdom could survive.
- *Territory*: It is the land in which the kingdom lies, defined by boundaries which were inherited or the king's own making.
- *A strong hold*: The king must have a fort or forts for the overall protection and defense of his territories.
- *An army*: A reasonably large army made of troops of chariots, elephants, horsemen and foot soldiers plus all assorted paraphernalia was one of the most essential components.

Above all there were the native people and other inhabitants of the territories with their possessions of land, wealth and skills; the acquisition or accretion of all this was what wars were all about. Or else the monarch had no role, there was no kingdom, no kingship, no need for an army and nothing and no one to protect.

Defence of the Kingdom

Having a kingdom and an army, six means of defence have been laid down in the art of war in the ArthaŚāstra (Kangle, 1972). These are mediation, war, marching, halting, stratagem and recourse to protection.

These were meant to protect the powers of monarchy and to provide the majesty, and dignity of the king's stature and his energy and counsel. Being well educated, well-versed in the religious dictats and in the art and craft and science of polity, the king further received counsel to tackle the enemy, for the enemy was ever present and could be inferior or superior, or equal in prowess and majesty and might. The attitudes to war also varied. Vyāsa counselled Dhritarāshtra in *Mahābhārata* that victories could be achieved by exercising one of the four policies or *nītis* (Sen Sarma, 1975, p. 19): *Sama nīti* – by negotiations, to avoid war, *Danda nīti* – through treaties it was a better method, *Bhēda nīti* – through diplomacy was also good, and finally *Yuddha nīti* – going to war. This was the lowest grade and was resorted to only when all others methods failed. Yudhishthira is believed to have said that it was 'better not to have a war at all'.

Two types of war were recognised. First was the *Dharma* or *Nyāya Yuddha*, known to be an honest and just war. It was conducted strictly by honour and was governed by codes; and then there was the *Kūta Yuddha* or unethical war, where the ruling maxim was 'nothing was unfair in war'. *Kūta Yuddha* was repulsed by both the saints and the soldiers and was considered to be a cowardly, despicable and immoral act (Sen Sarma, 1975). Kautilya excelled in *Kūta nīti* from all evidence.

Many means were resorted to, to cause injure to the enemy. The ancient treatises in describing the maxims of war have also enumerated the clever means by which a king and his army could take advantage of the adversary. Prominent among the advice given is the subject of spies, spying and resorting to unethical means. Many of the methods suggested by Kautilya on secret war must have been in practice from before his time and seem like an echo from the early Greek and Roman times. In the Vedas too there are quite gory and cruel sounding methods to injure the enemy and for besting the enemy on the battlefield and off it. There are blood-curdling hymns to be uttered to hasten the defeat and annihilation of the enemy. The considerable attention given to defining the various means of inflicting injury in ancient texts is evidence of its enthusiastic accreditation of the polity and permission from the monarch. One of the major ways of war was the *Aupanishadikam*. Kautilya's *Kūta nīti* fully advocated and endorsed taking recourse to every means fair or foul to wrest an advantage from the enemy. He described some really gruesome ways a war could be fought not just with the army but using methods of warfare which today would come under severe international strictures and public outcry and rebuke.

Aupanishadikam* – *Secret Means of War: Poisoning of individuals and small populations or soldiers with chemicals in the battle zone has been practiced in the ancient times. Also rampant was the poisoning of community wells and water bodies so that people die either from the water or from a terrible thirst, both being awful forms of practice of the Athenians in around 413 BC. Alexander's soldiers are believed to have jumped into wells wearing full body armour only to drown, so crazed were they with thirst. Shooting poisoned arrows covered in snake venom is mentioned in the *Ṛg Veda* and was common in India. Unconventional weapons unhesitatingly used in war or at any other time to gain advantage over the adversary in ancient times are described in the *ArthaŚāstra* rather quaintly as means to injure an enemy. The means were secretly decided, plans hatched, weapons prepared, delivered, and administered. It was part of the *Kūta nīti* advocated by Kautilya and described under *Aupanishadikam*. Even as some methods were revolting and fearsome, there were other means by which pain could be tolerated. Liniments could be prepared from an awful combination of live and dead substances that a traveller going long distance or the soldiers going on long expedition marches could apply on their feet for endurance. Smoke for instant death, slow death by smoke inhalation, potions to wish illnesses on enemies, potions for pain tolerance, for endurance and many magical acts have been described in gory detail, all of which employed plant and animal parts and their liquid extracts and their dried powders in combination with some metals. Used in the form of acrid smokes, blazing fires, poison arrows and poison drinks to name only a few gave unfair advantage in war but were permissible in '*Kūta nīti*' (AS, Book 14). For tolerance to pain, preparations were applied on the body or parts of the body as pastes, oils, and ointments which would make men burn but not hurt. Such applications apparently helped one walk over hot fire as though on a bed of roses! For endurance, it was suggested that a man going on a journey wear shoes of camel skin smeared over with a serum of the flesh of an owl and a vulture and covered with leaves of the banyan tree. With this, he was believed to be able to walk 50 *yojanās* with no fatigue. For an even longer journey covering 100 *yojanās*, he could apply (on his feet presumably) the fat or serum from roasting a pregnant camel with *saptaparna* (lechites) or from roasting dead children in cremation grounds. How much more gruesome could it get?

The Roman law also recognised wars as just and unjust according to motive and occasion. Sen Sarma (1975) explained that if rebels went on a rampage it was unjust or '*bellum injustum*' and those defending the attack could claim that it was *bellum justum*. The ancient Greeks and Romans were no more hesitant than the ancient Indians to use such tactics where poisoned arrows, poison potions and many such unethical means had been employed.

Preparing beverages in the form of potions using plant and animal extractives, generating deadly vapours by the burning of poisonous plants and substances to pollute the air over battle fields all find mention in both Eastern and European literature. Adrienne Mayor's book (Mayor, 2003) describing the vile arts, crafts and technology and the various forms of biological and chemical warfare employed in Greek and Roman times is a chilling recapitulation of the crookedness in war practices and the fact that the warring instincts were not noble at any time in history in any part of the world.

Army – the Enabler of Kings

The sages (*Śukranīti*) have said that 'without the army, there is neither kingdom nor wealth, nor can there be prowess or territory' (Sarkar, 1914).

To keep an army establishment and maintain it from one year to the next, ensuring its loyalty and preventing any treachery and revolt, the state had decreed who were the fit persons to be taken into the army. It also resorted to the payment of salary, given a guideline for prescribing a certain amount of food entitlement or instead of these two, had dangled incentives like permission for looting as compensation and announcement of rewards and prize money after victory. There were different categories of soldiers and different entitlements of pay and rewards within the army (see section on salaries and rewards, etc).

Śukranīti, besides detailing the duties of the Crown Princes, the King and the state officials, describes the general rules of morality, of social customs and institutions and instructions on how to locate, build, equip and guard fortresses (Śukra 4.6). The Army (Śukra 4.7) has been defined as the group of men and animals equipped with arms and supplies. Two kinds of armies have been mentioned: one was *swagama*, that which proceeds independently and the second *anyagama*, which resorts to vehicles (Śukra 4.6, 2–4) and both these armies could belong to the gods (*Devas*), the monsters (*Asuras*) or human beings. Clearly the infantry would be the *swagama* type and the army using elephants, chariots and horses of the *anyagama* type. Sukracharya emphasises that the strength and physique of the soldiers were to be promoted in the interest of hand-to-hand fights by means of tussles between peers, by exercises, parades and adequate food (Śukra 4.7, 32–33).

(a) **Minimum army strength for a king:** The science of polity was such that a king who did not possess a good treasury and army was directed by Kautilya to strengthen the safety and security of his territory and more specifically safeguard the fort, (the haven of the king and army) where according to Kautilya (AS 5.11), both treasury and army could be kept safe. It is in the fort that secret wars, the upkeep of the army, reception of the allies and driving out of the enemies can be successfully practiced (AS 8.1).

Also with a certain level of annual income (of 1 lac *karshas*), according to *Nītiprakāsika* (Oppert, 1967), the king was advised to have one unit of military establishment every year – a reserve force of 1000, all of the same age, well accoutered, and decently equipped with weapons and missiles; 300 foot soldiers armed with lesser firearms and guns/cannons[1], a moderate number of horses, a few elephants, a small number of bulls and camels (Śukra 4.7, 22). A prince with an income of 100,000 *karsha* should have 300 foot soldiers armed with lesser firearms and guns, 80 horses, 1 chariot, 2 larger firearms or cannons, 10 camels, 2 elephants, 2 chariots, 16 bulls, 6 clerks and 3 councilors (Śukra 4.7, 47–52; Śukra 4.5, 26). In a state yielding a revenue of 1 lac rupees (*karshas*), the highest official received a pay of 100, and the clerk 16 *karshas*. Whether this force was meant to serve as the royal body guard or used only for ceremonial purposes or to add majesty to his position as king and ruler is not clear. The expenditure on this unit amounted to 8300 *karshas* per month, inclusive of personal expenses (enjoyments and charities), salaries for all men at different pay scales (out of which they would presumably procure their own food and other necessities), on feed and fodder for the animals as well as on procurement of firearms (Śukra 4.7, 58; Śukra 4.5, 26).

The army should be so managed, equipped and provisioned that a thousand could be called in for service in an instant (Śukra 4.7, 76–78). They were to be responsible for their personal arms, uniforms and their own food. And it is here we get to see what this instant readiness meant (other than weapons and training) i.e. food, water, a vessel measuring one *prastha* and a vessel in which food for many might be cooked (Śukra 4.7, 75–76). Why would a trooper carry such a large vessel to cook food when a small one would have sufficed for his own food? Perhaps he had to prepare food for others as well as fetch water for camp mates. Obviously the sense of service and sharing which was inculcated into the troops is a reflection of the culture and social customs of those times.

(b) **Fortification:** The selection of the ground, its location and the plan for construction of a fort including the layout of roads, houses and the palaces etc. have been explained in detail in ArthaŚāstra. There are precise instructions on how the royal roads were to be laid – four in number, three going west to east and one going from south to north. There would be twelve gates provided with both land and waterways. Separate roads would lead to different areas of the country, pasture grounds, military stations, garden lands, forests, towards elephant forests and other places of community activities and ceremonies. The royal kitchens and the storehouse faced east to south. Since the people lived within the fort among the important amenities, there would be a water well for every ten houses. And what should be kept and stored in the fort? These would be all the essential requirements for human and animal subsistence and nourishment and health. Food materials such as grains, oil, sugar, salt, dry fish and vegetables, dried flesh, medicinal articles, meadow grass, hay stacks for the animals, metals, skins, charcoal, firewood, and strong timber and tenders, fibrous garments for various uses, weapons, armour, stones, bamboo and even poison for war use (AS 4).

Kāmandaka (Ganapati Sastri, 1912) explained that the property of a king depended on making his land as fertile as possible and that he should strive to 'adorn' the land with crops, possess rich mines and minerals and other commodities for trade, a land 'copiously watered', abounding in woods swarming with elephants and also for irrigation and trade have/plan/lay out 'inland and navigable communications' so that one did not have to depend on the rains for agricultural purposes (Kā.4.51–52). Even inside the garrison there would have to be an abundant supply of drinking water and provisions so that they would be able to hold out while the besiegers would slowly die away from famine. The importance of water in strategic planning of yore is also in evidence with the maxim that a king's fort would have to be located on a desert soil so that the besiegers would be compelled to back off and give up out of desperate shortage of food and water (Kā.5.59–61).

As for the quantity of food stuffs, arrangements were to be made for their availability – either within easy access or as baggage carried by the army itself, or obtained from allied/enemy land.

Provision was also made for the families of fallen soldiers and, according to Kautilya, certain quantity of food rations were given to the sick, the wounded and even out of work soldiers. In provisioning the army in the field, allies and friendly neighbours played their role effectively. The encampment was kept supplied with all essentials by traveling traders and their pack mules and bullock carts which collected stuff from the villages nearby and brought them to sell to the army personnel.

The practice of stockpiling of animal and vegetable foods in fortresses in anticipation of long sieges reflected the advance planning and preparedness for all eventualities. One clear statement about war and siege preparedness goes on to say that all these above items must be stored in the fort in such quantities that they can be enjoyed for years together without any shortage. Obviously long sieges of the fort were not uncommon and therefore, provision and supplies were meticulously planned for. There is an injunction to continuously watch the quality and use of each object and keep replacing old things with new. The existence of an inventory system, and accounting by scribes, was in evidence. Kāmandaka too in his writings on *Nītisāra* put down maxims embracing all subjects under the polity. Among these were comprehensive dissertations on military expedition, an account of the system of encamping, the use and employment of various expedients, the various modes of warfare, the movement of generals, the element of surprise and the arrangement of troops as well as the functions of elephants and horses. These ideas and maxims parallel those of Chānakya propounded in the *ArthaŚāstra* where responsibilities were assigned to officials in the army and in related departments.

(c) **Responsibilities of officers:** The responsibilities have been described variously as,

- Activity of the Commandant of the army (AS, 10.33.51),
- Of superintendent of the armoury, (AS 2.18.36),
- War preparations (AS 9. 2. 3–10),
- Ascertainment of the relative strength and weaknesses of the enemy (AS 2.1. 135–136),
- Duties of a C-in-C in addressing the ranks and announcing the rewards to the soldiers (AS 10.3.152).

In that period, the king would also appoint superintendents of chariots, foot soldiers, and horses and elephants whose responsibilities were set down and described in considerable detail.

(d) **Food procurement:** Food procurement was carried out by state officials and comprised such tasks as knowing all about agricultural produce, revenue accruing to the country, and the purchase, barter, bargaining, and borrowing of the produce. The official for agriculture was required to collect the various kinds of foodgrains grown in the king's territories. Regarding food for the troops, the only direct mention is that 'should the army be disbanded or should any member give up undertaking (to fight) due to sickness, the balance of the grain and perhaps other items allotted to the men should be disbursed on their return from the expedition' (AS 2.15). The foods available to the populace in the fourth century BC and in common use by them were: grain, fats (butter, oil, suet and marrow), sugars (treacle, jaggery, unrefined sugar), salt (from Indus-land, sea salt, *bida* salt, saltpeter, borax and salt from saline soil), honey (from bees and that made by juice of grapes), several types of fruit juices, fresh and dried fish and meat, bulbous roots, vegetables, curds (yogurt), sour gruel, spices, etc.

Kautilya further elaborated on the agricultural superintendent's duties saying that these included setting apart one half of the foodstuffs for times of distress so that the people may get adequate food at all times. Further, the official should see to it that the old stock was periodically replaced with new.

Kāmandaka too had recognised the importance of holding ample stocks of every commodity in the fort garrison such as drinking water and provisions in preparation for a long siege. The situation where troops were well fed, when the inmates of the fort or camp were cheerful, and when the elephants were 'sufficiently mad without imbibing intoxicating liquors' – would indicate that every effort had been made to prepare for war so that no famine should undermine their will to hold out. It was also customary before a battle that the elephants be fed intoxicants to make them more spirited and take part in the fight.

The Superintendent of the Magazine (Stores In charge) who was enjoined to know about agricultural produce, revenues from the countryside, purchase, barter, bargaining, bartering, and labour in place of taxes, income from other sources, returns from expenditure and any additional income. He was not only authorised to stock various foodstuffs, but have them processed, keep count of the yields and supervise the distribution of authorised quantities.

(e) **War wisdom and preparations:** While Śukra believed that a monarch would guard and secure his wealth, treasury and army by well-planned fortification, Kāmandaka warned that during army expeditions, the treasure was carried along with the kings, and it was loaded on the elephants and guarded by lighter troops, for royalty depends on treasures (Kā.19.16). The marching army would also carry all sorts of essential elements of warfare and encampment. But in the strategies of kings to conquer an enemy land, the foremost was that of capturing the land with a wealth of corn (standing or harvested) for it was deemed a sound policy to deprive the enemy of his food supply. Destruction of corn thus captured was said to add to the strength of the invaders' own army. Corn may have been a casual term for grain and did not necessarily refer to maize (Kā.15.4). A standing crop was an invitation to the enemy to either capture it for their own use or destroy it to deny the rightful owners of the harvest. Both were tactics of war to starve the enemy one way or the other.[2]

Two things that were considered to be of importance and were given much thought before going to war were the climate and the economic situation. Seasonal climates were important to the kings to proceed without impediments on the way, the principal one being the monsoon rains. Marching to the new territory for war, moving a large army and planning of encampments enroute would be nightmares in the slushy mud. Likewise, the summer was not considered a good time to plan a war because of the intense heat and the drying up of water pools.

Water was important for men and animals, especially elephants. Elephants were the prized possession of the kings; one well equipped war elephant trained for battle and ridden by a brave person was believed to be capable of slaying 6000 horses (Kā.15.11). The elephants also played a lead role in army marches. For want of water the animals became distressed, and deprived of drinking water in the scorching heat they went blind. Therefore, marching with elephants was best when one saw rain clouds and in the rainy season. Since the elephants, horses, camels, bullocks, mules, etc. were a part of the huge ponderous armies of the Indian kings, water, fodder and green grass were needed in enormous quantities – water for the elephants to bathe in and cool off and feed and fodder to care for all the animals.

Other seasons were good for horses and in general for a military expedition. The best season was when it was neither too hot nor too cold, neither rainy nor dry or when the Earth was covered with corn.[3]

The best seasons to go to war are clearly enunciated in the 'art of war' propounded by every military thinker whose treatises form the basis of military strategy, tactics and planning adopted in different parts of the world. The 'Art of War' by Sun Tzu in China (Griffith, 1963, Giles, 1999), 'the Art of War' as described in Kautilya's *ArthaŚāstra*, the art of war of Clausewitz (Graham, 1908, Matthijis Jolles, 1950, Rapoport, 1996), the art of war by Jomini (Jomini, 1996) and even the writings of Machiavelli in the sixteenth century reflect the fundamental principles of war and battle engagements. The theories are usually based on practical considerations, observation of climate and conditions of the road, experience and intuitions and also drew from previous commentaries. The mention of a convenient time for going to war depended on which part of the world the author belonged too.

After season and climate come the economic considerations. Sen Sarma (1975) has summarised these from *Mahābhārata* as the time of harvest of the standing crops since the farmer and his land were a protected entity, and the condition of the terrain and its roads and mountains must be good and would facilitate movement. Lastly, the existence and flow of rivers which would allow navigation to be considered.

In the epic age, wars were geographically limited to the battlefield and were well away from the civilian population who had no role or say in wars and thus, on principle, were never to be harmed. The 'attack and kill' was limited to those directly taking part in the war. The final aim of such battles was to kill the enemy king and annihilate his entire army and thus claim and possess the land. The Kurukshetra war was said to have caused great devastation in the entire land – presumably in the areas geographically close to the battle and the kingdoms concerned. Millions of men were said to have died. There was just one *aksauhini* (this denotes strength) still standing on the *Pāndava* side, out of their initial seven, and four were left on the *Kaurava* side, out of their initial eleven *aksauhinis*. According to Yudhisthira's own estimate, some sixteen *crore* men were killed (10 million = 1 crore). In the *Rāmāyana*, on the other hand, there existed a single battle objective – to rescue Sita by defeating and killing Rāvana and teach him and his cohorts a lesson in honour and righteousness.

(f) **Marching the troops:** It was no mean task to organise an expedition or mount a war with the king's huge retinue. Accompanied by the treasury and his army of monumentally big contingents, which was extremely unwieldy in composition, there seemed to be a greater number of non-combatants and camp followers than combatants and their paraphernalia. The entire procession progressed very slowly. It was as if a whole city marched with the king, taking its people and animals, its businesses and its provisioning system.

In the front, the leader took his place; in the center stayed the king and his harem and the ladies of the court. On the sides, they had protective cavalry and bodyguards. The elephants and surplus army were positioned at the extremities in circular array. And all sides were occupied by the army habituated to forest life. Other troops followed the camp and the commissariat while the army of an ally and its followers selected their own road to advance and find suitable positions to render the best possible help.

Art of War in Ancient China

The art and tactics of war practiced in ancient China find some parallels to ancient Hindu military thoughts and codes. In both civilisations from an ancient ritualistic point of view, hostilities were prohibited during intense agricultural activities like planting and harvesting. After all every land had to grow its own food and the bulk of the army was assembled from the recruitment of agricultural workers and other citizenry freed from farm and other work (for the duration of a specific war). It was their duty in a system of fiefdom. Thus, wars were seasonal affairs and after a successful expedition or campaign the king and the army returned to their own land, fort, and territory and got on with their own specific roles in their society until the next war. There were other military dictats common in both civilizations – such as not to strike the elderly or the injured in battle and not to massacre cities. In stark difference, while in ancient China, no righteous prince was allowed to deceive or take advantage of his adversary, Kautilya described every trick and turn, cunning ways of spreading disaffection among the enemy to gain advantage. A most readable treatise on the art of war of ancient China came from the pen of a Chinese individual, Sun Tzu, in the sixth century BC (594 BC and thus it must predate Kautilya's *ArthaŚāstra* and Kāmandakīya *Nītisāra*; *Śukranīti* is said to predate both these). It first came into the hands of one father J.J. Amiot, a Jesuit missionary in Peking (Beijing) whose interpretation and translation was first published in 1772. Samuel Griffith (1963) translated it and provided ample commentaries and interpretation.

A more recent work is by Giles (1999) whose knowledge and command of the Chinese language provides, a more thorough and elaborate translation. He also gave details of Sun Tzu's life and times. Clavell (2005) rendered an abridged version of each chapter.

Sun Tzu, whose personal name was Wu, was a native of the Ch'i state. He was a thinker, an observer and found it necessary to put down his thoughts and suggestions on how to conduct wars. He wrote the 'Art of War' in 13 chapters which brought him to the notice of Ho Lu, King of Wu. Sun Tzu demonstrated how to control and handle an army during a specially arranged inspection drill of troops for the benefit of the king, after which he was appointed a general. He then proceeded to defeat the king's enemies, the State of Ch'u which lay to the west, put fear into the states of Ch'i and Chin which lay to the north and attained fame and might together with the king.

Sun Tzu also referred to as Sun Wu (Giles, 1999, p. XI–XVI, introduction) is believed to have been in Ho Lu's service some time during 512 BC and is believed to have died of a wound somewhere in 496 BC before his patron king Ho Lu.

His original work may have been much larger than the 13 chapters contained in 82 *pien* or chapters, with diagrams in 9 *chiian*, a collected edition in itself (Giles, 1999, p. XVII). The writings comprised several hundred thousand words but apparently Ts'ao Ts'ao, the Emperor of Wu Wei pruned away all repetitions and condensed it to bring out the essence of the whole to a single book of 13 chapters (Giles, 1999, p. XIX).

Commentaries on Sun Tzu were written by others; many later authors produced different versions of the subject material as commentaries or as condensed or plagiarised works. Giles (1999, XXXIV–XLII) lists some 11 commentators starting from AD 155 to AD 220 through the eighth and nineth centuries, to the eleventh century where scholars prepared compendiums of information on ancient warfare, making special reference to Sun Tzu's 13 chapters. Ts'ao himself wrote a book on war probably using surplus material from Sun Tzu. According to Giles, the 13 chapters are mentioned in the Shih Chi. Thus Sun Tzu's work was already in existence. It was also well known in Ssu-ma

Chi'en, almost in the same form as we now find it, according to Giles. This book and Wu Chi's Art of War are the two books of common reference material for military thought and action.

Wu Chi's name is always associated with Sun Tzu's, even though he came a century or more later (born 430 BC and executed in 381 BC). He had a colourful and eventful life, falling in and out of favour with the ruler of Lu, then the marquis of Wu. He then fled to Ch'u. During this time he wrote the art of war in Lu, and was busily engaged in the reorganisation of the administration in Ch'u. Using strict measures to abolish the very severe abuses rampant in the kingdom, he earned himself foes all over the place leading to his death after king Tao's death (Griffith, 1963, p. 150). Griffith states that the work ascribed to Wu Chi (condensed into 6 chapters with many sections) was a compilation prepared after his death. Although differing greatly from Sun Tzu's titles of contents, Wu Chi arranged his military thoughts under:

- Planning operations against other states,
- Estimating the enemy,
- Control of troops,
- A discussion of generalship,
- Responding to changing conditions, and
- Encouragement of officers.

Battles in Ancient China

The battles of ancient China have been described as primitive melees producing usually no decisive results (Griffith, 1963, p. 33). The two sides camped on opposite sides or waited for days on end to be told of the arrival of the auspicious moment by sooth sayers who divined the right time by studying the situation, and after the commanders conducted sacrifices to propitiate their gods!

The description of the battles that ensued provide a picture of 'amateur theatricals and staged shows' in the words of the author. The entire battle array entered the fracas with roars, simultaneously killing and getting killed, pursuing the remnant army half-heartedly for a short distance, gathering any plunder of value but rarely exploiting the victory. The essence of such engagements was to carry out limited operations and achieve limited objectives.

Just as in the case of ancient India, the campaigns in ancient China were seasonal and hostilities were suspended during the seasons of planting and harvesting (Griffith, 1963, p. 31). Winter was too cold to fight and the peasants hibernated in thin mud huts; summers were too hot.

Ethics and codes of conduct in war: It was also forbidden to strike elderly men or further injure an already injured person. Massacring of cities, ambushing of enemies, or keeping the army over the season was not considered honourable and human hearted. A righteous prince did not stoop to deceit nor did he take unfair advantage of his enemy/adversary. In this connection, Griffith (Griffith, 1963, p. 31–32) narrates the outcome of a long siege of the capital of Sung in 594 BC by king Chung of Ch'u.

His army ran short of provisions even as there was no end to the siege in sight. Worried, he wondered if he would have to abandon or abort the siege and return home empty handed. But to find out what was happening to the men inside the besieged fortification, Chung sent his minister of war Tzu-Fan to climb a hillock and observe the situation. He was intercepted on the high mound by Hua Yuan, the minister sent by the Prince of Sung. In the conversation that ensued and the exchange of information that followed between the two ministers, Tzu-Fan learnt that the state of Sung was exhausted, and that they had no food reserves left; so much so that they were resorting to 'eating their children'. Since this was a beastly and unthinkable thing to do to one's own children, they overcame their squeamishness by exchanging their children; they spilt the bones and cooked those too (Griffith, 1963, p. 30).

When Tzu-Fan also mentioned that according to his own knowledge, when faced by such extreme straits the besieged parties had been known to present a bold face by gagging their horses after giving them grain and sending out the fat ones to meet the enemy, the latter would believe that their adversary had plenty of grain for the animals, which were well fed, and/or that the troops were also abundantly provided with food supplies and could outlast the intended siege. He was surprised at the candidness with which Sung admitted to the real state of affairs by giving an accurate account of their desperate straits. In Hua Yuan's reply here, we see an example of an integral part of waging war in ancient China; Hua Yuan said the reason he had been frank was because he had heard that 'a superior man seeing another's distress had compassion for him while the one who was mean rejoiced in it', and since he believed that Tzu-Fan was a superior man, he had decided to be frank. Upon hearing this Tzu-Fan also confessed that they were actually left with only seven days rations! When the king Chung learnt of the desperate conditions in the besieged kingdom he was all set to go on the offensive immediately. But he was reminded by Tzu-Fan that they being the superior force could not be seen to be mean when a state as small as Sung had a subject who did not practice deceit. His highness was persuaded to end the siege and go back with his army. By telling the truth, it was possible to raise the siege, make peace and keep their respective fortunes intact. Truth, honour and the righteous thing to do were the dictums by which life seemed to have been lived then.

The Old Feudal System and the New Disciplined Army

By around 500 BC, it is said that war, which was ritualistic until then, became ferocious, barbaric and cruel between feudal armies, which were disintegrating. A different period and different society provided opportunities to those with talent. The feudal system until then had ensured that individual loyal armies were assembled for any war that the lieges waged. There were levies imposed on the lesser war lords and fiefs. These were temporary measures and considered to be rather unreliable, inefficient and inadequate.

The armies in ancient China were private just as they were in feudal Europe and India. The command of the army of Chin state around the time of 573 BC had been monopolised by a few great families. When required by their sovereign, the nobility were expected to provide a certain number of chariots, horses, carts, oxen, armed foot men, grooms and even cooks and porters (Griffith, 1963, p. 32). The size of such contingents, made up of peasants, mostly depended upon the holdings of the families and amounted to several thousands in strength.

A peasant had little value, and was not considered even as valuable as an ox or a horse, and thus his welfare was of no concern at all to his superiors! The foot men were expendable and of little use in battle except to group themselves around the horse-chariots carrying a driver, a spearman and a noble archer. The fighting infantry were men who would march ahead of the chariots or even cavalry and be the first to be cut down by bows and arrows. Only a few selected men carried shields of woven bamboo or the more cumbersome and crudely tanned ox or rhinoceros hide. Their weapons were daggers, short swords, bronze tipped spears and hooking and cutting blades tied with leather to wooden shafts. The nobles however carried the bow. Only the guards had helmets, a body armour, crossbows (a Chinese invention of the fourth century BC) and feathered arrows.

The need for disciplined well trained standing armies was felt. Conscripts from the peasant lot aged between 16 and 60 years also formed a section of the new armies. Sun Tzu had appeared on the scene around 500 BC. Military commanders applied Sun Tzu's art of war during the reigns of the Chin and Han dynasties, though they did nothing special to perpetuate it properly. It was said to be Wei Wu, as mentioned earlier, who first wrote a commentary on it (Giles, 1999, p. XXXI). This period saw the first of such armies, headed by elite shock troops possessing courage, skill, discipline and loyalty.

The new army was better trained, better clothed and better equipped. Their training enabled them to march 300 *li* (about 100 miles) without resting. It is said that the guards of Chin were dressed in armour and helmets, their weapons were crossbows with fifteen feathered arrows, extra arrow heads, swords, and a three day supply of parched rice to sustain them. Thus, the equipped armies did not have to confine their operations to certain seasons but could go on attack at short notice. No hot headed, rash and reckless show of individual prowess was tolerated, unlike in previous times. The elements of the new armies became capable of performing according to prepared detailed plans. Special attention was required to be given to this professionally trained lot in terms of morale and feeding. Rewards and punishments were equitably administered (Griffith, 1963, pp. 34–35).

Sun Tzu's art of war (Giles, 1993) was governed by five constant factors – the moral law, heaven, earth, the commander, and method and discipline (Sun Tzu, 1.3–4). Drawing upon each of these factors separately, which affect morale, a general or commander was required to be familiar with every aspect. The method and discipline were concerned with marshalling of the army in its proper subdivisions, with the gradations of rank among officers, the maintenance of roads by which supplies may reach the army and the control of military expenditure (Sun Tzu, 1.10–11).

If there is a lesson to be learnt from Kautilya's *ArthaŚāstra* on using 'every means' to obtain victory, there is a similar *Kūta Nīti*, Chinese style, from Sun Tzu, which hails that all warfare is based on deception (Sun Tzu, 1.18–25). Feigning attacks, holding out bait to entice the enemy, seeking to irritate, attacking when the enemy appeared to be unprepared and at a place least expected were some of the crafty devices to be adopted.

Force Strength and War Expenditure

China used chariots in that period but there is no evidence of cavalry as such having been a part of the army. For waging war, Sun Tzu suggested using 10,000 swift chariots, and perhaps a 1000 heavy chariots and 100,000 mail clad (protective metallic body armour of ancient warriors) soldiers. The war chariot was important as a nucleus a round which foot soldiers were grouped, may be 75 foot men to a chariot, while a heavy chariot was surrounded by 25 foot men. The army would be divided into 1000 battalions, each consisting of two chariots (one swift and one heavy perhaps) and 100 men (Sun Tzu, 2.1).

For such an army the expenditure at home and in the field, plus entertainment of guests, small sundry items spent on maintenance of chariots and armour was estimated to reach some 1000 ounces of silver a day. Armies of the size of 100,000 men mentioned by Sun Tzu were unknown in China before 500 BC. Such large armies were very well organised, trained and commanded, led by professional generals. Finances, supplies and replenishment were major issues with the commanders.

(a) **Supplies for the marching army:** 'No country ever benefited from a prolonged war' was one of Sun Tzu's maxims (Sun Tzu, 2.6–8), and therefore, perhaps the skilful soldier was not expected to raise a second levy for war materials nor load his supply wagons more than twice. Neither wasting of precious time for reinforcements nor turning the army back for fresh supplies was desirable in the attempt to conclude a speedy war. Wisely therefore, it was recommended that the war material should be taken along from home the first time but it was preferable, in fact necessary, to forage in enemy territory so that the army was well supplied and stocked with sufficient food for its needs (Sun Tzu, 2.9–10). Astutely, Sun Tzu observed that contributing to the maintenance of an army in the field at a distance impoverished the people. Clearly, as Giles observes, this might have a reference to the farmers having to send in their contributions of grain (corn) to maintain the army, which would have been a tremendous burden; the peasantry would be drained by such heavy demands and become exhausted. Prices would go up and people's homes would be stripped bare, their incomes having disappeared. Keeping these consequences in mind, a wise general took to foraging on the enemy (Sun Tzu, 2.10–13) because he knew that 'one cart load of the enemy's provisions was equivalent to 20 of one's own and likewise a single 'picul' of his provender was equivalent to 20 from one's own store (Sun Tzu, 2.15). Food could figure as a strong point as well as a weak point in tactics of warfare. It was quite easy to harass an enemy who could be starved out if one was well supplied with food (Sun Tzu, 6.4). Manoeuvering with a disciplined army could be advantageous if only one did not have to wait to equip it fully. But on the other hand, to undertake lengthy marches without proper supplies was also not approved (Sun Tzu, 7.6). Nor did Sun Tzu recommend making forced marches without halting day or night, and covering 100 *li* (sometimes 300 *li*) within 24 hrs instead of the normal 30 *li* for any supposed advantage. The object was to arrive with most of the army intact and this was possible with a march of 30 *li*/day when at least two thirds arrived without falling into the enemy's hands or dropping back due to exhaustion. A profound observation regarding marches pertains to the fact that 'an army without its baggage train is lost; without provisions also it is lost as well as without supply bases' (Sun Tzu, 7.11).

(b) **Spoils of war:** And who took the spoils of thc plundered land? The maxim was to let the spoils be divided amongst the men. And when a territory was captured it was to be cut up into allotments and given to the soldiers too (Sun Tzu, 7.20). The soldiers should make the land their own farm, should sow and plant. These decisions would yield their dividends much later as the Chinese carried out very memorable and successful expeditions penetrating for example the Caspian and populating the conquered land with their own people.

In selecting the right moment to attack as a part of a studied maneuver, it was essential to assess how keen the soldiers were. It was a fact that morning was the best time, when the soldiers were keen and raring to go, provided they had breakfasted (Giles, 1999, p. 66). When the enemy is struggling and toiling and famished with hunger, to be well fed was considered to be an art of preserving and caring for one's strength (Sun Tzu, 7.31). But how much emphasis and effort were necessary to feed the soldiers? Adequate but not too much, because in assessing military advantages, over-caring for the men invariably exposed a General to worry and trouble (Sun Tzu, 8.5). Not that he should be careless of his troops, but it did not mean that situation of strategic importance could be sacrificed for the comfort of his men (a short-sighted policy indeed) because in the long run the troops were bound to suffer more from defeat or from a prolonged war than from hunger in the field.

Sun Tzu expressed definite thoughts on marching and encamping and was fully aware of the treacherous mountains and mountain warfare as well as river warfare. These aspects of war are not found among the maxims of ArthaŚāstra.

Marching through salt marshes presented its own difficulties from lack of fresh water and poor quality of green fodder (Sun Tzu, 8.7). The emphasis on the welfare of the troops was given great importance because one finds frequent references to the necessity of finding suitable places for camping in terms of locating fresh water and pasture land which were essential, where the animals could be turned out to graze (Sun Tzu, 8.12). Some of Sun Tzu's priceless maxims pertain to this aspect of war. 'Utter weariness and faintness of the troops could be gauged by the way they leaned on their spear, tired and spent and their extreme thirst was indicated when those who were sent to draw water began to drink themselves' (Sun Tzu, 8.29). Also, during marches when an army fed its horses with grain and killed its cattle for food – these were extreme straits, ordinarily it would have been so, that the men ate the grain and horses the grass (Sun Tzu, 9.34). Desperate situations of war also could be understood to have arisen when one found that 'the men did not hang their cooking pots over their camp fires', indicating that they would not be returning to their tents and were determined to fight to the death. On terrains that were accessible and traversed by both sides, Sun Tzu recommended that one should occupy the higher sunny side first and that supplies should be well guarded to derive the best advantage in the fight that would ensue (Sun Tzu, 10.3). Such high sunny places also protected the army from disastrous floods.

On the nine situations confronted by the army, the invading forces had to show solidarity and move as one body, using tactics appropriate to the type of battle ground. The general should make forays into the fertile country in order to supply food to his troops (Sun Tzu, 11.20). A skilful tactician was likened to *Shuai-Jan* a snake found in the Chang Mountains and characterised by rapid and sudden movements (Sun Tzu, 11.29). Some commentators have described the lessons that could be learnt by an army from imitating *Shuai-Jan* (Giles, 1999, pp. 128–129). Continuing discussions on how to act on different types of grounds, Sun Tzu said that on desperate grounds a discerning general must proclaim to his soldiers that the situation was hopeless and that their lives could not be saved. Interpreting the maxim, a commentator said that it was then that the orders were given to 'burn the baggage and impedimenta, throw away stores and provisions, choke up the wells (of water), and destroy the cooking stoves' (Sun Tzu, 11.50). It was, as it were, a signal to the troops to fight to the death.

(c) **Burn everything to the ground:** Tactics for attacking by fire targeted first of all the soldiers in the camp, who were to be burnt. The second target was their stores and provisions such as fuel and fodder; the third was to burn the army's baggage trains; the fourth objective was to burn and destroy their arsenals and magazines; and the fifth was to hurl dropping fire among the enemy (Sun Tzu, 13.1). The Chinese diligently followed these tactics through the ensuing ages. Sun Tzu's words are interpreted by scholars to say that to attack by fire, a means must be available, which indicates the presence of traitors in the enemy camp, favourable circumstances such as wind which would not be blowing towards them but towards the enemy and dry weather to set everything afire (Sun Tzu, 12.2). One may imagine the catastrophe caused by a fire attack – burning to cinders everything – from men to their stores, baggage trains and weapons.

War always demands a price. Sun Tzu was conscious of the great devastation a war caused, and of the fact that raising an army of 100,000 men and marching them over great distances entailed a tremendous loss of men and materials, that it was a drain on the State's resources, that the daily expenditure amounted to nearly 1000 ounces of silver and that there would be great unrest and agitation among the people everywhere and also that some 700,000 families would be impeded in their labour, (Sun Tzu, 13.1). After all, the peasantry tended the land which was divided amongst them. One plot of land was made up of nine separate lots of fifteen acres each. Each of eight families cultivated one lot of fifteen acres, while the centre plot was worked on behalf of the state. In war, one man from each of the families was conscripted into military service, each farm gave up at least one able-bodied man. Food production was affected; the conscripted men had to be looked after by the state; they got killed in the war, or if wounded, were unable to return to work. The land and the people became impoverished. The words 'the true object of war is peace' were uttered by Prince Chuang of the Ch'u State as early as 597 BC (Sun Tzu, 13.3). Military might and skill were viewed as the means of repressing cruelty, for the preservation of the 'appointment of Heaven', for the firm establishment of merit, for returning the people to a happier state of affairs, creating harmony between princes and for the diffusion of wealth. The objective, therefore, was to conduct a speedy war and end hostilities in the shortest possible time.

China after Sun Tzu

In all this one gets a picture of feudal and imperial China employing a large number of peasantry as soldiers who were provided, on an individual basis, with so very little by way of armour, clothing and weaponry that one cannot but come to the conclusion that such 'mundane' things as their food and well being would not have made the rulers pause even for a moment in thoughtful consideration. Collectively, however, as a body of fighting men, provision was made for them to access food and get adequate rest; the latter it appears was more for the sake of their animals, allowing them to graze and drink.

One could attempt to extrapolate from these readings what the life of an ordinary soldier might have been. The poor soldiers had to look out for themselves. Poverty does not lend itself readily to observing any niceties or proper codes of conduct. They could die for glory. The men were ferocious and fought with everything they could muster. In the observations of Mo-Tzu, who lived sometime between 497 BC (death of Confucius) and 372 BC (birth of Mencius) and was a high official in the state of Sung, may have been a disciple of Confucius and was skilled in defensive strategy; the behaviour of the soldiers was thought to be atrocious. The ferocity of the Chinese army was such that, disregarding every code of conduct and maxim of war advocated by Sun Tzu, they attacked and fought with an innocent state, dealt with the vanquished in a merciless way and went on a rampage. The soldiers who were regarded as the teeth and claws of rulers, would begin cutting down the grain crops as soon as they entered the borders, whether by boats or chariots. Felling of trees, destruction of walls and fortifications of moats and ponds and setting on fire ancestral temples of state seemed to have been routine acts. They slaughtered the sacrificial animals and massacred the people irrespective of their strength or age and carried off all the boats and treasures. Mo-Tzu further observes that the soldiers were urged to die in the line of duty to gain the highest honour of the land. In the second rung of honour came killing a large number of the enemy with their spears, bows and short daggers and the lowest credit went to those wounded in skirmishes and battles. No mercy was shown to any soldier who broke ranks and fled from the scene of battle, for whom the only penalty was death. Thus did the fearsome Chinese warlords' rule flourish until the triumph of Chin and the unification of China.

Sometime after Sun Tzu, in 350 BC people of feudal China were subjected to countless and continuous wars and longed for peace. The first Emperor of China (246 BC) put an organized centralized government in place. He carried out reforms and standardisation in China's ancient laws, currency, roads, weights and measures, axle-lengths, written language, and straightened out the army and unified all the seven states. For his army, there was the large, poor peasantry—trained in peace times and rewarded for bravery in war.

A remarkable find from excavations in Mount Li of the Emperor's tombs is the unearthing of 3210 terracotta figures of foot soldiers of an infantry regiment facing eastwards, some wearing armours, some un-armoured. Except for Chin officers, in these times, men wore no protective helmets. They had spears two meters long. The armoured men carried bows but the majority had crossbows with a 20 metre and 65 feet range. There were chariots endowed with special functions, and chariots with drums and bells, the striking of which signalled an advance or retreat. A more detailed appreciation and description of the terracotta findings in the pits can be found in many newspaper articles, in the National Geographic magazine and a book on the topic by Cottrell (1981).

The Roman Art of War

Before Baron Carl Von Clausewitz (Prussian) and Jomini (French), both of whom served in Napoleon's army independently wrote their own interpretations and versions of Napoleon's method of war, there was Niccolo Machiavelli – not a general exactly but a Florentine citizen of the sixteenth century (AD 1509) and secretary to the patrician Lorenzo di Filippo Strozzi. Machiavelli was known for his witticisms and clever comments and quotations appropriate to every occasion. He wrote and reported on many aspects of life, state, governance and war. Among his works titled *Prince* (3 volumes) there is one on 'art of war'. Seven books in volume 2 (Gilbert, 1965) serially numbered from 1 to 7 dwell on the art of war. As Machiavelli wrote in the preface to his work, these contain the jottings he made of the friendly interactions when he would sit and participate in the lively conversations which would ensue between Lord Fabrizio Coloma and his own friend Cosimo Rucellai in the latter's garden. He thought it fit to make a note of the direction in which the conversation was moving and interspersed his own pithy comments on the Roman armies of the past and certain ailments of modern armies.

Rome, a small city state, often fought (753 BC–338 BC) for its existence with those who were considerably more powerful in the Mediterranean. However, by 133 BC Roman civilisation and the state, had brought its arch rival, Carthage, on the African coast, and all of Italy as well, to heel. It then reigned supreme for the next 500 years (Mckinley, Howland and Dann, 1994, pp. 8–12). Within this epoch, the aristocratic Roman government introduced reforms in public life, providing just and fair life, good education, equitable opportunities and justice and a very well organized army structure. In this period some of the great classics of literature – Virgil's 'Aeneid', Livy's 'the history of Rome' and poems of Horace and Ovid were produced. From an understanding and appreciation of Roman tactics of warfare, said Machiavelli, there is much for us to learn about their army organization, logistics, provisioning and food rationing.

Machiavelli found that in early sixteenth century Italy, the army was more dissolute and drunken than in the times of the Roman Republic. Not only Italy but all of Europe was yet to fully emerge from the throes of the 'dark ages'; all of the older civilisation, culture and infrastructure having been practically wiped out. In the context of incessant wars and warring states, it is not hard to visualise the commiseration of the learned citizens on the state of the army and give voice to their disenchantment. It would have led them to compare the various features of the army as it was, with that which existed in Imperial Roman times and that is probably how the writing of the art of war came about.

Machiavelli's writings touch upon the same 9 to 13 aspects of war (as embodied in the ancient Hindu and Chinese works) in the seven books. Machiavelli dealt with citizen soldiers, provisions in Roman armies, the disposition of the booty, how the pay should be handled, the principles of encampment of a model army, stratagem and psychological warfare, winter campaigns, even considerations of health and supply in choosing a campsite, assuring adequate food supplies in camp, food for the besieged city and how to send out messages from a besieged city etc. Finally, he also provided diagrammatic representation of seven types of army organization and particularly how to form a normal battalion. Every topic covered in this work which drew examples from the Roman Empire (250 BC–AD 500) is much the same as can be found in *Śukranīti*, Kautilya's *ArthaŚāstra* (fourth century BC), *Kāmandakīya Nītisāra* and *Sun Tzu* (fifth century BC), all of which predated Machiavelli by some 2000 years and more!

The sum and substance of the art of war as enunciated by Fabrizio and Machiavelli emanated from Roman strategies and practices of war lost in the past and long since forgotten.

The Roman Army and Organization

No Roman was forced against his will to serve as a soldier because according to Machiavelli, 'a well governed state has only citizen soldiers. When Rome turned to professional soldiers, she fell' (Machiavelli Book-1, pp. 576–577).

The Roman army structure and organization was constructed on the strength of citizens of the Republic who had political privilege and military obligation. The Roman army was made up of infantry and cavalry formed into legions. Their weapons were pikes, swords, javelins or piluses or throwing spears tipped with three inch long points. For protection there were the pike men and the musketeers.

The younger and poorer citizens drawn from the peasantry served as *velites* or light troops – the fourth line who were actually arranged up front and who screened the main body of the legion.

Composition of a Roman Army: The Roman army consisted of the infantry with shields (o), infantry with pikes (ó), regular light armed men (r), irregular light armed men ($) and the light cavalry (y). The seven arrangements described by Fabrizio for Machiavelli's benefit were designated with symbols and the precise positions were described, of the infantry and the armed men as well as of leaders of ten men (x), the centurions (c), the constables of the battalions (ɔ), the head of the battalions (ф), the captain general (ẅ), the music (s), the standard (z), the men at arms (□), the light cavalry (y), and the cannon (θ) (Machiavelli Book 2, pp. 612–614). These formations could have been used at different times in the same battle or in different battles. Machiavelli drew diagrams to depict exactly how the various elements were to be arranged in camp and in battle.

The concept of formations found in the Roman formations (significantly there were no elephants) and the concept of formations or arrays known as the *vyūha* employed in the Kurukshetra war during the 18 days it lasted are similar, where several battle arrays – one for each day of the war and named differently – had been deployed.

The Roman hierarchy drew its inspiration from the power of the senators – the *Imperium*. Any one who aspired to become a senator usually had to belong to an aristocratic family and also possess considerable wealth. Money was needed to spend on elections – for money changed hands as much then as at any time in history for favours received and conferred.

A Roman formation is shown in Table 3.1. At the top of the pyramid was a *legionis*, a man of senatorial class who commanded the legion and who was ultimately destined for a political career. A legion is comparable to an army brigade. Under him came a young senator designate, a tribune as well as five assistant tribunes of equestrian rank below the senator. In the absence of a legionis and senior tribune, a centurion took charge, commanding a century or a company of 80 men, who could be designated a camp prefect. There were 60 prefects to a legion, graded in seniority. The prefect was also known as Pilus and the most senior of the prefects was known as Primus Pilus.

Table 3.1: A legion of the Roman empire

Roman Grouping	*Strength*	*Modern Equivalent*
Conterbernium	8 man grouping	Squad/Section
Century	80 men	Company
Cohort	6 Centuries	Battalion
Legion	10 Cohorts	Brigade

Source: Keegan and Homes, 1985

The first legion was extra strong with five double centuries. The Roman legion was divided into brigades of infantry and cavalry. According to Machiavelli, expounding on the art of war, one Roman legion of the past (equal to one brigade) had 6000 infantry and 300 serviceable cavalry. The army was further divided into battalions as per arms. It was immaterial what numbers constituted the formations because it was a simple matter to double the soldier strength without affecting the formations described.

In every two Roman legions in a Consular army, there would be 12,000 infantry and 600 cavalry plus another 12,000 infantry as auxiliaries enrolled from friendly states and cities. They did not believe in having more foreigners in the infantry than Romans but it was acceptable to have foreigners in the cavalry. All these were auxiliaries which would be placed only in the flanks enclosing the legions in the centre. Fabrizio's concept of increasing the number of men in the army followed this Roman formation precisely, even in the camp.

If a general found it necessary to camp an army comprising 24,000 infantry and 12,000 cavalry (half of infantry strength), the army could be divided into four brigades, two composed of his own people, the Roman citizens, and two made up of foreigners. If the number had to be increased it was achieved by doubling, and their disposition would follow exactly the same pattern (Machiavelli Book 6, p. 680). Machiavelli observed that it was always strategically important to keep two brigades of one's own people and two of foreigners. Kautilya had also decreed that the standing 'Moula' armies should always be in greater number than the mercenaries (foreigners or professional soldiers) because the former were more loyal (own people).

The Roman army was a citizen's army of the Republic. In the first century AD all legionaries were recruited from outside Rome and Italy. These legions had numbers and honorific titles such as Legio III – *Augusta pia fidelis,* Legio IX – *Hispana.* While fighting Hannibal, their legions formed three main lines known as Hastati, Principes, Triarii and one extra known as Velites. This fourth division was made up of younger and poorer citizens to screen the main body (Keegan and Homes, 1985, p. 58).

Billeting soldiers in cities and their food arrangements followed a code of practice. Since long before Charlemagne's time, from before the Christian era began, it was the practice for soldiers to be in the city. In elaborating about the billeting treatment and conduct of soldiers who did duty as civil soldiers and who were not actually in combat, MacMullen has quoted numerous original texts from AD 300 which mention that, 'some of the larger units, legions and vexillations were in cities, probably also in permanent barracks. The motile units of the palatini and comitatenses except when actually in combat, at which time they lived under canvas, were normally billeted in cities'. Further, there was a Theodosian code on billeting which, among other directives, states that soldiers both proceeding to or returning from combat were to 'occupy the ground floor rooms of each tower of the New wall of the Sacred city' (MacMullen, 1988, pp. 209–215).

Soldiers, officers and the cavalry garrisoned in different civilian city homes and localities had ample access to a variety of food ingredients in sufficient quantities. Under the very casual, relaxed discipline, as well as the extra rations sanctioned, they never felt any shortage of food or drink. Historical records also tell of *valens* sending supply ships from the Black Sea up the Danube for the troops stationed in the cities nearby (Richi, 1973, p. 217).

On the subject of citizen soldier in the Roman armies of the past we have another Machiavellian observation. He was of the opinion that after toiling so much, an army was entitled to rest and refresh with food. In the ancient past, to make their expedition (combat) successful, their prince commander, who was also travelling with them, had the task of making his army obey. He was very clear that by reverting to the practices of the past, 'many troubles and hardships' of the army could be removed and a general could be thus relieved and their expeditions and undertakings made so easy (Machiavelli Book 5, pp. 670–671).

Pay and rewards: While no specific figures for the payment of a Roman soldier have been found, to ensure that the soldiers were not rendered penniless at the end of it all, it was customary to make the soldiers deposit one-third of their pay with the standard bearer who kept the money safe and returned it only when the war was over. It served both to prevent reckless spending by the young men and to take care of the standard bearer (the standard or the flag was a visible beacon of where the commander was in the field and therefore a rallying point; a fallen standard spelt doom and defeat even in ancient India), a practice that was regretfully dispensed with in the modern Italian armies (Machiavelli Book 5, p. 672). Since a standard bearer was of great importance for the morale of the army, he was doubly precious and the soldiers took great care to protect him and in turn were courageous but cautious, brave but economical in the way they fought.

When booty and plunder or prisoners' ransom was to be collected from the defeated army's lands, Machiavelli was explicit that it was not to be left in the hands of the soldiers. Since wars were meant to be won and to occupy more land and add to the country's riches, the plunder by soldiers led to extreme loss of such wealth to the treasury and encouraged the soldiers to continue to ransack the city, both of which caused a grave situation. In Roman times, all the booty taken belonged to the public. The Roman armies had *quaestors* or finance officers (of senatorial rank) with whom all the ransom, war chests and booty had to be deposited. It was the latter who had the authority to distribute and from here they managed to pay the soldiers regular pay, provide for the care of the wounded and provision the army with its requirements. Sometimes, the entire booty was collected in a central place from which the Consul distributed rewards to each Roman according to his rank, thus encouraging legions to win the war and not resort to robbing. It was not the practice for the infantry to pursue the enemy by breaking the ranks in the formation. Pursuit was the sole responsibility of the cavalry and it did that exceptionally well, together with light-armed soldiers who did not belong to the legion. Since no man was permitted to own the booty, no one who was not authorised pursued the retreating enemy; there was no confusion in the army, and every Consul who triumphed brought back substantial wealth and 'the Roman state grew rich'.

Camp selection: The Roman generals paid great attention to the health and supply aspects in choosing a camp site during preparations for war. As in the other treatises on 'art of war', the Romans had also made certain that the place chosen for encampment was healthy, the terrain was suitable and it was at a location where the enemy could not cut off any approach road leading to water and access to the supply magazines. By looking at the pallor of the inhabitants, it was possible to determine if they were sick or healthy and hence the suitability of the place chosen. A general who was well informed of the topography would see to it that the soldiers remained healthy (Machiavelli Book 6, p. 692). To prevent a possible siege it was important for the general to select a proper place of encampment with prior knowledge of the respective stations of friends and enemies.

For ensuring the health of the soldiers and proper amenities, they were to sleep under tents, camp under shade giving trees, and in a place where there was plenty of firewood to cook their food. They were never allowed to march in the heat during summer (or only before daybreak). In severe snow and ice during winter, they must have the means for fire-making and proper clothing to keep themselves warm, they were not to drink bad water, and when sick, they were to be cared for by physicians. The army was also kept healthy with daily exercises.

Machiavelli proceeded to describe the method and plan for proper and functional camp layout in some considerable detail. Inside a camp there were well laid out streets, officers' quarters, market place, the irregular pike men and velites, and artillery carefully placed in quarters separate from the non-combatants. The numerous tradesmen were assigned to specific streets. Sheep and cattle herders with their animals and wagons of supplies were assigned separate streets. The major and important streets were 60ft wide, and not to be occupied. They were the market street, front street, a middle street (North-South direction) cutting through the market street and an inner street along the irregular pike men and velites. Wide streets, open spaces, ditches to place the artillery, guard duties and strictly enforced discipline were the distinguishing features of the Roman encampment (Machiavelli Book 6, p. 686).

Foods and supplies: Provisioning and food supply was carried out by army traders of every description. Carpenters, ironsmiths, horseshoe makers, cobblers, engineers, canoneers, skilled artificers, public wagons for living and for maintaining/repairing equipment had to be accommodated on streets not less than 60 feet wide. In the temporary but quite elaborately planned township, everything an army and the soldiers would need when away from home ground were made available in the market streets and within the encampment. The descriptions of the layout of the Roman encampment are reminiscent of those found in the *Mahābhārata* and the *ArthaŚāstra* and which were emulated in the great princely armies and in Mughal times as described in *Ain-I-Akbari* (Sallami, 1939).

Food in a besieged city could be a problem. To be well prepared before a siege began was the smart thing to do to stave off starvation, particularly when the siege was likely to last long. It meant keeping the city store houses well stocked with every conceivable article. *ArthaŚāstra* and *Śukranīti* very clearly describe the stores, food and other articles of everyday use and the quantities in which the king should charge these to be stocked within a fortified city; the quantities and the intent signifying that the war preparedness catered for truly long sieges even perhaps lasting a few years. The fort cities in ancient India were prepared for sieges over many seasons during which agriculture continued and the forest produce was gathered and stored and life went on within the embattled walls. In extenuating circumstances, to deny the enemy any food, grain was burnt in the granaries and in the standing crops. There have been clever ways in which starvation of the population was brought about and deceptive ways to announce that there was plenty of food and the besieged city could outlast the enemy outside. Kautilya and Sun Tzu both expounded on it. And it was the custom also in Roman times to be equally well prepared for such eventualities. There were ways to send food under dire circumstances. If a river ran through the territory, there was a possibility of sending some food down via the water ways. There was one instance where nuts were thrown into the water which were carried by the stream to help the Romans in Cassalino which was under siege by Hannibal (Machiavelli Book 7, p. 711). The Romans also adopted methods similar to those described by Sun Tzu where a few steer, well fed on grain, were let out of the starving fort and allowed to be captured. The enemy would inevitably catch and slaughter the animals only to find them full of grain. This told them that there was sufficient amount of the precious grain within the fort to not only feed the people but to feed the animals as well. This was supposedly meant to discourage further extension of a siege which usually succeeded by starving out the city. Food was used as a clever means of sending messages to friends out of a besieged city. Cipher messages were put in the dough and baked into bread (as in the Chinese fortune cookies) which the messengers took with them as their own food.

The essence of planning was also to ensure that the enemy did not cut off food supplies. This meant that friendly neighbours had to be cultivated who would provide food daily, which the camp official would issue in judicious quantities to each man and who must then make use of it without wasting. It was easy for an enemy to defeat an army safely and surely by causing hunger, even though it was not an honourable thing to do. There were other camp stratagems to avoid hunger, which dictated that what was given out must be used up and eaten at the same time, when the commander directed. No one was to eat except when the general did. No chance there of hoarding, or extravagant eating or going hungry as a consequence. It was a discipline very strictly enforced.

Starving out a city had been a common practice in the ancient civilisations. It was a question of endurance and of who would first feel the want and crumble, for it was not always easy even for the enemy outside to sustain his army endlessly outside the city and wait out the consequent surrender. He was running short too and friends would not perhaps continue to support him through a very long siege.

The Roman ways of provisioning during marches centered on providing flour, lard and fat. The men made this flour into bread using lard/fat and vinegar for flavouring. Machiavelli has specifically mentioned that wine and particularly baked bread were the most difficult to supply to the army. Thus each soldier's supply of rations consisted of parched grain or flour (to make his own bread to his satisfaction), lard or fat and condiments to flavour the bread and 'keep them strong', and vinegar to flavour their drinking water in lieu of wine. In addition they could be carrying cheese, fish extract (always in the legionary's diet) and maybe salted and cured or dried meat as the principal rations

(Keegan, 1993, p. 305). Included in his supplies was barley – for the horse. A large herd of all sorts of animals tagged along with each army on the march which was fine because the animals did not have to be carried and some of them would be slaughtered for fresh meat. With such light weight pack rations which they could take along, the ancient armies could march for days on end through very difficult places, experiencing no hardship for food. Their horses received barley, as did the herds of animals which followed, carrying their own grain and any other fodder (Machiavelli Book 5, p. 671).

In comparison to the armies of the past, Machiavelli believed that the modern armies i.e. in 1509 AD were degenerate. Machiavelli's comments show in no uncertain manner what he thought of the modern army and its vexing demand for baked bread and wine! Bread could not last long on a march and the army would go hungry, and if it had to be supplied continuously, great expense would be incurred. In fact, he felt very strongly about it and expressed his concern about the difficulty and cost of supplies during the Pisan war in a letter he wrote dated May 18, 1509 to the 'Commission to the Army before Pisa'. He sounded suitably aggrieved in this letter when he mentioned that 'it was the most burdensome and difficult task to keep the army supplied continuously with wine and bread and the soldiers often had to go hungry.' If he were allowed to have his way he would rather go back to the ancient Roman army practice of giving flour, etc. with which the men could make their own bread. He believed the modern army had become decadent and degenerate (Machiavelli Book 5, p. 671) and therefore, the soldiers should be brought back to the old Roman way of living, that they should 'eat no bread except what they themselves baked; and if there was no wine, the soldiers should go back to the earlier practice of flavouring their drinking water with vinegar and that they be given other provisions as in their ancient past'. On the matter of wine, he said that, 'he had no objections to the soldiers drinking it but the army and the commanders should take no specific trouble to bringing it and supplying'.

The Roman Supply Chain and Management

The army of the Roman Republic from 260 BC for more than two centuries was engaged in constant spats with neighbouring states and fought campaigns far and wide while moving large armies. They resorted to two ways to acquire food. One way was to live off the land, which every army in civilisation has resorted to, the difference being the way the Romans would estimate and ensure that the land they passed through or halted in would provide the necessary amount of food for the huge numbers of men and animals for a designated period. Such estimates reconstructed by Erdkamp (1998, p. 19) provide an example of how much food could be extracted from a place with limited population. Another way was to create supply bases and stock them in advance of the marching army.

(a) **Live off the land, Roman style:** In a small area measuring 800 square kilometers and sparsely populated with some 8000 people, according to the times, enough food could be produced in the season to feed the village for one year. It meant that from stocks in that village 8000 people × 12 months equalling 96,000 (or rounded off to 100,000) could be fed definitely until the next harvest, barring of course unpredictable circumstances such as agricultural and weather problems that might come in the way. This quantity of food meant to last for one year for the local population would be requisitioned by the army to feed in one month 12 times that number of men or a proportionately lesser number over two or three months presuming that the villagers would yield up and surrender the quantities commandeered. Erdkamp speculated that to obtain sufficient food quantities for about 34,000 troops for three months, the available resources (for two months) were supplemented by plundering. As for occupying the land and spreading the men around, it seemed to work out at 20 persons per square kilometer. So an even distribution of 20 men and their animals in one square kilometer would be a nice spacious occupation of the land to find food, feed and fodder for the army. One does not know the fate of the local inhabitants who would have had to yield their entire food supplies for the year to the encamped soldiers and further suffer the plundering.

(b) **Establishment of supply bases, magazines:** Another way of provisioning was to transport the food and the feed and organize supply bases within the Roman Republic and in allied land. The supply magazines were established in quickly erected fortifications in a location that could be easily defended. These magazines were meant to be granaries and store houses, provide shelter to the troops and their animals and were also usually accessed by roads, rivers and ports (Erdkamp, 1998, p. 47). The purpose of the magazines would have been twofold – to serve as winter quarters and to provide during field operations in the endless wars that were waged in Italy. Detachments of troops were located all along the supply routes. Roman towns served as bases wherever possible and, at other times, towns under the allies were relied upon.

Transportation of supplies was by road, by sea or inland rivers. Goods were laden on pack animals, horse drawn and ox drawn carts, and on the shoulders of out-of-work agricultural labourers. Pack animals carried the bulk of supplies to the magazines while the carts and wagons moved heavy war materials and siege equipment to and from magazines. The wagon trains able to carry loads of 900 kg were meant to follow the troops even in rough terrain (Erdkamp, 1998, p. 74). The pack animals and the wagon trains by their very nature were not swift and therefore could not cover long distances in one day. The oxen were slow movers too and could cover some 25 km while the mules could go for 70 to 80 km (an average of 40 km when on continuous duty). Considering the few round trips the mule-drawn wagons and the pack animals could make between the magazines, taking time off to graze, a vast number of animals were needed. For an army of 40,000 men and 4000 horses, and army train of 3500 pack animals, the shuttle transport between the forward army and a magazine located 100 km away, one estimate showed that 3000 to 4000 mules would have been required (Erdkamp, 1998, p. 73).

And the question then arises: 'how many days supplies could they carry'? At the rate of the army's requirement of 1680 tons a month, it would require 40,000 mules accompanying the main body, an impossible number. They would consume most of the feed they carried and eat more than the tonnage needed for a month! To cut the number of mules to 3000 would mean taking only five days' supplies. If more food had to be taken for a longer period, of 10 days perhaps, the soldiers and the servants themselves had to carry part of their own rations. But even so, it meant that, transporting at the rate of five kg barley per day for one horse and two kg for a mule (with perhaps no opportunity to obtain supplies of green fodder) most of the carrying capacity would have had to be devoted to animal feed! (Erdkamp, 1998, p. 75). Therefore, the Roman armies found it imperative for the men to carry their own rations for longer periods in order to take food for longer stretches of operations.

Scholars differ on the matter of how many days' rations were issued to the men at a time. Some have quoted sources where it was found to be 17 days (in some campaigns in Gaul) and others believed the issue was made every 20 days and yet other scholars mention 15 days and 30 days.

But what certainly seems to have been done was for the soldiers, not the light troops, to take along rations for a definite number of days to guarantee regular food. A soldier's gear on his shoulder is estimated to have been 50 kg (food, vessels and weaponry combined).

The carrying capacity of ships was also an important consideration. When the stores were sent by sea, a large number of coastal ships were needed as well as conducive sailing conditions. Here again a *guestimate* by Erdkamp throws light on the volumes and tonnage involved. Taking again the example of an army of 40,000 consisting of 8000 non-combatants and 4000 horses and 3500 mules. These would consume 1050 tons of wheat and 810 tons of barley (plus green fodder for the animals) per month. Wine, at perhaps 250 ml per day, would amount to 3000 hectoliters per month and olive oil at 50 ml per day would be 600 hectoliters per month.

In the times of the middle Republic, large ships able to carry huge quantities were to be found only in small numbers. More often than not there were small ships of 350 ton capacity, or even less, of 100 to 200 tons. To load all of 1850 tons of the grain, and the 15,000 amphorae (each of 20–30 liter capacity) for wine and oil, 20 to 25 ships of average size would have had to be found. And after that there would arise the real task of requisitioning so many ships at one time on a regular basis to make frequent trips over a period and a distance as well as finding adequate number of civilians to unload the weighty cargo. It is also not known whether the state owned the fleets of sea going cargo vessels or whether they were contracted from businesses or used captured ones (Erdkamp, 1998 pp. 59–60).

River boats found everywhere were plentiful but not as many in the Mediterranean region (where there were fewer navigable rivers) as in France, Holland and England. But where the rivers proved to be very useful was in the internal trans-shipment of goods brought in by sea. Armies of Caesar and Marius had benefited by this method. River navigation by sailing and towing or rowboats brought the water crafts to the ports. It is in this connection that we come across the mention of rations for the prisoners who were taken to row the boats and for the galley slaves who rowed the sea going ships, both types being very hard work.

Endnotes

1. Since the *Śukranītisāra* is said to predate Kautilya, who belonged to Chandragupta Maurya's time, and we learn from other sources that gun powder was invented by the Chinese in the thirteenth century AD and brought to India by Babur who invaded and attacked with guns and cannon, the term guns in Śukra's writing may allude to some other form of firing weapon device. While on the subject of gun powder it would only need a small digression to point to another interpretational study of weapons, army organization, etc. in the ancient Hindu tradition which is very illuminating (Oppert, 1967). Oppert referred to two ancient works in Sanskrit – the *Nītiprakāsa* or *Nītiprakāsika* of Vysampāyana and the *Śukranīti* of Usanas or Śukrāchārya. The *Nītiprakāsa*, an extract from a larger work devoted to Nitisara is ascribed to Vysampāyana to whom is also ascribed the *Yajurveda* (which also embodies Dhanurveda). The existence of gun powder was inferred thus. The war machines of ancient Hindus were made of metal or stone out of which iron and lead balls were hurled at enemies.

   The application of smoke balls or *nalika* were really made of gun powder and *Dhūmagulika* was explained by *Ćurnagola* or powder ball. Oppert observed (1967, p. 44) that though the invention of gun powder is ascribed to different persons belonging to different countries and since the correct authorship and antiquity is debated, he would go ahead to prove that the oldest documents giving descriptions of gun powder and its application to the discharge of missiles are written in Sanskrit and found in India. In his opinion, no Chinese work in respect of antiquity can be compared to Śukranīti and even if the parallel Chinese claim of being the first to discover gun powder were to be true, it could not have been anterior to the invention in India. Evidence seems to be available for India to claim the first invention of gun powder long before the thirteenth century AD Chinese discovery.

2. Barley on the other hand seems to have been the main food crop – as we learn from *Atharva Veda* (AV. I, Book 7, Griffith, 1896, p. 142). Water is another important consideration: water for the elephants, for want of which the animals get distressed and deprived of drinking water in the scorching heat they go blind. Therefore marching with elephants is best when one sees rain clouds and in the rainy season. Other seasons are good for horses and for a military expedition – the proper season is when it is neither too hot, nor too cold, nor rainy, nor dry or when the Earth is covered with corn.
3. The repeated emphasis on corn by Kāmandaka as opposed to Kautilya's usage of the term rice makes an interesting digression on the staple grain of that period. As mentioned earlier, *Kāmandakīya Nītisāra* is supposed to have been taken away by Hindus and practiced in the Island of Java, and when it was overrun by Buddhism, the people with the original texts moved to Bali (Ganapati Sastri, 1912: Synopsis). The *Nītisāra* is believed to have been preserved in its full original text, but all this does not explain the reference to corn as the staple grain of that period.

References

Clavell, James. *The Art of War: Sun Tzu*. Hodder Mobus, Noida, Delhi, 2005.

Cotterell, Arthur. *The First Emperor of China (The greatest tomb find of our time),* Macmillan, London, 1981.

Dikshitar, V. Ramachandra. *War in Ancient India*, Macmillan & Co. Ltd., Madras, 1944.

Erdkamp, Paul. *Hunger and the Sword: Warfare and Food Supply in Roman Republican wars (BC264–320)* J.C. Gieben Publishers, Amsterdam, 1998, pp. 10–80 and Chapter 3: Magazines and Transport.

Ganapati Sastri, T. (Ed). *Kāmandakīya Nītisāra*. Commentator Sankararya. (English translatior-Anon). (Original Sanskrit version by Rajeshwar Sastri: 1886). Trivandrum Sanskrit Series number 14. Trivandrum 1912 Kā: Synopsis and Books 4, 5, 15, 19.

Gilbert, Allan. *Niccolo Machiavelli: The Chief Works and Others*. Vol 2. Chapter: The Art of War. (Translated). Duke University Press, Durham, North Carolina, 1965. Books 1,2,5,6,7 (pp. 561–727).

Giles, Lionel. *Sun Tzu: On the Art of War* (translated from Chinese, with note) Heian International Inc. Torrance, CA. American Edition 1999. pp. Introduction p. i–xLii and chapters 1, 2, 6, 7, 8, 9, 10, 11, 13.

Graham J.J. *On War: Carl Von Clausewitz*. (Translated) Keegan Paul, Trend Trubner & Co. London 1908.

Griffith, Samuel B. *Sun Tzu, The Art of War* (Translated) Oxford University Press. 1963. pp. 30–150.

Griffith, T.H. *Atharva Veda*. Volumes I & II Translated, with commentary. E.J. Lazarus & Co. 1896. I, Book 7: 59,142.

Jomini, Baron Antoine Henri. *The Art of War*, Greenhill Books, London, 1996.

Kangle, R.P. *Kautilya ArthaŚāstra*. 2nd ed. University of Bombay. Motilal Benarasi Dass 1972. AS: Books 2, 4, 5, 8, 9, 10, 14.

Keegan, John and Homes, Richard. *A History of Men in Battle*. Elisabeth Sifton Books, Viking Penguin Inc, New York 1985.

MacMullen, Ramsay. *Corruption and Decline of Rome*. Yale University Press, New Haven and London 1988. pp. 140–215.

Matthijis Jolles, O.J. *On War, Carl Von Clausewitz*. Infantry Journal Press, Washington DC, 1950.

McKinley, Albert E., Howland, Arthur C. & Dann, Mathew L. *World History*. Volume 1. Atlantic Publishers & Distributors, New Delhi, 1994, pp. 8–12.

Oppert, Gustav. *Weapons, Army Organization and Political Maxims of the Ancient Hindus* (with special reference to gunpowder and fire arms). First Published 1880. The New Order Book House, Ahmedabad, 1967, pp. 4–108.

Rapoport, Anatole. (Ed) *On War, Baron Von Clausewitz*. Penguin Books, London, 1967.

Rice, Lewis. *The Amarakosha of AmaraSimha*. 4th Ed. Asian Educational Services, New Delhi, Madras, 1988.

Richi, Pierre. *Daily Life in the World of Charlemagne*. (Paris, Libraire Hachette, 1973) Translated and copyright 1978 by JO Ann McNamara. University of Pennsylvania Press.

Sallami Abu l-Fazl Gallami. *Ain-I-Akbari*. Translation. Royal Asiatic Society of Bengal, Calcutta, 1939.

Sarkar, Benoy Kumar. *Śukranīti – The Sacred Book of the Hindus*. The Panini Office, Bhuvaneshari Asram, Allahabad, 1914. Chapter 4: Sections 5, 6, 7.

Sensharma, P. (Major, retd) *Kurukshetra War: A Military Study*. Dhiren Roy Darbari Udyog. Ganganagar, 24 Parganas, 1975.

Shamasastry, R. *The ArthaŚāstra of Chanakya* Books I–IV. Mysore Review, Mysore 1906–1908.

Shamasastry, R. *The ArthaŚāstra of Kautilya*, Books V–XV. Bombay British India Presss, 1910, Book 14.

Shamasastry, R. *Chanakya's ArthaŚāstra – The Science of Polity*. Chapter XXX. Mysore Review, Mysore, 1906–1908.

4

Vedic and Epic Wars

The Vedas on Wars

Several references to wars, their conduct and the techniques employed in them may be found in the Vedas and the Purānās. L.M. Singhvi, in his foreword to one English translation of the *Ṛg Veda* (Satya Prakash and Vidyalankar, 1980), said that in the Vedic vision of human society, men were not seen to be aggressive, oppressive or predatory in nature, but rather they were under an obligation to protect and preserve and to aid and comfort mankind everywhere. A Ṛg Vedic hymn talks about togetherness which shines down on a fractured and fragmented world out of whose womb the new world order is struggling to be born (Ṛg 6.75.14 and Ṛg 10.101.2). But it is noteworthy though, to find how persistently, sonorously and prayerfully the Ṛg Vedic Samhita calls upon the cosmic forces to accept the sacrifices being offered and ensure that enemies are subdued in war.

The gods are described as being well equipped for war with transport, weapons, armour and the strength and intent to slay the enemy. The heavenly architects and technicians – *Rbhu, Vibhu* and *Vaja* were associated with roadways, airways and waterways respectively (Ṛg 40.4.33, 9.34.1). *Rbhu* (a word derived from Uru) was associated with Indra, i.e. with mid space (both airways and spacecraft). *Vaja* was the artificer of the gods, looking after them as well as the roadways and chariots. *Vibhu* (from *Vaibhava* meaning rich and powerful) was associated with Varuna or the oceans i.e. waterways and ships. The missiles in battles were *Uparatati* meaning stone, glittering lances, bows and arrows. They were mounted on brilliant, strong wheeled chariots drawn by strong horses and rode on clouds and rain-bearing winds. When they burst forth in all their glory and luster on the islands, they agitated both heaven and Earth, and caused the waters to rise and tremble with their approach (Ṛg 9.8.1–40).

These readings lead us to suppose and then accept that though the Vedas, whose knowledge was not intended for a particular race or a country, and which believed that man was on Earth to protect, nevertheless had realistically portrayed the necessity for preparedness for war with weapons and transport, should there be any.

Also, the Vedas gave thought to what might happen in wars and recommended that several sacrifices be made and prayers and incantations be chanted to guide the human species through troublesome times of war and uncertain peace.

Myths and Legends of Celestial and *Asura* Wars

In *Vishnupurānam* 4.4, (Dutt, 1894, pp. 258–259) Parāsara narrates the story of Khatwānga also called Dilipa (son of Viswāsaha and grandson of Ilavile). Khatwānga was invited by the gods to join them in a terrible war against the *Asuras* and successfully destroyed a number of them. For performing this act he earned a boon from the celestials. The seven celestial *rishis* (sages) blessed that he would be such a king that no one would ever equal him on Earth. Thereupon, he came from heaven, dwelt an hour and became united with the three worlds by means of his liberality and knowledge of truth. King Dasaratha, father of Sri Rāma, was a descendent of Khatwānga. The glorious god from whose navel the lotus springs was born for the protection of the world as the four sons of Dasaratha (Rāma, Lakshmana, Bharata and *Shatrughna*). From their life story springs the epic Rāmāyana.

Another tale of terrible combat that involved Soma, (son of Atri who was the son of Brahma, the Creator of the Universe) and Vrihaspati assisted by Rudra, a pupil of Vrihaspati's father Angiras. There was enmity due to the licentiousness and haughty behavior of Soma who stole Tāra, wife of Vrihaspati, the preceptor of gods. In this combat, all the Daityās and Dānavas and other enemies of the celestials joined Soma while Indra and all others assisted Vrihaspati. Rudra and the *asuras* hurled weapons at each other and the gods were becoming overwhelmed with the ferocity of the fight. This was a cataclysmic war between gods and demons, so the Universe sought protection from Brahma and begged him to intervene. The latter then called a halt to this war. It was this same Soma who had celebrated the *Rājasūya* sacrifice and derived much glory because of it. All these successes were enough to alter his behaviour, make him arrogant and unmindful of any other consideration. This combat is rightly known as Tārakamāya or Tāraka war.

If such were the earliest wars mentioned in our Purānās, the warring gods and the celestials who resided in the heavens and the *asuras* of the nether world seemed to require no support to conduct the war. Neither did they need any sustenance in any form like we do on this Earth. The celestials did not need to wait for the right moment to begin a war or even to choose a territory more advantageous to them. These were mystical creatures imagined and created by the Aryans and earthly rules did not apply to them.

The reasons for all these wars usually originated with the desire of the demons (the evil) for dominance over the celestials (the good) as the Aryans saw. Their weapons were the bows and arrows, powerful whirring wheels (*chakra*) and probably maces too. They rode in chariots amongst the clouds in the skies and vanished as quickly as they appeared after hurling their weapons. Their art of war was simple, straight but magical. Incantations for the destruction of a hostile army and prayers for aid and victory in battle abound in the Atharva Veda (AV. XL. 9–10; XVI. 7–8; XIX.13 and 28, Griffith, 1896). One hymn (AV. XL. 9) carries some blood curdling words, calling on the vultures, ravens, kites and crows and every carrion bird to feast on foes if even one on other side has suffered any injury. Another verse (AV. XL. 10) incants to let each greedy beast of prey, and fly and worm regale itself upon the human corpse if even one of the opposition is pierced!

There is a prayer for protection from arrows (AV. I. 19), for punishment of enemies (AV. I. 23), a counter charm against the incantations of an enemy (AV V 31), a charm for destruction and plunder of enemies (AV. VI. 66 and 67), to remove the enemy (AV, VI. 75), a charm calling for banishment beyond mankind, even a prayer to strengthen a war horse (AV VI. 96) and of course a charm to ensure victory in battle (AV. VII. 85). A particularly harsh hymn (AV. VI. 66) has many verses raining down what appears to be curses and awful threats on the enemy. When translated, it reads as:

- Handless be every foeman who comes to fight against us.
- Dash them together with great slaughter, O Indra! and let their robber chief run pierced with arrows and having wished all sorts of amputations on the enemy,
- Let us part among ourselves, in hundreds, Indra! All their wealth.

This indeed is staking claim to the plunder and booty taken in war fought as ruthlessly as can be imagined!

Wars in any era had reasons to justify them. The pre-Vedic people were peace loving resident farmers able to grow crops, engage in trade and practice skills and crafts. The wandering pastoral Aryans who first ventured on expansion of their holdings eyed the granary stocks of the Indus people. In the Epic age, the Rāmāyana tells us the story of how Rāma, to whom valour, honor and obedience were the essence of an Aryan prince's life, was dishonored by Rāvana by stealing Sita (his consort) away. To retrieve Sita, avenge himself and reclaim his honour were the chief causes of Rāma going to war against Rāvana.

The primary cause of the Kurukshetra war was land – a dispute for land between the Kauravas and Pāndavās. Other causes according to SenSarma (1975) are said to be usurpation of kingdom, seizure of territory, carrying away cattle, arrogance, etc. Wars for political hegemony, ideological, socio-economic and other reasons would emerge in the course of the history of India and the world; each wrought its own havoc on the land and the people, their culture and traditions and their ways of life and freedom. Selecting a proper season and climate to launch a war have been important considerations but equally important were economic considerations. Sen Sarma, while discussing the battle of Kurukshetra has summarised the economic considerations of war as discussed in Chapter 3.

Invasion in the Indus Region, Food Raiding and Food Management

The excavated town of Mohenjodaro (referred to as Duryona in the *Ṛg Veda*) was a town fortified and reputed to have had great granaries. The Aryans wandered into or purposefully sought the land of the Indus people (known as *Dāsa* or *Dāsya* or *Dāsyu*) eyeing their stocks of food. The Indus people belonged to a thriving civilisation which practiced farming, animal husbandary, mining and many skills and crafts. The river Sarasvati, called *Vajnivati*, meaning possessed of food, made its banks fertile and lush with vegetation and grain crops. Thus there was always plenty of grain, standing crops and animal wealth consisting of cattle and horses. The town of Mohenjodaro had as its Chief, one Sushna whose name suggests an individual who seemed to have exploited the people and collected taxes in the form of farm produce and acquired great wealth and power.

The Indus people, *Dāsyas*, had great wealth, extensive overseas trading and a great number of fortified towns. The Aryans captured all these after killing them. The *Ṛg Veda* is replete with *richas* referring to the *Dāsyas* as the aborigines of India – having great hoards of wealth, which was coveted by the Aryans who constantly and severally invoked the gods for obtaining bounteous gifts, great wealth, food, cows and the rest.

There exist many references, at least 13 *Richas* in *Ṛg Veda*, about the wars waged for food, as summed up in the Melkote Documents (2004, pp. 219–224). It was easy to capture the corn crops (corn here probably meant barley) in the fields and chase the farm animals with lighted torches. In one such battle of invasion between the Aryan Angiras with Kutsa in the lead and the Dasyu Sushna, the latter was felled and killed and the great stocks of food in the enemy land were captured. Kutsa is referred to as a '*kavi*' or a poet, probably a composer of *Richas* as well as a warrior. All the early pioneering Aryans were composers and fighters, i.e. before the emergence of the class (Varna) system. They regularly attacked the Indus people. Harappa (Hariyapiya in Ṛg Veda) was attacked for food and a great granary was found here. Kutsa is also referred to as 'Dashoni' the owner of ten towns. Owning ten towns with granaries and other possessions was wealth indeed and therefore it bestowed very high position to the owner.

An important Ṛg Vedic *Richa* (3.30.22) is about the war for food and has been repeated at least ten times in various forms in other *Richas*. This invokes Indra in praise and in prayer to help gather the fruits of the battles for food. Since it was the Aryans who composed the *Richas*, they described the struggles of their fore fathers who lived centuries before them and of the events that happened in a far away time. The struggles occurred between the Asuras who possessed wealth and the Aryans who were called the *Suras*. *Sura* also means bright and white as the Sun, meaning white and fair complexioned, and the native Indus *Dāsyas* who were dark or black complexioned were called Asura (the opposite of Sura). This justification of nomenclature is provided by one of the authors in the Melkote Documents. This explanation seems plausible, when we observe how conscious the majority of the Indian populace is on one's skin complexion and which is also one of the causes of the north-south divide based on the Hindi words *gorā* (fair) and *kāla* (dark) and the obsession of the majority with fair skin colour.

Wars and Confrontations in the Rāmāyana

Rāmāyana, the *ādikāvya* or the first poem, was the first recorded specimen of genuine classical Sanskrit poetry, and its composition is attributed to Vālmiki. It was first recited by Sri Rāma's twin sons Lava and Kusa. It is narrated in six chronologically progressing sections known as *kāndas* viz. Bālakānda, Ayodhya *kānda*, Aranya *kānda*, Kishkindhā *kānda*, Sundara *kānda* and Yuddha *kānda* (Sastri, 1935).

Rāma, the scion of the line of *Ikshamaki* and the eldest of the four sons of King Dasaratha of Ayodhya was expounded by Narada as 'like Vishnu in valour, Kubera's equal in bounty and like another Dharma in truthfulness'. The Ayodhya princes are described in Tulasi Das's *Rāmacharitamānas* as being well-versed in the Vedas, the martial arts and the essentials of the four modes of conduct embodied in the art of governance and the art of war. They were experts at *Sama* – friendship, *Dāna* – gifts, *Danda* – punishment and *Bheda* – sowing dissension, all at which Sri Rāma demonstrated and effectively employed in various situations during the progress of the epic story (Hill, 1952). Even as a mere boy prince of less than 16 years of age, sage Viśwamitra demanded the presence of Rāma to defeat and annihilate the skilled and valorous *Rākshasas* and Māricha Subahu (Rām. Bāla *kānda*). Dasaratha offered his entire Aksauhini army and pleaded with Viśwamitra, pointing out that Rāma was but a lad who was raised in the luxury of the palace and though well trained and taught about battles, knew only the stories of wars between celestials and Yama which had been narrated by Vaśistha (Mitra, 1891 Ch. 8, Utpathi *kānda*). Viśwamitra did not relent and still preferred Rāma over Dasaratha's entire army. They had grown up on gory tales describing a mythical war where fact and fiction cannot be separated as Vaśistha explained the outcome of a ravaging war among the gods and demons. This war seemed to have been conducted with elephants, chariots and cavalry drawn in long lines, along with the traditional musical drums and conch shell calling the troops into specified battle arrays of armoured warriors and in the array of Garuda Vyūha in particular (Mitra, 1891, Ch. 32, 1–21). The goddesses watching this battle in heaven needed to see it the better and so ascended imaginary *vimānās* or aerial cars which took them up higher in the sky to a quieter region. We have at once a commingling of the celestial, the magical, the Earth bound and very human. The descriptions in the Yoga Vaśistha Rāmāyana are fiery and imaginative, taking the readers across time warps, and provide no clue as to whether Vaśistha had foreseen a future battle such as Kurukshetra with his clairvoyance and described it in its entirely to Rāma or whether Kurukshetra already had happened and its knowledge was a part of lore and legend.

In Upāsana *kānda* (Mitra, 1891, Ch. 93, p. 1199) there is emphasis on spiritual knowledge. Vaśistha instructs Rāma saying that the wise have no taste for delicious fruit, nor do they hunger after dainty food of any kind; the wise do not thirst after delicious drinks like milk, curd, butter, ghee or honey, nor do they savour the taste of sweet liquors, hot food or wines or any beverages at all. The wise one only hungers and thirsts for eternal life.

With such instructions embedded into the mind of the young prince in his early formative years, it is little wonder that throughout *Rāmāyana*, we find little to pad up our thesis on foods used by Sri Rāma in his wars against various enemies. Thus begins the Prince's induction into war, using his bows and arrows, which were the only weapons of that time to be used against Tāraka and others. He also employed the powerful '*Manavastra*' to kill some *Rākshasa* possessed of magical arts. After Rāma was banished to the forests, he was taken in a chariot and deposited in the wild to make his home with Sita and Lakshmana. Here he met the sage Bhāradwaja at the confluence of the rivers Ganga and Jamuna (Mitra, 1891, Rām. Ayodhyā *kānda*). His brother Bharata rode a long distance on horses and was accompanied by brigades of soldiers who went searching for Rāmā. Their horses were exhausted and their noise frightened the elephants in the forests. Learning of his father's demise Sri Rāmā performed oblations in the river as per tradition. Later he met the sage Atri in the forest (Mitra, 1891, Rām. Aranya *kanda*). Here the forest dwellers who were mostly Brahmins offered roots, flowers, fruits, etc. and beseeched him to protect them from the Rākshasas who destroyed their sacrifices. Against the established principle of not entering a battle without justifiable provocation, Rāmā felt it was his duty to protect the weak and the pious. Here the sage Agastya, who was well-versed in Dharma encouraged Rāmā and presented him with a bow ornamented with gold and gems to attain victory (Mitra, 1891, Rām. Aranya *kānda*). They proceeded towards Panchavati passing the river Godavari where they met a great vulture known as Jatayu, son of Syeni. This bird played an important role later in the poem. Even as the Princes and Sita lived by themselves in a peaceful manner, there were frequent confrontations with the *Rākshasas* and interference in their hermitage. These demons came from Lanka. The story of Sita being kidnapped by Rāvana, the King of Lanka, unwinds itself from here. Sri Rāmā goes to rescue Sita and along the way finds allies, sends search parties and spies to Lanka, wins over enemy dissidents and declares war on Rāvana. In all this effort, Rāmā possessed no human army and no weapons other than his own bow and magical arrows (Mitra, 1891, Rām. Yuddha *kānda*). According to Vālmiki Rāmāyana, says Rajkumar, (2004, Vol. I, pp. 81–82) the expedition to the south was an extension of the Aryan sphere of influence over the lands of Vānaras and the *Rākshasas*.

The war in Rāmāyana was fought with an army of willing monkeys and bears, *Jāmbavants* (Fig. 4.1), who were among the forest dwellers and who, unlike the tribals, could hop from tree to tree, cross riverine hurdles and live off the forest produce such as fruit, nuts, honey, insects and the rest. It is a mythical tale of war between *mānavas* – the upright, handsome entities and the hideous and horrendous *rākshasas*. One scholar has equated the former with the Aryans progressing slowly southwards from their northern territories and the latter with the native tribes who had prior claim to the forest land and resisted any attempt at subjugation and domination by the priestdom of the Aryan culture (Krishnamachariar, 1937). In a more fanciful comparison, Rāmā's brigade of monkeys is likened even to the more friendly forest tribes of the southern region – whose colour, stature and unprepossessing facial characteristics reminded some of certain forest apes (Mann and Zachariae, 1892, p. 192) in a poetical, perceptual, fanciful representation of the aboriginal. Since Rāmā marched through a large territory of native tribes and was accompanied by the monkeys, there was really no necessity for him to organise and provide for their food. And when there were forest tribes who

Fig 4.1: The fighting army of monkeys and bears in a pitched battle against the mighty army of Rāvana where the warriors were astride chariots and horses is graphically depicted in the central panel of the nineteenth century 'Rāmāyana Shield'. The shield is silver plated brass plaque and narrates scenes from Rāmāyana in several panels decoratively surrounded by flowers sacred to the Sun. It was designed by Ganga Baksh of Jaipur.

Source: Albert Hall Central Museum, Jaipur

participated in the forest wars they were quite self-sufficient, independent and looked nowhere for any largesse. They carried their own provisions and could obtain other food from the forests.

Rāmā with his monkey troops at last came to a halt at the sea shore when confronted with the mighty and roiling ocean. Confronting the ocean, *Sāgar,* who actually is believed to be an elder in the family of Rāmā's own lineage and thus his ancestor, Rāmā is told by Vibhishana that the ocean would find a way to bridge them all across the waters to Lanka even though Rāmā could easily cause it to dry up (Mann and Zachariae, 1892, p. 361). So they waited by the ocean for three nights. In *Narasimha purāna* (Jena, 1987, Chap LII) it is mentioned that the ocean felt terrified of Sri Rāmā who waited with flaming missiles of Agni. Here the legend says that the ocean at first did not manifest even after three nights, making the divine Rāmā wait in anticipation of having a path opened in the ocean for them all to cross. Rāmā was so enraged as to be provoked to cause the drying up of the ocean by hitting it with missiles emitting flames of fire! Thereupon the ocean manifested himself seeking Rāmā's pardon for causing the delay. Rāmā mollified, ordered the ocean to build a bridge.

How Nala's and Nila's (two monkey brothers) engineering skills (gifted by a seer long ago) crafted the land bridge with the ocean's help between the edge of the forest on the seacoast on one side and Lanka on the other is another legend, glorified by narrations of '*Sethu Bandhan*'. The stones that were used, which normally should have sunk by their own weight actually floated like boats – by the power of Sri Rāmā. The bridge was now firm and strong and the army marched on it (Hill, 1952, p. 368). All the creatures of the sea came up to see the Lord – crocodiles, alligators, fish, serpents and other creatures with enormous bodies 300 leagues in length. It is said that the throng of monkeys was so great that some literally flew through the air; others mounted on the sea creatures to cross over. Then on the far side of the ocean, the legend continues, Rāmā pitched his camp and then commanded his troops to go and eat. The bears and monkeys went every way to find fruit bearing trees. And such was the power of the Lord that regardless of the season all the trees bore luscious fruit and so the troops climbed every tree and ate its fruit to their full satisfaction. They also shook and hurled the trees at the roving demons; biting off their noses and ears and sent them screeching. It was indeed a magical army and a divine way to wage a war.

Rāmā's art of war: The principle elements of the art of war – which are to be found in the treatises on the subject (*Śukra, Kautilya, Kāmandaka*) seem to have been the guiding principles applied during Rāmā's progression through the forests in search of Sita after her abduction. Rāmā is known to have taken sides in a feud between Sugriva and his brother Vāli, and used guile and trick to kill Vāli, (Sastri, 1935, p. 58). He (Rāma) made allies with Sugriva after causing dissension. He also met Vibhishana, the pious and righteous brother of Rāvana and befriended him. Mārut was sent as a spy to discover the whereabouts of Sita in Lanka. He marched long distances and camped on the coast until the ocean bowed and after crossing to Lanka he laid siege to the city and went into fierce battle according to Narasimha *purāna* (Jena, 1987).

Rāvanā's army: While clubs and maces were the weapons used by Rāmā's army and archery his own chief weapon, Rāvana possessed a conventional army – not of monkeys but of humans; the commanders rode in chariots and fought with bows and arrows and maces. Ten thousand elephants, 10,000 chariots, 20,000 horse men and one crore *Rākshasas* was the strength with which Rāvana joined battle with Rāma and his monkeys as quoted by Thapliyal (2002) from the Yuddha *kānda* (37.176, 93.33–33 and 95.27–28).

So how could these many fighting men and their commanders, the thousands of animals and their keepers be fed and kept supplied with food, any sort of food, is a question that has found no direct answers. Fortunately though, Rāvanā's army did not have to travel very far, it did not have to fight on difficult terrain or alien territory and did not march, and the climate was supposedly not hostile. These factors lead us to presume that the services in the encampments (if not the palaces) in Lanka catered to Rāvana and his senior commanders and that the women folk kept themselves busy with cooking for their men in the field in the same manner and made similar foods as might have been in daily use in the southern lands.

There was no dearth of any kind of food in Lanka. Hanuman himself discovered a great variety of meats and other foods in Rāvāna's palaces when he went in search of Sita (Rām. Sundara *kānda*). Cooked meats from deer, buffaloes, peacocks, peahens, fouls and pigs; salted and curd soaked, dried and processed meats of a special bird known in Sanskrit as *vārdhranasa* (cited in Vishnu Dharma); meats of porcupines; cooked meats of *krakara* birds, *chakoras*, goats and fishes, different types of herbal *lehyas* or *Choornas*, beverages and liquors and also marinated acidic food preparations known as *ragashadaba* indicated in Soopa Śāstra. But as given in the book '*Pradeepa*', *ragashadaba* is a mixed preparation of sugar, honey, grapes and pomegranate (*raga*) and *shadaba* is the distilled liquid of *raga* (Alasingacharya, 1919, Vol 6 pp. 62–64).

At the end of the fearful slaughter and defeat of Rāvana, and after Sita was subjected to purification through a fire ceremony, Rāmā, Sita, Lakshmana, and Mārut (Hanuman) returned to Ayodhya, emplaning in '*Pushpaka*' – the aerial vehicle or *Vimāna* that belonged to Rāvana. This *Pushpaka Vimāna* must have been magical and huge. It could accommodate the entire surviving army of Rāmā as well; and if it had a pilot no specific reference can be found in the Vālmiki *Rāmāyana* (Sastri, 1935). The chronology of *Rāmāyana* poses certain difficulties. Sri Rāmā is believed to have been born in the *Treta Yuga* or as some believe, 7000 years ago. From all scientific evidence, the agricultural man is dated to around 10,000 years ago, the domestication of cereals and even animals followed in the next few thousand years, after which the wandering tribes of the world established civilisations as we know them. The invention of the wheel 5000 years ago in Sumeria and that of the Cuneiform script followed. The Indus Valley civilisation flourished from 3200 BC to 2000 BC and beyond. The war methods of the pre Vedic Indus people and those of the Tamils in the southern regions of India have been discussed briefly. The wandering Aryan tribes invaded India and are supposed to have come to the Indus region and wiped out the Indus valley civilisation by about 1800 BC. From the available Sanskrit literature reviewed by Krishnamachariar (1937), the *Purānas* and from other works we learn that there were many kingdoms, ruled by dynasties all over the country. Where there are kingdoms, there are wars, and the Indian treatises of polity and war and particularly the Kautilya *ArthaŚāstra* were believed to have been produced in the Mauryan period, 320 BC. The Aryan Prince Rāmā, as per legend, is believed to have been born 7000 years ago in Ayodhya, a recognised geographical region and an established kingdom, but it is an established fact that the Aryans came to India several thousand years later and brought the Vedas with them. The basis of all learning in Rāmā's time must have come from oral teachings of the sages who were disciples of other sages because the Vedas had not yet appeared unless they came from one of the previous Vyāsa. Even for this to happen, they would have had to be in existence at the same time as Sri Rāmā. As a Kshatriya prince he became adept in the many forms of martial arts, the art of governance and the essence of Dharma befitting a future monarch. He was learned in the Vedic principles of the conduct of life, in the principles of war as propounded by Śukrā, Kautilya and Kāmandaka which were written in another millennium or even later than the Aryans' advent; these tactics were employed by Rāmā during his forest tenure and the war with Rāvana. The *Vymānika Śāstra* of Bhāradwaja is said to have been written sometime in the *Dwāpara Yuga*. The mention of the aerial vehicle, the *Pushpaka Vimāna* to fly back to Ayodhya in the *Treta Yuga* is another instance of a time-warp state. But one may also argue that the science and art of building the aerial vehicles was known but happened to be written down in the *Dwāpara age*.

It is therefore rather difficult to reconcile all the many accepted-on-faith but anachronistic facts associated with Rāmāyana and assign a definite period for its occurrence.

Kurukshetra, the Great Indian War

Mahabharata tale is based on, and is supported by, the active life of the soldier belonging to the Kshatriya class whose principle duty was to protect the order of society by enforcing the caste structure (Minor, 1982, in introduction). The tale is a significant departure from the earlier Vedic literature which surrounds the sacrificial alter ceremonies and Vedic instructions. It focuses rather on the royal courts and battlefields. And though Lord Krishna, the Gita and tales of valour, honour and duty make their appearances there is no continuity to suggest that they were all linked. The author, Robert N. Minor, believed that, 'the majority of Mahābhārata is an epic tale, a series of narratives and a collection of legends, fables and stories. Gita on the other hand is strikingly different and its teaching as a whole is not completely consistent with the non-didactic portions'. Krishna referred to as a Lord of Lords in the Gita, is forgotten as one in the rest of the Mahābhārata and remains a hero, a prince but not the highest of the gods, though now and then admitted to have descended from God Vishnu.

Nonetheless, here we have human faces, characteristics and qualities that are at war with each other, exhibiting *dharma* along with human compulsions, weaknesses and jealousies. The human armies with their strengths and capabilities use materials and equipment made on the Earth and there are no magical or celestial interventions to win a war to reclaim lost possessions and kingdom.

As has been stated elsewhere in this book, the armies of the epic age had nine types of formations, the *patti* being the smallest unit of ten (1 chariot, 1 elephant, 3 horse and 5 foot soldiers) and the *Aksauhini* the biggest (a total number of 2,18,700). The Kauravas marched with eleven *Aksauhinis* and the Pāndavas with seven *Aksauhinis* (Thapliyal, 2002). The Pāndava army on the march was accompanied by carts, transport cars, all kinds of vehicles, the royal treasury, weapons, other mechanical devices and implements, physicians and surgeons, the invalid, the weak and the powerless. The traditional army of four divisions – the *catarunga* proceeded as an irregular body amidst war music, beating of drums, the boom of conch shells and the war crier. In the vanguard rode Bhima and other knights and kings dressed in their armour, followed by Phabhadrakas and the Pānchalas. The King, who rode in the centre, was surrounded by various carts, wagons filled with stores, provision, tents, treasure chests, arms and machines. Behind the King came the main army headed by their princely knights and commanders. (Rajkumar, 2004,Vol. I, p. 85). Similarly, the Kauravas marched well equipped, with countless tents spread over 5 *Yojanas*. The pavilions were stocked with provisions for the several thousand soldiers and the numerous non-combatants. Not only these but the elders and the allies made up a considerable contingent by themselves. There were all sorts of medicines and equipment for the doctors to treat the sick and the wounded. It seems that plenty of food, fodder, water, chaff and firewood were carried. Honey, ghee, pounded lac were important constituents of the stores. In the camp were bards, poets, priests, panegyrists, vendors, women of rank and prostitutes. Both Dikshitar (1944) and Rajkumar (2004) have quoted liberally from *Mahabharata's Udyoga Parva* chapters 151 and 152.

War materials: The requirements for materials in war are plenty – food to sustain the warriors and the troops and the thousands of non-combatants, and materials to replenish the lost and broken weapons, to repair the damages to weapons and chariots. There must have been quite substantial food arrangements since Chanakya had specified that foodstuffs and provisions be carried in double the quantity of what may be required for any emergency (Shamsastry: AS. 10.2). Duryodhana's army therefore went furnished with all requirements needed for a large force comprising eleven Aksauhinis. In a list of war supplies, described by Dikshitar are included materials for repair of chariots, tiger skins to cover the chariots, spare spears and blades, sticks, spare quivers, different kinds of ropes, oil cloth, sand, inflammable materials, skins of leopards, oil, molasses, ghee, water, syringes and pots of poisonous snakes.

A division of the army commissariat has been mentioned (Dikshitar, 1944). In the epics, the duties of the commissariat, which had a particularly important role during the marches, lay chiefly in supplying clothes and arms and taking care of the wounded men and animals. It was the commissariat's responsibility to co-operate with the management and to see to the conduct at the huge bullock transport trains which carried foot soldiers, war supplies and fodder for the cattle. The commissariat also oversaw the functioning of the grooms for the horses, mechanics and forgers and their smithy works and carried along the physicians and the astrologers. The gongs and drums – instruments for heralding and announcements in war and state occasions were also carried by the commissariat.

The Kurukshetra war lasted just 18 days, starting on the new moon day of *Agrahayana*, which fell in the period November-December. On the eve of the war, the Pāndavas left Matsya and started for Kurukshetra (Sen Sarma, 1975, pp. 89–90) and Yudhishthira selected a flat, cool, grassy land which provided plenty of firewood – to camp his army. Plenty of water was available from the clear streaming river Hiranbati. Thousands of tents were pitched and trenches dug. In each tent plenty of food, water, weapons, resin powder, grass husk and honey were stored. Apparently, the tents of the five Pāndavas and their allies were similar in all respects. And promptly all the administrative establishments and ancillaries were set up (Udyog Parva, Ch. 150). The Kauravas too arrived, scouted for the most appropriate locale to camp and ensured that they were well shielded from the enemy. It is said that even though both the antagonists were deployed on flat and even ground, they were very well aware of hills and forests around them and the art of fortification. Fortification has been described in a very detailed manner in the *ArthaŚāstra* which included the encampment, formations, field preparations and battle arrays of the Kurukshetra war. Sen Sarma (1975) provides details of the battle arrays. While discussing the disposition of various establishments and the placement of personnel in the work tents, he says that the royal kitchens, store houses and the elephants' stables were located on the south-eastern side of the camp.

The vast Kaurava army was distributed throughout the hills and forests of Pānchala, Kurujangala, Marupradesha, Ahichchetra, Kalalkuta, Varana, Vatadhana as well as on the banks of the rivers Ganga and Jamuna. The commanders of this army built lines of communication and tracks for carrying food and other essentials from the camping area to the front lines which were well protected from enemy interference and attack (Sen Sarma from Mhb. Udyoga Parva, Ch. 151).

Face to face battle between opponents riding on chariots or horses ensued. Stone carvings depicting such a battle scene can be found in old temples as shown in Fig. 4.2.

Fig. 4.2: Stone carvings from Hoysala period, Somnathpur Temple, 800–900 years old, near Mysore. Arrows are flying in a close formation battle scene between chariot warriors, backed by foot soldiers.

Battle arrays: The various battle formations or *Vyūhas* employed in the *Mahābhārata* were of several types, arranging the chariots, elephants, horsemen and footsoldiers and the positions of the various kings and commanders riding on chariots. Graphic drawings of the various *Vyūhas* and Vedic battle arrays provided by Thapliyal (2002, pp. 150–155) are in three types of linear arrays and by Sen Sarma (1975, pp. 175–178) in the shapes of a mace or a weapon, birds, half-moon, fish, circular and pear shaped, etc. These *Vyūhas* were adopted on different days of the battle (Table 4.1). Sen Sarma claims that his drawings are in agreement with *Vyūha* patterns given in Dhanur Veda. There were two variations of Sarbatomukha (the second one was said to have been adopted by Bhishma on the second day of the battle), two variations of *Bajra Vyūha*, *Garura Vyūha*, two variations of *Ardhacandra Vyūha*, *Makara*, *Sakata*, *Cakrasakata*, two variations of *Kraunche*, *Syena* and Sringata and variations of ocean like *Vyūhas* – adopted by the Kauravas and the Pāndavas in the 18-day war.

Table 4.1: Names of the battle arrays or Vyūhas employed in the 18 days of the Kurukshetra war presented in the narrative and imaginary descriptive form.

Vyūha	*Description*	*Formed by*	*Employed on battle day*
1. Sarbatomukha or Maha Vyūha, (Dangerous)	face like or circle like	Bhishma Salya and Dronacharya	day 9 18-day day 2
Bajra	mace like	Krishna/Arjuna/ Abhimanyu	–
2. Garura	Garuda bird	Bhishma	day 3
Ardhacandra	Half-moon	Pāndava, Royal gentries	day 3, 12 and 16
3. Syena	large-winged bird	Pāndavas	day 5
4. Krauncha	a large bird – heron standing eagle-like	Pāndavas and also Bhishma	day 2 day 6
5. Ocean like	solid masses of soldiers arranged in parallel rows	Bhishma	day 8
Ocean like		Karna	day 17
Suci Vyūha	like a needle	Drona	day 14
Mandala Vyūha	circular	Bhishma	day 7
Cakra Vyūha	circle	Drona	day 13
6. Sakata	like a table, 'T' shaped	Dronacharya	day 11
Cakra, Sakala, 20 miles side, stalk 48 miles long 20 miles wide, stalk 48 mile long	7 petals/or a lotus or pitcher-shaped	Dronacharya for Kaurava Royal gentries	day 8, day14
7. Makara	Whale or crocodile like	Bhishma, Karna	day 5 day 16

Source: Sen Sarma, 1975, pp. 161–178.

Each array or *Vyūha* deployed the army elements on all four sides and cleverly mixed bow men, the infantry, the cavalry (the mounted archers and lance men), the elephants and the chariots. The arrangements were meant to carry out a massed attack from up front but give protection in the rear and the sides. The formation would lead with a charge of cavalry, but to protect the flanks with the elephants, encircle and protect the standard bearer, and arrange the music bands so that the latter could effectively enthuse and signal the troops to take appropriate positions and action. The formations were so intricate and complex that it was not easy for the enemy to breach the formidable arrangement from any side except with prior knowledge. Legend says that Abhimanyu, son of Arjuna had acquired such knowledge '*in utero*' when Arjuna described *chakravyūha* – the circular formation to Draupadi. What may be taken as a battle formation with elephants aligned in a circular form can be seen in the stone carvings on a temple (Fig. 4.3).

Fig. 4.3: Stone carvings from Hoysala period, Somnathpur Temple, 800–900 years old, near Mysore. War scenes depicting elephants, chariots and horses are common features of temple carvings. This particular scene appears to represent perhaps the artist's conception of battle formation in a circular fashion – chakravyūha. A chariot warrior and foot soldier to the left and a spearman holding a shield to the right are also seen.

Pitched battles took place where elephants and men all seemed to pile up on each other and a warrior perhaps dislodged from his mount had to fight off an elephant single handedly (Fig. 4.4).

There is no mention whatsoever of what the food was and how it was made and conveyed to the soldiers in this war. But from reading of the traditional practices one may learn this aspect of the war.

Camp life in the battlefield: In a fortification protected by high ramparts and having different types of defensive installations, one finds in the Purānas that the location of the royal residences and the army barracks were to the east, the armoury and the arsenal to the west, the traders and merchants towards the southeast, the Brahmins to the north and the dancers, artists, camp followers to the south. It was a mobile township, however temporary it may have been, and life went on as usual. Since the soldiers were paid salaries and received extra allowances on the eve of an expedition, and the traders and merchants formed a part of the army on the march, it is to be assumed that brisk selling and buying of all essential goods including food stuff was carried on. The soldiers downed their weapons at night fall and the artisans and crafts men and mechanics their tools and

Fig. 4.4: A battle scene where the elephants are milling over each other and the figure of a warrior holding a mace is seen warding off or attacking an elephant. Stone carvings from Hoysala period, Somnathpur Temple, 800–900 years old, near Mysore.

implements. It was time for clean up, refreshments and entertainment – bathe in the pools and rivers as well as take the elephants and horses for drink and bathing, the grass cutters were busy throughout the day gathering green grass and fodder and the grooms of the horses attended to the feeding of the animals. The women camp followers cooked the food in their tents and either served them there or had it sent forward to where the soldiers were, if they were unable to return to the tents. It is not clear how and when the food was conveyed to the soldiers in the battle front or into the remnants of that day's battle formation (still encircled by outer protective lines). By historical accounts, the formations would disintegrate at the first sign of the falling of its commander and his standard. All those many thousands of men, elephants and horses to be fed and rested and made ready for the next day's battle engagement must have been a formidable task. To appreciate how formidable a task it might have been, we only need to learn of the huge numbers that formed the *Chakravyūha* on day 14. This formation took the form of a lotus flower; the length of the stalk was 48 miles while the diameter of thc lotus like *Chakra* was 20 miles (Dikshitar, 1944, p. 111). Within the centre, Drona organised a *Suchi* (needle) *Vyūha* – with 100,000 cavalry, 60,000 chariots, 14,000 elephants and 21,000 armoured infantry! Just imagine the massed crowd and the resulting slaughter in the near hand to hand combat.

References

Alasingaracharya, Pandit Devashikhamani Vaalmikimaharshi Praneetha. *Srimad Rāmāyanam – Sundara Kandam* (Kannada).Venkateshwara Publishers, Madras, 1919, Volume 6, pp. 62–64.

Dikshitar, V. Ramachandra, *War in Ancient India*. MacMillan and Co. Ltd., Madras, 1944, pp. 1–120.

Dutt, M.N. *Vishnupurānam or Dharmasastra*. Elysium Press, Calcutta, 1894, Part 4 Section 4.

Griffith, Ralph T.H. *Atharva Veda* (Translated, with commentary). E.J Lazarus and Co. Benaras, 1896. AV. Books I, V, VI, VII, XVI, XIX, XL.

Hill, W. and P. Douglas. *The Holy Lake of the Acts of Rama*. English Translation of Tulasi Das' Rāma charita mānas. Oxford University Press, London, 1952, pp. 1–370.

Jena, Siddheswar. *The Narasimha Puranam*. Study text with English Translation, Sloka Index. Nag Publishers, New Delhi, 1987, Chapter L II.

Kangle, R.P. *The Kautilya ArthaŚāstra* 2nd ed. Motilal Benarasidass, Bombay, 1972.

Krishnamachariar, M. *History of Classical Sanskrit Literature*. Tirumalai Tirupati Devasthanam Press, Madras, 1937.

Mann, John and Theodor Zachariae. *History of Indian Literature*. Vol. I. Keegan Paul, Trench & Trubner & Co. Ltd., Pasternaster House, London, 1892, pp. 192, 361.

Melkote Documents: Indus Civilization, ṚgVeda and Hindu Culture in '*Food Preservation in Ancient India*'. A Compilation of documents from various sources provided by Academy of Sanskrit Research, Melkote, 2004.

Minor, Robert N. *Bhagavad-Gita*. Heritage Publishers, 1982, Introduction.

Mitra, Viharilal. *The Yoga Vaśistha – Maha Rāmāyana of Vālmiki*. Translation from original Sanskrit. Banneriee and Co. Calcutta, 1891.Chapter 32, pp. 1–21, Chapter 93: p. 1199.

Rajkumar (ed). *Encyclopedia of Military Systems in India*. Vol. I. Ancient India. Commonwealth Publishers. 2004, pp. 81–85, 151.

Sastri, P.P.S. *Vālmiki Rāmāyana* (condensed) In Poet's own words. English translation. G.A. Natesan & Co. Madras, 1935.

Satya Prakash Saraswat, Swami and Satyakam Vidyalankar. *Ṛg Veda Samhita*. Vols. VIII, IX; Books 6,8,9,10,33,40. (English Translation). Veda Pratishthana, New Delhi, 1980.

Sen Sarma, P (Major). *Kurukshetra War: A Military Study*. Dhiren Roy Darbari Udjog, Ganganagar, 1975, pp. Introduction, 1–180.

Shamasastry, R. *The ArthaŚāstra of Chānakya* Books I–IV. Mysore Review 1906–1908. Books V–XV. Bombay, British India Press, 1910, AS 10.2,159.

Thapliyal, U.P. *War in Ancient India – Concepts*. Section I. In Volume X, Part 3: *Historical perspective of Warfare in India*. Some Morale and Material Determinations. S.N. Prasad (Ed). In *History of Science, Philosophy and Culture in Indian Civilization* Serie. General Editor - D.P. Chattopadhyaya. Published by Bhuvan Chandel, Distributors Motilal Benarsidass, New Delhi. 2002, pp. 43–67.

5

Rise of Armies in Ancient Times

Armies in the Fertile Crescent

The Fertile Crescent, bounded by mountains in the north and desert to the south gave birth to civilisations in Egypt and Syria, and Mesopotamia and Babylon in the Tigris and Euphrates Valley. Primitive nomadic tribes are known to have organised themselves into small groups for governance and mutual aid. When they fought, their methods depended on surprise and individual strength and bravery. The brave were considered to be champions and there were others who were followers of these champions. If one champion fell, his followers were also slaughtered or enslaved.

No military organisations existed at that time. Even in Egypt's Early Empire, around 3000 BC, there was hardly any military force except for the small militia which the kings maintained for defense against marauders. The Middle Empire of 2000 BC was engrossed in seeking knowledge and developing maritime commerce. The art of fortification was well developed, which was adequate for self protection. It also kept them isolated from outside contact.

Although the Egyptians were not known to be warlike, the Old and the Middle Empires had companies of archers, heavy infantry armed with spears and shields, and light infantry carrying smaller shields and battle axes. It was not until the New Empire in 1500 BC, in the time of the nineteenth dynasty, that there is any significant mention of a massed army or a battle.

Mercenaries were recruited from Greek immigrants with whose strength Ramses II planned to conquer Palestine, then held by the Hittites of the Anatolian civilisation. He gathered a force of 15,000 men in infantry, and horse drawn chariots but there was no cavalry. He organised pack trains for supplies and repaired the wells and tanks enroute to cross hundreds of miles of desert and land, and encamped in Kadesh. The description of his encampment depicts a rectangular fortified area well laid out with parks and posts separating the tents, which is similar to the way armies made camps throughout the history in Rome and in India. When Ramses's army went into battle, the king or the commander or the champion rode in a horse drawn chariot with a driver and an archer riding with him. The Hittites had three people riding in the chariot, the third one carrying a shield. The description of war elements from the time of Homer is no different from that in Egyptian times. A tight formation of heavy infantry walked closely behind the chariots. The light infantry of archers, slingers and skirmishers followed the heavy foot soldiers (Spaulding and Hoffman, 1994, p. 17). Sumerian sculptures depict fighting forces consisting of spear and shield bearing heavy infantry, covered in helmets for protection, forming a phalanx of the Assur, a kingdom in the Tigris Valley (Spaulding and Hoffman, 1994, p. 29). This territory, which was blessed with a conducive climate and was lush with wild game, good crops and animal herds required a strong army for its own defense from marauders and wild beasts.

The Assyrian kingdom which was an absolute monarchy lasting for 1000 years from 1500 BC to 600 BC launched many expeditions to its east and west, towards the regions of Babylon, Euphrates, Hittites and the Mediterranean. Much before this, around 2000 BC, Babylon was beginning to decline and thus became an easy target. The Assyrian King's sovereignty ruled much of Asia beyond Asia Minor. He was the military chief and led his army personally, on chariot or even walking on foot.

The army had infantry made up of the peasantry and chariots for the nobles and horsemen. A similar type of an organisation is found to have been in use during the time of the Epics in India. The charioteers and the infantry both had archers while the infantry also had spear bearing men. Whenever required, the archer from the chariot would dismount along with his shield bearer and fight side-by-side with the infantry archers and spearmen working in pairs. The cavalry which mounted the archers and later the lancers appeared later in time after the use of chariots declined. The men were however equipped more for skirmishing than for carrying out a solid massed charge.

At one time, the Assyrian strength in a coalition army was estimated to have been 77,900, comprising 3940 chariots and 1000 camels against the Sargon Dynasty. The latter had an estimated 50,000 to 100,000 fighting men plus another 50,000 auxiliaries. It was never a centralised army and each chief led his own men in his own fashion.

History tells us that it was the Median King Cyaxares of Aryan descent from Iran, which was under Assyrian rule for a long time, who first organised the Asian troops according to the arms and formed separate companies of spearmen, archers and horsemen, the bow becoming the principle weapon of combat. He attacked Assyria but had to turn back because of the Scythians – a marauding tribe of horsemen wielding sabers and coming from Southern Russia, according to Herodotus I, 103–104 (Green, 1987). For almost a century, the Scythians ran amuck in Mesopotamia, Syria and even came near Egypt, plundering and looting the country as they went but leaving no one in charge to govern the conquered lands.

The Persians organised the army with highly skilled mounted archers being the chief arm. The chariot had been sidelined by this time but in the battle of Thymbra (Spaulding and Hoffman, 1994, p. 29), Cyrus introduced a Camel Corps, camels being already employed as pack animals. The camel section led the whole army, the infantry supporting it and the cavalry following. Hugely surprised by the unexpected sight of camels, the enemy's horses baulked and their cavalry became disorganised. Taking advantage of these developments, the Persians on their mounts began a face-to-face combat with the archers and spearmen. Advance planning and strategic arrangements with neighbours and allies by Cambyses, organisation of a government at the centre and in the states and bringing the military system under the control of the central governance by Darius, building a strong garrison in each province in the kingdom along with a system of checks on civil and military affairs were major advances in military science for that time. It was Darius who mounted an expedition to the upper Indus region with a heterogeneous army. The cavalry was the main wing, the heavy infantry firing bows from behind wicker shields. Darius used land contingents from his empire and the Greeks as the maritime force.

Indus Valley and the Aryan Armies

There is little to be learned about military organisation in the Indus Valley. From archaeological excavations in the Harappa-Mohenjodaro digs, finding of male heads representing warrior types and other artifacts, a picture emerges. This shows that the Indus people had armies, had built forts, colonised the sites and had erected barracks for the fighting men and produced weapons. The principle weapon of war was the bow and arrow; its use must have been pretty well developed because archery went on to become an art form by itself in later times. However, these Indo-European people from 2000 BC up to 600 BC in the Ṛg Vedic times did not seem to have troops on a scale comparable to the Assyrians during 3000 BC to 1300 BC, who marched 100,000 men to the peripheries of their borders across Mesopotamia (Dupuy and Dupuy, 1993, p. 365). Their army consisted of archers, cavalry and spearmen. In ancient Egypt too (1200 BC), the army of Ramses was known to have employed some 20,000 men and 2500 chariots in the battle of Kadesh in what is now the central Palestine (SenSarma, 1975, Dupuy and Dupuy, 1993).

Though little is known about armies in Vedic times, there are hymns in Atharva Veda recited as chants, charms and prayers for protection against the enemy, on how to destroy enemies, about chariots in an army and prayers to aid victory in battle (Griffith, 1896, AV Books XL, XVII, XIX). The Vedic armies had two well-defined elements: the foot soldiers or *Padatee* and the chariots or the *Rathas* (SenSarma, 1975). They erected scores of forts and occupied large territories. The foot soldiers were also called the *Maruts* and were organised in units and led by commanders (Thapliyal, 2002, pp. 68–103). For war, the field formations were organised in tens and multiples of tens, according to the *Ṛg Veda*. The smallest units of tens were known as the *Dasagrah*, of hundreds as the *Satinah* and that of 1000s as the *Sahasriyasah* (Fig. 5.1).

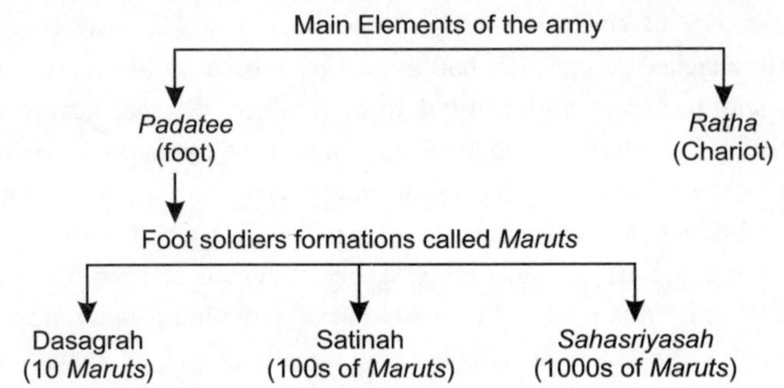

Fig. 5.1: The Indo-European Vedic army strength in Sahasriyasah

Source: Chattopdhyaya, 2002 pp. 68–103

The Ṛg Vedic Aryans occupied numerous small territories or states and were engaged in localised wars even when their armies were small. The need to define several aspects of preparing to deal with the enemies and destroy them is evident from the hymns in *Atharva Veda*. The hymns invoke Lord Indra and contain all manner of chants, charms and prayers and these also mention the chariots in an army (AV. Vol. II, XL, 9–10; XVI, 7–8, XIX, 13 and 28). While reciting hymns invoking the gods to protect against enemies (AV. Vol. I, Book V), there are also references to how to protect oneself against diseases (AV. Vol. I, Book II) and even about antidotes and prayers to counter the ill effects of poisons (AV. Vol. I, Book IV) and prayers to aid in victory in battle.

The Tamil army's formations by contrast were named differently. Their army had two elements, *Padai* and *Tanai*. These were divided into divisions or groups known severally as *ani, undai* and *otter*. The foot soldiers were formed into two ranks. The front ranks were known as *akkam, kodippadai, tar, tusi* and *nirai.* The back ranks were called *Kular* (Aiyangar, 1995, p. 39).

In the post-Vedic times, by tradition there was a four-fold division of the army – the classical *catarunga (chaturanga)*: it was formed with the infantry, cavalry, chariot and elephants (Dikshitar, 1944). The foot soldiers or the infantry were recruited from all in the social order, and even foreigners. Their numbers were considered more important than their quality. The infantry was a very important division in both the epics and the *purānas*. The hero, called the *Rathi*, fighting from the chariot (*Ratha*), was an important personage whose skill and bravery would be decisive in a battle (Rajkumar, 2004, Vol 1, p. 85).

The *sadānga* of Kurukshetra was a six-fold classification of the army which included the *catarunga* plus – the Commissariat (5th division) and the Admiralty (6th division). In other places, even an eight-fold division has been mentioned (Table 5.1) which included the four in *catarunga*, plus the Commissariat or the *visti* the 5th, Transport and Admiralty the 6th, the spies or *cara* the 7th and the division of elders and advisors or the *desika* the 8th division (Dikshitar, section VII).

Table 5.1: Organisation in other armies – divided into 8 divisions

Cataranga	– 1–4 divisions (Padatee, Ratha, Ashwa, Gaja)
Commissariat (*Visti*)	– 5th
Transport, Admiralty	– 6th
Spies (*Cara*)	– 7th
Elders (*Desikan*)	– 8th

Source: Dikshitar, Section VIII

For transport purposes, bulls and camels were employed. While expounding the role and duties of a king the sage Śukrācharya said that a king should have an army of such proportion and strength that the infantry should be four times that of the cavalry, the number of bulls should be one-fifth the number of the horses and the number of camels should be one-eighth of the horses. He further defined that the number of elephants should be one-fourth the number of camels and the number of chariots to be half the number of elephants (Sarkar, 1914). In addition, Śukranīti also mentions cannons, which should be twice the number of chariots. Thus, there should be a predominance of foot soldiers, medium quantity of horses, small number of elephants and bulls and camels to be equal in number (Śukrā 5, 41–46). There were nine levels in the Indian army formation. The smallest unit of the army was a *Patti* and the largest *Aksauhini*. One *Patti* consisted of 1 chariot, 1 elephant, 3 horses and 5 men in the classic *catarunga*. All subsequent larger units were successively trebled. The basic principle of trebling was adopted by the kings of India till the time of Tipu Sultan in 1780s. According to *Nītiprakasa*, which Oppert referred to (1967), and *Amarakosha* of Amar Simha (Rice, 1988), each unit formation in the nine stage army carried a clear identity namely, *Patti*, *Sena mukha*, *Gulma*, *Gana*, *Vahini*, *Prtna*, *Camu*, *Anikini* and *Aksauhini* (Table 5.2).

Table 5.2: The nine stages in the ancient Indian army formation in a *catarunga* and the strength of each stage

	Chariot (*Ratha*)	Elephant (*Gaja*)	Horse (*Ashwa*)	Foot (*Padatee*)
Patti	1	1	3	5
Sena mukha	3	3	9	15
Gulma	9	9	27	45
Gana	27	27	81	135
Vahini	81	81	243	405
Prtna	243	243	729	1215
Camu	729	729	2187	3645
Anikini	2187	2187	6561	10935
Aksauhini	21870	21870	65610	109350

Source: Nītiprakasa–VII, 5; *Amarakosha*, II, 48–49

The 9th formation, called the *Aksauhini* was considered to represent the whole army. However, further to the original *Patti* of 1+1+3+5 composition, another ratio of the individual elements of the *Patti* was also employed. This ratio was shown to be composed of one chariot (*a*), with a retinue of 10 elephants each (*b*), or which was accompanied by 100 horses (*c*), and 1000 men (*d*). Thus, each elephant had a retinue of 100 horses and 1000 men, each horse was followed by 1000 soldiers and each foot soldier had 10 followers. The number of men, animals and chariots in the 9th formation of *Aksauhini* (Table 5.3) could thus be truly colossal and mind boggling.

Table 5.3: Higher proportion of the component elements in the composition of a nine stage army

	(*a*) Chariot (*1*)	(*b*) Elephant (*a x 10*)	(*c*) Horse (*b x 100*)	(*d*) Foot (*b x 1000*)
Patti	1	10	1000	100,000
Senamukha	3	30	3000	300,000
Gulma	9	90	9000	900,000
Gana	27	270	27000	27,00,000
Vahini	81	810	81000	81,00,000
Prtna	243	2430	243000	243,00,000
Camu	729	7290	729000	729,00,000
Anikini	2187	21870	2187000	2187,00,000
Aksauhini	6561	65610	6561000	6561,00,000

The armies in Mahabharata were huge, and the *aksauhinis* were commanded by many kings and feudal lords. The Kurukshetra war was said to have been fought between seven *akshauhinis* of the Pāndavas and eleven *aksauhinis* of the Kauravas. One *aksauhini* could have been either roughly equal to or a little more than 100,000 as shown in Table 5.2, or was a larger formation of 656 million (>65 crores) as depicted in Table 5.3.

Where camels and bulls were employed, the former were war animals and the latter were baggage cart pullers. Their number was also defined in proportion to the chariots, elephants, horses and men. A more plausible and reasonable distribution of these components in aggregate military units provided for a ratio of 5 chariots to 10 elephants, 40 camels, 64 bulls, 320 horses and 1280 men (Śukrā *5*, Slokas 20, 21).

On a comparative basis, it may be noted from Table 5.4 that one *Patti* – the smallest sub unit of a *catarunga*, had four mixed elements which totalled 10 in number. This could be equated to one section of any modern army. One *Senāmukha* of 30 mixed elements could be compared to a platoon. One *Gulma* of 90 comes nearest to a company of 120. Other higher formations cannot be directly equated to any other stage. One *Gana* of 270 cannot be equal to a battalion; the latter is nearer to the next higher grouping of *Vahini*. *Prtna* (2430) comes closest to a brigade. *Camu* (7290) has no equivalent modern grouping: it has less than half the number in a Division. *Anikini* with strength of 21,870 may be ranked as a Division (20,000 men). There are no comparable units to stand for Corps and Army in terms of numbers but one *Aksauhini* could be somewhat like a group of less than two armies.

Thus, although there are nine successive stages of formations in both the ancient Indian and modern armies, not all organisational units are exactly comparable.

Table 5.4: Comparison of the organisation of catarunga with that of a modern army (In a catarunga, the strength is trebled in the successive stages of organisation)

Unit/element organization in 9 stages	*Ancient Catarunga*					*Modern Army*	
	Ratha (chariot)	*Gaja* (elephant)	*Ashwa* (horse)	*Padatee* (foot)	Total strength	Unit name	Total strength
1. *Patti*	1	1	3	5	10	1. Section	10
2. *Senmukha*	3	3	9	15	30	2. Platoon	30
3. *Gulma*	9	9	27	45	90	3. Company	120
4. *Gana*	27	27	81	135	270	–	–
5. *Vahini*	81	81	243	405	810	4. Battalion	1000
6. *Prtna*	243	243	729	1215	2430	5. Brigade	4000
7. *Camu*	729	729	2187	3645	7290	–	
8. *Anikini*	2187	2187	6561	10935	21870	6. Division	20000
–	–	–	–	–	–	7. Corps	60000
–	–	–	–	–	–	8. Army	180000
9. *Aksauhini*	21870	21870	65610	109350	218700	9. Group of armies	

In Dhanurveda, the *Aksauhini* is not the highest formation. In the Kurukshetra war, ten *Akshauhinis* together formed one *Maha-Aksauhini* (SenSarma, 1975, pp. 202–203, quoting sloka from Sadāsiva Dhanur Veda). The *Aksauhinis* themselves differ in total strength from 21,8700 of the *catarunga* to 656 million. By this measure, one *Aksauhini* could amount to anywhere between 200,000 to 6,560 million (65 crores). What might be the strength of a *Maha-Aksauhini*? And this was only one full formation. The Mahabharata war involved seventeen *Aksauhinis* pitted against each other in the 18-day battle. Crores were said to have been killed. No modern army has ever equalled such numbers.

Composition of the Troops

The composition and description of the troops in itself is very interesting and is revealing of the quality and character of the army. Regarding the composition of troops, Śukrāchārya mentions two categories – the *Moula* army which has existed for many years and the *Sadyaksa* which did not. There were apparently six types of troops in the service of the king according to Kāmandaka (Kā. 240–249) and Rajkumar (2004, Vol.1, p. 123). These were:

- The long standing troops called the ***Moula***, who were energetic, confident, faithful and more reliable than the *Bhita*.
- The ***Bhita*** or the mercenary troops who depended on the king for livelihood, but were more reliable than *Sreni bala*.
- The ***Sreni bala*** which possibly consisted of the rank and file and was given to excessive drinking and soon became incapacitated in service.
- The fourth type was called the ***Mitra bala*** – the allied forces, composed of allies and 'friends' who waited to turn against the king at an opportune moment.
- The fifth group consisted of those people belonging to the enemy but who have been weaned or turned over.
- Finally, the forest tribes, the ***Atavika*** troops or auxiliaries who sat at the lowest rung of reliability and were considered to be faithless, greedy and sinful.

The relative strength of the armies in the Indian continent from the time of Alexander the Great's invasion shows the continuing dependence on the foot, the cavalry and the elephants until the time of the second arrival of Mahmood of Ghori, although chariots ceased to be of much import soon after the defeat of King Porus (Thapliyal, 2002 b). According to Megasthanese, there were no chariots in the war machinery of the Mauryans and thereafter. The elephants went out of the Indian army during the British Raj.

Military Salaries in Ancient India

For smooth functioning of the state, salaries were disbursed to state employees on fixed scales. There were several chiefs of military 'corporations', chiefs of elephants, horses, chariots, infantry and commissioners of departments, who each received 8000 (*karshas*) with which they could lead a respectable life.

Besides the chiefs, there were superintendents of the infantry, cavalry, and chariots and of elephants, even guards of the timber and elephant forests, who were paid 4000 *karshas* each. A trained soldier was paid 500 *karshas* (Kangle, 1972, AS.5.3). This payment would have enabled each class of state employee to provide comforts and life for himself and his family.

The payment of salaries was effected from the treasury. 'From the treasury, the army comes into being. From the treasury and the army, the earth is obtained, with treasury as its ornament', so says Kautilya (AS 2.12.37). Thus, without a well stocked treasury a king and his kingdom would be most ineffectual.

The king's treasury had its sources in the mines, the forests and the farming land, in their yields and produce and of course in the commercial trade. From the working of the mines and their yields were determined the price, the share, the surcharge, the monopoly tax, penalty, duty, compensation, fine, inspection fees and manufacturing charge for twelve kinds of metals and commodities made from them (AS 2.12.35–36). The superintendent of the mines was the individual responsible for the functioning of the mines and other activities. The superintendents of agriculture and of forest produce were responsible for all that could be grown, harvested, collected and for levying and collecting state taxes (AS 2.13.17 and 24). All these added to the wealth of the state and in expanding the king's power, influence and might. However, even though one gets an impression that all this must be the king's property, it was not so. Kangle explains that the goods and objects, land, gifts and all else became the property of the state and Kautilya's policy definitely did not recommend any kind of aggrandizement of the monarch at the cost of the welfare of the subjects or the state.

The maintenance of state employees and a huge army was firstly, a necessity to run the state machinery and secondly, was important to impress the neighbouring empires of the power and might possessed by the monarch. To keep all of the employees loyal and happy, the state undertook the business of paying salaries commensurate with their importance in the scheme of things, their rank and their own powers and individual valour.

Śukranīti, Kautilya *ArthaŚāstra* and Kāmandakīya *Nītisāra* all provide precise salary scales and the value of gifts to be paid by the king to the troops and their chiefs. There must have been standing armies professionally trained and equipped by the state for these ancient writers to have codified this aspect of state governance and employee maintenance.

Chakravarti (1972, p. 87) quoting from *Mahābhārata*, (Sabha parva 5, 48–49) mentioned that a sage asked a king, "do you give your troops sanctioned rations and wages at the appointed time? Or, do you cause resentment by withholding them? Do you know that the irritation caused by arrears of pay and irregularity in the distribution of rations may goad them to mutiny?". There is a similar query in *Rāmāyana* (Ayodhya kanda, 100. 32–33). Yudhishthira paid 1000 coins to every *rathina* (charioteer). Bhishma (Mhb. Aranyaka.16.21–22 in Thapliyal, 2002a, p. 47 quoting Bhishma in Mhb. Shanti Parva.58–59) is said to have emphasised the supreme importance of keeping the army contended and gratified to avoid danger to the state emanating from disgruntled troops and advised Yudhishthira to raise the salaries (SenSarma, 1975, p. 71; Chakravarti, 1972, p. 87). Chakravarti also found statements from the Agni *purana* (239, 31) where regular payment to the soldiers was considered to be a very important factor in building a strong army.

The important dispensations and distribution of pay had to emanate from the strength and stability of the ruler's income. Śukrāchārya indicated (Śukrā 4.6, 53–58) how a king's income was to be distributed when it was 100,000 *karshas* per annum (Table 5.5).

Table 5.5: Rulers' Income Distribution under different heads

Recipient Category	Pay in *Karshas, k*	
	Per month	Per annum
King's own personal needs, enjoyments/charities	1500	18000
Clerks, 6 no. @ ~16 k per man	100 each	1200
Councillors, 3 no.,	300 each	3600
On Family	300 each	3600
Learning, Education	200	2400
Horse and Foot soldiers	400	4800
Elephants, Camels, Bulls, Fire Arms	400	4800
Savings shown	1500	18000

Source: Śukrā 4.6, 53–58; Srakar, 1914

After spending on self and family frugally, although more than on any other account, there were still considerable savings of 18,000 *karshas* per annum. The sums expended on the horse and foot soldiers seem awfully small, only 400 *karshas* per month. And there were a sizable number of these in a standing army. The same amount is shown against all the stable elephants and all other animals put together. This amount seems rather small too. But there is another source for feeding the animals. Fresh green grass, fodder and hay were obtained from the forests. It is also likely that in the feudal system, the king was not required to maintain the entire army, only his own personal guard

In Mauryan times, scholars say that there was no precise pay structure although Greek writers have observed that the soldiers were paid liberally by the state but lived frugally (Thapliyal, 2002b). Kautilya who belonged to the same period, had held definite ideas in this regard (AS 5.3.34). He observed that the salary of state employees exhausted one quarter of the state's revenues if the principles of *Dharma* and *ArthaŚāstra* were to be followed (AS 5.3.1–2). The recommended pay scales or the pay entitlements in the army during this period differed from Śukrā's recommendations (Table 5.6).

Paid in *panas*, the pay scales appeared to be comparatively high in every cadre. The Commander-in-Chief was the highest paid officer with a huge sum of 48,000 *panas*. The pay scales declined with decreasing importance of personages in the scheme of things. All the four top ranking positions carried high pay scales. After that, the next in importance were the chiefs of chariots, elephants, cavalry and infantry. They were each paid 8000 *panas*. Everyone who had a significant role in the

Table 5.6: Pay scales of Army Personnel as per rank in Kautilya's time

Rank		*Pay per annum (panas)**
1	Commander-in-Chief	48,000
2	Chief of Palace Guards	24,000
3	City Commandant	12,000
4	Director of Factories	12,000
5	Chief Commander of a Division	
	Chariot	8000
	Elephant	8000
	Cavalry	8000
	Infantry	8000
6	Deputy Commander of each Division	4000
7	Camp Superintendent	2000
8	Physician of the army, horse and elephant trainers	2000 each
9	Chariot warrior	2000
10	Battalion Commander	2000
11	King's Charioteer (Rathika)	1000
12	Superintendent of Armoury	1000
13	Patti Commander	500
14	Elephant Driver	500
15	Trumpet blowers	500
16	Stationary Spies (*samsthah*)	500
17	Other specialist soldiers (Pattika)	1000
18	Staff and Accounts writers	500
19	Ordinary soldier	250
20	Servants leading the spies	250

*1 *pana* was assumed to be equal to 1 English shilling (Chakravarti, 1972).

conduct of war was entitled to be paid according to the list shown in Table 5.6. The foot soldiers true to their treatment throughout history were among the lowest paid although their numbers were huge in all the armies and were the main body of the army though not as important as the chariots, elephants and horses or their riders or drivers.

Yet another set of salary scales figure in the *Nītiprakāsika*: VII, 6–8, according to Oppert (1967, pp. 4–8), which differed from the values found both in *Śukranīti* and *ArthaŚāstra*. *Nītiprakasika* is said to be an extract from an even larger work devoted to *Nītisara* and is ascribed to Vaisampayana (who transcribed *Yajur Veda* and recited the contents of *Mahābhārata* to Janamejaya, the great grandson of Arjuna). Vaisampayana, says Oppert, is introduced in the *Nītiprakasika* as the one describing and explaining the *Dhanur Veda* and discussing weapons and administration of the kingdom to Janamejaya at Taksasila in Punjab. Thus, it appears to be anterior to Kautilya *ArthaŚāstra*.

In this work, the pay was said to be in *varvas* and *niska*. *Varva*, we are informed is a very ancient coin, the value of which remains obscure. Oppert's discoveries on pay scales as found in the *Nītiprakāsika* are tabulated in Table 5.7. Here too, it is evident that the royal princes and the senior most commanders received far higher remuneration, because they hailed from royal lineages and commanded a sizeable number of troops.

There is a progressive reduction of salaries from what is paid to the crown prince and Commander-in-Chief which is 5000 and 4000 *varvas* respectively to that of a private (5 *suvarnas*). *Nītiprakāsika* (VII, 32–42 in Oppert, 1967) goes on to state that 15 *varvas* each were to be paid to an elephant driver, a charioteer and an ensign bearer, a superintendent of wheels, an officer in command of 300 infantry troops, a camel express, a messenger, the head gatekeeper, the chief bard, the chief singer, the chief panegyrist, the head storekeeper, the army pay master and the muster master. Apparently, they all occupied a position of similar importance.

Table 5.7: Ancient pay scales in the armies as per Nītiprakāsika

Rank	*Pay in varvas or gold coins*
1. Crown Prince usually next in command to the King	5000
2. Commander-in-Chief	4000
3. Attiratha or 1st Charioteer, a Royal Prince	3000
4. Maha Ratha	2000
5. Rathika	1000
6. Gaja Yodhi	1000
7. Ardha Ratha	500
8. Eka Ratha	300 niskas*
9. Leader of an elephant	300 niskas
10. General commanding the whole Cavalry	3000 niskas
11. General commanding the whole Infantry	2000 niskas
12. Officer commanding 1000 Infantry men	500 niskas
13. Officer leading 1000 troopers	1000 niskas
14. Officer commanding 100 small Pattis and who must ride on a horse	7 varvas**
15. A private	5 suvarnas***

*, **, *** The significant differences between these denominations have not been provided by Oppert. These currencies can only be less than the *varvas* since pay seems to decrease progressively with lower ranks. However, *suvarna* means gold. A private is shown to get 5 *suvarnas* but an officer above him 7 *varvas* and even higher cadre officers seem to have received payment in *niskas*.

Source: Oppert, 1967, pp. 7–8

One cannot but agree with Oppert's observations that if in the lower echelons this scale of salaries were indeed correct and were diligently disbursed, one would have to believe that an extensive gold currency existed in ancient India and was liberally dispersed among the state employees.

We must also remember that when the king left for an expedition, he was accompanied by his treasury and a monumental entourage consisting of almost everyone mentioned above plus hordes of non-combatants, highly placed women, artisans and craftsmen, traders and entertainers, etc. To have to pay the troops and others enroute would have been no mean task by any estimate.

The scales of pay were obviously very high according to Chakravarti (1972, p. 88), who assumed, based on other scholars' work, that 1 *pana* was equivalent to one English shilling. By this reckoning, a Commander-in-Chief was paid 48,000 shillings (*panas*) equal to pounds sterling 2400 per annum. Similarly, the lowest in the rung – an ordinary rank soldier received 250 *panas* or 12.50 pounds and a specialist soldier some 25 pounds. Also, we find that the pay scales of the army personnel by this reckoning were considerably higher than those of civilian state employees.

Food in lieu of cash pay: A major chunk of the state's budget was spent on maintaining the army. For all this war machinery in the form of personnel, huge numbers of arms, weapons, animals and chariots, the empire must have been very prosperous and the price of food, commodities and articles absurdly cheap. Even so, a great amount of cash was needed. Where was so much cash to be generated from and accumulated to disburse salaries in this manner? Wise men, thinkers and others at the royal court had decided that grain should be substituted for cash. We have seen that 1 *adhaka* of grain was thought to be sufficient for one Aryan male (AS 2.15.43). To use grain in lieu of cash, a formula was applied – where for an annual salary of 60 *panas*, 1 *adhaka* of grain per day (i.e. 365 *adhakas* per annum) was allotted. Kautilya gave certain figures (Table 5.8 A) that help to understand the purchasing power of the currency. One *adhaka* cost three-fourth of a *pana* although there were different ways of measuring the liquids which were priced differently (Table 5.8 B and C). Ghee or clarified butter was the principal cooking fat. It is obtained from heating churned butter till all the moisture is expelled. The yield of ghee from a quantity of butter therefore was going to be more costly, taking into account the decrease in weight of the yield. Similarly, oil was expressed in seed presses. Not only was there a surcharge for the process (if one used the public presses for processing) but the product itself was priced (if purchased) in *varakas* and *ghatikas*. These are again new terminologies for which appropriate equivalent modern currency has not been provided by the interpreters. There was barter trade by weight or volume and price in negotiable currency of the times (Table 5.8 E and F). One *dharana* in trade was greater than one *dharana* in revenue measure. Articles meant for the servants were measured by a different value than the ones for the harem (of the king). There was brisk barter for many items of everyday need and as Table Table 5.8D shows, several different kinds of quantity measures and corresponding pricing values were in use for solids, liquids, grain, grass, and even for payment to different classes of people.

Table 5.8 A–F: Price of goods

A: For Price of dry solid material		
1¼ *pana*	– price of a *drona*	
¾ *pana*	– price of an *adhaka*	
6 *masakas*	– price of a *prastha*	
B: For liquids prices are doubled for measures		
1/32 part is surcharge for heating clarified butter		
1/64th part in case of oil		
1/50th part is the flow from the measure in case of liquids		
C: 1 masaka – price of a kuduba		
½ *kuduba*, ¼ *kuduba* and ⅛ *kuduba* measures		
84 *kudubas* of clarified butter		= *varaka*
¼ of these or 21 *kudubas* of clarified butter		= *ghatika*
64 *kudubas* of oil		= *varaka*
16 *kudubas* of oil		= *ghatika*
D: Measure: Wt/vol market price		
*1 *prastha*	– 450 g – ¾ *pana*	
1 *pala*	– ½ *prastha* = 28 g = 0.02825 kg	
1 *kuduba*	– 1 *masaka*	
1 *dharana*	– 16 *mashas* = 3.388 g in silver weights	
E: 1 gunja	*= 2 grains*	
1 *drona*	= 128000 grains (Wt)	
or	= 500 cubic inches	
or	= a little less than ¼ bushel	
or	= 2 gallons	
1 *vaha*	= 37½ bushels = 1 cartload	

Contd.

Contd.

F: 3 *tulas* would weigh up to 902½, 810 and 722½ *dharanas* instead of 1000 as in the *Ayamani*
Dharana of trade is greater then revenue measure by 1/20th ....5 *palas*
That for servants by 2/20th ....10 *palas*
And that for harem by 3/20th ....15 *palas*
From 100 *palas* amounts of 5, 10, 15 *palas* respectively were given out. The smallest measure is for delivery to the palace.

**Silver weights:*
2 *rattis* = 1 *masha* = 0.218 g (then 1 ratti = 0.109 g)
16 *mashas* = 1 *dharana* or *purana* = 3.488 g
Source: Data for A–D: AS 2.19.36–46; for E: Kangle, 1972, p. 136; for F: AS 2.19.28–30

In the absence of specific figures, it is assumed here that perhaps 50 per cent of the salary was paid in cash and the rest as grain. A Commander-in-Chief receiving a princely sum of 48,000 *panas* (or shillings) per annum would be entitled to 384 *adhakas* per day, while an ordinary rank soldier (at 250 *panas* per annum) would get paid 2 *adhakas* per day. It is very likely that the soldiers going into battle preferred only a fraction of their daily grain entitlement to be paid in the field and the rest to be given to their families if they were left behind. It was customary to have a large number of non-combatants accompany the army when it marched, who, if not in the state's employ or if they did not earn by their own craft and trade, would be dependent on the soldiers and other employees. These camp followers would then eat part of the grain rations given to the soldiers, and the soldiers would spend part of their cash salary to buy other essential goods.

In the Roman army, it was a practice to make every soldier bank part of his salary with the pay master when in the field. This ensured that the soldier did not spend all the money received every pay day and had something substantial to take home. Whether a similar practice existed in the Indian armies is not known.

Rewards and gifts as incentives: Mookerji (1958) commenting on the local government in ancient India has said that there were several types of guilds such as craft guilds, trade guilds and military guilds. These guilds had their own laws and the military guild (which is also referred to in *Mahābhārata*) bore arms and possessed military resources as it controlled the partnership in plunder when and if the guild was deputed to plunder the enemy's country. These and other guilds were highly efficient in finding means to guard themselves and their villages from any attacks from within and outside. They also formed their own military strength which was sent off to plunder for profit and go on expeditions, they functioned so efficiently that apart from religious grants for acts of rural heroism, they were conferred bravery awards for repelling cattle raids and robbers and of course for their role on the battlefield. One-sixth of their plunder went to the king. The remainder was divided as follows: four shares for the leader of the freebooters, three shares to the one who exhibited special heroism, two shares for the one who was specially energetic, and whatever still remained was equally distributed to the other associates (Chakravarti, 1972, p. 87). These rewards for the blood spilt, unlike the cash distributed, came in the form of land grants inscribed on stone and copper plate (Chakravarti, 1972, pp. 294–295). However, bearing arms in peace time when no apprehension of danger existed was considered an offense against the king and a menace to peace (Chakravarti, 1972, p. 216).

However, in anticipation of spoils of war every king, feudal chief and soldier felt enticed. The very gods had vied with each other for bounty and a share in the booty. Many forms of treacherous gifts have been mentioned in the *ArthaŚāstra* (Shamasastry, 1906, p. 80). *ArthaŚāstra* (7.3) suggested that very high rewards be given for slaying the king, the heir apparent and the chief of the army, all of whom were the highest dignitaries in the land and whose death in a battle would materially affect the outcome of war. The Commander-in-Chief was required to address the troops ahead of war and announce the rewards. The enemy king carried the highest price on his head and in a descending order were the prices for killing the heir apparent, the foremost warrior, and for the destruction of various people, elephants and chariots (Table 5.9).

Table 5.9: Spoils of war – the rewards of victory

Act of War	* *Reward (Panas)*
Slaying of enemy King	100,000
Slaying Heir Apparent	50,000
Chief of Army/Foremost Warrior	10,000
Destroying 1 elephant or 1 Chariot warrior	5000
1 horseman	1000
Chief of Infantry	100
Bringing a head	20

*This reward plus twice the pay in addition to whatever was seized.
Source: ArthaŚāstra 7. 3

The field observations and reports from mates and some corroborative evidence in the form of eye witness accounts might have aided in establishing the correctness and credentials of each claimant. There was also the severed head which was raised at the end of spear or sword and shown to all. Beheading a fallen warrior and raising the severed head on a petard seems to be a very gory and blood-curdling method of announcing a win but in the Vedic chants there is sufficient material denoting the extremely determined and rather cruel methods advocated for gaining victory. The ancient armies assiduously followed these customs of war. Beheading a fallen warrior was mandatory to prove a brave's victory and to further assert his position in the army hierarchy.

All through the descriptions of the ancient wars, the foot soldiers were said to have been of inferior quality and were considered to be of no great importance, though they were recruited in large numbers, mostly from the poorer classes, peasantry and even barbarians and foreigners. Chakravarti (1972, p. 15) says that these footmen followed the knights in their chariots as *pādānugah, anugah* or *anucarah*. They hardly ever exhibited any individuality or initiative and perhaps they were not expected to.

The foot soldiers and the standard bearer rode close to the king or alongside the king or the knight. The moment a king or a senior commander fell, the foot soldiers fighting around him went into disarray. They either fled the scene or were slaughtered. The next commander had the task of regrouping them into a cohesive fighting unit. In the epics, the foot soldiers were mere decoration for the knights, reflects Chakravarti. It was therefore very essential to first guard against having the king or a prince or a commander taken prisoner or killed, and secondly, to be able to regroup very swiftly to continue the battle. The consequences of losing a king were very drastic and heralded the quick end to any war. His slaying was an important objective of the war and thus this act earned a very big prize if accomplished. *Kāmandaka* (Ganapati Sastri, 1912) also advocated rewarding a difficult task and expected that the king would liberally remunerate the warriors who were aware that loyalty to a liberal king would fetch just rewards. The figures mentioned here are the same as in *ArthaŚāstra* except that the terms are different and the values are ten or more times higher. A royal antagonist's slaughter fetched 10 million *barnas* to the slayer, 5 million for the destruction of the royal prince or a general, 10,000 for the chief of a brave detachment of heroes, 5000 *barnas* to destroy an elephant and 1000 when an archer or a foremost soldier was killed (Kā 19.17–21). It is not clear whether *barna* is a distorted form of *varva* or a much smaller coinage in denominational value. Anything captured belonged to those who conquered. Thus, a lot of the war spoils like gold, other metals, gems, etc. came to the share of each brave as well as a score of cows.

In the Jataka, salaries were given as 100,000 coins per annum to an expert archer. Under exceptional circumstances an archer could be given even higher remunerations like 1000 coins per day (Thapliyal, 2002 b). *Karsha*, *Pana*, *Barna* or *Varva* were monetary denominations in use in different parts of the country over a period of time. In ancient Kashmir, Kalhāna, writing in his *Rājatarangini* (Vol 2, Verse 4.495, Stein, 1961), mentions *Dinnara* or *Dinara* (derived from the word denarius) in the state's monetary system. Large sums of *dinaras* or *dinars* were paid, once thought to be of gold but unlikely considering the huge quantities involved and therefore probably made of copper. Over a period of time, all the above terms began to be used to represent cash, and not any specific denominations. Thus, *karsha* or *karsh* or *kash*, *pana* and then *dinar* or the present day Kashmiri term *dyar* signify money.

Among the Chola kings (1001 AD), army organisation and training were rudimentary. The warrior families owned ample means of livelihood and maintenance. These kings, who ruled Sri Lanka and Maldives, seemed to have made regular payments of wages to their own men and also to those from Kerala, who enlisted into their armies. The tax revenues were collected in the form of huge amounts of paddy and gold but the wages were given as paddy every month. Since this wage disbursement was carried out in the capital Tanjavur, or in other central places, there must have been a very well-oiled system for collecting, transporting, stocking, accounting and distribution (Sundaram, 2002, pp. 184–208). The vastness of Chola armies mentioned in literature reveals that they had several categories of troops and each category was maintained by those who raised them, particularly the hereditary troops. They could however request more aid from the king. Obviously, these were feudal in nature and thus joined the king with their own contingents and a truly vast retinue – all of which had to be supported. The Cholas in fact were in the habit of travelling light, limiting the train to the bare minimum and used to rampaging. It is said that when Rajendra Chola defeated Someswara II of the Chalukyas in 1054 AD, his troops had no need to transport any stores because all of it could be easily taken from store houses or from their own people.

Coming closer to the beginning of Mughal times, Babur (Hiro, 2006) was no less clever at recognising the importance of pleasing everyone, including the members of his army, although the major chunk of the treasures confiscated from the vanquished side went to his own kith and kin and nobles and allies who fought with him and supported him. For example, in the Battle of Panipat (Table 5.10), everyone in the army was rewarded. The non-combatants, like the traders and students who accompanied the army also received appropriate gifts after the victory. His largesse was bestowed even on those who did not fight such as his younger sons, relations, holy men in Mecca and Medina, and every soul in Kabul from where he set out to conquer Hindustan (Babur, pp. 279–280).

Table 5.10: Distribution of treasures by Babur in Agra after the Battle of Panipat, 1526

	Those who fought	
1.	To son Humayun	70* lakhs, and a treasure house (unvalued)
2.	Some *Begs*	10 lakhs
3.	Some *Begs*	8 or 7 or 6 lakhs
4.	Suitable Money gifts to the whole army, to every tribe – Afghan, Hazara, Arab, Baluch etc, according to his position.	
5.	Every trader, student, every man coming with the army	ample portion and share of the bounty and largesse

Contd.

Contd.

To those not with the army	
1. Kamran (Babur's younger son)	17 lakhs
2. Mohammed Zaman Mirza	15 lakhs
3. Son Askari, son Hind-al and a whole lot of relations, younger children	gold and silver coins, and jewels, slaves
4. Relatives in Samarkand, Khurasan, Kashgar, Iraq	valuable gifts
5. Holymen in Samarkand, Khurasan, Mecca, Medina	large offerings for God
6. Every soul in Kabul and the valley of Varsak in Badakshan – male, female, young, old, bonded, free.	1 shahrukhi

* One lakh (or lac) is 100,000. Whether this currency was *taanks* or Shahrukhis is not mentioned. Since revenues of Hindustan were enumerated by Babur in taanks (Babur, 277) presumably the victory gifts were also bestowed in taanks.

Source: Hiro, 2006, BaburNama, 277–280

Animal Strength in War and Veterinary Care

The Aryans were adept at employing animals in warfare. Ṛg Vedic kings and their chiefs fought from top of elephants, though the army fought on foot (Raychaudhuri, 1963). Their chariots were pulled by highly bred horses and elephants, and formed a mighty and formidable force. Their horsemen i.e. the cavalry made up a large segment of the army and then there were camels, bullocks, pack horses and mules as well to pull carts and wagons and carry loads and supplies. In the epics, the chief strength of the army was based on elephants.

In *Mahābhārata* many animals were employed for military purposes. *Kurus*' eleven *Akshauhinis* and Pāndavas' seven were composed of chariots, elephants and horses. In *Rāmāyana*, though Sri Rāmā fought fierce battles with Rāvana on Lankan soil, there is no record of his having taken army formations nor did he need any forces except for the brigades of monkeys and bears. But Ravana's army certainly was a large and mighty one consisting of chariots, elephants and horses. Highly skilled mounted archers were the chief arm in the fourth century BC. However, we learn from Kautilya, several Greek writers and from the writings of more contemporary historians that Indians used any type of animal that could be tamed and thus they came to rely heavily on elephants in warfare. Aside from the *Mahābhārata*, elephants have been employed from the time of King Porus, who faced Alexander, up to the time of Tipu Sultan, who challenged the British forces. The cavalry and elephants became the main divisions of the army, the epic and Greek style chariots pulled by horses were dispensed with by the time of Kannauj (AD 600) and there were no war chariots at all in Mohammedan India. The invading Mohammedans and the Mongols relied entirely on horses; they rode like the wind and swept through the land in frequent attempts to loot and conquer.

The sheer size of the *Moula* and feudal armies with their cavalry, chariot and elephant divisions in ancient India and the number of animals in them, was noted by Megasthanese and Huen Tsang in their own observations and records on the strength of armies in various kingdoms. There were no chariots in Chandragupta's time; these were truly unwieldy armies. The Vijayanagar Empire was also famous for having large armies. In the battle against Bijapur, Golkonda and Bidar, King Krishnadevaraya joined battle with 129 *ghattams* of elephants and 60,000 horses, apart from 500,000 foot soldiers. All references to the strength of ancient armies appear to draw upon the estimates shown in another historical work 'The invasion of India by Alexander the Great' (McCrindle, 1974).

Both Chakravarti (1972, pp. 8–12), and the Military Systems of Ancient India (Rajkumar, 2004, pp. 295–296) have referred to this work. Figures shown in Tables 5.11, 5.12 and 5.13 are taken from these secondary sources.

Table 5.11: Strength of the armies – elephant and horse strength in the military might of some Indian states at the time of Alexander's invasion

King/State	*Infantry*	*Cavalry*	*Chariots*	*Elephants*
Massaga	38,000	–	–	–
King Porus	30,000	4,000	300	200
	50,000	3,000	1000	130
The Malloi and the Oxydraki	90,000	10,000	900	–
Agrammes, King of Gangaridae and the Prasii	209,000	20,000	2000	3000

Source: Chakravarti, 1972

Table 5.12: Information gathered by Megasthanese at the Mauryan court of Pātaliputra

Name	*Infantry*	*Cavalry*	*Chariots*	*Elephants*
Mauryan Empire, Chandra Gupta	600,000	30,000	–	8000 or 9000
The Calingae	60,000	1000	–	700
The Madubae, Molindae, Uberae	50,000	4000	–	400
The Andarae	100,000	2000	–	1000
The Megallae	–	–	–	500
The Pandae	150,000	–	–	500
The Gangaridae	60,000	1000	–	700

Source: Chakravarti, 1972

Table 5.13: The strength and might of medieval Indian states, from the accounts of Huen Tsang and early Mohammedan historians

State	*Event*	*Infantry*	*Cavalry*	*Elephants*	*Reference*
King Harsa of Kannauj AD 606–647	eve of battle for conquest.	50,000	20,000	5000	pre Buddhist records
	after battle	NA	>100,000	60,000	
Pratihara, King of Kannauj AD 956 (Al Masudi)	had positioned four armies in the four directions	Each 700,000 to 900,000 strong	NA	NA	Elliot, (1877) I.23
Jaipal, Rajah of Bhatinda, AD 1001, (Al Utbi)	against Sultan Mahmud	30,000	12,000	300	Elliot, (1877) II.25
King Gonda	against Mahmud's invasion into Cadella	*145,000	36,000	390	Tabqat-I-Akbari from Briggs, (1870–1872) I,64
		**45,000	36000	390	
Prithvi Raj Chauhan or Rai Pithora, AD 1192	leading Confederate host	Numerous	200,000	3000	Ishwariprasad, (1928) pp. 8–121
	2nd Battle of Tarain	Numerous	300,000	Numerous	

NA – not available; *, ** two different estimates
Source: Chakravarti, 1972

The fact that in any given battle, the kings of ancient and medieval India were able to assemble such seemingly impossible numbers of men and war animals reflects on the readiness and willingness of men to join in battle. This was perhaps for glory but certainly for the bounty and rewards earned by the victorious side and definitely for the opportunity to loot and plunder the vanquished land. The numbers only swelled from one dynasty and kingdom to the next. The medieval armies were even larger with hundreds of thousands of men and animals which curiously became even more massive with each regrouping or a second round of battle. That there were battle ready soldiers waiting to enlist is one possibility. There is also the other possibility that, it being a feudal period, the peasants and other rural folk would have had no choice but to take up arms at the command of their lieges and march into battle with their own animals. Since it has been repeatedly stressed by experts that the common folk, and particularly, the peasantry were not troubled in their daily pursuance of farming activities and were largely left alone to grow food and tend to animals, one presumes that countless men could still be spared for war without affecting the farming work. There must have been hordes of men in every kingdom and allied territories who were kept awfully busy raising and rearing the monumental number of animals. The cost of such an enterprise would have been astronomical but there has not been any particular mention of this aspect in historical writings. Huge pasture lands were needed for grazing the animals, large forest ranges for the elephants and large tracts of water for drinking and to bathe the animals – especially the elephants which had to have their skin kept cool by submerging in water or mud.

Veterinary practices and care: The *ArthaŚāstra* (AS. 30) devotes considerable space to the various features and physical characteristics of the best horses and best elephants. Even though there was a superintendent for the horses, the elephants, the cattle, chariots and carts, just as there was a superintendent for every department in the state, there is no specific mention of chariots in warfare in the Mauryan period, and these do not figure in the strength of the armies depicted in the tables here.

The best horses were believed to originate in Kambhoja, Sindhu, Aratter and Vananyn. The second quality of horses came from Bahlika, Papeya, Sanvira and Taitla while horses from any other place were graded as of ordinary quality (AS 30.1). Based on specific quality characteristics, a distinction was made between the best, the middle and the ordinary horses. For example, the face (*mukha*) of the best horse should measure 32 *angulas*, its length five times its face (160 *angulas*), its shank 20 *angulas* and its height four times its shank or 80 *angulas*.

Elephants abounded in the jungles of India and the art of trapping and taming them must have come from long practice and the skills must have been finely honed. Noticing how many elephants were employed in post-Vedic armies for millennia their development and training must have received as much special attention as that for the horses. The elephants were locally found animals, well adapted to jungles, therefore they could find their way in thick forests; they were intelligent and faithful and it was believed that they were also capable of reading enemy tactics, gauge direction, climb with great facility to heights up to 12,000 ft when necessary and could be maintained at relatively low cost (SenSarma, 1975). The best elephants – based on physical stature – were those which were 7 *aratnis* high, 9 *aratnis* long and 10 *aratnis* in girth.

In the Kurukshetra war, the elephants made up the central column of the advancing army, each one well protected with various types of armour covering called *Kavacas*. One elephant carried 6 men, weapons and two mahouts or drivers. These animals were so highly regarded in their war worthiness that one elephant was considered equal to 6000 men according to SenSarma.

ArthasŚāstra was eloquent on the diets and veterinary care to be given to the animals (AS 30.47.18-24). Physique, physical work and food requirement seemed to determine the diet and rations for the horses. There was a special diet for the best horses (Table 5.14) and lesser rations for the middling and lesser horses. A draught horse or a stallion of middle size was given the same food as the best horse; and similar horses but of lower size received the same food as a horse of medium size. Though all food allotment must be related to work and utility of each category of horse, the physical stature of the animal commanded better rations and larger quantities. A fact of great interest is that a considerable quantity of meat was fed to the horses as part of the daily rations and also milk. This practice has not been mentioned in the context of rearing war animals any where else in later literature. From the descriptions of the rations, it appears that it was no small expense to feed and care for the animals.

Table 5.14: Animal rations – horses

For the best horse:

Feed

2 *dronas* of salli rice, vrihi rice, barley or priyangu – either dried
or half cooked, or half cooked meal of mudga
or *musa* and a *prastha* of fat
5 *palas* of salt
50 *palas* of meat
1 *adhaka* of juice (~ 3.51 kg)
or 2 *adhakas* of curds for moistening the lumps in dry food

Drink

1 *prastha* of liquor (may be about 48 handfuls)
5 *palas* of sugar
or 10 *palas* of milk

For a fatigued horse:

1 *prastha* fat as clyster
1 *kuduba* fat for the nose (12 handfuls)
½ *bhara* green fodder (~ 56.69 kg)
or 1 *bhara* grass
or bundles of grass 6 aratnis in circumference

For other classes of horses:

Less by ¼ for the middling horse (i.e. ¾ of the above quantity)
¼ less of middling horse rations for the lowest type

Special veterinary care and tending was given to a fatigued horse for revival, such as after a long journey or after carrying heavy loads and for a foaling mare (Table 5.15) for 14 days after the birth of a foal. Not only this, the just born foal was nurtured under strict veterinary care till the age of 4–5 years. When it was fully developed and grown up it was then graded and taken for training as a warhorse, or a chariot horse or a draught horse as the case may be.

Three types of horses could be trained for war depending on whether they were furious (*tiksha*), mild (*bhadra*) or stupid or slow (*manda*) and presumably put to work as appropriate to their nature, comments Shamasastry (1910, p. 165).

Table 5.15: Veterinary care

For a just foaling mare
Drink – 1 *prastha* of ghee for 3 nights
Feed – 1 *prastha* of barley meal
An invigorating drink of fat and medicines
Then ½ cooked barley or beans
Green fodder
And a diet according to season
Nurturing a Foal
After 10 nights after birth to age 6 months,
1 *kuduba* barley meal
¼ *kuduba* ghee
1 *prastha* milk
Till age 3 years
½ *prastha* increase in barley meal every month
Till age 4 years
1 *drona* of barley
After 4 or 5 years
Considered fully fit, developed then classified as best, middling, lower and feed as per fixed rations

Those who cared for the horses, such as the trainers, the grooms, and the veterinary surgeons were also permitted a share of the rations which were known as *patisvadabhajat*, though how much came to each one's share is not specified.

In the *ArthaŚāstra*, the rearing of elephants as well as the nourishment to be given to them has been explicitly described. Since elephants naturally lived in forests, even the tame ones were perhaps left free in a demarcated area and they fed on non-poisonous bushes and trees found in the surroundings; their feed did not have to be transported, unlike for the horse. Even though these animals fed on jungle plants, in the course of their rearing and training they were entitled to get the best of feed and greens. Hence there were food rations for the elephants which were determined on their size, measured in *aratnis*. These elephants belonged either to the king's retinue or were being trained for war or other work.

The rations meant for each *aratni* of the best elephant and for other lesser category of elephants are depicted in Table 5.16. Here too one will notice the liberal use of meat, milk and fat in the diet. One inescapable feature in these animal rations was the administration of liquor.

There were other animals which performed various tasks and their well being and care was supervised by the state. The pack trains and supply lines were run with load carrying mules, donkeys, bullock carts and camels. Dairy farming flourished and hence the care of cows and cattle became important. The superintendent of cows, cattle and other animals had the responsibility to oversee their timely and proper feeding as per the prescribed ration scales (Table 5.17). The superintendent of cattle who in addition supervised the preparation of curds, churning of butter and the making of ghee, had the task of bringing solidified curds as food for the army, and giving butter milk to the dogs and pigs (AS. 2.29.27). The Chief of Commissariat looked after the feeding arrangements when the army was marching. There were grooms, elephant drivers, grass cutters, etc. who attended to their specific duties of looking after the animals and feeding them.

Table 5.16: Elephant rations

Best elephant
Feed – For each aratni in height
1 *drona* rice grains
½ *adhaka* oil
3 *prasthas* melted butter
10 *palas* salt
50 *palas* meat
1 *adhaka* of juice
or 2 *adhaka* of curds to break dry lumps
Drink made of
1 *adhaka* of liquor
10 *palas* of sugar
or 20 *palas* milk
For massaging
1 *prastha* of oil for smearing on limbs
1/8 *prastha* of oil for the head and also for the lamp
2¼ *bharas* of green fodder
2¼ *bharas* of dry grass
limitless quantity of leaves and plants
For 8 aratni size elephants beyond rutting
same food as above
For middle/low types – 6 or 5 aratni elephants or 25–30 yrs age
the ration is reduced by ¼ successively

Table 5.17: Feeding and nurturing of pack and farm animals

Bullocks (driving at the speed of a gentle horse)
Feed/fodder
½ *bhara* green fodder
1 *bhara* grass (a weight equal to 2000 palas or one load)
1 *tula* oil cake from the press
or 10 *adhakas* of broken grass and bran
5 *palas* of rock salt
1 *kuduba* of oil (for the nose)
1 *prastha* of oil as drink
1 *tula* of meat
1 *adhaka* of curds
1 *drona* of barley or half cooked masa beans
Drink for health
1 *drona* of milk
or ½ *adhaka* of liquor
1 *prastha* of fat
10 *palas* of sugar
1 *pala* of ginger
Mules, cows, donkeys:
everything less by ¼ amounts
Buffalos, Camels:
everything twice the amount
Working bullocks:
feed according to working time
Suckling cows:
depends on milk yield

Source: AS. 30.47.18–24

Even by encamping on terrains with plenty of water, tree cover, grass lands and bushes, with forest animals and birds and aquatic fauna as source of meat, the king would have had to depend perforce on the village store houses in the friendly neighbourhood, and from allies, to supply and replenish grains, beans, milk and milk products.

From the quantity of daily rations described for each class of animals, a rough estimate has been made, of the grains, fat, oil, curds, milk, meat, liquor, salt and sugar combined. It provides the weight of food items required per day amounting approximately to 43 kg for a horse, 28.34 kg for an elephant and 70 kg for a bullock, not counting the unlimited quantities of green fodder and grass for the elephants and grazing requirements of the other animals. While the Mauryan army went to war with 30,000 cavalry and 8,000 elephants, Prithvi Raj assembled an even mightier force of 200,000 cavalry and 3,000 elephants. The cavalry horses alone in each of these two armies would have had to be provided with 1,290 metric tons and 8,600 metric tons respectively of animal food everyday. Fighting animals were not made to carry any load, for which purpose there were pack animal trains – loaded with their own food, the food for the cavalry horses, elephants, and the grains, etc. for the men and all the war related paraphernalia too. How long and wide would this train have been? How did such an unwieldy contingent of animals, chariots (where used), men and equipment progress at all on the primitive roads of India? But march they did and covered vast distances at their own pace. That is why war expeditions were always long. It has been recorded that a chariot horse could cover anywhere between 6 to 12 *yojanas* on the road per day where as the riding horses covered less distances – either 5, 7 ½ or 10 *yojanas* per day (AS. 2.30.39). In later times suttlers and traders who joined the marches provided this service of obtaining essential goods and selling them at the campsite.

Mercifully though, the wars even in the epics were of short duration. Sri Rāmā's Lanka war, scholars speculate, lasted anything between 4 to 39 days and this would have been a trying period for Rāvana to keep his huge army fed and in order. The Kurukshetra war lasted 18 days according to SenSarma's reckoning and the pitched battles and wars in the various Indian states did not last any longer than perhaps three to four weeks. The battle arrays were themselves arranged on a massive scale and some were said to have been nearly 7 miles wide and 46 miles long as described in the Kurukshetra war. Historians quote Herodotus on the strength of the fighting Persian forces at Marathon and Plataea. According to him, the army of Xerxes had 5,100,000 men and sufficient number of cavalry. They marched on such narrow paths between mountains and passes that the last man could only reach Susa, beyond Tigris, when the first wave arrived before Thermopylae. The Vijay Nagar Empire as given in *Rāya vacakamu* (Aiyangar, 1919, pp. 113–120) also fielded impressively massive and unwieldy armies against Bijapur, Golkonda, and Bidar. King Krishnadevaraya is said to have taken 129 *ghattams* of elephants, 60,000 horse and 500,000 foot soldiers (SenSarma, 1975).

These dimensions give us a sense that it would not have been possible to just get up and go to war at the whim of a monarch. Time, effort, financial resources to gather men and materials, to provide training and gather all the animals required necessitated advance planning. The state had to be rich with an immense treasury, territory and farm produce and trade. Some order and method were required to maintain and monitor the various permanent armies and look into the logistics and actual mechanics of going to war and strategies for every stage of battle. Therefore, it is no wonder that the 'Art of War' encoded by the early political and military thinkers of ancient India placed special emphasis on the means of assembling a fighting force, the importance of support of allies, selecting the season for war and selecting suitable ground for encampment after selecting an appropriate battle ground. Both forest lands and pasture lands were equally necessary to find green fodder and grasses for the animals. Large tracts of water were essential for drinking and to bathe the animals.

Both the men and the animals marched on their stomachs, carrying with them what they could, foraging from the forest where and when they could and requisitioning or rather commandeering on king's order from the villages of the allies and the vanquished enemies.

References

Aiyangar, Krishnaswamy. *The Sources of Vijayanagar History*. Madras, 1919, pp. 113–120.

Aiyangar, P.T. Srinivasa. *Pre Aryan Tamil Culture*. Asian Educational Services, New Delhi, 1995, p. 39.

Briggs, John. *Ta'rikh-i-Farishtah*. Translated. 3 volumes. London 1870–1872. I, 64.

Chakravarti, P.C. (Ed). *The Art of War in Ancient India*. Oriental Publishers, Delhi, 1972, pp. 8–295.

Dikshitar, V. Ramachandra. *War in Ancient India*. Macmillan and Co. Ltd., Madras, 1944, Section VIII.

Dupuy, R.E. and Dupuy, T.N. *The Harper Collins Encyclopedia of Military History*. Harper Collins Publishers, New York, 1993, p. 365.

Elliot, Sir H.M. *History of India as Told by Its Own Historians*. Vol. 2&3. Ed. John Dawson, (Vol. 1–8). Allahabad, Kitab Mahal, 1877. I, 23; II.25.

Ganapati Sastri. T. (Ed). *Kāmandakīya Nītisāra*. Commentator Sankararya. (English translatior-Anon). (Original Sanskrit version by Rajeshwar Sastri : 1886). Trivandrum Sanskrit Series number 14. Trivandrum 1912 Kā: pp. 240-249, Book19,17–21.

Greene, David, Herodotus. *The History*. (Translated) The University of Chicago Press, Chicago, London, 1987, I.103–104.

Griffith, Ralph T.H. *Atharva-Veda*. Translated with commentary. E.J. Lazarus and Co. Benaras, 1896. Volume I: Books II, IV, V & II; Volume II: Books XVI, XVII, XIX and XL.

Hiro, Dilip. *Babur Nama: Journal of Emperor Babur*. Abridged and edited version of original translation by Annette Susannah Beveridge. Penguin Books India Ltd., 2006.

Prasad, Ishwari. *The History of Medieval India*. Allahabad, 1928, pp. 118–121.

Kangle, R.P. *The Kautilya ArthaŚāstra* 2nd edition. Motilal Benarsi Das, Delhi, 1972, AS Books 2 and 5.

McCrindle, J.W. *The Invasion of India by Alexander the Great*. Today & Tomorrow's Printers & Publishers, New Delhi, 1974.

Mookerji, Radha Kumud. *Local Government in Ancient India*. Second Edition. Motilal Banarsi Das, Varanasi 1958 (First printed 1920).

Oppert, Gustav. *Weapons, Army Organisation and Political Maxims of the Ancient Hindus* (with special reference to gun powder and firearms). First published 1880. The New Order Book Co., Ahmedabad, 1967.

Rajkumar (ed). *Encyclopedia of Military Systems in India. Vol. I. Ancient India*. Commonwealth Publishers, Delhi, 2004, pp. 85, 123–124.

Raychaudhuri, S.P. *Some aspects of agricultural practices in ancient India (3250 BC–800 AD)*. In Symposium on 'The History of Sciences in India'. National Institutes of Sciences of India, New Delhi, 1963, pp. 107–117.

Rice, Lewis. *Amarakosha of Amara Simha* 4th edition. Asian Educational Services, New Delhi, Madras, 1988, Section II.

Sarkar, Benoy Kumar. *The Śukranīti – The Sacred Book of the Hindus*. The Panini Office Bhuvaneswari Asram, Allahabad, 1914. Chapters 4 & 5.

SenSarma, P. *Kurukshetra War: A Military Study*. Dhiren Roy Roy Darbari Udjog, Ganganagar, 1975, pp. 2–205.

Shamasastry, R. *The ArthaŚāstra of Chanakya*. Books I-IV, Mysore Review. 1906–1908*a* pp. 80.; AS 2.29.27.

Shamasastry, R. *Chanakya's ArthaŚāstra – The Science of Polity*. Chapter XXX. Mysore Review, Mysore, 1906–1908*b*, AS–30.1.

Shamasastry, R. *The ArthaŚāstra of Chanakya*. Books V–XV. Translation. British India Press, Bombay, 1910, p. 165.

Spaulding, Oliver Lyman and Nickerson Hoffman. *Ancient and Medieval Warfare,* Constable & Co. London, 1994, pp. 17–29, 103–104.

Stein, Sir Aurel N. *Kalhāna's Rājatarangini: A Chronicle of the Kings of Kasmir*. (Translated, commentary, appendices.) in 2 volumes 1900. Motilal Banarasi Das, Delhi, Constable & Co., London, 1961, Vol 2, verse 4. 495.

Sundaram, J. *Chola and Other armies – Organization. In Volume X, Part 3: Historical perspective of Warfare in India – Some Morale and Materiel Determinations*. S.N. Prasad (Ed). History of Science, Philosophy and Culture in Indian Civilization. Series. General Editor–D.P. Chattopadhyaya. Published by Bhuvan Chandel, Distributors Motilal Benarsi Das, New Delhi, 2002, pp. 184–208.

Thapliyal, U.P. *War in Ancient India – Concepts. Section I: In Volume X, Part 3: Historical perspective of Warfare in India – Some Morale and Materiel Determinations*. S.N. Prasad (Ed). History of Science, Philosophy and Culture in Indian Civilization. Series. General Editor – D.P. Chattopadhyaya. Published by Bhuvan Chandel, Distributors Motilal Benarsi Das, New Delhi. 2002a. pp. 43–67.

Thapliyal, U.P. *Military Organisation in Ancient India. Section I: In Volume X, Part 3: Historical perspective of Warfare in India – Some Morale and Material Determinations*. S.N. Prasad (Ed). History of Science, Philosophy and Culture in Indian Civilization. Series. General Editor – D.P. Chattopadhyaya. Published by Bhuvan Chandel, Distributors Motilal Benarsi Das, New Delhi. 2002b, pp. 68–103.

6

Wars from the Purānās to Panipat and Plassey

The four *purānās* – *Vāyu*, *Matsya*, the later *Vishnu* and the still later, *Bhāgavata*, according to Bhandarkar (1985) contain information about several dynasties who ruled at different periods as well as the number of princes belonging to each dynasty and the length of each one's reign. For example, the duration assigned to the Mauryan dynasty founded by Chandragupta is recorded as 137 years.

Western scholars believed that the history of India was chronicled and recorded only after the Mauryan dynasty began and was written by travellers from outside the land.

In the Mauryan dynasty, there were 9–10 princes according to Maxmueller, deriving chronological information from Alexander's time (Bhandarkar, 1985, p. 30). King Asoka (273–232 BC) of the Mauryan dynasty was the greatest of all the ancient emperors. His might and rule extended from Kapurdigir in Yūsafzai country to Dhauli in Cuttack, from Tirhut in the north to the Gujarat peninsula in the west. His concern for his subjects and his warcraft were said to have been phenomenal. However, little remains of the history of his time. There are only rock edicts to go by after he spurned his Hindu religion and violence and entered a life of piety and peace under Buddhist order. Due to this shift to another religion, the Hindus declined to keep any record of his reign in India (Mitra, 1969, pp. 407–426). He was thought to be a renegade from the religion of his ancestors and since Buddhists were also expelled from the country, Asoka's name and fame could not be kept alive.

After the decline of the Mauryan dynasty, the Sunga family was founded in around 185 BC producing around ten rulers and reigning over the next 112 years as per all the purānās (Bhandarkar, 1985, p. 30). The Kanvas or Kanvayanas began their dynastic rule (73 BC) and reigned with four princes for 45 years. At the same time came Andrabhrityas (Satavahanas and Salivahanas) in Maharashtra, who lasted for around 411 to 456 years or even 460 years, bringing great prosperity to the land by way of trade, commerce, better administration by trade guilds (Bhandarkar, 1985, pp. 41–42).

There is virtually no mention or description of wars in these chronicles but by this time Kautilya *ArthaŚāstra* and his description of the art of war had been in existence for some centuries and one supposes that throughout the reigns of the various dynasties, the principles and the codes of war enunciated by Kautilya were followed. For our purpose, we should perhaps look at the Chalukyas (Chalika or Chalukya), the life of whose legendary Prince Vikramaditya was described by Bilhāna in his *Vikramānkadevacharita*. Copper plate grants indicated that the Chalukyas descended from Hariti and belonged to the Mānavya Gotra. The god Kārtikeya led them to prosperity and they fought under a standard showing a boar and were successful in subjugating all kings. Bilhāna's writing and the copper plate engravings from Yevur and Miraj both agree that Ayodhya was the original seat of the family, which in course of time established a branch in the South (Bhandarkar, 1985, p. 48). In the reign of King Pulakesi (son of Kirtivarman) from 535 *saka* or AD 611, there was an attack by a prince probably belonging to the Rashtrakuta race. Though the latter attacked with his army of horses brought in from the northern areas, his strength did not match Pulakesi's powerful army and therefore chose to become his ally. There were continuous battle engagements all across the south, first with the Kadambas reducing their capital Banavasi, then with the Ganga family of the Chera country (near modern Mysore) and then the head of Alupa holding the provinces of Malabar, vanquishing both and forcing them into becoming allies. There was a powerful navy in war, where hundreds of ships launched an attack on Puri (called the Lakshimi of the western ocean) which was probably the capital of the Mauryan king of Konkan and afterwards of the Silaharas (Bhandarkar, 1985, p. 51 and footnote 4). Pulakesi also defeated the kings of Latu, Malava and Gurjara and became their siege lord. The king of Kannauj, a powerful monarch in the north took up arms along with his huge army of elephants against Pulakesi in an effort to occupy the southern country below the river Narmada, but was unsuccessful. From copper plate grants, it is found that Pulakesi kept a mighty and strong force on the banks of Narmada to guard the frontiers. It is said that the kings of Kosala and Kalinga feared him. His large army also marched against the Pallava king of Kanchipuram (or Conjeveram) and laid siege. Crossing the Kaveri river he invaded the kingdoms of the Cholas, the Pandyas and the Keralas. Having established his supremacy, there was peace in his empire. Inscriptions indicate that this career of conquest ended in AD 643.

The Kalinga kingdom under the Eastern Gangas (Orissa) held sway from around AD 900–1200. They followed the law of primogeniture – the eldest son by the chief queen succeeding the throne. They kept big armies – several thousand infantry to man the elephant corps. They employed trainers known as *sahani* – *gaja sahani* (elephant trainer), *aswa sahani* (horse trainer) and are said to have been in battles against the kings of the east and the north. Archery was the way of warfare and *kumta* and *khadga* (sword like weapons) also came into use by the twelfth century. The invading armies of the Chola king coming in search of the Kalinga king are said to have indulged in untold atrocities, plundering, pillaging and burning townships, even though such acts were not sanctioned in the art of warfare (Rao, 1991). The movement of troops however proceeded on military roads or *rājapatha.*

Huen Tsang, the Chinese Buddhist pilgrim visiting India during this period described the bravery of Pulakesi and his continued independence as a much loved king and benefactor who remained unvanquished and unsubjugated by the repeated attacks of Harshvardhana and his mighty alliances from the east and west. Huen Tsang was much impressed by the warlike habits in this vast kingdom (Maharashtra) covering 1200 miles (6000 li) in circuit. He described the climate as being warm and the people as being tall, haughty, but simple and honest. They were helpful but would bear no insult in silence and readily use their spear to avenge themselves after giving due warning to the enemy. Their battle manners were described thus: 'though the fugitives were pursued they were not slain upon surrender. A general who had lost a battle was made to wear women's clothes in shame and in sacrifice of his own life', a very different sort of punishment indeed. There were hundreds of champions maintained by the state. In preparation of combat, they drank wine to the point of intoxication and became so spirited that they felt they could defy 10,000 men single handedly! They also fed the elephants these intoxicating potions to make them fierce. They could kill a man on the road and not be punished. On the commencement of the campaign, these brave champions marched in the vanguard to the beat of drums. They trampled everything under their feet. They would frequently come to blows under the influence of strong liquor (Bhandarkar, 1895, p. 52).

Pulakesi was succeeded by his second son Vikramaditya I, who has been called the favourite son or *priyatanaya*. Vikramaditya was a brave and able man and was able to curb the rebellion in the kingdoms of Chola, Pandya and Keralas. Vikramaditya II, the great grandson ascended the throne in AD 733 and launched himself against Kanchipuram's Pallava king – their hereditary enemy (Bhandarkar, 1895, pp. 56–57). After the defeat of Nandipotavarman who fled from the battlefield, a large amount of war spoils were captured in the form of rubies, elephants and instruments of martial music. He however did not destroy the temple town of Kanchi, but donated a good amount of money to the Brahmanas and restored the temples.

The pivotal point for the citizens in the upper classes of society in ancient India was their king. They all tried to imitate him and his luxurious style of living. In comparison, the life of the poor people was dismal in every respect; dressed in rags, they could only afford to eat rice and paste made of black lentils fried in foul oil. The king neither had time for the sufferings of his people nor did he show any interest in them. Immersed in self gratification of every kind, pursuing amusements – except on special occasions when they might condescend to announce celebrations where all may join – the kings of that period are said to have totally ignored the poor and the peasantry and violated all norms of social behaviour. Many kings come across as having forgotten the ancient code of the kingly Kshatriyas, what it meant to be a king and to take a king's responsibilities towards his subjects seriously. They indulged in excesses of every kind including incest; they were weak and abusive and did pretty much as they pleased in conducting the business of the state (Dhar, 1991). This description of the kingly life in Kashmir could apply to many other parts of the country.

In Kalhāna's *Rājatarangini* (Stein, 1961) one finds the chronicles of the kings of Casmir (Kasmir or Kashmir). In the time of King Uchchala of Kasmir, there was not a single festival that was celebrated in a bloodless manner. The celebrations were violent. The king used every woman available freely, gorged on food and drink and had no time at all for governance. One has to wonder how they were able to raise and maintain armies and fight wars. One may also imagine the fate of the soldiers in the royal army because most of their numbers would have come from the poor stock and they joined the army because they hoped to get paid or at least get rewards after victory. King Harsha (AD 600) was the last of the great emperors of this period.

Islam was established in Delhi and the countries of Hindustan by a pardoned martyr Sultan Sa'yid, the son of Bah-ud-din-Sam around AD 1173 as mentioned in the *Tarikh-i-Mubarak Shahi* by Yahiya Bin Ahmed Bin Abdullah Sirhindi (Beveridge, 1910). In AD 1174, Sultan Muizz-u-din took control of the vicinity of Ghaznin and marched towards Gujarat. The Raja of Gujarat, Rai Bhim Deo's large army of infantry and elephants defeated the Muslims. Again from AD 1179 to AD 1198 fresh attempts were made to conquer the fort. In one such encounter, Pithor Rai with his numerous cavalry, foot and elephants routed the Muslim invaders and pursued the fleeing sultan but failed to capture him; so he marched against the fort of Tabarhindah being defended by Ziauddin Tulaki who had been installed as governor for 13 months. The fort held out for 13 months but due to the dire situation created by the inability of the new recruits and lack of supplies and fodder, negotiations began, truce was sought and then the fort was vacated. The history of Muslim rule in India commenced in the year AD 1260 according to Elliot and Dawson (1877).

The Muslim period in India is painted with scenes of bloody wars, slaughter of the vanquished, looting of wealth from every temple and land, and burning down of every hamlet, farm, and standing and stored crop. From the detailed accounts in Elliot and Dawson (1877) of the chronicles of the Mohammedan period in history, one gets a sense of the determination with which they attacked, the suddenness of it and the chilling depravity of the invaders, of the irreconcilable and petty rivalries and jealousies of the fragmented kingly states, of deceit and connivance against each other to gain favour for the preservation of their own land and fortunes from the conquering Mohammedans.

And the invaders once having gotten a foothold, spread all over the country and into the Dekkan, creating dynasties. There were Hindu states in the north and south but these different dynasties ruled supreme in their little corners till the arrival of the Mongols and the establishment of the Mughal Empire.

Mughal Invasion and Rule

India was open to the world of nomads in the west only through the Khyber Pass in the Afghan mountains. The inhospitable lands to the north and northwest of India were inhabited by Turks, Turcomans, Khirgiz and Mongols – all pastoral tribes but really the most cruel, violent and pillaging horsemen (Braudel, 1993, p. 164), and the target and victim of their aggression was India. Although trading colonies had been established on the Malabar Coast as early as the eighth century, the spread of Muslims was slow (Braudel, 1993, p. 232). In the early thirteenth and fourteenth centuries and again in the sixteenth to seventeenth centuries, the repeated waves of destruction accompanied by clash of civilisations produced large-scale massacres. Several thousand Mongol cavalry were repelled by the heroic battle with the far fewer but very brave and skilled horsemen of the Indian army. In the *Shah Nama-I-Hind* of Isami (Mahdei Husain, 1898), the author describes that the Mongols who came charging in AD 1200 were so terrified of the Indian army led by Malik Khamush that after barely two days of fighting, their camps were found to be deserted.

Timurlane and Babur

Emir Timur Beg also known as Timurlane of Samarkand (AD 1370–1405) captured Delhi in AD 1398, sacked it thoroughly and withdrew (Babur Nama, p. xviii: Hiro, 2006). Emir Timur was a nomadic Muslim, who conquered 2.15 million square miles of territory but died a violent death. Leafing through the account of Timur's invasions, one learns of long marches through mountain passes, finding winter quarters in fortressed towns to sit the winter out, long sieges of forts, which made both parties go hungry in large numbers. The allowing and ordering the massacre and slaughter of the vanquished and even claiming the wife of a captured enemy were the tactics that characterised Timur Beg's war exploits. However, beautifully laid gardens, camping meadows, growing excellent fruits and greens also goes to Timur's credit. Samarkand was beautified after its fort was captured. He had gone as far as Bhira and further into the interiors. On his return he left several of his territories, from Kabul to Chirab, in the hands of his descendants. The great grandson Sultan Masood Mirza Kabuli and his sons reigned over these regions but eventually lost Kabul and Zabul in the period AD 1452–1466 (Babur, p. 212).

Zahiruddin Muhammed Babur (AD 1483–1530) is known as the founder of the Mughal Empire, and is said to have descended from the dual lineages of Timur and Chengiz Khan (AD 1162–1227). Babur's claim to having founded the Mughal lineage comes from his own parentage. His mother was a half Chaghatai and half Mughal and therefore Babur considered himself to be half Timuri-Turk (on his father's side) and half Chaghatai (his mother) (Babur, p. 350). Babur led an eventful existence from very early on (Babur, p. xviii). At the Battle of Panipat in 1526, his army was very small but he possessed parbque bases and field guns whose carriage wheels were secured with chains to resist possible mounted charges while on the battlefield (Braudel, 1993, p. 233). Babur, whose victory was considered a victory for Islam, expanded his army with mercenaries from Kashmir, Iran, and other Islamic countries and also from the west.

Babur's own memoirs, *Babur Nama*, provides details of his several expeditions and campaigns. In it, he describes a Mughal custom laid down by Chengiz Khan which he followed in the matter of battle order (Babur, p. 87). Each clan had its place and position which its ancestors had always occupied. The most reliable men (equivalent to the ancient Indian Moula army) went to the extreme points of the right and the left, Chiras and Begchik clans always took the point on the right. Disputes to claim this honour were settled with swords. One would take the highest place in the battle array and the other in the hunting circle. Then they all went hunting and afterwards merry-making. He describes Mughal fashion of dress and bearing (Babur, p. 91) – Mughal caps, long coats of Chinese satin embroidered with chain stitch, Mughal quivers and saddles of shagreen leather, Mughal horses decked out in a unique style. When a sultan paid a visit to another, or a son visited his father, he took a small number of men, 1,000 to 2,000. Very stylised manoeuvres on horses were carried out before dismounting and paying respects to the waiting sultan.

On Kabul, he waxes eloquent, praising it in every way. The trade between the neighbouring countries and Kabul in the period AD 1504–1520 was lush with goods coming in from Khurasan, Kabul and Kandhar. There were two trade markets coming via the land route between Hindustan and Casavang from Kashgar, Fergan, Turkistan, Samarkand, Bukhara, Balk, Hissar and Badakshan. It was certainly more profitable to conduct trade right there than to go looking for goods in China or Turkey. Thousands of horses, 8,000–10,000 at least, were brought in every year. 15,000 to 20,000 loads of household goods, white cloth, sugar candy, refined and common sugars and aromatic roots came from Hindustan. The slave trade was rampant too. Hefty profits rolled in by all these methods. Kabul's climate was so conducive to growing a wide variety of fruit and tree nuts, even lotus flowers, tulips and sugarcane that all these were planted in the specially laid gardens (Babur, pp. 125–126). Rice and corn also grew in abundance (Babur, p. 129).

It was a rich land by all accounts. From crops, land toll and from the travelling nomads (traders perhaps), 8 lakhs (800,000) of *shahrukhis** used to be collected, annually perhaps or at other specified times (Babur, p. 135; *2 *shahrukhis* = one Indian rupee). All this was on irresistible lure for the Turks, Afghans and Mughals.

Babur's second expedition from Kabul to Hindustan followed soon after he took the Bajauri fort in a campaign against Haider Ali Bajauri, which was on his route. Bajaur's army in the fort was made up of footmen equipped with bows and arrows, stones and swords and very likely lances as well, but they were no match for Babur's army of horsemen and swordsmen equipped with mantlets, ladders, axes and other objects to climb over the fort walls, to break them and capture it, and matchlock guns as well (Babur, pp. 205–206). Babur's attack was so successful that the fort was captured, in his own words, 'in two or three astronomical hours'. The Bajauris were non-Muslims inimical to Islam and were therefore massacred, their wives and children captured. Of more than 3,000 men killed in that battle, there were many who were beheaded. It was a common practice to behead those soldiers who were unfortunate enough to be surrounded and caught (Babur, p. xxxii). Babur himself, as those who preceded him, committed massacres and slaughters – his diary records the killing of his enemy in battle and capturing the wife as booty. Babur and his troops, at the end of the day, returned to their own camp and he bestowed the territory to Khwaja Kalan along with a large force of warriors.

With battle matters settled to Babur's satisfaction, it was time for merriment, entertainment and sport, with wine, intoxicating confections, fruit and equipped with hunting eagles they went after black deer (Babur, pp. 207–208). Replenishment of their supplies during the march from Kharaj valley on their way to Bhira came in the form of raids carried out even during a snowfall in the mouth of the valley. The local Afghans deserted their homes when they saw the troops. There was plenty of corn in their homes, which were halfway up the valley, all of which were captured for the men and their horses.

Kabul was his base but Babur set his mind to raid Hindustan (Babur, p. 209); the soldiers hoped for some really valuable plunder – for this purpose, they had to be better organised. The horses which had already travelled as far as Bhira were hardly capable of going any further. This army that was proceeding to strike against Hindustan had to go past the Indus river and dense forests. Here they found wild game rhinoceros. The army composed of horses and baggage camels crossed the waters while the camp bazaar and foot soldiers made it across on rafts. But events turned against him even after he negotiated with the Bhira head man, for a price of 400,000 *shahrukhis* (Indian rupees 200,000, or US$ 100,000), for peace and dominion (Babur, p. 213). Treachery and untimely malaria together conspired to make Babur abandon his march to Hindustan once again (Babur, p. 221).

In his fifth expedition to Hindustan, the Battle of Panipat was fought in 1526. From Lahore came 20,000 *shahrukhis* in gold sovereigns and silver *tankas* (Babur, p. 245) brought over by Nour Beg when Babur's party reached, Baran River. His purpose to march eastwards was to tackle Ibrahim Lodi who sat on the throne of Delhi. Lodi's army was 100,000 strong, buttressed by 1,000 elephants. Babur was on his way from Ambala, bestowing gifts of towns, keeping close watch on Lodi's movements, sending smaller detachments to meet head-on Lodi's own military collector. At close encounters, first a group of 100–150 warrior scouts engaged with the enemy and then when the huge army of Humayun appeared, the enemy could not escape and was surrounded. Some 100 men were beheaded and the rest of them were taken prisoner along with seven or eight elephants (Babur, pp. 256–257).

Battle Preparation – Panipat

Babur began his battle preparations much in advance. His force did not seem to have been larger than 12,000 in number. In the camp, every man was ordered to collect carts whichever way he could. They gathered 700 carts including the baggage carts of the army. These carts were to be joined in 'Ottoman' fashion with ropes made of rawhide. Between every two carts, five or six mantlets were fixed. The matchlocks were to be fixed from behind these and all work was to be completed in five to six days. Battle plans were made and on a consensus it was decided to keep the crowded town of Panipat on one side and carts and mantlets ahead of the infantry and matchlock men on the other. They marched forward camping only one night on the way to assuage the anxieties and restlessness of the soldiers on a strange land who had been on the move for a long time.

It has been said that the astrologers had foretold Lodi's defeat and added to that his army suffered from low morale. In the fierce battle that ensued, his 100,000 strong force (at least that much if not double, which he could have collected as levy from his lands) was no match for the 5,000–6,000 contingent of Babur that was thrown in under the leadership of various Begs in preliminary encounters. In the main battle which engaged from dawn to past noon, which Babur describes in detail, men, elephant riders, archers, cavalry, field cannon shots were all involved in manoeuvres in which Lodi's men were encircled. Babur offers praises to God saying that due to his mercy and kindness, the battle was made easy and won in half a day (Babur, p. 262). On first count, 5,000 to 6,000 men were found lying dead close to where Lodi had been.

The conquerors estimated that 15,000 to 16,000 men may have been killed all over the field, but found later on from statements given by Hindustanis in Agra that perhaps 40,000 to 50,000 died in that battle. A detachment sent to capture Lodi who fled towards Agra instead found his body on a heap of the dead. True to their custom, he was beheaded and the head presented to Babur (Babur, p. 263). Babur then saw to it that Ibrahim Lodi's body was bathed and prepared for burial and a tombstone ordered to be erected.

The Mughal Empire was born, and as Braudel (p. 233) says, founded its luxury on India's general poverty in the midst of fabulous riches and a series of famines. The whole of Muslim Rule in India from the beginning was characterised by terror, cruelty, heavy taxation despite failed harvests juxtaposed with the opulence and splendour of the land. The Kohinoor diamond came into their hands after Lodi's defeat, offered by the Rajah of Gwalior to Humayun who then gave it to Babur upon his arrival in Agra.

The Beginning of Mughal Times

Babur, much as he was enthusiastic about entering Hindustan after defeating Ibrahim Lodi, found little to recommend the place. He was a keen observer and recorded all that he did and saw on a daily basis. His notings on the life and customs in Hindustan are quite acerbic and pungent, pointing out numerous defects and its unpalatable customs, its people, its weather, and almost everything except its riches and the industry of the people. He records (Babur, p. 275) that the 'country had few charms'. However, he also recorded the way Indians categorised their seasons and months, aligned with the 12 zodiac signs; the names by which each week day was known then are the same as the names in the Hindi language now in use. He noted how time was divided and how to tell the time of day, the various weights and measures for trade and currency purposes (see Annexure 3, Table A 3.7) and the very important matter of how numbers were counted at that time which are much the same as now.

Babur's son and heir, Nasiruddin Mohammed Humayun was even more of an art and literature lover than was Babur. He loved the floating palaces with bazaars and gardens as well as the music although he was not particularly different in his military approaches. His idiosyncrasies (stars ruled his life and actions) and frivolities were also many. Categorisation and systematisation was a mania with him. Humayun is credited with the innovation of devising the prefabricated portable bridge. He organised and streamlined his administration, his courtiers and the government departments which were classified into four categories based on the four elements, each under a minister who had to wear clothes suited to his department. For all these administrative initiatives, his army lacked training and discipline, it lacked good leaders and was at best a rabble that gathered under his standard and was defeated time and again by Shershah. In 1540, when Humayun met Shershah outside Agra, his army appeared to be mighty impressive with firepower of 700 swivel guns, 21 heavy cannons, and a battalion of about 5,000 musketeers (Eraly, pp. 46–48). Humayun was himself not said to have been a great leader, and since his amirs (those who had not perished in Bengal in the battle with Shershah) had 'no prudence or knowledge', he could not whip this big force into an able fighting one. There was disinterest in the camp, among the officers and the troops who were all disorganised. Waiting on the banks of the Ganga, his army became restive and demoralised which led to mass desertions. Shershah's intense desire to drive the Mughals out of Hindustan and wipe their rule out of existence was realised, and Humayun, leading an army of 40,000 (even after it was thinned down) was routed in Kannauj and fled to Kabul, the home and retreat of the Mughals, but from here too he had to move to Persia.

Shershah of the Delhi Sultanate, a hard working Sunni, comes across as a somewhat accommodating but very pious potentate for many Hindu officers were in his service; the infantry was predominantly so, as were his musketeers. He was charitable to the extent that several thousand horsemen and private followers were fed out of his kitchens. Humayun could make a come back only 15 years later and then only after Shershah's death. In the interim, Humayun retreated to Persia and lived there as a fugitive from India and Kabul.

The royal entertainments in Persia, till his return in AD 1554 included a lavish style of living at the expense of the Shah, who entertained him with courtly hospitality and pomp and ceremony (Eraly, 2000, p. 105). Each day, in his honour, no less than 500 dishes of different foods were presented and the Shah specified that no less than a total of 1,500 items (foods, beverages, desserts combined) be prepared everyday and served on *langari* dishes known as Muhammad Khani.

Even though Persia was rich with food, jewels and wealth, one must wonder how the fugitive Humayun's welcome stay could have been supported in such a lavish style. But Humayun, treated like a royal, fell readily into the lap of pomp and revelry and adopted the style of Persia. This must have left a lasting impression on the Mughal for when he returned to Agra, his style of living and functioning was definitely different. His knowledge of and interest in various subjects contributed to the development of arts, architecture, music and poetry.

Akbar, his son who succeeded him, was raised under these cultural pursuits and though his acquisition of book knowledge was severely limited, he had an instinctive feeling for good things, a kind approach and the right ways.

We know little of the Mohammedan 'art of war' and how it was conducted beyond the evidence of their pillaging and destruction and later of their single-minded pursuit of conversions to Islam, which left its lasting imprints on the conquered land by a succession of Muslim rulers. Babur was no different, nor was Humayun.

We have some insight into this aspect in Emperor Akbar's time from consulting the chronicles of Akbar's rule known as *Ain-I-Akbari* (Sallami, 1939). Akbar had appointed a *Sipah salar* or commander of the forces (a sort of provincial viceroy to His Majesty) and a *Faujdar* – the commander of the forces for each province (Ain: 1, 2). *Sipahi* is the Hindustani name for soldier – a term which became better known as *Sepoy* in the British Colonial rule and *fauj* stands for the army.

The duties of the *Faujdar* included constant inspection of the force's accoutrements and suppression of any rebellion. He planned for the troops, provided horses where necessary at the expense of the state and furnished a tour of the troops particularly because there were 12 *subahs* (areas or districts) spread far and wide. His responsibilities also extended to supervising the pitching of camps in the neighbourhood of a body of rebels and inflicting loss upon persons. There was a clear direction not to use the cavalry, should the infantry suffice. There were definitive instructions given and ethics involved in dealing with the enemy, which can be gauged from the warning that the camping place should be well beyond bowshot and for the army not to be rash in attacking a fort. Gathering spoils and loot in war has been a way of warrior life since Alexander's time and it was no different now, but Akbar being fair and just, wished that equity be scrupulously observed in the distribution of spoils. Fighting in the name of the Emperor, one-fifth of the war loot must also be reserved for the royal exchequer (Ain: 1, 2).

There is no specific mention of any type of care or rations or food entitlements for the soldiers. This is not surprising and in fact is to be expected. In matters of food, the soldiers ate what their culture and tradition dictated. One may also remember that the vast majority of the soldiers – the *sipahis* coming from the various provinces or *subahs* were the responsibility of the *Subahdar*. They belonged to the villages of the chiefs, and were perhaps looked after by the latter. Even otherwise, they belonged in the villages and ate what they normally ate in their communities – not lavishly but simply and wholesomely.

Food service in the Imperial Mughal kitchens: The food for the nobles, chiefs and commanders who belonged to the higher classes and the aristocracy as well as the soldiers in the emperor's entourage came out of the Imperial kitchens.

The Imperial kitchens in Mughal times were of a class by themselves. Not forgetting the early exposure of Humayun to Persian elegances and his enjoyment and penchant for lavishness and pomp, a very elaborate protocol for food preparation and service was designed and operated whether it was in the palace or in the encampments. Firstly, there was no fixed time for a meal but the servants always had to have things ready so that within one hour after the order was received for food to be served, the Imperial kitchen served up more than 100 dishes (Ain: 23). Cooks recruited from all countries prepared a great variety of foods with grains, greens, meats, oily sweets and spicy dishes, under the supervision and control of a sincere, loyal and trustworthy man appointed as *Mir Bakamal* or master of the kitchens. He was assisted by numerous upright and sincere persons i.e. the *Bakamals*. Special provisions came from all over the land. There were numerous ingredients and staples which went into the preparation but a note from Mir Bakamal and Diwan-i-buyulat (Superintendent of stores) was necessary to lift any stores needed for food preparation. There were such items as *Sukhdas* rice from Bharaj (Bahraich), *Dewzira* rice from Gwalior, *Jinjin* rice from Rajori and *Namlah* and *Ghi* from Hisar and Firuza, as well as ducks, waterfowls and some vegetables from Kashmir.

The sheep, goats, fowls, ducks etc. were fattened by cooks; fowls never kept for less than a month. The king and his force commanders dined on the same grandiose scale with a spread of food and service comprising various kinds of breads, sauces, curds, plates of pickles, fresh ginger, limes, and various greens. Foods were prepared and dished out under Mir Bakamal's seal of inspection and approval and under his hygiene and safety control. It was mandatory for the cook and Bakamal as well as the palace servants to taste the food at different stages of preparation. Babur in his memoirs (Babur, p. 286) records an attempt to poison him. During one lunch, meat, fried carrots, bread, dried hare meat and buttered fritters were served to him. The bread he had eaten had been sprinkled with poison powder. Babur fell violently sick but survived. His antidote was milk in which stamped clay was dissolved which had a laxative effect. After this episode, it was made mandatory for the food to be tasted by the cook, the subordinate cook and the head taster before serving to the monarch.

There is an interesting reference to the practice of keeping some victuals in 'half ready' state should they be needed in short order. Copper vessels, coated with tin (tinning), were the preferred choice of cooking vessels and food was served in gold, silver, stone and earthenware and ceramic plates and pots and cups. A fanciful range of flavoursome recipes are mentioned like *zard birinj* (spicy rice with meat and nuts – sweet or savory), *Qubuli* (rice with meat, *Ghi* and condiments), *biriyani* (using a whole Dashmad sheep) which used to be made in the Mughal kitchens (Ain: 24) and which are still popular today. The use of spices and condiments in a special way and the particular way foods were prepared have earned the cuisine the name *Mughalai* style.

Mindful of the messiness involved in animal slaughter, butchering was carried out in specially constructed slaughter houses which were far away from the royal kitchens. This ensured cleaner surroundings.

More than any rations that might have fallen to the soldiers share and although some amount of food might have been given out of the imperial kitchens to the officers and servants attached to the stables, it is the specific food allocations for horses, camels, cows and mules, (Ain: 53–70) which are very interesting; these rations were quite precise, much the same way as mentioned in the *ArthaŚāstra*.

The royal exchequer directly bore the expenses of all this luxury but the expenditure on the daily maintenance of troops amounted to a fixed salary and was the responsibility of the different *subahs* to which they belonged.

Akbar's court was huge and his army housed anywhere between 50,000 to 200,000 men in Delhi alone, composed of cavalry, musketeers, gunners, light field guns (stirrup artillery) and heavy cannon, reserves of horses and elephants, soldiers, grooms and servants. Their leaders received pensions and profits (Braudel, 1993, p. 234) which allowed them to live in a lavish style. Each leader resplendently riding an elephant or sedan chair or palanquin or dressed and decked out in splendour was a sight to behold – with 100 servants in tow (in the field these were non Muslims, of a darker skin) carrying various articles like toothpicks, spittoons and drinking water. The Delhi contingent had Rajputs led by their own Rajahs, who raised their own native armies against neighbouring Persians or Pathans or Muslims from Bengal or against Hindu or Muslim princes of the hostile Deccan.

A constant thorn in the side was Shivaji – the great Hindu Maratha warrior. He was fully versed in war preparedness. Shivaji devoted much effort to fortify his estate and each fort was kept in a most efficient and performing manner under a garrison of faithful soldiers. This involved a vast expenditure and additionally a large supply of stores, equipment, ammunition and food to be maintained for emergencies. He needed funds to make payments to his army and to obtain war materials. He was rapidly spending the revenues collected from estates. He was the master of southern Konkan but he ambushed as easily to capture money and baggage trains proceeding towards Bijapur (Puri, 1980 p. 79).

Aurangazeb, who sent his armies against Shivaji, experienced the kind of warfare which the Marathas carried on for a long time to come. Shivaji was daring and had no compunction to order his followers to attack and plunder the baggage of Amir-ul-Umara's army wherever they met up. Upon learning this, a cavalry force of 4,000 horses with experienced officers was detailed to march and protect the baggage (Pringle, 1904, p. 425). Typical ambushing tactics were adopted by Shivaji's daredevil *Dakhinis* who appeared suddenly pouncing on the train and made off with horses, camels, men and whatever else they could carry away, and having achieved what they wanted, vanished as quietly when they saw approaching troops. And it would not be wrong to say that the plundering soldiers provided for themselves all the food and any other supplies required and that there was no other special mechanism of food distribution while engaged in such guerilla war.

Between Aurangzeb's death in 1707 and the Battle of Plassey in 1757, when the East India Company took over, was a period during which the once great Mughal Empire was declining. Delhi was seized by Afghans and the Deccan kingdoms were once again left to their own devices. Long before the British, Portuguese trading dominated Calicut and then Goạ. There was also a French and Dutch presence in the southern parts in the way of factories. The British nonetheless began, in the name of expanding trade, insidiously to build force strength and occupy portions of land in the provinces of Bengal and Madras. Jafre (1998) gives us an insight into this transformation from Mughal to colonial rule.

The British Empire spread gradually in stages and was complete by 1849 when it conquered the Punjab (Bruadel, 1993, pp. 236–237). There were several native autonomous states, each independent, (real or virtual) which pursued their own skirmishes and wars. In the south, there were pliable rulers as allies or collaborators but also there were some fiercely independent minded ones whose defeat at the hands of the British brought the almost complete subjugation of India.

Hyder Ali and Tipu Sultan

One notable phase in India's warrior tradition came with the reign of Hyder Ali and Tipu Sultan of Seringapatam (now called Srirangapatnam), who waged wars against British domination on one side and against the Marathas on the other while repulsing both Nizam's and Maratha troops from their territories. Hyder Ali knew when to strike a blow against the British. In 1769, he launched his first war against the British in a raid with 6,000 horses on Madras and dictated peace terms to the Governor (Kirmani, 1958, p. 144). One must try and imagine the march with such a large cavalry on primitive roads and through thick woods and forests. There are no specifics on how the troops fared during their march and intermittent encampment. Hyder was defeated in his last war in 1781 and killed. Tipu, his son, made peace with the British but was in a continuous state of battle with the Nizam, the Marathas and the Coorgis in turn. When he struck Travancore, which was an English ally, though successful initially he came up against the British who struck against his own territories. Bangalore fell in March 1791 and Seringapatam Fort itself was threatened by February 1792. One major shortcoming in those times was the situation of supplies and sickness among the troops. In war, powerful allies are a great help in providing support, supplies and other necessities. Tipu did not seem to have entertained any such closeness. Commenting on those times, Michaud tells us that Tipu was a staunch Muslim who hated all infidels alike (both Christians and Hindus), listened to none, lacked judgment and kept his own counsel and thus precipitated the alienation of the Nizam's and Peshwa's troops, who might have all come together against the British (Menon, 1985).

Tipu scholars in India differ with this view of Michaud. Certainly, Professor Sheik Ali's (a renowned Tipu scholar) assessment of Tipu's reign does not support such a view (Sheik Ali, 1982). Others have gathered evidence to support the view that Tipu was tolerant, showed great respect to Hindu seers and temples and paid heed to the advice of his counsellors among who were Poornaiah, his Chief Minister and a Hindu. Scholarly papers read at a recently held national seminar highlighted Tipu's tolerant view of the Hindus and provided a rationale for his confiscating vast tracts of land and temple revenues that belonged to the Brahmins (Tipu Seminar, 2006). According to Prof. K.K.N Kurup of the University of Calicut, another renowned scholar, Tipu was not only a good administrator but believed in equitable distribution of land and wealth among his subjects, both in Carnatic and Kerala regions. He paid special homage to the Sringeri Śankarāchārya and returned the temple lands belonging to the religious establishment after a court ruling. Tipu is believed to have brought about reforms in finance, military and civil administration and organisation in the state, and in fact was the first ruler in the South to separate civil and military administration, even as his contemporaries were steeped in medieval beliefs. According to Joseph Sebastian, Professor of History at the University of Mysore, Tipu developed an alternate model for feudalism that was rooted in eighteenth century Asia. Ali (1982) states that since Tipu knew that the British had come to India for trade he made efforts to improve trade with other countries, particularly France and Turkey. What might have happened if Napoleon had come to India? We might have fallen under French rule instead of the British for the flag always followed trade.

Tipu is considered by the experts to have been a seasoned soldier who understood the utility of artillery, sophisticated guns and missiles for the destruction of fortresses. Nevertheless he kept a large number of high bred horses in his army. He is said to have instituted a proper recruitment of soldiers by the state and paid the soldiers promptly. His astuteness also extended to issuing special regulations to organise a navy for which he chose Bangalore as the Headquarters. He believed that a navy was absolutely necessary to resist the colonial powers and thwart their insidious expansionist intentions. None of the historians however discussed Tipu's military organisation or supply logistics. These were considered micro-details and hence outside their area of interest, which was economy and modernisation of the state under Tipu.

Mysore Troops and Warcraft

While the modern Indian scholars are silent about Tipu Sultan's manner of carrying out wars, Michaud was more forthcoming, very explicit and commented at length on it from a generalisation on how Indians made war to the fall of Tipu's empire in Mysore (Menon, 1985). It was a time when, after two centuries of progress in Europe, some of the newer concepts got injected into Hyder Ali's thinking. Europe's great success lay in the realm of new war craft, which was very much advanced as compared to the practices in India. Hyder Ali, helped by the French Governor, had formed his armies after the European style thus making him a formidable match for the English. Mysore troops, like other native troops elsewhere in the country, were essentially composed of irregulars who had no skills training. Also, their principal task was to act as escorts to convoys, block the transport of the enemy and attack essentially when the enemy was in flight.

They were ill-clothed, ill-equipped and carried a sword and a very long country made musket, difficult to load and fired with a match. Their skills lay in firing balls for a machine called matchlock (the same which more than two centuries ago won Babur the battle of Panipat), and using bows and arrows and spears and discharging rockets at the enemy cavalry while the latter was passing a defile. Rocket scientists in India acknowledge that Tipu was the first ever to have conceived of a rocket-like missile and had some built which he used against the British forces (the only known existing sample piece is on display in a London Museum). In this respect, Tipu was far ahead of the British or the French in his war technology and craft, however archaic and anachronistic the rest of his army and war machinery.

The regular infantry soldiers, though small in numbers, were well cared for, well trained, well paid and disciplined but in actual battle engagements much confusion reigned. They used a European design musket (with bayonet) which in fact had been passed on by the English themselves as their army arsenal discards. The English surmised that this weapon could not be dangerous in the hands of these troops since they only used defensive tactics, stood too far and never used the bayonet. The way these native armies waged war was more like guerilla attacks. Tipu's army also had bullock cart drawn artillery obtained from French foundries and gunpowder from Indian manufacturers.

Pay and Camp Food

Each soldier was well paid and a horseman even better, up to Rs. 200/- per annum. The horsemen always had a servant man to care for the horse, cut grass and fodder for the animal. The soldiers' own supplies and household articles were carried on a bullock. In essence, the soldier's family and household followed him and helped pitch camp and cook and care for him. The tent was a piece of cloth and even palm-leaf sun shelters were put up quickly. If there is no one specific account that can be found referring to supplies and provisioning during marches and in wars fought in the various Indian states in our history, it would be because for the kings and commanders everything was arranged as befitted their position and status by the large retinue of personal attendants and servants that accompanied them. For the soldiers and the rest of the contingents, there were large bazaars accompanying the armies that acted as supply chain for food and other necessities. These bazaars were set up in the entrenched encampments in designated locations by civilian traders who stocked every conceivable article required by the soldiers, commanders and non-combatants. The contractors supplied food and forage and the soldiers purchased their own food. For the king's pleasure and personal service, there were the *Peshkhanas* (advance tents in preparation of the journey) in the style of the Mughals (Eraly, 2000, p. 112) whether during an expedition or while just shifting residence. This manner of travel was an ancient practice observed by the native rajahs and maharajas and all the Muslim dynasties and Mughal kings that ruled India. When war expeditions marched out, the armies were attached to this civilian umbilical cord of supply and could not stray too far out or away while they were on the move.

In keeping with the tradition, Tipu's armies were accompanied by large contingents of non-combatants and it is said that while his *zenana* (palace ladies) was huge, in Hyder Ali's tents one did not see any women. Descriptions of such entourages indicate that each soldier was accompanied by his family (both immediate and extended) and his belongings, his animals and his cart or tumbrel. Probably the entire village emptied itself out if sufficient number of soldiers belonged to that village. People living inside the forts may have felt more secure to leave their families and belongings behind. In either case, for replenishment of the supplies, food or forage, the countryside was ransacked.

Tipu is known to have kept many fortified towns in his territory well stocked with essential goods – arms, weapons, animals, feed, forage, grain and other articles to be accessed during his marches. But before marching, it was customary to take a good strong dose of opium mixed with food in the form of a preparation known as *bhang*, which gave them a sense of courage and made them impetuous and ferocious. That the armies took copious amounts of such substances to bolster their courage before battle is learnt from the descriptions of battle preparedness during the Kurukshetra war and the battle of Tunga.

In the time of the invasion of Mysore in 1799, the British had gathered a force strength of 40,000 combatants and true to the native tradition, four or five times this number of non-combatants. Wellington had the singular job of getting adequate number of pack animals to organise his baggage trains. There were moving columns of the army marching from Bangalore containing numerous soldiers, their followers in the 'follow train', thousands of animals and huge quantities of supplies to last them for the anticipated period of march and battle. It was a four-sided formation 3 miles wide and 7 miles long, hollow in the centre filled with the commissariat's transport animals and masses of supplies. It was imperative that supplies be taken along because the countryside had been stripped bare.

If Tipu's *zenana* was huge, the senior British officers travelled no less grandiosely. The officers had humble quarters, but the generals had more lofty tents and their entourage was characterised by the accompaniment of numerous followers of all sorts and a number of women, reminiscent of Napoleon's winter campaign in Russia which witnessed a huge encumbrance due to the army's followers and which immeasurably slowed down both his progress and retreat. That Indian troops followed some very archaic methods is seen from the resemblance between their fortresses and those of Greek and Roman fortifications. Tipu's warcraft too relied on some ancient customs such as the classic battle array, where the leader or the king was mounted on the elephant flying the banner and rode in the centre of a formation. A great value was placed on the cavalry while the footmen were used only as front line fodder. History shows us that the infantry was always advantageous in conquering the enemy as it was able to disperse and scatter quickly.

With Tipu's fall in 1799 came the British occupation of Mysore.

Battle of Tunga, 1787 – The Day of Battle

The battle of Tunga between the Rajput confederacy and the Marathas serves as an example of the massing of armies and the pre-battle preparations (Saksena, 2002, pp. 370–374). The Rajput confederacy's strength has been estimated as 54,000 where different Rajas pitched in with their own troops as was the custom, and the combined strength of this force being 40,000 (or 30,000 troops according to some records), while the others in the confederacy contributed some 20,000.

The Marathas gathered a 46,000 strong army from disparate sources − Sikh mercenaries, Baji Rao's two battalions of de Boigne, Naga monks, Rajdhar Gujar, Madhaji and Rane Khan.

Customarily the battles were fought from sunrise to sunset hence battle preparations began early − three hours before sunrise. A *naguarra* (drum) was beaten as a wake-up call to get ready; it announced to the encamped troops that battle would ensue in the morning. *Choubdars* moved from camp to camp telling the troops to 'get ready' for war which meant completing morning ablutions, bathing and strapping on the battle gear. Those whose responsibility was to cook had already begun their work. Men moved with huge quantities of meals and distributed them. At the same time, gunpowder was also distributed.

Meals were consumed quickly. The commander or the ruler ate only when he was informed that all the men had eaten. It has been mentioned here that opium was being used; whether it was consumed along with the meal or was carried on the person is not known. It is likely that the narcotic served to give a certain amount of courage (however false it might be) if taken before battle, and if taken upon being injured, it decreased the pain of injures received in the battle. It was customary to pray before battle, the commander of the forces worshipped and invoked divine graces for victory and success. The *naguarra* was sounded a third time, which signalled the cavalry to mount their horses, and off they went into the battle deployed as per the predetermined battle array − usually a hollow square.

The East India Company

It was Vasco da Gama who first landed on the Indian coast of Calicut in 1498, just four years after Columbus discovered America and two years before the Portuguese discovered Brazil. Babur's Mughal Empire in Delhi was on its way to establishing a glorious future for itself from the 1520s though Babur himself had a very brief rule from 1526 to 1530.

The Portuguese had taken San Thome. St. Francis Xavier's ascendancy at Goa and Sir Francis Drake's voyage round the world in 1577 were heralding events. Akbar, by then, had come to ascend the Mughal throne and was to become the greatest Mughal Emperor ever. The Portuguese, Dutch, English, and French all sought and demanded trading rights with India. While the Portuguese came early in Babur's time, it was the lucrative Dutch spice trade in the East Indies which the English wanted a slice of and could not get. Indian spices were the next best (Woodward, 1978, p. 25), therefore the English looked towards India. Competition with the Portuguese and the French was their original and primary objective. They captured a Portuguese ship containing cargo from India in 1592. It was full of articles of every description, from gems, jewels, silks, calicos, carpets, quilts, dyes, porcelain vessels, to rare objects like ivory and even coconuts. Their value was estimated to be more than £1,50,000. This was the incentive for them to start trade in the East which led to the formation of a trading company. So in AD 1600, the East India Company was founded in London, to establish trade with India and if possible to capture a good bit of the spice commerce. They wanted a Royal Charter to trade and in return promised large rewards (Woodward, 1978, p. 19). Queen Elizabeth I gave them the charter. The Company of merchants of London who traded in the East Indies became the Honourable East India Company.

The beginning of one of the greatest mercantile enterprises ever founded began with trade in the port areas of Bombay, Madras and Calcutta. Its business presence expanded rapidly, moved inland and became very influential. These areas later became known as the Presidencies of Bombay, Madras and Bengal. Their trading stations were known as factories (Gaylor, 1992, p. 1).

From the early days of settlement the Company employed sepoys to guard and protect their properties. These early soldiers were nowhere like the well-drilled sepoys of the East India Company of later times. They were ragged, ill disciplined bandit like lot. The two people who are given credit for transforming this ragged bunch into an efficient infantry are Robert Clive and his Commander-in-Chief General Stringer Lawrence, the latter is also called the father of the Indian Army (Woodward, 1978, p. 119).

Not long after that, the Company established itself in 1619 in Surat, Masulipatnam, and Armagon successively. The Madras history begins when the first Fort St. George was built in Madras by Francis Day in 1640. He was convinced that a sandy strip near the sea was an ideal place for a settlement. And there began the tussle between the British and Mir Jumla for the Fort. The French captured San Thome but had to yield to the British but then attacked Madras and regained the territory. The Mughal Empire fell after the death of Aurangzeb around 1707. New currency called the New Star Pagoda was minted.

Robert Clive did not appear on the Indian scene until 1743. He was a clerk, not a solider but managed to get a commission and joined the fight to take Madras back from the French in the campaign at Trichinopoly in 1746 (Reid, 1999, pp. 69–77). Clive's career rose steadily; he prospered and acquired status and then a position as the Lt. Governor of Cuddalore before the age of 30.

In 1756, Madras was confronted with the news that Nawab Siraj-Ud-Daulah had captured the Company's settlements at Calcutta and that some 146 Europeans had been taken prisoner and were confined in a small space for one night. During this operation, 123 of them had died – an incident that came to be known as the Black Hole of Calcutta (Reid, 1999, p. 26). The situation called for reinforcements, not found in Bengal and not adequately obtainable from Bombay. Therefore, Clive was dispatched in command of the land forces while Admiral Watson sailed in command of his naval fleet. The land forces of Clive were composed of 600 men of the 39th Foot, 300 of the Company's European Regiment and 1,500 Madras sepoys. In a very brief time, Calcutta was retaken.

The Battle of Plassey and After

Eighteenth century India or Hindustan, as it was known under the East India Company, was a veritable land that promised huge revenues as land taxes from Bengal to the Carnatic, and from Punjab to Assam and was the battling ground for the British and the French in the South. Both had armies made up of Indian soldiers beginning to be drilled and trained and armed in the European fashion. Both Robert Clive and the French Commander Duplex had become quite knowledgeable about the Indian way of warfare and believed that only a handful of imported ruffian white troops would be sufficient to cause terror and instill psychological fear into the Indian soldiers by wielding the European flintlock muskets. In Bengal, the Company was establishing its presence by building forts, abusing local traders and nawabs and cornering their revenues. Bengal, that rich land where the flailing Mughal Nawab Siraj Ud-Daula reigned became a battle ground for Clive to quell any second thoughts that Siraj might be harbouring against the East India Company. The early history of India during the British reign has been the subject of scholarly works by several recent authors like Edwards (1963), Lawrence (1994), Metcalf and Metcalf (2002) and Wolpert (1993).

Commercial privileges enjoyed by groups and companies almost always seem to turn into political ambitions if only to retain a hold on commercial interests. It was no different in Bengal. The East India Company took every possible advantage and brazenly began to show its true colours. When the Nawab who was the natural inheritor of the state and who until now had cordial relations with the British felt obligated to declare war, seeing the obvious spread of the British presence, he was swiftly defeated and Calcutta was seized (Lawrence, 1994, p. 127). The English Company needed its revenues no less than the restoration of its prestige. The revenues would support the war effort in the Carnatic against the French. It was Bengal, says Lawrence that was the main source and strength of the Company.

The beginning of the strangle hold of the East India Company on India may be ascribed to the Battle of Plassey.

Plassey, India's nemesis and Clive's trained military muscle and success were the proof, if one sought it, that the East India Company was to be a force to reckon with. Siraj was not easily cowed down by his defeat at Clive's hands, so he re-grouped his army yet again. In the historic battle that ensued, Clive's army was small in numbers, 3,000 men by this time – 1,000 European troops, 2,000 sepoys and 8 small caliber cannon and howitzers compared to the typically loose and ponderous huge Indian Army of 40,000 infantry, 18,000 cavalry and 50 heavy guns mustered by Siraj Ud-Daula, along with a large train of massive bullock drawn cannons. Clive encamped near the river Bhagirathi, close to the village of Plassey. On June 22 at 6 am, the British army crossed the river and reached a place called the Mango Tope. From daybreak on June 23 until dark, the battle raged. The Nawab's army was apparently no match for the totally reliable and disciplined English troops, the majority of whom were Madrasis. The Nawab's troops, huge in number as they were, had become a demoralised lot, Clive having prepared for five months, shaking their and their generals' morale with subversive tactics. Many of the troops never fought at all. These are stated to be the actual facts of the battle of Plassey (Reid, 1999, pp. 26–28). In the battlefield they fled in fright and were found to be disorganised. All that the European army had to do was to shoot the beasts, the bullocks and the elephants and roar at them (Lawrence, 1994, p. 128). The resulting stampede and chaos and falling commanders caused Siraj's army to flee. Bengal was now in British hands and expansion by coercion became a policy and a pattern of their occupation and rule. Much administrative energy was devoted to collecting all the land revenue from the rural peasants. In the late eighteenth century, native men of substance had been empowered to collect taxes from Bengal, Orissa and Bihar. These people came to be leaders only in name. Mir Jafir was installed as the Nawab.

Advantages of being in the Company: For the Englishmen, being in Company pay or being associated with it in other ways was lucrative. Even the lowest employee looked forward to accumulating some sort of wealth from the dealings, gleanings and takings of different kinds.

Military power increased enormously and fortunes were made from war profits, gifts received and from corruption. Clive and several other officers received large gifts from Mir Jafir. Every Company official saw an opportunity to make money. Tax collection officers began to pocket revenues. Fortunes were made from war profits.

Robert Clive, from a class of minor gentry in Shropshire, became a soldier of fortune and not a soldier by training. Clive made 44,000 pounds sterling from 1744 to 1753 as war loot as a junior commander and then received gifts of appreciation from Mir Jafir to the tune of pounds sterling 200,000. Altogether, between 1757 and 1766, he was said to have earned pounds sterling 234,000. Junior officials were ready to sail to get into action – not necessarily for glory but for possible chances of promotion, extra campaign allowances and a chance to grab loot and prize money.

In this way, many officers of the military made tidy sums from campaign allowances and from loot and prize money, enough at any rate to provide annuities for their families at home and still save enough and get a pension to live like the gentry and lead a life of ease upon their return.

Many soldiers grabbed what they could, when they could since procedures for money distribution were not only slow but mostly favoured the senior officers (Lawrence, 1994, p. 130). It seems that after the fall of Bharatpur in 1826 after a long siege, the soldiers watched cartloads of gold and silver being auctioned off and also saw others carry off gold ornaments, jewellery, and camel hair shawls, while still others were seen to dig up floors to hunt for buried cash. War and looting such as this was happening for decades and could not be controlled by the officers.

Thus a son in the Company's army meant lucrative gains for the family back home. But such officers and men were still looked down upon by those in the King's army.

The Sepoy Army

Napoleon had once said that there were no bad troops, only bad officers and that the morale and efficiency of a unit reflected on their officers. According to military historians, Indian soldiers in this respect had been exceptional; all that they required was professional and dedicated officers to lead them. The British seemed to have held this view throughout the regime of the East India Company. There was no native commissioned officer in the Company's rule; a Subedar was the highest rank, upgraded to Subedar-Major that an Indian could aspire to become (Rajkumar, 2004, p. 65).

However, the bulk of the three Presidency armies, Bombay, Calcutta and Madras were filled with Indians. There were three arms – the artillery, cavalry and the infantry. There were no native forces in the artillery battalions which numbered six in all. They were all manned by Europeans. Together with cavalry and infantry, there were 19 European manned battalions to 167½ native manned battalions. There was no cavalry arm in the Bombay Presidency army. All the armies however, had Lascars. In 1785, the total army strength was 73,000 (Rajkumar, 2004, pp. 60–61). For the next 72 years, the identity of the three Presidency armies was kept distinct and though never united into one army, they were required to fight together. The complete history of the military system of the East India Company lists the full details of the strength of the army as well as the Nizam's army, of Hyderabad, which came under British protection in 1798. Much later, in 1849, the Punjab force – Sikh cavalry and infantry was raised, whose strength reached 70,000 in 1857.

The Bengal army was somehow given a greater prominence and it formed almost fifty percent of the total Company army strength, 323,623 being the total strength of the Combat Arms (Rajkumar, 2004, p. 189).

At the time of the Sepoy mutiny, while the Europeans in the Bengal Army numbered 59,486, the native strength was put at 170,000. And why not? Apart from the fact that the native forces, in the words of Sir Thomas Munro, were 'quite orderly and easily managed, the native officers were well acquainted with their duties, and conduct almost all the interior details and leave but little for the European officers to do'. Further, 'they might become insolent and careless when left to themselves and European officers are absolutely necessary to direct them but not many are required. One (officer) to a company is quite enough for a useful purpose'. There was the equally important consideration of finances. For one thing, it was cheaper to finance even European troops in India; an individual's pay was just Rs. 36/- against the equivalent of Rs. 185/- in England. One European earned three times as much as a native and the Royal troops were even more expensive (Rajkumar, 2004, p. 59), Balancing economy with safety, the British of course compromised minimally with the artillery arm. A native artillery was raised in Madras during the Mysore war in 1796–1799. The success of the native troops in various British campaigns during 1856 reinforced their fears of putting guns in the hands of the natives and especially so after the 1857 mutiny.

To move the necessary guns and artillery, animals were needed. Men had to drag it all the way to Calcutta due to non-availability of transport animals. One estimate of the number of horses required for moving horse artillery, heavy guns, thousands of rounds of ammunition, tumbrils, forge wagon and stores carts gives a figure of 546 (Rajkumar, 2004, p. 103). For operations in the South, they could not obtain suitable or good quality animals, which became, the main reason for their debacle in the confrontation between Lord Cornwallis and Tipu Sultan in May 1791. During the several droughts, animals died, there was bad weather, the Maratha army failed to turn up, the guns could not be fired and so they were abandoned. There were no cattle or drivers in the employ of the army. Hiring and firing was done on an *ad hoc* basis in the Madras Army. But finally better sense prevailed and eight companies of drivers and draught bullocks were raised. The Madras Army consisted of Naidus, Mudaliars, Panickers, Pillays: Hindus as well as Muslims and Christians who joined the army and were found to be hard working, minding their own business, well disciplined, intelligent and efficient. A common bond existed between them which was characterised by closely working together without any animosity. They ate the same kind of food too (Reid, 1999, p. 41).

The strength of one troop unit varied between the years 1749 and 1752 and there was as yet no native cavalry in Government Service (Wilson, 1882, p. 37). *Peons* were the name given to the First Native foot soldiers and in 1747 there were some 3,000 of them employed at Fort St. David. Over 900 were armed with musket. The Government considered 1,300 men to be adequate to protect all its persons in Fort St. George (600 men), Fort St. David (600 men) and Devicottah (100 men) (Wilson, 1882, p. 72). The Bengal Native Army was raised in 1802. Bombay, Madras, and Calcutta were the main centers of British rule, each with its own forces and Commander-in-Chief but the Commander of the Bengal army was the supreme authority in all matters military. The men who were recruited at first into the native armies belonged to the lower castes but there were also Afghan and Turkish mercenaries. But eventually, to give the armies a national flavour, peasants and the sons of large land owners were taken in increasing numbers. Many new entrants were Brahmins and the Bengal army in particular was almost entirely made up of high caste Brahmins (Edwards, 1963, p. 20). The General Service Enlistment Act introduced as a measure to make the Indian sepoy accept service anywhere in the home provinces or abroad (mostly Burma) became very unpopular. A caste Hindu would not wish to cross the seas. But service abroad was essential to keep the military garrison in Burma well supplied with troops. Since troops of the 38 Regiment had refused orders to proceed to Burma in 1852, the enactment of the Bill now made it mandatory to serve abroad or in any of the home provinces (Wolpert, 1993, p. 232; Metcalf and Metcalf, 2002, pp. 99–100).

The transition from Mughal to British colonial rule went in stages. One by one the hitherto independent states were taken, the last was Oudh which was annexed after the Mutiny; Emperor Bahadur Shah was exiled and Nawab Wajid Ali Shah forced to abdicate (India Today, 2000, p. 19).

Lifestyle of the Neo-English Nawabs

The life and living standards of the English people employed at senior levels was in direct contrast to their lifestyles in England and the status of both commoners and Indian sepoys.

The retinues in civilian and military households of the English people in India were phenomenal. A quiet elderly civilian couple needed no less than 57 employees. Some had more than 60 servants, even as many as 110 to serve a family of four! What did these servants do? Apart from being a *dhobi* (washerman), a *darzi* (tailor), cowherd, shepherd, poultry man, carpenters, gardeners, grooms, coachmen, hairdressers, wig-bearers, valets, *hookah-bunder*, ladies maids, children's *ayahs*, cooks, bakers, dog watchers and dog walkers, there were just too many waiting at the tables.

A military officer, a captain who took part in the Mysore war of 1780, had an impressive number of staff comprising his steward, cook, valet, a groom and a groom's assistant, a barber, a washerwoman, fifteen coolies to carry his baggage, his wine, his brandy, his live poultry and milch goats. These servants in turn had their families with them (Woodward, 1978, p. 137).

As someone who was there and had witnessed the British and their army life in particular, the account given by Sir Otto Trevalyan provides an accurate picture of the times (Trevalyan, 1992).

From 1775 onwards, the East India Company had kept a brigade in Cawnpore (Kanpur) for the defense of Oudh; the forces maintained by revenues from the rich and extensive land. In 1801, Lord Wellesley foreclosed the mortgage on Cawnpore and acquired it for the Company, according to Trevalyan. In 1857, there were three regiments of sepoys, the First, the 53rd and the 56th Bengal Infantry, the 2nd Cavalry and a company of artillery men; the total native force numbering around 3,000 against a little over 1,000 of Europeans or persons of European extraction, Eurasians or Anglo Indians. There were about 300 officers and soldiers of English birth attached to the various sepoy battalions. Cawnpore was also host to what was called the covenanted civilians – the so called aristocracy of Indians, certain lesser officials attached to the post office, the public works and the opium departments, people in the railways, merchants and shopkeepers.

At Cawnpore, there was a first class military station. The cantonment area was the unique military quarters for the Englishmen and entirely distinct from the native quarter. There is the sense that an English officer of the Bengal Army, even the lowest ranking subaltern, was a man of abundant leisure whether he was posted in Calcutta or Cawnpore. He was free to indulge in anything that took his fancy and had the time and means to do so; from just lazing about to playing not too strenuous games, growing fruits and vegetables, visiting libraries, attending races and dinners given to passing dignitaries or attending the Free Mason's gatherings, or visiting the Breakfast club and Ice club, etc. He had nothing more vigorous to do than gaze at his own horses or at the Patna sheep belonging to the station Mutton club, and lazily attempt to gain a little insight in to the hateful 'Eastern Languages' from a native tutor. He dressed in fine silk and linen to keep him cool in the night.

The Fresh Food Ice Club membership was an essential feature which enabled the English to procure fish and codfish that came from the Canadian lakes and New Foundland and apples from Pennsylvania, all embedded in crushed mass of ice. Therefore, there was no dearth of fresh food. The 'Ice House' located on the beach in Chennai was built to house the ice brought in from Boston in the 1700s. It is a place of deep gloomy corridors and rooms at different levels. It now houses the Swami Vivekananda Memorial. Every Presidency had its ice arrangements for the comfort of the Europeans in the Army and the civilian English families. They could purchase anything – locally sold fish, flesh, fowl, at what they considered low prices, but which the Anglo Indians found to be rather steep for mutton at 6 pence a pound and a fat turkey at 3 shillings a piece. There were other indulgences such as quail, wild duck, snipe and black partridges also to be tried at low prices (Trevalyan, 1992, p. 11). There were exclusive military posts (Trevalyan, 1992, p. 29) such as in the Departments of Adjutant General, the Quarter Master General (QMG), the Commissary General and the Judge Advocate General.

In Trevalyan's descriptions, these officers were high ranking and lived befitting as they perceived it to be their station and position in the Company. Whatever may have been their rank, the Englishmen made their homes with no regard to economy or space.

The British hierarchal system functioned with a small cadre of officers at the top in administration. It was no different in the army. An officer of the lowest rank enjoyed perks and luxuries in India far beyond his imagination. These included spacious accommodation and a horde of servants to do his every bidding and to anticipate his needs and pleasures.

Each lived in a stand alone house surrounded by three to four acres of paddock land with a sort of ditch marking the boundaries. In Calcutta, the residence of a bachelor or subaltern was a single storey brick house with two or three bedrooms, shabby, cobwebby, minimally furnished but well served with a personal staff such as a tailor, a *punkah*-puller (a *punkah* is a ceiling fan made of ruffled cloth strung and fixed to a horizontally hung pole fixed high on the wall near the ceiling; the pole is pulled to and fro manually by a rope, which duty befell a boy or a man exclusively employed for the purpose), and a personal madras valet to spread butter on *sahib's* bread with a greasy wing of a fowl! Drinking water came from the row of jars of porous clay which cooled it. A table full of soda bottles, playing cards, chessmen, *Hindustanee* dictionary, books, revolver, cigars, regimental book club volumes and some 8 or 10 chairs, plus a couch completed the furnishings along with a list of men in the officer's own company. The personal effects of the officer included the sword, buggy ship, rifle and shotgun. In the kitchen department, there would be several boys, assistants for clean up, cook, cook's assistants for food preparation, footmen to bring food and serve and a *khansama* (butler) to supervise service.

Married quarters were rather more grandiose than this but were still somewhat shabby. Description and sketches of the lifestyle lived by the English family men provided by Woodward (1978) depict a vast number of personal and family servants, probably one each to carryout a specific task. Naturally, all the servants – men, women and boys were all natives. Whether these people belonged to the family of the sepoys or were outsiders is not mentioned.

A life of plenty and leisure marked the every day routine of the British military officers and men. That they could pursue this lifestyle was fully owed to the native sepoys and Subedars of the Bengal Army who did the brunt of the work associated with the regiments and the barracks.

The officers came to depend greatly on the subordinates (mostly native Indians) in the army, the tiers of subordinates clouded the administrative and moral responsibilities but who in turn served with loyalty and a serene system of mutual comfort and faith was established, said Trevalyan who had witnessed it all (1992).

Under these circumstances, it was never imagined by the British army that their so faithful and obedient sepoys and subedars would rise up against them in revolt, as they did in the mutiny of 1857. This was the last major Indian uprising against the British and though it began with a bang, it ended with a whimper.

Cantonment Quarters of Native Troops

The quarters of the native troops and officers were quite separate from the European sector and they lived in Sepoy lines. These lines were long rows of huts made from mud and bamboo and thatched with straw. Everyone had his own cabin, inviolable and out of bounds. In these accommodations lived numerous relatives, mostly female. The officers lived in their own dwellings at the end of each row/line. Each house had a small courtyard with a few feet high mud wall as fence. Each regiment had a bazaar peculiar in its way, with suttlers pandering to every whim, fancy and taste of the native troops, from food, clothes and ornaments to entertainers and even drugs.

The Brahmin battalion was completely staffed with Brahmin officers and their hierarchal structure in the army ran as follows: in every regiment (Trevelyan, 1992, p. 33) there was a Subedar major (spelled Soubhadhar) or a native colonel and in every company was a Subedar who reported to a European Captain, and a Jemmadar who answered to a European Subaltern. These were the commissioned officers wearing sword and sashes, who sat on courts-martial and were saluted by the ranks. They also carried the musket. But there was no pretence of friendship between the English and the native officers. The native equivalent of the British Army sergeant and corporal were known as *Havildar* and *Naick.*

There was a hierarchal system among the sepoy tribes too and this was based more on cultural/traditional habits and customs than merely on rank. Since most people originated from the villages, even in the matter of food, the customs of their individual village, community, caste and family prevailed. All the sepoys and their head sepoys (Subedar) practiced elaborate rituals. Each would bathe and make ready for prayers in the orthodox Hindu way, and sit in a cleansed/purified place in his house or barracks to eat food (also prepared by observing orthodox methods) served to him by his underling, who would not eat until his master had eaten. Everything was made fresh and the main foodstuffs came from his village. The fare depended on the riches and luxury and the status he enjoyed in his village and community.

Army Emoluments in the East India Company

It has been mentioned previously that the pay of an English soldier in India did not amount to more than Rs. 36. Discussing the origin, propagation and equipment of the British army, and the expenditure incurred by the Crown on army officers and transport in England contemporary to the British Raj, Scott (1880) of the British army provided some figures calculated on per diem basis.

Emoluments of the officers of the Trayn (Train) Ordnance corps amounted to 38 pounds 8s 10d, while not specifying the number of officers. For the hire of 1,500 horses, Rs.150/- was expended per diem. The pay of 532 drivers was 39.18s and the cost of 60 country wagons was £600 per *mensem* (month). The horse feed, apart from all else, also included meat which for the 1,500 horses cost 112.10s. This is the only other time apart from the ancient ArthaŚāstra where a meat ration has been indicated for horses.

In India, the officer cadres of the Artillery of course did far better, and for a princely sum varying between £150 p.a. for a first captain and chief engineer and second captain, second engineer of the Artillery to £100 p.a. and £75 (and progressively less to £60 and £50) to the Director of Laboratory and first lieutenant worker.

The pay packets of the sergeant Bombardiers and corporal Bombardiers were fixed at 2 shillings and 1s 6d per diem respectively. The gunners and drummers received 1s per diem (Wilson, 1882, p. 45).

In 1747, one Capt. Alexander Delavaux was appointed as a chief engineer and as a captain of all the settlements and captain of all the Train of Artillery at £200 per annum and as per the Court of Directors' advisement, the Madras Govt. was to provide Capt. Delavaux this sum. The native soldiers' pay was calculated sometimes in fanams and pagodas and cash in the Madras Army and at other times in rupees (Rs.), anna (a), paise (p), and c (meaning cash which came to be known as *casu* in later times). Till the introduction of the decimal system in India in 1954–55, rupee, anna and paise were the currency (there were 16 annas to a rupee or 192 casu or cash/paise per one rupee).

Perks for Englishmen in military service: An officer's special perquisites upon his arrival in India included a suitable residential apartment in the fort, diet money, a *pallankeen* (pallanquin), and servants, just as these benefits were allowed for the members of the Council of Directors. In addition, the Captain was to be given travelling charges at company expenses whenever he travelled from one place to another on company business (Wilson, 1882, p. 45). Like Captain Delavaux of the Laboratory, there would have been several such high ranking officials deriving not only super-pay but all manner of benefits in the service of the Company.

Pay for the natives: It must be remembered here that the native commanders were subordinate to even the European subalterns and their allowances were small in comparison. In 1759, when the appointment was created, the total emolument for a Subedar was Rs.114/- of which Rs. 60-per month came from rank pay as Subedar and Rs. 54-as allowance for the position of command. For reasons not known nor explained, this pay was revised to Rs.127/- in 1766 and remained so till 1785 when the appointment itself was abolished (Wilson, 1882, p. 369). One account given by Wilson in the 'History of Madras Army' of the pay of a private soldier provides a figure of 2½ pagodas at 8 shillings to a pagoda to just about 1 pound sterling per month or 75 fanams (at the rate of 30 fanams per pagoda) (Wilson, 1882, p. 114). (Note: a pagoda was later valued at 42 fanams at the rate of 12 fanams to one rupee.) In the Native Artillery at Madras, the total monthly pay check of 107 personnel amounted to no more than 255 pagodas (p) where as the only subedar was paid 16 pagoda, 2 Jemmadars were paid 6 p each, 6 Havildars got 4 p each, 6 Naigues (Naiks) 3 p each, one Drummer and one fifer got 2½ p each. The 2 *Bhesties* (water carriers) got 2 p each and the 88 privates got 2 p each too (Wilson, 1882, pp. 345–346).

The pay and *batta* of the artillery drivers of the draught cattle in the Madras Army, when it came around to appointing regular drivers under the control of the officers commanding the companies of foot artillery, also had to be provided for. It varied from *Darogahs* to a driver. The monthly pay of a *Darogah* was Rs. 17 of a chowdry Rs. 12 and of a driver Rs. 6 and 8 annas(a). Since they were the backbone of the army's mobility, they were also paid daily *batta*. For the three categories mentioned above, the *batta*, respectively, was 2a 5p 87c, 1a 10p 40c and 1a 2p 93c (Rajkumar, 2004, p. 105). The terms rupee Re/Rs., anna (a), paise (p) and casu/cash (c), were in usage until the middle 1950s. After the decimal system was introduced, the term rupee was retained as well as paise where 1 Re = 100 p).

Although pay scales in the other armies have not been mentioned, it is presumed that in all the Presidency armies, the pay scales were the same or very similar. At Fort St. David on the Coromandel Coast, a military garrison was settled under the command of a major, a captain and commander at pounds 250 per annum, paid in pagodas. In the same settlements, the per diem payments for one Capt. Lieutenant were 5s, for one engineer 4s, for 1 adjutant 5s, for the 4 sergeants 1s 8d, for the 4 corporals 1s 2d, for the Drum major 1s 8d, for the two drummers 1s 2d each and for the 70 or 80 private sentinels 10d. In another Company, the captain got slightly more i.e. 10s and a lieutenant 5s (Wilson, 1882, p. 69). Such a disparity in pay has not been explained.

As the century of British rule progressed, life for the ordinary folk seemed to be a humdrum affair, no excitements of public celebration, pageants or spectacle as in the days of the rajas. The Sepoy on the other hand found that his pay of 7 rupees (14 shillings) a month was raised by one rupee after 16 yrs of service or by two rupees after 20 yrs of service! Since they lived together in a Company, there were expenses towards clothes, (up to five rupees per year), towards washerman, barber and sweeper to be shared. These deductions amounted to less than six annas per man per month. The Sepoy in the Bengal Army sent at least 3 rupees, sometimes even 4 home to his family living in the villages of Oudh and Bihar from where most or all of the recruits originated. (The modern army sepoys, now called jawans, on the other hand have their families living with them in certain peace postings and training establishments).

After all these deductions from his month's pay there remained just three rupees or often even less (only one and half rupees) in the sepoy's pocket (Mason, 1974, p. 199).

While these were the salary scales on regular pay, the troops were often moved during operations and were paid their daily *batta* until 1755, presumably in addition to the regular pay but one fine day, the government in its wisdom decided to discontinue payment of the outstation *batta* and the commanding officer alone was exempted because he incurred expenses while entertaining travellers (Wilson, 1882, p. 118).

Food purchasing value of money in the mid 1700s: It must be clear to the readers that there were no free meals and rations given to the troops and the pay they received had to suffice to meet personal and family needs of food, clothing and shelter. Discontinuing the daily batta in outstation manoeuvres brought great hardship to the soldiers. What would they eat on their own? How would they eat on their pay packets which would have to be stretched to give them adequate food? How much cash could they really carry outstation to allow them to buy food from local markets? The readers of today may be better able to appreciate this dilemma of the late 1750s by glancing at the market price of provisions and other necessities in the rural southern bazaars. The European soldiers were harder hit perhaps but they were trained differently.

A market survey was carried out in Trichinopoly on March 6, 1755 by a Major Kilpatrick. He later represented to the Government to reintroduce *batta* on the basis of the market prices prevalent at the time. He backed his petition with a prepared price list (Table 6.1) which was submitted to the Board of Directors of the Company. Even though by today's reckoning the prices seem to be incredibly low, the sepoys had a hard time living practically hand-to-mouth on the remnants of their pay packets. Food was not the only thing they needed.

Table 6.1: Market Price of provisions in Trichinopoly, 1755

Rice	: 12 seers* for 1 rupee
Wheat	: 2 ¼ seers for 1 rupee
Mutton	: 6 seers for 1 rupee
Beef	: 10 seers for 1 rupee
Firewood	: 8 small bundles for 1 rupee
Fish	: Not available

* One Seer or ser carried different values. In the old Madras Presidency, one seer was equal to 8 palams of paddy or rice.
Source: Wilson, 1882

They needed other necessities such as shoes (which wore out pretty fast), which cost 2 quarters per pair, coarse shirts cost Re. 1 and 2 each, a coarse cloth waistcoat cost Re. 1. The washerman and the barber had to be paid for each service at half a rupee. And the soldiers could be compelled for long stretches of time to buy him daily food and necessities. Barely 2 or 3 rupees a month were all that he could save if he did not send any money home.

How could he budget his money? He purchased 1 seer of rice for 13½ cash, 16 cash worth of mutton or beef, scraps of fish perhaps, about 6 cash worth of ghee or butter oil and small amounts of pepper. Salt perhaps for 2½ cash, a small amount of buttermilk for 4 cash and firewood to cook his food for 8 cash (Wilson, 1882, p. 114).

Their simple food was made up of rice, fat, meat, buttermilk and condiments and while probably being adequate enough in quantity and major nutrients, the diet seems to have been devoid of any fresh vegetables and fruits. If the men did buy or scrounge for such dietary accompaniments, it is not mentioned. But basically his eighteenth century diet looks to have been a deficient meal both quantity and nutrient wise.

Further, this partly nutrient deficient meal cost the soldiers 2 fanams and 12 cash per day (@ 20 cash to a fanam), around 78 fanams which was much above their monthly pay of 2½ pagodas, or 75 fanams not counting other necessities.

Even as the twenty-first century reader is awed at the 1750s price structure of commodities, for sepoys of the time it would have been a hardship of no small order when deployed out in campaigns and with no additional *batta* to help stretch the budget.

On an average, a man is supposed to consume 2 lbs of grain per day. While we will not argue over the correctness of this figure given by Mason (1974, p. 200), there are different types of staple grains in North India such as rice, wheat and millets, eaten in that order by the rich folk, common people and the peasants respectively. This is a long tradition and practiced till date. Rice was more expensive than wheat and the millets gave a dark, coarse or bitter flour and therefore were not readily accepted grain both by people and livestock. There are of course vegetable preparations to accompany the staple cereal for which spices, salt, ghee, etc. are used.

Around the 1840s, the cost of grain – 60 lbs per month (at 2 lbs per day) for a man was two and half rupees. A special allowance was sanctioned in 1847 to cover the cost of grain if it rose beyond this level. Usually at that time, one rupee fetched 50 per cent more millet as wheat, thus for two rupees one could purchase 60 lbs of millet. So a pay packet that after deductions left about three or two rupees plus to be spent on food would seem to be sufficient to feed a man with the basics. Rice was the staple in the South but in the Bengal Army, the Rohillas and men from Oudh would eat only wheat and if this was not affordable, then millet. The supplies were purchased from regimental shops whose business it became to stock and store all sorts of grain.

But as facts stood in the mid 1800s and well into the 1900s, even in England, the peasants did not make more than 10 shillings a month and could not afford to eat meat except at harvest time. A British soldier in India in the middle 1800s received just 9 rupees a month after deductions.

A grass cutter is said to have earned 2 rupees in the early twentieth century. A land worker on the farm received nothing but food and protection from the landlord whose land he tilled and 2 rupees in cash every six months or so (Mason, 1974, p. 201). By these standards, 2 or 3 rupees in the 1800s would seem to the men of that time to be a fairly decent amount.

By comparison, soldiers today in independent India are paid full salaries plus compensation for hardship areas, they are provided with free nourishing meals, they are clothed and shod appropriately, fully equipped and given vehicles with fuel when on duty.

Army Pension

For those sepoys who were on pension, even if it was Rs. 3 (after 1796), it was a sum very welcome after 20 years of service. It was revised upwards in 1836 as per Lord Bentinck's proposal to Rs. 4 after 15 years of service for a sepoy; after 40 years retiring as Subedar he would get Rs. 40 a month; and a sepoy retiring as Jemmadar Rs. 20. During service, the sepoy was paid five and a half rupees and a Subedar Rs. 52 on long home leave or furlough. Allowances were paid to the sepoy's families when he went on overseas service and a pension to the nominated heir if he was killed. Administratively all these provisions and paper work were checked and monitored every quarter (Mason, 1974, p. 202).

Such pay, provisions and facilities did not exist in the feudal and imperial system in India. The hereditary troops owed allegiance to their feudal lords much as it was in medieval Europe and the troops or mercenaries were hired for a specific campaign. Neither regular pay nor a pension figured in the scheme of things with the Mughals or the Marathas. They took no responsibility for the men after they left the army.

Therefore joining the army of the Company was a prospect that enticed all the Brahmins and the Rajputs, the Muslims and the Sikhs, the Nairs and the Mudaliars, and the Marathas in all the three Presidencies. And with the level of pay and provision for pensions as described, it was surely the cheapest army to be maintained anywhere in the world.

References

Beveridge, H. *The Tarikh-i-Mubarak Shahi Yahiaya Bin Ahmed Bin Abdullah Sirhindi* Translated from Persian. Low Price Publications, first printed Delhi, 1910.

Bhandarkar, Ramakrishna Gopal. *Early History of the Dekkan: Down to the Mohammedan Conquest.* 2nd ed Asia Educational Services, New Delhi, 1985 (First published 1895, First reprint, 1979). Asian Educational Services, New Delhi, 1985, pp. 30–67.

Braudel, Fernand. *A History of Civilization*. Penguin Books, 1993/1995, pp. 164, 232–240.

Dhar, M.K. *Royal life in Ancient India*. Durga Publications, Delhi, 1991.

Edwards, Michael. *Battles of the Indian Mutiny*. B.T. Batsford Ltd, London, 1963.

Elliot, Sir H.M. *History of India As Told By Its Own Historians*.Vol II & Vol III. Edited by John Dawson (volumes 1–8) Allahabad, Kitab Mahal, 1877 in Volume II.

Eraly, Abraham. *Emperors of the Peacock Throne: The Saga of the Great Mughals*. Penguin Books. New Delhi, 2000, pp. 46–47, 61–105, 112.

Gaylor, John. Sons of John Company; *The Indian and Pakistani Armies – 1903–1991*, Spellmount Ltd., Turnbridge Wells, Kent, 1992.

Hiro, Dilip. *Babur Nama: A Journal of Emperor Babur*. Abridged, edited. Penguin Classics, New Delhi, 2006, pp. xviii, xxxii, 125–350.

Husain, Agha Mahdei. (ed). *Futuhu's Salaten or Shah Nama-I-Hind of 'Isami'*. Vol. II. 1898. Asia Publishing House, New Delhi, 1977, p. 898.

India Today, 'Come Home To History – Past 1000 years'. The Millennium Series Vol. 2. June, 2000, p .19

Jafre, Saiyid Zaheer Husain. *Studies in the Anatomy of Transformation of Awadh from Mughal to Colonial Rule*. Gyan Publishing House, New Delhi, 1998.

Kirmani, Mir Husain Ali Khan. '*History of Tippu Sultan. Being a Continuation of the Neshani Hyduri*'. Sushil Gupta (India) Pvt. Ltd. Calcutta, 1958, p. 144.

Lawrence, James. *The Rise and fall of British Empire*. St. Martins Press, New York, 1994, pp. 120–130, 220–221.

Mason, Philip. *A Matter of Honour: An account of the Indian Army, its officers and men.* Jonathan Cape London, 1974, pp. 199–202.

Menon, M.K. Raman. *Michaud's History of Mysore under Hyder Ali and Tippoo Sultan*. By P. Michaud. (Translated from French), Asian Educational Services. New Delhi, 1985.

Metcalf, Barbara & Metcalf, Thomas, R.A. *Concise History of India*. Cambridge University Press, Cambridge, UK, 2002, pp. 99–100.

Mitra, Rajendra Lala. *Indo Aryans*. Vol II Early Life of Asoka. Antiquarian Book Sellers, Delhi, 1969, pp. 407–426.

Pringle, Kennedy. *History of the Great Moghul*. Anmol Publications Pvt. Ltd. New Delhi. 1904, p. 425.

Puri, R. C. (Translation) '*Shivaji: The Great Patriot'*. Lala Lajpat Rai 1st edition-Urdu. Metropolitan, New Delhi, 1980, p. 79.

Rajkumar. Editor, *Encyclopedia of Military Systems in India*. Volume 6: Military system of East India Company. Commonwealth Publishers; 2004, pp. 60–190.

Rao, N. Mukund Kalinga. *Under the Eastern Gangas*, Ca 900-Ca 1200. B.R. Publishing Corporation, Delhi, 1991.

Reid, D.M., (Col). *The Story of Fort St. George*. Asian Educational Services. New Delhi, Madras, 1999, pp. 26–41, 69–77.

Saksena, R.K. 'The Battle of Tunga'. In *War in Ancient India*: In Volume X, Part 3: Historical perspective of Warfare in India. Some morale and materiel Determinations. S.N. Prasad (Ed). History of Science, Philosophy and Culture in Indian Civilization. Series. General Editor – D.P. Chattopadhyaya. Published by Bhuvan Chandel, Distributors Motilal Benarsidass, New Delhi. 2002. Appendix 2, pp. 370–374.

Sallami, Abu-l-Fazl Gallami. *Ain-I-Akbari*. Translation. Royal Asiatic Society of Bengal, Calcutta, 1939, Ain: 1–70.

Scott, Sir S.D. *British Army: Its origin, propagation and equipment*. Volume III – From Restoration to the Revolution. Cassel, Petter, Galpin and Co., London, Paris, New York, 1880, pp. 31–346.

Sheik Ali, B. *Tipu Sultan*. Geetha Book House, Mysore, 1982.

Stein, M.A. *Kalhāna's Rājatarangini*: *A Chronicle of the Kings of Kasmir*. Translation, introduction, commentary, appendices, Motilal Banarasi Das, Delhi, A. Constable, London, 1961.

'Tippu Sultan – State, Economy and Modernization'. National Seminar. Organized by History Department University of Mysore and Directorate of Archeology, Government of Karnataka, Mysore University, Mysore, February 23–25, 2006.

Trevalyan, Sir George Otto, *Bart. Cawnpore*. Indus Publishers, New Delhi, 1992. An Imprint of Harper Collins Publishers India Pvt. Ltd. First published, 1865, New Delhi [also published by Macmillan and Co. Ltd., London, 1907], pp. 1–33.

Wilson, W. J. Lt. Col(Retd). *Madras Army: History of the Madras Army*. Volumes I & 2, Madras, E. Keys printer, Government Press Printer, 1882, Vol 1. pp. 37– 45, 69–72, 114–118, & Vol. 2. pp. 345–369.

Wolpert, Stanley. *A New History of India*. Oxford University Press, USA, 1993. p. 232.

Woodward, Peggy. *Rise of the Raj*. Midas Books, Speldhurst, Kent, 1978.

7

Modern Armed Forces of India

A major change occurred after the Sepoy Mutiny in 1857. The East India Company ceased to exist as such; the European troops merged with the Imperial British Army and the Indian troops were re-organised.

The Indian Army before Independence

Grouping based on class and religion were the main features in the army. In the re-organisation, after abolishing some and amalgamating the others in the then existing British and Indian regiments, the ratio of Indian troops to English troops was 2 to 1 in the Bengal army and 3 to 1 in the Bombay and Madras armies. Even the recruitment patterns changed. While earlier there were mixed regiments in Bombay (men from different parts of the country), the Bengal and Punjab army men of different classes and religions were now grouped into separate companies of the same regiments. The native officers of these Companies belonged to the same class and religion. Thus Sikh, Rajput, Brahmin, Punjabi, Muslim, Pathan, Dogra, Gurkha, even Pioneer with *mazhabi* Sikh Companies came into being and existed as water tight entities ostensibly for cohesion and efficiency. There was also severe curtailment in the recruitment of high caste Brahmins and Rajputs, who until then had filled the ranks of Bengal Army. A chasm may have appeared between the different classes and castes grouped in the name of efficiency to avoid any further subversion in the army. Such separate entities continue to exist till today (Gautam Singh, 1966, pp. 241–242).

Strangely the people of the South, Central and East who were loyal and fought valiantly alongside the British were now downgraded as of little military worth. Keegan (1979) wonders whether this feeling of identifying with race, community, religion, caste and local affiliations would ever be banished (Keegan, 1979, p. 309). Another upshot of this policy was to induct others from the North and Northwest – the so called 'martial races' – Muslims, Sikhs and Gurkhas of proven loyalty.

In the two subsequent re-organisations that quickly followed, the number of English officers was progressively reduced in the regular cavalry; artillery and infantry regiments were kept to 6 per unit. The Company's European infantry, artillery and cavalry regiments were transferred to the British Line under various nomenclatures like Regiments of Foot, Royal Artillery, and HM's cavalry. There were multiples of these regiments: 42 cavalry, 142 infantry, 9 artillery and 3 Sappers and miners. The Madras Army had classes labelled as Christians, Muslims, Marathas, Brahmins, Rajputs, Telugus and Tamils. But if one considered the food related issues of the soldiers of that period, the one advantage seen of such a classification, is in the matter of food preferences. People of one so-called 'class' hailing from the same background and region eat similar types of food; similarly, they observe and practice similar rituals. Getting together in one company, there would be less dissension and disagreements when a common menu is to be decided upon. But communal eating in a mess was still to come.

In 1878, the army's strength was 200,000 including 65,000 British troops. By deft rearrangements into different regiments, the Crown sought to cut expenditure and improve efficiency. The ordnance department and transport services also saw significant changes. New Commissariat Regulations were applied to the whole of India. The term 'native' was abolished in respect of regiments and corps. Another significant change was to put the pensioned off sepoys on a reserve list, who would return to attend a month's refresher training to be made fit for war readiness if required. There was now India Command and Burma Command. The Hyderabad contingent was broken up. New numbers designated the army units. The Gurkha units were separately numbered (Mason, 1974, p. 246). The Presidency Staff Corps were merged into the Indian Staff Corps, a new term, to which all the officers of the Indian army now belonged.

Sons of John Company Unified

The armies of the East India Company have been called the 'sons of John Company' in India and Britain.[1] By 1895, the three Presidency Armies were merged into one Indian Army which was to function administratively under four commands – the Punjab Command which included NW Frontier, the Bengal Command, the Madras Command (including Burma) and the Bombay Command (including Sind, Quetta and Aden) (Rajkumar, 2004, p. 6). There was only one Commander-in-Chief, not one for each Presidency. The Indian Staff Corps was abolished in 1902 under the C-in-C Lord Kitchner and the Viceroy Lord Curzon. All officers would now be gazetted directly to the regiments. The cavalry and the infantry lines were renumbered but the Bengal units were preferentially allowed to choose and take the first numbers, a point that was resented by both the Bombay and Madras armies. Another re-organisation in 1908 divided the entire army into the Northern Army and the Southern Army. In the beginning of World War 1 in 1914, the total strength of the fighting forces of India was 150,000, which rose to 1.5 million in 1918 (Gaylor, 1992, pp. 1–4). For military efficiency and reasons of economy, other structural changes were introduced. The once too many cavalry units were whittled down, all of which were amalgamated into re-formed linked pairs (Gaylor, 1992, p. 11).The infantry and the Pioneers were also put through similar changes and re-grouping. Both contained British and Indian officers and Indian ranks.

Indianisation and Indian Military Academy

The rewards of fighting in the many campaigns of the First World War in France, in Gallipoli, in the Middle East and East Africa, and protecting Hong Kong, Singapore and Malaya in the East and keeping vigil on the Northwest Frontier are said to have come about in the form of the Montagu-Chemsford Report. The Indian Army with British officers was to be Indianised. Ten gentlemen cadets were to be admitted to the Royal Military College, Sandhurst. The graduates would be commissioned and called the King's Commissioned Indian Officers, posted for the first year overseas in the same way as their British counterparts, before joining an Indian regiment. Of course there were several phases in this Indianisation process (Gaylor, 1992, p. 22), which were slow. A few among the first batch of the newly commissioned officers refused to transfer from the Indian Army units to which they had been earlier attached.

It was found that there was a thirty per cent failure rate among the Indian cadets in the Royal Military College, even given their educational status and British Public School backgrounds. Surely Sandhurst could not be harder than a somewhat comparable training establishment, the Royal Indian Military College, RIMC, at Dehradun, which was established in 1922. Studying at the RMC Sandhurst was a drain on the family's finances and resources even after graduation because of the abysmally low pay while there was no doubt that those who chose to join the ICS, medicine or law became self-sufficient. Therefore, another academy was thought to be essential to improve the availability of Indian Officers (Gaylor, 1992, p. 24). Accordingly, the Indian Military Academy, IMC, was established also in Dehradun, in 1932 with an initial intake capacity of 100, but by 1938, there were 56 officers who passed out each year. No Indians needed to go to Sandhurst. The Royal Indian Military College came to be the premier feeder institution of cadets seeking entry into the armed forces whether by preparing them for Sandhurst, the Indian Military Academy, the Joint Services Wing or the National Defence Academy (Singh and Mishra, 1997).

While the squadrons of the cavalry and the infantry continued to be commanded by British officers, the troops and the platoons had the Viceroy's Commissioned Officers (VCO). These VCOs were regarded as being important in assisting the British officers with problems of a local, ethnic and cultural nature. They were now phased out and in their place, the newly commissioned Indian officers would command the troops. At the end of World War II, there were 8,300 Indian officers among the total officer strength of 41,500. When the partition occurred, both India and Pakistan got officer corps.

Of the many princely states in 1914, 29 participated in the Imperial Service Troops providing cavalry, infantry, artillery, Sappers, Signals, Camel Corps, and Transport Corps. Out of a total of 22,479, 18,000 served overseas (Gaylor, 1992, p. 51). After World War I, there was a decision to arm and equip a number of the State Force units which were named Field Service Units on the same lines as the Indian Army in order to provide better training and for uniformity of the troops, but at the time of World War II, these units required re-training.

Commissioning into the Indian Army

There were Risaldars, Subedars and Jemmadars – the Junior Commissioned Officers of the erstwhile Indian Army, and which have no equivalent titles in the present day, but which could be equated to the master Warrant Officer, Master Signaler Risaldar and Risaldar class I RVC and Master Engineer (Rajkumar, 2004, p. 347). These were the VCOs. Commissioned Gurkhas were Gurkha officers. But almost all had gone up the ranks. Although in a strict sense not officers, they were nevertheless bestowed with the respect and social considerations befitting an officer. They were recognised as *sahibs* by even the British officers, and were the only link between the latter and the Indian soldiers in all matters of army discipline.

Those VCOs who passed out of Sandhurst, and others who were capable, the non-commissioned officers like Jemmadars and those who distinguished themselves were granted the King's Commission. In 1926, there were 42 King's Commissioned Indian officers (KCIO), who passed out of the Royal Indian Military College, Dehradun. By the time World War II was declared in 1939, this number had risen to 600. Those who volunteered to join during the war were given Emergency Indian Commissions (EIC). The demand for officers having increased steeply, officer training schools opened in Mhow, Bangalore and Belgaum. When the war ended, there were 14,000 officers as KCIOs, ICOs (Indian Commissioned Officers) and Emergency Indian Commissioned Officers.

The matter of pay: There was a very visible pay disparity between the officers, not just by rank alone but by where they passed out from and what commission they held (Gautam Singh, 1966, pp. 267–268). Sandhurst graduates naturally were at the top of the scales; no less than a difference of Rs. 100/- to Rs. 150/- existed between KCIOs and ICOs up to the lieutenant's rank, of Rs. 160/- to Rs. 360/- in a Captain's rank, and Rs. 300/- at the Major and Lt. Colonel's level. There was also an additional package for married officers to the tune of Rs. 100/-.

In July 1947, a revision of scales saw a second lieutenant getting Rs. 350/- and a full General Rs. 3000/- and incremental scales in between inching by Rs. 150/- to 250/- with every next higher rank and only showing a steeper increase (about Rs. 650/-) from a Brigadier's pay to that of a Major-General.

Three other important Corps were established as the need arose. These were the Royal Indian Army Service Corps, The Remount and Veterinary Service Corps and the Indian Catering Corps. These Corps, as will be shown later, became the indispensable elements of the supplies and transport chain and food preparation and service in the garrisons and field messes.

Emergence of the Modern Armed Forces

> 'The safety, honour and welfare of your country come first, always and every time. The honour, welfare and comfort of the men you command come next. Your own ease, comfort and safety come last, always and every time.'

Thus spoke Field Marshal Sir Philip Chetwood, the Commander-in-Chief of the Indian Army at the inauguration of the Indian Military Academy in December of 1932 (Lachman Singh, 1997, p. 46). The Empire is no more, the Indian Army split into two at the time of Indian independence. India became a vibrant democracy and a republic. The title of C-in-C passed from a military general to the President of India, a civilian.

The officer class and other ranks of the present day Indian Armed forces include anyone who is physically fit and of the prescribed age, possesses the basic minimum education prescribed and has the preparation, grit, tenacity, determination and intelligence to go through the entrance tests and qualify in the Service Selection Board's interview (officers) and district level interviews (for other ranks). It is a multi-ethnic, multi-religious, multi-denominational, multi-lingual, multi-regional class, its members hailing from families of the traditional soldier class, the so called martial races or others such as priests or traders or farmers or Gurkhas (though all of them may have to struggle to achieve the same standards of education and physical fitness necessary). All of them consider service in the armed forces as soldier or officer, a matter of honour for the individual member, for the immediate and extended family and for the community and even for the village as well. Until very recently, joining the military service was an important option in the career choices of a young aspiring man. A life of dignity, honour, respect, while serving your country and deriving reasonable benefits as pay, allowances and perks was not to be had in the service of the government outside the Indian Civil Services. Now that there are far more career choices with better financial packages, infinitely less dangerous and equally or more glamorous, there is no special call to a particular religion or caste to send members into the Armed forces. An officer or a soldier belonging to one religion is no more or no less than the one belonging to another except of course as per their rank. While in India there is still a strong family tradition of enlisting or opting for the Armed services, following in the footsteps of fathers and grandfathers, there is no such thing as Hindu or Hindi soldiers nor does such a distinction exist in India as against the 'Islamic soldier' of Pakistan (Lachman Singh, 1997, p. 67) where the entry to the officer class came from the sons of JCOs and NCOs, of landlords, government officials, Army Officers and other well-to-do families, although officers in both countries claim their legacy from the British Army.

Many authoritative treatments have been written on the subject of the Indianisation of the Army in India, and on its re-organisation and structure, tracing the Army's history and evolution (Venkateswaran, 1967, Lachman Singh, 1997, Rajkumar, 2004, Keegan, 1979, Elliot, 1935–1945,

Gautam Singh, 1966). What emerges from all that they have said is that the rabble, the ragged, the haphazardly trained and rather casually disciplined sepoys recruited to protect the properties of the East India Company and fight the battles of expansion were brave and loyal, and under British discipline and training and under officers as leaders and mentors, got transformed gradually over a period into a tightly knit, reliable and extremely able fighting group. It seems therefore that readily accepting the European discipline and adopting their method of warfare only added to the warring capabilities of Indian sepoys, who by tradition were raised and functioned on the tenets of the Indian art of war. They not only performed in an exemplary fashion in various frontier wars but also in World Wars I and II. There were 2,500,000 men of all classes in the Indian Army in World War II (Keegan, 1979, p. 30). Major General J.G. Elliot in describing the story of the Indian Army during 1939–1945, gave particular accolades to the contributions that both the Gurkhas and the Indian soldiers made to the British elements. They were frugal, which was a standard for everyone to learn, they expected hard times and made the best of them and they moved light. The English man brought his priceless gift of easy bonhomie; all three races of fighting men came together naturally because all possessed in liberal measure of that unfailing catalyst – a sense of humour (Elliot, 1945, p. 11).

Organisation at the Time of Independence

At the time of independence, the Imperial army which was 500,000 strong was divided, one-third going to Pakistan and two-thirds to India. While in India, in its secular nature, unit identities were preserved and posting of soldiers of different religions between units resorted to for homogeneity, in Pakistan no non-Muslims were accepted in the army (Keegan, 1979, p. 303).

From August 15, 1947, the organisational set up showed that the three wings of the Armed Forces were headed respectively by the Flag Officer Commanding Royal Indian Navy (FOCRIN), the Commander-in-Chief Army, Army Headquarters and Air Marshal commanding Royal Indian Air force (Air HQrs), all falling under the Defence Ministry headed by a Defence Minister in the cabinet of the Governor General as well as the Constituent Assembly (Legislative) (Rajkumar, 2004, p. 42). There was a Chief of Staff or Chief of administration, five naval commands located at Bombay, Cochin, Madras, Vizagpatam (now known as Visakhapatnam) and Calcutta. In the army, there was the Chief of General Staff (CGS), Adjutant General (AG), Quarter Master General (QMG), Engineer-in-Chief, and Military Secretary (MS) as well as three commands – Southern, Delhi and East Punjab (created after partition) and Eastern. In the Air force there were two equal wings under a Senior Air Staff Officer and Deputy Air Commander as one and under an Air Officer-in-charge Administration as the second. These two officers looked after the operational group and training group respectively.

On March 25, 1955, the Indian Prime Minister, Pundit Jawaharlal Nehru informed the Lok Sabha (Indian parliament) that the heads of the three Services would henceforth be known respectively as the Chief of staff of the Army, of the Navy and of the Air force instead of Chief of Staff and Commander-in-Chief, not to lessen the authority but only in keeping with the provisions of the Constitution. The British officer of the Royal Navy who would succeed the Naval Chief at that time would be the last British officer to command and thereafter his successor would be an Indian (*The Hindu*, March 26, 1955, reproduced in *The Hindu*, March 26, 2005).

The Supreme Command of the Armed Forces is now vested in the President of India. The only time the Armed Forces collectively salute the President is on the Republic Day, the 26th of January every year.

The restructuring of the Army under the British Raj paved the way for its modernisation. Today it is a force to reckon with, its mobility and effectiveness comparable to European and other western armies. Today, India has the second largest Armed Forces in the world. Internally, some vexing border issues continue to exist even as new and pressing demands are made on the force's physical presence for active protection and peace-keeping purposes in international situations arising in geographically far away lands. There have been serious battle engagements on the borders with Pakistan (1948, 1965, 1971, and 1999) and with China (1962) as well as other conflicts in 1969 and 1978. The regions of Jammu and Kashmir, the western borders, the northeastern terrains and Arunachal Pradesh need intensive patrolling, army deployment, mobility, equipment, supplies and support.

India's Force Strength

The modern Indian defence forces are structured and organised as three wings of the Armed Forces – the Army, the Navy and the Air Force falling under the jurisdiction of the Ministry of Defence, Government of India, and the Paramilitary and Central forces coming under the Ministry of Home Affairs.

The strength of the Forces has steadily grown since independence by recruitment, modernisation, skills training and weaponisation. From the 1970s to 2004, the overall picture has changed as shown in Table 7.1.

In the regular Armed Forces, there are 1,298,000 active personnel in the three services combined who are all volunteers with 1,100,000 personnel in the army alone of which 800,000 are available for combat formations (Bennet, 2001). The Air Force has 145,000 personnel and the Indian Navy 53,000 (including 5,000 in naval aviation, 1,000 marines and 2,000 women). In addition, there are reserve personnel – 300,000 in the army, 46,000 volunteers in the territorial army, and 140,000 in the Air Force and 55,000 in the navy. These statistics differ slightly according to Singh (Jasbir Singh, 2004) from those given elsewhere.

Table 7.1: Strength of the Indian Armed Forces from 1979 to 2004

In 1979 (after Keegan, 1979)	*In 2004 (after Jasbir Singh, 2004)*
Between 1975–1979	
Army 950,000	1,100,000
Navy 46,000	
40 major vessels 1 aircraft carrier, 2 cruisers, 8 submarines, 375 smaller craft	53,000 (+ 5000 naval aviation + 1000 marines + 2000 women)
Air Force 100,000	145,000
670 combat aircraft	701 combat aircraft
Paramilitary Forces: 300,000	~ 900,000

The role of the army: The army exists to safeguard the territorial integrity of the nation against external and internal threats, and in peace time to assist the civil authorities during natural calamities (Rajkumar, 2004, p. 303). A far more specific purpose and role for the army has been defined in the Kargil Review Committee Report (1999, p. 81). The primary role of the army is to safeguard the national borders against external aggression and to protect the integrity and sovereignty of the nation. It goes on to express threat perception and states that the threat assessment for any theater of operations is made at the highest relevant level and covers not only the total forces available with the adversary in a particular sector but also the forces that he can specifically apply within the limitations of his logistic capability and the terrain. 'On this basis, the formations are tasked and provided necessary resources', it concludes.

Under the overall authority of the Chief of the Army Staff, there are the Vice Chief, two Deputy Chiefs of the Army Staff, the Adjutant General and the Quarter Master General. A very elaborately structured organisation functions under the Office of the Army Headquarters (Rajkumar, 2004, p. 304). By the present nomenclature, the latter is known as the Integrated Headquarters, Ministry of Defence (Army).

The strength of the Army as of 2009 is shown in column one of Table 7.2. Today, there are six Operational Commands or field armies viz. Southern, Eastern, Western, Southwestern, Central and Northern Command and one Training Command, equivalent to field armies and under a General Officer Commanding-in-Chief (GOC-in-Chief) who is of the rank of a Lieutenant General. The Army is placed under the overall command of the Chief of Army Staff (COAS) of the rank of a General actively supported by the Vice-Chief of Army Staff (VCOAS), a Lieutenant General.

For the uninitiated, the organisation within the army has formations called the commands, corps, divisions, brigades, battalions, companies and platoons, the last being the smallest unit (Fig. 7.1). A formation has three subordinate formations or a unit has three subunits.

Army
↓
5 commands
↓
2 to 3 corps to each command
↓
*2 to 3 divisions under each corps
↓
**3 brigades normally in each division
↓
3 infantry battalions in each brigade
↓
4 rifle companies to each infantry battalion
↓
3 rifle platoons to each rifle company

Fig.7.1: Organizational structure of the army

Organisation in the Army follows a three-tiered system generally (Verma, Hiranandani and Pandey, p. 14, 2008)

*An infantry division consisting of brigades, artillery, engineers and ASC is the smallest organization which is fully self reliant.

**A brigade is not independent except in case of a few mountain brigades entrusted with small tasks.

There are 10 Corps Headquarters. Each Corps' major formations are armoured divisions, mechanised infantry, infantry divisions (each again self contained with brigades of infantry, artillery and an armoured regiment), mountain divisions, independent combat brigades (a composite comprising of armoured, infantry, mountain and parachute/commando units) artillery brigades, air defense brigades and engineer brigades. The mountain divisions were formed in 1963 following the war with China in the Himalayas in 1962, after the bitter experience of deploying an army not geared for mountain warfare.

The current global perception about Indian military strength is that it has a sophisticated defense industry able to build Soviet tanks, Swedish Bofors under license and that its science and technology

Table 7.2: Organization and Strength of the Indian Armed Forces, 2009

Army	*Navy*	*Air force*
Commands: 6 regional + 1 training	4 Principal + 1 submarine + 1 naval aviation Commands	5 Principal +2 Maintenance and Training (Support)
Strength *Active* 1,100,000 *Reserve* 800,000 (300,000 within 5 years and 500,000 until age 50)	55,000 (includes 7000 Naval aviation, 1200 marines, 2000 women)	1,25,00
Territorial Army Volunteers-40,000 in 48 battalions	8000 in Coast Guard	
13 Corps (with 3 Strike Corps)	9 Bases* 2 Fleets 16 Submarines	
Combat units- 68 armoured Div, 319 Infantry battalions, 300 artillery regiments (3 Armoured Division (Div) 10 Mountain Div, 4 Rapid Div, 18 Infantry Div, 2 Artillery Div, 355 infantry battalions (25 mechanized, 11 Para, 2 SF Commando, 300 Artillery regiments with SSM Prithvi and Agni.) 3 Engineer Brigades), 22 helicopter squadrons 18 Air Defence Brigades	***Surface Combatants*** 1 aircraft carrier 8 destroyers 11 frigates ***Patrol and Coastal Combatants*** - 49 (include corvettes, off shore and inshore patrol craft, mine sweepers, Amphibious crafts, support vessels like tankers, tropedo recovery, tugs, survey and hospital ships) ***Naval Aviation***, combat aircraft-35, Helicopters-97, plus 15 squadrons for Air attack, Antisubmarine, maritime, Transport and Communications, Search and Rescue	***Combatants*** 565 Combat Air craft 20 armoured helicopters 39 squadrons – fighter ground attack and fighters (Migs, Su-30 MKI, Mirages, Jaguars 4 sqdr (AWACs, recon tanker, maritime attack,) 2 sqdr-attack helicopters 13 sqdr Transport aircraft 19 sqdr Helicopters Isquadron for VIP flight craf 237 Training aircraf 5 Unmanned aerial vehicle (UAV) Nishant
Weapons System Main Battle Tanks, MBT-3928 (consisting of T-55, T-72, Vijayanta, Arjun, T-90, & PT-76, many types of guns, rocket launchers 2 SAM Groups	***Weapons Systems*** Prithvi (ballistic) cruise/Antiship; SAM (Barak and others); AAM, ASM, ASCM, Torpedoes, Main guns, Air Defence guns, ASW Rocket Launchers of various kinds	***Weapons system*** SSM, ASM, AAM, SAM

The total strength of the Armed Forces is shown to be 1,288,000 (active) and 1,155,000 as reserves. Compared to figures available for 2004, there have been changes in all the three Services in respect of personnel strength and combatant units; and an attrition of some 36,000 personnel has been recorded in the 2009 estimates against the 2007 figures.

Source: Jasbir Singh, Indian Defence Year Book, 2004, 2007, 2008, 2009

* A new integrated Naval Base is getting ready on the western seaboard at Karwar in Karnataka, the INS Kadamba, said to become India's fourth Naval Command Headquarters. It will be the biggest such base this side of the Suez. It will have a huge anchorage, a long wide jetty, berthing facilities for 10 ships, logistics to administer and accommodate more than 1000 officers, sailors and their families as well as a modern repair shipyard. Currently, 5 ships of the Naval Surface fleet are based out of INS Kadamba. Eventually in phase II, it will be able to house 300 officers, 2500 sailors and allow large ships like Admiral Gorshkov (rechristened INS Vikramaditya) the aircraft carrier (*The Hindu*, Sunday, May 20, 2007).

SAM-Surface to AirMissile. SSM-Surface to Surface, ASM-Air to Surface, AAM-Air to Air.
BrahMos missiles are expected to be made ready for all the three Services.

base has developed and produced a main battle tank *Arjun,* missiles like the medium ranged SAM-*Akash,* quick reaction low level SAM- *Trishul,* a 250 km range tactical SSM *Prithvi* and a 3rd generation fire and forget ATGM *Nag*. Further, very soon the small arms will be replaced by Indian designed 5.56 rifles, carbine and machine guns presently at the prototype stage (Westhorpe, 1991). Three Corps under Western Command HQ in Chandigarh are meant for mobile armoured warfare operations on the western borders. The Northern Command HQ, Udhamour, controls three Corps deployed in the climatically hostile mountain ranges in Kashmir on the ceasefire line and in Ladakh on the Chinese border. The Eastern Command HQ, Kolkata, faces both extremes of weather and terrain and threats of insurgency from Nagaland and Assam and of Chinese incursions across the mountains. A large number of mountain divisions and Special Forces are deployed in this area. The Central Command HQ, Lucknow, has a strategic role with its one Corps held in readiness to support the Eastern Command. The Southern Command HQ, Pune, is assigned different tasks with its Strike Corps on the western borders and another Corps for security operations in Southern India. The Southeastern Command HQ is in Jaipur.

Counter Intelligence and Jungle Warfare School (CIJWS): The army's job in the Northeast is difficult in the rain washed dense jungles of Manbhum in Arunachal Pradesh infested with militants and insurgents. Different skills and the art of jungle survival are essential for tackling the brutal traps and ambushes laid by insurgents from Myanmar, Bangladesh, China and Bhutan and the ULFA militants with their daring and cruel raids and gunfire annihilations of civil populations. The Army's Counter Insurgency and Jungle Warfare School in Mizoram provides skills training for men who are posted in these regions (www.Bharatrakshak.com/land-forces units/institutions/91.cijues.html).

High-altitude training: A fallout of the Kargil conflict was also a realisation that the troops needed to be especially trained for high altitude (HA) combat. In what way would this training differ from how the troops are prepared for Siachen posting? Only selected volunteers are trained for mountain operations and acclimatisation to the intense cold and high altitudes of Siachen. They man the gun perches and live in bunkers on selected locations and their job is to keep vigil. They spend not more than three months in one tour of posting. In Kargil, there was a different situation where a number of troops were required to be deployed suddenly and quickly. And to do this, it was felt that there were not enough troops and battalions specialised in mountain warfare. It was a definite handicap.

The HA commando school or the *Parvat Ghatak* at Tawang, Arunachal Pradesh, very near the Indo-China border, situated at 15,000 ft is the highest place in the world to accord the necessary training to operate under temperatures at −20°C and below. Run by the Tawang-based Korea brigade, a hand picked platoon of one officer, one JCO and 26 other ranks are subjected to an intensive four-week training capsule to toughen them up, develop skills, craft and capabilities to go behind enemy lines, carry out subversive acts, commando raids and learn the art of survival under such extreme conditions. This training is preceded by a pre-training sojourn at different altitudes for acclimatisation. Men posted to Kameng sector must go through this process which proceeds with first halt for six days at 9,000 ft of which there are two days of rest, two days of short walks and then two days of longer walks of 5 km each; the second halt at 12,000 ft also sees a similar protocol but may be of a little shorter duration. After this the men are considered ready for the activities at 15,000 ft. The training here consists of physical exercises like long distance walking, jogging, running early in the morning followed by theory and technical lectures and demonstrations, direction finding, compass reading, walking the rope bridges laden with heavy clothing, parka, boots, solar protective goggles, gloves, cap and backpacks (www.Bharatrakshak.com/landforces/articles).

Special Forces: From the time of World War II (Bennet, 2001, p. 145), there have been Indian Special Forces in the form of commandos fighting the Japanese in the mountains and jungles. This tradition of Special Forces was carried on in India after independence. Now the paramilitary commandos formed after the 1965 Indo-Pakistan war are among the premier Special Forces. The first battalions participated in the invasion of Bangladesh in 1971 and went as part of the Indian Peace-Keeping Force in Sri Lanka in 1988.

The Red Devils Parachute, another unit of the Special Forces was formed in 1990. The Para commandos are highly trained in combat skills in HALO (High Altitude Low Opening) and HAHO (High Altitude High Opening) parachute techniques. Dressed in black, bedecked with gadgets and tools and superbly equipped with combat necessary devices, they can be deployed in many different kinds of missions – counter insurgency, anti-terrorist and others. Their tasks include provisioning of the elite infantry's battle groups as well as clandestine operations. On regular training along with other armies and special courses abroad, the Special Forces unit is a highly capable, powerful and adaptable section of the Indian Army.

Joint Exercises: Indian contingents have periodically participated in simulated field maneuvers with the armies of other countries. Such events are said to enhance learning by experiencing various simulated combat situations helping to hone the skill and performance of units in alien situations. Living and working together and acting out as adversaries in a competitive but friendly atmosphere, such occasions provide opportunities to not only observe the use of new equipment and gadgetry and methods but they also provide opportunities to learn from and improve each other's performance. Besides, such close encounters build understanding and appreciation of each other's capabilities.

Much in the news in December 2007 was the joint Indo-China military exercise carried out by 100 selected crack Indian Special Force members on Chinese soil with Chinese troops. Nothing more has been reported in the media. Both sides, required to perform on high altitude borders as a matter of course would have exhibited their skills and knowledge and picked up the subtle nuances of a foreign unit in operation never to be learned otherwise. Such an exchange has not been envisaged between India and Pakistan.

The Role of the Navy: India's vast land mass is ringed by a 7,562 km long coastline served by several (9) major ports or harbours and more than 100 ports. India's territories in terms of far distant islands in the Bay of Bengal and the Arabian Sea and India's assets like the offshore oil wells, her international maritime boundaries reaching as far as Indonesia and Thailand and as near as Myanmar, Sri Lanka and Pakistan necessitate a Navy that is able to protect India's territories, its economic interests and prevent or repel any attack from the seas. From the first initial unit of the Honourable East India Company's Marine Force which was officially instituted in 1612, the Navy in India went through phases of being named the Bombay Marine, the Royal Indian Marine during World War I and the Royal Indian Navy during World War II. At the time of the latter, its vessel strength was 117 and it took part in operations in the Persian Gulf, Red Sea and Burma (Raj Kumar, 2004, pp. 312–313). The prefix 'Royal' was deleted after India's independence in 1947 and attaining the status of a republic thereafter.

The Indian Navy's role is to safeguard the maritime interests of India and planning and executing combat operations. Apart from establishing supremacy in its role of providing maritime safety, its responsibilities also include keeping trade routes open, denying the use of trade routes to the enemy during hostilities, thus cutting off the latter's supply lines, provide safety to merchant shipping ferrying oil, armaments and ammunition, and launch counter attacks on enemy ships, submarines and aircrafts. More recently its role has been extended to patrolling to prevent piracy on the high seas.

The navy maintains air and electronic surveillance, patrols the surface along shipping routes, transports and lands the ground troops of the army through amphibious maneuvers, and supports them till they are fully and independently established. Their role of search and rescue (SAR) at sea, both in peace and war, involve answering distress calls from small crafts. It came into prominence during the Tsunami disaster in December 2005. Here, the Indian Navy played a key role in assisting the civil authorities in rescue operations. At other times, it has rendered assistance by being actively helpful in rescuing stranded people during floods which periodically afflict several regions of the country and carries out evacuation of Indian civilians from war afflicted countries as happened recently in Lebanon and from pirate hijacked merchant shipping in Somali waters during November 2008. Among its many maritime related technical responsibilities, the navy carries out hydrographic surveys of the Indian waters and publishes almanacs and tide-tables for various ports (Rajkumar, 2004, p. 314).

Strength and organisation: A 2009 estimate (Jasbir Singh, 2009) of the strength of the Indian Navy (Table 7.2) puts a figure of 55,000 including 7000 naval aviation, 1200 marines and 2,000 women.

There are four principle commands – Western, Eastern, Southern and Andaman and Nicobar (under joint command) in Mumbai, Visakhapatnam and Cochin respectively and two sub-commands (submarine and naval air) with 9 bases, 2 fleets and 16 submarines in the Indian Navy. It also has principal surface combatants, one aircraft carrier, 8 destroyers and 15 frigates. Besides these, there are patrol coastal combatants, naval aviation crafts as well as many other support craft and personnel.

Coast Guard: The Coast Guard now falls under the Navy's ambit. The Coast Guard ship 'Sagar', one among the marine fighters is equipped with a super gun to enhance its capabilities in patrolling the coastal waters. It has 8,000 strong personnel, 50 shore patrol and coastal boats, 24 transport aircraft and 17 helicopters.

Challenges: There have been plenty of maritime challenges in all Indian waters, from the Liberation Tigers of Tamil Elam off the Rameswaram coast (until their recent defeat), and from smugglers landing contraband, straying fishermen and terrorists in Gujarat and Kutch zones. These waters are patrolled by the Navy and Coast Guard.

An indigenously built warship, INS Kolkata, belonging to the destroyer class, was recently launched from the Mazagon Dock in Mumbai. This new, complex and multi-role destroyer is reported to be the largest and the most lethal combination of stealth and strength. It can operate two multi-role helicopters and is fitted with advanced weapons, sensors and integration system (*The Hindu*, April 1, 2006). It has the supersonic BrahMos missiles. The soon to be obtained Barak missile system, originally developed for the Israeli Navy and presently installed and operated successfully in the warships of several navies, is meant for the defense of naval vessels against anti-ship threats which include aircraft, missiles, smart weapons and unmanned aerial vehicles. A highly advanced system, it is the ship borne anti-missile – missile point defense system as well as an anti-air, anti-surface gunnery control system. According to one media report, its flexible modular architecture allows tailoring according to the size of the warship (*Deccan Herald*, October. 13, 2006).

The Indian Navy has plans afoot to expand both vessel wise and capability wise. It currently has 49 ships, 16 submarines and 142 aircraft – including helicopters, combat aircraft, anti submarine but desires to augment the fleet strength by acquiring 32 new ships. The aircraft carrier 'Admiral Gorshkov' purchased from Russia is currently being refitted to suit the Navy's specific requirements and is expected to be delivered in a few years. The Navy also plans to lease a nuclear powered submarine from Russia as well as procure new long range reconnaissance planes which can be used over the vast stretches of the west coast of Africa to Southeast Africa and Australia. Their sea harrier fighter strength is said to be depleting, which needs alternatives such as the naval version of the LCA. Their Sea King helicopters also require upgradation (*Deccan Herald*, December 9, 2007). A recent addition is the nuclear powered submarine INS *Arihant.*

Joint exercises by the Navy: The Indian Navy is also assiduously honing its man power skills. In 2006 alone, two exercises were undertaken in Indian waters. The first of these was in April, when both India's and France's navies, supported by their air forces, went on week long manoeuvres involving their aircraft carriers (Varuna II and 'Charles de Gaulle' respectively), and their destroyers and submarines off the coast of Goa. The purpose of the war games was that 'the defence forces of the two countries should know each other for any future emergencies' and to be absolutely certain of 'their inter-operability', meaning either familiarity with drills and procedures or agreeing to certain procedures under given circumstances (*The Hindu*, April 3, 2006).

In October 2006, the Indian and US navies practiced expeditionary manoeuvres off the Konkan coast and carried out a simulated joint semi-urban counter-terrorism exercise in Belgaum, Karnataka. They also carried out anti-submarine operations, maritime interdictions, weapons firings, visit-board search and seizure operations, dissimilar air combat, cross-deck flying and simulated war-at-sea. Joining the US marines in the semi-urban exercises in Belgaum were the infantry from the 21 Battalion of the Punjab Regiment under code name 'Shatrujeet' 06 (victory over enemy) who worked together in intelligence sharing, communications and weapons and equipment usage.

Practicing war in simulated conditions is important as part of training exercises and war readiness. The war games that each branch of the forces engage in are dictated by the kind of response each is expected to provide. Indo-US interactions in this area materialised as four previously conducted war games in the nature of practicing for war or *Yudh Abhyas* in wooded mountains. Special Forces from both sides participated in para drops and mock assaults (*The Hindu*, October 27, 2006).

The Role of the Air Force: The Indian Air Force celebrated 76 years of its existence in 2006. Indian pilots have made a name for themselves in the air battles of World War I, even as aviation itself was in its infancy. This led to a reluctant formation of an Air Force, manned with Indian officers in 1933. Their first operational test came in 1937 against Waziri and Afridi tribes in the North West Frontier Province. They flew Lysanders, Hurricanes and Spitfires in the Second World War. They were deployed not only in NWFP but also against the Japanese in Burma.

At the time of partition, India inherited six and a half squadrons but most of the Air Force's permanent stations became a part of Pakistan. In the immediate aftermath of partition, the Air Force went into action to save Srinagar in the very first war between India and Pakistan over Kashmir in 1947 (Rajkumar, 2004, pp. 324–325). As there were no bomber aircraft, it is reported that the bombs were rolled out by hand over target positions. Today, the Indian Air Force possesses modern aircrafts as well as very sophisticated and advanced support systems.

The Kargil Review Committee Report (Subramaniam, 1999, p. 442) reiterated the chief role of the Indian Air Force as being the protection of the Indian State against threats from hostile Air Forces, which includes the detection of hostile or unfriendly aircraft, counter air operations, achieving air superiority or favourable air station over a designated region or area to allow freedom of action to land forces and air defense of vital assets. The Indian Air Force simultaneously provides support to land battles by destroying enemy tanks, defense positions, enemy's logistic infrastructure and targets, especially if they are beyond reach of artillery.

The Air Force, had it been deployed in the 1962 Indo-China border war, would easily have helped India win according to Air Vice Marshal Tewary – by rapidly stemming the Chinese advance, 'neutralise its military successes' and by running interference with the Chinese supply lines which were stretched thin. Not having proper assessment of the opponent's strength, it was feared that the Chinese Air Force might bomb Indian cities in retaliation. India went to the US asking for 12 squadrons of star fighters F-104 and 4 squadrons of B-47 bombers without consulting the Indian Air Force as reported in The Hindu (October 6, 2006). Therefore, one must realise the enormous military strength and strategic advantages of deploying the Air Force at the right time. Kargil gained definite advantages because of this very approach and the Air Force won accolades from the former Chief of Army, General V.P. Malik for its role (Malik, 2006).

The Indian Air Force has five major roles – strike missions, close support for the Army, air lift and strategic and tactical reconnaissance (Rajkumar, 2004, p. 326). It also participates in humanitarian services and goodwill missions air lifting huge amounts of supplies as it did in the aftermath of an earthquake in Islamabad (December, 2005), in relief-rescue operations in Indonesia (June, 2006), in Maharashtra, Gujarat, Andhra, Chattisgarh, MP and Rajasthan (*Deccan Herald*, October 8, 2006).

Structure and organisation: There are five air commands located in different zones: Western Air Command (New Delhi), South Western Air Command (Jodhpur, Rajasthan), Eastern Air Command (Shillong, Meghalaya), Central Air Command (Allahabad, UP) and Southern Air Command (Trivandrum, Kerala). There are several squadrons in the Air Force fighter ground attack, fighter squadrons, for transport purposes, several helicopter squadrons and other crafts for miscellaneous use (Jasbir Singh, 2007). In addition, there are two support commands, Maintenance Command at Nagpur and a Training Command in Bangalore (Table 7.2).

The Indian Air Force's strength is 125,000 with another 140,000 personnel as reserves as shown in the Indian Defence Book 2009, (Jasbir Singh, 2009, p. 223). The force is broadly divided into three categories: (i) administration, (ii) logistics and training and (iii) flying branch. Operationally, the force is divided into five operational and two functional commands. These can again be categorised under air defense, strike, training, reconnaissance, transport and helicopters.

In 2004 (Jasbir Singh, 2004), there were said to be 701 combat aircrafts, in 2009 there are 565. 22 (now 20) armed helicopters, 30 (now 33) squadrons of fighters – MIGs, Mirages and Jaguars for ground attack, 9 fighter squadrons of MIGs, all with electronic counter measures and electronic intel, 12 squadrons of transport craft, 19 squadrons of helicopters, 2 squadrons each of attack helicopters and reconnaissance craft, training squadrons and VIP flight squadron as well as two unmanned aerial vehicles. Though the acquisition of 126 multi-role combat aircraft has been mentioned, there was little development till 2006. There are also missiles such as ASM – Prithvi, Kerry, AAM and SAMs.

The new face of the IAF: The most recent additions to the Indian Air Force are the Russian made Sukhoi-30 MKI deep penetration fighter bombers. The Su-30 MK multi-purpose fighters can carry long, medium and short range missiles for close fighting as well as accommodate anti-radar missiles, TV-guided missiles and other such precision weapons. The aircraft is a long range interceptor and has a range of 3,000 km extended to 5,000 km with built-in fuel tanks and with in flight re-fuelling features. The first new-generation multi-role Su-30 MK in the Air Force can be used for long range patrolling, tracking and what is called 'radar loitering', and training high accuracy weapons etc.

The custom made multi-role Su-30 MK plane for India is labeled Su-30 MKI (Rajkumar, 2004, pp. 335–337).

Mid-air refuelling is said to be 'a big force multiplier' for enhancing the range and endurance of the existing fighter fleet of the IAF. The Su-30 was a collaborative venture between India, Russia, France, South Africa and Israel, but the integration of the system was done in Russia.

To further enhance air defense capabilities, the indigenously developed Akash system and the Indo-Russia jointly developed BrahMos missile will be integrated with the Sukhois. (*Deccan Herald*, June 6, 2006). Eighteen new Su-30 MKI planes will replace the used Su-30 K. The used Su-30 K are said to have exhausted their pre-overhaul flight limit of 1500 hours flying and will be taken back to Russia at a price of $12 million per aircraft (*The Hindu*, April 13, 2007). At the same time, the upgradation of MIG-29 and Mirage-2000 fighters was going to be done in order to retain India's cutting edge air capabilities (*The Hindu*, April 10, 2007).

The IAF's new plans include some major ambitions – global combat reach, exploit space assets for military purposes even as it plans to retire the last of the MIG-25 planes, which is one of the two planes in the world that has the capability to fly at stratospheric levels to take reconnaissance photographs of good quality (*The Hindu*, April 7, 2007).

Joint exercises: Army, Navy and the Air Force regularly conduct and take part in joint exercises with foreign countries' forces. The joint exercises are also a part of global reach to learn, understand and benefit from the multi-lateral exercises because each country has different tactics, languages and processes (*The Hindu*, April 7, 2007). Such joint exercises can be likened to the periodic 'in house' and international intellectual seminars and scientific and practical workshops conducted by academic and scientific research organisations which serve as the means to learn about novel ideas, advanced techniques, innovative approaches and developments emerging in various countries, and meet and interact with the people associated with such activities.

In October 2006, the Indian Air Force and the Royal Air Force took part in the first ever joint exercise in 43 years (the last one being in the 1960s) between India and UK. India, expecting to receive the AWACS – Airborne Warning and Control System, used this exercise to familiarise its pilots and senior officers with the British AWACS (*The Hindu*, October 14, 2006). Ever ready to explore, test, accept and induct new technologies and systems, the first step is to become acquainted with and participate in joint exercises with the force that has it or can show it; it is the best precedent to acquiring.

A new aspect of joint exercises in the Indian Defence forces is to perform manoeuvres jointly with the Army and the Air Force. One such manoeuvre was conducted on March 19, 2008 in the Thar desert at the Pokhran firing range. Code named 'Brazen Chariot', both the forces showcased their combat prowess, engaged their latest array of weapons in a mock (simulated) air-land battle just 75 km away from the Indo-Pakistan border. It was a display to demonstrate the synergy achieved, to themselves and to the world at large. The participants were the Army Southern Command and the Air Force South Western Command. There were reported to be more than 100 foreign observers from 59 countries and more than 37,000 personnel took part in the war games/manoeuvres. The impressive Army showed up with T-90 tanks, SMERCH long range missiles, spy drones, the latest air defense gun systems and fighter jets. The Air Force displayed its might by sending fighters, transport aircrafts, helicopters, SU-30, MiG-21, MiG-27, IL-76, AN-32, Mi-17, Mi-35 aircraft raining down firepower from a variety of weapons. Since these events were reported, other exercises have been carried out by the Army, Navy and the Air Force.

The paramilitary forces: India's paramilitary forces are of several types and numbered some 944,000 in personnel strength as shown in Table 7.3 (Westhrop, 1991; Bennet, 2001) but an update (Jasbir Singh, 2009) estimates that not only is there an increase in the types but also in force strength. Each type of force has specified tasks allotted to it as shown in the table although increasingly it is found that the Army is being brought in to assist with state and internal law and order situations and to deal with insurgency.

Table 7.3: Indian paramilitary forces – strength and function

Force	*Strength*	*Tasks*
NSG (National Security Guard)	7357 (5,000)	Anti-terrorism
CRPF (Central Railway Protection Force)	229,699 (90,000 regular)	Internal security
BSF (Border Security Force)	208,000 (250,000 reserve)	Border patrol, deserts
Assam Rifles	63,000 (40,000)	Border patrol, NE, and Myanmar border
Ladakh Scouts	(5,000)	
ITBP (Indo-Tibetan Border Police)	36,324 (141,000)	Policing India-China border
Special Frontier Force	10,000 (8,000)	Border security
CISF (Central Industrial Security Force)	94,000 (70,000)	Security of government/major installations, VIP protection
Defence Security Force	31,000 (30,000)	Security of defence installations
RPF (Railway Protection Force)	70,000 (70,000)	Railway protection
PAC (Provincial Armed Constabulary or State Armed Constabulary)	450,000 (250,000)	Policing
SPG Special Protection Group	3000	VVIP Security
Rashtriya Rifles	60,000	Security in Jammu and Kashmir
Sashatra Seema Bal/Seema Suraksha Bal	31,554	Border policing and security
Civil Defence reservists	500,000	Trained for towns, cities (several states), also for NBC
Home Guards	487821	

Source: Indian Defence Year Book, 2009. Data complied from Westhrop, (1991) showing some changes that have taken place in the last two decades.

The task with the Indian paramilitary and the central police forces is perhaps more broad and wide, encompassing not just internal security but also to patrol, guard and protect our vast borders in the west, northwest, north and northeast. These specially formed forces, like the Rashtriya Rifles, deal with terrorist infiltration such as from Pakistan. In the central police forces, we have three border guarding forces – Assam Rifles (AR), the Border Security Force (BSF) which is also known as the *Seema Suraksha Bal* (SSB), the Indo-Tibetan Border Police (ITBP) as well as Special Service Bureau (SSB).

Further, we have the Central Reserve Police Force (CRPF) which acts as the main assault force to assist in law and order, the National Security Guard (NSG) which acts in specialised form of counter terrorism and anti-hijacking operations, and a Rapid Action Force (RAF) which is a specialised wing of the CRPF dealing with riots and communal disturbances. The Assam Rifles falls under the operational control of the Army even though it has the primary duty of guarding borders in the Northeastern region. Another very important and essential functional organ of the Government of

India is the Border Roads Organization (BRO) which has been engaged in building and maintaining well laid and all weather roads, a lifeline linking important and distant sectors in the northern belt of India. Without its active role in maintaining the infrastructure of the roads, all supply and transport links could be imperiled, access to national highways and mountain strongholds, surface link in the Kashmir valley and the rest of the country cut off. BRO is also rendering yeoman service in Afghanistan and Iran (Jasbir Singh, 2004, p. 371).

One may now gauge the strength, spread and reach of our Defence forces within the country, the varied duties they perform, the massive deployment of the number of personnel necessary in each region at any given time, but mostly simultaneously in all places and wonder how the entire force is made to function like clockwork. Necessarily therefore, the Indian forces must remain highly motivated, well trained and disciplined, well armed and well supported in every respect.

Force Strength – India's Neighbours

We have neighbours whose borders march with ours and with whom we are in continuous engagement of one kind or another. Hence, their force strengths matter to India. In comparison to India, the total active military manpower of China, whose People's Liberation Army is 80 years old now (Aiyar, 2007), is estimated to be 2,274,000 (being reduced now) in which the Army strength is 1,600,000, the Air Force's 250,000 and the Navy's 255,000 (Table 7.4). There are some 500 to 600,000 reserves.

Pakistan on the other hand had 620,000 army personnel (with reserve strength of 513,000), 25,000 navy personnel (naval air and marines numbering 1,200 and maritime security agency numbering 2000) and its air force has 45,000 personnel and Bennet's figures also showed (Bennet, 2001, p. 141) that there were 550,000 personnel on its active strength with 400,000 available for combat units. Table 7.4 presents, more recent figures. Unlike the Indian Army, the Pakistan Army plays a political role even as its main focus rests on organising and arming itself for border war situations. Pakistan's paramilitary forces are 294,000 strong, whose primary task of course is to maintain internal security.

Table 7.4 : Comparative strength of the armed forces of India, Pakistan and China

		India	*China*	*Pakistan*
Total				
Active		1,288,000	2,270,000*	NA
Army:	Active	1,100,000	1,600,000	550,000
	Reserve	3,00,000 + 500,000	50,000–600,000	5,13,000 ++
Territorial Army		46,000	NA	NA
Navy		55,000 19 submarines Surface 26 combatants	2,55,000 + 10,000 marines + Naval aviation 26,000 62 submarines 75 surface combatants	24,000 10 submarines 6 surface combatants
Air Force		1,25,000 565 combat aircraft	250,000 19,00 + combat aircraft	45,000 360 combat aircraft
Paramilitary Forces		1,300,586	294,000**	304,000

*NA = Data not available

Source: Indian Defence Year Book, 2009. Data for * and ** from Westhorpe, 1991. Data for ++ from Indian Defence year book 2008

Pakistan's Army, Organisation and Command Structure

The organization of the modern Pakistan Army is similar to that in India, and equally manpower intensive.

There is one Chief of the General Staff and one Vice-Chief or Deputy Chief (when appointed). There are seven branches under the Chief of General Staff which are named: General Staff Branch (Br. for Branch), Adjutant General Br., Military Secretary Br., Master General of Ordinance, Inspector General Training and Evaluation, Quarter Master General (QMG) Br. and Judge Advocate General (JAG) Br. Under the General Staff Br. fall the three Directorates of Arms and Services. There are nine Corps numbered 1, 2, 4, 5, 10, 11, 12, 30 and 31 and presently all are controlled and commanded by GHQ, Rawalpindi. These nine corps consist of 21 divisions. The army is said to be well balanced and capable of quickly regrouping along the northern border and Siachen sector to meet any threat (Cloughley, 1998, pp. 342–343).

One important and noteworthy item of the Pakistan Army is that ammunition for many weapons in its armoury can be produced by Pakistan Ordinance factories, which makes the hundreds of thousands of rounds of firing definitely cheaper than it is in India.

Under the Constitution of Pakistan, the role of the Armed Forces was defined as 'to defend, under the direction of the Federal Government, Pakistan, against external aggression or threat of war and subject to law and act in aid of the civil power when called upon to do so'. It also provides that the validity of any direction issued by the Federal Government under clause (1) shall not be called into question by any court (Cloughley, 1999, p. 373).

These provisions apparently were not considered to be adequate by the powers and thus, by 1998, an ordinance was signed to legalise pretty harsh and draconian measures to try and punish any offenses deemed to be illegal such as strikes, lock-outs, destruction of state property, creating civil commotion etc.

Force strength: During the partition, the British Indian Army was split and one-third of the share came to Pakistan. According to the 2007 data (Jasbir Singh, 2007, pp. 258–263), Pakistan's force strength is made up of 1.2 million personnel including 513,000 reserves in the three branches. The Pakistan Armed Forces personnel and combat strength in the Army, Navy and Air Force are summarised in Table 7.5.

Pakistan's long land borders with India, the confluent coastline on the Western seaboard and until 1971, the East Pakistan Coast, have required deployment of its forces. There have been three border wars with India since independence. The continuous engagements in the Siachen sector since 1984 and in the region of Line of Control (LOC) in Jammu and Kashmir, together with the fight against terrorist Taliban elements on the Northern and Western borders and an incessant flux in the Baluch region would necessitate the deployment of forces in the length and breadth of the country. When such numbers are actively deployed in scattered locations, the question of their support logistics comes into prominence.

Nothing noteworthy or specific is known about Pakistan's logistics aspects but since after Partition, much progress has been made in modernising the Armed Forces and in equipping them with new types of weaponry and missiles, armoured vehicles, ships, and modern fighter and transport aircrafts. It can be assumed that much progress would have been achieved in the support systems as well and that there must be an efficient system in place for support logistics. In the 1950s, Pakistan (West and East combined) was reported by a nutrition survey group of the NIH, USA, to have 7000 miles of railroads. A good railway transportation system between the major cities and well laid roads nearly

Table 7.5: Strength of Pakistan's Armed Forces

Army	Air force	Navy
Strength *Personnel* – 5,50,000 *Reserves* – 5,13,000	*Personnel* – 45,000	*Personnel* – 24,000 (Naval Air, Marines 1400, Maritime Security Agency 2000)
Paramilitary forces – 294,000 (National Guard, Janbaaz force, Mujahid force, NCC, Coast Guard, Northern Light Infantry, Frontier Corps, Rangers, Maritime Security Agency		
Organisation 9 corps HQ	3 Regional Commands 11 Major Air Bases	5 commands, 3 Bases major base at Karachi,
2 Armoured divisions (div) 18 infantry div, 1 command area div, 36 brigades armoured artillery, machanized, engineer, Recon regiments 1 Special Forces group of 3 battalions and 16 Aviation sqdrs	415 combat aircrafts 5 Fighter Ground Attack Squadrons 10 Fighter Squadrons 1 Recon Squadron 1 Training sqdr 7 Search and Rescue helicopter sqdr 25 Transport aircraft 184 Training aircrafts 15 Helicopers -Utility	8 submarines 6 frigates at surface combatants. 6 patrol and coastal combatants, 4 Missile craft 3 coastal patrol 11 inshore patrol 3 Mine Counter Measures 9 Support and Miscellaneous **Coast Guard** 28 boats and crafts **Naval Air** 17 combat Aircraft 18 Helicopters 1 Anti submarine squadron plus transport aircraft, and search and rescue anti submarine helicopters etc.
Weapon systems – 2461 main battle tanks MBT SSM, ASM, SAM, AAM	SAM and Different types of Missiles (ASM, AAM, SAM)	Not specified

Source: Jasbir Singh, Indian Defence Year Book, 2009.

58,000 miles long as well as 2,630 miles of navigable waterways (in East Pakistan) were ample to move men, materials and stores. Passenger air connectivity was already in operation as noted by a group of American scientists who were there on a NIH project (National Institutes of Health, USA, 1959) to carry out nutritional evaluation of Pakistani soldiers.

Special Forces: Pakistan's Special Service Group (SSG) is an elite commando unit created in 1954 as 19th Battalion Baluch Regiment. Since 1964, it has been enlarged to 24 companies, each having specialised units for operations in deserts, mountain ranges, underwater warfare and intelligence gathering, all done with the assistance of US Army training teams.

The Musa company was added in 1970, originally as a combat swimmer unit but now a dedicated anti-terrorist unit. The personnel are skilled in heliborne insertion, combat shooting, and parachute techniques of both HAHO and HALO kind. The unit is variously equipped with weapons to be used in any situation. SSG was deployed in deep penetration operations in strategic locations in India within disputed areas of Kashmir, against LTTE in Sri Lanka and for covert missions in Afghanistan. SSG plays a role as air marshals in VIP flights and in hostage rescue in air hijack and providing high level security for nuclear research facilities.

The 3rd Commando Battalion of the Special Forces was deployed in 'Operation Search Light' to suppress the political and civil unrest in East Pakistan beginning with the search and capture of Sheikh Mujibur Rahman, the Leader of the Awami League.

China's Force Strength

According to Bennet (2001), even though China currently does not possess adequately trained personnel, specialist weapons and technology expertise support, plans are afoot for the next five years to raise increased numbers of Special Forces. The counter terrorist units known as Immediate Action Units are controlled by State Police, with personnel from special OPS units, trained and equipped by the army. The Long Range Operations group formed in 1999 for airborne reconnaissance and amphibious warfare, located in Southern China, is known by the name 'Sword of Southern China'. A brigade-sized unit and more superiorly equipped group, it is staffed with mostly college-educated and staff college trained officers unlike the shambling mass of soldiers. Their duties pertain to counter insurgency operations and terrorism, and tackle religious and ethnic unrest in interior China.

Electronic warfare is another facet of Special Operations of the Chinese army involving intelligence gathering, close range signal interception and jamming. In close approach missions, electronic signal blocking is carried out so that targets as close as 550 yards suffer tremendous signal losses.

While every army aspiring to raise its standards and achieve a high state of modernisation wishes to posses such electronic warfare groups, China is the one listed by Bennet to have such a group among our three neighbours.

The Wars

While the Indian Army's dedicated mountain divisions face Pakistan and China in the bitterly freezing cold mountains of Kashmir, Ladakh and the Northeast, the armoured and mechanised divisions stay ready for tank battles in the dry hot deserts of Rajasthan. Meanwhile, the special forces' jungle warfare-trained infantry brigades carry on counter insurgency engagements in the hills, dense valleys and jungles of Assam and Nagaland.

There have been notable battle engagements between India and Pakistan ever since they attained independence. The October 1947 Kashmir War was precipitated because of disputed borders. It was sudden, unexpected, bloody and bitter. At the time of ceasefire in 1948–49, the eastern portions of Jammu and Kashmir were held by India and the Western Azad-e-Kashmir portion was held by Pakistan. A portion in northern Kashmir known as Aksai Chin came to be held by China. The Lahore-Punjab border witnessed major armoured battles in 1948 and after that again in 1965 and 1971, the latter leading to the defeat of the Pakistani Army and the creation of Bangladesh. Since 1984, there has been a continuous force deployment in the Siachen sector and a war in Kargil heights. An uneasy truce of sorts exists all around. The northeastern regions with porous borders with Bangladesh, China and Myanmar are threatened constantly with infiltrations, insurrections, militants and terrorists of various hues. The weather conditions are very bad if not outright hostile in some places, infrastructure and connectivity is lacking in other areas, and local food production is quite insufficient to feed even the local inhabitants. Therefore, massive efforts are required to coax anything out of the soil and to transport foodstuffs and supplies over long and treacherous terrain. Although the guns on Siachen and on the China border are silent now, there are constant encounters, often mortal combat between the army or the paramilitary forces on one side and insurgents and terrorists on the other.

Recruitment to the Modern Indian Armed Forces

The East India Company hired sepoys for guard duty and for the protection of its property. These men were ragged looking, pathetic and ill-disciplined, more like bandits (Woodward, 1978, p. 119). The three efficient Presidency Armies – Bombay, Madras and Bengal which had been formally incorporated by 1750 under the leadership of Robert Clive and his Commander-in-Chief General Stringer Lawrence, also recruited the so called 'other' upper caste Hindus and the sepoys' strength was far greater than the British strength.

The reason that made the men join the army was that it offered good money for that time; it was a place that, in the minds of the village people, offered work with honour, gave them importance in the eyes of the others as well as prestige and position. Their entry in large numbers into the Bengal Army can only be explained on the assumption that they considered it to be a special honour and privilege. Reminiscences of an old hand Subedar Sitaram Pandey of the British Army confirm these facts and sentiments (Lunt, 1970).

There is no conscription in India. Service in the Defence Forces is voluntary and every citizen of India above the age of 16 years is eligible to seek enrollment subject to certain provisions. There is no compulsory National Service (military) in India as it exists in Israel, Switzerland, Singapore, Finland, and Taiwan. The Chief of Army Staff expressed his opinion on January 14, 2007, (Editorial, *Deccan Herald*, January 17, 2007) that it may become necessary to overcome the serious shortage of military manpower. Every year, some 60,000 personnel of different ranks are said to retire from the services. These people could be as young as 28–29. Several thousands are needed rather desperately to keep the force strength up. Presently, the forces are said to be short of some 14,000 officers. The General does not include women in his statement. In Israel, women are obliged to do military service but in other countries such as United States and UK, it is voluntary for all. The United States and Australia did have compulsory military service during the Vietnam period.

The personnel recruited into the Indian Defence forces come from all the states in the country unlike in the past. In the time before independence till at least the time of re-structuring of the armed forces, only certain ethnic groups were chosen preferentially for specific branches of the services or regiments as a hangover from the feudal and British colonial times (Westhorpe, 1991). This did not happen until the governance of India passed from the hands of the East India Company to the Crown after the 1857 war. People from all strata and walks of life elected to join the army for various reasons, most because of the promised pay and pension. Joining was not an arduous job either and there were no great selection criteria applied in India or Britain.

Today, in a highly competitive environment, it is no longer possible for one to walk into the Armed Forces, nor is it any easier to clear the tests administered for physical, educational, and psychological assessment. The armed forces depend increasingly on technology, on high level of inherent abilities and on skills acquired by training individuals who have attained a basic level of education at the time of joining. Dunnigan (1982) observed that from World War studies it was found that the most effective infantryman was a man with average intelligence or above, with good mechanical skills, and the kind of person most wanted in the artillery or to run a tank. He also said that with stupid and inept recruits, a good infantry could not be had. Even to cook, the recruits need to have had some basic level of education from where the excellent training imparted to them will make them either into top class chefs or just run of the mill every day *langar* cooks.

Young men and women opt to make a career by joining the Armed Forces in various capacities. All the three services – the Army, the Navy and the Air Force periodically call for enlistments in both non-technical and technical streams.

No officer may find his way into a commission irrespective of what his lineage or affiliation is unlike in the British times. Officers and cadres must go through examinations and a rigorous selection process. For the officer cadre, the Union Public Service Commission's selection procedures apply by way of the UPSC's Combined Defence Services (CDS) Examination, which is conducted twice every year. Only graduates are eligible to apply. There is a need for people with all kinds of specialties from lawyers and doctors to all branches of engineers, languages, sciences and computer and information technology specialists. Those seeking admission should be between the ages 17 and 23 years and should be unmarried.

For enrollment to the Army ranks, periodic rallies are conducted in different districts after due advance publicity is given via newspapers. The eligibility criteria are based on age, educational qualifications and physical fitness and men may then appear in person and go through the selection procedures on the spot. For the Navy and Air Force, where the required qualifications are technical in nature, there are calls for applications published in national newspapers. The candidates may then apply on paper by providing the information requested. No application forms are issued and no agency for recruitment is appointed. Thus, all recruitment is directly conducted by the three services (*Deccan Herald*, May 2, 2007). In the Air Force, there are career prospects for candidates between 16 years to 23 years in the Flying branch with 10+2 education and any graduatation with Physics and Mathematics. In each service, there are age-related weight, height and fitness criteria. In general terms, fitness requirements consist of a 1.6 km run to be completed in 7 minutes, 25 squat ups and 10 pushups.[2] Medical standards include a minimum height of 157 cm and correlated weight, and proportionate chest expansion of 5 cm, good medical and physical health, free from disease and disability of any kind, no cardiac, dental, ear, psychiatric and neurological conditions and possessing colour perception at CPII. There are visual standards of 6/6 or no worse than 6/9.

Training in manners and etiquette: While drill and basic military training is all that is imparted to the fresh recruits in the soldier category, things are quite different with the officer cadets. They are made to go through the process of unlearning and discarding their mannerisms and attitudes to life, emulate gentelemanly behaviour towards each other, cultivate courtesy and politeness in general and towards women in particular. While it has been rather easy for men to adopt quickly to the western style of dressing, eating and socialising and while some are inherently mannerly, others baulk at having to 'climb down', so to say, by showing gallantry towards women and particularly outside of the Service environment.

In a guide to customs and services in India, the author of an instruction booklet for the officers (Kapur, 1988) describes the do's and dont's about the customs and dress code for the mess. They learn western style table etiquette and are told to give precedence to the president of the mess in sit down dining and wait for the senior most to be served first and that service would proceed clockwise.

Women's recruitment into the Forces: Joining the Armed Services is a calling for some and a platform for a good career for others. In Vedic India, though wielding weapons and receiving military training of sorts, women did not participate in wars. Non-Aryan women joined the profession of arms in large numbers because men did not regard it as ungallant to war with women. In fourth century BC India, Greek accounts describe women as being active in war in some states in the Northwest (Thapliyal, 2002c, p. 93). However, at the present time in India, women are never taken into the combat arm; they can only join in a technical capacity in the support branches. There are women in medical services, in ASC, perhaps in JAG and other non-combatant areas. No women are posted on a ship; the Navy while training them for a variety of technical and non technical responsibilities restricts the women's compliment to shore postings. The Air Force, which is also a highly technical branch provides more scope for women with technical qualifications. Crucial ground duties apart, since 1992 women have also found entry into the flying arena. They are allowed to fly only transport aircrafts. The Air Force offers training to graduates in many areas – flying, technical training, security training, meteorology training and of course medical training. Applications are vigorously scrutinised and meritorious candidates are called to appear before the Service Selection Board. The shortlisted candidates are put through vigorous training at one of the Air Force training establishments (*Deccan Herald*, May 3, 2007). Women are appointed only on a short service commission of five years, which may be extended to ten years or more.

The fate of women aspirants to the Armed Forces at present seems to be uncertain with the recent report that the Defence Council does not view their presence favourably in any capacity in any branch let alone the combat branches, the reason being that women are said to be most vulnerable to various atrocities if taken captive in active combat zones. In other capacities, their unsuitability is being highlighted saying that they expect, ask and demand preferential treatment in their work and postings, that they are very stress prone and complain of gender bias, that their marriage and family commitments come in the way of discharging their duties.

This subject has been contentious. There are those who are totally opposed to the idea of women in the forces like the former Vice-Chief of Army, Lt. Gen. S. Pattabhiraman who said as much in 2006. There are others who feel that the women are useful to have in certain disciplines and only in non-combatant positions, and not in others such as infantry and combat duties, or in ships, submarines and in diving, and only as pilots flying transport aircrafts and helicopters. Except for these bars, women are recruited to serve in the Army, Navy and the Air Force. Since 1992, women have been inducted into the three Services in other than medical fields (Jasbir Singh, 2007). The highest ranking woman officer in the forces Lt. Gen. Puneeta Arora is a medical doctor who defended categorically the stand of the Armed Forces saying that there was no gender based discrimination in the Services and that women did not necessarily have to wear the combat fatigues because there were plenty of other avenues open for them in the Forces. More girls are opting for commercial pilot training because of the job opportunities in India and elsewhere. There are women only in the officer cadres, not in the ranks. As such, each one is a qualified graduate in Law or Sciences or Humanities and other professional courses such as engineering, medicine, nursing, management, computer science and technology and applications. There is no woman in any of the musical bands of the Services! It is wholly staffed, played and conducted by men. For the present the women are non combatants and there they are likely to remain for quite sometime. The recent news that women constables would be posted to the India-Pakistan border in the BSF may lead to changes in other areas too.

At present, women constitute only a very small fraction of the Indian Armed Forces, the maximum percentage being employed in the Navy (5.4 per cent), although in actual numbers, Navy has 703 and the Army more than 900 (2.56 per cent). In the Air Force, in technical capacity and as pilots, there are 225 women (2.8 per cent). In comparison, the figures for some other countries are quite high. As per the Indian Defence Year Book (Jasbir Singh, 2007), Israel has employed women and welcomed them into the Armed Forces and also sent them into combat and treated them on par with men. Women's representation in the Israeli army is 83 per cent where as in the United States of America it is 15 per cent. It had 71,500 women in 2001, 22,000 of whom were deployed for frontline service as pilots and in the capacity of soldiers as privates and sergeants in combat zones. The British and US Armies have women as privates and sergeants; the British Navy has women sailors, one of whom was captured in March 2007 along with a group of 14 sailors by Iran while their ship was believed to have transgressed the territorial waters of Iran. They were all set free later. USA never had a woman President, but India, UK and Israel have had women at the helm of their nation's affairs (Indira Gandhi, Margaret Thatcher and Golda Meir and now Chancellor Angela Merkel of Germany and a woman President of India too). Pakistan and Bangladesh also had women Prime Ministers (the late Benazir Bhutto, Begum Khaleda Zia and Sheikh Hasina) and Sri Lanka had two women Presidents (Mrs. Bandaranaike and Chandrika Ranatunga). But except for Israel, USA and now UK, the rest of the countries baulk at the thought of women cadres in combat zones; no women are mentioned as being members of Pakistan, Sri Lanka and Bangladesh forces.

Pay and emoluments

The pay for the ORs (Other Ranks) during the initial training period is Rs. 4,500/- pm and on completion of training ranges from Rs. 5,300/- pm to Rs. 16,000/- pm depending on rank and years of service. During the entire period of training and thereafter, the technical cadres are given books, reading material, uniform, food and accommodation free of cost. There are many benefits such as Leave Travel Concession for self and dependents, Group Housing Benefits, other privileges, Insurance cover of 750,000 at nominal premium of Rs. 750/- pm, 30 days casual leave and 60 days annual leave as well as one free railway warrant every year. There are benefits for post retirement stage as well.

The pay for officers is commensurate with rank and is the same in the tri services, subject to certain benefits, additional allowances that are associated with nature of work and the area of posting. Officers' salaries in the Armed Forces can be gauged from what the Chief of Army Staff gets – a fixed amount of Rs. 30,000/- (Verma, Hiranandani and Pandey, 2008, p. 62). These are in no way comparable to other civil servants and the corporate sector who receive quite gratifying pay packets and perks beyond an ordinary person's imagination.

More details about recruitment and pay structure may be found in Verma *et. al.* (2008). However in all the Services, both for officers and ORs alike, the entitlements include free rations as per scale, accommodation and services at concessional rates, free medical facilities for family, group housing, concessional travel, canteen facilities and many other such benefits. Officers are also encouraged to take up courses for resettlement and are given study leave etc.

Officers ranks in the three services: Table 7.6 depicts the designation of comparative rank names in the ascending order used in each of the services. The Army is mentioned first since in

India, the Army is ranked the senior service, and then comes the Navy and then the Air Force, possibly for reasons of strength, operations and areas covered. Earlier, the order of seniority used to be Navy, Army and Air Force.

Table 7. 6: Equivalent ranks of officers in the three Armed Forces

	Army	*Navy*	*Air Force*
1.	Lieutenant (Lt.)	Sub-Lieutenant (Sub Lt.)	Flight Lieutenant (Fl. Lt.)
2.	Captain (Capt.)	Navy Lieutenant (Navy Lt.)	Flight Lieutenant (Fl. Lt.)
3.	Major	Lieutenant Commander (Lt. Cdr.)	Squadron Leader (Sqdr. Ldr.)
4.	Lieutenant-Colonel (Lt. Col.)	Commander (Cdr.)	Wing-Commander (Wg. Cdr.)
5.	Colonel (full) (Col.)	Captain (Capt.)	Group Captain (Grp. Capt.)
6.	Brigadier (Brig.)	Commodore (Cmde)	Air-Commodore (Air-cmde)
7.	Major-General (Maj.Gen.)	Rear Admiral	Air-ViceMarshal (AVM)
8.	Lieutenant-General (Lt.Gen.)	Vice-Admiral	Vice-Marshall
9.	General	Admiral	Air-Marshall
10.	Chief of Army Staff (COAS)	Chief of Naval Staff (CONS)	Chief of Air Staff (COA)

The junior most rank of an officer is of a lieutenant/sub-lieutenant/flight-lieutenant and the highest is that of a General, Admiral and Air-Marshall respectively. The three Service Chiefs are placed under the Supreme Commander of India who is the President of India.

Recruitment to the Paramilitary Forces: Central Police Forces

The Central Police Forces comprising the Border Security Force (BSF), the Central Reserve Police Force (CRPF), the Central Industrial Security Force (CISF), the Indo-Tibetan Border Police (ITBP) and SSB assist the Central Government in solving complex issues and protect the country from external aggression. Entry into these branches is said to be tough, requiring physical stamina and fitness. There are women in the State's and Indian Police Force and the CISF (Patil, 2006, in a newspaper interview).

The woman contingents of CISF are visible in places of tourist interest, and airports. In 2006, a woman's contingent of the Rapid Action Force was sent as part of the UN Peace Keeping Force to Darfur, Somalia.

In the Central Police Force, there are a few women. We have some prominent and accomplished women IPS officers such as Kiran Bedi and Jija Madhavan Hari Singh. It is a sad commentary that only these names come to mind out of the millions.

Recruitment versus Nutrition Concerns

An average Indian's diet recommendations based on weight, height, age, gender, and physical activity has been calculated by the All India Institute of Medical Sciences, Department of Cardiology (www.foodpyramidindia.org). On a 2,000 to 2,200 Kcal per day pattern and a physical activity of 30–60 minutes, the daily diet recommendations provide for 260 to 280 g of cereals, 60 g pulses, 200 g green leafy vegetables, 300 g of other vegetables, 500 ml milk (full or skim), paneer 30 g, cooking oil 15 to 20 g, nuts from 5–8 g to 15 g and sugar between 25 to 35 g. This pattern is said to provide between 1,990 to 2,190 Kcals of energy, from 321 to 346 g of carbohydrates, 66 g of protein and 46 to 56 g of fat. Paneer is a substitute for 75 g of chicken (for non-vegetarians). The quantities indicated for the cereals, pulses, vegetables and meat are on raw basis (www.foodpyramidindia.org). The majority of the soldier ranks derive from rural agricultural families living off their land; they are the not so well to do rural and urban youth belonging to large families and able to get only minimal education. The more educated among them aim for technical cadres. The Navy and the Air Force require more technically-skilled people to carry out various ground duties and on-board jobs. The enlistments come, not necessarily from the socially disadvantaged class but due to economically strained circumstances and generally from those who cannot support further higher education beyond middle and high school and need to find a secure and reasonably weli paid job for the qualifications acquired. The youth who flock to the army recruitment camps must possess the physique and physical performance capabilities that will approach the physical standards laid down for the purpose. The socio-economic background of the hopefuls does not support a living standard that will be able to provide nourishing food to the children. The recent nutrition survey of India, according to media reports, has shown that more than 50 per cent of the children in India, both in rural and urban settings suffer from various degrees of malnutrition.

Then there is the question of their educational status. The rural youth number among the maximum middle school dropouts. They are just passably literate at this level. How many hopefuls would be left to clear the class 10 exams and how many among these will pass the required class 12 or pre-university course, given the high failure rates at each level? Mathematics, Physics and Chemistry are not subjects that can be learnt without proper teaching and perhaps coaching. There is yet another hurdle to cross for those aspiring to join the technical cadres and officer class, which is the English language – spoken and written. Education in our country being what it is, there is a serious dearth of reasonably well educated youth with reasonable knowledge levels or technically capable high school and college graduate material who can clear the various levels of testing required to pass the Service Selection Board examinations and interviews for officers.

At an average of about Rs. 30/- per day (Rs. 32.35 for officers and 32.16 for other ranks) spent on the daily authorised rations, the country's exchequer expends approximately Rs. 43,268,000 or Rs. 4.33 crore a day for providing free rations to the active strength of the Armed Forces. This amounts to Rs. 15,792,820,000/- or Rs. 1,579/- crore per year. In the 2007 budget, the Union Government allocated some Rs. 8,000 crore for Defence.

Endnotes

1. The remains of the John Company can be seen in the vestiges of four units in Britain. These are (a) 10 (Assaye) Battery which in 1803 was No. 3 Company, Bombay Artillery, (b) 38 (Seringapatam) Battery which in 1799 was No. 4 Company, Bombay Artillery, (c) 129 (China) Battery, known in 1840 as a C company of 2 Battalion, Madras Artillery and the last (d) 137 (Java) Battery formed in 1778 but qualified for the honour title in 1811 as No. 1 Company, 2 Battalion, Bengal Artillery. Their own arm badges depict elephant (a and d), a tiger (b) and a dragon (c). These Batteries not only survived but made their presence felt by their participation in the 1991 Gulf war. The British legacy in the matter of the two armies is evident in regiments with British origins and bearing British titles whose officers and men still wear the same kind of uniforms and carry the colours as per the British pattern (Gaylor, 1992, p. xi). The legacy is also displayed clearly in the way the regimental centers are maintained.
2. Running, push ups and squat ups are the basic and simple fitness tests administered to recruits for screening. A research report (Parker-Pope, 2008 for *New York Times*) on exercise physiology says that pushups reveal fitness level. To perform pushups, strength and endurance are required. It tests the whole body engaging muscle groups in the arms, legs, abdomen, hips and legs.

References

Aiyar, Pallavi. 'The PLA turns 80 today'. *The Hindu*, p. 13, 2007.

Bennet, Richard, *Fighting Forces: An Illustrated Anatomy of the World's Great Armies*. Barron's Educational Series, Inc. New York, 2001, pp. 140–145.

Cloughley, Brian. *A History of the Pakistan Army: Wars and Insurrections*, 2nd ed. (with a new chapter on the Kargil issue). Lancer Publishers and Distributors, New Delhi, 1999, pp. 342–373.

Deccan Herald. March 12, 2008 date lined article by Tara Parker-Pope in New York Times.

Dunnigan, James F. 'The Poor Bloody Infantry' in How to make War. *A Comprehensive guide to Modern Warfare*. Arms and Armour Press, London, 1982, p. 19.

Elliot, Sir J.G. (Maj.Gen. Retd). *A Roll of Honour: The Story of the Indian Army 1939–1945*. Army Publishers, New Delhi, p. 11.

Gaylor, John: Sons of John Company. *The Indian and Pakistan Armies 1903–1991*. Spellmount Ltd, Turnbridge Wells, Kent, 1992, pp. x–xi, 1–24, 51.

Jasbir Singh R.K. Lt. Gen, PVSM (Ed). *Indian Defence Year Book 2004*. Nataraj Publishers, Dehradun, 2004, pp. 261–278, 337, 371.

Jasbir Singh, R.K. Lt. Gen., PVSM (Ed). *Indian Defence Year Book 2004*. Nataraj Publishers, Dehradun, 2007, pp. 258–263.

Jasbir Singh, R.K. Lt. Gen., PVSM (Ed). *Indian Defence Year Book 2009*. Nataraj Publishers, Dehradun, 2009, pp. 210–233.

Kapur, Nand Lal (Brig.). *Customs of the Services in India: A Guide for Officers*. EBD Educational Services Pvt. Ltd, Dehradun, 1988.

Keegan, John. *World Armies*. The Macmillan Press Ltd., London and Basingstoke, 1979, pp. 30, 303–309.

Lehl, Lachman Singh (Maj. Gen. Retd). *Missed Opportunities: Indo-Pak war 1965*. Nataraj Publications, Dehradun, 1997, pp. 46–67.

Lunt, James (Editor). *From Sepoy to Subedar, Being The Life And Adventures of Subedar Sitaram Pandey, A Native officer of the Bengal Army*. Vikas Publications, Delhi, 1970. (First English Edition –1873). (Written and related by himself) Translated and first published by Lt. Col. Norgate, of the Bengal Staff Corps at Lahore 1873. Illustrated by Frank Wilson, pp. xxvi, 15.

Malik, General V.P. (General, Retd). *Kargil. From Surprise to Victory*. Harper Collins Publishers India, New Delhi, 2006.

Mason, Philip. *A Matter of Honour: An Account of the Indian Army, its Officers and Men.* Jonathan Cape, London, 1974, p. 246.

Metcalf, Barbara & Metcalf, Thomas R. *A Concise History of India*. Cambridge University Press, Cambridge, UK, 2002.

National Institute of Health, 1959, 'A Nutrition Survey of the Armed Forces of Pakistan'. Inter departmental Committee on Nutrition for National Defence, National Institute of Health, Bethesda, Madison, USA. The J. Nutr, Vol 68, Supplement 2, May Aug, pp. 1 64.

Patil, P. (Former IGP and Director, Karnataka Police Academy). In *Deccan Herald* March 16, 2006.

Rajkumar. (ed), *Encyclopedia of Military Systems in India*. 'Military System of Independent India', Vol. 8, Commonwealth Publishers, 2004, pp. 6–42, 303–314, 324–335, 337–347.

Singh, Bikram and Mishra, Siddartha. *Where Gallantry is Tradition: Saga of Rashtriya Indian Military College*. Platinum Jubilee Volume. Allied Publishers, New Delhi, 1997, pp. 3–7.

Singh, Gautam Lt.Col. *The Indian Army Through the Ages*. Allied Publishers Pvt. Ltd., Bombay, 1966, 1969, pp. 1, 241–268.

Subramaniam, K. 'From Surprise to Reckoning'. Kargil Review Committee Report, Sage Publications, New Delhi, 1999, p. 81, 442.

Thapliyal, U.P. *Military Organizations in Ancient Period.* Section I: pp. 68–103. In Volume X, Part 3: Historical perspective of Warfare in India. Some morale and material determinations. S.N. Prasad (Ed). 2002. In *History of Science, Philosophy and Culture in Indian Civilization Series*. General Editor-D.P. Chattopadhyaya. Published by Bhuvan Chandel, Distributors Motilal Benarsi Das, New Delhi, 2002 *b*.

Trevalyan, Sir George Otto. *Bart. Cawnpore*. Indus Publishers, New Delhi, 1992. An Imprint of Harper Collins Publishers India Pvt. Ltd. First published 1865, New Delhi [also published by Macmillan and Co. Ltd., London, 1907], pp. 1–33.

Venkateswaran, A.L. 'Defence Organization in India (since Independence)'. Publications Division Ministry of Information and Broadcasting, Govt. of India, 1967.

Verma, Bharat (Capt), Hiranandani, G.M., Vice Admiral (Retd) and Pandey, B.K. Air Marshal (Retd). *Indian Armed Forces*. Lancer Publishers, New Delhi, 2008. pp. 1461–63, 235.

Westhorpe, Chris. *The World's Armies: An Illustrated review of Armies of the World*. Salamander's Book Ltd., London, 1991.

Woodward, Peggy. *Rise of The Raj*. Midas Books, Speldhurst, Kent, 1978.

Section – II

Food

8

Origin of Food Habits, Diets and Beliefs

Evolution and Food Habits

Food consumption is the basic instinct of all living things. The first life on the planet was microbial in nature, emerging and living in the primordial soup that was the ocean, also inhabiting rock, the deep Earth and the soil. They developed mechanisms and metabolic profiles to fit the environment they inhabited. Anaerobic systems and archaebacteria existed without Oxygen. Vegetation and photosynthetic cycle with the oxygen and carbon dioxide exchange mechanisms caused an atmosphere where a variety of fauna grew abundantly, both small and big. The herbivores ate the vegetation while the predators killed the herbivores as well as creatures placed lower in the food chain.

In the evolution of man, that began some six million years ago, from the time of the early hominids until the period of settled living followed by the agricultural revolution, food was what could be hunted or foraged and gathered from the wild (Gore, 2003). In the interim, from around two million years ago during the Pliocene, *Homo habilis* devised tools to hunt but active hunting began with *H. erectus,* which was better endowed with the capability to utilise nature's bounty. Acquisition of the skills of fishing came later sometime between 190,000 and 130,000 years ago in Eastern Africa during the time of major glaciation (Oppenheimer, 2003, pp. 76–77). While *H. habilis* still ranged, modern man appeared. According to some writings, fire was domesticated much earlier, at least 700,000 to 800,000 years ago and with the discovery of fire came the appreciation of cooked meat and adapting a less strenuous way of eating and digesting the same food (Nestle Report). But Oppenheimer makes no mention of this special ability in the hominids of less than a million years ago. Not until 45,000 years ago did the anatomically modern man appear in the near East and Europe (Oppenheimer, 2003, p. 81). The Ice ages had great effect on their food sources, as the vegetation dried up and they were forced to move out of their original land looking for larger animals. The migration of the species had begun.

Pre-agricultural man ate some 200 species of plant foods such as wild grass seeds, tubers, tree nuts as well as many kinds of meat and fish (Cordain, 1999).

The agricultural epoch dawned in the Fertile Crescent in the Middle East and Central Asia. Oases helped in cultivation and irrigation. Excavations in Nabta Playa, now a rainless desert dating back to 12,000 years ago on the Egyptian-Sudan border provide evidence of domestication and exploitation of plants in the Saharan region which can be dated to 8,000 years ago. Starch analysis techniques applied to excavated remains of seeds point to an early transition from foraging to root crop cultivation in Panama's tropical forests (Piperno et al., 2000). History of plant domestication of Southwest Africa reveals that pulses and cereals began to be used intensively in many areas around 12,000 years ago and shortly after domestication varieties of peas, lentils, barley and Emmer wheat came into use. Though some areas still depended on wild grasses, by 8,000 years ago both domesticated wheat and barley had come into general use (Wendorf, 1992). One by one several crops were domesticated and horticulture began to be practiced.

The First Farmers

It was established from the stone artifacts found in Mount Carmel on the Mediterranean that cereals became an important dietary substance. Pits for storage and for roasting grain have also been discovered in these areas. The cereals in the diet were wild barley and different kinds of naturally occurring wheat. These people were perhaps the earliest of plant breeders in the way they seemed to have practiced generations of selective planting so that more food was produced by 8,000 BC.

Students of agricultural sciences, plant genetics and breeding and biotechnology would know that the wild wheat known as Wild Einkorn (*Triticum boeticum*) and wild goat grass (*Aegilops speltoides* and *A. taushii*), diploids having two sets of chromosome were the original starter specimens which gave rise to the domesticated Emmer wheat (*Triticum monococcum*) with tough ears and certain other hybrids. The wild Emmer wheat (*Triticum dicoccoides*) obtained from back crosses was a tetraploid in nature (four sets of chromosomes) but also possessed tough ears. Further crossings produced Emmer wheat (*T. dicoccum*), the hexaploid (six sets of chromosomes) hard wheat (*T. durum*), spell wheat (*T. spelta*), bread wheat (*T. aestivum*) and club wheat (*T. compactum*). The hard wheat, bread wheat and club wheat were domesticated. These species possessed not only tough ears like their wilder ancestors but also free threshing seeds (Hunter, 2003, pp. 20–21).

The First Shepherding

The earliest people as we know hunted wild animals like the gazelle, boar, deer etc. for food. It is not easy to tell when they took to breeding the animals in different parts of the world. Wolves were domesticated to dogs around 11,000 BC. Mouflons became sheep; aurochs or wild cattle became cows. Gazelle meat along with wild cereals became an established major diet by 9,500 BC. Sheep and goats entered the farming cycle soon after, followed by the domestication of the pig (7,500 BC), cattle, (7,000 BC), cat (7,000 BC), chicken (6,000 BC), llama (5,000 BC), donkey (4,000 BC), horse (4,000 BC), camel (3,000 BC), guinea pigs (2,000 BC), rabbit (1,000 BC) and turkey (300 BC). Much of the domestication happened in the region of West Asia (or Middle East), Central Asia and Arabia. Other places where domestication of animals has been found to have occurred were as diverse as Spain, China, the Andes, Peru, Mexico and Russia (Hunter, 2003, p. 23). Sheep and goats were particularly important in farm economy, for they produced meat, milk, hide, fur or fleece. The settlers thus had grain, meat and milk for food and hide and fleece to clothe and protect them from the severe cold.

Not until 2,000 years ago was any agriculture practiced among the Puma Indians and the Papua New Guinea tribes; it is also significant that there are many peoples who still live as the pre-agriculture man did (Cordain, 1999). Two immediate examples of such a lifestyle may be found among the Australian Aborigines and the Jurawa and Onge tribes in the Andaman and Nicobar islands (Chakrabarty, 1998) all of whom belong to the Australoid group.

Our Palaeo Diet and Basic Foods

It has been determined that while our pre-human ancestors of 3–4 million years ago who lived in the warm wet African forests subsisted mainly on fruits and tree nuts along with animal food in small quantities, the bipedal hominid of two million years ago began to turn carnivorous during the Ice age. This happened because the freeze resulted in the drying up of the planet; more grasslands sprung up which supported many herbivores that ranged freely and were easy game for the hunters. As mentioned earlier, *Homo habilis* made stone tools and *Homo erectus* took to active hunting and thus ate large amounts of meat. The Neanderthals who appeared somewhere around 250,000 years ago (*H.neanderthalus*) coexisted with modern *Homo sapiens* in Europe between 28,000 and 40,000 years ago (Oppenheimer, 2003, pp. 104–105) in the region of Germany, France, Russia, the Middle East and Africa. This portion of archaic history is found in France in Chauvet cave engravings, drawings and brilliant paintings (Clottes, 2001). Many bones of large animals have been discovered in the vicinity of early habitation of this species indicating that they had been used for food in the cold climate.

Some 40,000 years ago, the Pima Indians hunted really big game like the Siberian mammoth and their diet was derived entirely from meat with hardly any carbohydrate content except for the seasonal berries and from small quantities found in the liver and gut contents of the hunted kill. The Australian Aborigines of 50,000 years ago continued to hunt seasonal animals, shellfish and gather plant food. The Eskimos who relied on sea animals for their food seemed to have no absorbable carbohydrate at all in their diet. Civilisation has touched most of these tribes and is responsible for changing their eating habits due to ready access to a variety of processed foods.

The Island tribes inhabiting the Andaman and Nicobar islands (there are some six to seven of them belonging to this group of palaeolithic ancestors of not less than 40,000 years ago) hunt for food in a way reminiscent of the archaic lifestyles. Recent findings reveal that these tribes are more similar to some African people in respect of their DNA profiles. Exposure to civilisation of these Andaman and Nicobari tribes is already habituating them to look for quantities of cereal (cooked rice) and starchy-sweet food (ripe bananas). Now they demand these foods before they consent to be sent back, herded in closed vans[1]. The change in food habits brought about due to change from hunting and foraging in the wild to reaping a regular harvest in the post-agricultural settled life pattern and domestication of animals, profoundly affected the dietary composition of the human species in respect of consumption of carbohydrates, protein and fat (Brand-Miller and Colagiuri, 1999). Data compiled originally by Hirsch (1995) and discussed by these authors trace the estimated changes in the carbohydrate, protein and fat intake that have occurred in the last one million years.

Very low dietary calories from the slowly absorbed non-starch polysaccharides or fructose, 80 per cent of energy derived from high protein, or high fat characterised the pre-agriculture diet from a million years ago until 10,000 years ago. This was in sharp contrast to the significant increase in diet of carbohydrate content from agricultural cereals which provided 90 per cent of energy in the last one thousand years and a steep decline in protein and fat calories. This changed pattern of dietary intake has been progressive from the time of evolution to the time of the Industrial Revolution. In fact, just in the last 100 years or so, when modern food processing came into its own, the carbohydrate (cereal) intake as well as of fat were seen to rise and the protein consumption fell below the level of pre-agriculture diets. Simopoulos (1999), discussing the genetic variation in relation to nutrition observed that there was a significant difference in the diet of the hunter gatherer and the western diet and summed it up as follows:

- the hunter gatherers consumed low-energy dense, high protein (mostly from animal source) food which also had,
- low to moderate carbohydrate content but had,
- high fiber and low fat (vegetable and animal) which presented a low ratio (2.4) of omega 6 (w-6) to omega 3 (w-3) fatty acids in contrast to the highly energy dense, low (or moderate)

animal/vegetable protein, low fiber, high fat (especially the saturated type from animal sources) and high (12.0) ratio of w-6: w-3 containing western diets.

The hunter gatherer exhibited high physical activity and we know that the average modern man generally indulges in low physical activity. In an actual worldwide survey of 181 hunter gatherer diets, it was found that the energy from plant food contributed 35 per cent of calories and the animal foods 65 per cent. The Paleolithic human diet is estimated to have contained 37 per cent protein, the Eskimo diet 45 percent, and the Australian aborigine diet 54 per cent. Physiologically, maximum protein intake should be 50 per cent (i.e., 300–375 g) per day. Carbohydrates in animal derived diets range from 1–17 per cent i.e., from 1–125 g from sources like milk, organs, gut contents and fat content in such diets would be 34–54 per cent derived from animals and tree nuts. After examining the metabolic parameters in regard to sports nutritional aspects, Chen (1999) arrived at the conclusion that the levels of physical activity/energy efficiency (PA/EE) in the modern version of our species is the lowest ever in our evolution. To site an example, *Homo erectus* of 1.7 million years ago with a body weight of 53.1 kg and *H. sapiens* of 45,000 years ago with a body wt. of 57.0 kg exhibited total energy expenditure/resting metabolic rates (TEE/RMR) ratio of 1.8; their daily foraging, gathering and hunting range was indeed wide covering several kilometers. A Kung tribesman was lighter in weight (46 kg), his TEE/RMR was 1.71 and he walked 14.9 km a day. The Aches of the tropical Paraguay were heavier (59.6 kg). Their TEE/RMR was 2.15 and they would cover an average distance of 19.2 km daily in search for food and hunting. A modern day athlete with a body wt. of 70 kg showed TEE/RMR of 1.7, (the same as the Kung tribe who is much lighter) and could run 12.1 km/day (probably in training). Our average office worker of today (average wt 70 kg) walks 0 km/day and has a TEE/RMR ratio of 1.18 which is the lowest ever, just as Chen (1999) observed.

For this transformation to have been effected, the agricultural humans would have had to settle down, lay down roots, till the land, plant and watch over cropping harvest, learn to store and process grains, meat, fruit and vegetables. According to Eaton and Konner (1985), evidence till date has indicated that the human genes have changed very little in the past 40,000 years and our nutritional needs were also determined then. Since that time, from a predominantly meat eating species we became cereal consumers in large measure. While our genotype adapted to carnivorous habit and insulin resistance has remained practically unchanged since 40,000 years ago as Cro-Magnon man, our modern high cereal/carbohydrate consumption pattern has resulted in hyper-insulinemia (Brand-Miller and Colagiuri, 1999). We are essentially carnivorous in nature as a result of evolutionary adaptations in diet and our antique genome is maladapted to deal with the onslaught of high carbohydrate diets.

More sedentary habits developed from acquiring skills, art and craft, language, script, technology and trade. It would be right to say that once they were out of Africa, the human species wandered in archaeologically and genetically traceable migratory patterns across the world. That the major civilisations established themselves by the side of the great rivers – the Euphrates, the Nile, the Indus and the Yangtze was no coincidence, but was indicative of the stage of evolution the species had reached and the intellect that became inherent. No doubt there were still the wandering nomadic tribes which moved with their animal herds from one region to another in search of new pastures. The history of our civilisation has been explained and discussed in great detail by several scholarly works. One such beautifully detailed work on the subject was produced by Will and Ariel Durante (1965) in the form of 'Story of our Civilization' in several volumes.

Foods, Diets and Rations in Ancient India

It is necessary to scroll through the entire treatise of ArthaŚāstra to glean material relevant to food in general. There is more information to be had on the rations for horses, elephants, camels, bullocks and mules than anything near ration entitlements for men as soldiers. All one can be expected to learn about food here is how much food (as grain) should comprise the meal of an Aryan male, of a child, of females and men of lower classes.

The Aryans who came in to the Valley region were pastoral people and their diet consisted of whatever could be obtained from the land such as grains, milk from the cattle herds, butter, ghee, wild game meat, oils from oil seeds, various kinds of fruits and vegetables and extractives made from them as flavourings, beverages, and sweets, etc.

Grains: The most often mentioned foods in the *Ṛg Veda* are *apupa*, *karambha*, *saktu* and the *dhanas* all of which were made from barley, when rice (*vrihi*) was still unknown (Melkote Documents quoting Ṛg III, 52.1; VIII 91.2; VI 57.2 pp. 62–63). Using different types of grains in combination with milk, meat and with ghee as fat, a great variety of common and sacrificial foods were made in sweet and other forms. Parched rice *Parivapa*, mixture of five grains *pancaudana*, milk preparation *Ksiradana*, meat preparation with grains *mamsaudana*, a gruel like *purodasa* for ritual offerings have been mentoned in the *Ṛg Veda*.

Grain processing and yields: A noteworthy feature was the record of yields from different grains. In the *ArthaŚāstra*, three types of rice are mentioned in this context. *Kodrava* or *vrihi* rice was said to yield only half of substance (meaning perhaps that 50 per cent is removed as inedible husk while processing paddy). From *Sali* rice, the yield was one-half less than that (25 per cent only of the original) and from *varaka* rice, one-third less. *Priyangu* millet also yielded only half of substance. There were different processes too. *Udaraka*, barley and wheat gave the same mass when pounded; sesame, barley, *mudga* and *masa* (these two are beans) when 'rubbed' also retained the same mass. Frying was a process where wheat and barley increased by one-fifth of their mass. Flour from grains and pulses obtained by the grinding methods then in practice also find mention. When milled into flour, *kalaya* meal yield was three-fourths of the original, *mudga* meal even less. The legumes yield was also 50 per cent of the original where as the lentils (this distinction is not clear) were said to yield one third less of the yield of legumes, (Kangle, 1972: AS.2.15.42).

These figures had been provided as guidelines to the Superintendent of the Magazine who was enjoined to know about agricultural produce, revenues from the countryside, purchase, barter, bargaining, labour in place of taxes, income from other sources, returns from expenditure and any additional income. He was not only authorised to stock various foodstuffs, but have them processed, keep track of the yields and supervise the distribution of authorised quantities. Animals were fed different kinds of grain and it was essential to clarify how much of the unprocessed grain would be sufficient to yield adequate amounts for each animal. To feed a young elephant, the 12 *adhakas* of rice it was entitled to, (eleven for a vicious one and nine for a war elephant), the starting quantity before processing should be several *dronas* of *Sali* rice. This upon processing would most likely yield the reported 25 per cent of rice grain. Their caretakers were also authorised a portion of 68 *adhakas* of rice coming into the stables.

Oil seeds: The oil seed sesame was in common use as well as its oil *Taila* (oil mentioned in *Atharva Veda*), usually stored in big earthenware jars. However, *ghee* was the principle medium for frying.

Milk and its products: Many milk products and drinkable milk of cow and buffalo were common in *Ṛg Veda*. No reference to butter or *navanita* from buffalo finds a place although buffalo meat was a common food item. Creamy butter *phanta, mastu* (sour curds), *vajina* (mixed milk) and *ghee* were common in Ṛg Vedic times but not *amika* or clotted milk.

Alcoholic drinks: The consumption of alcoholic drinks followed certain rules, which for some classes of people were stringent (Majumdar and Pusalkar, 1955). Manu and Yajnavalka forbade the three upper classes to drink certain wines although for the Kshatriya and Vysya castes, a degree of relaxation of the rules was permitted. The three kinds of *suras* made from (a) rice flour, (b) molasses and (c) honey or grapes or *Madhuka* flowers were totally forbidden to the Brahmanas. The Kshatriyas and Vysyas were allowed two kinds. It is said that for the Brahmanas found guilty of drinking, rice wine particularly, invited death as punishment, and for drinking other types penances were required to be performed by the guilty. The rules for drinking also implied that there were proper seasons for drinking. A commonly made beverage *Hemantha* was consumed in the cold season along with pork and newly husked rice. For the summer heat, the essence of quails and deer and wine mixed with water were considered to be delicacies appropriate for the weather.

Use of wines, liquor and opium in war: Consumption of alcohol is a conspicuous practice among the troops of today, not that it is confined to them only, although persons in the know say that drinking alcohol and eating meat is on the wane among the armed forces in general and among those deployed at higher altitudes in particular. Drinking as a custom and as an essential part of any meal and in war time in particular has existed since Vedic times. It seems to have become quite popular by the sixth century BC. Alexander and his army used hard drinks and the Iranians, the Greeks, the Śakas and the Kuśanas were equally fond of this beverage. Greek historians observed and recorded the consumption of alcohol during the Mauryan period and noted that it was a popular drink of the times. Many types of wine were produced under state management for local consumption and trade, as revealed in ArthaŚāstra (AS. 2.25; 12.4.4). India has witnessed a long period of foreign invasion, and with each successive conquerer, alcohol consumption became gradually more popular.

Wine and liquor was drunk as a habit, sipped and enjoyed for relaxation, swallowed by the warriors and the brave for mitigating fatigue, reverently offered and consumed for enhancing prowess and for making one fearless or even joyously and copiously consumed for the celebration of any event and victory.

Drinks were taken before joining a war to boost the spirits of the warriors and troops and after the end of the war to soothe the nerves according to ancient custom and practice (Rice, 1988: Amarakosha 2.8.103; Thapliyal, 2002). A similar use is attributed in *Raghuvamsa* of Kalidasa and in *Sundarakānda* in *Rāmāyana* (Raghu 4.65; Rām.sundara. 62) as pointed out by Majumdar and Pusalkar (1955). Here the soldiers of the land sat on deerskins and surrounded by wine creepers drank to remove their exhaustion after victory. In fact, the rulers must make the soldiers drink invigorating wines before joining battle according to Śukrā's advice (Thapliyal, 2002b, p. 91). Not only men but when women soldiers (known as *saktis*) felt acute thirst during a battle, it was *madira-sindhu* (ocean of liquor) which came to their aid, showered them all with the beverage and quenched their thirst. As per a legend in Brahmanda Purana, by the mere fragrance of this act the weak might become strong and even the dead might come alive!

War elephants, which formed an important and significantly strong division of the army, were known to become temperamental, tired, non-responsive or fierce depending on the circumstances in war. In the beginning of an engagement they were fed with intoxicating drink as recorded by Hiuen Tsang during his travels in India (Thapliyal, 2002c, p. 144).

Many types of wine and their production have been described in Panini's time (Thapliyal, 2002b, p. 91). *Soma* and *Soma ras* were cult things in ancient India and Iran for thousands of years, observes Hildebrandt (1891, 1899, 1902) in his book on Vedic Mythology.

Soma Ras and its Preparation

Spirituous drinks of ancient India (Mitra, 1969, pp. 389–421) includes Soma Ras using juice of the soma creeper plant – *Asclepeas acida* or *Sarcostemma viminalis*, barley meal (malted) and clarified butter and the meal of wild paddy (nivdra). This Soma rasa or beer made of Soma appears to have had a low keeping quality. It is said to be able to bestow a great amount of exhilaration both in men and the various gods Indra, Agni and others. There were several other fermented liquors viz. from Jujube, Aniseed, etc. which were very popular and copiously consumed. Soma was never made for sale, comments Mitra but has been intimately associated with the early history of Aryans even before they separated from the Persians. The only people specifically barred against alcoholic beverages were the Brahmanas.

North and South Indian Food Habits in Ancient Times

Food habits of people in the Tamil land and in Aryan India seem to have been very similar as recorded in the *Ṛg Veda* and *Atharva Veda* (Iyengar, 1985, p. 61). Meats of all kinds were equally relished. Animal milk mixed with wild honey, ghee, butter and curds were common to both people. Among the grains, although rice, barley, beans and sesame were the principle foodstuffs, there is a mention of corn, probably depicting grains in generic. Whereas the Aryans consumed wheat and barley, barley was not used in the South. The rice was hand pounded and the grains were milled in mill stones and kept in earthen vessels in the homes. Their method of food preparation appears to have been similar too. Parched grain meal made into gruel, boiled with curd or milk and cooked meat formed a good part of the meal; these were prepared fresh and served on leaf platters (lotus leaf was common). Skin bags and jars of stone were used to keep honey, curd etc.

Meat and drink: The supposition that Indians have been mainly vegetarians is not supported by history. Indians loved meat and enjoyed it when available. This was true both of the northern Aryans and the southern Tamils. The hunted game was never wasted or thrown; however, meat was never their staple food as it was for people in other regions of the world where cereals were not produced in sufficient quantity. Rice and wheat as well as millets were eaten with vegetables and meat in the form of a curry. Iyengar (1985, pp. 57–58) provides a description from *Porunarrupadai* (103–107) of a feast hosted by a Tamil royal patron which consisted of well boiled loin of a ram fed with bundles of *arugu* grass, big chunks of it roasted at the end of iron spikes. Milk and fried meat were also served. The guests ate meat night and day until their teeth became blunt and they were disgusted with the (thought of) food. In the old times, both meat and vegetables were boiled with black pepper. The Greeks and the Romans (*Yavanas*) loved the spice and its sharp 'boiling' taste, which gives the black pepper its name *yavanapriya* meaning 'dear to the Yavanas'. They also mutilated the vernacular name *miriyal* for pepper and called it *pippali* and hence *pepperos*. Pepper is actually long pepper or chilly fruit and hot pepper. However the name stuck. Pepper was imported from India into Europe by Venetian and later Dutch traders during the Middle Ages – not for eating but for preserving meat. The steep increase in the price of pepper seems to have been the core issue in European markets controlled by the Dutch. The price of pepper was the causative element that pushed English traders to found the East India Company in 1599 in order to circumvent the avaricious Dutch merchants' demand of a high price for this commodity. Could it really have been that India went under British colonial rule for two centuries for the sake of pepper?

In regard to meat eating, no taboos were mentioned in Vedic mantras as far as the flesh of horses, bulls, buffaloes, rams and goats were concerned and there existed slaughter houses for the express purpose of butchering these animals. Fish and birds also made appearances on the menus as found in Satapatha Brahmana (iii 1.2.21) (Iyengar, 1985, p. 59). Meat was available and eaten by all people until after the Vedic times. Boiled, spit roasted, fried, cooked with rice or grains, with spices and salt or with spices and sweetening agents, meat in several forms was relished. Meat of many animals, including beef, was used in sacrificial rites and for propitiation to gods. Obeisance to the sages and hospitality to the visiting guests was not considered complete without animal sacrifices and offerings of their meats, particularly beef. Flesh was offered to a guest of status in a special rite was known as *madhuparka* (Mitra, 1969, pp. 354–388 and Melkote Documents). There are ample references in the Vedas to this effect explains Mitra, while discussing the idea of beef in ancient India. One of the food habits of the Indo-Aryans was to kill a fatted calf and serve the meat of cattle – a valuable food offering and a mark of generosity, hospitality and respect to honoured guest(s). There were no compunctions of conscience to cattle slaughter; beef was a highly esteemed food, not only fit for guests but deemed to be absolutely necessary by pious Hindus in their funeral ceremonies. A supply of beef in the journey of a pious Hindu from this world to another was ensured by way of killing a cow and burning it with the dead. This sacrifice or '*Gomedha*' enjoined in the Vedas and practiced in the age of Rāmāyana and Mahābhārata was so shrouded in incomprehensible and unintelligible utterings that the general public never realised the facts about cow slaughter. The *slokas* and *mantras* chanted were so mysterious to the uninitiated in Vedic ways and meaning that truth did not become evident. It was thus believed by the people at large that the slaughtered cow would somehow revive itself immediately and therefore its meat was fairly acceptable (Mitra, 1969, pp. 354–355). Valmiki threw a reception for his brother sage Vashistha, who was a prominent Vedic personage (Vashistha is believed to be the author of the original law books *Smiritis*). For this reception, a lot of cattle calves were slaughtered for the entertainment of the guests. Mitra (1969, p. 356) quotes an entire passage from *Uttara-rāma-charita* describing this event.

Consumption of all animal food was authorised by Manu, who also cautioned that it would not be considered wrong or a sin if it was consumed after worshipping god (Mitra, 1969, p. 358). It has been stated in Satapatha Brahmana that a big bull or a ram was cooked for a king or a Brahman. Yajgnavalkya said that he would eat the flesh of milch cows and bullocks only if it was tender. Horsemeat was relished too, according to *Ṛg Veda*. Venison or deer meat did not get the label of acceptable food until the sixth century BC. Other animals sanctioned by wise legislation as lawful meat foods were the hedgehog and porcupine, lizard *godha* (guana), *gandaka* (the rhinoceros), tortoise and the rabbit or hare among the five-toed animals. Also included among lawful food as meat were all quadrupeds (except camel) which have one row of teeth (Mitra, 1969, p. 359 quoting Manu V.18). In the Sutra period, (*Bharadwaja Srauta sutra*, IV, I.ff) Vedic Aryans did not seem to have used fish. However, in the *Mahābhārata* (Adiparva 28.21), eaters of fish are mentioned wrote Dange (Melkote Documents, p. 61).

Asoka's First Rock Edict reveals that in the big temple of heaven for the beloved Emperor Priyadasi, 100,000 animals were sacrificed every day (Mitra, 1969, quoting another source) and although no species were mentioned, Mitra speculates that Asoka, who was a pious Hindu and adherent of the Sastras, could not have confined the slaughter to goats and sheep alone when the Vedic ways enjoined cow slaughter for rituals and food.

Spit roasted meats of animals, beef and birds, and carved into pieces, various types of liquor, sauces and adjuncts made from tamarind, pomegranates, sweet basil, sub acid herbs, ginger, asafoetida and radishes as well as sweet and savoury cakes of rice, or rice and coconut etc. were specially popular in what has been termed as 'picnic' foods in ancient India (Mitra, 1969, pp. 422–443).

Manu had ordained that fresh meat purchased from a butcher's stall was pure and fit for consumption by pious Hindus (Mitra, 1969, p. 382). The animal slaughter did not seem to require the presence of a priest to chant prayers as a ceremonial rite of slaughter. However, traders were required to sell meat without bones of deer and beasts freshly killed. Meat of several animals were permitted and accepted as food and offerings (AS 2.26.7) but the calf, the bull and milch cow among animals were neither to be killed nor to be tortured in anyway. Both these forbidden acts attracted severe fines of 50 *panas* each. Most meat came from cattle that were beyond productive age and from forest animals. There were reserve sanctuaries for many animals under state protection where killing, binding or even injuring of deer, beasts, birds and fish brought down an imposition of the highest fine from the Superintendent of Slaughter houses (Kangle, AS 2.26.1). Several lake birds and sea fish were also protected against violence of any sort. Any kind of poaching was a crime.

The quality of meat sold was an important consideration. The sale of meat that was swollen or without head, feet and bones, or meat that was foul-smelling or from a naturally dead animal was especially forbidden (Kangle, AS.2.26.12).[2]

Until the late Vedic age, as given in Satapatha Brahmana (iii 1.2.21) (Iyengar, 1985, p. 59), there was no objection to beef eating in North India. Since even the sage Yajnavalka (probably in the first millennium BC) had no fear of eating beef 'if it be tender', the total ban on beef eating and feelings of disgust of beef eating among, the Hindus cannot have predated his writings.

The reverent sentiments leading to the banning of beef eating emerged as a result of thinking that the benign cattle which were said to be the divine Bhāgavati's representative on Earth, were needed for agriculture, for their milk and milk products. The meek and the gentle eyed animals evoked love and affection. Since the cow and the ox, believed to support everything on this Earth were bestowed with all good features and vigour of other animal species, they were therefore in turn worthy of protection from destruction; eating of their flesh would be a grave sin punishable by re-birth as a strange being, *brunhathi*.

Meat and drink appear to go together but as has been mentioned, *Soma Ras* and many other alcoholic beverages were popular and those that were allowed to drink, indulged in it. The ancient Tamils drank hard liquor which was known by several names. Iyengar provides at least 60 references in Tamil language to substantiate the statement that liquor was brewed from honey and matured in bamboo cylinders. One name for the sweet-rice liquor was *toppi,* which was said to be brewed in the homes. People drank the rice liquors and ate the meat of the strong bull cut up in the field. That they often drank themselves into a stupor with intoxication is suggested by the description of the beverage formula used to clear the morning hangover! The exotic potion was concocted with pounded white nuts (ejected from over-ripe jack fruit found floating in rivers) mixed with butter milk, and juice of sweet-sour tamarind fruits (which has a white rind) in which was cooked white rice (matured in bamboo tubes). This seems to have been a guest offering too, served by pretty and flower decked *kurava* girls (Iyengar, 1985, pp. 62–63).

Since drinking was a common pastime of men and drinking intoxicants was advocated in battle/combat and it has been described in ancient texts that the armies of the past (up to the time of Napoleon) marched with a huge paraphernalia in maintenance and supply line including the women folk, it is logical to conclude that the various camp followers not only gathered the ingredients to make the liquor and prepare food and serve it but were also required to 'detoxify' the drunken men with a hangover in the morning and make them fit for another day's battle!

Vegetarianism as a practice is said to be anterior to 600 BC chiefly because so many cereals, pulses, fruits and vegetables had become available. Achaya (1998, pp. 40–44) has described several cooking concepts in the Orthodox Aryan rituals called *'Kachcha* food' of which there are the boiled rice, boiled *dal*/lentils and *chapattis* eaten everyday at home and prepared fresh for each meal, and the '*Pucca* foods' which were fried in ghee to be shared with others, also for taking on long journeys without fear of contamination or spoilage.

Cereals: Various varieties of rice grown in the five different regions of the South were the main cereal and staple food of the time. These were mountain rice, bamboo rice, white rice and red rice. Parboiling was the normal method of processing, though raw rice was usually popular. Pounded rice boiled in water, sometimes with (legumes) pulses (as in *khichadi*/*pongal* form), different forms of porridge like rice water (starchy *ganji*) etc. were prepared. The ancient way of primary processing also extended to making parched rice known as *pori* in Tamil.

Wild honey gathered to go with many dishes was a favourite, as was jaggery, manufactured by boiling down sugarcane juice to molasses and cooling it down in pots and wooden moulds. Curdled milk (Curd), churned butter, and ghee were the chief milk products. The ancients realised that butter could not be kept in the prevailing warm climate without becoming rancid. Therefore, it was melted down soon after churning out.

Fruits, vegetables and their products: Extensive use of vegetables and fruits is recorded in the Tamil litreature (Iyengar, 1985, p. 62). Tender fruits were used as vegetables and preparations were made with leaf, stem, root, tuber and mature fruit and pulp etc. All have specific and various names either in pure Tamil or synonyms borrowed from Sanskrit such as for jack fruit, mango, unripe plantains, brinjals etc.

Before the age of fire matches, fire was built in the forest areas in the mountains by rubbing one piece of wood on another and firewood was brought in from the forest by elephants. In the plains however, a constant fire was kept stoked in earthen fire-pots. The way the Jorawa tribes in the Andamans carry fire is reminiscent of this. Salt mining was known and it was an extensive industry-salt being needed for various preparations (Iyengar 1985, pp. 64-65).

Grain Rations for Different Classes of People

What was the daily food of people in ancient times? ArthaŚāstra provides some information regarding quantities of different ingredients, which are recommended for individuals. Grains, then as now, formed their staple food and we have a formula of sorts to cook rice.

Military personnel, royals and nobles: The portion of authorised entitlements of grains to be given to the chiefs, queens, princes and kings was successively less by one *adhaka* of that given to an infantry man (AS 2.15. 42). These were as follows:

- 8 *adhakas* for infantry men,
- 7 for chiefs,
- 6 for the queens and the princes,
- 5 for the kings or 1 *prastha* of rice grains, unbroken and cleaned.

Giving an infantry man 8 *adhakas* or 160 *seers* seems to make no sense what so ever, unless it was meant for a longer and unspecified period (but certainly not for one day). Here one should again take note of the weight of one *adhaka* in kilograms. One *adhaka,* according to Sircar's Epigraphical glossary (see Annexure 3), was 20 seers, which can be assumed to be equal to 20 kg (1 seer = 1 kg approx). This amount would suffice for 33 days at 600 g per day (approximately the same as the current Standard Ration Scale in the Services and nearly the same as recommended by ICMR 1998). By this reckoning, eight *adhakas* of grain to an infantry man should last him about 8–9 months. The daily energy content of 2,400 Kcal would be derived from this grain ration. Entitlements for other food items are not known.

These particular weights in grams differ from those discussed in Chapter 2 (Table 2.4 and Annexure 3, Table A3.3). By Kangle's estimate (commentary on ArthaŚāstra), the value of one *adhaka* is taken as 1.81 kg; then 8 *adhakas* or 14.5 kg (or more precisely14.48 kg) at the rate of 1 *prastha* (0.452 g) per rice meal of an adult Aryan male (assume here an infantry man) would last 32 meals of smaller portion sizes. If any rice preparation was eaten once a day or once made, eaten at different times, this could be ration for 32 days. There could have been many other items of food and other meals of the day to accompany rice. Once cooked, this quantity of rice was perhaps meant to last the entire day, even though the amounts of rice prescribed for one person as given in Table 8.1, column 1, were said to constitute one meal for an Aryan male. That amount (0.452 g) of cooked rice would make an enormous single meal.

Food for the commoners: There were four food items recommended for commoners (AS.2.15.42–46). These items were rice, broth, salt and butter or oil. The term 'broth' is not further specified, but it could mean a liquid ingredient or water extract, its quantity seems to be inadequate to prepare boiled rice or even a *pulao* preparation, unless it was rice flour which was cooked into a porridge or a gruel like mass. One can only assume that with butter, small amounts of oil and salt present, this had to have been some kind of rather dry preparation.

The recommended food rations as depicted in Table 8.1 decrease by half for children, lesser by one quarter for women and lesser by one-sixth for the lower classes. Children's and women's food intake understandably would be lesser than an adult male's in general but why there was a reduction in the quantity for the 'lower classes' (presumably only the males) has not been explained.

Table 8.1: Grain rations for one meal of an Aryan*

Food	*Man Quantity, g*	*Women Quantity, g*
Rice	1 prastha or 450 g	¾ prastha (337.5 g)
Broth	¼ prastha or 112.5 g	¾ of ¼ prastha (84.37 g)
Salt	1/16 of broth or 7 g	¾ of 1/16 broth (5.25 g)
Butter/oil	¼ of broth or 28.1 g	¾ of ¼ prastha (21.0 g)
Food	*Arya child Quantity, g*	*Males of lower classes Quantity, g*
Rice	½ prastha (225 g)	1/6 less of main ingredients (375 g)
Broth	1/8 prastha (56 g)	93.75 g
Salt	1/32 of broth	Not available
Butter/oil	1/8 of prastha of broth	½ of ¼ broth (14 g)

* Weight in grams in each column corresponds to one *prastha* or its fractions
Source: AS.2.15.42–46

Meat and vegetable preparations: Some kind of processing of meats and vegetables was in practice from the very ancient times. In *ArthaŚāstra* some recipes for their preparation are described. It is a little surprising that a work of such a nature should concern itself with a recipe description. Since Kautilya was given to describing minute details of many aspects of polity and governance, it is assumed that for ensuring proper trade practices in selling prepared foods or perhaps even for instructions to the cooks, these directions may have been thought to be helpful. It is also possible that it was the way the foods were prepared and Kautilya simply noted it down for his records.

Preparations using both fresh and dried meats and vegetables were in vogue. Although no specific entitlement of either foodstuff has been discovered for men and women, a recipe described (AS.2.15.47–49) for a meat or vegetable preparation provides us with some insight. There were separate instructions and ingredient quantities for fresh and dried meat and vegetable.

To cook meat in quantities of 20 *palas*, fat, salt, sugar, spices and curds were required as the chief ingredients (Table 8.2). For cooking 20 *palas* of vegetables, one and a half times more of the main ingredients were used. Both dried meat and vegetables were in common use for which the same ingredients in different quantities were to be added as depicted in Table 8.3. The dried vegetables were made with a larger amount of spices and curds than the meat.

Table 8.2: Ingredients used for fresh meat and vegetable preparations

Food item	*Fresh meat*	*Fresh vegetables**
Fresh meat/vegetables	20 palas	20 palas
Fat	1 kuduba	1½ kuduba
Salt	1 pala	1½ pala
Sugar	1 pala	1½ pala
Spices	2 dharanas	3 dharanas
Curds	½ prastha	1½ prastha

*Vegetables were cooked in one and half times more of the same ingredients.
Source: AS.2.15.47–49

Table 8.3: Preparations with dried meat and dried vegetables

Dried meat (everything twice as that for fresh meat)			*Dried vegetables (everything twice as that for fresh vegetables)*		
Meat	–	20 palas	Vegetables	–	20 palas
Fat	–	2 kudubas	Fat	–	3 kuduba
Salt	–	2 palas	Salt	–	3 palas
Sugar	–	2 palas	Sugar	–	3 palas
Spices	–	2 dharanas	Spices	–	6 dharanas
Curds	–	1 prastha	Curds	–	3 prasthas

Source: AS.2.15.47–49

Achaya (1998, p. 55) has also reported finding a somewhat similar recipe for meat where 20 *palas* (700 g) were cooked with 1 *kuduva* (250 g) curds, 1 *pala* (35 g) salt and 1/5 *pala* pungent spices; this food, he found, was sold in the prepared form.

Spices and condiments as flavorings: There were a variety of ingredients – sweet, sour, salty and spicy. 'Juice' in a food preparation probably meant any one of the following: sugarcane juice, melted jaggery, honey, treacle, juice of jambu fruit, or *panasa* fruit (jack fruit) infused with decoction of something called *mesarangi*, and long pepper (presumably red chilli), kept for 1 month or 6 months or even up to 12 months and then mixed with *cidbhita*, *urvaruka*, sugarcane stalk, mango fruit and *myrobalan* (or separately in unmixed form) constituted the group of fermented juices (AS.2.15.17). Several souring agents were derived from the juice of fruits such as tamarind, *karmada*, mango, pomegranate, *myrobalan*, citron, *kola*, *badara*, *sauvirka*, *parusaka* (AS 2.15.18). The group of sweet ingredients included treacle, jaggery, and unrefined sugar and honey made by bees and juices of grapes (AS.2.15.14). Butter, oil, suet and marrow constituted the fats (AS 2.15.13). Sea salt, *bida* salt, salt petre, borax and salt from saline soil and salt from Indus land were in common use (AS.2. 15.15). Sour liquids included curds and sour gruel etc. The group of spices were made up of several items – long pepper, black pepper, ginger, cumin seed, the bitter kirata, white mustard, coriander, *coraka*, *damanaka*, *maruvaka*, stalk of *sigru* etc (AS.2.15.17).

Food stocking and storage: Awareness about the importance of food reserves in ancient times is also evident. The stocking of foods and ingredients as well as keeping and issuing of dried fish, dried meat and vegetables such as bulbous roots, fruits, etc. was the direct responsibility of the Superintendent of the Magazine. There was a specific directive on being prepared with stocks of food and grain. It was mandatory that half of all available food should be set apart for use during times of distress faced by the country's rural folk and only half should be given out. That the stocks of food could become stale or spoiled or inedible after a period of storage was well understood since the Superintendent's duties extended to periodic replacement of old stock and keeping the storehouse replenished with fresh stocks at all times.

Goods sold in the marketplace or offered for barter by weight and volume included food substances – raw or in prepared form. There were surcharges for clarifying butter to butter oil or ghee. The price of items (AS 2.19.36 –46; 2.19.28–30) was paid in *panas* and *masakas* and there were different prices going for solids such as grains or flour, measured in bushels and *prasthas* and liquid materials like oils or butter even in small quantities, measured in *kudubas*. There were separate charges levied for grain delivered to the palace, to the king's harem and for servants as shown in Table 5.8A to 5.8F.

Foods for Aerial Pilots

The *vimāna* or an aerial vehicle was used in various celestial wars. A treatise on the science of aeronautics and its engineering aspects known as the *VymānikaŚāstra* (VS) existed in ancient India (Rao, 2003) and though its antiquity cannot be ascertained, it is definitely an old document attributed to the Sage Bhāradwaj. A section in Chapter 2 spanning several sutras pertains to diets and foods for the pilots or the *Akāsha Yoddha* (aerial warriors). It is Bodhananda's interpretation and descriptions in the sutras V.S 7–125 written by Joyser (1973) and translated by other scholars into English that are discussed here.

Bodhānanda explained that the food of the pilots as per *Kalpasutra* was of three kinds and was determined according to the seasons, the entire year having been assigned to three periods of four months each: (a) spring and summer (b) rains and autumn and (c) winter and snow. For each season there are specific recommendations for liquids, grains and type of meat to be eaten as shown in Table 8.4. Goat's milk (now recognised as having certain unique properties) and barley and sparrow's meat were meant for winter months only.

For the pilots belonging to the three *Dwija* castes (Brahmin, Kshatriya and Vysya), the food would not include flesh. This stricture was a significant departure from the prevailing custom and habit of meat eating in the normal course by all people including the three castes mentioned. It has already been discussed in the previous section that the Vedas and the ArthaŚāstra provided ample evidence of meat-eating practices. Achaya (1998, pp. 56–57) also noted that vegetarianism became widespread only in the Buddhist and Jain periods and even here it was the animal sacrifice in sacrificial rites that were banned. This is borne out by the Asokan Rock Edicts on Dharma (Nikam and Mckean, 1962). Somewhere along the progression of the *yugas*, the priestly class of Brahmins was also enjoined not to eat flesh and drink spirituous liquor. However, in this principle of diets from *Ashaanakalpa* of *Kalpasutra*, flesh eating was prohibited particularly for the pilots of the three classes. For lack of any reason, it could be speculated that it was more to do with fitness, safety, alertness and endurance than for religious or social reasons. In the absence of meat, the foods meant for the four months of winter and snow has not been given. There were three kinds of pilot foods in liquid, grain and meat form recommended for spring, rainy and winter months as shown in Table 8.4.

Table 8.4: Pilot's food according to seasons as mentioned in Bharadwaja Sutras: Aaharah kalpabhedat

Period	*4 months* *Spring, Summer*	*4 months* *Rains, Autumn*	*4 months* *Winter, Snow*
Liquids	Buffalo milk, curds, butter, ghee and its products	Cows milk, curds butter, ghee and their products	Goat's milk, curds and its products
Grains	Adhaka or Turdal rice and products	Wheat and black gram Green gram and products	Yava or barley and black gram, wheat, green gram
Meat	Flesh of sheep and its products	Flesh of cocks and hens, and their products	Flesh of sparrows and products

Sources: Hanumanta Rao and Ananda, 2004; Narayan et al., 2004

Diet rules: A more interesting explanation bases such prohibitions on the strength of ancient beliefs that alteration of the diets in different seasons was meant for the purpose of warding off the evil effects of 25 kinds of '*Bhedinee*' or poisonous maleficent forces which tended to paralyze the pilot's physical efficiency (V.S., Sutra 8**)**. The seasons apart, even meal timings have been specified for pilots (Sutra 9). According to Shaunaka, family men should take food twice a day, or once a day. Ascetics should eat only once a day, while the others may eat four times a day. Air pilots should eat five times a day, and yogis may eat as often as they wished. Diet rules purported to be given in *Lalla-kaarika* (Sutra 9) also mention different meal times for different classes of people. The day was divided into three hour periods called '*yaama*'. Family men were advised to eat at the end of the second *yaama* in the day and at the end of the first *yaama* in the night; those who would eat only once a day, had best do it during the third and the fourth *yaamas*. From these statements one cannot say to which class these pilots belonged. The labouring classes were to eat three times during the day and once in the night. It would seem that all those who were employed in a hard day's work in the farms and fields, at various skills and crafts, in manufacturing and soldiering were required to fortify themselves through the day with meals at regular times. For some inexplicable reason air pilots belonged to this category and were asked to eat three times in the day and twice in the night.

Diets and foods: The ancient people were aware of the properties and nature of foodstuffs and the requirements for people. Sutra 10 that according to the *Ashaanakalpa,* there are five kinds of food that are nutritious and wholesome: cooked rice or grain, gruel, cooked flour, flat baked bread and preparations made out of essence (extracts) from food material; this last in particular is considered to be the most superior of all types of foods. The art of cooking describes what we recognise to be steps in primary processing and value addition – dehusking of grains and separating non-edible parts and grinding the grain into flour. This flour was cooked in a 'suitable' vessel and when it reached the eighth degree of reduction, essences, sweets, condiments and ghee were added, and made into food balls, 'having nice flavour and delicious taste and being nourishing to the body'.

Bodhananda went on to further clarify the dietary recommendations made in Sutra-10 saying that preparations made from edible roots like potato and other bulbous vegetables and from fruits were also considered to be suitable as food. These mostly starchy roots and fruits may be eaten when grains are not available. These may be ground up into flour or used as sugar candy, jaggery, and honey. Milk and ghee, and oily products constituted a good part of the diet. There are said to be some 56 different roots and berries, which are said to be sweet, salty, pungent, acrid and alkaline in taste. Such type of roots should be cleaned, powdered, cooked and made into balls.

In particular there were 16 kinds of bulbous roots and 32 kinds of fruits for food purposes. Their products made excellent foods. Food from roots was particularly recommended as they were said to help develop the brain, nourish the body, strengthen bones and give virility – the food from bulbous roots was said to promote brilliance, bodily vigour and strengthen the life current. Preparations made of fruits nourished the mind and intelligence, blood, flesh and vital liquids. All these were alternatives to the grains and flesh and other normally available foods, and these alternatives are also recommended for pilots of the 'Vimanas' (Sutra 11). Bodhadananda's interpretation states that even grasses, herbs and shrubs could be made to yield food (Sutra-12). Though finding the colloquial names for these food sources was difficult, some scholars (Hanumantarao and Ananda, 2004, pp. 59–60) have attempted to find English and Latin names for some of them (Table 8.5). There are six kinds of *durva* grass, six kinds of *munja* hemp, six kinds of *darba* or long grass, six kinds of shoundeera, six kinds of *ashwakarna* or Sal, (or *Primordica charantia),* three kinds of *shatamoolas*, and some plants known as *Kaaruvellee*, *Chandra vellee*, *Madhuvellee*, *Varchulee*, *Makutee vellee*, *Sugandha* and *Soorya vellee*, all of which can be used to prepare foods which are nutritious and bracing.

Table 8.5: Grasses, roots and creepers as food sources in Vymanika Sastra

	Sanskrit	*English*	*Latin*
Grasses	*Durva*	Millet grass	*Cynodon dactylon*
	Munja	Pin reed grass	*Saccharam officinarum*
	Kusa	–	*Ergrostis cynosoroides*
	Yava usira	Barley godhuma	*Veriveria zizanioeles*
			Triticum sativum
Rhizoids and Tubers	*Saundira*		*Pipeus longum*
	Satamula	–	*Asparagus racemosus*
Creepers	*Sugandha*	–	*Cymbopogon martini*
	Somavalli	Soma plant	*Cocculus cordiofolius**
	Chandrakanta	White water lily	*Nelumbo nucifera*
	Punarnava	–	*Boerhavia repens*

* This Latin name for Soma plant differs from the names by which others like Hildebrandt have called it which were *Anquetil duperro* or *Amomum/Sarcostemma viminalis* (or *S.intermedium*).

Source: Hanumanta Rao and Anand, 2004

Persons possessing such knowledge selected these grasses and other vegetation from the wild. The various plant parts such as flower, shoot and leaf were properly cleaned and cooked to prepare solid or liquid foods considered to be satisfactory substitute food for the pilots. For obtaining foods with long shelf life, according to *Ashaanakalpa*, preparations based on plants such as *Somavellee*, or moon plant *Chakrikaa Rasavallika, Kooshmanda vallee, Ikshuvallee Pishtavallaree, Sooryakanta, Chandrakanta, Meghananda Purnarnava, Avantee, Matsyaakshu, Rukma* and many more have been recommended. Their extracts or concentrates were mixed with condiments and made into candy and consumed along with milk, ghee and honey. These preparations were considered to be highly nutritious foods and were believed to enhance the longevity and the potential energy as well as increase and nourish the intelligence of the pilots.

One is left wondering once again at the detailed manner in which not only the descriptions are given for the construction of several types of highly sophisticated crafts from millennia ago but, also that recommendations and suggestions for appropriate foods were made for giving proper nutrition to the pilots to enable them to carry out their very arduous tasks.

Diet in Roman Times

Roman legions were stationed all across the empire. The soldiers served wherever their bosses – procurators or legates were posted, whether it was London and Lyons or Carthage and Caesarea. In wintertime they lived in the cities and the suburbs, scattered in different streets and alleyways. There was no physical demarcation to the units for the bulk of the army. During Diocesan time, there were frontier troops posted to wherever there was construction of small forts on riverbanks or war in the deserts but most of the time the army lived with the civilians (Macmillan, 1988, p. 146). Cities with any concentration of population greater than or around 5,000 appeared to provide almost permanent lodging for the troops. Thousands of soldiers thus lived alongside civilians and the cities became very vulnerable to ruination by the military. They were so isolated from the emperor that deception, threats, fraud, challenge to any authority etc. were commonplace occurrences.

Under these situations, it was but natural that the soldiers were left to their own devices and helped themselves to whatever they wanted from the civilian homes, including food. We gain some insight to the nature of food habits in that period by reading about the daily life in the time of Charlemagne in around AD 800. The writings of Anthemia, a physician who wrote '*de observations ciborium*' around AD 511–534 were consulted by the Carolingians for planning diets. A '*diet ciborium*' was prepared and addressed to King Thierry, King of Austria. The dietary advice given to a convalescent bishop (who generally ate rather well) by his colleague included injunctions to avoid excessive fasting, recently caught fish and freshly killed poultry. Beans cooked in fat possessed purgative properties.

Seasons and their observances were important. Suggestions to brave the winter healthily said (a) 'eat hot food in winter and (b) exercise, (c) avoid frequent washing of hair and (d) purge continually (e) take bath in March, (f) and no bleeding' (It was a regular medical practice known as phlebotomy). In April, all the fresh meat could be eaten but not 'roots'. There were injunctions never to drink beer and never water on an empty stomach during May. Sage (a herb) was not to be eaten in June but a glass of water upon rising as well as boiled milk were allowed. In July, it was advised to desist from sexual relations to avert any 'humors' to the brain (Macmillan, 1988, p. 170). Medical knowledge was poor compared to the Byzantines and Arabs (and Indians and Chinese).

Apart from these special food instructions for possibly those who were in the habit of indulging themselves, a sample of what the monks ate in the cloisters would provide a glimpse into what the common people ate. The monks practiced very frugal food habits by virtue of following a monastic way of life and religious pursuit.

There were months of food shortage, fears of hunger (by rich and poor alike) before harvest and not all were able to lay down stores for lean periods. The peasant was better placed since he could at least pick some vegetables from near his house and scour the countryside for other foods (roots, fruit, game, mushrooms etc.). However, the soldiers boarded with them and despite strict injunctions against making excessive demands, their presence was a threat to the peasants.

Bread and meat: In the Abbeys, the monks ate a pound of bread and ¼ to ½ litre of wine or twice that amount of beer every day. While no fruit or lettuce was allowed, each meal consisted of three dishes of dairy products and vegetables. On feast days and special occasions such as royal anniversaries etc., stuffed chicken, geese and cakes also appeared in the food basket. In the Benedictine order, the monks would each get one meal per day in winter and two in summer, which were a *Collatio* at noon and *Cena* in the evening. On the other hand, the ascetics of Breton partook of a more frugal fare – only barley bread mixed with ashes, bowls of gruel and vegetables and no fish or shellfish either. Some other holy people accepted only some salt, bread, leeks (shallots, green onions stalks) fish and wine.

The princes and aristocrats ate meat daily and always preferred roasted meat to boiled meat as well as spicy dishes. Meat of deer, cattle, sheep and goats was favoured, particularly pork, the consumption of which was very high (about 600 pigs/year) at one refectory where 50 pigs were reserved for the abbot alone. Smoking and salting of pork were the means adopted to make the meat last through the winter. There were *lardariums* for smoking bacon in every abbey. Fish were eaten when the meat rations had to be guarded. There was an abundance of eggs, geese, moorhens and chicken brought into the kitchens of aristocrats both within and outside the church. One estimate for around AD 893 provided by Richi (1973, p. 174) was of 200 farms producing nearly 20,000 eggs/year for the Abbey of Prciini.

While white bread was meant for the privileged classes, monks and canons, the servants got only rye bread and the peasants ague and barley. At one monastery, nearly 450 loaves of bread were baked everyday and at another a 1,000.

Among the vegetables, legumes were growing in the fields such as beans, lentils, peas, green beans, chick peas and other edible herbs and roots. Herbs and flavourings grew in the kitchen gardens and included leeks, garlic, onions, carrots, etc. The bishops' gardens yielded common vegetables like leeks and beans for the canon's table. Fresh herbs came daily from the tenant peasants of the abbey. Obtaining dairy products was rather more difficult. The commonest were butter and cheese. Cheese often substituted for fish in Charlemagne's time and it is said that the king so liked the cheese after once tasting it at a bishop's table that he directed the abbey to send him two cart loads of it every year! Monks too loved cheese and the tenant farmers of the abbey of Saint-Germain-des-pres provided them with 160 pence of cheese (each pence = 75 lbs approx.).

Meals using honey, gruel and butter were also cooked in the monasteries. Carolingian cuisine depended also on using large quantities of spices and condiments such as pepper, cumin, cloves and cinnamon. Fruits including apples of every kind from the orchards and grapes from vineyards were much in demand and there was not only a store house for fruit but also a *customs pomorum*, an in charge of fruit storage as well.

Alcoholic beverages: Alcoholic drinks flowed and it is said that every class of society drank heavily. Abbots and bishops, soldiers and officers, nobles and peasants and the lay people drank to the point of intoxication and senselessness. Richi (1973) aptly called it an age obsessed with wine. Though condemned by moralist civil-religious law, people drank any time of the day and on every occasion and for any reason or otherwise. Vintage in the monasteries were carefully guarded and hidden, needing wine for church rituals and for serving at meals. Wine was drunk at the tables of the rich and the church while beer 'cervisia' was popular in northern and eastern regions. Breweries and malteries functioned with the advice and instructions of the abbeys. Neither wine nor beer could be kept for long but had to be produced to meet the demand. Other drinks like cider (from wild apples or pears), mulberry wine, and hydromel (from honey) were also made.

Water: The good qualities of pure drinking water in lieu of beer or wine were also extolled by the more knowledgeable, although many people drank water and the abbots and bishops did display their concern for provision of good clean drinking water. They would organise the diverting of river water to flow through conduits to the cloister or kitchen fountains. There were water fountains in the courtyards of the abbey. In a beautifully executed tapestry from fifteenth century Netherlands exhibited in the 'Cloisters', Metropolitan Museum of Art, New York, titled '*Unicorn is found*' which is one of a series of seven tapestries titled 'Hunt for the Unicorn', a water fountain is a centre piece (Fig. 8.1) of a hunting scene. The scene shows several men clearly belonging to the elite classes accompanied with a crowd of armed men bearing spikes cornering a unicorn near a circular

Fig. 8.1: A fifteenth century tapestry 'Unicorn is found'. The mythical animal unicorn appears to have been cornered at the drinking fountain.

Source: Cloisters, Metropolitan Museum of Art, New York City, a gift of John D. Rockefeller Jr., 1937.

water fountain in the midst of wooded trees and other foliage. Unicorn is a mythical, white horse like animal with a single horn on the head. Water is seen coming out from the side of this well or fountain where the unicorn appears to be headed. This structure has a tall ornate pillar like projection in the middle and has two faucet like outlets from which water is pouring out. In all probability the unicorn, exhausted after the long chase by the men and the hunting dogs may have stopped for a drink as did the other forest animals. The fountain may have been intended for travellers.

Grain Measures in the Third and Early Second Century

In the Roman army, the grain allotment to the soldiers described by Polybius was calculated on the basis of a measure known as *Attic medimnus* of wheat per month. The smallest measure was, according to a nineteenth century scholar, a *cotylae*, 32 *cotylae* making one *modius* (8.62 litres) and 4 *modii* making up one *medimnus* (equal to 128 *cotylae*). One *medimnus* measured approximately 34 litres (actually 34.48 L). The Roman wheat of the time was estimated to have probably weighed 0.722 kg per litre, the 34 L thus weighing 26.5 kg (Erdkamp, 1998, p. 28). Further, the pre Julian Roman calendar month was either 29 or 31 days, but for convenience sake, a figure of 32 days was assumed by Erdkamp for further calculations. This worked out to a daily ration of 4 *cotylae* (based on 4 *modii* or 1 *medimnus* a month) which was equal to two measures of a metal drinking cup (2 *cotylae* volume capacity) that every soldier possessed. There were other terms such as *choenix* employed in grain measurements as shown by Erdkamp, who summarised data from various sources such as Herodotus, Thucydides, Sallust, Polybius and Cato.

Briefly, the rations mentioned in these ancient European works (Erdkamp, 1998, p. 43) were somewhat similar over a period of time. The army of Xerxes is said to have been given one *choenix* of wheat per day per man which amounted to 24 kg per month. The Spartan army received almost double this quantity: 2 *chonices* per day of alphita (coarse barley) which would be 43 kg per month. In addition, they also received an unspecified quantity of wine and meat everyday. For the Roman army of the mid Republic in the first century BC, a grain ration of 2/3 *medimnus* or 4 *modii* of wheat per month was prescribed. This came to about 26.5 kg in a month. There is no mention of any other supplementary food. This trend seems to have continued for a century because in the second century BC, Cato's agricultural slaves were also provided 4 *modii* (26.5 kg) of wheat per month in winter and 4.5 *modii* in summer. Though slaves, they were nevertheless given wine, olives, olive oil and figs. On the other hand, the Roman prisoners appeared to have been given only 5 *modii* (33 kg) grain per month.

Weight equivalents: To convert the Roman measures into modern equivalents, each *cotylae* measured 0.269 litre by volume or 0.194 kg by weight (at 0.722 kg per L). The 4 *cotylae* of daily rations therefore would be equivalent to 0.776 kg (776 g) and more than 1.0 litre. (Erdkamp's sources would have it that it was 0.830 kg based on another estimate of the weight per litre of Roman wheat thus making a difference of 54 g per day in calculations). Roughly speaking, 4 *cotylae* or 776 g are nearer to the Aryan grain rations as per ArthaŚāstra and to the modern scale of around 600 g of cereals recommended by ICMR (1998) and provided in the Indian Armed Forces ration scales. Cato's agricultural slaves, performing a hard day's farm work, received about the same quantity but the prisoners who were made to row the boats and do very hard work in the mines were given higher amounts, though from other readings one gets an impression that the prisoners were the worst off.

Different Ration Scales

In the main army, an infantry man's ration of wheat consisted of 2/3 of an *Atticus medimnus* a month which would be equal to 85.33 *cotylae* or 22.66 litres or 17.66 kg (Erdkamp, 1998, p. 27). So this quantity would not be equal to 2 cup measures a day but only about one and a half cups.

A cavalry man who came from the upper classes received 2 *medimni* a month. It is not as if he ate more than the infantry man but the cavalry men of the upper classes usually were also accompanied by one or two servants who went to war with them (to provide personal services and to take care of the horse who had to be fed) which explains their higher wheat ration. Their horses were provided 7 *medimni* of barley. The practice of taking servants along to war remained a distinctive feature of the feudal society in Europe and came right through the nineteenth century into the twentieth century in the form of an officer's batman/valet (Every officer in Britain and India was assigned personnel drawn from the ranks that was a member of the regimental unit anyway but was fed and paid by the army and not by the officer. The modern Indian Army has retained this custom).

There were always allies and mercenaries who joined the army in the fighting wing. For them the rations were again different. Polybius records that (Erdkamp, 1998, p. 27) the infantry man received the same amount as the soldier in the main army which is 2/3 *medimnus* of wheat; the allied and other cavalry men's share was 1 *medimnus* of wheat per man and 5 *medimni* of barley for his horse. At different periods in the Roman Republic, the upper class cavalry man's servants were maintained either with the issue of extra rations or directly looked after by the commissariat, but in the allied and mercenary units from Africa, men got rations for themselves and their horses but not for their servants or for their pack animals (Erdkamp, 1998, p. 28).

Ration issue: The soldiers were issued 16 days wheat rations at a time. To take the required amount of rations for any operation, they only had to measure out 2 metal cups (or 1 ½ cups) of wheat for each day of manoeuvres. It is presumed that they carried the necessary paraphernalia for preparing bread, biscuit, gruel or any other food commonly eaten in those times. Presumably too, meat and other food items (wine, olive oil etc.) were provided to them, either daily (fresh meat only) or at regular intervals (cured meat, sausages and other types known in Roman times), in unspecified quantities. We know, however, that Cato's agricultural slaves got wine, olives, olive oil and figs etc. To make estimates of food shipments for logistic purposes, Erdkamp based his calculations on the daily rations for the men and horses from which we find that wine was calculated at 0.25 L per day and olive oil, their principle cooking medium, at 0.05 L per day (Erdkamp, 1998, pp. 55–56).

In early modern armies as per Pliny's writings, bread and biscuit rations appeared in lieu of wheat. The *Panis militaris* or military bread weighed about 1,100 g (made from 830 g of wheat and water). The biscuit rations weighed 2/3 of the bread i.e. about 733 g. *Roman citizen's rations:* Certain scholars have suggested that the rations had been increased from 4 *modii* to 5 *modii* per month by first century BC. In the first century BC, every Roman citizen above the age of 14 years was entitled to 5 *modii* of grain (33 kg) – wheat or corn per month amounting to 1.4 kg of bread per day. Therefore it is assumed that even the soldiers got the same amount of grain, which was one *modius* more than the scale in the second century BC. But it has been also suggested that the ration given to any one male individual of 14 years and above also had to suffice for his dependents. A family consisting of one man, one boy of 14 or above, one woman or more, and may be one or two children – which could have been the average family size at a conservative estimate would thus have to subsist on 10 *modii*. Whether this was sufficient is not known. However, each soldier received his own rations, and sometimes cash payment of 5 denari per month.

In this respect the adult Roman male's ration differs from an Aryan male's food entitlement described in *ArthaŚāstra*. In the latter, it was pointed out earlier that there were specific ration scales for boys and for women as well as for people of the serving classes, albeit in much reduced quantities.

Other classes of people such as agricultural workers (of Cato as we have seen previously), prisoners, galley slaves (those who rowed the ships and boats) and slaves received individual scales of ration, more or less in similar quantities, with some minor differences, i.e. between 4 to 5 *modii* per month (Erdkamp, 1998, p. 43).

The Traditions of Food Classification

In the Ancient scriptures of the Hindus, food was revered as god, as an offering to the gods and as the blessings of gods; ***'Annam Brahmam'*** was the 'Food for Eternal Life'. In the Upanishads (PU III, 1–2; 6–100 as mentioned in Melkote Documents) it is expressed thus:

Brahman is food
Do not disparage food
Do not dispose food
Produce abundant food
Deny none hospitality of food
From food indeed are creatures born---
For truly food is the first of all beings---
And therefore it is called the universal remedy.

Those who worship Brahman as food assuredly obtain all the food they need (Melkote Documents).

In Samkhya philosophy, the *Triguna* or the three qualities that constitute *prakriti* (nature) are taken to be *Satva* – purity, *Rajas* – activity and *Tamas* (inertness, darkness). The Aryans attributed these three *gunas* to different types of people which also served to classify foods they ate (Kilara and Iya, 1991). The descriptions of the three categories are quite distinct. Caraka (Charaka), who is believed to have belonged to Northwestern India (Valiathan, 2003, p. 10), used, in his *Caraka Samhita* (dated between second century BC and AD first century), the same terms to denote psychic *doshas*, which bind a person to different modes of conduct. These are explained in the following three ways:

Sātvic – is described as being virtuous, noble, and pure and *Satvic* food was designated to be consumed by Brahmins and allied castes. *Rājasic* – is embodied in passionate and luxurious nature and the food is considered semi pure – diets of leaders, warriors, for princes and others of Kshatriya class; it is purported to impart masculinity, brawn and power. Only garlic, beef, pig and fish were forbidden in their food. *Tāmasic* – is a nature that is poor, coarse and the food without taste. From Vedic, Ayurvedic, yogic and Gita literature, there is much to learn about the benefits and dangers from foods. Ayurvedic principles of food intake believed to be based on scientific findings prescribe when, what, how and how much food to eat and what to do after eating; and what the various incompatible foods are which cause several disorders of the skin, intestinal tract or otherwise exert adverse effects, toxic manifestations, some of which may lead to fatalities. Combinations such as milk and sour fruits, milk and fish, milk and horse gram (*Dolichos biflorus*), pigeon flesh fried with mustard oil, honey and ghee mixed in equal quantities, milk with radish are also shown as being incompatible, (Reddy, 2004, pp. 32–36) as well as meat of peacock roasted on castor stick in castor oil, hot curd and such combinations (Haridasan, 2004, pp. 52–56).

The yogic concept of foods while applying the same three *Guna* categories also recognises *Tāmasic, Rājasic* and *Sātvic* food. In the *Gita* (Gita 17.10), as explained by Nagaratna and Nagendra, (2004, pp. 41–45), *Tāmasic* foods are stale, tasteless, stinking, which have been cooked the day before, and thus unfit for human consumption. Boiled rice kept soaked in water overnight (southern rural practices in some areas till date), fermented drinks, cooked foods kept for several days fall into this category. Eating *Tāmasic* food makes a person less alert, hazy, lose vitality. These authors very interestingly point to the facts of processed food, modern high powered lifestyle habits as leading to the *Tāmasic* state.

Rājasic foods are said to stimulate the nervous system and speed up metabolism. These foods are rich and tasty and are meant for the Kings. A pushy aggressive activity is associated with the rulers and Rajputs (sons of rulers or kings) as well as for the fighting classes, the military forces, and politically active persons. Rajputs were allowed to consume meat and wine but a scholar, teacher and a priest was forbidden *Rājasic* foods.

Sātvic foods, according to the *Gita* (Gita 17.9), are those which increase life and vitality; *Satva* or purity, *bala* (strength and stamina) and confer health, happiness, cheerfulness and love. Such foods are savoury, oleaginous, substantial, agreeable. These foods are fresh, wholesome, and natural, of good quality, mildly spiced, cooked as they should be, lead to calmness yet alertness and a state of quiet energy.

Sātvic foods give strength from within, *Rājasic* foods provide strength to muscles and give a feeling that the food consumed is providing all the energy. Whereas fresh cow's milk is *Sātvic*, buffalo milk is *Rājasic* and sour or curdled milk acquires *Tāmasic* character.

Further, in the Aryan way of thinking, each category of food became associated with a certain class/caste of people over the millennia. Thus, eating *Tāmasic* food (of the lowest order) was felt to be degrading to people in their social hierarchy. The indigenous people were not restricted in eating anything because they were outside the Aryan fold! Such beliefs have been harboured by our people for thousands of years, without paying much heed to the actual nutritional value of the foods falling into these three categories. Purely based on Śastras, such a categorisation is believed to have had its effect on dietary habits causing nutritional deficiencies in various segments of the people.

The *ArthaŚāstra*, which precedes Caraka from the Kuśana period by some three centuries, had laid down stringent laws about management of illnesses arising from excess consumption of unwholesome food. It must be said here that the diets of the Indian people – kings, nobles, soldiers and all others stemmed from these basic principles and beliefs and every attempt was made to adhere to such dietary habits as were common to each class of people/section of society both in peace and war. Therefore, India's food and dietary practices are rooted in millennia of custom, ritual and history; say Kilara and lya (1991). Vegetarianism in its present form was adopted by Brahmins but not the Kshatriyas. The same authors observed that the system of caste and the status derived from belonging to a particular caste applied to all parts of India, with some regional differences. Not only food but who cooked it and how it was made became equally important. Separate kitchens existed for the castes and of course separate cooks and cooking utensils. Kautilya (AS: 11.15.26) has also listed essential equipment for kitchens – weights and scales, grinding stone, mortar, pestle, winnowing basket, broom and a basket. Weights given in *ArthaŚāstra* are said to be different from those used by Caraka (Valiathan, 2003, p. x).

A variety of spices (salt, long pepper, turmeric, mustard, cloves, black pepper, asafoetida, cumin, dry ginger, myrobalan) have been known to be used during the first to fifth centuries AD in the Buddhist and Jain periods. Preservation of fruits and vegetables using vinegar and oil and with spices also dates back to 300 BC to AD 100. The same is true for several other preserves like jams, jellies etc. Syrups and the use of fresh herbs for flavouring was in vogue too.

Food and drink had been recognised in the science of Ayurveda to possess therapeutic value (Valiathan, 2003, pp. Lxxvii–ix). According to this, a good physician had to be very knowledgeable about the nutritional aspects of food in order to prescribe therapeutic diets. Caraka's diets were rich in content and variety and included many kinds of meats and fermented drinks and a large number of vegetables, fruits and greens, indicating that he was well aware of the significance of a varied diet due to the abundance of nutritive qualities in these foods. In his time and country, there was no prohibition on animal killing for meat. Rice, bird meat, cow's milk and sesame oil were favourites among the individual food categories. Caraka is believed to have prescribed a vegetable preparation along with a meat dish whenever the latter was intended as a treatment. Caraka's classification of foods recognised ten groups (Valiathan, 2003, p. 110):

- One each for grains with husk (*Sukhadhanya*),
- Pulses (*Samidhanya*),
- Meats (*mamsa*),
- Vegetables (*saka*),
- Fruits (*phala*),
- Greens (*Harita*),
- Alcoholic drinks (*madya),*
- Water (*jala*),
- Milk and milk products *(gorasa*) and
- Sugar cane products (*Iksu*).

One can easily feel the similarity between this classification and the grouping of certain foods today based on their nutritional significance.

Caraka also elaborated the names of individual foods in each class, their qualities and effects on *dosas* and on the body (Valiathan, 2003, pp. 111–137). Since, according to Ayurveda, there are three *dhatus* of the body such as *vata, pitta* and *kapha*, there are specific directives on using post-prandial drinks, both alcoholic and non-alcoholic, of such type that their properties are opposed to the properties of the food consumed, but not opposed to the *dhatus* (Valiathan, 2003, p. 138).

In Ayurveda, food is placed into four categories – as eatables, drinkables, lickables and chewables according to a summary given by Bhajandasji (2004, pp. 46–51).

In the Indian land, there has been the ancient custom of observing six seasons or '*Ritu*'; *Hemantha Ritu* (cold), *Sisira Ritu* (also cold but transition to dry season), *Vasantha Ritu* (intense heat), *Greeshma Ritu* (hot and very dry season), *Varsha Ritu* (rainy season) and *Sharad Ritu* (end of rains; cold begins). *Greeshma*, *Varsha* and *Sheeta* or *Sharad* are dominant seasons while the other three are transitional periods. Specific foods and beverages were advocated for consumption in each season to suit the three different *doshas* of *kapha*, *vata* and *pitta* (Table 8.6). A person in whom all the three are in balance is said to be a healthy person.

Table 8.6: The foods recommended for each of the six seasons

Hemantha (Cold)	*Sisira (Cold – Transitional)*	*Vasanta (Spring)*	*Greeshma (Hot and dry summer)*	*Varsha (Rainy)*	*Sharad (End of rainy season)*
Good digestion		*To avoid poor digestion*			
food should be heavy, substantial, oily, sweet, acidic, salty, forms of milk.	same as in Hemantha	not eat heavy greasy, acidic or sweet.	large amounts of sweet tasting.	avoid parched grain flour mixed with river water.	sweet foods, pungent tasting.
halva, laddu, almonds		should drink hot water after morning exercises	almonds, white rose flower, Brahmi, Sanka pushpou combination to cool the body	eat acidic, salty, ghee containing foods	rice, wheat, barley, green pulses, banana, papaya, white gourd, tinde
sugarcane juice preparations		eat barley wheat, gram garlic, ginger in food		old wheat, barley rice, pulses with curds, sweet tasting fruits and vegetables.	

Source: Bhajandasji, 2004

The food consumed is believed to transmit and impart several properties to determine physical fitness and mental personality.

In the Vedas, apart from water (preferred drink), *Soma* juice finds an elaborate mention. In ArthaŚāstra, as already discussed, a very detailed method of preparing the *Soma* juice using several ingredients has been described. However, post 300 BC, routine alcohol drinking was discouraged according to some writers. *Soma* was an intoxicating drink and was believed to inspire confidence, courage, faith, trust. The authors Kilara and Iya (1991) cite two references where they say the Vedas did not condone alcohol consumption though in Caraka Samhita, a wine (*madira*) especially for therapeutic purposes was recommended. The consumption of intoxicating beverages referred to in the Epics was seen as fit only for lower classes and not for those with high status, presumably the Kshatriyas and such.

Endnotes

1. This was witnessed by the author accompanying a visiting group during 1998 (in a trip to the interior region of the Andamans which was specially arranged for certain officials by the concerned authorities). The Andamanese tribesmen carried fire in the form of burning wood or charcoal wrapped in leaves and tied to their waists near the bikini line. In a group of some ten men, at least three were seen to carry the fire.
2. It is much the same even now where temperature abuse in warm climates causes spoilage of fresh meat (here perhaps denoted by the term swelling as well as foul-smelling). The presence of head, bones etc. helps to identify the animal species without which one can hardly tell what meat one was buying. 'Cold slaughter, a modern term used in meat science and technology, denotes the slaughtering of an already dead

animal, a malpractice reportedly indulged by some traders. Being not just against the good sensibilities of people this is also not a desirable meat as its quality undergoes rapid deterioration. That practicing all these fine aspects of wild life protection, safety observations and quality assurance of slaughtered meat existed then should not come as a surprise to us, considering how everything else with regard to the daily practices and administration of the state had been scrupulously laid down as guidelines.

References

Brand-Miller, Janette C. & Stephen Colaguiri 1999. 'Evolutionary Aspects of Diet & Insulin Resistance'. In Simopoulos, A.P. (ed) 'Evolutionary Aspects of Nutrition: Diet, Exercise, Genetics and Chronic Disease'. *World Review of Nutrition and Dietetics.* Basel, Karger. Vol 84: 74–105.

Clottes, Jean 2001. France's Magical Cave Arts. *National Geographic*. August, 200(2): 104–121.

Simopoulos, A.P. 1999. 'Genetic variation and nutrition'. In Simopoulos, A.P. (ed.) Evolutionary Aspects of Nutrition, Health, Diet, Exercise, Genetics and Chronic Disease. *World Review of Nutrition and Dietetics.* Basel, Karger, Vol 84: 118–140.

Hirsch, J. 1995. 'Role and benefits of carbohydrate in the diet: Key issues for future dietary guidelines'. *Am J Clin Nutr*, 61: 996S–1000S.

Wendorf, Fred 1992. 'Saharan Exploitation of plants 8000 BP'. *Nature*, Oct 22, 359: 721–724.

Achaya, K.T. *Indian Food: A Historical Companion.* Oxford India Paperbacks, Delhi, 1998, pp. 40–44, 55–57.

Achaya, K.T. *Story of Our Food.* Universities Press, Hyderabad, 2000, pp. 56–57.

Chakrabarty, Sukhendu, 1998. 'Modern Andaman & Nicobar'. A Report for the Guha Research Conference. 198. Symposium on 'Biodiversity'. Port Blair, November, 1998.

Chen, J.D. 1999. 'Evolutionary Aspects of Exercise'. In Simopoulos, A.P. (ed). 'Evolutionary Aspects of Nutrition, Health, Exercise, Genetics and Chronic Disease'. *World Review of Nutrition and Dietetics.* Basel, Karger, Vol 84: 106–117.

Cordain, Loren 1999. 'Cereal Grains: Humanity's Double Edged Sword'. In Simopoulas, A.P. (ed). Evolutionary Aspects Of Nutrition, Health, Diet, Exercise, Genetics and Chronic Disease. *World Review of Nutrition and Dietetics* Basel, Karger, Vol 84: 19–73.

Durante, Will & Durante, Ariel. *The Story of Our Civilization.* Simon & Schuster, New York, 1965, pp. 62–63.

Eaton, S.B. and Konner, M. 1985. 'Palaeolithic nutrition: a consideration of its nature and current implications'. *New Engl. J. Med*, Vol 312: 283–289.

Erdkamp, Paul. *Hunger and the Sword: Warfare and food supply in Roman Republican Wars (264–30 BC).* J.C. Gieben Publishers, Amsterdam, 1998, pp. 27–43.

Gore, Rick 2003. 'The Rise of Mammals'. *National Geographic Magazine*. April, 203(4): 2–37.

Hanumantarao, H.S. and P. Ananda. 'Studies of Ancient Indian Food Science and Technology with particular reference to pilot food mentioned in Bharadwaja's Vymanika Sastra'. In 'Science and Tradition of Food: India's Heritage of 5000 years'. First National Convention. July 25–27, 2004. Proceedings of a Symposium. Academy of Sanskrit Research, Melkote and CFTRI, Mysore, Souvenir, pp. 57–60.

Haridosan, A.P. 'Food in Ayurveda'. In First National Convention on 'Science and Tradition of Food: India's Heritage of 5000 years'. July 25–27, 2004. Academy of Sanskrit Research, Melkote and CFTRI, Mysore, Souvenir, pp. 52–56.

Hildebrandt, Alfred. *Vedic Mythology* (Vedische Mythology) in three volumes 1891, 1899, 1902. 2nd edition in 2 volumes 1927, 1929, translated from German Vol I by Sreeramulu Rajeswar Sarma. Motilal Benarsidass, Delhi, 1980.

Hunter, Erica C.D. *First Civilization.* Updated by M. Corbishley. Facts on File Inc., New York, 2003, pp. 20–23.

Indian Council for Medical Research Dietary Guidelines for Indians – A Manual. National Institute of Nutrition, ICMR, Hyderabad, 1998.

Iyengar, P.T. Srinivasa. *Pre Aryan Tamil Culture*. Asian Educational Services, New Delhi, 1985, 1995, pp. 57–65.

Joyser, G.R. 'Vymanika Sastra – Aeronautics of Bharadwaja' as propounded by Subbaraya Sastri. Translated, edited. Coronation Press, Mysore, 1973.

Kangle, R.P. *The Kautilya Arthasastra*. 2nd ed. Bombay University, Motilal Benarasi Das, Delhi, 1972. AS. Verses from Book 2, Chapter 1–25 and Book 12, Chapter 4.

Kilara, A. & lya, K.K. 1991. 'Food and the dietary habits of the Hindu'. In 'Religious and Philosophical Bases of Food choices: An Overview – Outstanding Symposia in Food science and Technology'. *Food Technology*, October 1991-92.

Macmillan, Ramsay. *Corruption and Decline of Rome*. Yale University Press, New Haven and London, 1988, pp. 146–215.

Majumdar, B.C. & Pusalkar, A.D. 'The History and Culture of the Indian People.' Vol. IV. The Age of Imperial Kannauj. Bharatiya Vidya Bhavan, Bombay, 1955.

Melkote Documents (Anon): 'Food Preservation in Ancient India'; in a Collection of Documents From various sources: Cultural sources from the Veda (by Dange, S.A.). Academy of Sanskrit Research, Melkote, Received August 2004 from the Academy.

Mitra, Rajendra Lala. 'Indo-Aryans: Ancient and Medieval History, Vol. I Beef in Ancient India' & Vol II: 'Spirituous and Fermented drinks', Antiquarian Book Sellers and Publishers, Indological Book House, Delhi, 1969; quoting *Asiatic Society Journal,* Vol. VII, p. 249.

Nagarathna, R. and H.R. Nagendra. *Yogic concept of Food.* In 'First National Convention on Science and Tradition of Food: India's Heritage of 5000 years'. July 25–27, 2004. Academy of Sanskrit Research, Melkote and CFTRI, Mysore, Souvenir, pp. 41–45.

Narayan, S.H.S.N. Hanumantha Rao and R.K. Narayan. 'Seasonal Foods for Pilots'. In 'Science and Tradition of Food: India's Heritage of 5000 years'. First National Convention, July 25–27, 2004. Proceedings of a Symposium. Academy of Sanskrit Research, Melkote and CFTRI, Mysore, Abstract MP-37, Souvenir, pp. 92.

Nestle Report: Two Million Years of the Food Industry. Nestle SA, Switzerland.

Nikam, N.A. and Richard McKean. *The Edicts of Asoka*. Edited and translated. University of Chicago, 1959, Asia Publishing House, First Indian edition, 1962.

Oppenheimer, Stephen. *The Real Eve: Modern Man's Journey Out Of Africa*, Carroll & Graf publishers, New York, 2003, pp. 76–81, 104–105.

Piperno, D.R., A.J. Ramere, I. Holst, & P. Hansell. 2000. 'Starch grains reveal early root crop horticulture in the Panamanian tropical forest'. *Nature*, 407: 894.

Rao, M.P. 'Aviation Science in Ancient India'. Proceedings in Symposia on '100 years since first powered flight and Advances in Aerospace Sciences'. December 2003, Bangalore. Aeronautical Society of India. R. Balasubramanian. Ed, pp. 74–83.

Reddy, P. Sudhakar, 'Health and Food-Ayurvedic prescriptive.' In First National Convention on Science and Tradition of Food: India's Heritage of 5000 years. July 25–27, 2004. Academy of Sanskrit Research, Melkote and CFTRI, Mysore. Souvenir, pp. 32–36.

Rice, Lewis. *The Amarakosa of Amara Simha*. 4th edition, Asian Educational Services, New Delhi, India, 1988, 2.8.103.

Richi, Pierre. *Daily Life in the world of Charlemagne*. Translated Paris@Libraire Hachette, 1973, Copyright 1978 By Jo Ann McNamara. 2nd print University of Pennsylvania Press, p. 174.

Sastri, P. P. S. *Valmiki Ramayana*. In poet's own words, Text in Devnagari and English translation. G.A. Nateson and Co, Madras, 1935.

Swamy Bhajandasji. 'The Indian Concept of Food in Ayurveda' in 'First National Convention on Science and Tradition of Food: India's Heritage of 5000 years'. July 25–27, 2004. Academy of Sanskrit Research, Melkote and CFTRI, Mysore. Souvenir, pp. 46–51.

Thapliyal, U.P. *Miltary Organisation in Ancient Period.* In 'Historical Perspectives in Warfare in India'. Vol X. Part 3 Editor. S.N. Prasad (ed). History of Science, Philosophy and Culture in Indian Civilization (PHCSPIC). Series General Editor-D.P. Chattopadhyaya. Published by Bhuvan Chandel. Motilal Benarsi Das, Delhi, 2002b, pp. 68–103.

Thapliyal, U.P. *Early Indian Heraldry and Ceremonials in Ancient India.* In Volume X, Part 3: Historical Perspective of Warfare in India. Some morale and materiel Determinations. S.N. Prasad (Ed). History of Science, Philosophy and Culture in Indian Civilization. Series. General Editor-D.P. Chattopadhyaya. Published by Bhuvan Chandel, Distributors Motilal Benarsi Das, New Delhi. 2002c, pp. 134–156.

Valiathan, M.S. *The Legacy of Caraka.* Orient Longman, Hyderabad, 2003, pp. ix, x, 1xxxviii, 110–138.

9

Modern Food and Nutrition

Modern Concepts of Nutrition

Modern scientific discoveries and accumulating knowledge about nutrition and health have brought greater understanding about the right and the wrong ways of eating; modern studies have examined several present diets of peoples and compared these with that which existed before modern developments had occurred in the food and agricultural area. In spite of such new information being available, in general, the people tend to adhere out of habit to some preconceived notions which rely on superstitions that have little to do with nutrition or health.

In the modern thinking, nutrition is defined as a science of food as it relates to optimal health and performance (Bogest, Briggs and Calloway, 1973). Essential nutrients in adequate quantities must be present in the foods we consume for physical health and growth and physiological performance, to spur mental alertness and even help in emotional stability. Inside our body, the forty or fifty essential nutrients ingested through food give rise to thousands of other substances more complicated chemically than the original nutrients, all of which are necessary for life and fitness. Some of the new tenets examine the composition of foods to determine its utility, its suitability, when and how much to eat, the pitfalls of eating too little or too much of one or more foods or the wrong foods, the concept of diets and the balance (in respect of various nutrients) that should be achieved in planning daily meals, and healthy diets. These also venture into the realm of appetite and hunger regulation and the functions of taste and smell that help in food intake.

The broad lines on which food is regarded according to the current understanding relate to food types and grouping, their chemical and nutrient compositions and content. Also, food is considered according to its energy content which allows muscle work to be performed; the recommendations from scientific studies (of the quantities deemed essential or adequate based on various parameters), the novel thoughts on what are ideal diets and more beneficial food ingredients and certain unfolding research data that lead to the better understanding of nutrition matters. These also form the basis of our understanding of military foods and rations. To students of nutritional sciences, these descriptions will seem to be superfluous but for the others it would help in understanding the basis of defining food content in meals and rations.

Nutrition for Optimal Health and Performance

The effects of the food that is habitually consumed by culturally different people are reflected in their stature and stamina. Also, the instinctive selection of foods does not always lead to good nutrition. These facts are borne out by two examples. One was that of a study by McCarrison (1922) on the early diets in India. The southern people or tribes who ate milled rice, fruits and vegetables with little or no milk were small in size, inferior in strength and short lived in comparison with tribes in the farther north. They ate un-milled rice or wheat and consumed goat's milk and butter, had splendid physiques and enough stamina to make good soldiers. Other tribes in the Himalayas who ate frugally but consumed fresh and sun-dried apricots, vegetables, goat's milk and meat on occasional feast days were very strong and healthy and lived long, as are the long lived Balkan people who too eat little meat but include whole grain cereals, cheese and fermented milk called koumiss.

Another example provided by Bogest *et al.* (1973) is that of African tribes which showed differences in build and strength depending on whether they are subsisting largely on corn and sweet potato (the small sized Akikuyu) or meat and milk (the taller and the heavier Masai tribe). It provided a brief glimpse into the traditional eating habits of different people/tribes, physical stature and fitness. Since then of course numerous other investigations and studies have been carried out worldwide and data have been gathered from epidemiological sources as well as from volunteer studies on the relationship between behaviour, work capacity and underfeeding.

Major nutrients in foods: The major nutrients in food are identified in chemical terms as carbohydrates, proteins and fats known as macronutrients since they are required in large quantities. Several essential nutrients like vitamins and minerals are known as micronutrients since they are required in small amounts.

These classes of nutrients are present in different quantities in various foods. Cereals and millets, pulses, egg, meat/chicken/fish, milk, roots and tubers, green leafy vegetables, other vegetables, fruits (variety), sugar and oils and fats are the basic foodstuffs which supply all the major and micronutrients that the body requires for its growth, health and fitness.

The modern understanding of these foods has caused them to be classified into different categories. Conventionally, four food groups are recognised as (a) cereals, millets and pulses, (b) vegetables and fruits (c) milk and milk products, egg, meat and fish and finally (d) oils and fats together with nuts and oil seeds. The same foods listed in the four groups can also be classified according to the major and minor/other nutrients they provide. This classification recognises three main categories, namely, energy rich foods, body building foods and protective foods (ICMR, 1998, pp. 12–13). Combining these features the foods can be categorised as follows:

- Carbohydrates and fats are energy rich foods which belong to the first category. These include (a) whole grain cereals, millets contributing carbohydrate, protein, fiber, minerals, such as calcium and iron and B-complex vitamins, (b) vegetable oils, ghee and butter which also contribute fat soluble vitamins and essential fatty acids; (c) nuts and oil seeds which are oil-rich and also sources of proteins, vitamins and minerals and (d) sugars which provide empty calories and have no nutrients.
- In the second category, the body building foods are the protein and other nutrient rich foods such as (a) pulses (legumes), nuts and oil seeds contributing B-complex vitamins, invisible fat and fibre, (b) milk and milk products which essentially supply protein, fat, calcium, vitamin A, Riboflavin and vitamin B12, (c) meat, fish and poultry which are also the major sources of proteins, B-complex vitamins, iron, iodine and fat.
- Under the category of protective foods supplying largely vitamins and minerals are (a) green leafy vegetables rich in antioxidants, fiber, carotenoids, (b) other vegetables and fruits rich in fiber, sugar, antioxidants, vitamin C and others, and again (c) eggs, milk, milk products and flesh foods which essentially give us protein and fat, calcium, lecithin, B-complex etc.

People all over the world eat these same basic foods in one form or another and while in some cultures, animal products constitute a large part of the meals, in other places more refined cereals and millets dominate and fruits and vegetables receive less importance.

However, in the common Indian diet, all these food types are used in varying quantities and are prepared differently. The vegetarian's food consists more of pulses and their products along with cereals, milk and milk products, fruits and vegetables while the non-vegetarians consume occasionally or to the extent affordable, meat, poultry and fish together with cereals, milk, vegetables and fruits.

Accessibility and affordability of the different food types are the two major factors in the context of food security and nutrient sufficiency of diets in India which govern the total intake of one day's energy and nutrient needs. The Indian Council of Medical Research, (ICMR) a Government of India body, has determined and laid down guidelines for nutrient intake for adults – men and women (including pregnant and lactating women) and children. The determination of energy and nutrient needs are based on gender, age, body weight, growth requirements and the extent of physical work performed.

Definition of work categories and energy requirements: The nature of work done is described under three classes.

- Sedentary work like sitting, office work, computer work, teaching, writing or just ordinary moving about during a day's work.
- Moderate work includes activities such as continuous housekeeping work, gardening, cycling, jogging and walking.
- Hard work involves activities like road building, construction/manual labour work, military troops carrying out arduous field duties, intense physical fitness exercises, vigorous swimming, some adventure and team sports, tennis, athletics, distance running, etc.

The three kinds of work require different amounts of energy for performance. The energy for doing so is obtained from the energy rich food consumed and is defined as the number of calories obtained from one gram of food. What is this energy? The human energy exchange is expressed as heat, which is generated from different types of bodily activities carried out in 'sleep' form or 'awake' form, and depending on physical exertion, the corresponding amount of heat is generated by way of mechanical work. Most of this heat of energy is dissipated or lost, while only a small percentage (10–30 per cent) of energy (effort) is applied to external load. By international convention, the unit for energy is a Joule (J) or its derivative, the Watt (W). The British Thermal Unit (BTU) for measuring heat is also used but for nutritional and physiological expression of this energy exchange, the unit kilocalorie (Kcal) is used. The relationship between the terms is shown in Table 9.1.

Table 9.1: Energy conversion factors

1	Kcal	=	4184 J or 4.184 Kilojoules (KJ)
1	Kcal· min^{-1}	=	69.7 W or 238 Btu.h^{-1}
1	KJ	=	0.25 Kcal
1	Kcal·h^{-1}	=	1.16 watt (W)
100	W	=	1.43 Kcal·min^{-1} or 341 Btu· h^{-1}
100	Btu· h^{-1}	=	0.42 Kcal·min^{-1} or 1046 W

Source: US Military Nutrition Research Report, 1983

The energy content of foods: The energy content of major food groups is determined by a thumb rule formula: any kind of carbohydrate will contribute 4 Kcal/g, any protein will also provide 4 Kcal/g and any oil or fat will add 9 Kcal/g.

The food that we normally eat is moist i.e. it contains water to different degrees. The water on the planet (75 per cent) is present prominently in the biological systems as life is not possible without water. Water is the universal solvent and it is the medium in which all cellular metabolic reactions take place. Thus all biological tissues in plants and animals, both terrestrial and aquatic, contain water in leaf, stem, trunk, root, flower, fruit and all the body organs. All chemical substances are dissolved in water. Unless dehydrated (partially or fully by parching) in the sun or by other technological means to remove its water content, every food must be reckoned to have certain water content. For example, fresh fruits and vegetables in general contain almost 94–96 per cent water, which is to say a fruit weighing 100 g has 94 per cent or 96 per cent water and the rest (i.e. 6 or 4 per cent) would be dry solids comprising of carbohydrates, vitamins, minerals, fiber, natural colours, antioxidants and all the other good things put together.

Recommended Dietary Allowance (RDA): The daily nutrient requirement or the recommended daily allowance, RDA, refers to the quantities of various nutrients that should be consumed through food and which are commensurate with an individual's physiological needs. The RDA according to ICMR is the nutrient estimate that should be consumed daily to ensure nutrient delivery in all individuals in a given population (ICMR Manual, 1998, p. 13). The recommended level depends on the bioavailability of nutrients in a diet. The RDA represents the suggested averages per day.

Recommended nutrition and dietary guidelines: Dietary guidelines or allowances for Indians (men, women and children) according to their age, body weight and physical activity are expressed in terms of net energy or Kcal per day food and have been prescribed by the Indian Council of Medical Research (1998, annexure 1, p. 65). These allowances depict net per day consumption of energy in Kcal/g of protein and fat per day and milligrams (mg) of calcium and iron as well as 8 vitamins – vitamins A, thiamine, riboflavin, nicotinic acid, pyridoxine, ascorbic acid, folic acid and vitamin B12, in micrograms. The bulk of the calories are derived from carbohydrates, the weight of which in a food substance is only expressed by the difference (from protein and fat combined).

The RDAs for Indian men and women and the quantities (in grams) in terms of protein and fat, milligrams of calcium and iron as well as total calories for a type of work as determined by ICMR (1998) are given in Table 9.2.

Table 9.2: *RDA for adult Indians: total calories, macronutrients and minerals based on work performance

Group	*Work*	*Body Wt (Kg)*	*Net energy (Kcal/d)*	*Protein (g)*	*Fat (g/d)*	*Ca (mg/d)*	*Iron (mg/d)*
Man	Sedentary	60	2425	60	20	400	28
	Moderate		2075				
	Heavy		3800				
Woman	Sedentary	50	1875	50	20	400	30
	Moderate		2225				
	Heavy		2925				

*RDA values refer to per day.
Source: ICMR Manual, 1998, p. 65, recommended by the Nutrition Expert group, 1968

The revised values are marginally different from the Nutrition Expert Group's recommendations. In terms of vitamins, 600 μg of retinol and 2,400 μg of beta-carotene as vitamin A, 40 mg/d ascorbic acid and 100 μg/d folic acid and 12–20 mg/d nicotinic acid are essential. The other vitamins are needed in very small quantities – less than 2 mg/day. The recommended dietary guidelines for

Indians also say that the diet should contain an adequate amount of cereals, milk and pulses, liberal quantities of green leafy vegetables and other vegetables and fruits, a moderate quantity of eggs, meat, fish, cooking fats and spices and only sparse quantities of highly sweetened foods, juices, jams, ice creams, etc.

Balanced diets: A balanced diet is one that contains different types of foods in such quantities and proportions that the need for calories, minerals, vitamins and other nutrients is adequately met and a small provision is made for extra nutrients to withstand short durations of leanness (Gopalan, Rama Sastri and Balasubramaniam, 1971). A balanced diet thus should be one, which provides 60–70 per cent of total calories from carbohydrates, preferably starch which is complex and not highly refined, about 10–12 per cent of calories from proteins and between 20–25 per cent of the calories from fat. A balanced diet should further contribute non-nutrients such as dietary fiber, antioxidants and phytochemicals which promote health. The commonly known antioxidants which protect the body from free radical damage are vitamins C and E, beta-carotene, riboflavin and selenium and other phytochemicals like polyphenols, flavones, etc. Our generous use of spices in cooking, where turmeric, ginger, garlic, cumin, coriander, cloves and cinnamon added in different preparations enrich the food with antioxidants which these spices contain.

To design any diet which would provide adequate scales of different food items, one must know the principal or macronutrient content or the nutritive values of the major foodstuffs. For this purpose, the values for the energy and nutrients obtained from individual portion sizes have been provided by the ICMR (ICMR manual, 1998, p.72), which are indicated in Table 9.3. Rather than give the values for 100 g of each, the items are designated as a portion, 30 g for cereals, pulses etc. and larger or smaller portion sizes for the others. Generally a 'portion' equals 30 g, or one ounce (oz) unless otherwise mentioned for cereals and 100 g for fruits and vegetables. It must be borne in mind that most foodstuffs have all the three major nutrients but in different amounts, some significantly high, some only in very small amounts.

To read the values as depicted in the table, one portion of 30 g cereals will be seen to provide 100 Kcal of energy from its constituents which are 3 g protein, 20 g carbohydrate and 0.8 g of fat.

Table 9.3: Portion size of foods uncooked and their macronutrient content

S. No.	*Food group*	*g/portion (minimum)*	*Energy* (Kcal)*	*Protein (g)*	*Carbohydrate (g)*	*Fat (g)*
1.	Cereals/millets	30	100	3.0	20.0	0.8
2.	Pulses	30	100	6.0	15.0	0.7
3.	Egg	50	85	7.0	–	7.0
4.	Meat/chicken/ Fish	50	100	9.0	–	7.0
5.	Milk toned, (ml)	100	70	3.0	5	3.0
6.	Roots and tubers	100	80	1.3	18	–
7.	Green leafy vegetables	100	45	3.6	–	0.4
8.	Other vegetables	100	30	1.7	–	0.2
9.	Fruits	100	40	–	10	–
10.	Sugar	5	20	–	5	–
11.	Fats and oils (visible)	5	45	–	–	5

*In common use, the calorific values for carbohydrates are taken as 4 Kcal/g, for proteins 4 Kcal/g and for fat 9 Kcal/g.

Source: ICMR Manual, 1998, p. 72

Balanced diets (for one day) for adults and portion sizes of various items are planned with nine basic food sources by using multiples of minimum portion sizes which are spread over three meals (and sometimes a fourth one meant as a snack meal).

Based on the nutritive value of Indian Foods, Gopalan and co-workers (Gopalan et al., 1971) of the National Institute of Nutrition, Hyderabad have suggested the composition of an ideal ration scale as given in Table 9.4 (ICMR, 1998, p. 74) for men and women engaged in sedentary, moderate and heavy work. It may be seen that the portions vary in number from as many as 14 (for cereals) to as little as 1 (for fruit or vegetable).

Table 9.4: Number of portions in a balanced diet for adult men (M) and women (W) based on the nature of work

S. No.	*Food Group*	*g/portion*	*Sedentary*		*Moderate*		*Heavy*	
			M	*W*	*M*	*W*	*M*	*W*
1.	Cereals and millets	30	14	10	16	12	23	16
2.	Pulses	30	2	2	3	2.5	3	3
3.	Milk	100 (ml)	3	3	3	3	3	3
4.	Roots and tubers	100	2	1	2	1	2	2
5.	Green leafy veg	100	1	1	1	1	1	1
6.	Other veg	100	1	1	1	1	1	1
7.	Fruits	100	1	1	1	1	1	1
8.	Sugar	5	5	4	8	5	11	9
9.	Fats/oils	5	4	4	7	6	11	8

Source: ICMR manual, 1998, p.74

As this discussion is a preamble to talking about food and nutrition for the actively performing soldier of the Armed Forces, it would be appropriate to see exactly how much of food in terms of weight in grams is being apportioned to each category. Taking the example of the cereal portion, it can be seen from Table 9.5 that its portion size (in grams) varies with the nature of work done and with gender. The maximum amount 650 g of cereal entitlement goes to males performing heavy work and the smallest amount, 360 g, is recommended for a woman who is doing sedentary work. All vegetarians are recommended to take more milk (200 ml) in place of the flesh and egg foods. Non-vegetarians, on the other hand, are apportioned a smaller amount of milk (100 ml) because they will get 30 g each of meat and egg.

It stands to reason that a moderately active man or woman would expend more energy and thus will need to consume more food from the groups of cereals, pulses and fats/oils than those whose life is sedentary. Men or women doing a heavy load of work are recommended to take even higher amount of cereals, sugar and fats. Here, sugar serves purely as a source of energy and confers no other nutritional benefit.

From the data obtained from extensive surveys of diets carried out all over India, a 'Diet Atlas of India' was published by the National Institute of Nutrition, Hyderabad. Wide regional variations occur in the intake of different foodstuffs, say Gopalan *et al.,*1971 (p. 40), but basically the bulk of the diets are cereal based and it is from the cereals that the nutrients are obtained, specially by the socio-economically disadvantaged people. An average diet in the survey revealed that it consisted of 540 g cereals, 12 g pulses, 7 g of greens and other vegetables, 80 ml of milk, 5 g of meat, fish and eggs put together, 15 g of fats and oils, 13 g of sugar and just 5 g of fruits, which together provided 57 g protein, 24 g of fat, 490 g carbohydrates and 2400 Kcal of energy. Calcium, iron, vitamin-A, thiamine and riboflavin were deficient. It is noteworthy though, that the protein content was not low at all but in fact quite significant. However, the authors felt that these diets were not adequately balanced and therefore needed urgent improvement in order to improve general health and to prevent deficiency disorders from taking their toll.

Table 9.5: Balanced diets for young adult Indian men (M) and women (W) for vegetarians (V) and non-vegetarians (NV) (Food quantities in grams based on ICMR, 1998 recommendation)

S. No.	*Foods*	*Sedentary work*		*Moderate work*		*Heavy work*	
		M (g)	*W (g)*	*M (g)*	*W (g)*	*M (g)*	*W (g)*
1.	Cereals, g	400	300	475	350	650	475
2.	Pulses (dals), g	70	60 (45 NV)	80 (65 NV)	70 (55 NV)	80 (65 NV)	70 (55 NV)
3.	Green leafy Vegetables, g	100	125	125	125	125	125
4.	Other Vegetables, g	75	75	75	75	100	100
5.	Roots/Tubers, g	75	50	100	75	100	100
6.	Fruits, g	30	30	30	30	30	30
7.	Milk, ml	200 (100 NV)	200 (100 NV)	200 (100 NV)	200 (100 NV)	200 (100 NV)	200 (100 NV)
8.	Fats and oils, g	35 40 (NV)	30 35 (NV)	40	35 40 (NV)	50	40 45 (NV)
9.	*Meat and fish, g	30	30	30	30	30	30
10.	Eggs, g **	30	30	30	30	30	30
11.	Sugar and Jaggery, g	30	30	40	30	55	40
12.	Groundnuts, g	–	–	–	–	50^{+}	40^{+}

*,** only for non-vegetarians and eggtarians
+ Additional 30 g of fats/oils to be included in place of groundnuts

As part of the dietary guidelines for Indians, the ICMR has also described a food pyramid (ICMR manual, 1998, pp. 10–11). A website, www.foodpyramidindia.org, is a useful source of information and provides directions to calculate an individual's energy and other requirements according to gender, age and activity level.

Meal defined in terms of energy content: It is customary to define a meal by its total energy/calorie content. In a well-balanced meal where carbohydrates, proteins and fat are present in the recommended amounts, each component will contribute towards the total energy content. Based on scientific study it has become an accepted norm in dietary nutritional practices to recommend that carbohydrate, protein and fat contents should, in general, contribute to the daily total energy intake not less than 50–55 per cent, 15–20 per cent and 25 per cent of calories respectively. These values provide a guideline to create balanced menus of meals spread over the entire day. The same values are used by dieticians, nutrition experts and food scientists in their respective fields of work.

Thus a higher carbohydrate containing item such as rice is balanced with a protein rich preparation like dal or meat curry, the requisite quantity or 'portions' accompanied by vegetables cooked in a little fat would work towards balancing a meal. Of course dal is not exactly the same as meat/chicken/fish curry in protein content or quality. The quality of the proteins differs in vegetarian foods from those present in flesh and other animal products. Vegetarians need to supplement their protein intake with milk and/or milk products such as yogurt/dahi, cheese, etc. (known as lacto vegetarians) or along with egg (known as ovo-vegetarians). Those who eat both milk and eggs are known as ovo-lacto vegetarians. There does not seem to be any specific name for seafood eating groups. There is a group known as 'vegans' in some parts of the world and perhaps in India too, who do not consume any animal product, not even milk and its products and probably not even natural honey.

The energy derived from the food and its metabolism is stored in the body in the form of 'body fuels'. These fuels are present in different quantities. In a man weighing around 70 kg, there are 12 kg of fat as adipose glycerides, 6 kg as muscle protein, small amounts of glycogen (0.07 kg in liver and 0.40 kg in the muscle) and 0.02 kg of glucose circulating through body fluids. Their total calorific content is 135,965 Kcal, adipose fat and muscle protein being the repositories of the two highest levels of energy (110,000 Kcal and 24,000 Kcal respectively). It is estimated that in an adult man, about 25–40 per cent of the body mass is fat (Cahill, Aoki and Rossini, 1979, pp. 1–70).

The mechanism for the body to obtain and spend energy derived from food is called the energy metabolism. Part of the nutrient energy is converted into chemical, mechanical, electrical or osmotic forms of energy. The chemical energy in the nutrients is known as the redox energy which is converted into Adenosine triphosphate i.e. ATP. This is the universal ingredient of energy metabolism. ATP is synthesised both aerobically and anaerobically. The energy metabolism for the whole body is primarily due to the Resting Energy Expenditure (REE). Macronutrients like carbohydrates and amino acids and fatty acids, the latter two derived from proteins and fats respectively, are broken down by different pathways – glycolysis, beta oxidation and amino acid pathways but glycolysis is the only energy yielding path able to produce energy (Fig. 9.1).

$$\text{Nutrients} \rightarrow \frac{\text{NADPH}}{\text{NAD}} \rightarrow \text{oxidative phosphorylation} \rightarrow \frac{\text{ATP}}{\text{ADP + Pi}} \rightarrow \text{energy dissipatio}$$

Fig. 9.1: Glycolysis yields energy

Note: NAD – Nicotinamide Adenine Dinucleotide; NADPH – Nicotinamide Adenine Dinucleotide, reduced; ATP – Adenosine Triphosphate; ADP – Adenosine Diphosphate; Pi – inorganic Phosphate

Redox potential is the amount of energy that can be released when 1 (or 2) electron(s) jump(s) from one compound (which will be oxidised) to another (which will be reduced). Phosphate potential is the amount of energy released when ATP is converted to ADP+Pi (adenosine di phosphate and inorganic phospahate).

Energy in the body is utilized for active transport of ions and substances across cell membranes, for the synthesis of new molecules and for the contraction of muscle fibres. In healthy adults, the REE is found to be 40 Kcal h^{-1} m^{-2} of body surface area (Gibney, Macdonald and Roche, 2003, p. 30).

The Concept of Glycemic Index and Glycemic Load in a Daily Meal

Carbohydrates exert an effect on the glucose levels in the blood, the more carbohydrates we consume in our food, larger is the effect on blood glucose levels. Under laboratory conditions, this effect can be determined by feeding volunteers with different kinds of foods and monitoring their blood glucose at regular intervals (usually in about 2 hours). The food is then given a number called the Glycemic Index or GI number. Low GI foods show a small effect which lasts over a longer period. High GI foods give a big kick very rapidly but the effect is short lived. On a scale of 1–100, low GI foods carry a number 1–55. The values between 55–70 are considered to be moderate GI. Any number over that is high GI. All pure carbohydrates like glucose, sucrose as well as sweet meats, cakes, pastries, sugared juices, jams, etc. fall into the last category. One could eat a small amount of such foods and experience a small GI. So eating low GI foods is good for all and especially for diabetics or those who are watching their weight. On the other hand, one could eat a lot of moderate category carbohydrate rich food and still get a high GI number. Therefore, it is not sufficient to know which foods have high or low GI but really how much to eat each kind to get a good balanced meal, to prevent excess carbohydrate load but get energy to work and perform. It is not easy to keep checking the GI number of every food article and work out the quantity that is ideal. Here, the term *load* is introduced. It is the total carbohydrate load/glycemic load or GL that determines how the glycemic index would show and how the blood glucose levels would dip or rise or maintain themselves. Meal plans can be worked out to include foods that belong to the category which have low GL numbers, 1–10 being small and GL 11–19 being moderate. Choosing a low GL diet for diabetics is said to make it easy to allow eating three meals and two snacks in a day without feeling hunger pangs. A number of foods common in western diets are identified with their GI and GL values. In the Indian diet, white rice would be one that would carry a high GI and a high GL number. Brown rice or wild rice, dalia (rough broken wheat), oats, barley pearls, probably other common millets like *Ragi* and *Jola*, greens, vegetables (not root), fiber rich fruits, whole grains, certain oil seeds like soya, linseed, almonds and walnuts, dry fruits like apple, fresh bean sprouts, lentils and other fresh and dried whole beans (*chana*, *moong* for example), toned milk in small quantities, non-fat yoghurt or *dahi* etc. for vegetarians and lean meat, fish, eggs, bacon for those who would eat them provide a choice of low GI/GL meal items which coupled with 30–40 minutes of brisk walking should keep the figures in check. White breads, pizzas, burgers, fries, fried snacks, Indian *mithai* (sweatmeats), ice-creams, jams, honey and any sweet fruit are not helpful and should be avoided or eaten in very small amounts for variety and pleasure on occasion.

One should remember that the human race ate very simple food, first foraging for wild nuts and fruit, then as scavengers, then hunted meat and beach combed for fish. Its carbohydrates came from the little fruit that it found and the gut contents of killed animals! Our genome is not geared to deal with the carbohydrate load that entered our food chain since the agricultural revolution and even more so after the industrial revolution. This takes us back to the beginning and our palaeo diets at that time consisted of mostly gathered plant foods and some amount of hunted meat and fish. Fruits, nuts, berries, wild honey, along with lean meat and fish sustained us in the highly physically active hunter – gatherer style of living. Evolutionary nutritionists and biochemists are of the opinion that our genome which was fixed some 40,000 years ago has not had sufficient time to adapt itself to this new situation and thus it is exhibiting the phenomenon of insulin resistance by a mal-adapted carnivore type genome.

Changes in Dietary Pattern

Our diet now differs vastly from early diets, which were not energy dense, therefore our energy intake was moderate. The protein content in the diet was high, mainly derived from animal sources. There was low to moderate amount of carbohydrate of the slowly absorbable kind but with high amounts of fiber contributed by the wide choice of plant foods available and used. The fat consumed in low amounts came principally from tree nuts. In the post agricultural revolution period, especially in the last 100 years and more particularly in the present western diet, (Simopoulos, 2003, p. 2) everything seems to have become reversed. Brand–Miller and Colaguiri (1999) traced the changing pattern of food intake from one million years ago till the present day. It clearly revealed the reversed pattern of intake with regard to the major nutrients. This can be explained by recognising that lifestyles gradually changed from active to sedentary, from low consumption of complex carbohydrates to high amounts of rapidly absorbed (refined) carbohydrates and thus a lot less fiber; protein ingestion from all sources became low to moderate and fat intake both from animal and plant sources rose far above those in the palaeo diet. With respect to several vitamins, (riboflavin, folic acid, thiamin, ascorbic acid, carotene retinal equivalent, vitamin A and vitamin E), a similar change is noticeable. Their intake was considerably less in the US diets than it was in the Paleolithic period.

Today, cereals together with other food crops represent only about 17 per cent of the plant species that our ancestors gathered and ate. Altogether, we depend only on some 30 major food crops as compared to the more than 200 species of plants in palaeo times. Our genes cannot cope with a large grain diet and that too consisting of large quantities of refined carbohydrates, because we evolved from carnivorous origins consuming little carbohydrate. In the 40,000 years since our present profile of genes originated, not much change has occurred in our genes, the background spontaneous gene mutation rates being very low. Nevertheless, our dietary patterns have changed since then. The data from Simopoulos (2003) and Eaton and Konner (1985) reconstructed and tabulated exemplifies this premise (Table 9.6). The appearance of insulin resistance and diabetes drew the scientists' attention to this fact first, the causes being attributed to the increased consumption of refined carbohydrates together with a sedentary mode of life. The protein content of food at present is generally on the lower side, and is derived mostly from fatty meat; it is even more deficient in vegetarian foods unless the diet is varied, wide and mixed. Fat intake has risen too. The fine balance that existed between complex carbohydrates, animal and fish proteins and fat from flesh, fish and plant nut sources altered drastically. The cause for all this is said to be the agricultural revolution that happened around 10,000 years ago in the post glacial period.

Table 9.6: The dietary patterns, 40,000 years apart

Characteristic	*Hunter gatherer in Paleolithic lifestyle*	*Western modern man in current lifestyle*
A. *Physical activity*	High	Low
Diet	Gathered and hunted	Processed, refined
Energy density	Low	High
Energy intake	Moderate	High
Protein	High	Low–moderate
Animal protein	High	Low–moderate
Vegetable protein	Very low	Low–moderate
Fiber	High	Low
Fat (Both animal and vegetable)	Low	High
Total Omega 6 + Omega 3	High (2.3 g/day)	Low (0.2 g/day)
Ratio Omega 6/Omega 3	Low (2.4)	High (12)
B. *Total dietary energy %*		
Protein	33	12
Carbohydrate	46	58
Fat	21	30
Alcohol	0	–
PUFA*/Saturated Fat ratio	1.41	1.00
Cholesterol, mg	520	300
Fibre, g	100–150	30–60

*PUFA, polyunsaturated fatty acid

Source: Simopoulos, 2003; Eaton and Konner, 1985

Scientists have also pointed out that in the new pattern of dietary intake, we are eating not only far too much fat (an energy dense food) but we are also eating more food than ever before. Further, we are eating such combinations of fats, particularly from vegetable sources, that contribute far less of one particular essential fatty acid known as Omega-3 and far more of the long chain Omega-6 fatty acid. This is quite evident from the data shown in Table 9.6. Both are polyunsaturated fatty acids or PUFA. The body cannot synthesise these substances and therefore these must be ingested in the form of essential fatty acids – Linoleic Acid (LA) which gives rise to the long chain Omega-6 fatty acid, and Alpha-Linolenic Acid (ALA) which gives rise to the Omega-3 fatty acid.

In Paleolithic times, the total consumption of Omega-6 and Omega-3 fatty acids was 2.3 g per day, where as now it is 0.2 g per day, most of which is Omega-6 fatty acid. The ratio of the two fatty acids is much higher now (12.0) than it ever was before (2.4) showing that the fine balance that existed between the two has been disturbed.

The blame, scientists point out, rests at least partly on the modern technology and especially on the vegetable oil industry, making more of every kind of vegetable oil easily available. The oilseeds are rich in LA (Omega-6 FA) whereas fish and fish body oils are rich in ALA (Omega-3 FA). The optimal ratio of Omega-6/Omega-3 FA is essential to maintain sound health. PUFAs play a wide variety of roles in body function. They are important in cardiovascular conditions, in inflammatory diseases, in cancer, in dermatological conditions, in the central nervous system, brain function and in cholesterol metabolism. While the ratio of 1:1 of Omega-6/Omega-3 FA would be ideal and optimal for coronary heart disease conditions, other ratios may be appropriate for other disease conditions. For brain and related functions, a ratio of 4:1 is found to be good, according to Yahuda (2003).

Omega-3 PUFA in particular possesses many health promoting and disease preventing characteristics in cardio arterial disease, cancer and inflammatory conditions. Excessive consumption of Omega-6 PUFA and a high ratio of Omega-6/Omega-3 PUFA promote disease conditions (Jing X. Kang, 2003). The ratio also plays an important role in brain related functions like production and activity of neurotransmitters, learning, memory, seizures, multiple sclerosis, sleep, stress and such conditions.

In today's lifestyle and dietary habits, knowing about the role of various dietary nutrients in health and disease and especially in the context of Omega-6 and Omega-3 PUFA, dietary fat and PUFA intake levels have been recommended for adults in the fervent hope that the trend towards epidemic lifestyle diseases and particularly the alarming appearance of Metabolic Syndrome (high blood cholesterol and triglycerides, hypertension and glucose intolerance) may be slowed if not reversed. Today our major dietary nutrients are recommended at energy levels of 12 per cent, 58 per cent and 30 per cent from protein, carbohydrate and fat sources respectively. Some cultures consume fat between 15 to 40 per cent, which is quite different from Palaeolithic times. Lacking sufficient data to calculate an estimated average requirement for the intake of fats and the two PUFAs, an international working group at the National Institutes of Health, NIH, Bethesda, USA has suggested a reference intake or what is referred to as the Adequate Intakes (AI) for adults. For a diet providing 2,000 Kcals per day, the working group has fixed the optimal limits for LA at 2 per cent of energy level or 4.44 g (3 per cent or upper limit of 6.67 g) and for ALA at 1 per cent energy level or 2.2 g, and for trans fat at 1 per cent energy level or 2.0 g (upper limit). The NIH working group also recommended that the majority of the fatty acids should be obtained as mono unsaturated fatty acids and that the saturated fats be less than 8 per cent of the total energy.

Giving nutritional supplements in the form of Omega-3 FA rich foods and special preparations, leafy vegetables like purslane, which is rich in ALA, fish and fish oil capsules to improve the Omega-3 FA intake is a strategy that is being tested along with diet modification. Efforts are being made to understand the gene function in order to attempt to convert the ingested Omega-6 FA to Omega-3 FA in the mammalian cells. At present, it does not happen because a gene encoding the conversion enzyme Omega-3 FA desaturase is missing, but virus mediated gene transfer strategy is betting on the possibility that such a gene transfer will eventually become available beyond experimental successes (Jing X. Kang, 2003, pp. 24–25). Yet another modern approach would be to genetically modify foods such as milk and egg to improve their ALA and thereby the Omega-3 FA content. There have been media reports that Omega-3 rich algae have been found which, if grown in substantial amounts, will meet a great amount of nutritional needs without having to wipe out the fish population.

Traditional and Healthy Diets

What makes a healthy diet is a quintessential question. Historical records and nutritional surveys are two of the tested means to learn and establish the suitableness of any diet. An examination of historical records of North and South American Indians, Eskimos, Asians, Africans and Australian Aboriginals and New Zealand Maoris has shown that the people of these cultures maintained and enjoyed good health, fertility, absence of tooth decay, fast and less painful child birth and minimal degenerative diseases compared to those in technologically advanced cultures (Cousens, 2000).

Traditional food thus comes across as the type most desirable for good health. The traditional food systems of the indigenous peoples are composed of items from the local natural environment, unprocessed and culturally acceptable. The variety of plant and animal species that form a traditional food system contribute towards complete diets providing adequate amounts of fiber, micronutrients and limited quantities of saturated and refined carbohydrates (Kuhnlein and Raceveur, 1996).

The example provided by a diet composed of corn, other cereals and sweet potato traditionally eaten by the Akiyuki tribe of Africa mentioned by Bogest et al. (1973) falls far short of adequate nutrition according to some authors (Orr and Gilkes, 1931). A parallel is drawn between those who are physically bigger and stronger and who eat whole grains and goats milk in the Northern reaches of India and the people of the South whose principal diet is milled rice, fruits and vegetables with little or no meat or even milk foods, who are inferior in strength, smaller in physique and short lived according to Bogest et al. (1973). The Central and South American countries where the main feature of the diet is based on beans and possibly corn and such cereals exhibit severe deficiency symptoms among the children who managed to survive and develop further.

In India, the vegetarian diets which comprise entirely of cereals and pulses and other plant foods have been observed to be deficient in vitamin B-12 in the studies carried out by Kumar and colleagues (1989). However, there is a certain intake of dairy foods in the form of *dahi* (yoghurt) and milk in their diets. This is characteristic of the agricultural man who became increasingly dependent on the cereals he cultivated. Although most cereals have vitamin B but not B-12, the different steps of processing, milling and cooking decrease their biological availability. In the first half of the twentieth century, epidemic forms of vitamin B deficiencies – *Beriberi* (Thiamine deficiency) and *pellagra* (niacin deficiency) occurred (Roe, 1973) in the Southern United States among corn eating populations. In India too such deficiency related epidemics have occurred. The literature on nutrient content and composition of traditional indigenous foods is growing and will surely form the basis for diet and ration formulations in the future. Until such time as traditional indigenous diets are fully adapted to modern technology without loosing their innate goodness, modern nutritionists have come to believe that there is one diet which can be called the most right for good health and good life. And this has come to be recognised as a model diet for healthy living.

A Model Diet

The honour of becoming known as the best diet for healthy living goes to the Mediterranean diet. This is described as the pattern of diet found in olive growing areas of the Mediterranean region and that which was prevalent in the late 1950s and early 1960s before the advent of the fast food culture. This diet consists of high intake of vegetables, legumes, fruits, nuts and cereals (which in the past were unrefined), high intake of oil such as olive oil but low intake of saturated fats, moderately high intake of fish and other seafood when living nearer to sea, a low to moderate intake of dairy products such as cheese and yogurt, a low intake of meat and poultry and regular but low intake of alcohol mostly in the form of wine accompanying the meals (Trichopoulos et. al., 2003).

The Mediterranean dietary pattern has been associated with better health and improvement in longevity. Both from evidence gathered from classic ecological studies and direct evidence, the facts of longer survival, of protection from myocardial infarcts, of protection from certain types of cancers (breast, colorectal and prostate area), diabetes, Alzheimer's, ageing and such other diseases associated with oxidative processes have been unequivocally established.

The rationale for this is that in an oxidative process taking place inside the cell, free radicals i.e. reactive oxygen are liberated which are damaging. There free radicals need to be scavenged by way of ingesting natural antioxidants. Vegetables and specially tomatoes have been recognised as some of the natural plant foods rich in antioxidants (Weisburger, 1999). The cultures whose normal traditional foods include these in one form or the other are at an advantage. The Mediterranean diet is rich in tomato usage. The Southeast Asian and South Asian diets include tea and vegetables. The presence of antioxidants in a food is determined with the help of biochemical methods used in the laboratory.

From epidemiological observations in recent years, Tur, Romaguera and Pons (2004) have gathered credible data through a cross sectional nutrition survey carried out in the Balearic Islands to conclude that such healthy eating trends are changing for the worse among the younger generation who are departing from the traditional Mediterranean diet and lifestyle. Older people and more women were seen to be adhering to the traditional diets. Increased consumption of animal products together with higher intake of saturated fats and reduced intake of basic foods based on vegetables were noticed in a nutrition survey in Spain between the years 2000–2004 (Trichopoulos et al.,2003; Trichopolous, 2001; Trichopolous and Vasilopoulos, 2000; Tur et al., 2004).

Except for olive oil and some other variations, the Indian diet appears to resemble in some ways the Mediterranean diet. Much the same plants and animal species enter their dietary patterns. Meat does not form a major constituent of the Indian diet. Fish and other sea food consumption generally occurs among those living in the coastal regions and near fresh water bodies, though several inland people in different parts also consume fish. Milk and yoghurt are considered important dietary components. Ghee (clarified butter) and cottage cheese (*paneer*) are the favoured and prized milk products. There are plenty of fresh vegetables and greens in the common middle class diet as well as seasonally available fruit in small quantities. It is the poor dietary intentions and/or poor diet compliances that fall short, not the diets.

The Indian diet differs greatly from the Mediterranean diet in the quantity of processed, refined polished rice that is consumed as bulk cereal in India. It was not so until modern rice mills began to operate and produce white rice. The refined wheat flour that had been the mainstay of wheat eaters for the past nearly fifty years is slowly being replaced again with whole grain flour but there is no such indication as yet of semi polished or unpolished rice replacing the white rice. A matter of considerable concern in both the affluent and the less affluent sections of the rural population is the increasing (and preferred) use of white rice; the rural folk who traditionally ate coarse cereals and minor millets and cottage level processed or hand pounded rice now have taken to white rice if they can afford it. White milled rice is available through the public distribution system in urban areas. Less milled and red and brown rice are out of favour except in niche sectors where people are aware and are diet conscious. These foods are also much more expensive than the commonly used rice because now they are found only in organically grown form.

Alcohol is not a beverage that accompanies any Indian meal as a tradition, though in villages it is an addiction and the urban lot imitates life in the fast lane. Consumption of hard liquor, beer and rum has passed beyond the limits of gracious social drinking and has become established as lifestyle requisites for the upwardly mobile younger generation. It has also reached alarming levels of habituation and addiction. The rural folk too, who had been used to drinking some form of fermented brew, the common beverage being the country liquor or *arrack* but in moderation, have now become big time drinkers. Poor nutrition due to poverty and/or lack of awareness regarding healthy food coupled with alcohol consumption, compounded by smoking is ringing the death knell among the rural folk. Whereas the abundance of disposable income and the faulty lifestyles among the upwardly mobile, availability of wines and liquor both made in India and imported from all over the world, consumption of high calorie nutrient poor diets either intentionally or also perhaps due to lack of awareness and lack of opportunity, time or intention for regular exercise are some of the reasons for the epidemic emergence of lifestyle diseases among the urban people all over India.

Globally, the increasing dependence on fast foods by practically all sections of the people everywhere depicts the changes that came in the twentieth century with technology. Changes in the lifestyle, changes in the old fashioned ritual of eating at least one meal if not all meals at home together, the fast paced life of both men and women who now work outside the home, the rich and the not so rich finding quick foods to suit their taste and match their pockets, foods prepared by someone else and offered at places convenient to them have all made life easier for most people. Street foods (Simopoulos and Bhatt, 2000) today provide a great many people everywhere in the world with a vast variety of quick foods which encompass a large variety of traditionally eaten items. Although they provide food conveniently, quickly at anytime of the day however un-hygienically prepared or however inadequate nutrition wise they may be, and also provide a livelihood to many in the business of selling, for some sections of the people this is the only way a hot meal can be had and the only source of subsistence of any kind. If a meal approaching the model diet could be sold out of the street vending system many people would benefit.

Mediterranean diet: Mediterranean diet specially the Cretan foods, is seen to be low in Omega 6 FA but rich in Omega 3 FA. A Mediterranean diet meets such requirements to reduce complications of heart disease. One diet was formulated to test its effects on heart attack or Coronary Heart Disease (CHD) patients in France in a study called Lyon Diet Heart study. This Mediterranean diet consisted of less than 30 per cent of total daily energy derived from fats, of which less than 8 per cent was obtained from saturated fats. The total intake of LA was kept to 4 per cent of energy and that of

ALA to more than 0.6 per cent of energy. This Mediterranean diet although custom designed to suit individual patients was made up of more bread, more cereals, more legumes and beans, more fresh fruit and vegetables, more fish, less meat (beef, mutton or pork) and less quantities of preserved or processed meats such as sausages, salamis and other cold meats which were replaced by chicken. The butter or cream were replaced with canola oil (erucic acid free rape seed oil) and canola oil based margarine chemically comparable with olive oil but which was enriched with LA or ALA. For salads and cooking, olive oil and canola oils were used. By these means the ratio of Omega-6 to Omega-3 of 4:1 was maintained.

Keeping in mind that not more than 30 per cent of the total energy should be derived from these fats, the specially crafted Cretan food has been found to be very effective in test subjects, decreasing total mortality by 70 per cent (De Lorgeril and Salen, 2003). Fish oils as a direct therapeutic source of Omega-3 FA is also recommended and has been tested in place of steroidal medications for inflammatory diseases like rheumatoid arthritis (Cleland and Proudman, 2003).

Benefits of eating fish, at least two servings of fatty fish per week, as a means of prevention of secondary heart attack by patients who suffered from myocardial infarction have been seen in a trial called the Diet and Re-infarction Trial (DART) by way of reduction of mortality by 30 per cent. The very long chain Omega-3FA such as DHA and EPA obtained through fish oils and fatty fish are believed to have an effect on the occurrence of ventricular fibrillation (De Lorgeril and Salen, 2003, pp. 65–66).

Indian versus Mediterranean foods: Naturally, with so much of scientific data accumulating on the role and effects of the Omega-6 and Omega-3 FAs, one compares the Mediterranean diet with other diets.

Chemical data for fatty acids and essential fatty acids of various nuts, meats and fish were obtained by DeLorgeril and Salen (2003) who found that peanuts and pine nuts contain the highest amount of oleate (23.8 and 21.5 g/100g). High levels of LA were also reported in these nuts and in walnuts. Walnut and linseed though lower in oleate contain high amounts of ALA. Salmon and mackerel and beef and pork have very little ALA. There is no ALA at all in the groundnut. Walnuts though more expensive than other dry nuts are available in India and are more commonly found and consumed in the North. Pine nuts or *chilgoza* are found in select stores in the North and is not a common dry fruit. Linseed is very much a dietary ingredient in rural Karnataka and possibly in other states too and may not be known widely as a food item. But it possesses the highest ALA content of all. By including walnuts in greater amounts and linseed in some acceptable form in the rations, the troops will derive significant benefits due to larger amounts of ALA according to this chemical data. Almond too is a special ration item but has little ALA compared to walnut. For the mountain troops posted in high altitudes, the dry fruits and nuts are given as special dietary items.

The Standard Service Ration Scales also list meats like pork (tinned ham, sausages) and fish such as tuna and mackerel. None of these items contain any significant amounts of ALA though mackerel does have a little more ALA than any other and salmon and pork have only small quantities of LA, and beef has more LA than the meat and fish foods according to the data of De Lorgeril and Salen (2003). The nutritive content of pork in respect of its oleic acid, essential FA and amino acids and folate content is the lowest.

In Indians, a higher prevalence of CHD was found in urban populations than in rural areas relative to their fat intakes but still much lower than in western populations (Pella *et al.,* 2003, p. 74). The rural populations of North and Northeast India traditionally eat different types of grains and use mustard oil for cooking because it is traditional and less expensive than ghee (clarified butter). The urban people prefer ghee but also liberally use vegetable ghee or hydrogenated fat and refined vegetable oils in their cooking and choose refined flour to make *chapattis*, *puris*, bread, biscuits and such other preparations. This dietary pattern, according to Singh *et al.* (2001) alters the Omega-6/Omega-3 FA ratio and makes it much higher than is considered appropriate for good coronary health. The authors Pella *et al.* (2003) call it a paradox because in spite of lower total fat intake (24.7 per cent) compared to the Indians resident in USA and UK (31–35 per cent fat energy intake) they found that the urban Indians have a high prevalence of Coronary Artery Disease (CAD), which they now attribute to the increased ratio (6.2) of Omega-6/Omega-3 FA in the urban diets than the lower ratio (2.3) in the rural diets.

It was clear from these dietary observations, that the urban populations exhibited higher CAD risk factors and Type 2 Diabetes, high BP, higher total and Low Density Lipoprotein (LDL) cholesterol, triglycerides and post- prandial 2-hour blood glucose and plasma insulin. The Indian immigrants in UK and USA exhibited similar characteristics. An Indo-Mediterranean diet Heart Study conducted over a two year period by Singh *et al.*, showed that the consumption of a diet rich in whole grains, fruits, vegetables, walnuts, mustard or soybean oil as source of Omega-3 fat, caused the mean intake of ALA and thus Omega-3 FA to be two fold greater. It is thus possible to modify even the vegetarian diets to lower the Omega-6/Omega-3 ratio.

The recommendations from the Joint WHO/FAO Expert Consultation on Diet, Nutrition and Prevention of Chronic Diseases state that Omega-6 PUFA intake should be kept to 5–8 per cent of energy and of Omega-3 PUFA at 1–2 per cent of energy resulting in a ratio ranging from as low as 2.5:1 to as high as 8:1.

Total fat and omega fat intake: There is no RDA for fat intake for Indians. In the vegetarian diet, there is no Eicosapentonoic Acid (EPA) and Docosahexanoic Acid (DHA) component. Very little of the LA and ALA are converted in the body to EPA and DHA, although attempts are being made to achieve such a conversion by toying with the enzyme concerned. No substitute is possible either. The best source for these is fish and fish oils. Such being the case, the rations for the Indian military personnel may also need to be further critically evaluated to determine whether they meet the new dietary health norms of lowered Omega-6/Omega-3 ratio and whether there is a need for modification. At least one can look at the possibility of modifying the existing diet to resemble more the Mediterranean diet. For this, a suitable combination of fats has to be determined by selecting the appropriate dietary sources in the rations. Presently, refined oils such as Sunflower, Sundrop (Dhara) brands of hydrogenated fats or oils, milk, butter, cheese, jams, sugar, atta, rice, bread (white), mutton, egg and chicken are the main ration items. Fish, generally is only a 'once a week' item. It is not known whether these rations have been examined to determine the Omega-6/Omega-3 ratio. But from other evidence (Pella *et al.*, 2003) one may deduce that the standard military rations using the above listed food items with a total daily calorie intake of more than 3,000 Kcals will have at least 8.4–8.8 minimum ratio of Omega-6/Omega-3 fats, and very likely far greater than this level.

To make combat ration packs and survival foods which are light in weight but more calorie-dense, introducing higher fat content in a formulation is one of the principal approaches, the other ingredients being carbohydrates mostly in the refined form, because saturated fats, especially the hydrogenated oil or vegetable ghee are not easily oxidised and therefore do not develop early rancidity and hence have better shelf stability. Palatability of long shelf life food products is an important quality criterion for acceptance before procurement and is important for compliance with consuming the designated amount of food. With the kind of oils (rich in PUFA) that could normally provide better Omega-6/Omega-3 ratios for maintaining better health, there are greater chances of food becoming rancid more rapidly. To prevent this development, more antioxidant substances must be added as preservatives. Under the provisions of the Prevention of Food Adulteration Act (PFA Act, 1954), the use of preservatives in processed food is strictly regulated. If any chemical must be used at all or in greater amounts, then it has to be examined under the provisions of the Act. That is a dilemma that will confront the food scientists when they proceed to replace stable saturated fats with unsaturated fats in order to obtain better Omega-6/Omega-3 ratios.

In the Indian domestic market, many brands of vegetable oils are sold. Not too long ago, Poly Unsaturated Fatty Acid (PUFA) rich vegetable oils in daily cooking used to be advocated vigorously by way of product advertisements and were claimed to be the answer to many prevailing health concerns. A limited survey of a small grocery department store in an upper middle class neighbourhood carried out by this author during February 2007 showed that manufacturers of the various single and blended oils are not only displaying nutrition information on the labels but are also proclaiming certain health advantages in respect of the chemical composition of their products (Table 9.7).

Table 9.7: Saturated (sat FA), monounsaturated (MUFA), polyunsaturated (PUFA) fatty acid contents of vegetable oils and blends in the Indian market identified by the brand name

S. No.	*Brand Name*	*Oil source*	*Nutrition composition, g. per cent of*			*Antioxidant*	*Fortified with*
			Sat. FA	*MUFA*	*PUFA*		
1.	Dhara Health	Refined sunflower oil (pure)	12	88	–	TBQH 0.018	None
2.	Crystal	Refined sunflower oil	NA	NA	–	Present	NA
3.	Sundrop super lite	-	12	88	–	NA	Vit A,D,E
4.	Sundrop Heart with Oryzanol	Sunflower oil Rice bran oil blend	21	46	33	NA	Oryzanol, Vit E
5.	Sun Gold	Agricultural marketing (AG Mark) quality	NA	NA	NA	NA	NA
6.	Sun Pure	Sunflower oil	Claims O Cholesterol			0.02 Tocopheral	–
7.	Nature Fresh Acti-lite	Refined vegetable oil	14.4	23.3	57.9	NA	NA
8.	Giva	Rice bran oil	20	45	35	0.02 Tocopherol	NA
9.	Nature Fresh Acti-lite	Refined Sunflower oil	–	–	–	–	–
10.	Dalda (Hydrogenated) oil or oil hydro	Soya, cotton seed, rice bran, mustard, rape seed, sunflower, Mahua, Palm, Maize, Sesame and others	–	NA	–	–	

In the market survey, sunflower oil was found to be the most commonly sold oil under different brands. It has very little ALA. Rice bran oil has more ALA than either sunflower or even olive oil. Rice bran oil which is sold as a pure product has a fatty acid profile which seems to approach, though not exactly the achievable target of 1:2:1 with 20 per cent saturated, 45 per cent monounsaturated and 35 per cent PUFA. In the blended form with sunflower oil, (called Sundrop Heart with oryzanol) a similar FA profile emerges. Coconut oil is the only oil containing the saturated FA lauric acid; all others contain small quantities of stearic and palmitic acid; palm oil has the highest palmitic acid of all. Comparatively, it is a less expensive oil and is used by sections of the population as it is distributed through the public distribution system to ration card holders and it is the principal oil in relatively less expensive and unbranded snack food preparation at the cottage and home industry levels.

The data provides some insight into the relative amounts of saturated FA, MUFA and PUFA found in the different oils. There is no further information provided about their respective LA and ALA contents. But data on composition of several edible vegetable fats – olive, linseed, sesame, soya, peanut coconut, rice bran, rape seed, canola, safflower (*karadi*), sunflower and palm oils reported by White (2000) indicated that only linseed, soya, canola and rapeseed oils have higher linolenic acid content. According to the currently held scientific belief, the best composition for a fat is a ratio where saturated fat (like lauric, stearic, palmitic): mono unsaturated fat (oleic acid): poly unsaturated fat (LA/ALA and other fatty acids) exist in 1:1:1 proportion. It is possible to achieve an ideal blend but the choice of oils would become limited. To achieve a ratio of 1:2:1 is more feasible according to scientist B.R. Lokesh, Head of the Lipid Technology Division, Central Food Technological Research Institute (Personal communication).

Rape seed oil is a low erucic acid containing variety similar to mustard oil but has high ALA as does canola oil. Canola oil is rape seed oil but without erucic acid. Mustard oil is very popular in the North Indian belt as a cooking medium. One hundred grams of Canola is said to provide 8 g of ALA, or two table spoons of canola provide 2 g of ALA. The mustard oil minus erucic acid could therefore be a suitable alternative and a good source of ALA. Soya bean oil also has higher ALA and was once very popular as cooking oil but now it seems to be used only in a blended form in making hydrogenated oil or Vanaspati.

There are regional preferences for these different oils in India. Experts believe that the varied dietary pattern among Indians with a healthy intake of cereals, pulses, fruits, vegetable oils, dairy foods, meat, milk and fish contributes intrinsically towards adequate amounts of invisible fats (and may be ALA too), and therefore one may not need to be alarmed about not getting enough ALA from the cooking oils in vogue. The largely vegetarian food consumed (either on religious grounds, or by choice or due to economic reasons) by the majority precludes the ingestion of Omega-3 from non-vegetarian (fish) sources. Though the total daily fat intake at a conservative level may be no more than 30 per cent on an average (could be higher or lower too depending on the economic status of the consumer), Indian diets definitely do not provide the ideal fat composition of 1:1:1 or 1:2:1.

As there is no RDA for fat, there are no formulae to be used to determine how much LA and ALA could be derived from mixing and fixing dietary ingredients. In India, more than two oils cannot be used in blends under the PFA Act (1954) although a smart blending of soya bean, mustard and linseed oils could give a very good blend. Olive oil, though not considered a source of ALA is important for its high oleic acid content and antioxidants thus it is less prone to oxidation. These are the only two reasons why olive oil is considered good otherwise it certainly is not a great source of ALA, and yet it is the main edible oil in the Mediterranean diet which is considered to be a model one. The problem with the Indian urban diet then could be (a) the higher intake of total fats not in the right chemical composition of 1:1:1, (b) consuming larger quantities of energy rich carbohydrates, (c) preferring the more refined flours over the more traditional coarse grains which do not give eye appealing and hedonistically attractive products to suit the emerging lifestyles and new taste perceptions and (d) the more frequent consumption of everything coupled with (e) sedentary habits.

Only long duration follow up and epidemiological observations will show how the high intake of total calories, fats and high LA will eventually manifest in the physically active and energetic individuals such as military personnel. Until then, the calorie and nutrient requirements will be determined on the well established nutrition norms of slightly higher energy intake versus energy expenditure. The issue of appropriate dietary Omega levels, their ALA levels in the Indian diet not being the only paradox, it exists in Japan and certain Israeli diets too, which have been dealt with at length by authors Hamazaki and Okuyama (2003) and Dubnov and Berry (2003) respectively.

Knowing how the various food items which are a part of every day diet contribute towards high LA may help in making careful, appropriate and intelligent choices and interventions. Dubnov and Berry (2003) provide some interesting examples in which the LA and ALA ratios in eggs are found to vary from one country to another – higher (50:1) ratio in USA than in Greece (2.3:1). Even the way the beef animals are fed (grass versus grain) appears to influence the LA and ALA contents and ratios in their meat. Grass fed animals showed a lower ratio than the grain fed ones.

Scientists have asked whether there is a way to fix an optimal Omega-6/Omega-3 ratio. One can only again cite the example of the Mediterranean diet with a ratio of 1–2:1, which as Simopoulos has said, is similar to what was obtained in our palaeo diet. But different countries differ culturally and in their dietary habits, patterns and traditions which influence the type and amount of fat intake. The European and US diets are rich in total calories consumed per day and range between 3,300 to 3,700 Kcals. Even Israel, which is a Mediterranean country consumes less olive oil but almost 85 per cent soya bean oil and shows a total per capita 3,100 calories consumption. Their fat ingestion levels range from 120 g/day to 160 g/day. It is not clear whether these many calories and this much fat are consumed by active or sedentary persons.

The average calorie content of the Indian Service Ration scale is around 3,000 Kcal, but could go as high as 5,000 Kcal at high altitudes, 27 to 30 per cent of which are derived from fat. At the 30 per cent level, the total fat calories consumed per day are assumed to be 1000, coming from 111 g fat (oil or oil hydro), meat, butter, cheese and other foods as intrinsic sources. This is low by comparison with the average western diets. The LA/ALA ratio of this ration is not known.

The dietary Omega-6/Omega-3 ratios in diets of different countries and the ratios recommended for improved diets were discussed by Dubnov and Berry (2003). The palaeo diet seemed to have a ratio of 1–2:1. In contrast, in every national diet the ratio is very high except the Mediterranean diet! To set the situation right, various nutrition bodies have made recommendations for maximum LA intake. The US Food and Drug Administration sets a figure of 4–7 per cent of total energy, the British Nutrition Foundation Task Force set a figure of 6 per cent and the WHO till recently had given a figure of 4–7 per cent.

To reduce LA intake until molecular biology and biotechnology can provide us solutions increasing the consumption of nuts, especially walnut, olive oil and fish would seem to be the proper strategy. Fish eaten at 15 g per day for just 2 weeks was seen to confer great benefit by way of improved serum lipid profiles, and reduced insulin resistance. Fish would also provide DHA and EPA directly.

There is one other nutrition concern in reference to fats. It pertains to trans-fats which are generated during the hydrogenation process and also during high temperature cooking, baking etc.

The trans-fatty acids are not otherwise expected to be present in natural conditions in foods other than dairy products. These substances only appear in foods made with hydrogenated fats or due to high temperature cooking and in baking. By this reckoning, fried foods and snacks and bakery products contain trans-fats.

In the light of the current knowledge, trans-fats at no higher than 0.5 g/serving of food is allowed by the FDA. A serving size could be 30 ml or 100 g. Since trans-fats are also present in animal fats such as butter, cheese, lard etc., there is a move to ban trans fat containing fats in any form. Therefore, the use of vegetable fats is recommended. In the *vanaspati* made in India, the trans-fat content was said to be as high as 40–50 per cent according to lipid science experts but with better methods it has been reduced to 10–15 per cent. If it could be further reduced to something like 2–3 per cent then it might be possible to achieve the prescribed limit of less than 0.5 g/serving.

Food intake is a behaviour that involves several systems internal as well as external to the body. Internally, there are the lipostat, leptin, neuropeptides Y, opioid peptides, nor epinephrine, galanin, benzodiazepam to increase intake as well as some neuro regulators to decrease intake. There are also our fine senses which draw us towards wanting to eat, taste, smell, flavour and aroma besides texture are important factors influencing intake. These sensory losses can seriously jeopardise compliance with the daily calorie intake.

For the Armed Forces personnel and others engaged in high performances activity, it interferes with the very basic purpose of their field deployment – that is to keep 24×7 hours vigil on the borders.

The problem of sufferance arises in troops deployed for long durations under adverse climatic situations, whose sense of taste and flavour perceptions have been affected as shown by researches carried out in High Altitude Warfare Institute. This has been observed in men after spending sometime in the Siachen sector where our troops have been operating since April 1984.

Food and Nutrition Research For High Altitude

Fatalities due to the cold weather and pulmonary edema are reported to be higher in high altitudes than deaths due to enemy firing. Dehydration due to the extremely cold and arid altitudes, freezing of all beverages, vegetables and other moist food due to the very low temperatures combined with an arrested or lowered ortho-retronasal perception system, aggravate the situation. A general feeling also persists among the troops that since they are at an elevation they are nearer to the gods and thus some of them forebear to eat meat and meat products. Another misconception generally nurtured by troops at high altitude is that canned foods (whatever may be the contents) are the cause of gastro-intestinal upsets – mostly flatulence. These are a combination of deadly forces exerting their influence to undermine the strength and morale that might be derived from food and nutrition. Even as several aspects of high altitude operations such as proper clothing and medical attention are being looked into by the concerned departments of the Indian Defence Forces and Ministry of Defence (MOD), even as Defence Research and Development Organisation (DRDO) laboratories carry out researches on smell and taste perception changes at high altitude, and even as Defence Food Research Laboratory (DFRL) conducted studies on incorporating antifreeze substances in food applications, the question of innovating by technology to make or incorporate unique substances, ingredients, etc. to enhance the reduced taste perceptions so that food may look, smell and taste more appetising, more desirable and thus more edible is something yet to be addressed seriously and effectively.

Some attempts have been made in this direction in making products called appetisers or appetite stimulants using a combination of spices and condiments long used in the Indian system of medicine as well as in home remedies (personal communication from DFRL researchers). Food science and technology is already much influenced by biotechnological advancements and has now gone into the realm of neuro-physiology with a bang.

High Altitude – An Extreme Condition for Troops

The Indian Armed Forces have been deployed and have been operating in the world's highest battleground – the Siachen since 1984. Their aircraft fly from and land on the world's highest airport at Leh in Ladakh, Jammu and Kashmir State, and the Defence R&D Organisation conducts research in life sciences in a laboratory which is at one of the highest locations in the world, also at Leh. Leh is situated at an altitude of 3,500 m or 11,480 ft. When troops are posted at altitudes above 10,000 ft in J & K sector, in the Siachen and such places their tenure is restricted to three months. There are various physical features which are not found at sea level but which characterise high altitudes – the most prominent being low oxygen pressure and very low temperatures in arid conditions. These exert a variety of physiological and psychological stresses on the human body and mind unaccustomed to living under such conditions.

The terrain at these altitudes when not clad in snow is a desolate picture. The Ladakh region is characterised by deep gorges and crevasses, vast steep rocky heights jutting with boulders and knife edge peaks, stark, naked and treeless but appearing smooth as weathered leather from a distance every where. There are ravines and crevasses crisscrossing the little flat ground that can be found. Most perches for the troop bunkers are rocky narrow ledges; bunkers are established to gain what protection can be found against the bitter winds. These bunkers are all-in-one living quarters for the men posted there while manning the guns.

During summer, there are some little streams flowing down the mountain sides (Fig. 9.2).

Fig. 9.2: At altitudes higher than Leh, it is still patchy green in September but it is scrub grass that grows by the side of the gentle rivulets. Sheep and yak have little to feed on and have to be kept moving in search of green grass before the snow sets in.

These deceptively tranquil little rivulets and the few other lakes give salt tasting water. These waters come from the snowmelts in the summer but freeze to rock ice in winter. Not a blade of grass can grow in winter or summer. At best there are small ground hugging thorny shrubs and plants with thick succulent leaves signifying the arid waterless conditions.

Man has been able to exist under extremes of conditions which obtain at high altitudes. The physical features of high altitude that must be reckoned with are low barometric pressure leading to low partial pressure of oxygen, cold and the wind chill, air absolute humidity and radiation solar, UV and ionising or cosmic (Hornbein and Schoene, 2001, pp. 44–53). However, exposure to high attitude (> 9842 ft, Health and Williams 1981 p. 6), stress factors which are hypoxia (low barometric pressure and low oxygen pressure), severe cold (upto –40°C), high wind velocity leading to high wind chill, extreme dryness and radiation (UV and cosmic) leads to serious medical conditions known as Acute Mountain Sickness (AMS) and HAPO (Hornbein and Schoene, 2001, pp. 840–841 and Health and Williams 1988, p. 9).

Hypoxia leads to High Altitude Pulmonary Oedema (HAPO), cerebral oedema leading to neuro pathology, high altitude retinopathy, photo-ophthalmia from solar and UV radiation, cold injuries like frost bite, anorexia due to loss of appetite, sleep and mental disturbances and exhaustion.

Responses to high altitude ascent includes rapid rise in hemoglobin concentration and polycythemia (Grover and Baertsch, 2001, p. 495) which is good from a survival point of view allowing an increase in oxygen carrying capacity of the blood. AMS which develops due to rapid ascent to high altitude is characterised by head ache, nausea, vomiting, insomnia, lassitude, and dizziness which in the benign forms usually right themselves upon rest and first aid. The sickness is thus self limiting. There are three stages to this sickness, stage 1 is AMS, stage 2 is HACE or High Altitude Cerebral Oedema (HACO) and then at stage 3 in its severe form is HAPO or HAPE (Baertsch and Roach, 2001, p. 731).

To maintain critical oxygen pressure required by the cells to function normally, a series of adaptations or acclimatisation must occur in the body (Vallotton and Dubas, 1991, p. 43).

The physiology and medical specialists of the DRDO and the Indian Armed Forces studying high altitude problems have evolved an acclimatisation protocol of 3 stages that recommends (a) a rest and quiet period of 7 days up to 13,000 ft, (b) another 5 days at 15,000 ft and (c) 15 days at altitudes higher than 15,000 ft. The troops being posted in high altitudes are rigorously put through this protocol so that they may function and discharge their duties ably. At Leh which is situated at a height of 3357 m or about 11,000 ft one full day of rest was recommended to get over the early symptoms of hypoxia (DRDO workshop on High altitude physiology, 2006)[1]

Therefore, diuresis is a mandatory part of acclimatisation now. Appropriate medication is prescribed to be taken beginning one or two days before ascent and then every day during the sojourn till acclimatisation sets in naturally. High altitude induced weight loss is mainly caused by malnutrition which is itself caused by hypoxia according to Selvamurthy and Singh (2003a, p. 487).

Energy, calories and nutrients: To perform various activities, energy is expended which determines the calorie and nutritional requirements. Normal sedentary life even at maximal work capacity at 4,500 m may not require more than 3,000 to 3,200 Kcal per day. Field observations have revealed that even with 3–4 days of acclimatisation, sub-maximal work can be performed (Sridharan *et al.*, 1995), not withstanding the fact that increased energy expenditure occurs at high altitudes because one is burdened down with the weight of warm clothing.

In a comprehensive review of human adaptation and nutritional requirements, scientists (Singh, Sridharan and Selvamurthy, 1999; Selvamurthy and Singh, 2003a) while discussing among other things the energy requirement for physical activity of different levels in temperate cold (less than 0°C) and hot (more than 30°C) environments pointed out that altitude energy requirements were similar to those obtaining for other environments for equivalent physical work. Their data showed that slightly more number of Kcal/kg body weight is needed in hot climate (maximum 62–75 Kcal for heavy work) than in cold (56–68 Kcal) and temperate climates (53–63 Kcal). Due to loss of appetite or hypophagia, which is quite evident in the first 3 days of exposure to high altitude, even with the best food made available, 40 per cent less calories are consumed at 4,300 m. The appetite regulator leptin is secreted and its levels maintained for hunger and satiety control on demand. At high altitudes, leptin levels are found to be significantly higher, falsely signalling that there are adequate stores of fuel available.

The energy cost of performing military manoeuvres in cold chilly terrains was found to be 4,281 Kcal in Mt Everest climbers at an average of 3,250 Kcal/day, and 3,500 Kcal for field manoeuvres at altitude of 7,000–1,000 ft. In the mid 1990s, the total calories in Indian troop's rations provided at 2,700–4,000 m high regions delivered 4,894 Kcal consisting of carbohydrates – 746 g supplying 2,887 Kcal or 61 per cent of the total, fat 147.9 g contributing 1331 Kcal, and the total proteins in the diet supplied 576 Kcal of which around 40 g were animal proteins (Sridharan, 1987, Sridharan *et al.,* 1995, Singh *et al.,* 1999). There are minor differences in these values reported by Sridharan and Rai (1984).

After a detailed investigation of the nutritional status of road construction workers engaged in work in the Western Himalayas at altitudes of 2,150 to 2,750 m and examining their capacity to work Sridharan *et al.* (1987) recommended that at an almost average daily expenditure of some 3,600 Kcal, their diet should consist of 3,750 Kcal for providing adequate energy, vitamins and minerals. Investigations also showed that nitrogen intake and excretion decreased progressively from sea level to increasing altitude at 3,500 and 4,572 m. Prolonged stay, however, stabilised the nitrogen utilisation. Fat is said to be digested or metabolised normally too but there is lower intake due to anorexia. It has been observed that high fat intake in the cold by a group of cross country skiers showed no harmful effects concerning cardiovascular risks. Even so, evidence suggested that carbohydrates are more important than fat during cold exposure and in fact, say Sridharan and Rai (1984) both mountaineers and short time sojourners at high altitude exhibit a craving for sugar and sweets, an observation which is also supported by the fact that native diets are rich in carbohydrates in the Andes and Himalayas.

Interestingly, in polar expeditions, viz. to the Antarctic, a mean caloric intake of 3,600 Kcal per man per day was observed of which 39 per cent came from fat and 48 per cent from carbohydrates, protein contributing only 12.7 per cent of the calories. Over all, in the several Indian Antarctic expeditions undertaken, a common observation according to Selvamurthy and Singh (2003a, p. 494) was an increase in body weight due to greater consumption of food, attributed by the authors to enhanced appetite, cold temperatures, emotional stress factors like loneliness, monotony and changes in the levels of physical activity. These findings are so different from those found at high altitude that special considerations must be given in respect of formulating suitable high altitude diet. While on the subject of nutritional requirements in high altitude conditions, one important consideration in diet composition that needs to be addressed is that of the quality of fat *vis-à-vis* the carbohydrate content. It has been observed that while the native Indian high altitude sojourners preferred high carbohydrate foods and though according to Sridharan and Rai (1984) carbohydrates are more important than fat during cold exposures, laboratory investigations on animals by scientists T. Ramasarma and colleagues of the Indian Institute of Sciences in their paper (Ravishankar *et al.*, 1999) have established that adaptation to cold depended on dietary fat and appeared to require additional PUFA. Their experiments revealed that a diet containing PUFA in significant amounts helps in adapting to the stress and survival in the cold. Peanut oil rich in PUFA was found to be superior to coconut (poor in PUFA) in experiments in survival in cold exposure. Fat free diets drastically reduced the survival rate. The researchers also drew attention to the possibility of PUFA – dependent lipid per-oxidation as an alternative source of heat in cellular thermogenesis. There is evidence from the studies of Hammer and Wills (1978) that Omega-3 fatty acid of PUFA in marine oils very effectively supported lipid per-oxidation. The fact that Arctic marine animals and fish store large amounts of Omega-3 FA lends credence to the possible role of Omega-3 FA in thermogenesis and possibly other vital functions.

In the cold of Northern America, populations were found to be partially deficient in essential fatty acids even when their diets were rich in other ways (Holman, 1993). This was attributed to the high turn over of PUFA. Ravishankar *et al.*'s (1999) findings also indicated that there was an inverse relationship between lipid per-oxidation and environmental temperature. The Eskimo diet is derived from marine sources with a fat content of 25 per cent but such a diet is not tolerated in warmer climates. Since the fatty acid composition of the tissues is controlled by dietary sources, adjusting the PUFA composition of food appropriate to the temperature of the environment may be a strategy to combat cold stress. In fact in preparation to a sojourn at high altitude, a suitable diet to preconditioning the system may be thought of and so formulated; this diet could be rich in PUFA and particularly in Omega-3 fatty acid.

Apart from the three major nutrients under discussion viz., protein, fat and carbohydrate, there are minerals like sodium, potassium and magnesium, iron, calcium, zinc, selenium etc., vitamins such as thiamine, nicotinic acid, vitamin A and other essential micronutrients, vitamins and antioxidants (vitamin C, E and beta-carotene) that are part and parcel of every diet at sea level and elsewhere. To compensate for loss of sodium and other salts through sweat and diuresis and as a result of generally reduced intake of these substances the diet must be so made up as to provide all of these and be enhanced with nutritional supplements. As scientific data are generated from continuing laboratory and field research on bio-medical aspects of cold and high altitude, the information is assessed and used appropriately resulting in revision of energy scales and formulation of diets and new recommendations. Taking various factors of malnutrition and metabolism into consideration, the following recommendations on energy, water and other nutrients were made (Brooks, 1996, p. 595).

(a) *Energy:* Intake should be increased by 500 Kcal per day above appetite levels emphasising carbohydrate rich foods to maintain body weight at high altitude.

(b) *Water:* Intake should to be greater than 3 litres per day to compensate for diuresis and insensible loss. Thirst is not the most accurate indicator of the need to drink more fluids in cold high altitude to keep dehydration away. At least 1.8 litres of water must be consumed by everybody under these conditions – either as water or beverages. Hot sugary tea with milk is a welcome drink in India and the troops are provided with quite adequate amounts of all three tea making ingredients in order to encourage fluid consumption (Sridharan and Rai, 1984, p. 432).

(c) *Other nutrients:* Despite the conclusions drawn by the Nutrition group of the United States Military Nutrition Research Report (1996) that no specific advantage accrued from any increased intake of vitamins and minerals except perhaps of vitamin E these may be needed as supplements. Maintenance of electrolyte balance in Indian troops appears not be a specific problem.

The diet of Sherpas consists largely of rice and dal (lentil soup). The Indian dietary pattern of those residing at high altitudes provides carbohydrates up to 60 per cent of energy. The troops' rations at altitudes of 9,000–12,000 ft were shown to contain 4,829 Kcal of energy, 144 g protein, 147.9 g fat, iron 91.5 mg, calcium 1.55 g, Vit A 6,279 i.u., thiamine 4.5 mg, riboflavin 3.8 mg, nicotinic acid 37.5 mg and ascorbic acid 247.6 mg (Sridharan *et al.,* 1995, p. 225).

The troops posted in high altitudes have to subsist almost entirely on canned or pouch foods and other processed items. The supply of fresh foods depletes rapidly in the 'road closed period'. Though sufficient stocks of processed foods are maintained, these are feared to suffer losses in vitamins to some extent due to processing and during storage. Even so, in a recent investigation by Sridharan *et al.,* (2004) it was found that up to 30 days at 3,660 m in the acclimatised subjects vitamin supplementation was not necessary. The tinned foods which were examined being found to be nutritionally quite adequate, the subjects had positive energy balance and were in excellent fitness shape. For extended stay such as of three months duration which is the maximum length of a tour of duty in the Siachen, vitamin supplementation is prescribed.

(d) *Taste perception:* Impinging on the various physical and metabolic complexities governing food intake and nutrition, altitude appears also to affect the human taste. Taste and aroma perception are integral parts of food acceptance and consumption and these characteristics are among those which define organoleptic features of a food. Jaded appetites can be stimulated to an extent with appetising aromas, flavours and tastes at sea level in those subjects who are able to perceive and in whom these sensory features function. Using individual substances representing respectively the first four tastes viz., glucose, salt, quinine, and citric acid among the five kinds of taste perceptions recognised (the fifth being *umami*) experiments conducted at high altitude – 3,500 m, revealed that while the taste thresholds of sugar and salt increased, those for quinine and citric acid decreased. The experiments concluded on the basis of the data that the high altitude hypoxia primarily caused such changes which may also be linked to anorexia followed by nutritional stress (Singh *et al.,* 1997 in *Compendium of Research,* p. 74). The inability to taste a bitter compound phenylthiocarbamide (PTC) at sea level in test subjects changed to PTC perception in a proportion of them. High altitude hypoxia again is said to be effecting certain hormonal changes altering the sensitivity to taste perceptions (Singh *et al.*, 1997, p. 85). PTC has been used for a long time in classical studies on population genetics to detect genetic variations in taste perception among large populations in towns and cities.

Extended stay in high altitudes would therefore have to take into consideration how best to continue to get the taste and flavour juices flowing in order to overcome the double whammy of anorexia and loss in some taste perception and increase in other tastes. The so-called craving for sweetness linked to carbohydrate requirement of the body may also be a reflection on the heightened threshold sweetness perception. Unless the food or beverage is extremely sweet, it may not be perceived as being sweet and hence not relished at all. The same argument perhaps could hold good for salt tasting or even spicy food. Inability to perceive odours, aromas, flavours and tastes to any degree or in low degrees is also symptomatic of advanced and progressive neurological condition in individuals, apart from being a genetic predisposition or the effect of high altitudes. Decrease or loss in taste perception at high altitudes therefore may have equally or more to do with intrinsic neuro-sensory changes brought about by several internal and external factors than the attribution of losses of the organoleptic features of food to mere failure of technology in preventing such losses during processing and preservation.

(e) *Digestion:* A word about digestion may not be out of place here. It has already been mentioned that fat is digested with no adverse effects. Even 32.0 g per day of fat consumed at 3,800 m appears to have been utilised up to 95.5 per cent. Fat as a concentrated form of energy is advantageous in delivering energy during strenuous exercises. Intestinal absorption of food as determined by gastro-intestinal function parameters (D-xylose absorption, pentagastrin stimulation, peptic activity) appears to be unaltered. But it has been gathered from conversations with those individuals who returned from postings at high and extreme altitudes and with medical personnel who attended to such veterans that flatulence and constipation were common experiences.

One reason could be that the rations include a variety of lentils or dals as alternate choices of which certain lentils notably *chana* or Bengal gram – whole, split or in flour form and several others are popular and preferred over some other kinds. Many of these are known to cause flatulence in general; some individuals are far more susceptible than others to abdominal discomfort after a meal containing certain of these lentils and preparations containing them, and however well cooked or prepared, there may be some individuals if not all, who are affected by these foods. Individual differences may exist though, in the extent to which they suffer from flatulence. To prevent flatulence due to such lentils, alternate items are suggested in the rations themselves. Units are free to select any of the alternatives.

Another reason could be that the troops' tinned rations, particularly the tinned meats, specifically the curries, are highly spiced with chilies, pepper, coriander, cumin, *garam masalas* and condiments like ginger and garlic. By themselves and in judicious combinations, these spices elevate even a simple common food to gastronomic heights. But the tinned ration items are found to be heavily spiced beyond normal limits. The purpose behind this practice is said to be firstly that the troops prefer it to be so and secondly to ensure overages to compensate for losses in storage of the strength and pungency of the spices: stock must last for longer than 6 or 9 months of shelf life in storage depots. The samples examined in the author's laboratory had reached the end of the declared shelf life but still smelled and tasted powerfully spicy. There were other chemical changes of course which do not apply here.

Since fresh foods – greens, salads, vegetables and fruits etc cannot always or on a regular basis be made available to units posted in base camps at 16,000 ft and none at all to pickets farther and higher up, it is very likely that depending wholly on ration items containing only processed foods and highly spiced items could cause flatulence.

According to medical specialists, constipation occurs due to lack of fresh fruits and vegetables in the diet and severe curtailment of physical activity and movement at very high altitudes. The non-existence of amenities and the very primitive 'back-to-nature' situation on the rocky precipices make constipation a more welcome development than would be believed. If there is any enclosed space at all designated as toilet then it is actually part of the living tent. The only other way at extreme altitudes a human body can void its fluid waste and faecal matter is by way of rappelling down a cliff side and hanging by a tethered rope. It would be understandable if a person is reluctant to do this everyday and may mentally switch off the prospect of facing this ordeal which won't help the situation. Many efforts are being made to develop portable or installable human waste collection and management mechanisms based on microbial consortia and specially designed digesters which can digest organic matter at very low temperatures. Until a suitable system is put in place for every picket post up on the icy peaks – a bleak proposition at best, troubles of this nature will continue.

Gastro intestinal micro flora plays an important role in intestinal functions. It is not known whether there are any changes in the intestinal micro flora occurring during residence at such high altitudes, leading to flatulence and other associated discomforts. A more physical phenomenon of expansion of gases in air spaces in the body under hypobaric conditions of high altitude could also be considered in the etiology of flatulence though direct evidence does not exist. Meanwhile the troops are pleased to attribute all their woes directly to the tinned rations/processed foods provided. The actual reasons may lie somewhere amidst all these facts, beliefs and conjectures.

Management, Therapy and Prophylaxis of Altitude Induced Conditions

Sustained research by DRDO scientists between the 1960s and 2000 (in DIPAS) on high altitude maladies and sickness has produced devices like the HAPO bag. This is a single man portable hyperbaric chamber used as a means of providing on-the-spot first aid to manage the high altitude pulmonary oedema till an airlift to a field hospital can be arranged. HAPO patients have benefited by this device during the Kargil war in 1999. Substances like nitric oxide (a mixture of 15 ppm nitric oxide and 50 per cent oxygen) have been developed and tested for the therapy of HAPO once the patient arrives at the field hospital situated at 3,500 m. There are other products in the offing for managing severe frostbite in the form of creams and decoctions for topical applications.

Mortality in troops due to high altitude stresses is said to be drastically reduced as a result of understanding and dealing with then. Living and functioning at high altitudes, we now realise, is an extreme stress situation. In the 1962 India-China border conflict and before high altitude physiology was understood and medical management mechanisms were developed to cope with operations in snow bound high altitude locations, causalities due to the extreme physical conditions were very high. At the start of the Siachen hostilities in 1984, a lot was yet to be learned – about physiology, psychology, medicine and the nutritional needs and appropriate foods and beverages needed in the stress environment.

Aids for adaptation: Adaptation and acclimatisation are essential to high altitude living and functioning. To help soldiers acclimatise, certain food supplements have been recommended by DRDO scientists. These supplements, called *adaptagens,* are prepared with various herbs and are known as Composite Indian Herbal Preparations or CHIP and *Panax ginseng.* Adaptagen is a chemical intervention to support the body's resources of adaptation like increased energy release and biosynthesis of nucleic acid and proteins. Both CHIP and ginseng are reported to reduce stress levels, increase oxygen saturation and facilitate fat utilisation (Srivastava *et al.,* 1993, Selvamurthy and Singh, 2003a, Singh *et al.*, 1999, *DRDO-Life Sciences Technical Literature*, 2005).

Adaptagens are infusions and extracts of roots of several medicinal plants (used in Ayurveda and probably long before that) and are orally administered. To make them more palatable and acceptable they are also incorporated into the juice of the yellow berry Seabuckthorn *Hypophae* spp.

A wild fruit borne on thorny shrubs (Fig. 9.3) growing abundantly in the high altitudes at Leh, Nubra valley and other regions, the Seabuckthorn berries are bright yellow in colour and taste extremely sour. The *Hypophae* plant occurs in four species and 9 subspecies and is a very rich source of vitamins A, B1, B2, C, E and K and many other antioxidants. It purportedly possesses other unique characteristics like anti-cold, anti-ageing and radiation protection and wound healing

Fig. 9.3: Seabuckthorn berries in the wild in altitudes higher than Leh

properties. Three of its species are found in India and extensive research has been conducted on this wonder fruit (DRDO Symposium, 2004). The juice does not freeze at sub-zero temperatures which is of great advantage in extreme cold and low temperature conditions. Stress busters like the drink made from Seabuckthorn and the adaptagenic beverage formulations such as CHIP would be a boon to the soldiers who must battle the fearful elements and the human enemy and insurgency threats simultaneously.

Clearly much time, effort and resources have been apportioned to studying high altitude problems, understanding the underlying phenomena and finding solutions and mechanisms for their amelioration. Devising a suitable nutrition package and food supplements among other things has played its role in sustaining the Indian troops at high altitudes.

Not only did several DRDO laboratories contribute to this effort, but the food and other industries have made their contributions by manufacturing the required products as per the prescribed specifications for quality and performance.

There are many diseases of high altitude such as Chronic Mountain Sickness (CMS) (Monge and Monge, 1966) that need to be addressed and understood; there are demographic and genetic influences bearing upon the lowlanders who sojourn at high altitudes and native highlanders who live there or move periodically from high altitude to low and back again which are also being investigated (Compendium, DIPAS Research, 2004, pp. 143–155).

With respect to nutrition in cold environments and high altitudes, many questions are being asked and addressed (Mil. Nutri. Report, USA, 1996). These pertain to the typical energy requirements for work at high altitudes and especially the precise carbohydrate intake which is essential, need for electrolytes like sodium for hard physical work, the relationship between fluid intake and food intake at altitudes, and the role of specific micronutrients such as vit C, Zn, Fe, Cu for enhancing performance (so far only tyrosine seems to be a candidate). Future research is definitely indicated to make sure that any rations that are specially developed for high altitudes will fully meet nutritional requirements in all respects and that there is better compliance with eating so as not to lose weight and undermine performance.

Endnote

1. Halting briefly at Changla Pass situated at 17,800 ft towards the China border on day 4 of high altitude sojourn, it may be said from personal experience that even a very short but quick walk up and down a gentle slope was very taxing and caused hyperventilation and then a brief spell of dizziness and blackout. The Border Roads Organization personnel all along the ascent from 11,000 ft were engaged in road repairs and construction work which is heavy manual work. If not native highlanders themselves, they must have been adequately acclimatised to carry out this very strenuous work.

References

Grover, Robert F. and Peter Baertsch, Blood, V. In '*High Altitude, an Exploration of Human Adaptation*'. Ed. T.F. Hornbein and R.B. Schoene, Marcel Dekker Inc., New York, Basel, 2001, pp. 493–523.

Trichopoulos, A., Costacou, T., Christina, B. and Trichopoulos, D. 2003. 'Adherence to a Mediterranean diet and survival in a Greek population'. *N. Engl. J. Med.* 348: 2599–2608.

Baertsch, Peter and Robert Roach, 'Acute Mountain Sickness and High Altitude Cerebral Edema'. In '*High Altitude, An Exploration Of Human Adaptation*.' Ed T.F. Hornbein and Robert B Schoene. Marcel Dekker Inc., New York, Basel, 2001 p. 731.

High Altitude Physiology – DRDO Workshop. FRL, Leh, Ladakh. September. 7, 2006.

Brooks, G.A. and G.E. Butterfield. 'Metabolic Response of Low Landers to High Altitude Exposure – Malnutrition versus the effect of Hypoxia'. In '*Lung Biology in Health and Disease*'. Vol 161: High Altitude. Ed. Hornbein, T.F. *et al.,* 2001. pp. 569–599.

Brooks, G.A., G.E. Butterfield, R.R. Wolfe, B.M. Groves, R.S. Mazzeo, J.R. Sutton and J.T. Reeves. 1991. Increased dependence on blood glucose after acclimatization to 4300m. *J. Appl. Physiol*, 70: 919–927.

Singh, Somnath, K. Sridharan and W. Selvamurthy. 1999. Human Nutrition at High Altitude. *Nutrition Bulletin* 89, 24: 195–202.

Sridharan, K. Mukherjee, A.K. Grover, S.K., Kumria, M.M.L. Arora, B.S. and Rai, R.M. 1987. 'Assessment of nutritional status and physical work capacity of road construction workers at altitude of 2150 –2750 (m on) two different ration scales'. *Nutrition Reports International*, 35 (6): 1269 –1277.

Holman, R.T. 'A long tale: The study of essential fatty acid deficiency at the University of Minnesota'. In 'Essential fatty acids and eicosanoids", (Eds.) A. Sinclair and R. Gibson, Vol. 12, pp. 3–17. Champaign, Ill, American Oil Chemists Society, 1993.

Singh, S.B., A. Chatterjee, M. Panjnani, D.K. Yadav, W. Selvamurthy and K.N. Sharma. 2000. Effect of high altitude on sensitivity to the taste of phenylthiocarbamide. *Int. J. Biometeorol.*, 44: 20–23.

Denby, Nigel, Michelucci, T. and Pyner, D., *GL Diet Made Easy: How to Eat, Cheat and still Lose Weight.* Harper Thorsons, London 2006.

Ames, B.N., Shigenaga, M.K. and Haggen, T.M. 1993. Oxidants, Antioxidants and degenerative diseases of ageing. *Proc. Natl. Acad. Sci USA* 90: 7915–922.

Bogest, L. Jean (late), Briggs, George M. and Calloway, Doris Howes, *Nutrition and Physical Fitness*, 9th ed. W.B. Saunders Company, Philadelphia, 1973.

Brooks, G.A., Butterfield G.E., Wolfe, R.R., Groves, B.M,. Mazzeo R.S., Sutton J.R., Reeves J.T. 'Increased dependence on blood glucose after acclimatization to 4300 m'. J. *Appl. Physiol.* 1991, 70: 919–927.

Brooks, G.E. 'Maintenance of Body weight at Altitude'. In search of 500 Kcal/day. In '*Nutritional needs in cold and high altitude environment'*. National Academy Press, Washington, DC, 1996, p. 595.

Cahill, Jr C.F., T.T. Aoki, and A.A. Rossini 1979. In '*Nutrition and the Brain*' series. Volume. 3. Ed. R.J. Wurtman, Raven Press, New York, pp. 1–70.

Cleland, L.G., James, M.J., Proudman, S.M. Omega-6/Omega-3, Fatty Acids and Arthritis'. *World Rev. Nutr. Diet*, 2003, 92: 152–168.

Committee on Military Nutrition Research. Activity Report 1994–1999. Food and Nutrition Board, Institute of Medicine. Mary I. Poos, Rebecca Costello and Sydne J. Carlson-Newberry National Academic Press, Washington D.C. May 1999: Appendix F-Conclusions and Recommendations from the Workshop Report on 'Nutritional Needs in Cold and High Altitude Environments'. March 1996, pp. 143–158.

Compendium of Research Publications of DIPAS on High Altitude, 1960–2004'. p. 85. Defence Institute of Physiology and Allied Sciences. DRDO, Ministry of Defence, Lucknow Road, Delhi, pp. 143–155.

Consolazio, C.F., L.O. Matoush, H.L. Johnson, T.A. Daws. 1968. 'Protein and water balances of young adults during prolonged exposure to high altitude (4300m)'. *Am. J. Clin. Nutr.*; 21: 154–161.

Cousens, Gabriel. *Conscious Eating*. North Atlantic Books, Berkeley, California, 2000.

De Lorgeril, Michel & Salen, Patricia. Dietary Prevention of Coronary Heart Disease: Focus on Omega-6/ Omega-3 Essential Fatty Acid Balance. *World Rev Nutr. Diet.*, 2003, 92: 57–73.

Dietary guidelines for Indians. A Manual. National Institute of Nutrition (ICMR), Hyderabad, 1998, pp. 10–13; Annexure 1 pp. 65, 72.

Dranov, Paula 2005. 'Follow your nose'. *Readers Digest*, June, pp. 133–137.

DRDO Life Science Laboratories Contribution to Troops, Technical literature, Directorate of Life Sciences, DRDO, New Delhi, 2005.

Dubnov, G., Berry, E.M. Omega-6/Omega-3 Fatty acid ratio: The Israeli paradox. *World Rev. Nutra. Diet*, 2003, 92: 81–01.

Eaton, S.B., Konner M. Palaeolithic Nutrition: A consideration of its nature and current implications. 1985, *N. Eng. J. Med*, 312: 283–289.

Gibney, Michael J., Macdonald, I.A. and Roche, H.M. (ed). *Nutrition and Metabolism*. Blackwell Science Publishing, Oxford, UK, 2003.

Gopalan C. *Diet Atlas of India*. National Institute of Nutrition, (ICMR) Hyderabad, 2000, pp. 28–40.

Gopalan C., Rama Sastri, B.V. and Balasubramaniam, S.C. *Nutritive value of Indian Foods*. National Institute of Nutrition (ICMR), Hyderabad, 1971.

Halliwell, B. Gutteridge, J.M.C., and Cross,C.E. 1992. 'Free radicals, antioxidants and human disease; where are we?' *J. lab. Clin. Med.* 119: 598–620.

Hammer, C.T. and Wills, E.D. 'The Role of lipid compounds of the diet in the regulation of the fatty acid composition of rat liver endoplasmic reticulum and lipid per oxidation'. *Biochem J.* 174: 584–593, 1978.

Harish, R., Divakar, S., Srivastava, A. and Shivanandappa, T. 2005, 'Isolation of antioxidant compounds from the methanolic extract of the roots of *Decalepis hamiltonii*'. *J. Agric. Food Chem.* 53: 7709–7714.

Heath, D. and David Reid Williams. *High Altitude Medicine and Pathology*. Butterworths and (Co Publishers) Ltd, London, Boston, 1989, pp. 8–15.

Heath, Donald and Williams, David Reid. *Man at High Altitude.* 2nd Ed, Churchill–Livingstone, Edinburgh, London, New York, 1981, pp. 4–6.

Hornbein Thomas F. and Robert D. Schoene, (Editors) 'Lung Biology in Health and Disease'. Vol. 161: High Altitude An Exploration of Human Adaptation. Marcel Dekker, New York, Basel, 2001, pp. 4–21, 44–53, 840–841.

Jing X. Kang. 'The importance of Omega-6/Omega-3 Fatty Acid Ratio in cell function'. *World Rev. Nutr. Diet*, 2003, 92: 23–36.

Kuhnlein, Harriet V. and Receveur, Oliver. 1996. 'Dietary change and traditional food systems of indigenous people'. *Ann. Rev. Nutr*. 16: 417–442.

Kumar, S. Ghosh, K. and Das, K.C. 1989. 'Serum B_{12} levels in Indian populations: An evaluation of 3 essay methods'. *Med. Hal. Sci.* 13: 1327–1333.

McCarrison, R. 1922. 'Faulty food in relation to gastro intestinal disorder'. *J. Amer. Med.Association*, 78:1.

Military Nutrition Research, Annual Report September 30, 1982–Sept 29, 1983. National Academy Press Washington DC, 1983. Appendix E: Energy and water requirements under considerations pertinent to Military Operations: A Bibliography of Abstracts, pp. 50, 82–85.

Monge, M. Carlos and C. Carlos Monge. *High Altitude Diseases – Mechanism and Management*. Charles C Thomas Publishers, Springfield, Ill. USA, 1966, p. 9.

Orr, J.B. and Gilkes, J.L. 1931, 'Studies on nutrition: The physique and health of two African tribes', British Med. Res. Council, Special Report no 155.

Pella, Daniel, Dubnov, Singh, R.B., Sharma, R., Berry, E.M., Manor, Orly. 'Effects of an Indo – Mediterranean Diet on the Omega-6/Omega-3 Ratio in patients at High Risk of Coronary Artery Disease: The Indian Paradox'. *World Rev. Nutr. Diet*, 2003, 92: 74–80.

Prevention of Food Adulteration Act, 1954; 1991. Directorate General of Health Services, Government of India.

Ravishankar, H.N., Bodlupalli, Sekhar S., Gaikwad, A.S., and Ramasarma, T. Survival of rats under cold stress depends on dietary fat. *Environmental & Nutritional Interactions* 3: 257–265, 1999.

Roe, D.A. *A Plague of Corn, the Social History of Pellagra Ithaca*, Cornell University Press, 1973.

Seabuckthorn: A Resource for Environment, Health and Economy. Seminar. Directorate of Life Sciences, DRDO. Held at INMAS, New Delhi, March 12–13, 2004.

Selvamurthy, W. and Somnath Singh. 2003a. 'Nutritional Requirements for Human Adaptation in Extreme Environments'. Proc. Indian National Sci. Acad., B 69 No. 4: 485–506,

Selvamurthy, W. and Somnath Singh. 2003b. High Altitude Physiology and Scientific designing of foods and beverages. In 'Symposium on Food Supply Systems for Special needs'. Technical Abstracts & Souvenir, p. 86. 5th International Food Convention, IFCON. 2003, 5–8 Dec 2003, Mysore, India.

Simopoulos, A.P., 'Importance of the Ratio of Omega-6/Omega-3 essential Fatty Acids: Evolutionary Aspects'. *World Rev. Nutr. Diet*, Basel, Karger, 2003 92: 1–22.

Simopoulos, A.P. and Bhat, R.V. 'Street Foods'. *World Rev. Nutr. Diets*. vol 8. Karger, Basel, 2002.

Singh, R.B, Dubnov, G., Niaz, M.A. Saraswathi, Ghosh, Singh, R., Rastogi, S.S., Manor, O., Pella, D., Berry, E.M. 'Effect of an Indo – Mediterranean diet on progression of Coronary artery disease in high risk patients (Indo Mediterranean Diet Heart Study): A randomized single – blind trial'. *Lancet*, 2002, 360: 1455–1461.

Singh, S.B., A. Sharma, D.K. Yadav, S.S. Verma, D.N. Srivastava, K.N. Sharma, and W. Selvamurthy. 1997. 'High Altitude effects on human taste integrity and hedonics'. *Aviat. Space Environ. Med.* 68: 1123–1128.

Singh, Somnath 1997. In 'Compendium of Research Publications of DIPAS on 'High Altitude 1960–2004'. pp. 74–85. Defence Institute of Physiology and Allied Sciences.

Speakman, John R. 2003a. Obesity part I. 'The greatest health threat facing mankind', *Biologist*, 50(1): 11–14.

Speakman, John R. 2003b. Obesity part II. 'The biology of body weight regulation'. *Biologist*, 50(1): 69–74.

Speakman, John R. 2003c. Obesity part III. 'Failed solution and new ideas'. *Biologist*, 50(3): 120–125.

Sridharan, K. and. Rai, R.M. 1984. 'Nutritional Aspects of High Altitude and Snow bound areas'. *Def. Sci. J.* 34(4): 429–441.

Sridharan, K. Ranganathan, S., Mukherjee, A.K., Kumria, M.L., and Praveen Vats. 2004. Vitamin Status of High altitude (3660) Acclimatized Human Subjects During Consumption of Tinned Rations. *Wilderness and Environmental Medicine* 15: 95–101.

Sridharan., K., J. Sengupta, K.B. Patil and K.K. Srivastava (1995). Nutrition at High Altitude In 'Biology of Highlanders'. (Eds.) A.K. Kapoor and Satwant Kapoor. Vinod publishers, Jammu, 1995, pp. 219–242.

Srivastava, K.K. et al. Stay in High Mountains and Panax Ginseng, 1993. A Report, Defence Institute of Physiology and Allied Sciences, DRDO, Ministry of Defence. New Delhi.

Swaminathan, M., Kantha, Joseph, Narayana, Rao M., Chandiramani, S.V., Subramanyam, Lalitha and Indira, K. 'Balanced diets and Nutritive value of Common Recipes'. Central Food Technological Research Institute, (CSIR) Mysore, 1981.

Tomohito, Hamazaki, Harumi, Okuyama. 'The Japan Society for Lipid Nutrition recommends to reduce the intake of linoleic acid: A review and critique of the scientific evidence'. *World Rev. Nutr. Diet*. 2003, 92: 109–132.

Trichopoulos, A. and Vasilopoulos, E. 2000 'Mediterranean diet and longevity'. *Br. J. Nutr.*, 84, Suppl. 2, S205–S209.

Trichopoulos, A. 2001 'Mediterranean diet: the past and the present'. *Nutr. Metab. Cardiovasc suplementa* 4, S1–4.

Tur, J.A., Romaguera, D. and Pons, A., 2004 Sept. Adherence to the Mediterranean dietary pattern among the population of the Balearic Islands, *British J. Clin. Nutr.* 92 (3) 341–346.

Vallotton, J. and F.A. Dubas. *Colour Atlas of Mountain Medicine* (Ed.) in collaboration with International Society for Mountain Medicine, Wolf Publishing Ltd., 1991, pp. 43.

Weisburger, J.H. 1999. 'Mechanisms of action of antioxidants as exemplified in vegetables, tomatoes and tea'. *Food Chem. Toxicol.*, 37: 943–948.

White, Pamela. 'Fatty acids in oil seeds'. pp. 209–238 in *Fatty Acids in Foods and their Health Implications* 2nd ed. Ed. Ching Kuang Chow. Marcel Dekker, New York, Basel, 2000.

Yahuda, Shlomo. 'Omega-6/Omega-3 ratio and Brain related functions'. *World Rev. Nutr. Diet*. 2003, 92: 37–56.

10

Evolution of Military Rations with Special Reference to India

"When everyone is struggling and toiling, famished with hunger, to be well fed is an art of preserving and caring for one's strength"

Sun Tzu 7.1

Food in Military Life

There are certain fundamental features in military foods and rations that differentiate them from civilian foods. The differences lie, not in the basic foodstuffs, staples and food preparations used traditionally in the diets of different people but in the manner in which the foods are defined and their portions or quantities fixed as daily requirements for work performance. These are based on scientifically determined guidelines for calorie content and nutrition profiles of various food items. It is made mandatory for the authorities to provide the daily entitlements for the personnel serving in the Armed Forces. For civilians, though similarly determined guidelines exist for good health and nutrition, these are in the nature of recommendations. Beyond this, there is no onus on anyone (the government or employer) to provide a civilian with either the recommended quantity of food or compensate in cash the cost of the food under the terms of employment. If the employer chooses to provide any food at all it is mostly in a subsidised form but never free.

Living in Barracks: Traditionally the men in arms have been housed in camps and cantonments separate from civilians in the belief that their interaction must be kept to the minimum for the soldiers to be effective in their job. All amenities and facilities were therefore provided to them within the confines of their barracks. Some of the best maintained premises can be found within the armed forces installations anywhere in the world. Every defense owned property and particularly military installations in India present a landscape of well laid out gardens, roads, buildings, internal amenities, efficient services, well provisioned and reasonably good kitchens and elegant mess halls and lounges (for the officers), sports for physical fitness, recreation facilities and other entertainments all enveloped in an aura of shining cleanliness, diligence, discipline and smartly attired people. They treat themselves well, take pride in their surroundings, and maintain them well because it is where they spend a good part of their working life when not engaged in field duties and combat. The Commandant has the absolute authority over a garrison. They are very protective of their rights and will not suffer any intrusion; civilians are allowed only by invitation or permission. The paramilitary forces are not fortunate in this respect, except superficially, in that they also have their working premises well laid out and maintained.

The men in arms are put through vigorous physical, educational and skill acquisition training from a young age. It is physically exhaustive, mentally demanding and challenging work which is very strenuous. They must also be combat ready in body and mind and by training. The young bodies (some of them are quite young and still growing) and minds require adequate and appropriate kind of food as nourishment, growth and development. It is best achieved in a structured way by defining the quantum of intake and ensuring proper access to food services. A central food service can only operate if the quantity of food per person per day is known and defined so that the right amount of the right kind of food is available at every meal. The food rations aim to do just that. Living together, training together, working together and eating together have unique advantages. It provides not only training of uniform quality but also helps to build a competitive spirit through shared activities, forming high morale and discipline and better skills acquisition and bonding and a special kind of camaraderie.

Having said that it must also be realised that military installations are scattered in different parts of the country – in urban areas, near cities, coastal ports, on islands, on mountains and in jungles, but also in places which are not easily accessible and sometimes in a foreign country. Since, irrespective of where they are, their foods must be made available to them and their only provider is their own military establishment, a unified system has been evolved which contains – based on scientific principles of how much food a man (or woman) should consume to keep healthy and fit to discharge all duties that he (or she) is called upon to do – a list of essential and recommended foods determine their appropriate quantities. These are fresh hot meals, prepared everyday.

The system of procurement, transportation and distribution of the various food items, cooked by trained people in proper kitchens will be described in Chapter 12. All together, the time span from purchase to actual use could be as long as six to nine months or more. During this entire period, the foodstuff must remain unaffected by weather conditions, changing temperatures, environment, handling, transportation and further storage in storage depots all over the country. All military stores and supplies therefore must be treated and packaged in such a manner so as to give them the essential shelf life of six to nine months and preferably much more.

For civilian consumers, fresh supplies are generally available for ready purchase (except under extenuating circumstances) and there is a rapid turnover of stock in the shops. No food product generally adorns a shelf for more than one to two months. The packaging provided for most 'rapid turnover goods' provides a shelf life of a maximum of three months and protection against moisture and infestation during this period.

The nature of military work is such that the personnel are deployed for different types of operational duties as part of large and small units, as detachments and as individuals. Fresh hot meals using bulk ingredients cannot be prepared every time the individuals or contingents are mobilised. There are different systems of feeding 'in transit' when the men are sent off on special assignments out of their units and are likely to be away for various lengths of time. And when they are in combat, they are expected to be independent of the supply lines and re-supply zones for a period and are equipped to be self sufficient for the duration which may be as brief as one day or as long as several days. At these times, they must carry on their shoulders or in their vehicles all the paraphernalia required for the task, for combat and for their own life support. The foods then come in conveniently packed form, generally of the processed variety, ready to eat or almost ready to eat. In this form they are known as 'operational rations' including 'Combat-type rations'. Their personal gear and subsistence must take into account weather and climatic conditions, terrain and the temperature in the region of deployment or action and the foods they carry must be appropriate for those conditions in terms of calorie, content, quantity, packaging and convenience.

In all the world's armies, fresh, operational/combat rations are used depending on the circumstances. While the former is entirely based on the national dietary habits, the latter two utilise the foods in the diet and convert them into more readily usable form depending on the level of innovation, science and technology and the industrial base in each country. Provisioning and supply of one or all types of foods is also dependent upon the logistics planning and preparedness for all eventualities. There are thus two main types of rations – the normal rations and the operational rations (and within the operational type there are many kinds). Normal rations comprise of a variety of basic foodstuffs and ingredients commonly used in the national diet. Operational rations originate from these foods but which have been tailored to serve operational purposes. The quantity and quality of food consumed provide energy calories for work and other nutrients to keep the body healthy and fit. Therefore, it is essential that adequate amounts of both be present in the food.

Energy/Calorie Intake

Exercising moderately or vigorously, doing daily work of an active nature causes energy expenditure. Different activities cause one to expend energy to different extents. Men and women doing different levels of work will need to replenish their expended energy by consuming foods with different calorific content. For Indian men and women, the Indian Council of Medical Research has recommended various levels of calorie intake commensurate with the nature of their work. This aspect has been discussed in Chapter 9.

On the same concept rests the recommended food and calorie intake of soldiers. By all measures, the personnel of the Armed Forces carry out physically demanding and strenuous tasks as a matter of routine, when deployed for operations. Their field of operations could well be deserts, tropical jungles, mountainous terrains or at high altitudes, anywhere between 9,000 to 22,000 ft above sea level, under the most adverse climate conditions which prevail in summer, tropical monsoons or blizzards and snow of very cold high altitudes.

Military jobs: Jobs involve marching, hauling personal gear, artillery, weapons, supplies, digging, trench making, road and bridge building, short range or long range patrolling, manning the weapons, maintaining communication lines etc. When engaged in actual combat, they go without rest or relief or even a reasonable halt for food and drink for days together. All that they can do is perhaps to snatch a moment to take a bite from their ready to eat rations.

The men on the seas and members of the navy are better placed in terms of their surroundings and access to food. Their daily routine engages them in physical work of different kinds – on deck and in engine rooms. Those serving in submarines are under a special kind of stress. People in the Air Force work under yet another kind of circumstance – long hard hours on aircraft maintenance and servicing, keeping the planes in flight readiness is one thing and then there's flying with skill and alertness in reconnoitering sorties, supply sorties and during fighter and bombing sorties. All these tasks are not to be taken lightly.

Physical strength, agility and stamina, technical skills and mental alertness, swift reaction to the unfolding and ever changing circumstances are some of the qualities of men in arms. Their daily expenditure of energy in the process of their duty is likewise high, substantially higher than what is recorded for an average worker. To compensate for this energy spent, their food intake is also recommended to be at a level higher than for average work.

Work dependent energy and food needs: The officers of the Armed forces in all the three Services – Army, Navy and Air Force combine both moderate and heavy work in the course of their duties and perform mentally more challenging work as compared to the jawans, sailors and airmen whose duties require them to perform intense, physically demanding tasks which may be called heavy work. The energy to perform these tasks must be wholly derived from the foods they consume. To supply energy through foods to the physically active men and women engaged in moderate to heavy work to the extent of 2,875–3,800 Kcals/day per man and 2,225 to 2,924 Kcal/day per woman, and keeping in view that a balanced diet is essential, the ration entitlements and ration scales have been determined by using portion size recommendations as discussed previously.

In the annual report from the Military Nutrition Research, National Research Council, Washington (1983, p. 50,) the findings of an earlier work by Pandolf, Giovanni and Goldman (1977) on energy expenditures are explained. These authors examined energy conversion factors in their experimental study with six men walking with different loads and at different speeds. In resting or sleeping, the energy turnover was estimated to be about 1.1 $Kcal{\cdot}min^{-1}$ or 77 w. In the intense exercise mode, it was 15 $Kcal{\cdot}min^{-1}$ or 1,046 w.

Energy expended in military work: Pandolf *et al.* also mentioned (1977, p. 86) various factors which affected energy turnover or exchange. Their list enumerated various physical, biological, emotional and environmental factors such as age, sex, body weight, body composition, body size (surface area), resting metabolism, fitness, muscular strength, movement efficiency, skill, emotional stress/fear, environmental factors like temperature, humidity, radiant heat, wind velocity, precipitation (rain, hail, snow) and terrain – hard surface, turf, mud, sand, gravel, rocks, mountains, snow, ice, low brush or high grass, jungle; and other factors such as acclimatisation, clothing and footwear, load carrying (weight, configuration, body attachment) task efficiency, vehicular transport, work/rest cycles.

What type of work can be classified as light, moderate and heavy? It has been shown by Pandolf and co-workers in the same article that in carrying out representative tasks, even simple ones such as sleeping or reclining in an 8 hr period, a man expends some 540 Kcal while a woman expends 440 Kcal of energy. A man performing very light work over 12 hrs (sitting, standing, painting, car/truck driving, lab work, typing, playing musical instruments, equipment cleaning and maintenance, expends 1,300 Kcal while a woman expends 900 Kcal). During 3 hrs of light work (walking on land, at 2–3 mph, garage work, electrical, carpentry, cook, mess hall helper 600 Kcal are expended (woman 450 Kcal). In moderate work lasting 5 hrs such as walking 3.5 to 4 mph, walking in loose sand or deep snow, loading and stacking rations, scrubbing floors, some 1,200 Kcal of energy are used by a man (960 Kcal by woman). Two hours of heavy work like walking with loads uphill, forced marches, work with trenching tools, dragging sleds or sustained firing of artillery pieces utilises 1,200 Kcal of energy per man (960 per woman). The rates of energy expended in each of these categories of work slowly increased from about 1–1.2 Kcal/minute in sleeping to 7.5 to 12 Kcal/min during heavy work.

There is a history of ration development associated with each country. The wars in the western world engaged hundreds of thousands of troops frequently and for long periods, thus necessitating the planning for feeding the large numbers. This perforce required that some sort of ration quantum be determined so as to enable the planners to prepare estimates and make arrangements for procuring or commandeering the required quantities of foodstuffs in strategically selected spots. The cavalry being an important wing of an army and pack animals being the sole carriers of goods, weapons, equipment and armaments before mechanised transports came along, feed, fodder and water for all the animals had to be found and provided for on the same footing as food (and liquor) for the soldiers.

The brief descriptions of wars and food logistics from earlier times to Europe during sixteenth to nineteenth centuries (see Chapters 6 and 14 for details) provide some understanding of the type of arrangements that existed for provisioning and the amount of food the Imperial, Continental and the British armies were given, though not as free issue. When the troops marched, even if most of the time their food was purchased with salary money paid enroute, it was purchased from traders and suttlers who accompanied the moving armies or from the requisitioned stores of the allies on the way. Much later, supplies were commandeered from the territories of allies on promissory notes signed by the king or the field commanders.

The purpose of defining a ration in that period definitely served to provide an estimate to those in charge of war, the officers in charge of logistics and the generals in the field of the quantum of food that would have to be found for the men and the animals in the camp and in combat.

Rations and Ration Scales

Before this discussion goes any further, it is necessary to define what exactly is meant by a 'ration' and 'ration scale', the terminologies by which all military food and quantities are defined. In the language of the armed forces the world over, rations are the food provided for the subsistence of one man (or woman) for one day. A ration scale is the nutritionally complete, or at least adequate, food necessary for one person to subsist for one day and consists of a tabulated list depicting the quantities of the various food stuffs and commodities comprising a ration. Each ration scale (and there are many types depending on the territory and the type of military operations) defines the legal entitlement of food and ensures nutritional adequacy within a known and procurable range of commodities (Service Ration Scales, Australia, 1962) and authorises issue of specific quantities of various foodstuffs for the feeding of each person. It also authorises 'alternatives' which are not only 'stand-in' foods but serve to add variety in daily eating. These are known as Service Ration Scales or SRS.

Basic ration scales: The demystification of military rations starts here. It has been shown in Chapter 9 by way of portion sizes in the dietary guidelines for Indians that a sedentary man's grain recommendation is 400–420 g rice/wheat where as for a man hard at work it is 650–690g. In the pre World War II rations for Indian troops as will be shown later, the quantity of wheat/rice was 24 oz or 720 g. In ancient India, Kautilya recommended that one Arya male was entitled to one *prastha* of grain. During the World War II period, Britain imposed civil rationing in India keeping in mind that a minimum quantity of staple food in the form of wheat/rice was essential for one person. Therefore there is no mystery or secrecy in looking at the military rations in modern India. Apportioning of various foods has been carried out on well established and understood scientific principles of nutrition and energy metabolism.

Using such guidelines, every ration is accompanied by its scale and the 'alternatives', which are also known as substitutes or 'in lieu of' items. These comprise both grocery type items to be cooked, and processed and semi-processed products (tinned or otherwise packaged) included as part of standard rations -- both for variety and for when a particular item is not available or is in short supply.

In the early history of rations, there was no great emphasis on nutrition or balanced food intake or the right kind of foods. Food was just something to fill the stomach with and it consisted mostly of bread or grains and meat and fat and a few condiments like salt and vinegar, alcohol to raise the spirits and morale, though this last effect could be debated. From time immemorial in Europe and in those nations springing from European stock, similar customs followed. India was no exception and neither during the Mughal times nor during the British was there any effort or intent to provide wholesome rations to the soldiers until the twentieth century.

The life, pay and allowances of sepoys in the East India Company and around the time of the late 1850s (see Chapter 6) reveal the nature of care given (rather not given) to the men. The health and the resilience of the native sepoys in fact seemed to be a little better than the English troops recovering from war injuries or other illnesses because it was seen that the diet of the sepoys naturally was varied and therefore more balanced than the food consumed by the English men. Throughout medieval history, we find that the soldiers coped with poor food or no food or improperly proportioned food. Providing food *per se* in the form of bread and meat and fat for cooking and perhaps wine or vinegar was the maximum that the planners and field commanders could think of and arrange for. There was neither the understanding of the necessity for other fresh foods nor the effort to find them. It was the fate of the common soldiers in Europe, America, and India too. They fended for themselves much of the time.

The earliest descriptions of rations that have been found belonged to the Roman and Kautilya's period. After the quite chaotic and barbaric dark ages in Europe and the incessant invasions in the medieval period from the west into India, and the continuous wars in China, the soldiers everywhere had no reason to be happy when they went to war. They were allowed to loot and plunder and they did that for food just as much as they did it for war booty and riches. Colonial times in America and India were the same. America was beginning to look at soldiers' food needs when it declared independence in an attempt to bring improvements. Information in English language relevant to the developments and progress in military rations exists for only some countries and which may well be outdated by now. Nevertheless some attempt has been made to find data on military rations for the Commonwealth countries, the United States of America, countries in Europe and Southeast Asia.

Indian soldiers, recruited at first to guard the warehouses and properties of the East India Company, fought many wars on its behalf. As mentioned earlier the native sepoys ate very much their own food using basic foodstuffs, which were purchased. Only in the twentieth century was there an effort to provide partial rations of some sort. Not having had rations on the lines that we understand now, the native Indian soldiers under the British were either paid a small sum towards food or issued rations like tinned meat, biscuits etc. To appreciate the evolution of rations in the post independence Indian context, it becomes necessary to review what the British rations were in the immediate past wars and how the inputs of science and technology helped develop foods and systems needed by the Indian army, navy and air force. The beginnings of military rations of both India and Pakistan are irrevocably linked and have emerged from the British times.

Rations in the Sepoy Army

In a meal, protein, fat and carbohydrates form the major nutrients, carbohydrates providing the maximum quantity, bulk and energy calories. An Indian meal consists of varied items prepared from rice, pulses, vegetables, clarified butter (ghee) or oil and meat, fish, poultry and eggs for those who will eat such fare. In the fixed rations allotted for Europeans, only meat and rice had been provided. One has to assume that there were seasonal vegetables and fruits included in the diet and that adequate amount of salt, spices and condiments were provided to make an acceptable meal. Salt is the only condiment mentioned but again one assumes (from another context) that Europeans had begun to get used to the various spices in culinary preparation and may have included a variety of spices in their own rations, although nowhere an actual reference to this effect has been found except in case of weekly dinner menus for gentlemen.

By this means each man was entitled to buy 1½ lb of beef or 1/8 of a sheep, ½ measure of rice, 2 drams of liquor, 5 billets of firewood and 1/16 measure of salt, the specific value or weight for salt and rice not having been further clarified (Wilson, 1882, Vol. 2, p. 345). The pay and allowances of sergeants, corporals, trumpeters, drummers, fifers and privates were increased by 3 d., 2½ d. and 2 d. in March in accordance with the terms of a Royal Warrant published in England on 5 July 1797.

The gentlemen and naturally officers ate much better than the men in the non commissioned and lower ranks.

Food and energy content of the rations: Rice and beef or mutton being the main ration items, energy and nutrients of the portions allotted can be ascertained. There was no mention of wheat or wheat flour for baking bread or of any pulses or vegetables. Only rice and meat were prominent because the rations mentioned were for the Madras Army.

(a) Rice measure: The Industrial Revolution not having yet visited British India in the late 1700s, there was no power milling. Paddy and all other grains were milled by traditional *chakkis* and by hand pounding. Rice therefore was of the hand pounded kind – rich in fiber and some amount of bran retaining most of the thiamine (vitamin B1), reddish or brown in colour and a little coarse – the quality, that modern holistic health proponents say is the best form of rice. One half measure of rice was the sanctioned scale. It may mean one half seer by assumption (1 seer roughly translates to about one kilogram or a little over 2 pounds) which would measure to 1 lb or around 450 to 500 g. Just about this amount of rice or a little more per day was taken to be adequate for one Aryan male's meal from the time of *ArthaŚastra*. Even in the modern Indian Service Ration Scale, around 600–650 g of grain as wheat flour only or wheat and rice combination or inclusive of other millets are provided. The energy calories obtained from carbohydrate source amounts to around 2,400 to 2,600 Kcals, or 60 per cent of the total daily energy requirements.

(b) Meat/beef quantity: Each man's daily entitlement was 1½ lb of beef or 1/8 of a sheep. Cattle are the source for beef and depending on the breed and rearing practices the live weight could have been at least 100 kg for a medium-sized animal (if not highly emaciated). A live sheep – of the variety generally found in the south of India (Bannur sheep as an example found in and around Mysore), would weigh 19 to 20 kg.

The carcass weight of a dressed animal is 50 per cent of the live weight. Hide, horns, hooves, offal-edible and non-edible are the by products. The meat to bone ratio of raw meat is generally 2:1, where 1/3 is the bone weight and 2/3 is flesh, not counting the yellow superficial fat or adipose. Raw meat is also full of moisture – about 80 per cent and its marbled fat content is less than 5 per cent, the rest is all protein. The beef ration of 1½ lbs or 670 g (where 446.67 g is flesh and 223.33 is bone) per day looks to be a very sizeable portion. Deducting the moisture content of 357.33 g @ 80 per cent and fat 20 g @ 5 per cent, the actual protein content is 69 g. A sheep carcass (50 per cent of live weight) weighing around 10 kg when dressed gives 2/3 of the weight as meat i.e. 6.66 kg. The ration of 1/8 of a sheep could mean live weight of 2.5 kg or dressed weight of 1.25 kg. If the dressed weight is taken to be 1.25 kg, the sheep meat is certainly more than 1½ lbs of beef. This amount of difference in the daily ration for beef and mutton is not explained.

Whether the rendered fat from cooking the meat served as the cooking medium or whether extra lard, ghee and other media were included is not known. Also not mentioned are the scale for wheat flour to bake breads and other bakery products but we learn from other references that at least half a loaf of bread (baked, presumably) formed a gentleman's daily meal.

As for the energy content of these ration items, calculations reveal that from the daily rice and beef/meat rations alone, a soldier would derive 2,950 to 3,150 Kcals of energy. In the current Indian SRS, the meat entitlement for non-vegetarian personnel is 110 g inclusive of bone. This is nearly 1/6 of what a European soldier was entitled to in the East India Company. From the fat calories @ 9 Kcal per gram and protein calories @ 4 Kcal per gram, the 670 g of beef per day provided 556 Kcal of energy.

On the face of it, the rations, though adequate in energy content and rich in both carbohydrate and proteins, appeared to be lacking in vegetables and fruits were bound to cause deficiencies of many vitamins and minerals. From the observations of company surgeons, the European soldiers' wounds healed much more slowly than those of the native Indian soldiers of the time. This indicates that though the natives somehow supplemented their food with fruits and vegetables, the Europeans soldiers perhaps did not because certain vitamins and minerals are important in many metabolic functions.

Royal British Army Rations of the Twentieth Century

In the British army an awareness that soldiers must be properly fed came about only after Alexis Soyer (1857) intervened to improve food utilisation and cooking practices in the Crimean war (see Chapter 14).

Under the British crown, the natives in the British Indian Army received no particular attention in this respect nor were any general guidance and nutritional advice provided to them regarding proper selection of foods in their daily diet for the sake of good nutrition and health. The British lived and ate very much in their own style while the natives followed their own inclinations and traditions. Fortuitously though, and certainly not through informed awareness or knowledge, advice or intent, and only because of their ingrained dietary habits and preferences (established in each religious and socio economic group through centuries of practice, tradition or convention) which included a good mixture of different kinds of locally available foods, the native sepoys ate (if they could afford to) reasonably well with a mixed diet of grains, fruits, vegetables, milk and milk products, meat, poultry, eggs and fish leading to a fairly good nutritive balance. The description of pay and food disbursements in East India Company and the living style of the Indian sepoys till the First War of Independence or the Sepoy Mutiny in 1857 provide glimpses of the state of food and nutrition and its manner of giving or its absence in nineteenth century India.

The British military rations appeared to have improved significantly since then and towards the time of World War I. The rations authorised for the British Expeditionary Force sent to France in 1914 and the changes seen by 1918 exemplify this fact (Table 10.1). There were no less than 20 items in the ration which must have provided about 4,000 Kcals per man per day, plus fuel, cigarettes and such items of comfort. Nutritionally, the food rations would have been quite adequate too, there were all the major and essential nutrient sources in the ration make up. This in itself may be taken as a great stride in modernising a military ration of the eighteenth and nineteenth century war time basics – of flour or hard tack, fat, salted meat, coffee and condiments and some dried vegetables.

Table 10.1: Rations for the British Expeditionary Force, World War 1, France

S. No.	*Food items*	*1914 Quantity, (lb or oz)*	*1918 Quantity, (g or oz)*
1.	Meat frozen/fish or	1¼ lb	8 oz and
2.	Meat preserved	1 lb	3 oz
3.	Bread	1¼ lb	12 oz
4.	Biscuit	3/4 lb	2⅔ oz
5.	Bacon	4 oz	3 oz
6.	Cheese	3 oz	2 oz
7.	Vegetables, fresh	8 oz	8 oz
	or	or	or
	dried	2 oz	2 oz
8.	Tea	5/8 oz	½ oz
9.	Sugar	3 oz	2½ oz
10.	Butter/margarine	–	1 oz
11.	Jam	5/8 oz	½ oz
12.	Oatmeal 3 times weekly	–	1 oz
13.	Rice	–	1 oz
14.	Salt	½ oz	¼ oz
15.	Mustard	1/20 oz	1/100 oz
16.	Pepper	1/36 oz	1/100 oz
17.	Milk, condensed	1/16 tin	1 oz
18.	Pickles, weekly	1 oz	3 oz
19.	Pork and Beans 4 × week	–	4 oz
20.	Meat-vegetable ration	2 oz	2 oz
21.	Tobacco, Cigarettes weekly	2 oz	2 oz

Source: Boileau, 1954

At the same time a comprehensive list of alternate or substitute rations had been drawn up. These consisted of fresh (12 oz) or dried (8 oz) fish one day a week in lieu of frozen preserved meat. Also in lieu of the frozen or preserved meat were baked beans and tomatoes (2 lb), or rabbits (one lb), or sausage (one lb), or frozen sausage (one lb) or sardines or other small fish (3/4 lb). For bacon (3 oz), there were alternative choices of meat and vegetable rations, or meat loaf (6 oz) or sausage (6 oz), or veal loaf (6 oz) or even butter/margarine (3 oz). For cheese (one oz) the alternatives were veal loaf (one oz), potatoes (4 oz) or potatoes (2 oz) plus flour/rice/oatmeal (one oz). A detailed account of the various war time rations can be found in the War Office's compilation relating to the Royal Army Services Corps (RASC) (Boileau, 1954, p. 434).

It is striking to find that already quite a few varieties of foods in processed form were available during this period so that it was possible to vary the diet and use different items without putting a burden on one kind or one source. All the processed items came in cans, the canning industry having established itself.

When World War II broke out in 1939, England was faced not only with the prospect of gathering her forces but also with the urgent necessity to address the question of feeding the force strength. The Indian forces alone mustered in at strength of 216,000 in 1939, which progressively increased to 223,000, then to 227,000 in 1940 and to 1.3 million by 1945. The Standard British Home Scale peacetime rations in 1939–40 consisted of a limited variety of items and therefore offered limited choices (Table 10.2).

Table 10.2: Standard Home Scale Rations – Peace Scale, 1939

S. No.	*Food item*	*Quantity, oz*
1.	Meat frozen (bone)	12
2.	Bacon	2
3.	Bread	16
4.	Butter/margarine	1½
5.	Cheese	1
6.	Jam	1
7.	Sugar	1½
8.	Tea	⅜
9.	Salt	¼

Source: Boileau, 1954

There were several types of ration scales during World War II. There were summer scales and winter scales using various commodities, and aside from the Home scale rations, there were the British Expeditionary Force 1940 rations (Table 10.3), and a Special ration E (probably signifying Emergency). When the rations came in the tinned form, there were at least 18 items to choose from (Table 10.4). The war front on the Middle Eastern sector rated different ration scales which were known as Middle East Field Service Ration for British Troops, Middle East Battle Rations for British and US troops, the Middle East Field Scale Service Rations for Indian Troops (Table 10.5), Middle East Women's Services Rations, Middle East Operational Ration Scale for Long Range Desert Groups, scales for Raiding. The Central Mediterranean Forces comprising the Allied Forces and the British had yet another set of rations. In addition there were Malta Defence Ration Scales and even Voyage Ration Scale for troops enroute from Malta to Sicily (meat, dates, jam and biscuits) and Gibraltar Siege Ration Scales.

Table 10.3: British Expeditionary Force Field Service Scale 1939–40

S. No.	*Ration item*	*Quantity, oz*
1.	Bread	16
2.	Meat, frozen	14
3.	Vegetables, fresh	8
4.	Potatoes	12
5.	Bacon	3
6.	Cheese	1
7.	Fruit, dried	4/7
8.	Tea	¾
9.	Sugar	3½
10.	Salt	¼
11.	Margarine	1½
12.	Jam	1
13.	Milk	2
14.	Pepper/mustard	1/100 each
15.	Rice or oat meal	3/7
16.	Flour	4/7
17.	Curry powder	3/8

Source: Boileau, 1954

Table 10.4: British Tinned Ration Scales, 1939–45

S. No.	Ration item	Quantity, oz
1.	Tinned ham and tongue	3/7
2.	Salmon	3/7
3.	Herring	3/7
4.	Biscuit	12
5.	Meat, preserved	12
6.	Meat extract	½
7.	Peas, dried	2
8.	Beans, dried	4
9.	Tinned tomatoes	4
10.	Tinned vegetables	4
11.	Tinned potatoes	6
12.	Preserved meat/dried vegetable or tinned potatoes, (meat and vegetable ration)	24
13.	Bacon/ham	2½
14.	Or meat loaf	2½
15.	Or beans	3
16.	Cheese	8
17.	Or chocolate (eating)	1
18.	Fruit	1

Source: Boileau, 1954

Table 10.5: Middle East Field Service Scale, Indian Troops

S. No.	Ration item	Quantity, oz
1.	Meat, fresh*	6
2.	Atta	20
3.	Ghee*	2¾
4.	Milk, tinned*	2
5.	Sugar	3
6.	Fruit, fresh	4
7.	Potato	4
8.	Vegetables, fresh	4
	Or vegetables + onions	2+2
9.	Onion	2
10.	Dal *	3
11.	Tea	1/3
12.	Salt	½
13.	Curry powder/garlic	1/12
14.	Ginger, turmeric, chilies	1/6 each
15.	Ascorbic acid tablet (vitamin C)	50 mg
16.	Herrings, tinned or salmon or sardine	6
17.	Atta	3
18.	and Rice (in lieu of Atta only)	10
19.	Oil, cooking or margarine/butter	2¾
20.	Fruit, tinned	2
	Or dried	4/7

*On medical recommendations various extras were provided such as dal, ghee, meat, fresh, milk tinned, chocolate and even tamarind

Source: Boileau, 1954

There were separate rations for the Africans and the Asians posted in East Africa and separate rations for West Africa. The list of rations designed by the British for this war includes at least some 31 ration scales (Boileau, 1954, pp. 433–519). It was an enormous exercise carried out during the war. Separate rations were called for depending on the nature and field of operations, to cater to ethnic differences in food habits, and due to shortage of all types of foods. Not every one of the participating Colonial armies got everything but only such minimum number of foods as was most available and preferred by them.

Getting ready for invasion, the Home Scales could not be employed. For the British Expeditionary Force in 1939–40, Field Service Scales had been drawn up providing a greater number of choices over the existing Home Scale rations so that the home front could gear up for procuring thousands of rations using whatever produce and products that could be garnered. Planning ahead, a wide range of tinned ration items and scales had also been made ready, for the progressive build up of reserves for operations overseas. These tinned rations and other ration stocks would be partly Compo-rations to be used not only for Northwest Europe but for either Europe or North Africa.

In 1941, a variety of stocks to last 90 days were to be held for 450,000 troops, of which the bulk rations were meant only for 25 days and Compo rations for 65 days. In a short time more bulk food (for 60 days) and 30 days Compo rations had to be provided for 660,000 troops. 24-hour emergency rations began to be stockpiled steadily from 1942 onwards for 1 million men and continued to be held at this level till July 1943.

These were known as the AFV packs whose requirement went up to 2.5 million by June 1944. And more than 2 million mess tin rations were required (Boileau, 1954, Appendix VIII B, p. 419). The tonnage of foods required for Operation Overlord's first 30 days covering D-Day to D+42 days was an estimated 210,000 tons, of which a definite 'Overlord' commitment itself was 56,000 tons.

While the British put their rations under a nomenclature that identified the troops and the particular region of their operations most of which could be classified as Operational or Combat rations, the US military rations were designated alphabetically like A, B, C, D and E where the C or combat rations under went several mutations through stages C-1 to C-3.

The purpose and aim of bringing about changes in rations and their scales is to:

- eliminate those items or products which would be impractical or uneconomical to provide on a continuous basis for large numbers,
- include such foods which are more acceptable than the ones being replaced,
- provide better nutrition,
- significantly increase handling characteristics during transportation, and enhance the shelf life of foods by choosing a variety of processed and safe items, and
- provide a great amount of convenience to the user wherever he may be operating.

Combat rations are distinguished by the inclusion of many ready to eat foods and a few which can be readily prepared with minimal facilities and fuss. Most combat packs also come equipped with some form of portable heater for heating up food and for preparing a hot beverage like tea, coffee or cocoa.

The practice of giving cash allowances to Indian troops as well as the JCOs and other ranks to buy food on their own and of their own choice continued until after the First World War.

It was during this time that elements of modern nutritional sciences were applied to assess the soldiers' diet and to evaluate the adequacy of the diet, both in quantity and quality from a nutritional standpoint. War inevitably causes food shortages and a country must make the best use of its resources. Keeping the soldiers fighting on the battle front and properly fed takes priority over all else after the essential combat requirements have been met. It is essential to know that the resources being diverted to the troops are doing what they are meant to, in this case, provide maximum benefit of energy and nutrition to keep them fit and fighting. Regarding the nutritional concepts relating to energy content, calorific value of foods and the role of vitamins in diet to avert deficiency diseases such as beriberi, scurvy etc.; the British rations of the period, to a certain extent, reflect this knowledge.

Lt. Gen. Puneeta Arora, SM, VSM, as Director General (formerly) of the Armed Forces Medical Services (DGAFMS) explained during a scientific talk (Arora, 2003) that the officer cadre of the Indian Army raised during World War II were given the option to take field scale rations provided to British or Indian troops wherever free issues were given.

After the war, in a modification to this it was decided to provide all soldiers a combination of rations and cash allowance; the cash allowance was paid directly to the units to obtain supplementary foods (Das, 1963). Disparities between the native troops and British troops however became glaringly apparent.

Free Rations: Let us examine the 'free ration' given to the Indians. The pre World War II ration scale was 24 oz of atta or rice, 3 oz of dal and 2 oz of potatoes, 2 oz of ghee, 1½ oz of sugar and ½ oz of salt supplemented by a messing allowance of 10 *annas* (@ 16 annas to a *rupee)* or about Rs. 19/- as given in Table 10.6.

The British troops, on the other hand were provided approximately 16 oz each of bread, beef, milk, 8 oz of vegetables, 10 oz of potatoes, 4 oz of onions, sufficient sugar, salt and tea. There was a supplementary allowance of 6 *annas* per day or about Rs. 11/- and 4 *annas* per month. In 1942 while the British troops were taken on a full Field Service Scale, no such scales were given to the Indians, except a paltry Rs. 3/- per month as messing allowance. Absence of vitamins and proteins in the Indian rations led to deficiency diseases. A higher monetary allowance did not help matters so it was abolished.

Table 10.6: The pre-war scales of the British and Indian troops in the Royal Indian Army

Per day rations pre war, British India Armies (Indian troops)*,**		British troops	
1. Atta	24 oz	1. Bread	16 oz
2. Rice	24 oz	2. Beef	16 oz
3. Dal	3 oz	3. Milk	16 oz
4. Potatoes	2 oz	4. Vegetables	8 oz
5. Ghee	2 oz	5. Potatoes	10 oz
6. Sugar	1½ oz	6. Onions	4 oz
7. Salt	½ oz	7. Sugar	NA
		8. Salt	Sufficient
		9. Tea	NA
* additional cash allowance 10 annas per month (16 annas = Rs.1/-)	NA (Not Available)	Additional cash allowance 6 annas per day	
** 1942, No field service scale till 1943, only Rs. 3/- per month cash			

Source: Das, 1963

The British troops in Britain until the time of World War II were drawing what were known as 'home scale rations' and were put on filed scale rations in 1939. These applied also to the British elements of the Royal Indian Army. For the native elements, modification of the service rations for field service came after four years of war in 1943. By a revision introduced the next year, a new standard basic scale of ration was given (Das, 1963, pp. 96–97). Even with all these modifications and revisions, what remained as a glaring fact was that the Indians' rations contained only about half of that authorised for the British; these differences are demonstrated in Table 10.7 (Das, 1963, p. 99).

Table 10.7: War time field service rations of the Royal Indian Forces – a comparison between the British and Indian troops

British Troops (4,500 Kcal)			*Indian Troops*		
1.	Bread	14 oz	1.	Atta and Rice	24 oz
2.	Bacon (tinned) or	2 oz	2.	Dal	4½ oz
	Eggs	2 No.	3.	Ghee	2 oz
3.	Beans or pasta dried	1 oz	4.	Milk, fresh	6 oz
4.	Curry powder/baking powder	1/3 oz	5.	Meat, fresh	2 oz or 6 oz every third day
5.	Briquetted almonds and raisins	4/7 oz	6.	Potatoes	4 oz
6.	Fruit, fresh	4 oz	7.	Vegetable, fresh	6 oz
7.	Fish (smoked) or	6/7 oz	8.	Onions	2 oz
	Eggs	2 No.	9.	Sugar or jaggery	2½ oz
8.	Marmalade/golden syrup	1 oz	10.	Salt	½ oz
9.	Margarine, unfortified or butter	1 oz	11.	Tea	1/3 oz
10.	Meat, fresh	14 oz	12.	Condiment	¾ oz
11.	Milk, tinned	2 oz		On medical recommendation only	
12.	Mustard	1/100 oz	13.	Fruit, fresh	4 oz
13.	Oat meal	1 oz	14.	Marmite	¼ oz
14.	Onions	2 oz	15.	Vitamin C tablet	25 mg (total)
15.	Oil, hydro	1½ oz			
16.	Pepper	1/100 oz			
17.	Potatoes, fresh	12 oz			
18.	Rice	1 oz			
19.	Salt	½ oz			
20.	Sugar	3½ oz			
21.	Tea	5/8 oz			
22.	Vegetables, fresh	8 oz			
23.	Flour	1 oz			
24.	Additionally, per week safety matches	2 boxes			
25.	Tobacco or	2 oz			
	Cigarettes	50			
26.	Toilet paper	35 sheets			
27.	Vitamin C tablet	1			
28.	Marmite	3/8 oz			
29.	Cocoa/tea with sugar	½ oz			
30.	Milk or	1 oz			
	Rum	20 oz			

Source: Das, 1963

Food shortages in India caused a reduction of rations for the Indians – 2 oz less of cereals and 1½ oz less of dal. In 1946, the cereal ration was further cut by 1 oz giving now a total of 21 oz. In the British ration also, there was a reduction of cereals by 2 to 4 oz, lowering their overall calorie content to 3,600 Kcal 900 less than before.

For the troops fighting in the Middle East, a slightly different set of ration scales were used as shown in Table 10.5. A significant difference in the rations from World War 1 to World War II was that staple foods such as *atta*/rice/dals and some vegetables were introduced in the later rations but still a great disparity persisted as can be seen from the foods in the British list which do not figure in the rations of the Indian troops. Only on medical recommendation were vitamin C tablets, fresh fruits or extra milk given and no marmite, tobacco or liquor or even matches. Bread or tinned meats were not the standard foods for Indians and it was necessary to provide them raw materials to prepare their own food their own way.

At this point in the British Raj, even as the Indian contingents fought in a war that was not theirs, there is no special source to confirm whether the native elements in the army reacted in any way to this disparity. However, the situation was quite different in the Royal Indian Navy (RIN). The disparity between the native and British pay, ration scales, not introducing the field scale rations until far into the war years, the general attitude of contempt and disregard towards the Indian elements, and the level of neglect shown by their own officers, the overall mistreatment of the Indian elements proved to be a source of disgruntlement and led to near mutiny among the Indian naval ratings.

Rebellion in the RIN: Trouble broke out in one ship after another from 1942 onwards, culminating in the mutiny on the ship 'Talwar' which erupted as an uprising in February 1946. In its own way, the succession of events leading to the Talwar outbreak is no less gripping than that of the Sepoy mutiny in 1857. Both stemmed from bottled up grievances pertaining to racial discrimination, inequality and insensitivity to the religious sentiments of the men. Now there was denial of access to canteens and allied Service Clubs, denial of decent treatment and edible food, denial of access to ordinary amenities and to dignity. Das, who researched the Talwar mutiny through official documents and depositions from complainants following the official hearings, comments that 'Talwar' stood for the rebellious RIN. As a colonial armed service it was built to protect the British interest, which was read as imposition of loyalty and devotion to the rulers and to their representatives on the upper decks. The Indian recruit had no identity beyond a number assigned to him upon entry into service. He was kept isolated from the civilians, every thing he did or thought or believed was scrutinised. Coercion was the rule of the times. It was altogether different for the British troops and seamen. Even those in transit and on ships were well fed as can be made out from the elaborate instructions, recipes and ration items included in the Patrol Service Cooks Instruction Manual 1943 issued by Flag officer, East Africa.

Indian Military Rations After Independence

It has been pointed out earlier that for the average Indian adult of body weight 60 Kg, the recommended energy level is 3,800 Kcal/day and for a woman 2,925 Kcal/day.

The first ration scales and menus were announced by Blackham in 1908. But the influence and application of modern nutritional science to military forces did not really begin until World War I when the energy expenditure of soldiers performing different types of activities was determined and the calorie value and composition of various foods for their energy, carbohydrates, proteins and fat contents were analysed according to Tilak and Bhadwar (1996, p. 42). These studies helped to formulate certain ration scales for the troops but at the time, knowledge in the field of vitamins was still very inadequate, causing epidemics of scurvy and beriberi in soldiers in the battle of Mesopotamia, even though the ill-effects caused by not consuming scorburates (or scorbutics) such as sauerkraut, fresh greens etc. had become well known from the experience of the Royal Navy and before that from the records maintained by Capt. Cook on his long sea voyages.

Various Considerations in Ration Formulation

The post-war, post-Independence face of the Armed Forces changed substantially, as well as its role. There were new frontiers to guard, they were spread out practically on all sides and the geography, terrain and regions of field operations expanded enormously. Climates, seasons and place access posed logistics problems. The composition of the forces also changed, showcasing the diversity and secular nature of the country. It became multi-regional, multi-religious, and multi-ethnic.

The dietary habits of the people of India are very diverse. The interests of the multi-regional composition of the Armed Forces can only be served best when all the basic foods are given for use in whichever way desired as per food habits.

The recruits at the time of entry into the military service are generally those who have experienced only their traditional foods specific to their own family and local traditions. The majority hails from rural backgrounds and therefore is only familiar with food of their own kind.

Bunking and eating together is the military way of life. It provides a chance to become familiar with others and their habits at close quarters. Mess food can be prepared with variety by mutual consent and thus the troops get to know about foods from other regions of India.

Though later rations emerged from the basic ration scale of the British times, they had limited scope and content to satisfy all. To address these issues, cognizance was taken of the fact that providing more grocery type foods from which different items could be prepared would be the obvious answer. Also, it may be noted that in 1947 the Indian food industry was not in a position to manufacture more than a very small number of processed products, none of which could be directly used as staples. And the Indian public in general was unaccustomed to processed foods.

The entrants of today have had better exposure to urban, exotic and other regional and international foods. The young folk everywhere are bold and take to new 'lifestyle' enhancing products readily and thus would readily accept variety at mealtimes but would still expect the familiar foods in their meals most of the time.

Rice versus roti: In the North Indian style, a lot of a particular combination of spices and spice pastes are used, unlike in the Southern style. Substantial amounts of carbohydrate calories are derived from *atta* (wheat flour) or rice, which are ration issues and it would take a good amount of getting used to for a southerner to eat *rotis* or *chapatis* (unleavened pan baked flat bread with wheat flour) every day in every meal. The rural folk do eat '*rotis*' and balls made of millet flour. Most army recruits from the South, East and Northeast would not have eaten '*chapatti*' except on occasion. Rice is their main meal. Potatoes are a must in the Northern food preparations but not so in the South. But amazingly we find that once in the army every new entrant adapts readily to the style of food preparation and the common messing facilities.

Although the military institution is a great leveler by drilling a wide, varied and a disparate lot into a highly unified and disciplined force, in the matter of food, giving everyone the same uniform food does not serve the purpose of unification. It probably is not advisable either in everyday practice. There would be time enough during actual combat when the exigencies of war curtail any elaborate preparation or food service. That is the time when anything edible would do to survive from one day to another and go on. But where a standing army (all wings included) is to be maintained in readiness and in fit condition, giving what the troops like most and which they would accept readily makes the best sense.

Service Rations and Manuals of Reference

In the pan-Indian face of the Armed Forces, to ensure that every one remains satisfied in the matter of food, i.e. besides giving adequate quantities, there is a standard Service Ration Scale (SRS) for officers and Other Ranks (OR), meaning the enlisted men. These rations and scales provide for certain basic foodstuffs which are usually the grocery kind so that northern, southern, western and eastern food items can be prepared. By and large the SRS consists of some 17 odd items, and barring substitutes for fresh items, very few are even semi processed and an even lesser number are fully processed. Unprocessed, raw, dry and fresh food ingredients make up the bulk of the rations. These include cereals like wheat and rice and sometimes other minor millets, dals of many varieties, milk (both are important source for proteins in vegetarian diets), eggs, meat/poultry meat, fish, fruits, vegetables, salt, sugar, spices and condiments, tea and cooking fat. Needless to say, the quantities fixed as entitlements are not only adequate for substantial meals for one day but also provide the required major and minor nutrients, antioxidants and energy recommended by military regulations for adult men and women performing physically arduous and mentally challenging tasks.

The Indian Army ration scales are contained, listed, described and catalogued in the 'Compendium of Army Instructions', Quartermaster General's (QMG) Branch, Army Headquarters. The ASC which is the main supply wing of the Supplies and Transport department in the QMG Branch also has its Reference Book of Ration issues entitled 'Scales of Rations and Supplies'.

The Indian Navy Book of Reference (INBR–14, 1997) and the Indian Navy Book of Rations Manual contain the instructions on Naval Victualing in ships and shore establishments. There is no doubt that this is sacrosanct for beginners, instructors, faculty, logistics officers and any one else who needs to learn about the system of supplies in the navy. A quick run through some of its contents reveals that it describes the victualing organisation, sources of supply of materials, method of demanding, indenting and procurement procedures, inspection of provisions, accounting of victuals, stock provisions to be maintained by ships and other establishments, scale and issue of entitled rations, extra issues, muster, payment issue of rations, packaging material, issue of Rations in Kind (RIK) to officers, stowage and preservation of provisions, survey of victualing stores, sampling victuals, messing, base victualing yard organisation, general system of governing contracts and disciplinary action against the contractors. Also described are the daily Standard Ration Scales for various categories of personnel and for various operations.

Substitute rations: An examination of the ration scales would show that there are many substitutes for most of items, and a list of those has been given under processed foods in the ASC Manual. There are definite instructions on how much of each alternate item may be given and how often.

When *atta* or rice is substituted with biscuits-service, it is because there is an existing stock which must be consumed; 540 g biscuits are given in place of 680 g *atta*/rice. It is called stock turnover. For the same purpose, some 60 g flour may be issued in place of 60 g *atta*/rice. Bread, where it is entitled, is not to exceed 230 g as part of the daily cereal ration.

There are a number of dals to select from; they can be substituted for each other so that the units may request (items in authorised list) any or all of them in different quantities, subject to the total not exceeding the quantity meant for a certain unit strength based on per head per day ration. Bengal gram flour *Besan* up to 40 g may be requisitioned as part of a ration.

Certain vegetables like *arvi* (*Colocasia* root) are not to be issued more than twice a week. When circumstances arise where the troops have to consume tinned vegetables more than 50 per cent of the time then germinated pulses must also be issued three times a week. This, as nutritionists will agree, makes ample sense in providing essential vitamins, which are lost to a considerable extent by the canning process followed by long storage. Salt, we understand, may be required in extra amounts and can be given on medical recommendations to a maximum amount of 30 g/man/day at any time of the year.

Meat (of goat/sheep) should be obtained after slaughter as per rites required in different religions. This instruction is strictly adhered to because of its sensitive nature much like the production of 'kosher' meat for those of the Jewish faith. Meat on hoof (MOH) or live animals is accepted on live weight basis and the 'out-turn' of the dressed meat yield is assessed at 2/5 of live weight. The by-product of slaughter is disposed off if such facilities exist, to the best advantage of the government and if not, these are destroyed under certification of the Commanding Officer. MOH rations are drawn as one week's quota and dressed meat is drawn as single/double/triple issue (110 g/230 g/340 g) or 2 eggs, whichever is desired in lieu of daily scale, and fish 210 g, or cheese 70 g, whichever are the allowed foods in this category.

For vegetarians, the daily ration of 220 ml of fresh milk or 90 grams of milk, tinned or 60 g of skim milk powder may also be similarly drawn once, twice or three times a week instead of drawing them on a daily basis. Rum as a substitute is given only in exceptional circumstances or when coffee/tea is not available. Ice is provided on recommendation of the force commander or by medical authorities duly approved by the commander at the rate of 37.2 kg per fighting vehicle in the armoured units.

Hygiene chemicals, some 25 of them to keep the camps clean, personal skin and lip moisturisers for use in winter and pest control substances for the general maintenance of surroundings, store houses, depots, sleeping areas are also authorised items in the Armed Forces. For water safety, there are designated chemicals for filtering, to remove taste, for sterilisation and for clarification of water. Water dispersible and powder form of DDT are very essential in carrying out the anti-malaria programme to protect field health sections, station health organisations, hospitals or units. The concentration and spraying frequencies are well established. Mosquito repellants are issued in operational areas or for those travelling through malaria prone areas as personal protective measures against mosquito vectors of malaria, filaria and other diseases spread by flies as well as against leeches. Mosquito disease control programmes in place are scrupulously implemented in cantonments and therefore personnel mosquito repellants are not for use in peace areas.

Newly established Basic Ration Scales: There are essentially two ration scales – one for the officers and another for the Other Ranks (ORs). Out of these, many other scales have emerged for special purposes and special categories. Any proposed change, either in the issue of an item, addition of a substitute, modification in the scale, passes through several rungs of evaluation, review and action. Recommendations are described in amendments to the existing scale of rations after Government approval. The Ration Scales are variously designed to provide a daily energy content (expressed as Kilocalories or Kcal or kcal) which range from 3,000 to 5,000 and contain different nutrients. When the concept of defined rations tailored to provide calories and nutrients originated in the twentieth century, it became a part of the establishment to see to it that these were provided as needed. This has been the custom since the British period where the garrison in charge or the Commissariat was given the responsibility to see that the troops had access to adequate amounts of food in the form of grains, flour, bread, meat and some form of fat (usually oils) and salt.

Ration Scales in the Army: There were common field scale rations until 1958. Separate field scales for officers were introduced for the first time in 1958 vide Army Instructions.[1]

After revision by DIPAS (Defence Institute of Physiology and Allied Sciences), this was adopted in 1972 vide another Army Instruction. But to start with, officers were not entitled to free rations in peace stations, only in field stations. It is in this way that the field ration scale was converted into Basic Ration Scale for all Indian troops (Table 10.8). Since independence these have remained essentially the same as before except for small and periodic modifications, additions and substitutions. It has taken some 40 odd years for the ration scales, which were deemed to be appropriate in the early 1960s, for the officers and ORs to be considered for review. Every official ration scale document examined till date continues to refer to the original authority of Government of India/Army order from the 1960s. However several addendums have been inserted, also by special letters of authority from time to time. But these are in the nature of suggestions for adding certain other *dals*/lentils, tinned foods as substitutes, authorising 'extras' for vegetarians and such other minor variations.

Table 10.8: The basic ration scale for peace areas – the basis of 3,760 Kcals per day per person (Figures in parenthesis are RDA given by ICMR for Indian Adult men doing hard work)

(a) Atta 600 g or rice undermilled/parboiled 400 g and atta 200 g (650)
(b) Dal 90 g (80)
(c) Cooking oil (vegetable oil/oil hydro) 70g (50)
(d) Milk fresh 230 ml (200)
(e) Sugar 90 g (55)
(f) Tea 8 g
(g) Vegetables fresh 180 g (125+100)
(h) Potatoes fresh 180 g (100)
(i) Onions fresh 60 g
(j) Fresh fruit 100 g (30)
(k) Salt 20 g
(l) Condiments 16 g
(m) Meat fresh with bones 100 g or milk fresh 190 ml for vegetarians (eggs 30 g and 30 meat, 50 g groundnuts)

Source: Tilak and Bhadwar, 1996

The calorific content derived from various ration items is shown in Table 10.9. Common to all basic ration scale are the same grocery and fresh foodstuffs described above. It may be noted that such a ration also satisfies the nutrition guidelines for adult Indians recommended by the Indian Council of Medical Research and actually closely follows the ICMR recommendations for a balanced meal providing 3,800 Kcal for a man performing hard work. Military work as described above falls into this category calling for even higher expenditure of energy. Therefore there are small differences in ration scales between the civilians and military personnel.

Table 10.9: Calorific content of the authorised ration items

S. No.	*Item*	*Authorised scale, g*	*As per Hygiene manual Kcal*	*As per ICMR Kcal*
1.	Atta/rice	600	2112.0	2047.8
2.	Milk	230	144.9	154.6
3.	Oil, hydrogenated	70	630.0	630.0
4.	Mutton – meat	100	154.4	155.4
5.	Dal	90	307.8	311.2
6.	Potato	110	81.4	106.9
7.	Onion	60	29.4	29.0
8.	Fruit, Citrus	50	34.4	34.4
9.	or Fruit non-Citrus	100	–	–
10.	Sugar	90	355.5	357.9
11.	Besan	15	54.5	55.8
12.	Vegetables, fresh	180	57.1	57.1

Using these basic rations, some 12 types of rations have been formulated (Table 10.10) There are sub categories again under Army, Navy and Air Force.

Table 10.10: Different ration types and scales in the Indian Armed Forces

1. In peace areas
2. Troops in field areas
3. Troops in high altitude – 9,000 ft and above
4. For officers – all services
5. For Indian navy and sub categories
6. For Indian air force
7. For cadets of NDA and IMA
8. Cadets for Rashtriya Indian Military College
9. For edentulous outdoor cases
10. Scales of diets for hospitalised patients
11. Special scales for officers of flying branch of Air force
12. Composite ration pack scales for operational conditions

Source: Tilak and Bhadwar, 1996

A further categorization of the SRS, INBR describes rations for all service personnel borne in the establishment of Inter Services Institutions, such as NDA, No. 1 and No. 2 Wireless Experimental Centres, Air Observation Post (AOP) Flights. The Navy, in addition uses several other ration types: SRS submariners – daily standard, MRE rations when SRS is not used, special rations to divers, landing party rations, composite pack rations, extra rations to personnel employed on survey work, rations for livestock (meat on hoof) in lieu of meat. Issue of milk to individuals employed in occupations involving risk of lead poisoning, special rations for Naval air crew when embarked on a carrier, Action Messing Pack rations, issue of extra milk to undernourished recruits, issue of extra rations to divers, emergency rations, submarines, issue of extra rations to rocket fuel handlers, diets and extras for hospitals/sickbays, special rations for Naval air crew (pre-flight meals), scale of rations for hostile and irregular forces taken prisoner by paramilitary forces, daily standard scale of rations for selected Services sportsmen. In addition, to all these there are special rations for Air Force personnel and emergency rations for pilots.

There is no uniform ration scale for all the three services though it was recommended by the office of the Director General Armed Forces Medical Services (DGAFMS). The principal differences in the scales, though minor in nature are seen in the entitlements of JCOs and ORs in respect of meat and chicken portions; the navy and air force get more of meat portion while the army gets a little more of wheat.

In the Army, while the JCOs and ORs were issued the peace scale rations as their entitlements, the officers in peace stations were not, as already mentioned. Rations and fuel scales for officers in the Northern and NEFA (war zones) provided for less *atta*/rice, bread, jam, butter, more choices of milled and processed products etc. (Table 10.11).

Table 10.11: Ration and fuel scales for officers in Northern and NEFA areas

S. No.	*Item**	*Quantity, g*	*Substitutes*	*Quantity, g*
1.	Atta/Rice	450		
2.	Dal	40	Peas, dried	40
3.	Oil hydrogenated	40		
4.	Sugar	90		
5.	Milk, fresh	250	Milk tinned or whole milk powder	100 30
6.	Meat, fresh dressed	260	MOH (and many choices)	640
7.	Vegetables, fresh	170	Tinned or curried or dry peas/beans	90 90
8.	Potatoes	110	Tinned, or other vegetables or dried	
9.	Onions	60	Spring green or dried	90 10
10.	Eggs, no	2	Vegetables or meat/fish	Various
11.	Tea	9	Coffee	28
12.	Fruit, fresh, Citrus or Fruit, fresh non Citrus	110 230	Jam/marmalade	~100
13.	Dalia and Sago/corn flour/ Ice cream powder/ custard powder	20 7	Corn flake or Semolina	30 30
14.	Butter	20	Oil hydro or tinned butter	30 20
15.	Condiments	20	Cash allowance or Vinegar, mustard, pepper, ground or cinnamon/cardamom & cloves	 140 ml 14 g 7 g
16.	Salt	20		
17.	Firewood or steam coal or Soft coke and	1400 700 900		
18.	Firewood or Charcoal for kindling matches, safety	200/400 2 boxes per wk for 45 men		

*Extra items provided over and above the scale were oil hydro (5 g), butter (14), sugar (70), whole milk powder (28), potatoes fresh (28), eggs, fresh (1) copra, dried (4), raisin's (4), pickles (15), jam (14), Rum (60) and Vitamin C tablets (300 mg) for some of which too there were substitutes like tinned milk, potatoes or other vegetables tinned or dehydrated, egg powder or tinned fish or meat, cashew nuts, tea or coffee for rum, and lemon or orange (drink) powder for vitamin 'C' (ASC Manual of Supplies).

For the ORs there was more of *atta* (680 g), of oil (80) and dal (90), no bread, jam or butter. There were special fuel scales for Dras, Kargil and Leh garrisons. The energy and nutrient content of some rations are shown in Table 10.12. The maximum energy content – 62 per cent is derived from carbohydrates (mostly cereals, sugar etc.). The food contains a good amount of proteins and fat as per the national nutritional guidelines.

Table 10.12: The energy from major nutrients in the various ration scales

S. No.	*Armed Forces*	*Total Energy* (Kcal)*	*From protein*	*From carbohydrate*	*From fat*
1.	Officers	3864	612	2028	1224
2.	JCOs/Other Ranks	4034	572	2436	1026
3.	Troops above 9,000 ft	4829	576	2984	1269
4.	Border Roads Organisation, Tradesmen and Pioneer	3528/ 3968	404/ 436	2332/ 2524	792/ 1008
5.	Submarine crew	3637	476	2036	1125
6.	Coast Guard Personnel	3740	448.4	2251	1040

*Carbohydrate – 62 per cent, Protein – 11–12 per cent, Fat – 25–28 per cent

Rations for high altitudes: Indian troops had barely sufficient opportunity to take stock of the volatile border situation soon after independence and were immediately embattled at high altitudes both in the Northwestern and Eastern Himalayan ranges. At the time of the Sino-Indian border war in 1962, rations for high altitude were formulated with two scales, one providing 5,500 Kcals for elevations of 9,000 ft to 14,000 ft (2,742 m–4265 m) and the second providing 6,500 Kcal for heights above 14,000 ft. These were the same basic items but with extras included to increase the calorie content. Both scales were empirical and adopted on an *ad hoc* basis. A study was conducted by scientists of the Defence Institute of Physiology and Allied Sciences (DIPAS) to rationalise these scales, according to the records of the Armed Forces Medical Services Nutrition Directorate, 1969. One study pertained to the *jawans* posted at 12,500 ft (3,800 m) and 15,000 ft (4,570 m) in Ladakh, Western sector and at 12,800 ft (3,900 m) in Sikkim (Eastern sector). Based on their findings a uniform scale was introduced on a trial basis for two years in 1965 vide Army Instructions.

Drawing attention to the various developments in the Indian Military rations Lt Gen. Puneeta Arora (2003) said that these ration scales recommended for *jawans* a calorific content of 4,680 Kcal at all altitudes above 9,000 ft, published vide Army Instructions 2/S/72. A review of the Officers rations for above 9,000 ft conducted about the same time showed that they were getting a higher calorie content (4,850 Kcal) than the *jawans*, although the actual consumption level was around 4,000 only. Downsizing the scale to correct this anomaly without compromising nutrition was examined in one exercise which produced a scale that delivered a more realistic energy content of 4,309 Kcals vide Army instructions SAI-3/5/72. It was only necessary to reduce the *atta*/rice component by a few grams, reduce the number of eggs and quantities of *besan* (Bengal gram flour), corn flakes and butter in a similar way.

In 1984, peace scales were abolished leaving only the field scales for both applications which according to Gen. Arora are still in force vide Army Instructions SAI 5/8/72. Efforts to evolve a common ration scale (peace scale) for the Army, Navy and Air Force conducted in 1968 brought out certain interesting facts:

- The rice to *atta* ratio for South Indians needed to be increased from the existing 2:1 (400g rice: 200g *atta*) to 3:1 (440g: 150g),

- That the potato and dal rations could be cut by 5 per cent each and that,
- In general the authorised cash allowance for condiments of Rs. 1.35 per person per day was totally inadequate for *jawans,* considering their penchant for highly spiced food. They required at least Rs. 2.25 per person on that account for a unit to be able to buy all the spices (that go into the condiments list or others not in the list) in adequate amounts.

There are some variations in rations in the three services. The Navy and Air Force personnel operate under different conditions and their nature of work is different and for this reason, even though a somewhat generalised basic ration scale exists for all the three services, these are not exactly the same as for the Army. Efforts to make a common uniform ration scale for all did not succeed.

Each Service has designated the rations by its own nomenclatures and reference numbers. For example, the Army's Basic Ration Scales for Officers in field situation carries a reference to a GOI letter dated 1988, while the Navy's Ration and Fuel Scales for Officers bears reference to an item each in the Indian Naval Book of Reference (INBR) and Navy Instructions (NI). Both are the same; the descriptions vary in places. Presumably the instructions in the Air Force Ration manual would bear yet another reference number but the SRS would be the same. Each Service has need for specific items in specified quantities to meet their own particular operational requirements. This leads to the enhancement of calories in certain rations for high stress related work or lesser calories for independent one day or short duration operations of the Special Forces. The Army provides fresh cooked meals or processed packed items as the situation dictates. The same applies in the Navy. The Air Force has little need for pack rations except as emergency foods or in supersonic aircrafts flying non-stop for 10 hours.

Ration scales in the Navy: The naval ration scales and procedures are laid down in INBR 14 or the Indian Naval Book of Rations. There are seven ration types. The ration guidelines are designated alphabetically A through N (skipping I and O which are not used at all because they could be mistaken for the numerals one and zero). The Navy Rations Instructions (1998) has classified many rations as enumerated earlier.

The Standard Ration Scales (SRS) in the Indian Navy as in the other two services consist of the basic 17–18 food items (plus some 20 odd more falling in the special category (dried and tinned stuff combined numbering some 40 items) under the category of cereals (*atta*/rice, flour/*suji* or semolina, semiyan or vermicelli or bread/biscuits) pulses (dals), meat, eggs, milk, vegetables, potatoes, fruit, cooking fat, butter, salt, spices and condiments, tea or coffee, sugar (see basic ration scales – officers). Submariners are authorised ration items such as fruit juice (liquid or powder), custard powder/cornflakes/jelly or ice cream powder, chocolate or almonds, walnuts or cashew particularly when serving in the submarines. There are many alternatives or substitute items under each category. As an example those who are vegetarians may be issued, in lieu of meat, any one of the following: milk (fresh, tinned or powdered), cheese (processed), or Nutramul or other milk beverage, oil (hydrogenated), fresh vegetable or ready to eat vegetables. For non-vegetarians there are many kinds of meats that may be provided depending on the supply position and operational requirement. Fresh MOH (live animal) is still listed as a substitute for fresh dressed mutton, or venison (it seems anachronistic and strange to retain it in view of the strict wildlife protection measures in the country), or tinned meat or fish, or eggs or chicken or tinned curried preparations. Similarly there are choices in vegetables from fresh, frozen, dehydrated to tinned in brine or in curry form. Potatoes are stand alone item separate from the other vegetables. Although in India it is considered to be one of the vegetables, it is a staple starch source in western diets and as a starchy item it contributes to the total carbohydrate content of a ration.

It is to be noted that the several substitute items for the main ration items are not issued in the exact same quantities. As an example, MOH is authorised at 640 g, in the dressed mutton form it is 260 g and in the tinned form it is 160 g. The net energy content of the officer's rations is 3,864 Kcal/day and that in men's rations is 4,034 Kcal/day.

The officers receive a higher quantity of meat ration (180 g) compared to the men and higher overall protein content (153 g) in their food as befitting those who perform more mental tasks. The medical, dental, and clothing stores scales of rations show small but significant differences based on the particular requirements.

Rations for sailors: Sailors, including boys, are given slightly different rations as shown in Table 10.13.

Table 10.13: Scale of rations for sailors (including boys)

Item	*Quantity (g)*	*Equivalents*	*Quantity*
1. Bread/*atta*/rice/ biscuits/flour/*suji*	600		
2. Oil, hydrogenated	80		
3. Sugar	70		
4. Tea		Coffee	
5. Salt, evaporated		Salt, refined	
6. Dal		Peas, dried or Gram, whole (Kabuli)	
7. Condiments		–	
8. Meat	180	Or Meat, tinned Or Fowl, live wt Or Fowl, dressed Or Fish or eggs (3 no.) or milk fresh and nutramul, or tinned milk or whole milk powder or chicken, curried; tinned, fish curried tinned or tuna chunks curried, tinned	Different amounts
9. Potatoes	110	Potatoes, dried/tinned, beans dried/peas dried/ vegetable tinned/flour/frozen vegetable/dal/sweet potatoes	
10. Vegetable, fresh	160	Peas dried/Lobia dried/Rajma/chana whole/frozen or dehydrated vegetable	
11. Onions	60	Onion spring, green or gandal or vegetable fresh	
12. Milk, tinned, sweetened	76	Milk fresh Or whole milk powder	
13. Fresh fruit, citrus	110	Fruit, tinned/ fresh fruit non citrus/ vegetable fresh/ vegetable tinned/ potatoes fresh/ frozen vegetable	

Submarine rations: The rations for officers and sailors on board submarines and those who are entitled to normal shore food are issued free rations in lieu of standard scale rations which are described in certain Navy instructions. When the submarine is at base port, the officers on board are not entitled to free rations but only when the sub is away from the base port.

The submarine crews live and work in an environment of greater hardship than a ship's crew. They are entitled to more bread, or tinned *chapatis*, or tinned *parantha/suji*/vermicelli/biscuits, oil hydro, sugar, tea, salt, condiments, dehydrated onions and special mixes of spices, more dal and a wider variety, but get fewer eggs and less potatoes; there are varieties of processed meats, Accelerated Freeze Day (AFD) meat or fish, egg powder or tinned milk, vegetables both fresh and dehydrated. They are also provided special items like chocolate or nuts, more fresh vegetables and fresh citrus fruit, jams, marmalade, pickles in addition to fruit juice and other such items.

It will have been noticed that the influence of technology is far more substantial in the Naval rations than on Army's rations. Processed foods figure largely in the breakfast, lunch or dinner menus particularly in the landing party rations and emergency rations for submariners, and to an extent in the Action messing meals. Emergency Rations for submarine personnel on board comprise fixed quantities of ready to consume items like boiled sweets or milk toffees or chocolates, fruit bar or mango flakes, refined seedless dates and raisins, cashew nuts, sweet biscuits, groundnut *chikki*, preserved sweetened milk or fruit milk, tinned butter or cheese, fruit juice, tinned milk powder or milk processed in cartons, as well as canned drinking water.

The landing party rations are special rations given to each officer and sailor in the landing party, which is on assignment or leaving the ship. The food provided is meant for 24 hours and is issued when the individual is not victualled from the ship. At such times, the 24 hr rations include tinned fruit and vegetables, or eggs, preserved meat or fish, biscuits, cheese, tinned unsweetened milk, sugar, tea, chocolate. The packs also include one hexamine cooker plus fuel tablets per party, tin opener, safety matches and water sterilizing tablets.

The landing party meals are made up of MRE items (Meals Ready to Eat) to provide breakfast, lunch and dinner and include corn flakes, meats or salami, or ham, omelet mix or egg powder, retort processed *Upma* or *Halwa*, preserved bread or *paranthas*, aseptically processed (tetrapak) fruit beverages or canned fruit juice, retort processed *pulav/biryani*, pre-cooked dehydrated vegetable curry, or retort processed *palak paneer* or *aloo-cholay* or a combination with curried dal or pouch processed *avial* or *sambar*, chicken/fish/meat curry, preserved cake, retort pouch *gulab jamun* or canned or pouch processed *rasagolla*, tinned fruit, dehydrated vegetable soup powder, or onion soup or chicken soup, instant rice, canned or pouch processed *kheer*, *chikki*, or custard powder. When the crew subsists upon ready to eat meals continuously for 7 to 14 days in a month one multi vitamin tablet/per man/per day is also authorised.

Rations for special category crews: There are special ration items for the Naval Air Crew. These are pre-flight meals for officers and sailors, the under-training air crew in the Air Force Academy, in the flying training units of IAF/Navy and civil flying clubs under control of DG, Civil Aviation. The extras include many items such as milk and milk products, tea, coffee, sausages/cheese, bread (Table 10.14).

Table 10.14: Special ration items for special categories in the Navy

S. No.	*Items*
1.	Tea
2.	Milk, standard Or whole milk powder Or milk fresh Or milk tinned, condensed
3.	Sugar
4.	Bread
5.	Butter fresh or tinned
6.	Jam
7.	Eggs Or whole milk powder Or milk fresh Or milk tinned condensed
8.	Cornflakes Or maida Or basin
9.	Sausages, tinned Or cheese tinned Or mutton/fresh/or sausages fresh or chocolate
10.	Potatoes
11.	Cooking oil
12.	Tomato sauce
13.	Salt
14.	Pepper

Divers also belong to this special group and after every dive, they are provided with extra milk and eggs. These extras are shown in Table 10.15.

Table 10.15: Special and extra rations to divers

Diver category	*Daily extra rations*	
(a) Clearance diving teams/units, (b) Divers – Clearance divers, Deep divers employed exclusively on diving duties on ships	Milk fresh or milk tinned or milk powder Milk tinned or powder only when the ship itself is using these items. Otherwise fresh milk is to be used	
(c) Staff and Divers under training at diving school	Eggs Or milk fresh Or milk tinned Or milk powder	2 No. 150 ml g, specified g, specified

Compo rations are given out for operational situations. There are slight variations among the compo packs described earlier (QMG/Army/66). Officers and sailors are issued these packs when normal food cannot be cooked such as during landing party operations. No normal rations or cash compensations are allowed at such times. The naval pack rations come as compo packs (Table 10.16), as landing party rations (Table 10.17) and as MRE packs (Table 10.18).

Table 10.16: Navy's Compo Pack Rations

S. No.	Item	Type A (non-vegetarian) (g)	Type B Vegetarian	Packing
1.	Biscuits			Paper, water proof
2.	Beaten rice			Polythene
3.	Sugar			Heat sealed alkathene
4.	# Vegetable, curried			Tins
5.	Pre-cooked dal	–	113	Tins
6.	* Mutton curry (chunks) or mutton curry (kheema) or fish	100	–	Tins
7.	Milk, toffee			Heat sealed pouch
8.	Milk evaporated			Tin
9.	Achar, dry (pickle)			Suitable container to exclude air
10.	Tea			Heat sealed pouch
11.	Salt refined			Sealed pouch
12.	Stoneless dates or raisins			Sealed pouch
13.	Cigarettes (number) or milk toffee for non smokers			Damp proof wrapping
14.	Multivitamin tablets	1 No.	1 No.	Laminated foil
15.	Matches, safety, box	3/5	3/5	Sealed pouch
16.	Tin opener, hexamine cooker and water sterilizing kit	1 per pack		

For vegetarians; * For non-vegetarians (Each item comes in specified quantities to provide the requisite nutrients and calories)

Table 10.17: Landing Party Rations

	Item	Vegetarian (g)	Non-vegetarian (g)
1.	Vegetable, tinned	220	4 eggs
2.	Fruit tinned #	110	–
3.	Biscuits	500	450
4.	Cheese		
5.	Milk, tinned unsweetened*	336	
6.	Sugar		
7.	Tea		
8.	Preserved meat or Fish tinned	–	450
9.	Chocolate	–	
10.	Hexamine cooker with 7–8 tablets	1 number per party	
11.	Tin opener	1 number per party	
12.	Matches, safety	2 numbers per party	
13.	Water sterilizing kit	1 number per party	

#,* Less milk and no fruit for meat eaters

Without obtaining fuel, no food can be cooked anywhere. Therefore, fuel rations are also specially mentioned in the ration scales. The main fuel is kerosene, steam coal and LPG gas, and where none of these are available then firewood. These are allotted as grams per head per day to the officers and ORs depending on where they are posted. The sports persons too receive a daily quota. On ships far more fuel is required than in other establishments. Similarly at high altitude the fuel consumption is far greater than anywhere else.

Table 10.18: Composition of one variety of MRE rations in each pack

	Item
1.	Cup 'O' Noodles*
2.	Biscuit
3.	Farsan Puri (Puffed rice)
4.	Chivda (beaten rice/poha)
5.	Groundnut Chikki
6.	Roasted chana
7.	Mango flakes*
8.	Roasted ground nuts
9.	Pickle

* These are meals ready to eat in a typically traditional Indian style except for the cup 'O' noodles and Mango flakes. Mango pulp is traditionally sundried and is formed into shelf stable fruit bars.

Ration Scales in the Air Force: Since there are separate but unified ration scales for the officers and men in the three Services, the same basic staples, fruits, vegetables, meat, milk, eggs etc. together with substitutes are provided in the Air Force. Personnel serving at high altitudes are also entitled to the HA rations but some interesting differences are noticeable. Their meat ration (180 g) is higher than for the army men (110 g). Bread is given only to officers but eggs are common for both officers and other ranks, whereas the *jawans* get them only in peace stations.

Extra rations – flying: Flying crews in the Air Force, Navy and the Army are given special rations. Preflight rations conform to another scale. Preparations with bread, eggs, butter, and jam, corn flakes and tea, coffee are the norm. Compliance is poor for an early morning meal and in a preflight situation whatever be the time of the sortie, it is absolutely essential that the pilots consume some meal so that their blood sugar levels are not low. Therefore eating a meal at least 1 to 1.5 hr before flight is mandatory. Another reason for preflight meals is that physiologically glucose tolerance is said to be lower on an empty stomach. Therefore, Air Force rations also include certain extra items especially for the flight crews. These are provided in the form of extra cheese sandwiches and quick snacks for an early morning sortie before breakfast. The breakfasts are usually sumptuous and filling and adequate to sustain the crew during the flights, which are usually not longer than a few hours. Leh is the highest Air Force Station at 10,000 ft. And here the standard High Altitude rations prevail. Special care is taken to avoid foods that might cause flatulence.

Emergency flying rations: Emergencies occur in every line of work and in the Air Force, these amount to life threatening problems during flight. An engine failure, malfunctioning in the intricate electrical/electronic control systems, leaking and loss of fuel, a direct hit in combat, inability to maintain proper altitude are some of the emergencies. In the aircraft, pilot seats are constructed with safety mechanisms such that in an emergency, the pilot could eject out of the aircraft. In the escape system, the aircraft canopy flies off and by pulling a handle the pilot seat elevates itself. The seat as well as the person strapped in it eject out of the open canopy. When it reaches a certain altitude, a parachute is deployed and the pilot separates from the seat. There is an emergency pack fixed under the seat which goes along with the pilot. Until rescue can be affected, a quantity of food and water must be made available. The Emergency flying ration serves such a purpose; it is an energy pack of some 1,000 Kcal/day. Operational features in the pilot's seat and in the ejection mechanism preclude putting anything more than the bare minimum, which must include not just food and water but some emergency first aid kit (containing bandages, pain killers, anti-allergens, morphine injection) and to help in search and rescue, flares and transmitter as well.

The emergency rations are actually no more than small handy energy food bars that fit neatly into the designated containers placed in a niche and strapped under the pilot seat. On the premise that the crash victim may not survive (normally does not) for more than 72 hours and is given up for lost if not found by rescue teams within this period, the rations are only sufficient for this period. *Supersonic flight foods*: Pilots flying long hauls need oral fluids and food to counteract the fatigue that will set in from hunger and thirst. In any flight that is expected to last longer than four hours, rations must be carried.

Special rations are required for feeding pilots when they are strapped into the seat of Sukoi M30, supersonic aircraft flying at altitudes of > 2.5 km and are practically immobile for the many hours of flying. Specific criteria have been developed by the Institute of Aerospace Medicine of the Air Force for foods, beverages and their packaging in order to select such items which serve physiological and/or nutritional needs, amenable to ready access and consumption during flight.

The energy content of the day's food does not exceed 1,000 Kcal/day as compared to a whole day's normal calorie intake of 2,800 Kcal. Fluid or water intake of some 1,000–1,200 ml is recommended in the form of 4–5 gulps (100 ml) every hour. There are fruit juices, coffee, water, etc. as well as palatable, freshly prepared snacks familiar to the Indian palate which are packed in user friendly pouches that may or may not be of the self heating kind. Convenient but sturdy packaging is necessary to keep the food safe and a container to house them securely in their place of storage.

Eating is done only at 2.5 km altitude and not below; when the cabin's altitude reaches an estimated 7,000–8,000 ft the face mask can be taken off and normal breathing can take place. The pilots can eat or drink while on autopilot. A pre-flight meal eaten one hour before an air sortie helps to stave off hunger and maintain the requisite blood glycemic levels. Such foods however must ensure low roughage because voiding bowel movement during flight is not on the cards, although there is provision to pass urine and collect it while sitting in the pilot seat.

There are operational, biological and physical criteria for foods, their safety levels, degree of convenience, shelf life, packaging, ease of eating, etc. which determine the IR fitness for use by the pilots of supersonic aircrafts. These criteria are very similar to those meant for astronauts on manned space ventures.

The food package must come equipped with essentials like napkins, eating implements, fluid packs for single or multiple drinks, an organised system to safely tuck away each food item in its proper place, for easy and quick access or removal without complicated manoeuvring or causing spillage.

Revision of Ration Scales in the Twenty-first Century

The nutritional requirements of various groups of individuals were reassessed in a recently completed review by DIPAS (Table 10.19).

Since there are different ration scales depending on the environment of work and the kind and amount of work that is performed, the yard stick for measuring is the biochemical estimation of the daily energy expended physiologically by an individual as against his calorie intake through the rations provided and examination of the various biochemical parameters to determine nutritional sufficiency. The ingested amount of food may be more or less than the actual rations authorised. The total calorie content (estimated and computed values) may be increased or decreased by suitably adjusting the composition, content and quality of the rations.

Table 10.19: Revised scales recommended since 2004

*Energy of Macro and Micro *nutrient in service ration scales*	*Energy Kcal/d*	*Protein g/d*	*Animal Protein g/d*	*Fat g/d*	*Carbohydrate g/d*
1. Officers – all services	3864	153	77	136	507
2. Men – all services	4034	143	43	114	609
3. Submarine crew	3637	119	40	125	509
4. Troops at 9,000 ft or above	4829	144	40	141	746
5. Coast guard personnel	3740	112	38	116	563
6. Border Road Organisation Personnel	3528	101	22	88	583
7. Tradesmen and Pioneer	3968	109	26	112	631
8. Glacier scale	5554	154	–	214	751

* Micronutrients like Vitamin A, thiamine, riboflavin, nicotinic acid, ascorbic acid, calcium and iron are also delivered in adequate quantities through rations. Wherever deemed necessary, vitamin supplements are issued.

The recently completed investigation involved personnel of the Army who were (a) recruits in basic military training, (b) men working in the plains and deserts (at sea level) and (c) those working at high (9,000–15,000 ft) and very high altitudes (above 15,000 ft). It was pointed out previously that there used to be two scales of rations for high altitude in the early 1960s which were modified to one uniform scale for high altitudes. The other groups examined were (d) navy personnel – Marine Commandos (MARCOS) and sailors in the ship and submarine and (e) Air Force personnel – both officers and other ranks.

Energy expenditure as expected varied with the type of work. The infantry recruits under rigorous training (maybe in a desert area) expended 4,670 ± 345 Kcal as against those in other Training Centers, where energy expenditure was considerably less at 3,800 ± 348 Kcal. The young men under rigorous training required substantially more calories than what they were getting through rations; these extra calories were being made up by way of foods and snacks from home. It was therefore found advisable to upgrade their ration scale by another 1,000 Kcal.

Two levels of ration scales were considered for high altitudes in this investigation – 4,664 Kcal for HA-I (9,000–15,000 ft) and 5,779 Kcal at HA-II (above 15,000 ft). While the energy expenditure profiles were found to be 3,880 ± 474 Kcal and 4,270 + 550 Kcal at HA-I and the base of HA-II respectively, the energy intake was similar to the computed figures at HA-I and the base of HA-II. However in the pickets of HA-II, the intake was significantly lower (3,698 + 322 Kcal) than at base. The decreased intake is the cause of weight loss of 4–5 kg in a 3 month period. Their rations also appeared to be far richer in fat (39.1 per cent) than the rations at HA-I (27.7 per cent) whereas higher carbohydrate intake had been actually recommended for such heights in previous studies.

Navy sailors and submarine crews expended similar amounts of energy, 3,313 ± 578 Kcal and 3,168 ± 282 Kcal respectively in their course of work but the MARCOs and divers expended much more: 4,055 ± 465 Kcal. As they already receive different ration scales with extra items, these special ration items have been considered to be adequate to compensate for the extra energy expended.

In the Air Force, the airmen and officers in this study in general expended less energy – 2,889 ± 320 Kcal and 3,615 ± 199 Kcal respectively and their intake was quite sufficient to balance the energy expended. The pre flight rations provide 1,540 Kcal of extra energy over and above the standard 4,088 Kcal per day.

Except for the men at HA-II who consumed less, and registered weight loss all others were seen to consume sufficient food and calories one way or the other. The recruits made up the short fall by snacking and the preflight crews are entitled extra meals as part of their rations. Based on these findings the young infantry recruits in military training have been recommended 1,000 Kcal extra per day. The extreme altitude picket dwellers must be made to eat more food and particularly more carbohydrate calories than fat calories.

Ration Scales and Free Rations during Training

Besides the many types of free rations being provided to the units deployed in different places, there are ration categories for young recruits and cadets under training. These are laid down in official manuals of the ASC. The ration scales for cadets in training are slightly different from the basic service ration scale. Many fresh entrants – boys and cadets, while qualifying for recruitment, are found to be undernourished. It is rather tough for an undernourished person to compete with more sturdy and physically stronger candidates. This is more obvious in the boys aspiring to join at the jawan's level and who usually belong to the economically disadvantaged strata. And because of that reason they are also educationally not qualified for admission as cadet officers. The rations given to them as well as cadet officers (if found undernourished) during training takes into consideration their extra nutritional needs. The realisation that the young lads require higher energy content, more bulk to satisfy hunger and better nutrition for their growing bodies has come a long way from the attitude of the concerned authorities in the Royal Military academies in England and the pitiful food given to the cadet officers.

In the Armed Forces of today, modernisation has occurred in the matter of rations to the recruits and cadets and the food is sumptuous, nutritious and filling when compared with food served in the past. A brief historical retrospective will make it obvious how fortunate the present day general recruits and officer cadets are and how much care has been taken to see that the still growing young lads in their teens and the very young cadets, once they have cleared the hurdles of recruitment, are well nourished during training so that they become strong and fit for military duties.

Food in training academies – Britain and India: There are military academics in India and private schools (in Dehradun, Pune, other places) which enroll students and impart a type of basic training for boy cadets who might eventually enter the Defence Services. Through this venue, cadets enter the National Defence Academy, Khadakvasla, under the Ministry of Defence and administered by the Armed Forces. By all accounts, their training is first class and they are truly well looked after and groomed to be made over from cadets to gentlemen and then officers. Their housing, environment and other facilities are of high standard and their food follows the pattern of rations and ration scales laid down by the Nutrition Advisory Board of the Directorate General, Armed Forces Medical Services, Government of India. Their basic training includes not only military craft and academic subjects leading to a Bachelor's degree in Military Sciences but also physical fitness, adventure sports, social etiquette as well as table manners as obtained in the western culture. For many cadets, perhaps sitting down at a table with a group of peers for a formal meal and eating off china plates and using knives and forks is a first time experience by itself although we presume that today's youth is well exposed to these manners because of their having observed and experienced such services in the abundant public eating places, up market restaurants and hotels that provide fine dining.

But what of the cadets of earlier generations? The various public schools (a quaint term for the very expensive private schools in India), were run for the education of the sons of princely states, for the scions of the landed rich and famous families and given training in many arts and crafts along with a dose of academics that were considered essential ingredients in the making of a well born westernised Indian, before they were sent off to another such public school in England as a finishing touch. These schools were meant to prepare students for the life of gentlemen. Eton and Harrow are two such exclusive schools in the UK. Pundit Jawaharlal Nehru, India's first Prime Minister was a student of Harrow. From there they went their various ways – to Oxford or Cambridge. Those Englishmen who intended to enter the Armed services went to one of the military academies – the Royal Military Academy at Woolwich or Sandhurst. The male members of the Royal family of England went to Sandhurst in a tradition of military training.

Before India's independence, there were few Indian officers in the Royal Indian armed forces who had trained at Sandhurst (*The Hindu*, January 29, 2005, p. 9). From 1923 on, when the Academy began admitting people from the colonies, General Sri Nagesh (appointed Chief of Army and Commander in Chief, Indian Armed Forces in 1955) was among the first batches of Indians to be deputed to Sandhurst. After passing out of the Academy, officers were given Viceroy's Commission and were designated VCO – Viceroy's Commissioned Officers. But we digress. A graphic account of the life of a British military cadet in the 1860s at the Royal Military Academy at Woolwich and Sandhurst is given by Sheppard (1980) in his eminently readable book entitled '*Sandhurst: the Royal Military Academy*'. The state of food in that place cannot have inspired any one to join.

Both the Sandhurst and Woolwich academies were highly and tightly budgeted by the Treasury because of the Government's policy of reduced fees and extra free places in direct commissions, which cramped the existing space.

The entry of cadets into Woolwich was done by nomination, by examination and by transfer from Addiscombe and Sandhurst. Those entering were in different age groups and had received no training but different levels of instruction. Like any boot camp, there were also young corporals with power, eager to yield it on the hapless cadets. The cadets got big punishments for small misdemeanours like smoking. If matters at Woolwich were bad, they were no better at Sandhurst. Although it was intended to increase accommodation for 100 single cadet rooms, officers quarters etc. the War Office was planning for 500 cadets in the already cramped space housing 375 cadets, 93 officers, professors, other ranks and servants.

The new accommodation provided rooms for Under-Officers but cubicles for the cadets, partitioned to within 2 foot 9 inches (84 cms) from the ceiling and bitterly cold. The circulating hot water heating system was elementary and inadequate and the place was drafty and freezing with windows open. Washing with cans of water lead to the flooding of the bathrooms and the stairs.

A cadet officer's misery in the British army: Food related grievances and this unhappy state of affairs lead to mutiny by the cadets in Woolwich. The grouse was that grown men were being treated as school boys and that the food was miserable and utterly inadequate and unsatisfactory. Apparently a Sandhurst cadet got a better deal than the one at Woolwich.

Mutiny at Woolwich Academy

The recollections of a college servant John Parrant (Sheppard, 1980, p. 65) around 1862 succinctly describe the cadet's food as being awful. Only a small portion of meat and bread were given to each cadet with no chance or hope of second helpings. The coffee that came up in pails was poured into basins. 'The whole table service and meals were rough and ready, and not at all comfortable' states Parrant, who was fully familiar with the services befitting gentlemen as he was himself a private servant to the Lieutenant Governor of the College. By the early 1860s, a new diet for the cadets had been decided.

In a daily routine that began at 7 am, there was time for breakfast at 8 am for 25 minutes, for dinner (the afternoon meal or lunch) 30 minutes between 2 to 2.30, and for supper 30 minutes between 6.30 to 7 pm. At 8.30 pm they were locked in for the night. For breakfast they were given bread and butter, coffee, sugar and milk. For dinner there was meat, vegetables, pudding, bread and a small beer. For supper, breakfast items were repeated but with tea this time. The entire daily diet cost a princely sum of 1 shilling and 8 3/8 pence (1s. 8 and 3/8 d) a day! And this diet was supposed to sustain the young cadets, all in the age between 20 to 22 years (20 years for infantry, 22 for cavalry cadets.

Cramped space where more than 1,000 occupied the space meant for 500, meager food, absence of any basic amenities and recreational facilities were the burning issues. Their outrage found expression in various ways. The cadets, some of whom were dubbed militants, stuffed a bread loaf down a field gun and fired it on the Governor's House. After much enquiry into the causes for the unrest and finding suitable redress in the military fashion, some improvements were suggested in the daily routine of the cadets. Better facilities and recreational opportunities were to be created, 'smoking allowed' zones were designated and a canteen for sale of beer and light refreshments was to be established on the premises. No doubt all this involved expenditure to the state but one Colonel Halliwell pressed for these modest reforms. During all weather, there was a Tuck Barrow (a vending cart) which came from the village, carrying all sorts of refreshments and beer to sell to the always hungry youngsters. There was sufficient ground space to run a canteen within the premises, offering all sorts of popular foods, such as cold fowls, hares, meat pies, sweets, ices and lemonade and beer, the last two being drunk as one beverage. The improvements in the daily cadet diet are not indicated but they cannot have amounted to much if a canteen was going to sell nice meaty, interesting and high caloric stuff for money!

Care and feeding of cadets today: Recruits today receive the full scale of rations. Cadets at the Rashtriya Indian Military College, Dehradun, are given 430 g of *atta*/rice/bread/flour, where the bread is limited to 280 g: several times a week *dalia*, a few times semolina and once a week cornflakes and milk (500 ml), as befits the needs of young adults. Butter, corn flour to make puddings, 2 eggs, (or bacon or liver or kidney,) cheese or cream, fresh meat four times a week, fresh fish twice a week, chicken (dressed) once a week and of course all the other essentials such as oil hydro, potatoes, dal, fresh vegetables and fruits, condiments like onion and garlic and tea or coffee or chocolate. Adequate quantities of meat, fish or poultry meat are provided to satisfy most young appetites. There are also compensations with milk, cheese and or eggs for vegetarian cadets, extra rations of coffee, sugar, and fresh milk or vitamin tablets are issued on medical recommendation to counter fatigue or bad weather conditions. Boys (Boarders) of Military Schools get rations at the rate of *atta*/rice/bread/flour not more than 400 g, of which there could be 200 g of bread. All other items are much the same as above and are issued at similar scales. For the cadets – day scholars of Military School, the cereal ration is almost half of the standard scales (230 g), out of which again, almost 50 per cent is the bread allowance. There are also lesser amounts of potato, oil hydro, etc. Drinking chocolate, baked beans instead of dal, pickles or chutney or vinegar in lieu of other condiments, golden syrup in place of fresh fruit with sugar are some of the variations.

For cadets at the National Defence Academy and the Indian Military Academy, the ration scales seem to be higher than those for the others shown above. The *atta*/rice/bread/flour amount is 510 g where not more than 310 g of bread is to be issued. Three times a week *dalia*, twice a week semolina, corn flakes once a week, and sago or vermicelli once a week, makes for an interesting yet filling breakfast foods. The daily allowance of standard milk (550 ml) is substantial in quantity to allow for its use at breakfast and as *dahi* or desserts in other meals.

Eggs, butter, bacon/ham/liver, cheese, jam or marmalade, syrup or fruit with sugar all appear to be part of a sumptuous breakfast meal or are used at any other time in part or whole. There are fresh vegetables, fruits, tea or coffee or drinking chocolate as well as different types of condiments as in the full troop's rations. Fuel allotment and matches also meet the same ration scale standard.

The rules regarding the issue of alternates are the same for all rations except that the tinned substitutes may also be used for training camps, during outdoor exercises and organised hikes. There are some establishments known as the Inter-Service Institutions and units where the Army, Navy and Air Force personnel are posted together such as the NDA, Wireless Experimental Centers and several AOP flight squadrons. Those who are entitled to free rations and fuel receive 600 g of *atta* or 450 g and 140 g respectively of *atta* and rice, 60 g *dal*, 90 g of oil hydro, 200 g meat fresh, 220 ml fresh milk and all other items at generally the same level as in the standard rations.

An interesting feature of providing rations at all times is the arrangements for food service during troop movement when the troops are aboard troop trains and troop ships. Troops in all ranks in all the three Services are entitled to get free rations, whether they are in peace or field garrisons, whether they are on route marches, traveling in troop trains or being transported on Indian Navy ships and commercial ships on Indian charter. Since dry rations cannot be utilised by the units on most of these occasions cooked food service operates.

Elaborate directions are followed in arranging food for journeys. For rail journeys, whenever possible, normal rations are provided at stations en route. This is arranged by giving advance information to the supply officers about the precise requirements. Cooked meals await the arrival of the men on the train – either a whole troop train or just a military coach. When troop specials proceed with no kitchen car attached or when there is no halting or when troops are travelling by road, where normal cooking facilities are not available in a journey lasting more than 24 hours, rations for the period are issued prior to the journey for a group of ten or more. But when normal rations or rail/road rations can be issued, no ration allowance or daily allowance is admitted.

The special travel rations for road and rail movement read differently from the normal issue. They contain *atta* or bread or beaten rice (450 g), biscuits (110 g), sugar (85 g), tea (14 g), oil hydro 70 g (if *atta* given) or butter (with bread) or sweetened condensed milk tinned (70 g); if only beaten rice is provided, milk tinned evaporated (110 g), vegetable tinned (140 g), salt (14 g), bread or beaten rice but more (42 g) with *atta*, jam or marmalade (60 g), eggs (2 no.) or *chana* roasted (100 g in lieu), fruit tinned (140 g) and pickles (28 g). Firewood is stated to be the fuel – 900g if *atta* is to be used and 450 g if bread or beaten rice! And yes, one does need matches, therefore 2 match boxes/per week for a group of men up to 45 in number, are issued, and for numbers more than 45, one extra match box for up to 25 men.

Some practical directions are also issued which say that eggs must be cooked before starting on the journey (these would be mostly boiled), and that *chapattis* could be prepared beforehand too, with 6 per cent salt added to *atta*, so that they could be preserved for up to 7–8 days. And for packing the cooked food, two polythene bags – 8 inch square, 300–400 gauge are sanctioned per head, which may be drawn from the supply depots.

Ice is supplied to military coaches at the rate of 37.2 kg per container per eight men in a III class coach at the start of the journey and then replenished. Hospital compartments and officers' compartment each get one container of ice filled with the same quantity as above. If a kitchen car is attached, there is one container of ice for it too or the ice is issued once in the morning and once in the late afternoon. Men on duty on roads are authorised both ice (910 g/man per day) and four water bottles/man/day between 1 April and 15 September; presumably each bottle holds one liter of water.

Fuel/firewood (depending on the nature of ovens) is supplied at predetermined levels to prepare food. At present, all fuel needs are met by LPG and oil kero (the terminology by which kerosene is known in the Services).

The normal peace scales of troop rations prevail in ships other than naval ships, but when the troops are on naval ships, naval ration scales apply.

Other conditions for those entitled to free rations and engaged on duties involving strenuous exertion such as in physical training schools, recruiting centers or when work is done in severe climatic conditions – rations are supplemented with extra amounts of *atta* or rice, oil hydro, sugar, dal and salt.

There are hospital diets and extras which fall under different categories. There are special diets for patients on fluids, for convalescents and for those being treated for Tuberculosis. There are other patient types who are not actually on any diet but nevertheless are entitled to certain extras varying in quantities – *atta*/rice are standard along with bread, cereal for pudding, breakfast cereals, fresh milk, butter, eggs, cream, fresh meat and chicken as well as fresh or tinned fish, fresh vegetables and fruits and all other items such as tea, cheese, sugar, jams, salt, cooking fat as oil hydro, pickles and condiments. The extras such as aerated water, fresh lime or lime juice cordial, ice, barley water etc. are provided on 'as is required' basis since 1971.

Edentulous patients awaiting the fitting of artificial dentures or whose dentures were withdrawn for refitting or those who suffered maxillo-facial injury are given a scale of rations where rice and bread are the main cereal forms and a higher quantity (660 ml) of fresh milk, butter, eggs or leafy vegetables, fresh potatoes and fresh citrus fruits are issued along with multivitamin tablets for a period varying from 30 to 90 days depending on the nature of the requirement.

The NCC falls under both the Central Government and the State Government, each being responsible for different aspects of the Corps. The NCC is a non-military group involving students of schools and undergraduate colleges and was formed in 1952 to inculcate a spirit of discipline and leadership training among the youth of the country. Though non-military in principle, it consists of all the three wings of the Armed Forces, the Army, the Navy and the Air Force for the purpose of training that is imparted by military personnel posted on attachment. The Commandant is a senior army officer and there are other officers and other ranks in support of the specific unit. There are regional battalions for men and women. NCC cadets do not automatically enter the Armed Services but for those who may desire to do so, the regular general selection and recruitment process is open to all eligible applicants. There are several thousand students enrolled as NCC cadets in the age group of 17–20 in the length and breadth of the country.

Even though the cadets are civilians and not usually associated with any military training academies, they do perform strenuous tasks in the course of their training while pursuing their full time academic education and the government has provided for giving them some form of refreshment in every session. Therefore, all who have enrolled in the NCC are entitled to a certain amount of food or cash as food allowance depending on the nature of the training. There are said to be two kinds of training, one that takes place in the colleges and is thus institutional and the other which takes place in the annual camps. In the institutional training, the enrolled cadets assemble for training and practice sessions once or twice a week during the academic year. Each session may last between two to three hours at the end of which the cadets receive refreshment allowance in cash at Rs. 12/- per person per session. When there are larger groups of 70–80 attending the session, food is provided through contract cooking or by eating at a hotel. The principals of the colleges or the NCC officers of the units are at liberty to arrange food for the cadets in the manner that is most practical and feasible for the institution and which they consider the best. About the nutritional content and quality of such foods nothing much can be said. It is left to the reader to speculate what Rs. 12/- would fetch in the name of food or snacks in the present day. In a Class 2 city perhaps this amount could fetch a small snack but in larger cities, it is unlikely that anything substantial can be procured.

The training camps on the other hand are annual events lasting for some 12 days and there could be as many as 550 to 650 cadets participating. Here the feeding is centralised, the food for the participants coming out of a central kitchen facility created near the camp, and which functions under a committee consisting of NCC officers. This committee prepares the 'bill of fare' or in lay terms the menu plan for all meals and for all the 12 days. It assumes the responsibility to procure the necessary food items, engage the cooks and supervise the food preparation and its service. Cooking in bulk is advantageous; adequate quantity and variety of food can be provided to every one with the cash allowances pooled together.

The allowance for the cadets' food could vary from state to state; some states, e.g. Karnataka, provide as much as Rs. 40/- per capita per day, some allocate smaller amounts (may be only Rs. 20/- or so) depending on how the state regards the NCC in terms of its importance and priority in the scheme of things. This amount of money must suffice for three main meals, early morning tea, and afternoon tea and snacks.

Though no definite ration scale as such has been found to exist, from talking to NCC officers it was gathered that the organisation makes sure that by purchasing all food items in bulk and at whole sale rates, the cadets get not only adequate food but that which is also fairly well balanced in its nutritional content by including milk, rice, wheat, dals, fruits, and vegetables etc. Foods are prepared in the traditional way to appeal to the regional palate of the cadets in the camp; when the camps are held in north India or for the largely north Indian Cadets the cuisine is north Indian in taste and when the cadets hail from southern India the foods prepared for them are South Indian.

A word about the service officers posted in NCC units around the country is not out of place here. When they are posted to places in proximity to the ASC supply depots, they can draw their authorized rations from the nearest supply station. But when they are attached to units which are far away from the ASC's supply chain, they are paid in cash per capita per day. The rub of the matter is that the cash compensation in lieu of rations is quite inadequate.

At the revised rate, a service officer's daily cash entitlement in lieu of rations as per SRS is fixed at Rs. 32.65 (from around Rs. 29/- in previous years) which amounts to approximately Rs.

960/- per month. It is glaringly obvious that at the current market rates of many foods, fruits and vegetables etc., this amount of money will not buy them all the necessary items for food preparation in the prescribed quantities. What will then happen to their calorie and nutrients intake? Invariably the Service personnel spend out of their own pockets to supplement quantities of foods. That is an expenditure that cannot be avoided if one wishes to eat adequate quantity and quality of food in keeping with reasonably balanced meals and adequate nutrient intake. Needless to say, the men of the ranks would be even harder hit due to cash compensation compared to when they eat in a unit mess.

As mentioned earlier, only ORs were entitled to free rations and for the officers only when deployed in field areas. The cost of free rations for all is considerable to the National Exchequer. The daily military rations when converted into meals, are not comparable with a common man's meals. The everyday food at any meal time for a common individual is a very simple affair. The meals are frugal and eaten in a hurry or not at all, depending on financial status, time or facilities available for buying or preparing and even eating. The energy and nutrient adequacy of foods consumed or accessible to a daily wage labourer engaged in road works, in building and construction activity or other strenuous work does not ever come close to the recommended daily intakes by the ICMR and is far below that recommended for the Border Roads Organization personnel. The situation is of course different with young professionals and business chiefs and other affluent people.

The Cost of Free Rations

It happened to gladden the hearts of Service officers when on the eve of Republic Day, 1983 it was announced that free rations had been authorised by the Government for all officers up to the rank of Army colonel and equivalent ranks in the Navy and Air Force. They were now entitled to receive 'authorised rations'. This privilege was extended in 1984 to Brigadiers and equivalent cadres in the Navy and Air Force and by 1987 even to General Officers, thus covering all personnel.

Free rations are not really free in the sense that someone pays and that is the national exchequer. At the average rate of Rs 32.65/- and 32.16/- per ration (for officers and ORs respectively) a conservative estimate amounts to Rs 1,518 crores annually, for the 1.3 million strong force. And this is only the cost of the basic rations. Special food packs and combat rations, MRE etc. cost much more. A tremendous amount of effort and energy go into the procurement and delivery of the rations to different geographical and often impossibly difficult locations, incurring expenditure on transportation by rail, road, air, pack animals and even porters. The Service men themselves haul stores when and where required.

Rations of Other Countries

Rations in Pakistan's Armed Forces

In the post World War II period, the importance of nutrition in soldiers' health and performance was recognised by many countries which hitherto had not been known to have done so, at least consciously. The troops ate in war time what they always did in normal times but war time food supplies being uncertain and often scarce and the supply logistics situation in the various theatres of war having become even more uncertain, soldiers of certain countries generally got off worse than ever before and particularly so because the access to traditional foods, fruits and vegetables etc. with which they supplemented their meals, was cut off. The post war era was one of rapid industrialisation in some countries but presented a grim face on the agricultural and economic front in many others. No country was disarming and more countries were gaining independence from their former colonial rulers.

Pakistan, a newly independent nation had an Armed Force of some 150,000, inherited at the time of partition. Pakistan also retained practically the same ration scales as India, both of which emanated from the war time British field scale rations for Indians in the army. In the Indian Army, separate peace and field scale rations were designated, differing mostly in calorie content. In Pakistan, to build her force, recruitments were being carried out but apparently there was a high percentage of rejection (more than 55 per cent) on medical grounds for all of Pakistan (West and East Pakistan). Nutritional diseases leading to disabilities were attributed to be the cause. The malaise due to poor nutrition is the bane of most third world countries. Healthy young adults are required to swell the numbers in the Armed Forces and if the state of nutrition in the general population is subnormal, it will impinge on the recruitment level and lead to loss of man power.

Both China and Iran had some data generated by 1955 on the food and nutrition situation of their countries in general and of their Armed Forces in particular which was gathered by US researchers (Berry and Sandstead, 1955).

In the wake of successful investigations in several Middle Eastern countries, Iran included, the US Interdepartmental Committee on Nutrition for National Defence was invited by other countries to conduct similar nutritional surveys. Pakistan also desired that a nutrition survey be conducted and a nutrition service be established.

The survey of nutrition and the rations of the Pakistan Armed Forces conducted by the National Institutes of Health in the 1950s, the results of which appeared in a scientific article in 1959 (NIH 1959), were the only reliable source available in the public domain to learn about the military rations of Pakistan, as well as about the country's food procurement mechanisms and the food service systems in the early years. It may be recalled that Indian troops in the British Indian army received a poorer fare than British personnel before World War II and were not provided with the full field scale rations until 1943, four years after the war started unlike their British counterparts There were food shortages in India but the British field scale rations for British personnel belied this fact.

The nutrition survey conducted by the US team first examined the ration scale for the Pakistan Army (Table 10. 20) as found in a training pamphlet of 1951 (Pakistan Army Training, 1951, Catering in the Army, Military Training pamphlet No.11 Code No. GSP-1036 Section 2). It is very nearly the same as the full field scale rations of Indian troops but with some minor differences. The cereal component was 2 oz lesser, the meat portion was 1 1/3 oz larger, there was more ghee, and the rations included fruits without having to get a medical recommendation. These ration entitlements compared favourably with the Recommended Daily Allowances of the Food and Nutrition Board, USA

Dietary habits: Pakistan consumed wheat (in the west) and rice (East Bengal, now Bangladesh) as its staple food. The foods prepared with wheat, rice, dals, vegetables, fruits, milk, sugar and spices identified and enumerated by the survey team are reminiscent of Indian foods of the same name. As for meats, chicken was the most preferred, followed by fish, goat and sheep meat in descending order. Ghee was the principal cooking fat, partly supplemented with vegetable fat. Among some other characteristics was the widespread chewing of betel nut with *paan* leaves. Beef found no specific mention in this report. The actual intakes agreed well with estimated activity levels. Ration issues to the Navy and the Air Force were said to be larger than that for the Army (to what extent is not revealed) though actual consumption of calories by the men of all the three branches was generally similar (Table 10.21).

Table 10.20: Basic ration scale in the Pakistan Army (1956)

Ration items	*Authorized quantity*
1. Atta	22 oz
2. Atta and Rice	16 oz, 6 oz
3. Dal	3 oz
4. Sugar	2 oz
5. Meat, fresh	3½ oz
6. Milk, fresh	9 oz
7. Ghee, 3 × per week	2¾ oz
8. vegetable oil/or oil hydro, 4 × per week	2½ oz
9. Potatoes	4 oz
10. Other vegetables	7 oz
11. Onions	2 oz
12. Fruits, Citrus, 3 × per week or	4 oz
13. Fruit, non citrus 3 × per week	8 oz
14. Tea	1/3 oz
15. Salt, rock	½ oz
Supplements for fatigue or bad weather	
16. Cocoa or Tea	1 oz
17. Sugar	1 oz
18. Milk, evaporated canned	1 oz

Source: NIH Project, 1959

Table 10.21: Average nutrient intake per man per day in Pakistan Armed Forces, 1956

	Energy, Kcal	*Protein, g*	*Fat, g*	*Salt, g*	*Vit C, mg*	*Vit A, i.u*
Army	3478	87	107	12.5	49	1904
Navy*	3555	97	104	13.5	270	4298
Air Force	3300	89	98	4.9	69	5218

* Vegetarians consumed higher calories

The systematic survey by the NIH team revealed no serious nutritional deficiency among the soldiers, sailors and airmen who had been examined. Their medical profiles were satisfactory. The study found it to be important to recommend further studies on vitamin losses during cooking and ways to minimise them – particularly vitamin C in the many native vegetables and by various cooking methods and for increasing the dietary sources of vitamin C, riboflavin etc. Increase in the intake of milk and dal components was suggested to increase riboflavin in the diets at the time of the survey.

Whether any review and revision of the rations and the scales was undertaken in recent times is not known but considering that the Indian rations themselves were revised only in 2004 from the 1960s scales barring small amendments and additions periodically, it is quite likely that due to other pressing exigencies of the Pakistan State in the last few decades a revision may not have taken place and if it did, it was not made public via scientific reports. The information certainly has not been found in the public domains.

Evolution of US Military Rations

Nutritional adequacy was not always the objective of creating a ration entitlement. The food which soldiers should get, particularly in war time, was defined more to enable adequate procurement of bulk foods than due to any nutrition concerns. It had to be purchased from traders and transportation arranged to places where the men could buy food from the suttlers, paying with whatever cash allowance was the norm in field conditions.

In colonial America, there were frequent wars with the native Indian tribes where the troops had to ride hard into the un-chartered wilds and out of the British fortifications. The natives were crafty and carried their own brand of sustenance in the form of dry chewable food – mostly air dried strips of beef called *Pinole* and ground parched corn or wheat and whenever possible ate off the land. When colonial America fought to free herself from British domination and rule by going to war against it, the Revolutionary War or the American War of Independence broke out in 1775. Here we find the first mention of a daily ration entitlement comprising of beef, flour, rice, sugar, milk and beer as well as soap and candle (Table 10.22). This was not a good composition for nutritious food. At least these many items had to be available so that the soldiers could feed and maintain themselves. There was no centralised kitchen in any unit, the men prepared their own food using whatever firewood they could gather. Some 26,000 rations were needed by 1778. Introduction of alcohol – rum, brandy, whiskey came a few years later, more for overcoming fatigue, just as coffee and sugar were allowed as 'fatigue' beverages. In the next century America went to war with Canada (1812), with Mexico (1838), within own territories in a civil war (1861) and then with the Spanish. A gradual increase in the daily entitlements became apparent in the rations of these periods as well as the inclusion of more foods such as potatoes, yeast, dried beans, vinegar and pepper. Coffee was given in the green bean form, not as we now know it in the brown, crisp, roasted and ground form *(*www.qmfound.com/army/subsistance-history.htm).

Attempts by the Army to design an emergency ration early in the twentieth century came about in 1907. This was necessary because all the rations until then were provided in the fresh form to be cooked in the soldier's own mess kits and in the field encampments. The emergency ration was a mixture of powdered dried beef and parched cooked wheat very much like what the natives had subsisted on. When soaked for sometime and seasoned with salt and pepper it would make some manner of gruel or soup. Salt and pepper came in vacuum sealed tins. Sweet chocolate also became a part of this emergency food. Further modifications and improvements were seen in the US rations from 1922 onwards. None of these ration meals could claim to be balanced (nutritionally). They were calorie dense, with quite a good amount of meat, bread and sugar. Chocolate bars made with oat flour in 4 oz size provided 600 Kcals and at the rate of 3 bars per day (1,800 Kcal) would just stave off the worst hunger pangs for a while. This was called Field ration 1 in the middle 1930s.

The reserve ration of 1922 consisting of the same four basics – meat, hard bread, coffee and sugar got a face lift and reappeared in the form of prepared meals in cans such as beef stew and beef with noodles. Thereafter, gradual improvements in nutrition, meal size, content and packing led to the advent of Field Ration C when World War II broke out in 1939, but the way in which the ration was put together proved to be too bulky and heavy for mobile units. Therefore to make the ration more user friendly for mobile troops like parachute troops, tank corps and motorcycle riders, the same foods were provided in slightly less quantity and with different specifications; it was designated Field Ration-K and adopted in 1942. In this variety the calorie content appears to have been quite extraordinarily high (8,300 Kcals). There was another type known as Field Ration-B by 1943, specifically catering to battle requirements and which was designed for a meal box with food sufficient for one meal for a detachment of 10 men. This was later whittled down to a 5-in-1 pack. The mobile detachments could carry the meal box(es) along in advance of the establishment of a field kitchen. This was the principal subsistence ration for battle conditions.

Alphabet designated US rations – A, B, C, D and E: US rations have been alphabetically labeled; D was the first field ration, C, K and B were different versions for combat conditions;

Table 10.22: US Rations from the time of American War of Independence

1775 Revolutionary War	*War of 1812*	*Mexican War, 1838*	*Civil War, 1860- 61*	*Spanish American war*	*Armour ration WW–1 1914–18 ration*
1. beef 16 oz	1. beef 20 oz	1. beef 20 oz	1. beef 20 oz	1. beef 20 oz	sugar, butter…17 times
2. flour 18 oz	2. flour 18 oz	2. flour 18 oz	2. flour 220 oz	2. flour 18 oz	+ substitutions had a
3. rice 1.4 oz	3. salt 0.640 oz	3. salt 0.640 oz	3. potatoes 70 oz	3. potatoes 70 oz	variety, improved
4. milk 16 oz	4. vinegar 1 gill (4oz)	4. dried beans 2.4 oz	4. yeast 0.045 oz	4. yeast 0.045 oz	soldiers diet
5. spruce beer 1qt	5. rum 1gill (4oz)	5. vinegar 0.16 gill	5. dried beans 2.65 oz	5. dried beans 2.65 oz	only difference in Vit A.
6. soap 0.183 oz	6. soap 0.640 oz	6. sugar 1.92 oz	6. green coffee 0.24 oz	6. green coffee 0.24 oz	Higher cost than allowed,
7. candle 0.0686 oz	7. candle 0.24 oz	7. green coffee 0.96 oz	7. sugar 2.4 oz	7. sugar 2.4 oz	So bacon, rice, onion &
supposed to be well fed, 26,000 rations required by 1778	not well fed in 1785, rum/brandy/whisky reduced to ½ gill! - but additional ½ gill for western frontier - but this was again cut by 1795, - coffee/sugar substituted for rum	8. soap 0.183 oz	8. vinegar 0.32 gill	8. vinegar 0.32 gill	tomato, margarine/lard
		9. candle 0.0686 oz	9. pepper 0.04 oz	9. pepper 0.04 oz	
			10. soap 0.64 oz	10. soap 0.64 oz	
			11. candle 0.24 oz Ration & food better when supply available, but often no food	11. candle 0.24 oz 1899 – sugar increased 1908 – butter/margarine, lard and flavouring extracts added. 1901 – Congressional Act- 1st ration components promulgated for economy, health.	

Source: www.qmfound.com/army/subsistance-history.htm

then came the combat-E type which replaced the old C Rations and was said to be designed by combining the best features of both. The field-B rations were the operational type having many items of the processed kind providing 2,974 Kcals and adequate amounts of protein, minerals and vitamins. Mostly packed in cans and therefore non-perishable, these foods required no refrigeration. In World War II, this was one dependable ration when fresh foods could not be supplied to troops. It was also the nearest full meal substitute to the grocery type foods provided in Field-A rations.

Field-A rations are used where the full kitchen facilities and food service is available because most foods used in meal preparations are fresh or fresh refrigerated wherever refrigerator facilities are installed. Such a system works best out of military bases, cantonments, unit messes, large ships and troop ships. The menus in rations A and B are similar except that processed substitutes for fresh refrigerated foods are used in ration-B to turn out freshly made hot meals.

When small detachments move, they are away from their unit messes and on their own. They carry pack rations of all essential meal items (providing 4,000 Kcal per man per day), processed and packed in a convenient form (mostly cans) and sufficient for five men for one day. The meal pack weighing 27 pounds includes the appropriate cooking equipment and the whole carton is carried by one man. For individuals, there are combat-C rations with different menus. A set of food packets designed for more specific situations – emergency and/or assault – for use by individuals are also now available.

The wars in recent times in Iraq (1991) and Afghanistan (2001) and the war in Iraq which lasted till ceasefire was declared in August 2010 have created a situation where the US troops posted in these regions depended entirely on the sustenance rations shipped from home to their military bases, as there is little food of any kind that may be found locally in the war torn and ravaged countries (see more details in Chapter 14).

Japanese Military Rations

The third partner in the Axis in World War II with Germany and Italy was Japan. After the bombing of Pearl Harbour, perhaps their longest range flying mission in the war, they fought in the Pacific theatre on several islands, in Malaya and Burma, which were not any closer to home but probably manageable enough to have supplies sent over and also in a position to commandeer everything required from occupied territories. The information available about their rations in this war suggests that they lived on very frugal rations, particularly in comparison to the variety of ration types which the Allied armies had.

The principal staple in Japanese diet is rice with vegetables and some meat or fish. White polished rice is preferred as a status symbol. The pre twentieth century Navy suffered acutely from 'Beriberi', a disease now known to be caused by thiamin deficiency, which resulted primarily from the poor nutritional profile of the diets. We now know too that polished rice is the culprit in the absence of other nitrogenous food substances and that its long term consumption leads to Beriberi.

To Takaki in 1886 goes the credit of recognising the cause of the all debilitating and frequently fatal disease of Beriberi in the predominantly rice eating Japanese. It was he who formulated a diet consisting of 350 g of carbon and 20 g nitrogen after observing the insufficiency of the Navy diet and conducted successful and long trial voyages with a crew of more than 240 in a Navy vessel to prove his point. His clever diet consisted of nitrogen rich items like condensed milk and meat eaten along with the standard rice and other accompaniments (www.findarticles.com/mi-qa3912/Is-200604/ai-n163503/05/militarymedicineApl2006/AlanHauk.jap.in).

Hot meals and fresh foods: In World War II there was general agreement between the Army and the Navy about rations provided to them, other rivalries not withstanding. As with any Armed Force in the world, every effort was made to serve hot meals to the Japanese soldiers both in garrisons and in the field. When they marched, it was necessary to carry several days' worth of rations, some of which could be cooked fresh and some to be consumed directly. Hot cooked meals came out of central kitchens according to pre-determined menus. These rations prepared in garrison or field messes or on board ships were supplemented with vegetables, fruit and flesh foods obtained from local sources. Only when such fresh produce was not available were the tinned food used, vegetables added to the meal and tinned fruit eaten as dessert. Bean paste, flavoured Soya, Miso powder and seaweed are the other foods very dear to the Japanese and they formed part of the army rations.

Japanese cuisine utilises a variety of vegetables – cabbage, coconut, sweet potato, burdock, lotus root, taro, bean sprouts, beans in a pickled form; radish and cucumber and pickled plums. Scallions and ginger were the favourite flavourants. Fruits such as lychee, oranges, peach etc. were provided in cans or fresh when available, canned fish such as tuna, squid, bonito, crab etc. provided the compulsory flesh food.

Ration types: In that period food packaging in the majority of cases consisted of metal cans. Japanese food rations came in a variety of packaging; such as muslin bags, paper sacks for rice, cellophane wrappers, and cardboard boxes and of course metal cans.

The available information reveals that there were several types of Japanese rations labeled (a) Imperial Japanese rations, (b) Standard daily rations (both fresh) and (c) Special/preserved (Table 10.23). In addition, there were two types of emergency rations, (d) 'A' and (e) 'B', (f) compressed rations known as *'Assaku Koryo'* and (f) high nutrition ration under the name *Netsuryo Shoku* (Table 10.24). This last was claimed to be a high calorie item – a hard food bar made of peanut or sesame, akin to the '*chikki*'. The liquor ration was beer or sake and was issued upon occasion to boost morale.

Some measures for the rations are given in cups, such as for the Imperial Japanese rations, where as in other categories, quantities are given in ounces per day. Keeping in mind that the Takaki diet recommended at least 20 g nitrogen and 350 g carbon per day it may be assumed that the Japanese military rations met the required dietary standards for quantity and nutrition content. Seeing how their diet is rich in vegetables and includes some form of beans and fish, there would not be a great concern in respect of proteins, vitamins and minerals. The only significant point that strikes is the fat content of the ration. There is no scale for fat in the standard daily ration and the bulk of the expendable energy is thus contributed by the white rice component. To prevent beriberi in the troops, rice was issued together with barley. But this combination was never liked; it took longer to cook than plain rice and also required more water to cook; its flavour was very different and it spoiled faster than plain rice when soldiers had to carry the cooked food on their marches.

Cooking and eating: The soldier's mess kit included a metal canteen in the form of a shallow wide bucket with a loop and handle (like a slop bucket) in which the men cooked their rice rations. Where a long engagement or march was envisaged, there was an ingenious carry bag or a 'rice tube'. This was a long tubular canvass or silk in which cooked rice was packed like a long sausage and the tube slung over the shoulder bandoleer fashion.

Long tedious assignments on islands led to boredom, isolation, and monotony; soldiers had access to what were called the 'soldiers store' maintained by all Company and larger units. Known as the PX system in the Western armies, this store was adequate for stocking and selling a variety of 'comfort goods'– foods, liquor, snacks, chewy bars, candies, canned foods, preserved noodles, dried fruits, even some fast foods like buns and sandwiches, which were rice and fish wrapped in banana leaves.

Table 10.23: Japanese Armed forces rations in World War II

Imperial Japan, Rations in Tin boxes per day		*Standard Rations, Ounces/day*		*Special/Preserved Foods, substitutes for standard Rations ounces/day*	
1. Rice with barley	1 ½ cup	Rice or Rice with barley	28.0.	Compressed dried Rice	20.0
2. Canned tuna or sausages (and/or squid-locally found)	¼ cup	Fish or meat or flour	7.4	Canned/dried meat	5.3
3. Cooked cabbage and/or a variety of vegetables or fruits	1 ¼ cups	Pickled Radish	2.1	Fish	4.2
4. Pickled radish (pickled cucumber umeboshi, scallions, ginger for flavour)	3 tea spoons	Vegetables, fresh	21.2	Canned vegetables	1.6
5. Dried seaweed (issued in field for sushi making)	< 10 z	Bean paste	2.6	Dried plum	1.1
6. Or occasionally beer or sake for morale		Soya sauce	1.5	Powdered Miso	0.5
		Salt	0.5	Salt	1.0
		Sugar	1.0	Sugar	0.2
		Tea (usually green)	0.2	Tea (green)	
		Fruit etc.			

Source: www.findarticles.com

Table 10.24: Japanese Armed forces rations – emergency

Emergency 'A' Rations ounces/day	*Emergency 'B' Rations ounces/day*	*Compressed Ration or 'Assaku Koryo'*	*High nutrition ration or "Net suryo Shoku" (high caloric content)*
Rice 29.0 (825 g) Meat or Fish tinned 5.0 (~ 170 g) Miso powder 0.5 (15 g) Sugar 0.5 (15 g)	Kanpan (hard tack crackers) 3 muslin bags 8 Oz Arranged in 6 cellophane wrapped packs of ~ 100 g each at 200 g per meal. Ration to be consumed only upon orders.	Compressed rice Picked plum Dried fish Salt Sugar Each item individually sealed in cellophane bags and all packaged in metal containers.	Hard sweets and rice crackers in box Or Peanut/sesame bars vitamin enriched Two or three days' food in box and bar shaped rations.

Source; www.lonesentry.com/articles/intelligence-rep (Army rations from Intelligence Bulletin, Vol II (9) 1944)

An interesting feature of the rations were the food bars (high nutrition), eaten 200 g per meal. Whatever be their nutritional value, it may or may not have proven to be sufficient to fill the stomach. It is reported that the Japanese Navy's handbooks suggested that the bars could be eaten along with grass or seaweed with the purpose of adding roughage (in lieu of vegetables) and to stave off hunger till the next meal.

Korean Diet and Military Rations

Soon after World War II ended, a war in North Korea broke out. US troops were shipped out again, which involved some tremendous logistics planning to keep them supplied with food, weapons and equipment thousands of miles away from their home bases. Japan was a supply base for the

American troops in this war but nothing is known about the Korean army rations beyond the report of a nutrition survey of military foods and rations of the Republic of Korea (ROK). The nutrition survey of the ROK's Armed Forces was conducted in 1956 by the National Institutes of Health, Bethesda, Maryland, whose findings were published in the Journal of Nutrition in 1959 (Williams *et al.,* 1959). Efforts to obtain more recent information in the year 2007 from visiting scientists of the Nutrition Board in Seoul, Korea were unsuccessful.

The Koreans' national diet and the main dietary components are cereals (81 per cent), meat, fish, egg and milk (5 per cent), oil seeds and fats (4 per cent), fruits and nuts (2 per cent), white and sweet potatoes (4 per cent), vegetables and seaweed (1.6 per cent) and sugar (1 per cent). From these their daily diet derives 2,058 Kcals. For Koreans, food is synonymous with rice, it being the main item of their food and the main source of energy calories. Barley and grain sorghum are eaten by poorer sections. While no rice is eaten at all in some isolated areas, in most other places mixtures of rice with barley, sorghum and millet or beans or potatoes are common.

The cereals are eaten together with soup, various soybean products, fish, or when available, beef or chicken. Extensive use of vegetables characterises the Korean diet as it does other Eastern diets. A very unique food item that always accompanies a meal is known as 'Kimchi', which is a vegetable dish. Wheat flour is preferred as bread; Soybean as curd (tofu), or sprouts, mash, or sauce is very popular in Korea but not soy milk.

The Armed Forces in any country follow the pattern of their national dietary habits. The Armed Forces of the Republic of Korea (ROK) are no different. While the US troops in the Korean war of 1950–53 were well supplied with their own essential and favourite foods sent from home and commandeered from bases in Japan, the Korean forces would have depended on home grown produce and products. The ROK soldiers' basic food allowances are shown in Table 10.25. The chemical composition of the average food consumed from kitchen survey samples revealed that the intake from meals prepared with the basic ration allowances provided energy and nutrients – actual and expected (expected values are given in parenthesis) of 3,947 Kcals (3733.0), protein 117.2 g (122.7), fat 13.1 g (44.7 g) carbohydrate 841 g (733 g) and crude fiber 16.2 g.

The same items (rice, soup, sweetened soybeans, fish and kimchi) were served at every meal three times a day – breakfast, lunch and dinner and apparently similar amounts of these items were consumed by an individual at each meal.

The main Korean food items, based on which the Korean military rations are derived and which the Nutrition Survey found to be a simplified version of the civilian diet. The common Korean diet consisted of rice, wheat flour, soya, Khimchi (like sauerkraut), Takuwan, Army soup (mix of vegetables, soya, curd, and dry fish) and salt-pepper. Basically, the military diet provided two main items – cooked mixture of rice and barely, and thick soup served three times a day. These two wer served in separate bowls or mess kits (800 ml capacity) made of aluminium. Any additional foods like canned pork, buns or other types were pilled up on top of rice or items like biscuits (crackers) were issued in bags. At the time of the Nutrition Survey report, the team said that attempts were being made to develop a three part mess kit.

Actual food consumption data gathered from four army messes, three infantry battalions and one in the Army Replacement Training Centre, showed that there were some 22 food items (consumed per man per day) in the Training Centre compared to 12, 14, 16 respectively in each of the three infantry battalion messes (their location is not known). Items such as enriched wheat flour, corn meal, sugar, dried salted fish, salted shrimp, canned ham, kimchi cabbage, pickled radish, pickled garlic and seaweed were not issued in the infantry messes on the days of observation. Although this by itself does not signify any thing particular, one may just wonder whether the curtailed version of the daily food in these messes compared to that in the Training Centre was in some way suggestive of a menu more suitable perhaps for field conditions.

Table 10.25: ROK Armed forces, 1956: Basic food allowance

			Supply source
1.	Rice	676.8g (70 per cent milled)	ROK
2.	Pressed barley	163.8 (processed form)	ROK
3.	Biscuit	83.3g	Ingredients by US
4.	Cigarettes	10.0 (numbers)	ROK
5.	Secondary dishes*		
	Vegetables		
	Meat and fish		US (canned meat)
	Soybeans		US
	Soybean products		
	Vegetable oil		US
	Red pepper		US
	Salt		US

* Within a fixed monetary allowance of 57.91 huan per day per man. ROK Navy, Marine and Air Force purchased the perishables locally.
Source: Williams et al., 1959

Overall, the nutritional status of the 1,514 enlisted men established that there was no cause for concern due to any kind of nutritional deficiency and that adequate amount of calories (3733 kcal), 122.7 g protein and 44.7 g fat were being provided as evidenced by weight-height-age relationship in the Korean, Formosan and Filipino men and their nutritional status was in fact better in 1956 than it was in 1953 (William et al. 1959). Only in respect of vitamins was there evidence of suboptimal levels, and deficiency of riboflavin in particular and since the ration system did not ensure adequate amounts of all essential nutrients according to the conclusions of the survey findings certain changes were proposed.

No data were available for field and combat rations for a modern army of Korea.

Australian Defence Services Rations

The Australian military rations contain foods and products similar to those in the British and US rations. Dominant items are bread and cereal products, meats of different kinds, fresh fruits and vegetables and butter etc. These rations are meant for preparing meals in kitchens. Although every diet includes foods of common use, the list is still small compared to the Indian staples used in ration formulation.

The staple items in the Australian Army Rations food guide for normal kitchen use are shown in Table 10.26 (SRS Australia, 1962, p. 13.). It may be noted that there is less meat for women and cadets but more for Asians. Also, there is no specific scale for cooking fat. It simply says 'as required'.

There are essentially three types of rations designed to give 4,000 Kcals per person per day (SRS, Australia 1962, pp. 8–12). These are variously called Mainland rations, Field Service rations and Overseas rations for peace time (Table 10.27). Australian forces fought in World War II side by side with other Allied forces; they went to war in Vietnam; they have their internal territorial responsibilities and were also deployed in Iraq.

Table 10.26: Service Ration Scale – Australian Armed Forces, 1962

1. Milk and milk substitutes (fresh)	Minimum 12–14 oz, (5/7 oz in field rations condensed)
2. Bread and cereal products Bread, combination of flour, wheat meal, oatmeal, rice	Min 3 oz–10 oz (½ oz to 2½ oz)
3. Fresh Fruits and Vegetable Fruit, fruit juices, potato, onion, other Veg. Tomato puree	Minimum 12 oz, a combination of all these as available
4. Meats and meat substitutes Meat cooked Meat carcass Bacon/cheese/egg	Mininum 40 oz 16 oz (less for women, cadets, more for Asians if no bacon) assorted quantity
5. Butter and table margarine Butter Cooking Fat	 1½ oz as required

Table 10.27: Rations for the Australian Armed forces designed to provide 4000 Kcal/man/day for those on strenuous duty

Mainland Ration Scale (for full nutritional needs)	*Field service Ration Scale (War time)*	*Overseas Ration Scales (Peace)*
For Army, RAAF, certain personnel in navy, those in N. Australia, Asians, cadets, service women messing separately, extra commodities for special conditions, adolescent apprentices, band boys, Clerical trainees, all include many commodities plus many alternatives.	A complete scale has a number of basic commodities and alternatives, provision for cigarette, tobacco and matches. No supplementary ration/ allowance. • Objective is to supply as many fresh foods as possible • When this is not possible, or no refrigeration, then higher proportion of non perishables included, • Several conditions – all processed foods (no fresh at all) • Allowance for this in ration scale. • Other important features –acceptability, keeping quality • Small bulk for minimum refrigeration, hand damage resistant, infestation resistant. • Little preparation with minimum man power	Full nutritional needs, Max scale of issue. For those beyond mainland, where rations given by another country, more liberal than mainland rations on some commodities, have many alternatives.

Source: Service Ration Scales. 1962

Endnote

1. Introduction of new items, ration changes and other related matters come as approvals from the Army Headquarters. These are called Army Instructions.

References

Arora, Puneeta (Lt.Gen) DDG Armed Forces Medical Services. 'Nutrition in the Armed Forces-A historical perspective'. In Symposium on: 'Foods for Special Missions'. International Food Conference IFCON – 2003, November 5–8, 2003. CFTRI, Mysore, India.

ASC Manual: Scales of Rations and Supplies. A Manual Issued by the Army Service Corps. Part extracts referred to as ASC Manual.

Berry, F.B. and H.R. Sandstead 1955. Report on mission to Far East 4–28 April, on problems dealing with nutrition of Armed Forces and Civil Populations. Inter Departmental Committee on Nutrition for National Defence, National Institutes of Health, Bethesda, Md.

Boileau, D.W. (Col), late of RASC. 1954. The Second World War 1939–1945. Army Supplies and Transport. Volumes I and II, Vol I. p. 233; Vol II pp. 433–519.

Compendium of Army Instructions: Rations and Supplies. Quartermaster General's Branch, Army Head Quarters, MOD, New Delhi–15.

Chattopadhyaya, D.P. 'Medicine and Life Sciences in India' Vol. IV, Part 2. B.V. Subbarayappa (Ed). 'History of Science, Philosophy and Culture in Indian Civilization'. Series General Editor–D.P. Chattopadhyaya. Oxford University Press, New Delhi 2000, p. 587.

Das, D.K. Revisiting Talwar: A study in the Royal Indian Navy Uprising of February 1946. Ajanta Publishers, New Delhi, 1993, pp. 99–100.

Guide and Instructions for Patrol Service Cooks. Issued under the authority of the Flag Officer, East Africa, December, 1943.

Indian Navy Book of Reference, Govt of India 1997, Several Appendices.

Military Nutrition Research Annual Report Sept 30, 1982–Sept-29, 1983. Committee on 'Military Nutrition Research', Food & Nutrition Board, Commission on Life Sciences, National Research Council USA. National Academic Press, Washington, 1983.

National Institute of Health, 1959. 'A Nutrition Survey of the Armed Forces of Pakistan'. Inter departmental Committee on Nutrition for National Defence, National Institute of Health, Bethesda, Madison, USA. *The J. Nutr.* Vol 68, Supplement 2, May–Aug. pp. 1–64.

Pandolf, K.B., Giovani, B. & Goldman, R.F., 1997. 'Predicting energy expenditure with loads and while standing or walking very slowly'. J. *Appl. Physiol. Respirat. Environ. Exer. Physiol*, 43: 577–581.

Pennington, William, *Pick Up Your Parrots and Monkeys: The Life of a Boy Soldier in India (Last Days of the Raj),* Cassel, London, 2003.

Service Ration Scales and Ration Packs, 1st edition. 1962. Australian Military Board, Department of the Army, Directorate of Supplies and Transport, Food Service establishment, Melbourne, Australia.

Sheppard, Alan. *The Royal Military Academy*. Country Life Books, 1980

Sinha, S.K. (Gen, Retd, PVSM.). *A Soldier Recalls*. Lancer International, Lancer and Spandeck, London, Norwich Hartford, 1993.

Soyer, Alexis. *Culinary Campaign*. Routledge & Co., London, 1857.

Summary of Survey findings: Revision of ration scales. Personal Communication from Director, DFRL. Mysore, January 2007 and discussions with former scientist of DIPAS, Delhi.

Tewari, K.K. (Gen, Retd). *A Soldier's Voyage of Self Discovery*. Auroville, 1971.

Tilak, V.W. (Brig) and Bhadwar, R. (Lt Col). 'Ration Scales and design considerations and the ground level realities of meeting these requirements for the Armed Forces'. *In* 'Design and Supply of Foods for the Indian Armed Forces'. Proceedings of Services-Laboratory-Industry Interactive Conference, December 10–12, DFRL Mysore, 1996, pp. 41–54.

Williams, R.R., W.J. McGanity, G.F. Combs and Kertesz, Z.I. 'A Nutrition Survey of the Armed Forces of the Republic of Korea'. *The J. Nutr*. 68 May–Aug. Supplement 1, (June), 1959.

Wilson, W.J. (Lt. Col, Retd) Madras Army. *History of the Madras Army*. Compiled Volumes I & II, Madras, E. Keys printer, Government Press Printer, 1882, I: pp. 233; II: 345, 361.

11

Operational Rations and Combat Foods

Description of Combats

Military combat is defined as a violent planned form of physical interaction between two hostile opponents where one or both adversaries could be organised forces recognised by governmental or other authority. Their objectives are one or more of the following: to control the territory or people, to protect one's own territory or people, to dominate, destroy and incapacitate the opponent (Dupuy, 1987, pp. 66–69). These combats could take any form, shape and length of time. For the novice, the military terms such as action, engagement, battle, campaign and war may all mean the same but a military person will distinguish between these terms.

A tactical engagement between the opponents may last 1–5 days and is carried out by the smallest of units up to divisions and army corps under the command of line officers.

In a battle, the army corps and armies are locked for a few days to weeks and are led by sub-commanders. Some of the readers may be familiar with names like the Battle of Plassey, the Battle at Trafalgar, the Battle of Waterloo, the Battle of Jutland or the Battle of Midway.

Campaigns are operations lasting weeks or months for strategic purposes and involve armies, army groups or entire branches of the service such as Napoleon's Russian Campaign, the Peninsular Campaign, and the Burma Campaign etc.

An all out military war is an armed conflict showing great belligerence where the entire armed force (army, navy, air force) are participating in the combat under the direction of the Commander-in-Chief and lasts for days, weeks, months or years. World Wars I and II, Korean war, Vietnam war, Indo-Pakistan wars, Iraq–Gulf war, Afghanistan war fall into this category. However, the dividing lines merge between all these four levels of combat.

Dupuy (1969) explains that wars are fought for national goals, campaigns for strategic objectives and battles for operational missions. An engagement is ordered for a tactical mission. On a smaller scale is an action lasting 1–24 hrs, where battalion or squad level fight erupts to gain very local objectives.

Progressively larger numbers become involved at the behest of their countries' armies. They are fittingly equipped to carry out their tasks – overt or covert in nature. This includes providing them all with temporary housing, equipment, transport, weapons and ammunition, communication devices, medical services, clothing and food to carry which is appropriate to the circumstances in which they are expected to operate.

Operational Rations – Foods for the Combat Zone

The units in peace areas are surrounded by the amenities and facilities provided in the barracks which include well equipped kitchens, well trained cooks, and regular and timely delivery of fresh supplies and all ration items. The units posted in field areas are attached to the base camps which have their own supply depots, ration store houses and field cook houses. Some structures may be of a permanent nature, others may be temporary encampments. As long as the supplies reach their intended destinations and as long as the field operations are normal i.e., non-combat situations –

fresh food service at every meal is the norm. But often detachments of five to ten men or individuals are deployed on patrol duties, or other tasks; the period of absence from the main unit could last from a few hours to three to four days. In battle, for military efficiency, it becomes imperative that the individual does not spend time trying to make food in the midst of fighting. It becomes the responsibility of the Command to provide him with whatever food possible. When providing rations became an accepted military support practice, there arose a new set of situations where standard or normal rations were modified to suit the operations under way. These came to be known as operational rations and or combat foods.

The operational rations are required for situations outside the garrisons and base camps when the men are deployed on various duties including combat. They may get full rations (complete energy content) or partial rations (restricted calories) depending on the situation and duration of operations and field conditions. Soldiers are deployed out of units regularly on patrols; they are air dropped on points on the hills; they trudge on the snow or sand or in the jungles, climb long or short mountain ranges; and have to carry food in their backpacks. And because of this, the weight and content of the food package must necessarily be restricted. There are no 'B' echelons (a system of provisioning in the army) for them to catch up with. These foods are usually of two types – one is used in combat and the second is meant for survival purposes.

Admirable sentiments such as, '*We do not really pay attention to food*'; '*It is the least of our worries'; 'Nobody has time for food in the thick of battle'* where bullets and artillery fire are raining down are aired by every officer spoken to with battle experience. The body needs fuel because hunger signals will bombard the senses. And it is for that time, those moments, for that brief hiatus that there can be few things more welcoming than to reach for that food and a smoke. Smoking is a mere temporary fatigue relieving diversionary palliative like opium used to be. Food to get energy and strength and to go on is not on the same scale as a smoke or a drink. Also the maximum complaints of any kind in the army revolve around food. That alone tells food is important, battle or no battle.

Rations for War Zone – Some Early Examples

There were hardly any standing armies in the past except for small militias and contingents of King's soldiers and cavalry on guard duties. The soldiers were recruited in numbers when an expedition was planned. Even then it was not the state's responsibility to arrange for their food. They were paid a salary by their feudal lords or were promised a slice of the loot for their services.

Gradually it was realised that for efficiency, food must be provided in the camps so that men did not spend time foraging. In the Roman Republic, in Kautilya's time and much later in Napoleon's time as well, there were systems to arrange for and procure the requisite quantities of food, feed and fodder for the armies when they marched.

Food of a Rajput king in combat: In India, the Rajput kingdoms in western parts were under continuous attacks from beyond the western frontiers and from the Mughals. The hilly and rocky terrain, hill top forts and the surrounding forests provided protection while the thick thorny jungles and the large stretches of desert and sand dunes stood as forbidding frontiers. Outside the walls of the fort, provisioning the fighting men in such conditions would have posed enormous challenges. Long drawn out campaigns required a supply mechanism but the terrain often dictated what could be transported. Therefore, the minimal rations which were carried along into the war zone could be as frugal for the king as for his men. There is no specific account anywhere of what these foods were.

The soldiers camped in the forest areas that were abundant with tree cover, wild game, and water in the rainy season from a river or a stream. The kings and the commanders camped where they could and were served faithfully by their own minions in the field. The travails of a king are depicted in a vast canvas displayed in Mehrangarh Fort, Jodhpur (Fig. 11.1). Maharana Ajit Singh Rathore of Jodhpur-Marwar hiding from the Mughal Emperor Aurangazeb was forced to live incognito for 29 years (from his birth in 1678 till the Emperor's death in 1707). Wandering and living under the protection of his father, the late Maharana Jaswant Singh's loyal employees and friends, the infant king grew to adulthood while continuously trying to evade capture and confinement and lived off the land. He was accompanied only by a small band of faithful supporters until he could conquer Jodhpur once again. He was assiduously served during this entire period by his trusted lieutenant Veer Durga Das Rathore, heralded as the saviour of the independence of Marwar.

Fig. 11.1: Living in forests during constant combats and conflicts, Veer Durga Das Rathore stood guard day and night and ever vigilant and protective of his young Royal charge Maharaja Ajit Singh of Jodhpur. He would himself prepare the king's bread or 'bati' over a wood fire by using the tip of his spear. The king ate while still seated on his horse and while surrounded by mounted guards keeping vigil. A water bearer is seen fetching water in earthen pots.

Source: Mehrangarh Museum Trust, Jodhpur, Rajasthan.

Combat Rations in Europe

Soldiers in Europe were given finite amounts of grains, olive oil or lard or ghee, hard biscuits or bread, salt and salted meats, dried meat or vegetables, vinegar, wine and green coffee beans. When there was a lull in fighting, the soldiers gathered firewood, made a fire and cooked. Most of them were very often accompanied by their families and all household articles and children; the women helped keep a home fire burning and prepared food in the forest camps.

There were no separate foods meant for use during combat. Only the basic items were provided and the soldiers cooked their own food every evening. It was the same in America since the time of the Revolutionary war, and in India under the Mughals, the East India Company and then the British Crown till World War 1.

The very inadequate and pathetic war zone feeding practices in the Crimean war in the 1850s suggested that though campaign feeding received a thought or two from the English military planners, it was more in the nature of sending some provisions to cook a meal of sorts with minimal facilities and by unskilled men than a meal of substance. The French troops were better off. In late nineteenth century Europe, field rations for the troops were introduced in Imperial Germany and the Austro-Hungarian Empire.

The Imperial German Army rations: For a long time, no particular rations for the military were designated. The German food consisted principally of bread, pork, bacon, sausages of various kinds, cheese, potatoes, and sauerkraut, other picked vegetables like beet and cucumber, and as was the custom in every country, the same habits of the German people were carried into the Imperial Army's service rations. Till the late nineteenth century, the Prussian soldiers ate portable food which consisted of slices of bacon, dried beans, hard bread, cheese, salt, sugar and a little coffee. There were small distances to travel and pack trains sufficed to carry and convey supplies. Napoleon, during his reign, had not only specified rations but also admirably managed to provide them for his troops on their marches. But after that, in Imperial Germany, there was no standard ration as such. With the increasing importance of the railroad in logistics, and the threat from France, and with the possibility of soldiers having to travel farther away in campaigns, a standard emergency or durable food was sought.

The Army Research group of the Kingdom of Prussia came up with a winner – a patent owned by a factory owner in Berlin. It was for a formula of compressed soup and was the 'Erbswurst' or pea sausage. The product came as six tablets of compressed split pea soup packed into a tube or sausage shaped foil or wax paper pack. The soup itself was made of ground peas, bacon, spices and salt. One tablet mixed with 8 oz or ¼ litre of water and cooked for a while gave a soup. This was eaten with round biscuits called Hartkeks – which were like the English navy's hardtack but could be chewed with some difficulty and without soaking in water. On occasions, the troops were put on this hard ration and also given a little fruit or vegetables for weeks on end to evaluate its nutritional adequacy. This was the ration until 1888 through the Franco–Prussian War.

But Germany was in need of suitable individual rations for prolonged periods for the soldiers who were being deployed globally – in the Pacific, the Arctic, Asia and Africa. This search for better rations resulted in a contents list for the soldiers ration pack (Table 11.1). Except for the quantities mentioned for each item and bacon, this ration appears to be no different from the portable ration of the 1870s. These rations were a far cry from today's German combat rations for the individual, known as *Einmannpackung,* providing two substantial meals to every soldier, of which one is a hot cooked meal whenever possible. In the three menus for the other meal currently available in heavy duty foil trays, there are lentils with sausages, Italian pasta, Yugoslav sausages, Goulash, beef patties in tomato sauce and tofu stir fry; there are also smaller foil cans of bread spreads, varieties of dried sausages, rye bread slices, soup crackers or hard crackers, coffee and tea, fruit salad, instant cream of wheat, instant fruit juice powder, chocolate bar, salt, sugar, chewing gum, jam, water purification tablets, plastic bags, matches and paperwipes.

Table 11.1: The Imperial German Army rations

Prussian Army 1870–71	*Prussian Army Until 1888*	*German Army 1890–1914*		*Additional items for different deployment areas*
(Quantities not known)	Erbwurst – 6	Erbswurst	130 g × 2	*Pacific region*:
Bacon slices	tablets,	Hard bread	1250 g × 2	Dried potatoes – 125 g
Dried beans	Hartkek	Beacon	150 g	(loose or in waxed boxes)
Hard bread		Coffee	25 g	*Arctic region/winter duty*
Cheese		Or		Chocolate Or
Salt		Tea	3 g	Chocolate powder
Sugar		Sugar	25 g	Extra sugar
Coffee		Salt	25 g	

The modern German army also has a Class I support system which provides the subsistence support in peace time and during emergency operations (Koehler, 1980). Such support and provisioning are said to be the responsibility of six individually administered military districts – both meant for garrison administration and food management. The garrison administrative office procures rations and the military district office stores the provisions and rotates them. It is said that in emergency situations, something called the 'mass consumption goods' are given to Companies. These are food stocks which have been kept at Corps depots.

Austro–Hungarian Rations: The Imperial Army of Emperor Franz-Joseph was a mix of 11 ethnic groups. In the time of World War I, it was a challenge to cater to so many different tastes and food preferences. There were three standard rations labeled *volle portion*, *normal portion*, and *reserve portion* (Table 11.2). The volle portion was the full portion rations issued to troops in relatively well stocked rear areas and in static positions in World War I. The contents of the volle portion would

Table 11.2: Imperial Austro-Hungarian Army rations in World War I

Volle portion (full portion/issue)	*Normal portion (normal portion/issue)*	*Reserve portion (emergency portion/issue)*
Beef – 14.1oz (400 g)	Beef – same as in volle	Meat 1 tin – 7 to 10.5 oz
Vegetables – 5.0 oz (140 g)	portion	Zwiebeck – 7 oz (200 g: 50 g
Bread – 24.6 oz (700 g) or	Vegetables 3.6 oz (100 g)	× 4 packs)
Zwiebeck – 14.1 oz (400 g)	Bread – same	Salt (small box) – 10 z (30 g)
(round Army Biscuit)	Salt – same	Tobacco – 0.63 oz (18 g)
Supplements	Pepper – same	
Salt 1.0 oz (30 g)	Fat – same	
Pepper or Paprika 0.02 oz (0.5 g)	Coffee – same	
Fat or Lard 0.7 oz (20 g)	Soup seasoning – same	
Ground Coffee – 1.6 oz (46 g) each, 2 tins	Vinegar – 0	
Soup seasoning (dry herbs) 0.04 oz (1g)	Tobacco – 1 oz	
Onion or garlic – 0.17 oz (5 g)		
Vinegar – 0.67 fluid oz (20 ml)		
Luxuries:		
Tobacco – 1.26 oz (36 g)		
For officers only (cigars) – 5 or cigarettes 25		
Wine 16.9 fluid oz (500 ml)		

Source: http://17th division.tripod.com/rationsoftheageofempire/id6/html.

have provided a sumptuous meal and abundant calories and certainly not less than 3,000 kcal/day. The normal portion ration was a marginally reduced version of the volle portion − less vegetables and no condiments like onion and vinegar. This ration was apparently meant for cooking a quick meal in the trench kitchens during lull in action.

The third ration for emergencies and also known as *iron ration* was just tinned meat – roast pork with gravy or pork loaf (the quantity varying between 200 g to 400 g) and Zwieback consisting of either toasted bread or hardtack or semi sweet biscuits. The only condiment was salt.

No matter what item in the ration was eliminated, it would never be tobacco, though its quantity may be slightly reduced.

Twentieth Century Developments in Combat Packs and Field Feeding Systems

The fundamental desire for a fresh cooked meal after a hard day's work can not be questioned. Depending on the war time, field facilities and opportunity to cook and eat, all meals of the day were preferably cooked fresh. World War I was a trench war where elaborate trenches had been dug in at the front, with well connected living space for offices and lines of communications in the trench network. Full cooking facilities had been provided underground in the German rear trenches and for sending up pails of food through the tunnels to the soldiers. The tunnel also had officers' mess. During long lulls the soldiers could get quite a lot of 'off' time and even go on home leave for short periods and come back refreshed. There were also packed rations which every man carried in his kit along with his rifle and ammunition.

Fighting in East Africa where the Indian troops had been sent to fight the Germans, the Royal Indian ASC was the prime mover of stores, supplies and everywhere possible hot foods were served.

The far flung theatres of operations in World War II involving armies of different countries who had their own regional/ethnic preferences for foods necessitated ration planning and supplies on an unprecedented scale. There were several categories of field rations used by the British forces as described earlier as well as pack rations and emergency sustenance rations in use by the US Allies. The Japanese army also had certain curtailed versions of field/combat foods.

All rations of that period were un-inspiring and operational rations in particular were minimalist in nature even if convenient. The post war scenario began to bring some changes in this respect. Better nutrition and acceptability together with convenience were sought.

Operational Rations – Design, Content, Nomenclature

Military thinking on food planning appears to run on similar lines whether the planners are Indian or others. Friedl and Hoyt (1997), referring to the US military's operational rations, say that the criteria for designing operational rations are:

- cut calorie rations for each day,
- increase calorie density by using high energy sources,
- lower the moisture content for weight reduction and increased shelf life; and preferably also keep it to
- a single item which may be a sort of calorie packed meal by itself.

There are several ways food has been provided to the men in operational areas and in battle. One way is to provide field rations or combat rations. In understanding and terminology, such a ration is invariably a canned or prepackaged meal, quickly prepared and consumed, which can be carried by men in the battlefield or transported there. Their uniqueness lies in requiring minimal preparation time. Many technologies have been applied to make precooked foods and instant powders suitable for such conditions, chief among these being canning in metal cans or foil-plastic bags or thin flat cans – retort pouch processing, freeze dehydration, other drying methods, compression methods, confectionary methods etc. Practically all the armies of the world use some form of pre-packaged rations for their soldiers as per ethnic tastes.

Reading through the current list of contents of several combat rations, each one is described variously as combat meal individual, or 24 hour rations for one man. They contain breakfast, lunch and dinner and other refreshments and include foods made according to that country's own regional cuisine, packed in cans or more often in foil based pouches and or trays but the meal menus essentially contains protein from the main entrée: meat preparations of a great variety, some with and others without vegetables, starches from breakfast type cereals, compressed cereal bars, rice or pasta or both, potatoes, breads, crackers; main meal accessories in packs containing meat preparations that accompany a meal; one or the other kind of bread spread, butter, jam, salt, spices, sugar, invariably a chocolate bar or hard candy or caramel, instant soup powder, fruit drink powder instant coffee, instant tea, or cocoa powder, dry fruits or trail mixes or nuts or fruit salad, chewing gum, more accessories like plastic spoon, paper towels, wipes, water purification tablets, sometimes one aluminum cup, often a disposable stove, alcohol based fuel tablets, disposable lighter or matches plastic bags or boxes as containers, sometimes extra sealable bags for rehydration of instant drinks and drinking water in pouches or bottles.

Descriptions of combat rations provide ration details for certain countries; here they have been grouped as under: Latin American kind (Argentina – *Racion de Combate*, individual; Colombia –*Racion de Campana*; Mexico – *Soldados individuales diarios combaten comidas*), United States of America – *MRE*, Canada – *IMP*, European kind (Czech Republic – *Bojova Davka Potravin BDP and KDP or Konzervovana Davka Potravin*, Finland, France – *ration de combat individualle rechauffable*, Germany –*Einmannpackung*, Ireland, Italy – *razione viveri speciali da combatimento;* Lithuania – *MRE*; Netherlands – *Gevechtsrantsoen*, Norway and Sweden –*Strdsrasjon*; Poland – *Zestaw Zywnosciiowy Indywidualne Racji Suchen*, Russian Federation – *Individual food ration* more like the French rations; Spain, United Kingdom – *Operational Ration Pack, General Purpose*; Ukraine – like the earlier Russian rations; Portugal – *Racao Individual de Combate*; Greece – *Merida Eidikon Dynameon* for the Special Forces), Middle East (Israel – *battle ration* or *Manot Krav*, Saudi Arabia – small MRE pouches, United Arab Emirates – European style rations), Australia – *Combat Ration One Man*, Peoples Republic of China – dehydrated items, Singapore – *Muslim, non-Muslim* and vegetarian labeled combat rations, Sri Lanka – *jungle ration 24 hr pack*, South Korea – ready to eat pouch foods and freeze dried single meal ration, New Zealand – *Operational ration Pack MRE*; Asia (Brunei – using Muslim dietary norms, Indonesia – *24 hr Composite rations*, Malaysia and Japan – canned and precooked pouch foods).

Pasta, beans etc. feature in the South American and Mexican foods, more fish and vegetables in the East Asian diets and meats dominating in Europe, USA and Middle East. Olives, more vegetables, fish etc. are included in Israeli and Greek diets. The Greek rations interestingly come in meals prepared with meats and meals without meats. Norwegian, Swedish and Korean combat rations are the only ones using freeze dried foods for the main/only meals; all others use the precooked and packaged moist foods. Most rations are available in multiple menus, weigh perhaps less than 2 kg and provide from 3,000 to 3,800 Kcals or sometimes even slightly more per man per day.

How long can a soldier subsist on such packed rations and continue to remain healthy, physically fit and perform as per expectations under conditions as varied as sleep deprivation, intense physical activity, climatic extremes and even hypobaric hypoxia? These were the questions that needed answers while considering military nutrition in the context of operational rations.

Friedl & Hoyt (1997) also pointed out that while the average daily energy calorie through foods amounted to 3,000 Kcals and sometimes less through operational rations, the energy expenditure during typical field training was determined to be in the range of 4,000 Kcal/day. There was thus a shortfall of 1,000 Kcals/day which was a substantial amount and must be provided in a form which was more acceptable and palatable than the operational rations.

The United States military operational rations evolved from the individual 'C' rations of World War II to MRE meals introduced in the 1980s. Troops are the same every where when it comes to poor compliance with consuming the designated rations that must be eaten to gain any benefit. Monotony, un-palatability of the rations and even anything not familiar to them take their toll and as Friedl puts it, the soldiers would rather go hungry and fall sick than eat.

The 'K' ration, which was the first packed ration for emergency use by the US military ever to be brought out, left an unforgettable imprint on the users and the researchers. The 'K' ration biscuits containing among other ingredients a heady concoction of brewer's yeast, soybean flour and liver extract emanated peculiar odours and flavours guaranteed to put off the appetites of even the most daring of animals let alone men. It seems even the desert rats avoided the discarded biscuits! Closer to home, in a post war scenario, a comparable instance where men dislike a ration item can be found in the unanimous aversion of the Indian troops to whole milk powder given as a substitute for fresh milk and a few sundry other items such as certain tinned meats.

With all due regard to nutritional planning, it is important that food science and technology keep pace with other modern developments, otherwise the troops in the field will suffer. The biomedical and nutritional assessments of the rations provided are important criteria to ascertain whether the said rations are serving their functional purpose. The military nutritional scale must therefore reflect the amount of energy calories, protein, fat, carbohydrate contents as well as the quantities of various vitamins and minerals.

The food items provided to the US army in combat are a pointer to the general advancement of the US food processing industry and have come a long way from the days of World War II. When in the 1950s, the Korean war broke out, an alternative to the can was sought. Radical thinking and R&D produced the 'Retort Pouch processing' and the right type of plastic 'Mylar' to withstand high temperatures and pressures of steam sterilization (Lampi, 1977). 'Kevlar' was also invented around the same time as a sturdy bulletproof material.

With the introduction of retort pouch technology into the commercial food processing sector, it has been possible to produce 'ready to eat' foods and assemble them into 1-day, 5-day or larger ration packs. Juggling with different cereals, pulses, vegetable and fruit based preparations, the semblance of a balanced meal can be and has been designed, supplemented with multivitamins.

Today, there is a great variety of food products and packs that form a part of field rations and operational and combat rations. This has come about due to the advances in technology, from greater understanding of nutritional principles as well as greater awareness among nation states of the need to look after their soldiers better and the willingness to act on it as a policy and by installing logistic systems for procurement and supply and budgetary allocations to make it financially possible. And above all, the technological developments leading to many food processing and preservation techniques and numerous food products with assured shelf life have made it possible to improve vastly the quality and variety of foods in combat packs. The grocery type rations have given way to ready to eat foods; iron rations have been replaced with nutrient sufficient meal packs; cans are gone and their place taken by the flexible polymeric pouches for ready to eat items and snacks; there are tetrapak cartons for ready to drink beverages, PET bottles for drinking water, instant dry ready mixes in portion size sachets meant for quick rehydration such as soups, juice, crystals, tea/coffee/ whiteners/sugar combinations – all falling under the nomenclature Meals Ready to Eat or MRE.

Every Armed Force has its own version of the MREs introduced in the 1980s but US, Canadian, British and Australian food habits and preferences being somewhat similar (or so we presume) if not exactly the same, their MRE menu items are meat based entrees, side dish, crackers or bread, butter or cheese spread, dessert, instant coffee/tea, sugar and creamer. Matches, spoon, a heater and toilet paper are also included along with the food packs.

The variety that can be found in the entrees, side dishes, crackers, breads, desserts and beverages and the convenient packaging in the various MREs is a testimony to the vast food technological-industrial base of these countries and the popularity of all such food items among the civilian consumers.

Operational rations of the US Army: In modern times, rations for cooking and easy to carry combat ready foods are not only different but a lot more care and concern have been shown in making each type of food in terms of their availability and quantities. In the United States military parlance 'A' rations (Quarter Master Museum web pages) are the various components that constitute the entitled daily issue of rations (as in the Indian SRS, which are grocery items) with which fresh cooked meals are prepared. When logistically convenient to deliver the 'A' rations – a mixture of dry rations, fresh chilled and processed items are transformed into standard meal menus in well appointed kitchens by the unit cooks and served by the food service people. All meals served at unit levels will use the 'A' type of rations. Feeding is carried out at three levels as depicted in Table 11.3: (a) for preparation and service in the unit, (b) for small detachments on the move in tanks or on patrols (five in one rations requiring heating with the mess-gear the men carried was believed to be the most acceptable operational ration) and (c) rations designed for use by troops engaged in air, amphibious, patrol or outpost action, (and were actually a replacement of the World War II K-rations) meant for individuals during combat when each person is on his own and must eat out of a pack and when there is no possibility of re-supply for some time. There are several aspects to be considered here which pertain to the nutritional quality of food, the body's physiological and biochemical parameters, and overall acceptability. There are other points that should be addressed such as the weight of the packets, whether it is possible to transport them without damage and loss in quality, the shelf stability and for how long it can keep without spoiling under variable climatic conditions. The various types of rations available for these purposes are shown in Table 11.4.

Table 11.3: Feeding at three levels for the troops

Unit	*Detachment*	*Individual*
Normal situation Kitchen equipment Ration supply	Tank crews Patrols Weather stations Siachen pill boxes no normal kitchen facilities	Active combat Amphibious landing-hostile strong no re–supply

Source: www.qmfound.com/historyofrations.html

The ration types and especially those used in war zones by the US armed forces as depicted in Table 11.4 range from the 'A' and field 'B' (using some non perishable foods in cans) and C-series packs. Combat E type rations replaced the earlier version of 'C' and the 'K' rations. Sandwich meals with coffee/juices, soups, paper wrapped fruit and candy stood for flight rations. Nourishment to the individual did play a part in designing these rations especially when the packs had to be small for operational situations. C-rations had appeared in seven versions numbered C1–C7, with choices of 11 meat components-beans and frankfurters, spaghetti and meat, beans with pork, ham burgers with gravy-pork sausages, patties and gravy, ham and lima beans, meat and noodles, chicken and vegetable, beef stew, corned beef hash together with canned fruit and chocolate, coffee crackers, jam, condiments.

Another set of rations go under the nomenclature of emergency rations, assault packs, survival packs (Table 11.5). These are not full rations, nor are they nutritionally complete but provide energy to function and carry on for one day or at most another day, until such time as normal food is accessed. Supplementary items not usually given are provided under special circumstances for fatigue relief or for sustenance in the theatre of operations or in the hospitals.

The Special Forces such as Delta Forces and Commandos are not like the other soldiers in the Army. As they cannot and do not expect daily re-supplies of food and water, careful thought is given to the weight and volume of the gear and food that they haul on their person. Further, they have no physical access to any facility for their own life support and waste management, meaning that when they are out on a mission, save for hi-fi communications, each member of the SF has to function as a totally independent unit from the time of starting a mission with no other supporting life line but what he can carry till the completion of the mission and his extraction. 'Extraction' in military parlance means evacuating/rescuing the individual or groups of individuals from the scene of action or a mission zone either when the mission is successfully completed or when it is abandoned or when the person has to be sent elsewhere. When they are in training and where there are kitchen facilities at the training base they eat the 'T' rations or fresh foods.

Each 'T' ration contains meat, starch (potato or bread or rice), and a selection of vegetables. These are pre-cooked meals filled and sealed in aluminum trays and irradiated. They are generally refrigerated for use beyond a few days. It seems two bottles of a special brand of Tabasco sauce was an absolute must for the soldiers, (as are the pickles, chilli powder, condiments etc., for the Indians) and is therefore included for every meal. The 'T' rations are ready to heat and eat, after being heated in hot water heaters. Fresh foods upon occasion are also obtained locally from shops and from the people of the areas where the SF are deployed. For water, they only use bottled water wherever available.

Table 11.4: Rations of different kinds in the US Armed Forces

Field A	*Field B operational*	*Small detachment*	*Combat E*	*Individual combat C-2 1948*	*Individual combat C-3*	*Air Force Flight Ration*
Best food from organized kitchens Present trend of study: seasonal/ regional preference environmental factors, racial/ economic food habits, food waste, nutritional loss Includes Components of grocery type, Cooking equipment even for detachment, field baking oven, insulated food containers, cafeteria trays.	Best substitute for A, where kitchen functions, but no refrigerator. Same menu as 'A' with nonperishable substitutes. Problem: study food acceptance, space available, with limitations Not used before WW–1, limited components during WW–2. - But became essential due to long lines of supply, lack of local fresh foods - therefore mostly canned/processed foods	5 in 1 small detachment foods components-for 5 men/1day All in one case weighs 27lbs. Carried by one man. Cooking equipment needed 5 menus- Canned meats Bread/v biscuits Pudding, Jam Vegetables, Sugar Milk, Beverage Confections, Cheese spread, butter spread, Cigarettes, can opener, toilet tissue, soap, water tab, sponge cellulose, Tape, paper towels 4,000 Kcal	Replaced old type C and K rations C and K were used interchangeably. So best features of both were combined in E.	Individual, packaged, pre-cooked. Maximum individual nourishment in smallest physical unit. Already modified 5 menus	Third revision of C. Hence C–3. ~5.5 5 menus of greater Variety 1. Meat+2 bread+3. Fruits. 4.Cigarettes etc Bread-cookie, sandwiches Premixed cereal 3cans–meat 3cans–bread/crackers sandwich and or cereal 1 unit jam, crackers, soluble coffee, sugar, cocoa disc, 1 jam & crackers also 1–12 oz can fruit for 1 meal, Field cooking equipment not required; provides better nutrition than 'C' *C–4- (recent) has 2 cans of fruit for 2 meals	In flight for feeding pilots flying > 3hrs 88½ oz in 8 cans. Sandwich type for 3-8 hrs flight, another for 8-16h flight; sandwich, fruit juice, coffee, sugar, soup, snacks, candy, canned fruit, wrapped in wax paper/ paper boxes, bags along with spoons, cups

Source: www.qmfound.com/army_subsistence_history. Notes from 1949 Conference on Rations.

Table 11.5: Types of food packets in US Rations*

Emergency packet Individual	*Assault pack*	*Survival pack*	*Ration supplements*	*Civilian vs. Military Food*
Not rations, just some calories	Individual use	Still being developed	Spice, condiments packs in combat conditions	Military objective – efficient Army so suitable food – responsibility of the command
Pre-cooked or prepared Where no kitchens	Easily carried and eaten hot/cold. Fuel tabs provided	Individual emergency as personal equipment on person for all military personnel active land/sea/air	Soldiers comfort items like toilet articles	Civil – individual's responsibility
Minimum weight and bulk	3 cans of meat 1 can of fruit	Something to eat	For hospitals and station – soups, beverages not normally given with ration, but only in theatre of operations	
– Provide less calories therefore not a Ration	1 can cookies 1 can confections in one place of battle, its use only for 23–30 hrs.		Sundries packs – comfort items as supplement to ration, field A & B for theatres of operations	

* After Civil/Mexican war, US soldiers did not have to fight on their own soil. It was always elsewhere that they went to fight. Their ration supply system to overseas theatre of operations depended heavily on ships and when necessary–air supply. The British too went to war not on their own soil but in other countries and continents.

Source: www.qmfound.com/army_subristence_history. Prepared by Quarter Master School for Quarter Master General. January 1949

However, these are more ideal conditions than what usually confront them. For this reason they carry packed rations. The universal packed rations now are the processed and pouch packed foods that make up the MRE and include freeze dried foods popular with the camping fraternity.

On Mission Mode: Special Forces can be sent anywhere and thus must be outfitted to function in any climate for stretches of time lasting from a few days to a week or more. Calorie content, nutrition, variety, convenience and taste aspects of the food components of their rucksacks receive much consideration (Clancy, 2001, p. 113). One stand-by for all types of operations are the MREs. MRE meals are fully moist and come packed and processed in thermal resistant plastic polymer pouches. Each pouch is then wrapped with a protective and sturdy outer packaging. It is not easy to cut open either the outer cover or the inner pouch. Although a small nick in the pack is supposed to help cut along the line. Individually processed foods are assembled into meals and contribute to considerable bulk. Each individual food item can weigh from 250 g (Indian MRE weighs much the same) but Clancy mentions a figure of 540 g for the US Army's MRE. There will be at least 2 to 3 packets per meal, and a meal is eaten at least twice a day if not more often. It would contain meat or vegetable, rice, pasta, and other variations in ethnic food, and mostly bread (Clancy, 2001, p. 113).

At a minimum, the food carton holding one week's food supply would weigh something like 7 kg (Indian food pack) and no less than 14 kg (US food pack). Welcome as the food will be because it is a long-life type of ready to eat food, such a cumbersome weight can only be a hindrance to mobility and a nuisance particularly in cold and hot weather action or in long range patrols. Other physiological reasons are said to be that the high calorie content and extra nutrients like vitamins present in these specially crafted foods make for pungent urine which will attract sniffer dogs in high security zones and during clandestine operations. That is not welcome.

Meal Cold Weather (MCW) and Long Range Patrol (LRP) Rations: Light weight rations can be a boon on packed weight considerations. Dehydrated foods are the answer as opposed to the fully moist retort pouch foods that go to make the MRE.

Dehydrated foods are produced by several technologies, but for the best retention of quality, nutrition and taste, Freeze Dehydration (FD) is the process of choice. FD foods have less than 3 per cent moisture, and as most of the weight of a food is due to its water content (between 60–95 per cent) and retort pouch food is no exception; FD foods by virtue of having very low moisture are featherweight in comparison. They only need addition of water to become rehydrated quickly before eating. Of course carrying or finding extra water for this purpose is essential.

Full meals can be assembled using FD food items from entrees, starch, and desserts to drinks and fruit bits. Freeze dehydration is many times more expensive than retort processing and the US military is said to procure only a small number of MCW and LRP rations which are available in 12 different menus, as against millions of MREs. FD food items are also popular with campers, trekkers and mountaineers. FD foods comprise a significant proportion of astronaut meals eaten in space crafts.

The US army utilises many 'off the shelf' foods. There are many varieties of foods available now in the market but the selected foods receive special packaging and safety evaluation. MRE items plus dehydrated foods go into the backpacks providing 3,000 Kcal. For group patrols, canned rations are made for four men and ten men units.

Presently for much of the troop feeding in the field of operations, the Army Field Feeding Systems (ACFFS) is brought in to service. It comprises of 'T' rations which are prepared foods in multi serve quantity, filled and processed in flat tray like cans. This kind of pack is amenable to quick heating and thus the troops get quick hot meals, prepared in Mobile Food Services Units (MFSU). This mobile service, mounted on trailers or trucks heats tray packs while on the move. When making halts at mealtime, the hot food comes out of the Supplemental Field Kitchen Kit (SFKK), which has equipment and a shelter that can be erected very quickly.

The army combat field feeding system emerged in response to the new challenges in a modern war and has been designed for mobility; it has the flexibility for big or small scale feeding of troops, it saves on labour, energy and water consumption and provides hot meals on demand.

Operational rations of United Kingdom: There are many types of operational ration packs designated four men and ten men packs which are nutritionally balanced and contain mainly canned items plus breads and biscuits. The rations provide 4,000 Kcal per man per day. In the individual 24 hr GS rations there is limited variety. Since the troops do not like canned foods, retort pouch foods are used. For variety, more seasoning mixes are included.

The special patrol rations of the Air Force meant to be used continually for 21 days are composed of 1.5 kg of balanced food made up of dehydrated foods at a level of 5,000 Kcal/day. The second type of operational packs is designed for restricted calories. The ultra light ration for the army is designed for 14 days use during which no re-supply occurs and provides 1,800 Kcal/man per day. On this restricted calorie diet, soldiers are physically fine and efficient for at least 10 days and there after some degree of weight loss occurs.

The Emergency Flying Ration (EFR) is truly a food for sustenance and survival under starvation. It is composed of protein 1 part, fat 2.5 parts and carbohydrate 5.5 parts. The EFR container measuring 130mm X 100mm X 55mm has to fit into the ejectable pilot's seat and thus the quantity of food that can be provided has to be limited.

Under modern warfare situations, one must be prepared to face nuclear, biological and chemical warfare threats. Protective clothing donned by those who are in the thick of rescue and evacuation work, decontamination, clearance and restoration of emergency facilities etc. have to be worn for long periods. Within the space-man like bubble suit, food and drink are consumed in the form of meal bars in special packaging and liquid vitamin glucose drink in retort pouch. The tubing to drink the liquid runs through the respirator pocket. The meal bars provide nutrients in a balanced way and sustain the individual for seven days.

C-ration series transformed – British version: There have been several versions of the combat rations originally known as 'C' rations 1, 2 and 3 denoting revisions since it was developed just before World War II and lasted until 1958 (www.en.wiki.org/wiki/c-rations#.2c_Individual_2c_combat.2cType_c.2c.28Revised29_281948_1958.29). The first or C-1 ration was designed to provide energy of 2,974 Kcals/per man per day with a protein content of 114 g and adequate quantities of vitamins and minerals. It had 3 cans of meat and vegetable component and 3 cans with crackers, sugar and soluble coffee.

The C–2 form contained packaged pre-cooked foods for ready consumption – hot or cold as the soldier may decide. A solid fuel portable stove formed part of the kit. This ration was meant to feed the individual trooper for a few days and at most for three weeks continuously. It came in five different menus and accessory packs which usually carried comfort articles such as tobacco, toilet articles, sweets, match box, and the like.

The next or the C–3 type also came in five full menus, each of which included bread, meat (any of ten different varieties), cookie, sandwiches, premixes, cereal, jam, crackers, coffee, sugar, cocoa disc (chocolate drink), a 12 oz can of fruit and one accessory packet. Each one man – three meal ration pack weighed 88 and 1/2 oz was distributed in eight small cans.

The modified recent version in the recent C–4 individual combat ration of the British Army provides fruit component in two meals in the form of two 6 oz cans instead of one 12 oz can. It seems the C–ration cigarettes were discontinued in 1972.

Meal Combat Individual: The C–terminology has been replaced with the term Meal Combat Individual or MCI. There is more variety in the MCI than there was in the C series rations and here 12 menus have been provided. The accessory packets provide cigarettes (any one of five brands), matches, chewing gum, toilet paper, coffee, cream, sugar, salt, one spoon, different sauces and flavourings to add to or enhance the taste and flavour of the food. This helps to break the monotony of the repetitive menus. There are seven menus in the GP pack. Keeping in mind the religious sentiments of different groups, three menus made with meat of the Halal type, three menus for Sikhs and Hindus and three vegetarian menus which are also kosher are features of the 24-hour ORP (Operational Ration Pack). In addition, there are four patrol rations which essentially comprise of light weight dehydrated reconstitutable foods. Within these there are rations designed for cold climates with rolled oats and for hot climates with additional fruit drinks.

Adequate and nutritionally balanced meals for one individual, these rations are meant to be normally used in the field. The hot meals are flexi-foil processed pouch foods. Each ration consisting of breakfast, snack, main meal, beverages and sundry items delivers 3,800–4,200 Kcals/day through protein 10 per cent, fat (maximum) 35 per cent and carbohydrates 55 per cent (www.mod.uk/dlo/catering/operating).

The ORP rations are packed in cardboard cartons, which are waterproof and purported to possess a shelf life of three years.

4-man ration pack: With four rations packed in one box, this 4-man ration pack is meant for crews in armoured fighting vehicles. It varies a little from the 10-man pack in that there is an extra savouries pouch and beverages but no pudding.

Within the MCI menus and within a menu again there is a wide choice for meals. Various items are grouped together in 'units' like B–1, B–2, B–3. For example, one menu includes beefsteak, pears, B–1 unit, crackers (7 No.), candy disc, peanut butter, and accessory packet. Each of the 'B' group (B1 to B3) contains four or more choices of meat. B–1 unit has a selection in cans of meats like beefsteak or ham and eggs or chopped ham slices or turkey loaf and fruit preparation like apple sauce, or fruit cocktail, or peaches and pears. The B–2 unit is made of larger cans with more selections like beans and wieners, spaghetti and meat balls, beefsteak and potatoes in gravy, ham and lima beans, meatballs and beans, crackers and cheese spread, processed caraway. B–3 unit provides small cans of boned chicken or chicken and noodles or meat loaf or spiced beef, white bread, cookies, cocoa beverage powder, a choice of apple, grape or berry jam. Further, there is a choice of chocolate, cream, coconut, fruitcake, pecan roll, pound cake and mixed fruit to select the confectionary for dessert. The British 24 hr 1 man ORP contents shown in Table 11.6 are an example of a combat pack including a variety of foods that are provided at present.

Table 11.6: Contents of British 24-hour 1-man ORP

1 boil in bag * Breakfast	1 sac wet Drinking chocolate mix 1 × 5g
1 boil in bag Main meal	2 sachet Coffee 2 × 5 g Sachets/Coffee
1 boil in bag Dessert meal	2 sachets dairy whitener 2 × 5 g Sachets
1 sachet of powder, Soup	4 sachets Instant white tea 4 × 5 g
1 ring pull can Meat pate	8 × 10 g sachet sugar
1 foil pack oatmeal biscuit	1 sachet orange or lemon drink powder (for 1 Liter Drink)
1 pkt. 6 Biscuit Browns	1 pkt Kleenex tissue
1 pkt. 6 Fruit Biscuits	6 no. water purifying tablets
1 bar Milk chocolate	10 pkt water proof matches with striker
1 bar Milk chocolate with raisins cereal bar	Variations in GP – ORP
1 pkt Boiled sweets	2 sachet orange/lemon drink powder (for hot climate)
1 pkt 5 sticks Wrigley's Chewing gum	1 sachet Rolled Oats mix (for cold climate)
	1 Kendal Mint cake bar (hot climate)
	1 pkt vegetarian Pate (spinach/lentils) (instead of meat)
	1 sachet vegetarian cheese Oat cakes – 4 no. (instead of Biscuit Browns)

*Food sealed in a pouch that can be immersed in water to boil or reheat

Source: www.mreinfo.com./greatbritish_24_hour_rationpacks.html.

In the same vein there are 10-man ORPs, a self contained ration to feed ten people for 24 hours introduced in 2002. It is meant for use by a cook with no particular skills but with access to a field kitchen. It contains breakfast, main meal and snack meal and may be supplemented with bread, fresh fruit and vegetables when supplies are possible. This ration has used commercially available products with shorter shelf life and more fresh rations. When last reviewed (2004) it had a good response.

Operational rations of Australia: A complete ration pack for the Australian forces usually provides an average 3,500 Kcals/day per man. Any increase that may be necessitated is done by issuing supplementary ration components; the supplementary pack by itself would serve as emergency ration, and together with main ration pack increases the calorie contents to 4,000 Kcal (*Australian Service Scales*, 1962).

The A, B and C versions of combat rations essentially were three choices, each with a fixed menu for breakfast, lunch and dinner, special ration packs in the form of light weight one man ration packs, patrol ration packs and emergency packs.

The rations are carried on a person when the packs are meant for one. Packs for 5–10 people known as 5-man as shown in Table 11.7 and 10-man rations are also used when a finite number move together for a specific period.

Table 11.7: Australian rations – combat, 5-man pack

Breakfast		*Lunch*		*Dinner*	
Baked beans pouch	500 g	Chicken Noodle soup pkt	50 g	Salmon and Pasta Mornay	500 g
Muesli bars		Potatoes (can)	450 g	Sweet corn	450 g
Biscuit, crisp bread (pkt)	5 × 32 g	Tomato soup pkt	50 g	Carrots	250 g
Biscuit, scotch finger (pkt)	5 × 35 g	Chicken pasta and veg, pouch	500 g	Cheese (can)	5 × 56 g
Tropical Fruit (pkt)	5 × 32 g	Green peas, pouch	500 g	Jams (tube) Raspberry/Strawberry	85 g
Forest Fruit pkt	5 × 32 g	Tomato sauce (can)	225 g	Curry powder, pkt	14 g
Beverage powders (lime, orange, tropical) pkt	5 × 12 g each	Butter concentrate	150 g	Coffee soluble	10 × 3.5g
Chocolate drink	5 × 20 g	Tea (pkt)	10 × 2 g	Sugar	20 × 7 g
Army chocolate, pkt	5 × 50 g	Sugar (pkt)	10 × 7 g		
Coffee soluble, pkt	5 × 3.5 g	Condiments, Salt, pkt	5 × 2 g		
Sugar (pkt)	20 × 7 g	Mustard, Soya sauce, Tobasco sauce, chilli sauce	5 × 10 g pkts		
Condensed milk (tube)	5 × 85 g	Chewing gum	4 pkts		
Vegemite tube	85 g	Fruit drink powder			

Note: There is variety and choice of items provided in three meals delivering 15,000 KJ/day/man or 15 MJ energy.
Source: SRS, Australia, 1962

The post World War II Australian rations were all packaged in cans of several different shapes – rectangular, tapered, cylindrical – for various items expected in the A, B and C ration types. It must be clarified that every ration pack contained breakfast, lunch and dinner items. The cans were divided into two sets – each set of cans placed in a high wet strength fibre board tray where the individual cans are prevented from rubbing by the fibre board and are placed in between the two trays (much like the modern egg container); the trays put again in an out pack.

A 10-man pack occupies a volume of 10 x 10 x 16 and weighs a staggering 41 lb to be carried as personal load. However heavy it may be, there are three meals a day for each man and that is something that ensures that the appropriate quality and quantity of food, free from spoilage and independent of the uncertain local sources (should there be any), is delivered to the troops right where they are.

Operational rations of Canada: There are two types of combat rations.

Individual Meal Pack: Combat rations for the Canadian Armed Forces are called the IMP or Individual Meal Pack. It provides three meals a day and 3,600 Kcals of energy, 10 per cent of which is derived from protein and 35–40 per cent from fat. Care has been taken to see that adequate amounts of vitamins and minerals are available through these meals. There is a great variety of meats, some egg and cheese preparations, soups, fruits, dessert, and starches in the form of cereals, oat meal, mashed potatoes, bread, puddings, cookies and crackers; for beverages there are hot chocolate, coffee, tea, herbal teas, and a variety of fruit drunks. It has been reported that between 1997 and 2004 there have been many additions to the menus, introducing a selection of five breakfast menus, six lunch/dinner menus and six supper menus in the IMP along with accessory packs. The food packs have come a long way from the field rations used in the World War II Normandy operations. Some of the most popular preparations used in the normal diets have found place in processed and stabilised form in today's meal packs.

Light Meal, Combat: Yet another variation of the Canadian IMP appeared in 2001 as a light meal pack. As of January 1, 2006 there are three menus in this curtailed version of the IMP. It contains four categories of items: (a) meat 50 g (b) raisins/apple chips 40 g, granola chips/chocolate chips, apple/cranberry cereal squares, triple chocolate, coffee, crisp chocolate bar, (c) hot chocolate 28 g and (d) Orange drink crystals for 250 ml drink in envelopes. There are also two beverage mixing bags as well for this purpose. (www.forces.ca/menu/maple, www.dnd.ca/admfines/subjects, www.marpae.dnd.ca/ottawa/newsfindings)

Operational rations of India: In the Indian Armed Forces every facility is provided to ensure that hot food is served to the troops whether the units are posted in peace establishments, base installations or deployed in the field as far as possible and convenient. When 4–6 people including JCO's go into the field in a vehicle, a cook goes with them and takes along the cookhouse paraphernalia – the Mess kit and the 'Men-set' meant for this small number (three 8" *degchi* (flat bottomed vessel) with lid, one small all purpose tea kettle, three assorted sizes of *parat* (a wok type pan), one folding spoon, one 3 L capacity pressure cooker, one *chapati tawa*, one tumbler and one small *katora* (a small cup without handle).

On patrol duty, each jawan carries his own plate, spoon, and glass, 1 L bottle of water in his backpack along with ammunition, equipment, a blanket and a mosquito net. The entire pack weighs some 18–22 kg. He would much rather carry the war equipment than be burdened with extra food. The soldiers of yester years are known to have carried much larger weights – up to 60 kg, which was mostly ammunition.

Types of operational rations: Operational or combat rations go under different nomenclatures. In the Indian Armed Forces, they are called Compo packs/rations. These are far more nutritious, convenient and modern than anything that was there during World War II or in the early Indo-Pak Wars or in the 1962 India-China border war. India's Defence Food R&D has focused on lines similar to the US Army's Food and Nutrition research. There are field versions of rations for the Indian Army, an early 1966 version of which was known as the 5-man compo-rations. It was a far cry from its first elementary 'avatar' and even this form may now be obsolete. Several other and individual pack versions – 1-man compo packs have been introduced since then based on two approaches to providing Indian military operational food and nutrition: one was to give a restricted ration for short operations – known as the Individual Mini Compo pack – light of weight and with limited items and meals (Table 11.8). On the face of it, this meal pack looks very unappetising; there is no cereal based staple item except biscuits. Beaten rice was really no substitute, Whole Milk Powder (WMP) used to be a dreaded item because of browning and rancidity problems associated with it.

Table 11.8: 1-man compo pack, India

Item	*Quantity, g*
Biscuits, Service	– 150
Beaten rice	– 425
Sugar	– 110
Vegetables tinned	– 160
PD* dal in tins	– 113
Mutton/curried kheema/fish	– 85
Milk toffee	– 57
Milk WMP	– 160 + 8
Milk	– 180
Achar, dry	– 28
Tea	– 9
Salt, refined	– 6
Cashew	– 85
Cigarettes	– 10 no. or milk toffee 35g
Multivitamin tablet	– 1
Matchbox	– 3/5 no
Tin opener	– 1
Hexamine cooker with 6–8 tablets	– 1 per pack
Water sterilizing kit	– 1

*PD – Precooked dehydrated

The second approach was to give a 5-man compo pack with complete meals for one day but which might contain some of the same items repeated in every meal. In both rations there were instantised dry mixes requiring reconstitution in boiling water.

The meal pack therefore included a hexamine stove and hexamine fuel tablets and matches. These compo packs contain processed and portion packed foods of convenience which are limited in quantity and variety. There was greater emphasis on delivering adequate energy and providing acceptable palatability through minimal weight, rather than on balanced meals. And therefore the question of about how long the troops perform as expected on such rations should be raised.

During certain critical operational missions, individuals work in very small groups, or are entirely on their own. That is when the 'selected foods' are put together as one man or 5-man food packs of various descriptions. Labelled as 1 man and 5 man compo rations, the instant food mixes are based on rice, lentils and wheat semolina. Foods such as spicy vegetable *pulav,* spicy *dal, khichdi,* curried dal, *suji upma* (savoury), and *suji halwa* (sweet) became very popular. The ration packs also contained portion packs of tea, dairy whitener and sugar (all of which are dry products).

These foods are generally familiar to the troops and therefore more acceptable. To produce the compo meal packs various technologies are employed. The principle kinds are hot air dehydration and retort pouch processing and both kinds are being commercially employed. Presently, the operational food a jawan gets is of the compo pack or MRE type. Such packs are manufactured and supplied as per requirement in conformation with the specified standards of quality, safety and packaging. These foods must provide adequate nutrition and not just calories because individuals could be away from base camp for 1, 7, 14 days or longer and would thus be deprived of freshly prepared foods and fruits and vegetables all of which are essential as energy and micronutrient sources.

From the 80's until recently, the army operational ration packs used by men on patrol consisted of a selection from precooked dehydrated items like vegetable *pulav* and *khichri*, rice, curried dhal, dry instant mixes for suji *halwa* and *upma*, groundnut *chikki* bar and tea mix together with stove, fuel, spoon, matches etc. There used to be 10 man or 5 man or 1 man compo packs depending upon the number of men in a patrol unit. The army now prefers 1 man 'Mini Compo pack' giving restricted number of items and lesser number of calories based on their altered logistics planning. For the Navy, it was MRE foods such as canned/retort pouch processed vegetarian and non-vegetarian curries and *pulavs, upma, halwa*, packaged nutrient bar, biscuits/chocolate bar, pickles, salt, tea/coffee. The total weight varied up to 2 kg. A 24 hr marine commando ration pack provides 3200 Kcal and offers varied menus for all meals.

Now in the new millennium commercial manufacture of retort pouch foods having been established in the civil sector, the army ration packs preferentially include pouch processed foods replacing the earlier forms of pre-cooked dehydrated items and quick cooking dry mixes.

Mobile Field Kitchens: For various reasons this concept has not really taken root although a prototype vehicle for food service on wheels was designed and fabricated out of a 1 ton truck in the early 1990s and developed by the R&D Engineers. It was a compact and reasonably self-sufficient system for dispensing quick and hot meals for troops on the move or in the field and undoubtedly its efficiency would have increased many folds by the use of better cooking and cleaning equipments and appliances and more processed or at least semi processed foods and more conveniences in the packaged foods which appeared as a result of new enterprises, new technologies and in the domestic market in the last decade. A demonstration or prototype mobile kitchen has been produced and is in limited use during training camps at the ASC Centre, Bangalore (described in Chapter 12). There is however, no evidence as yet that any such service vehicle is in operational use.

Survival rations: The army survival foods which used to be chocolate or candy or toffee now consist of 500 g of long life (at least 1 year), *chikki* bar providing 2,000 Kcal per day. The Navy's survival packs are designed for three days of rations per man providing 600 g for one day of easily digestible and low thirst causing survival food bar made up of low protein and high carbohydrate content as well as 400 ml of water, both possessing long life of up to three years. The emergency food for the Air Force is called the Emergency Flying Ration (EMF), which is made up of two small rectangular plastic boxes each containing 150 to 300 g of chocolate like flavoured high calorie food bar providing 1,000 to 1,320 Kcal/day and having 1–3 years of shelf life.

This requirement of very long shelf rations (up to three years) is warranted, it seems by their logic that there are 'wear and tear' maintenance schedules which periodically replace aircraft parts, and a major overhaul once in three years. For convenience's sake therefore, the food and water for EMF also should not need frequent replacement before the time for major overhaul, which would be three years.

The advantages of freeze dried foods were well known and the US Special Forces do get some FD foods in their meal packs, and astronauts and cosmonauts use these as space foods. Climbers have carried a variety of these in mountain expeditions and these are also much in demand by other adventure and camping groups in the West. In India, no commercial facility manufactures freeze dried meals and rations. However, in a limited way, a few cut vegetables and perhaps fruits, green pepper and shrimp were said to be freeze dried, the former for adding to breakfast cereal mixes and the latter for a niche domestic market and for export and as foods for mountaineers. However, FD foods have performed excellently in many special missions undertaken by various Defence and civil organisations and these requirements were fully met by the pilot scale processing facilities which exist in DFRL at Mysore. The Indian Army currently does not appear to be requiring freeze dried foods for any of its missions in cold weather or for long range patrols. Light weight hot air dried and dry instant mixes, which are long life foods were much the preferred ration packs in the 1980s and up to the mid 90s in the Siachen and the North Eastern and Eastern Himalayan sectors. Since these mixes require a few minutes of cooking in water, the portable solid fuel hexamine heater and matches always included in the packs would appear to be sufficient.

At this instant, there are six types of ration packs, which have been especially designed for Army, Navy and Air Force (*Product Information Brochures*, DFRL, 2005, 2007). These are:

(a) One man supplementary compo pack ration (Army) designed for short sustenance needs (400 g total weight, 1520 Kcal) and contains dehydrated rice *pulav* mix or *Upma* mix and semolina *halva* – both instant mixes (dry) together with three servings of tea, sugar, dairy whitener and a hexamine fuel based portable stove,

(b) One man complete meal compo pack rations provides one full day's meals, weighs 880 g and delivers 3,700–4,100 Kcals. Its component foods are also rehydratable dry mixes, a foldable field stove and fuel tablets. It is said to be a ration pack eminently suitable for use by the police and other paramilitary forces on patrol duty and for mountaineers, trekkers and others in adventure sports. As per the latest information obtained, the dry mixes have been replaced with retort pouch foods.

A recently described MRE ration for the Army (DFRL Brochure, 2007) is stated to consist of *suji halwa*, vegetable *pulav*, potato-peas curry, *chapatis*, soft bar and tea providing 3,300 Kcals. Each food for any meal is a portion pack and all the items comprising each meal are put in one individual polymeric pouch (Fig. 11.2). There would thus be three large pouches for the three individual meals – all put together in a bulk cardboard carton together with the heater and the fuel tablets. These, we are informed, are multi-entrée menu meals based on both vegetarian and non-vegetarian (meat or chicken) foods.

(c) Emergency ration for the Army are food bars.

(d) Emergency ration for the Air crew: they are compact high calorie food bars made of cereals and protein source and possess long shelf life and are meant to be replaced in the aircraft periodically. They are ready to eat and provide food for 24–48 hours only. Survival ration for the Navy, which

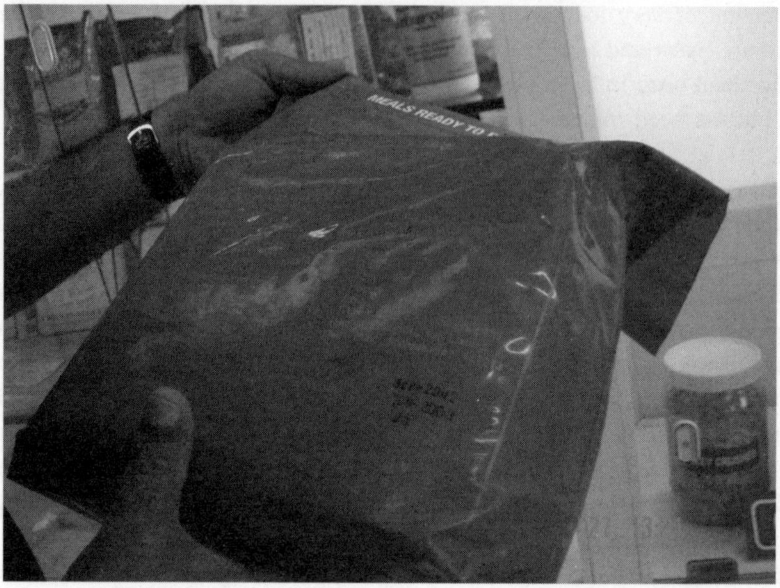

Fig. 11.2: Indian Army's Meals Ready to Eat – one man complete rations contain rehydratable products that can be quickly reconstituted in hot water in 10–15 minutes

are food bars high on carbohydrate but lower in protein content (to reduce thirst). The ration packs provide food for some five days to sustain the persons on the open seas until rescued and also contain long life water. Other types of emergency packs contain roasted *chana (*puffed Bengal gram*)*, fruit bar etc. Each menu delivers 3,300–3,600 Kcals per day.

(e) MRE rations for the Navy come in four types of menus, two with vegetarian items and two with meat containing items. The basic pack consists of *suji halwa*, Nutri-food bar, coffee/tea, biscuits, cashew nuts, cornflakes, electral powder (oral rehydration salts), vegetable *pulav/khichdi/chapatis*, potato peas curry and soft bar. The non vegetarian items such as chicken *pulav*/mutton *pulav* replace the vegetarian *pulav* and *khichdi* (DFRL, 2007).

(f) Commando pack rations are made up of three servings of tea (plus sugar, creamer), foldable stove and fuel tablets. The other contents of this ration are said to be somewhat similar to other ration packs, in a limited version and carrying more convenient and possibly ready to eat items, it does not however, provide hot meals.

The survival rations for all the three services are compressed food bars with chocolate, cardamom or other flavours and are mostly carbohydrate based. The bars are designed to provide around 2,000 Kcals per man per day, with three or four bars altogether, each bar individually packed in moisture proof, and safe packaging material. The Navy's survival bar contains more carbohydrates and lesser protein content than the other two types.

According to one source (www.frontierindia.net), there are also rations for men in the Main Battle Tank (MBT) and other armoured vehicles for up to 72 hrs. The first two days' rations weigh 2 kg each and provide 4,000 Kcal and the third day's rations weigh 1.5 kg and provide 3,000 Kcals. The food packets are of the ready to eat kind which include food bars. This has not been independently confirmed. It is possible that these packs are the same as the MRE rations for the army mentioned above.

The Commando pack rations were originally meant for the Navy. The Indian Navy found that the US Marine's Commando ration packs were made of ready to eat retort pouch foods and that the MRE foods would be eminently suitable for their own use. Therefore all the early rations for the Naval Commandos were designed with MRE foods by the Defence Food Research Laboratory long before the technology was commercially exploited. The Commando rations and the Navy's Landing Party Rations are all ready to eat foods – some are MRE type, some are food bars and other types of ready foods.

Until Kargil happened in 1999, the Army had expressed no particular interest in the MRE type ration packs and did not want any for their use saying it was too costly. But from the time of the Kargil war, the Army has been using MRE foods in various ration packs.

The most popular operational food types in India: In the early years, patrols would take with them the 'fried *puris* and potato curry' combos, ever the fall-back all-purpose and widely popular breakfast/snack/anytime meal which keeps better than most fresh preparations and is a favourite travel food. *Puris* are round, medium sized, rolled, unleavened wheat dough fried in fat or oil. They puff and brown slightly on frying and remain soft inside and are eaten with a semi-dry or wet curry. This item is easily prepared in the field kitchens and is generally well accepted. It is tasty, ready to eat, not messy or wet, can be packed in any kind of container or plastic bags in portion sizes to fit into uniform pockets or back packs. Veterans will also fondly recall that another fried but sugared snack known as '*Shakkarpara*' was an invariable stand-by in their survival kits; 'puffed *chana* or beaten rice' with jaggery were the other standby traditional snacks for any emergency subsistence requirements.

By 1984, the Indian troops had seen three border wars with Pakistan, one with China and were faced with a new unfolding situation poised for hostilities on the Siachen glacier at very high altitudes. Forces were deployed above 12,000 ft under 'Operation *Meghdoot*'. Faced with positioning enough troops in a hostile climate and precarious and inhospitable terrain on one hand and the need to carry out constant vigil and retaliatory military action on the other, the foods and their supply engaged the attention of the Army Headquarters after other combat necessities were addressed. All the existing mechanisms for fresh food supplies which had served the troops in the field areas until then in the Western, North western, Northern and Eastern sectors were found to be inadequate. The policy of ensuring that the jawans are provided with at least one hot meal per day, come war or routine patrols or operational exercises suffered in implementation in Siachen due to the very nature of the place and its environment. It is so cold up there and the altitudes and terrain so daunting and forbidding that the rations do not get collected from base camps to begin with, despite the most well established delivery system.

Siachen and high altitude deployment present their own peculiar challenges:

- Operational problems encountered in no other area of deployment (rarely if any is there a centralized cooking and hot food service),
- Adverse environmental pressure on body physiology and psychological effect (fear of the unknown, eyeball to eyeball situation with the enemy), aside from the 'always to be expected' problems due to breakdown of supplies which can happen anywhere. (Tilak and Bhadwar, 1996).

It is more than 20 years since the Indian military contingents began to be regularly deployed for tours of duty in these locales. The common public rarely come close to understanding, much less learn, about the tremendous physical, physiological and psychological challenges and consequences of high altitude conditions and service in the Siachen. For this reason, both issues have been discussed separately.

Energy dense products made with natural foods as sources and containing high amounts of carbohydrate (starch) and or fat have been introduced into the ration packs. Fruit beverages, dry fruits and nuts, chocolate, traditional sweet and savoury preparations made with milled cereals, and fat (and sometimes milk), different types of main meal items had been part of the rations. Every attempt was made to provide Siachen troops with the best products and such items that would find favour with the men.

Although some type of MREs specially produced for the services have been in use on trial basis in the Indian Navy and Indian Army for quite some time now, even before their commercial production began in India in earnest, the meal packs presently being made for the armed forces have provided the much needed fillip to the pressing need for special rations for operational purposes, a need that had been felt by many in the special action forces and security organisations in the country. While the Indian forces have expressed a guarded welcome to the introduction of MREs in special rations, according to Clancy (2001), the MREs are at best suffered by the US Forces and are not really popular. No packed ration will ever be able to replace a freshly cooked meal. But for the moment the MRE's are the nearest field alternative to fresh cooked meals and thus must be endured. While the US manufactured MREs are sold to its allies in other countries, Indian manufactured retort foods, some of which are used in MREs have become a commercial success on their own both in the domestic market and internationally, particularly among the Indian diaspora living in different parts of the World.

Hot meal out of box: Eating a hot meal can be the most heartening and enlivening experience for a person perched precariously on one of the sharp snowy ridges of the Siachen glacier or of other Northern and Eastern Himalayan mountains. The MRE packs, as much ready to eat as they are, can be quite depressing and daunting if eaten cold. The packs must be heated. The limited facilities and re-supply position in the cold and high attitudes do not always permit lavish use of fuel – kerosene. To help jawans prepare hot meals, a self heating system called therm-o-pack has been developed recently by Sabapathy and his team from DFRL (Sanjeev Kumar *et al.,* 2005).

Self heating pack system: It is a flexible double layered polymeric pouch in which certain chemicals are sandwiched between layers of plastic material. These chemicals placed in the outer pouch produce an exothermic reaction and generate heat. The food or beverage is filled and sealed into the inner pouch and does not come in direct contact with the chemicals. Heat is generated by activation with water and air within the polymeric layers and is conveyed to the food. The temperature of the food is claimed to rise from room temperature to a level that satisfactorily warms the food in about 8 to 15 minutes. It is not clear how long the process of heating will take or how warm the frozen food will become under the mind numbing sub zero temperatures at high altitudes. Since another vexatious situation in sub zero conditions is that of the freezing up of the water that should activate the heat generating reaction, informed sources have told this author that an anti-freeze substance has since been introduced into the chemical mixture to overcome this problem.

There have been several types of *in situ* patented heating systems in use by the US, Canadian and ANZAC forces. Some are in can form for heating canned foods while others come as pads for heating a pouch.

Operational rations in Bangladesh: Before the formation of Bangladesh, the rations would have been the common service rations and scales at Pakistan. No updates could be found for the current combat food types in Pakistan or about the present service ration scales in Bangladesh. It is possible that the same scales have continued. However the Bangladesh Operational Rations are an interesting mix of foods from the past and present. For a 3,400 Kcal energy/man/day delivery, the rations weighing 1,092 g consist of dry stuff like beaten rice (112 g) and jaggery (56 g), dal fried and salted (generally eaten as a savoury snack), traditionally made coconut-sugar bar (112 g) and *chikki*, (112 g), dal bar (112 g), *khichri* (cooked dal and rice) canned (450 g), soy biscuits (112 g), sweet drops – perhaps flavoured boiled sweets (28 g) and ingredients for two cups of tea – tea, milk and sugar (Arya, 1996). Beaten rice and jaggery often with roasted groundnuts or puffed Bengal gram obtained by traditional food processing have been subsistence foods in India for centuries. Beaten rice can be eaten as such or after briefly softening in water and seasoning it with spices.

Former Soviet Military Feeding System: The Soviet Union had very advanced Space Exploration and Manned Programmes and after the dissolution of USSR it must have retained the infrastructure to produce top quality foods for their cosmonauts. During one official visit to Moscow in 1984, this author was taken around the Soviet Space food packing facility which had a range of food/soup concentrates in tubes, bite size bread loaves in polymer packs, canned foods and coffee/tea packed in long bottle shaped flexible pouches with spouts and plugs for rehydration. After the dissolution of the USSR, it is not known whether the land, sea and air forces of its once constituent nations benefited in regard to rations and combat foods because of having these specially built up capabilities. But until then there were meal packs for three meals as described here.

The army primarily obtained all its supplies grown in military farms or produced in state controlled factories. Regiments obtained their requirements on cash payment. The quality and quantity of such food procurement was dependent upon the commander who determined what foods and how much of each to buy as per his own perceptions and understanding. The role of medical and supply officers is not very clear but the menus probably arose from the food stuffs available at any given time which were distributed at the rate of 2.5 kg per man per day, presumably for three meals in the order of 25 per cent for breakfast, 50 per cent for lunch and 25 per cent for dinner. Officers got better rations than men in the other ranks. The Soviet operational rations were of the 24 hr/per man type providing three meals, two of which come as hot meals even in combat. One menu for the ORs, as found in a source (Arya, 1996), provides a breakfast of 400 g (meat/noodles, bread, butter, tea and sugar), 1,600 g for lunch (cabbage soup, boiled meat, tomatoes, kissel and bread) and 400 g as supper (boiled fish, boiled potatoes, bread, tea and sugar).

The third meal is in the form of an operational ration pack which typically consists of one menu as shown in Table 11.9.

Table 11.9: Soviet operational ration pack

2 cans of meat each of 60 g
1 can barley 200 g
1 can of rice kasha 200 g
1 can of buck wheat kasha 200 g
1 can of pork fat 50 g
1 packet of dry bread or rusk 250 g
Tea and sugar

Source: Arya, 1996

The Soviet war machine employed mobile field kitchens to feed troops in combat. Versatile mobile kitchens mounted on trailers and capable of cooking for 120 men at a time were in use. The mobile food service systems also included a field bakery. Such an independent feeding system is useful for troops on the move as well as when radiation decontamination is in progress in nuclear radiation affected areas.

Little is known about standard or combat type rations of many other countries not discussed here partly because of reporting in languages other than English, partly because no one has reported it or perhaps because such information does not merit attention and importance due to other preoccupations.

A quick comparison of combat/operational rations of India, UK, USA and Soviet Russia (Table 11.10) highlight the diversity in the 24 hr ration types and the advances in field kitchen services available or in use.

Table 11.10: 24 hr operational/combat ration scales of different countries

	India	*UK*	*USA*	*USSR*
Total energy	3800	4000	3000	(2.5 Kg)
Content	960 g	BLD*	BLD*	BLD*
	1 man full meal Compo- BLD Supplementary Compo- simpler, 1500 Kcal (for 1-3 days) 1 man 24 hr marine Commando MRE (3200 Kcal) Survival ration Army 2200 Kcal 500 g. EFR 4str-2000 Kcal 125g × 2 boxes of toffees Special mission foods	Individual+GS rations (4000 Kcal) 4 men, 10 men GS rations (4000 Kcal) Ultra light wt rations (1800 Kcal) Special patrol- Air Force 5000 Kcal, 1.5 Kg Emergency Flying ration pack, size limitation not calories NBC situation feeding meal replacement bar + vitamin fortified glucose solution.	T rations MFSU** SFKK** ACFFS**	Operational ration 3-meal/24 hr packs. One menu of canned foods. MFK** on trailer/ Trucks for 120 men Semi mobile field bakery

* BLD refers to breakfast, lunch, and dinner. **The acronyms MFK, MFSU, SFKK, ACFFS represent mobile field service systems, units, and mobile kitchens.

Progress in Combat Food Development

MREs have made a tremendous contribution to the way operational foods are now designed. The US, Canadian and British, as well as the German, French and Dutch Armed Forces have a wide range of meal items for this purpose (www.mreinfo.com.w3) and there is a wide selection of menus. MRE is the main individual operational ration for many armies in the world. These are fully self-contained meals that deliver the required nutrition to a soldier away from the support of the unit. Primarily it refers to the retort processed and plastic polymer packaged moist foods, which are ready to eat (after reheating, if so desired); the total ration package also contains other and variously processed food items that are ready to eat. In a MRE kit, chocolates, biscuits, fruit bars, nutrient bars, cheese bits, buns, bread, sandwiches, fruit drinks and even *chapati* rolls can find a place. The kit comprises of the main course, desserts, snacks, beverage powder, eating ware and maybe a heater too.

What is required is meal planning – of breakfast, lunch or dinner with the food products available (from the manufacturers) and which are acceptable (based on nutritional, chemical, microbiological quality and safety criteria and found satisfactory by troop trials). Since World War II, any number of operational and field food packs have come into existence, first using only tinned items, then in the dehydrated reconstitutable form of foods and beverages, still later a mixture of moist and dehydrated foods and then the wholly pouch processed moist foods.

Between these two means of feeding the troops – freshly cooked with 'A' rations and the 'eat out of pack' compo or patrol rations, lies the area of innovation for future combat foods. What will the foods of the future be like? How will they differ from the present ones? What conceptual ideas are emerging in the innovations?

World War II veterans would note that what they had in wartime are simply not comparable to today's soldier meals. The main theatres of war then were in the Atlantic and the Pacific regions and partly in the deserts of Africa where battles were fought on ground, under sea, at sea and in the air. There were military bases from where the troops could be transported from, landed on and moved by mechanised transports.

The mobilised troops readied for the D Day Normandy landings had carried or had access to light weight 'K' rations, emergency D ration, food for one day like the C rations and also the mainstay emergency food which was two bars per day. When they were entrenched in fox holes during intense fighting they went without any food (www.qmmuseum/lee.army.mil).

The E-type rations used in Normandy landings as shown in Table 11.11, are not comparable with the present day IMP rations – Canadian or any other modern version, in content or in quality according to an article (web pages/Legion magazine, www.forces.ca/menu/maple).

Table 11.11: A comparison of World War II Rations with current Canadian Armed Forces Rations

Normandy, WW II	IMP, Canadian
E-type – 14 men	(3600 to 4200 Kcals per day)
BKF tea	BKF: ham steak with mustard sauce
Sausage – 2 tins	Sliced pears in syrup,
Biscuit – 1 tin	Honey – all grape beverage crystals
Margarine – 1 tin	Bread, peanut butter, hot chocolate, mix Gum
Lunch/dinner	Pork with herb and wine cream sauce
(Meat) haricot oxtail 12 tins	Apple sauce, peach beverage, bread, honey, instant mashed potatoes,
Vegetables 2 tins	Kit Kat chunky bar, lifesaver.
Pudding 3 tins	
Supper: Cheese 1 tin	Beef stroganoff, sliced peaches, orange beverage crystals, cream soup,
Biscuits	bread peanut butter, raspberry jam, instant mashed potato, sandwich with vanilla cream, lifesavers
	1200 to 1400 Kcals per meal
	$10–11.50 is the cost of each meal and it has a shelf life of 3 years.

Source: www.forces.ca/menu/maple

As technological advances unfold there will be changes in the food and its delivery systems. Scientists and technologists must constantly strive to understand the needs of the soldiers in the changing face of wars. They will need to conceptualise and design new products for application that are tenable and workable and harness the vast potential of the industry to mass produce foods and food packages, establish checks and quality assurance and monitoring criteria. It is then that the scientists will have done their part, hand over to the manufactures and other vendors, by way of transfer of technology the job of large scale manufacture and supply.

The means of waging wars have altered in the past few decades. There are no more large and wide battlefields where the opposing armies will begin massing as in the Kurukshetra war or Waterloo. Today's wars are fought from mechanised vehicles, from airborne craft, from the sea, from under the sea and in cyberspace too. The missiles discharged on the enemy are of the long-range kind making it unnecessary to face the enemy upfront. The troops are not marched in long winding columns taking weeks and months enroute (as Napoleon had to during his long march to Russia) but are moved, since World War I, in vehicles, troop ships and airlifts, along with every bit of gear and support system required in the temporary camps.

No troops from the US, Canada, Britain or Australia, Europe (except in Kosovo in the 1990s) have fought wars on their own territories since the last century and particularly since World War II. That is not so in India and the neighborhood and the Gulf region and especially in pockets of SE Asia, Africa and South America. In the twenty first century, the Middle East (West Asia) has become a region of constant war, strife, terrorism and sectarian fighting. The US and NATO allies have been engaged in retaliatory war against terrorism in Afghanistan and then in Iraq since 2002. They are supported with everything that modern technology can provide for fighting on a distant land. The Israelis typically fight from their own home bases but their area of operations is confined to the neighborhood. Similarly, Palestine, Syria and until very recently Lebanon rained down and received in turn, bombs and missiles of quite a sophisticated nature launched from home ground. These attacks cannot be called guerilla in nature, but could possibly be classed as hit and run or rather die-on-the streets type of war. Israel's war against these countries revolves a round aerial bombing. The forces of these countries need not be hugely mobile in the general sense and presumably have little need for elaborate logistics for supply and transport. West Asian food habits are quite distinctive, even frugal when necessary and their food can easily be cooked on campfire. There is no evidence available to determine whether they use any pre-packed and processed foods of their own during combat. However, the allies themselves share their special rations with the Iraqi troops who are involved in controlling the civil, sectarian and street fighting.

The Western countries with sound technological and industrial bases lead the world in equipping their Armed Forces with the best, the finest and the most modern. That goes for the food products in their rations and the feeding mechanisms in combat zones. So what kind of foods do the modern armies in the world require? Have the long awaited future foods arrived to suit the new style of waging wars? And whose job is it anyway? These are some of the questions that will be addressed here.

Combat Food Types and Dietary Preferences

There is comfort in finding familiar foods when under battle stress. So the approaches in designing newer food items and rations will be directed towards:

- Listing all such foods amenable to some form of mass manufacture, converting these items into portion sized, shelf stable, safe, processed and conveniently packaged form. The foods will be packaged for backpacks as well as for use in field kitchens.

- The innovations will include the use of such ingredients in product formulations which confer certain special benefits: by way of ergogenic effects, specific nutrients and antioxidants, bio preservatives, better nutrient balance, health promoting nutraceuticals and functional foods. All these are expected to aid in eliciting better performance, better endurance, better cognizance and responses, better health and immunity and greater stress reduction or stress alleviation.
- Energy and nutrient dense meal bars, pocket sandwiches, low fiber high protein snacks, refreshing beverages containing anti-stress substances for on the go use, or to consume in confined places as in tanks and submarines and during special operations, when riding in personalised armoured vehicles, and when flying in supersonic aircraft on long flights. Such items have already been thought of and are at various stages of testing and trials and some have already appeared as part of special rations. Combat feeding is carried out on considerations of whether it is to be done in field camps with kitchen facilities using normal rations at detachment levels or confined in a tank or at an individual level. In every case the foods provided must not only be palatable and acceptable but also meet nutritional and physiological criteria in a minimum weight, packaged sturdily and appropriately for the climate and weather conditions likely to be present and amenable for air dropping.

The Meals-Ready-To-Eat concept of yester years continues in the combat version of rations. Whether the meal is for one man for 24 hrs or for 5 or 10 men, to be made in a field kitchen with limited facilities and by men of limited skills or on the go, the emphasis is on quick access to proper food appropriate to the climate, and the nature of operations.

It is seen that western countries (inside NATO Alliance) presently engaged in combat situations have their own version of the MREs. These were introduced in the 1980s but US, Canadian, British and Australian food habits and preferences being somewhat similar (or so we presume), if not totally the same, typically their MRE menus utilise a wide selection of meat foods and there is a good amount of choice in the entrees, side dish, crackers or bread, butter or cheese spread, dessert, instant coffee/tea, sugar and creamer. Accessories are also included along with the food packs. It is a testimony to the vast food technological-industrial base of these countries and the popularity of all such food items among civilian consumers.

In India the choices of items in the MRE is limited by comparison and especially so for the meat items. Nevertheless, there is creditably adequate variety for the limited use MREs.

Despite the most modern field feeding systems that functioned in the Iraq war of 1991, the feeding of US soldiers reportedly was not found to be as satisfactory as expected. What more is needed? How much more needs to be done? What other or special foods are desired?

The presently available literature on the combat rations tells us that the so called 'future foods' conceptualised in the 1980s have already arrived. After all, men must eat a substantial quantity of food over a 24-hour period to derive sufficient energy and nutrients commensurate with the work done and to keep hunger at bay. There are no magic pills, potions and capsules that will assuage this need for any length of time although scientists will keep trying to minimise the 'food burden' on the troops and the Armed Force's logistics as a whole.

Water: One cannot ignore the problem of water; of carrying it, transporting it and supplying it in the field. While discussions usually pertain to food packs, providing water in the pack attains a great importance. Increasingly, operations are taking place in the hot baking deserts, in far away places of water scarcity and uncertainty surrounding its quality and safety. Logistics support systems provide for safe and clean water for all needs. Dehydrated foods included in pack rations require water for reconstitution. Every individual field food compo pack, emergency and survival packs must have a water component. Thirst will kill before hunger. Much research effort therefore has been devoted to this aspect.

In India's snow clad and isolated Himalayan border posts and in the Siachen glacier regions, melted snow and ice are the only source of water. Up in the border post's pillboxes, a great amount of effort goes into breaking up the ice and heating it in large cans over kerosene stoves. It will of course never reach a temperature of 100° Celsius and will not boil as we expect it to. It is a phenomenon of the high altitude. The maximum it can heat up to is to a temperature of about 70–80°C depending on the elevation. This must suffice for drinking, for preparing a hot beverage, and to rehydrate a dry food mix.

For manoeuvres in the desert, in the intense heat without any shade such as in the desert regions of Rajasthan or the Gulf, the human body would need around four times the normal requirement, roughly 2 gallons per day (1 gallon = 4.2 L). Each gallon of water weights 3.6 kg. The body looses water through perspiration and dehydration and must be kept well hydrated with as much water through drinking and eating as is possible.

There is really no easy way to carry volumes of water and food even for one week's mission. Several types of water containers and carrier systems for water sufficient for perhaps a day have been used in the past.

Prior to World War I, a canteen hung over saddle backs was the main source for water. Canvass covered metal canisters hung on the shoulder with canvass/cloth straps served during the World War II era. Gallon cans made of metal were used in the post war period till plastic and PET containers and bottles became common in the 1990s. The most recent types are known as 'Camelbak' hydration systems. These are of three types (Clancy, 2001, p. 117) and are reminiscent of flexible plastic polymer bags used for intravenous fluid administration, the fore runners of which were pouch bags carrying orange drink inside the space suits worn by NASA astronauts in Apollo missions.

The name 'Camelbak' is derived from the name of the company which manufactures these products as well as the early products specially meant for space crews and aircrews. The three presently approved models are the

(a) Storm, which fits into the existing back pack systems;
(b) The 'Thermobak' model is designed for high temperature/desert operations and
(c) The 'Stealth' model is meant for aircrews and vehicle drivers.

Ever popular with sports persons, a few types of hydration systems can also be found in specialty stores in the USA and Canada selling sports and camping gear.

They were not standard issue items but became so very popular with soldiers in the US Army that they bought these bags and then got them routed for issue through army stores. But from the year 2000, the Army itself has taken up the responsibility to provide the soldiers with the Camelbaks.

In the Indian Army there was no mention or evidence of any such water hydration system having been inducted for issue to special missions. It is also possible that need for such a device has not yet arisen in the Indian context. The only device that came closest to the present Camelbak system was an experimental IV administering bag which was a high density transparent polymer bag, long-oval in shape filled with potable water (1 to 2 L). It was variously processed (including gamma irradiation) to sterilise and impart sufficient shelf life for the express purpose of using it as part of a survival kit for aircrews. This was a laboratory level attempt and one is not sure whether it ever went up to the user trial stage. At present, only for the Indian Air Force, and particularly for the crew of the Sukhoi jets, there is need for specially constructed in-flight hydration system to drink 'hands off' from a glass or bottle.

Twenty-First Century Foods and Systems

Mobile field feeding systems: Since the Gulf war in 1991, the US Armed Forces which are superbly equipped in every way including field feeding, have continued to improve the level and quality of subsistence provided to their troops in the field. Already well prepared to serve hot meals fast through MREs and Tray rations (T-Rations) in the field using the 'Wolf mobile' (www.qmfound.com/food.htm) they have made further improvisations to provide 'eat on the move' capability to the marines and army soldiers. Individual meal menus or menu packs are put together in Unitized Group Rations or UGR to facilitate serving group meals in the field.

There are five breakfast and ten lunch/dinner menus. The UGR consists of 50 complete meals packed in three boxes along with eating ware, disposable cups and trash bags. The UGR comes in eight modules to provide 400 meals at one time. That is a very compact food delivery module system to feed hundreds at short notice. These are said to be 'build to order rations' which can be obtained from the vendor in 30 days.

First Strike Ration: 'First Strike' ration programme is one innovation which is a single ration per day containing food items that are conveniently packed, easy to use and consume (www.von.com/First_Strike_Rations). One example of such an item is a pocket sandwich with a three year shelf life which will fit easily into a man's combat dress pocket. Sandwich for breakfast, sandwich for lunch and sandwich for dinner in uniform packs – this ration comes along with three beverage mixes in three zip lock bags for '*in situ*' reconstitution of beverage and to directly drink from. A sandwich is made from at least two bread slices with a filling and is one of the commonest and most popular foods in the Western diet. It constitutes an 'anytime' meal or snack. Thus it is most familiar to every man, woman and child and most readily acceptable throughout the western and ANZAC countries and in fact has universal appeal like the pizza and Coca Cola. To carry a sandwich, which is soft and a little moist and packed neatly is not messy and it needs no further preparation. It is filling and satisfying and with suitable fillings it can be made very tasty, wholesome, nutritious and energy dense. To give such a food item a three-year shelf is truly an innovation, considering its moisture content (unless a dry form of bread has been used) and the property of the starch in the flour to stale (retrogradation). It is possible that the wrapped, prepared sandwiches have been irradiation preserved.

For pilots in the long range reconnaissance/surveillance aircraft U–2, clad in space suit type of pressure clothing, one easy-to-reach-for and eat food is 'Tube Food' developed in the early manned space ventures, this type of food is a pasty moist mash or a concentrate quickly expelled from the tube (metal or plastic) directly into the month. It was the most common form of food on Soviet space craft.

Yet another type of food is known under the name 'Hooah' nutrition booster bar. Calorie packed, it aims to provide high energy in the battlefield and is also part of the 'First Strike' ration.

The US's Combat Feeding programme together with Air Force Research laboratories has developed two newer foods specifically to overcome the stress factor of high altitude flying on long missions. Functional ingredients incorporated into the foods are reportedly beneficial in maintaining high level of alertness. These ingredients help in eliciting better cognitive performance and to get over lethargy and sluggishness of enforced physical inactivity in the cockpit.

Food science, food technology and the food manufacturing industry have made it possible to process, produce and pack these commonly consumed foods, snacks, beverages, confections etc. in safe, shelf stable and convenient form, the quality parameters of which are available for scrutiny and inspection. Only the appropriate selection and mixing of the food variety available is required to design a nutrient defined ration.

A ration so put together can be readily subjected to stringent evaluation by taste panels, and by field trials and any changes that may be necessary can be readily incorporated. If any special recipe is desired by the men or alteration to an existing one, it probably would not take very long to perfect it and manufacture it quickly.

Combat ration packs or the variety of individual constituent items are also used as convenient, wholesome, camp style foods by the Arctic and Antarctic explorers, as well as trekkers and trail walkers, high altitude mountaineers, adventure sports enthusiasts and paramilitary forces everywhere.

Spin Offs

The fighting forces required better rations, better preserved foods, better technology and processes for making long shelf life foods, safe foods, convenient portions and lightweight packaging, easy to open cans and pouches which meant more research in science and technology. All these requirements were met and one may go so far as to say that many major breakthroughs happened especially because of researches carried out for military application. And because of it, military research is credited with providing many spinoff benefits and continues to do so.

The invention of the pressure cooker, the development of food canning in the nineteenth century for Napoleon's troops, research in retort food technology for preserving food in thermo resistant polymeric plastic bags (Mylar) which received much impetus during the Korean war and which is now the backbone of the pouch foods included in the MRE, the use of freeze drying of foods used extensively for space food and campers food, developing dry fruit crystals for the well known orange drink 'Tang' and zip lock bags, both again for use on board manned spacecrafts in the twentieth century and the wonders of many other electronic, chemical and biological gadgets, aids and accessories are but a few examples of the urgent military needs driving inventions. Most of these have found everyday usage in civilian situations. None of these would have come about (at least not when they did) without intensive research by scientists or from experimentation by intuitive inventors.

The role of the food industry in all these instances is of no mean order. A most significant contribution to come out of the collaboration between NASA, the Army's Natick laboratory and the US food industry has revolutionised how we look at food safety and assurance of quality in manufactured foods. The Pillsbury Food Company in the US which, when charged in the 1960s with developing microbiologically safe food for space feeding, found that the major portion of the small quantities of test foods produced by them was being used up not in acceptability tests by trained subjects but through multiple sampling in the elaborate laboratory analyses set up for detecting various chemical, physical and microbiological hazards. To overcome this, they developed by 1972 a fail-safe quality assurance system for zero tolerance for hazards in food production. This has come to be known as the HACCP (Hazard Analysis Critical Control Points) system which is now mandated by the US Federal Government for certain key food manufacturing industries (meat, dairy, sea foods etc.) and which figures in the ISO food quality regulations. It is applied in food manufacturing in many countries including India and has been incorporated in the country's own Quality Standards and Certification protocols.

The description and discussion regarding the various combat rations presented here emphasise the fact that the military's subsistence in terms of foods and operational rations does depend on the advances in nutritional sciences, food science and technology and food engineering, polymer technology and that it should utilise the benefits of continued research and development in these fields and must encourage and include the manufacturing industry to be co-partners in developmental activities from early on.

Development of Rations – Whose Job is it?

While in some countries there are separate military research establishments for looking into the food and nutrition aspects of the military rations, in others perhaps such activities are carried out in cells within bigger projects. Availability of information of this nature is scarce in the public domain. In previous years, the periodic meetings of the Commonwealth Defence Science Organisation's member states would discuss the ongoing research and scientists would make technical presentations. The CDSO appears to have been wound up or at least Indian scientists no longer seem to be participating for quite some years now. As in other matters, publications and announcements in other language journals and magazines pose difficulties of translation.

In India: The emphasis continues to be laid on providing standardised rations according to Service Ration Scales (as advocated by the Armed Forces Medical Directorate) to the forces operating in every sector. Much energy and planning have gone into streamlining the nutrition delivery, food selection, procurement and distribution of food supplies.

Two Defence establishments namely the Defence Institute of Physiology and Allied Sciences (DIPAS) and the Defence Food Research Laboratory (DFRL) are the principal laboratories concerned with carrying out R&D in this area of life sciences, the former in the field of human physiology and nutrition requirements of men in the fighting forces based on physiological requirements, and the latter in developing specific ration packs, solider friendly foods, the associated preservation technologies and their quality assurance systems. Many foods, ration packs and beverage products and their processing technologies have originated from DFRL at a time when the domestic food manufacturing industry had not yet ventured into making processed (semi or fully processed) convenience meal items, ready to drink beverages and beverage powders for the Indian consumers. This laboratory's main focus continues to be the investigation and development of quality parameters, processes and innovative products and reintroduce such of those which lie in the realm of heritage or traditional foods in a modern processed and quality assured form. In this respect, its role is limited and does not appear to extend to participating in design and testing of field feeding and food service systems.

When a food product has been put through its paces (tests) in the laboratory and has been found to be satisfactory in all its physical, chemical, nutritional, microbiological, toxicological, organoleptic and packaging parameters, DFRL carries out field trials on troops using the food produced in its own pilot plants. Trial units are designated by the Army or Navy or Air Headquarters as the case may be.

From the results of the first field trials further action will follow with regard to any modifications or changes that may have been indicated or deemed to be essential. This process of taking the product through field trials for a satisfactory and totally acceptable outcome is a long one. The transfer of technology to a food manufacturing unit is vigorously pursued so that the item can then be made in large quantities. Specifications and standards in quality and safety are established and defined as a result of such investigations. Needless to say there are many a hiccup between concept development and technology transfer.

It is a telling point that the concept development for any operational food emanates from the food scientists. The inputs they work on are current scientific developments reported in literature, views and suggestions (and occasionally even the name or type of food) passed on by various units/force commanders during meetings or conveyed otherwise. The scientists are required only to apply their scientific knowledge in converting a desirable food or a recipe into a processed or stabilised convenient form. There is a compartmentalisation of the effort leading to dilution and delay of the final outcome. The food industry is at best a reluctant partner and often has had to be coaxed in to taking up test production. This situation has changed somewhat since the phenomenal success with the troops and in the domestic market of the retort pouch food technology after one early and bold entrepreneur took the first tentative step in manufacturing 'army required food' by this process.

In USA: The US, Army Food Service Programme of the 1990s, the present Combat Feeding Programme in the United States Military Establishment, the Army Natick Research Centre and the United States Military Nutrition experts together with the industry jointly are involved in the research and development of foods and systems in upgrading their quality and distribution as well as in the evaluation of the foods. The Combat Feeding Programme is said to undertake everything necessary for feeding the military forces 'from the deep sea to deep space' according to Phil Copeland of the American Forces Press Service (http://nsrdec.natickarmy.mil/about/food/index.htm).

The soldiers' food preferences and the desire expressed for a particular food are acted upon by the Combat Feeding Programme. Recipes are developed by food specialists and dieticians. These are tested by soldiers randomly formed into taste panels during development and once the recipe is developed it is subjected to field trials. The accepted version is then manufactured by food companies to preset standards and specifications.

The Army Field Feeding System's study devised the 'Wolf mobile' that is capable of serving fast foods in the field. This particular system was used in the Operations 'Desert Shield' and 'Desert Storm' in 1991. Subsistence training is provided by the Army Centre of Excellence in an effort to train and prepare the Army to feed the soldiers better, properly and adequately during future deployments (Quarter Master Museum, QM web). Despite all these establishments participating in developing and transporting foods into the field and employing field-feeding stations to serve hot meals in the combat zone, there were said to be lacunae in feeding troops in the 1991 Gulf war (www.af.mil/news/story).

This pertained to the Army's inability to provide the troops an acceptable level of quality meals. A quality meal does not just happen in the testing laboratories alone. It has to happen in the field in the actual area of soldier deployment and feeding. A very great amount of planning, preparation and positioning of different types of rations and the right types of equipment, transportation, and refrigeration and storage facilities go into the actual feeding in the combat zone. The entire supply chain and support system have to be geared to perform this task.

There is another but very crucial aspect to be considered before combat foods in convenient modules and other substances are given out as field rations. And that is the suitability of these foods in terms of nutritional adequacy, body physiology according to the climate and temperature, military efficiency and maintenance of good health, cognitive abilities and alertness.

Such questions have been posed as early as the 1980s when the MREs were introduced and evaluated by a series of controlled experiments on volunteers. The investigations carried out by various research groups including the US Army Research and Development Lab at Natick have been periodically reported in the Annual reports of Military Nutrition Research from the 1980s.

While the MREs have been a breakthrough of great impact on the way troops in the field can be fed, a question that needed to be answered was the effect of long term use of MREs.

It was shown that it leads to weight loss as determined from a 44 day laboratory study on volunteers fed with freshly prepared hot food made with 'A' rations in field training and those fed with pack rations. Students eating MREs three times daily consumed 3,000 Kcals but lost 1.5 lb while soldiers in field training given MREs consumed only 2,200 Kcal/day. Those soldier volunteers fed at least two fresh hot meals and one MRE lost 4.7 lbs while those subsisting only on MRE lost 10 lbs in a 30 day period. This was considered unacceptably high. Any such ration, MRE or other pack rations can at best be considered only for 'limited use'.

There are many types of operational rations in use; some are special purpose packs, some are suited to cold weather or hot weather; and yet other packs serving other functions. Meyer and Klicka (1982) discussing operational rations of the US Dept of Defence listed seven types. The main operational rations are:

- Standard B, provide 4,300 Kcals, meant for groups with organised food service facilities without refrigeration or resupply of perishables,
- Tray packs of breakfast and dinner −1,400 Kcal and 1,500 Kcal respectively providing high quality, nutritionally adequate hot food to sustain in the field under highly mobile situations; MRE (1,300 Kcals) for individuals on their own during operations,
- Special restricted rations like for cold weather called the 'Ration Cold Weather' (or RCW) which provides 4,500 Kcal/day to sustain an individual during assault, reconnaissance and such other situations where no resupply is possible,
- Light weight restricted rations (2,132 Kcal/day) for use up to 30 days for the sustenance of Special Operations forces during surveillance and reconnaissance,
- Long range patrol improved rations (1,570 Kcal/day) which is the extended life operational ration for personnel on initial assault and special operations and
- New generation survival ration (1,405 Kcal/g) for survival in any situation for up to five days.

These variable calorie rations contain between 18 (high) to 5 per cent protein, 30–41 (high) per cent fat and 49–60 per cent carbohydrates.

In a light weight ration, the calorie density is easily increased by incorporating fat at higher levels even as changes in carbohydrate content remain in a narrower range of variation.

In the survival ration mentioned here 41 per cent fat and 54 per cent carbohydrates were used with just 5 per cent protein. In the cold weather ration RCW – the fat and carbohydrate contents are 32 per cent and 60 per cent respectively while the protein was 68 per cent. The standard rations contain 13 per cent protein, 33 per cent fat and 54 per cent carbohydrates.

The rationale for using higher fat content in RCW derives from observing the cold region natives in North America. Traditionally these natives are said to subsist on a high fat diet. This is diametrically opposite to what the mountain people in the Himalayan ranges normally eat. At high altitudes, the native diet for generations has been rich in carbohydrates by preference and by long held belief that it is beneficial.

Nutritional needs in hot environments have also been elicited by such researches. It is important to ensure that a ration gets accepted to the level of 60–70 per cent of overall consumption (good) for maintenance of health. More carbohydrate and more water intake are encouraged by the addition of flavoured beverages to the MRE package. The adage that 'men will eat anything' does not apply. They would go hungry. There had been reports of weight loss of between 20 and 40 lbs in two months among soldiers fighting in the North Africa theatre of World War II due to continuous eating of Combat C or K rations for 67 days at a stretch (Friedl and Hoyt, 1997). Combat efficiency also fell seriously as a result of this.

In UK: The research into military food and nutrition requirements does not appear to be confined to any one or two organisations. Defence scientists no doubt have a great say in these matters as do the Nutrition Research Council and their Medical Research Council and other laboratories carrying out food research. The food industry in UK is well established and capable of manufacturing any requirement. Their combat rations are quite similar to the US rations as discussed earlier and are of the individual or group type.

Under the Defence Logistics Organization of the Ministry of Defence, various operations are listed (www.mod.uk/dlo/ipts/dfsipt/operations.htm). These are carried out by different groups or teams. The Operation and Commitments team addresses issues relating to current operations sustainability policy and the management of the storage and distribution of Operational Ration packs, as well as being responsible for operational requirements and policy and arranging for food supply to military operations. The procurement and distribution of the food are overseen by the Food Supply Management team, through what is termed the 3663 Food Supply Contract. The foods required by military garrisons for the British troops everywhere, even those deployed as far away as the South Atlantic theatre of Falklands or nearer home in the Gulf region and Afghanistan have been shipped under this contract.

The Food Supply contract team is meant to administer contracts for food supply including the Operational Rations packs. The 3663 is the name by which the prime supplier is identified with. This contract is renewed from time to time and a multimillion dollar contact was placed in 2006 (www.mod.uk/dlo/catering/ops/index, www.3663supplies.co.uk). It may have been further extended. The Food Quality Assurance team is the group that carries out QA of the contractor supplied as well as locally obtained provisions.

The production of the Operational Ration packs and the quality of the components that go into the making of the packs supplied by the DCG are also managed by the Food Supply management group in addition to managing the procurement of foods through the 3663 contract. All contractor-supplied foods are inspected and examined by the Food Selection Panel as to adherence to the quality specifications and obtaining value for money (www.practicalairsoft.co.uk/gp-menu.asp).

In Australia: The Defence Nutrition Research Centre of the Defence Science and Technology Organization of Australia based in Tasmania carries out the primary task of determining the nutritional requirements for fitness of the Australian Defence Forces personnel in the three services. Unlike in UK, USA, and Canada, the Australian climatic conditions are very different. It was determined that the troops under training and those who carry out exercises and arduous manoeuvres in the cold snowy mountains as well as in the hot tropical regions of this continent apparently were not receiving adequate amounts of energy. According to a five year long study, the nutrition guidelines used in Australia have been found to be inadequate for the dietary needs of men performing heavy outdoor work. The ration scales have existed since the 1960s (Department of the Army, DST, 1962). A Charles Stuart University release of information package states that the ration specifications are covered by document 'Sup man 4' of the Australian Defence Force Food Specifications which describes specifications for the ration entitlement or ration scale and the combat ration packs (http/ www.hsc.csu.edu.an.austarmy.htm).

In barracks as is common in every army, the Australian soldiers are fed through group feeding arrangements with freshly made food supplied from the kitchens. In the field, men are provided with combat ration packs – either individual or group. Field kitchens are set up by the Army Catering Corps wherever feasible to serve fresh rations (Quarter Master Museum, QM web).

The Future in Combat Rations

There are several questions that will need to be addressed before one can speculate about the combat foods to come in the future. How does one know what kind of combat foods may be required twenty years hence? How can the research community make reasonably accurate projections for technology? This would depend on the nature of future wars and the kind of military engagements the armies would participate in. What might be the art of war in future?

The answers obviously point to the need for concept development. Does the concept level of activities itself need to be improved? What new concepts are likely to emerge? Taking into consideration the fast and ever changing requirements for different types of operational rations, the ration designers must address the issue by factoring in consumer trends in food preferences and expectations, the range and depth of scientific information available or necessary on the various aspects of food, nutrition and human physiology, knowledge about appropriate technologies, testing tools, the merits of new and special ingredients and food formulae, and establish the suitability and appropriateness by experimentation and volunteer trials.

Nutrition is the first and foremost consideration in a ration alongside the amount of energy derived from it. It has been established that:

- On a scientific basis, combat rations must have a minimum of 1,200 Kcal/day, and if higher calorie content becomes necessary for specific operations, then the energy content should be appropriate for the designated temperature/climatic conditions. Therefore there should be adequate data pertaining to body physiology in relation to temperature, terrain and climate in the geographic area of operations. All these require quite elaborately gathered scientific information and experimentation.
- The main calories from food are contributed through protein, fat and starch (cereal) components which form the basis of any balanced meal. This calls for prior knowledge about nutritional requirements. Water is an important component of food but additionally it is consumed in the liquid form as plain water or beverage to keep the tissues well hydrated at all times and in a functioning metabolic state.
- Various ingredients are combined together into a semblance of recognisable food by food craft. The rations must be shelf stable and acceptable to the majority.

- Combat situations often develop quite suddenly, warranting speedy response. A well prepared force must be able to have rations ready and available for that occasion, or for a period, in a conveniently packaged form for easy transportation, painless preparation and quick consumption which means that on the technology front the matter of extending shelf life of a food sometimes as much as for three years, maintaining its nutritional, chemical and microbiological and hedonic qualities will have to be addressed by any technological means that is considered appropriate for the food and its acceptability.
- There is another important factor of consumer trends and preferences. What do the soldiers want, prefer, expect? Past experiences, new trends, modern day exposure to food variety and multicultural ethos should be factored in while contemplating the design or introduction of newer type of foods.
- In a general way there is a trend towards vegetarianism in the west, observes Nicole Belanger – Drapeau, Director of Project Management Office which is responsible for overseeing the Canadian Military's Combat rations (D. NET menu). Generally speaking, vegetarian menus in the western diets are based on salads, vegetable stuffing and vegetable containing soups, soya tofu and nuts and seeds usually added to multigrain breads and breakfast cereal preparations and a few vegetable toppings to pizza and noodle style foods. For extending the shelf life of all moist foods for long periods, steam sterilisation is the most acceptable technology. While the shelf life of foods is extended by this means by preventing any obvious spoilage, chemical deterioration *in situ* does take place after a period of time. Such changes occur in other processed foods also. It is reported that nuts and seeds used in vegetarian food preparations included in US rations lead to more rapid onset of fat rancidity in an atmosphere of oxygen. Various grains and seeds and nuts are added to multigrain breads which are important components of military rations. The challenge is to mitigate the adverse effect of oxygen even in the microenvironment of its package. To a large extent this problem can be solved by the use of oxygen scrubbers and scavengers/absorbers and specially treated packaging and changing the internal atmosphere by modifying it for storage. These inventions have changed the face of food preservation. Newer technologies using high electrical impulse, high pressure methods, have claimed a degree of success in preserving the freshness and flavour of fruit juices specifically and ensuring safety of food stored under refrigeration. Gamma irradiation, long in the running, is still confined to a few foodstuffs and products meant for commercial markets and for preserving certain foods only.

Introduction of new foods and novel methods: For the Indian Military rations, which are largely vegetarian in nature, the components are selected by the food advisory committee for procurement from the suppliers. Newer and special application products are developed by food scientists and evaluated extensively, first in the laboratory and then in user trails in field situations. Processed and semi processed products already seen on the domestic market shelf may be considered suitable as ration component, by specifying a different portion size, or different and better packaging and which are then obtained from the suppliers. The Indian food industry has neither independently developed nor manufactured any products (not since World War II) for military needs. It was rather difficult to convince any unit possessing manufacturing capabilities to turn to processing military food. However, in recent years, technology transfers from Defence Research laboratories have caused some products to be manufactured for general use as spinoffs, which come in very useful to the Armed Forces. There is now a wide range of food products available in the domestic market and under special circumstances the manufacturers perhaps may be able to make adequate quantities in the appropriate packaging expressly for the armed forces.

In both the US and Canadian Armed Forces, no food laboratories as such are said to be engaged in food product development activities. However, innovative approaches, investigating special topics in science and technology and engineering with possible military application are significant areas of their interest and focus. We may recall that the path breaking invention of retort pouch technology was investigated in great detail in the US Army Natick Research Labs. For processed foods, their food industries are constantly developing novel ingredients, products, packaging and processes. Almost every type of food ingredient and food such as breads, snacks, entrees, desserts, and beverages etc. commonly used in western cooking and meals are available in the fresh, refrigerated or processed and shelf stable and prepackaged form. There are numerous food industries doing their own R&D and producing the widest range of products imaginable. Full scientific and quality data pertaining to every item are also generated or gathered by individual manufacturers to support the claims of any special, specific or superior performance or quality attributed to the new products.

In the event that these are offered by the industry or suppliers as part of military rations, their suitability and stability in terms of operational, engineering and biological criteria are evaluated exhaustively. Their nutritional quality, appearance, texture, flavour, aroma and taste are prime considerations at this stage. Further testing is carried out by volunteer testers, the process of evaluation lasting 15 months or so. Appropriate and sturdy packaging being a very essential aspect of rations to maintain their shelf life, special evaluation of the packaging is carried out. The Center for Advanced Food Technology (CAFT) at Rutgers University has a pilot scale retort facility to evaluate the packing of commercially developed retort pouch foods. The Center however, is not engaged in developing any foods or rations.

During a brief visit by this author with the Director of the Ration Testing Facility, and while witnessing the operations in the retorting facility at CAFT it was given to understand that for acceptance of any products into the military rations system a process of quality evaluation is set in motion. The process is based on a questionnaire sent to the suppliers and data submission by the supplier. For this purpose elaborately designed software was in place for eliciting various quality parameters and safety features and which are evaluated against standards and the limits for acceptance and evaluation of parameters set up by scientists. Electronic submission of data aids in speeding up the evaluation and decision making process.

This had been developed with the joint efforts of the Army's Natick Laboratory, the CAFT and the US Army. A data eliciting questionnaire is first completed by the supplier group, the supplier/manufacturer bears the onus to generate the entire technical data pertinent to the quality and shelf life, nutritional profile, safety features and packaging information. Presumably there are other features, not revealed in the discussions regarding the proposed food product.

All requests for information and exchange of data are done electronically and only when the requisite criteria are found to be satisfactory is the new product(s) given a green signal of acceptance for further action. At times, CAFT undertakes to standardise packaging materials and processing parameters and conditions for retort processing of the products, probably meant for MRE.

There are great merits to this system. The food science research laboratories do not have to spend their human and financial resources in conducting researches that the food industry seems capable of doing pretty well on its own. The scientists are therefore able to devote their talent, energies, time and funds towards carrying out research in cutting edge science and technology.

The food industry is free to develop anything that in its perception will be accepted by the consumers whether it is a nutritional food or supplement, or products with new combination of ingredients, taste, flavour, texture, better presentation and packaging and shelf life, of different ethnicity, vegetarian or meat containing, specific for one religious group or another, lower or higher costing and is therefore not dependent on military orders alone for its survival or profits. All it needs to do is to conform to the US Food and Drug Administration's quality, safety and labelling criteria. The users i.e. the Armed Forces in this instance, should they select an existing or new product for their use, would get a product conforming to quality, safety and performance criteria acceptable to them. There are confidentiality matters in this tripartite evaluation system.

On the face of it, this system promises to be able to screen and evaluate a great many new product innovations brought out by food industry professionals. The industry also bears the responsibility to make quality products conforming to criteria and specifications laid down in military food rules and regulations in addition to adhering to FDA criteria. Once approved the production itself, in any quantity required, will not be a constraint because the product is already in supply to the civilian market.

Under the US Quarter Master Container Institute's catalogue method, every item, be it a food, food ingredient or a component (item name, portion size, weight, packaging), an article of clothing or shoes (size and quantity) or other items in specified quantity is identified with a code number. It becomes easier to place orders for an item coded X, which is identified with the item name as well as its quantity/portion/packaging. It facilitates digital information exchange between the concerned agencies and allows for easy monitoring by a centralised authority. A Canadian effort from July 1997 to streamline the estimation exercise of ordering food for troops in Haiti resulted in employing a system called Quattropro for data entry operations. It was successful in showing the author of this experiment W.O. Ray Deveault, a Canadian Food Service Officer how both the money and rations could be accounted for.

Clearly, several new concepts in addressing the issue of finding new products, ration procurement systems and quality and quantity monitoring methods had been developed by the year 2000. What will the scientific community project as possible technologies and tools for the coming decades?

The future weapons of war, the future ways of fighting (Alexander, 1999) and some futuristic foods and packs have received substantial attention from experts. Already, performance enhancing foods have made their appearance in the Western military provisioning. What next?

Since the trend in India seems to be revivalist and looking back to the ancient wisdom and knowledge, re-examination of cultural food practices and understanding tribal traditional practices, it is a safe bet to say that perhaps scientists will be digging deep into this fount to extract any hidden or hither to unrecognised sources of foods, medicines and even weapons. This last is already a subject of investigation for ancient secrets of effective stealth warfare and according to a report (Mayor, 2003, p. 9), Indian scientists in Pune are said to be studying Kautilya's formulae for powders from awful substances that were meant to cause madness, blindness or death among the adversaries. This could not be independently ascertained one way or another. Search for unique biochemical agents to confer special biological powers motivate researchers in other countries too. According to Mayor, US military scientists funded by the Defence Advanced Research Projects Agency, DARPA (www.darpa.mil) are reported to have initiated pharmaceutical and genome based investigations for special stimulants and agents based on genes in mice and fruit flies which would eliminate the need for sleep. Food, fitness and sleep, recovery from and resistance to stresses – these are major concerns in combat situations.

Even as high fangled research is trying to grapple with various combat related stresses and means to overcome them, there has been a more down-to-earth approach in recent times in India by the use of a fruit known as seabuckthorn (*Hypophae rhamnoides*) found in Himachal Pradesh and Ladakh a yellow coloured wild berry rich in vitamin 'C' content and other vitamins (see Chapter 9). It has been known to the locals for a very long time but had to await the attention of scientists for these many decades even though the plant and the Indian army both inhabited and occupied the high altitudes near Leh during all this time. This fruit is blessed with abundant quantities of different vitamins and anti-oxidants very important in general nutrition and as stress busters. In a seminar on seabuckthorn held in 2004 (Department of Life Sciences, DRDO, 2004) results of investigations conducted on this fruit were discussed. They point to its multifaceted qualities and as a source of vitamins, minerals, antioxidants and possible radio-protective features.

Energy substitutes in combat rations: Is it really necessary to provide a minimum of 1,200 Kcal/ day by way of food and beverage to a combat soldier? Not if we go by the information that there exist in Kerala, India, one forest tribe known as 'Kani' who have knowledge of a wild plant by eating a few leaves or fruits of which, tired persons are able to go on with renewed energy and stamina. Tribal knowledge of several wild plants growing in their own region, of the changes likely to occur in weather and climatic conditions or other natural events exists really from far back in time – 'Dream Time' as the Australian natives refer to their past. The indigenous people of every continent are the repositories of such ancient knowledge that has come to them by oral traditions or shown by practice carried on as a tradition. The discovery of this plant in Kerala was accidental and happened in 1987. A team of botanists went on an ethno-botanical expedition to the Western Ghats and took guides from the Kani tribe to show them the way in the thick jungles. They seemed to eat only some blackish looking fruits but exhibited remarkable stamina and endurance even after long treks. At one point they offered the fruit to the exhausted scientists. The effect, they say, was remarkable after eating the fruit which tasted like almonds. They felt a flash of energy and vitality and they could proceed on their trek. It required a great amount of persuasion before the Kani men would reveal the identity of the plant and show them the places where it could be found.

Scientists of the Regional Research Laboratory at Jammu and later the Tropical Botanical and Garden Research Institute, TBGRI, under the Botanical Survey of India, situated in Thiruvananthapuram, Kerala, have pioneered research investigations on this particular plant, examined its pharmacological features and pharmacodynamics, its captive cultivation and formulated products using its leaves and roots.

Identified as *Trichopus zelyanicus* Gaerth and later as *T. zeylanicus* ssp. *travancoricus* Burkill, ex Narayanan (family Trichopodaceae) it is known by its vernacular name *arogyappacha* and is said to exhibit health giving properties and possess anti fatigue, anti stress characteristics of a higher order than the Korean Ginseng (Pushpagandan *et al.*, 1988). Technical literature on the subject given out by TBGRI lists many wonder features of this plant. Its leaf extracts are said to be very effective too and its seeds have adaptagenic properties and act as anti stress and anti fatigue substances (Sharma *et al.*, 1993). Prevention of stomach ulceration induced by cold stress and aspirin is also seen. It is also found to be hepato-protective, immuno-modulatory and even exhibits aphrodisiac properties (Subramoniam *et al.,* 1999). Altogether this wonder plant is said to build stamina and also ameliorate old age related disorders. Protocols for protoplast regeneration have been established (Krishnan, Sudha and Seeni, 1995) and a patented product 'Jeevani' made with this plant material is commercially available. If this plant can be cultivated and processed in the quantity necessary to prepare the hunger dampening product formulation in sufficient amounts, one can only speculate about the immense advantages it will bestow on combat troops and Special Forces who are on the go. The wonder preparation eaten in small quantities before departure will obviate the necessity for immediate and frequent food consumption and permit the logistics planners to concentrate on providing more combat teeth and reduce their tail considerably. The troops can also thus dispense with carrying large quantities of food on their person and the need to scour the local resources if their food supply systems do not catch up with them or are cut off.

One does not need to carry more food than would be necessary for a day or so. From discussions in 2006 with Dr Rajasehkar, one of the scientists who conducted a great part of this research work, it has transpired that efforts made by the TBGRI to interest the DRDO in this plant, its product and its admirable characteristics drew no response or elicited no interest.

More is the pity because there is another wonder plant known to the indigenous tribes of the Kalahari desert of southern Africa, known as *Hoodia,* three species of which are currently the object of scientific interest. Eating a few leaves of the plant is said take away hunger and thirst. The plant contains an active ingredient identified only as P57. The three cactus like species are *H.gordonii*, *H.currorii* and *H.officinalis*. *H.gordonii* is bitter while the smaller looking *H.currorii* and the rarer *H.officinalis* are sweeter in nature and hence preferred by the indigenous Namibian tribes. South Africa's Council for Scientific and Industrial Research was instrumental in identifying the active component P57 and patenting it in 1996. *Hoodia* cultivation is being vigorously undertaken for export as dried *Hoodia* powder which sells as a supplement in health and herbal products stores in USA and is much in demand by weight watchers (www.google.com/Hoodia).

Another such wonder plant, *Morinda citrifolia (*www.chinaphar.com/1671/-4083/23/1127.htm), commonly known as Noni, or Indian Mulberry and found widely in the Polynesian islands, Fiji, Burma, Australia, is said to have both healthfood and medicinal value. The fruit is eaten by the natives and legend says that the Polynesian heroes and heroines survived famine by eating the fruit. Its therapeutic effects on a wide variety of infections, illnesses and disorders have been reviewed by Wang *et al.* (2002).

Stimulants: Tea and coffee are stimulant foods. Coffee has figured in military rations for at least the past 250 years in America and replaced wine in European rations. Tea and coffee are listed in the standard Indian military rations as well as the special issue items to relieve fatigue among the ship's crew and battle fatigued soldiers and anyone else in need of urgent refreshment. Alcohol in one form or another, usually wine, beer or rum has been ingested for millennia by soldiers as authorised daily rations and especially for fatigue and stress busting at the end of a hard day's march or battle. Opium has been known to be used from the ancient times in the eastern cultures as a pre battle morale booster and even war elephants in ancient and historical India were fed with a dose of opium before the start of battle.

From scientific evidence gathered over many years caffeine has come to be accepted as the number one stimulant without which people who are accustomed to it cannot get started or function properly. The principle beverages from which caffeine is derived are tea and coffee. The Europeans and Americans drink more coffee while the English seem to prefer tea. In India tea is more popular in the north and coffee in the south.

Coffee and tea are classified as stimulant brews under the Bureau of Indian Standards and caffeine is said to be addictive. It is seen to confer alertness in sleep deprived people and to cause withdrawal symptoms in the form of headache in people who do not get their daily dose or doses of hot cups of coffee. Caffeine has also had its name besmirched in regard to cardiovascular diseases. Coffee has been looked down upon in comparison to tea, especially green tea and black tea, in the matter of health benefits. The Committee of Military nutrition research of the US Army found that caffeine sustained mental task performance and recommended formulations for military operations (www.usmilitary.about.com, IOM, 2001). And now there is evidence which reveals (Kesavan, 2007) coffee's health promoting properties, especially its radio-protective role. Confectionary containing coffee extract and flavour are being sold in the domestic market as chewable toffee 'Coffee bite' and ice cold ready to drink beverage.

Energy boosting beverages such as Red Bull containing caffeine and taurine etc. sell for high prices in the domestic market in India. Many of these substances have been the subject of research by the Military Nutrition Research Board of the US Army.

Tea, not coffee is the preferred beverage included in the Indian military rations. Coffee is the 'in lieu' alternative to tea and is generally given to officers, though Other Ranks (OR) in the Navy and Air Force may also opt for it.

For the US soldiers in future wars, the foods will include Jolt, which is a caffeine-energy gum equal to 1 cup of coffee. It is expected to sustain a high energy level in the men in battle (http:\\ usmilitary.about.com).

Other Fatigue busters: Caffeine is not the only stimulant that can jolt a person out of sleepiness during long vigils and long distance drives. Many food flavourings and spices are found to possess properties other than spicing up the food. If what has been reported in the media from preliminary observations of scientists and if fully substantiated by further experimental proof, then peppermint and cinnamon whiffs are equally effective in warding off drowsiness and aiding stress relief. Flavoured water, beverages, chewables and sprays containing mint and or cinnamon may not be far away. Already there are mint flavoured herbal teas and many differently flavoured drinking water. There are many different kinds of mint flavoured confectionary items such as sweets, gums, chocolate etc. but all of them come with heavy lacings of sugar, and none of them claim to be anything more than what they seem to be.

Cinnamon is a popular food flavouring spice. It is used both in Indian cookery as a constituent of the mixed spices known as *garam masala* and in Western preparations such as cakes and dessert pies and stews. Its beneficial effects on diabetes are being revealed. Cinnamon would now be viewed in its new role as an 'alertness' causing substance.

Revelations of scientists at a conference of the Association for Chemical Reception Sciences suggest that wafting peppermint and cinnamon scents in the car can help reduce the level of frustration of the driver, relieve anxiety, lessen fatigue and make one more alert while driving. Inhaled at a rate of 30 seconds every 15 minutes, these odorous components added to low-flow oxygen moving at 1.3 litres per minute, exerted a remarkable effect on cognitive functions, wakefulness and mood. Both mint and cinnamon increased alertness (Raloff, 2004; www.sciencenews.org,/Conference of Association for Chemical Receptor Sciences, Sarasota, Florida/in Health Day News – Newsletter Health 24). Although examined from the point of improving driver efficiency and alertness for decreasing highway accidents, such simple, innocuous and pleasurable odorous inhalations may prove to be very valuable if included in a soldier's combat gear. Men driving transport and combat vehicles, battle tanks, supersonic aircraft and those keeping long and lonely vigils are likely to derive great benefit by these inhalations.

By traditional practice in India, ginger, lime, honey, pepper, turmeric and cumin are used in many combinations in food and in various Ayurvedic and home remedies. New research findings indicate that there is much merit to these practices. Formulated as pills and balls for sucking and chewing or incorporated into beverages and snacks included in the soldier kits and combat rations these condiments and spices could prove to be the most user friendly delivery systems for the wholly familiar and safe therapeutics. Such preparations which are apparently appetite stimulating or are digestives have been developed by both DFRL, DIPAS laboratories in India and are presumably undergoing field trials.

References

Alexander, J.B. Future War, Part II. *Non Lethal Weapons in 21st Century Warfare*. St Martin's Press, New York, 1999.

Arya, S.S., 1996. 'Food for the Armed Forces: National and Global Scenario'. In 'Design and Supply of Foods for the Indian Armed Forces'. Proceedings of the SLI Conference December 10–12, 1996, DFRL Mysore, p. 1–9.

ASC Manual: Scales of Rations and Supplies. A Manual Issued by the Army Service Corps.

Australian Service Ration Scales and Ration Packs. Issued by the Military Board, Canberra. First edition, 1962. Department of the Army, Directorate of Supplies and Transport, Food Science Establishment, Melbourne.

Clancy, Tom, with John Grisham. *Special Forces: A guided Tour of US Army Special Forces*. Berkeley Books. New York, 2001.

Committee of Military Nutrition Research. *Caffeine for the sustainment of mental performance.* Food and Nutrition Board, Institute of Medicine, National Academic Press, Washington DC, 2001.

Defence Food Research Laboratory, (DRDO), Mysore, Ministry of Defence, Government of India, Product Information Brochure, 2005 & 2007.

Dupuy, T.H. *Understanding War: History and Theory of Combat*. Paragon Publishers, New York, 1987.

Friedl, Karl E, and Read, W. Hoyt, 1997. 'Development and biomedical testing of military operational rations'. *Ann. Rev. Nutr*, 17: 51–75.

Hofschroer, Peter. 1815, The Waterloo Campaign. 'The German Victory: From Waterloo to the Fall of Napoleon'. Greenhill Books, London & Staple Books, Pennsylvania, 1999.

Kesavan, P.C. DAE – Homi Bhabha Chair, Distinguished Fellow M.S. Swaminathan Research Foundation, Chennai, in *The Hindu*, Thurs April 19, 2007.

Koehler, Walter L. 1980. 'Subsistence Support in the German Army'. 28 Nov. Technical Information Centre. TRADCO, APO, New York. http:\stinet.dtic.mil; www.stormingmedia.us/01/0140/E014057.htm

Krishnan, P.N., C.G. Sudha and S. Seeni. 1995. 'Rapid propagation through shoot tip culture of *Trichopus zelyanicus* Gaertn, a rare ethnomedicinal plant'. *Plant Cell Reports*, 14: 707–711.

Lampi, Rauno A. 1977. 'Flexible Packaging for Processed Foods'. *Adv. Food. Res.*, 23: 305–427.

Mayor, Adrienne. *Greek Fire, Poison Arrows and Scorpion Bombs: Biological and chemical Warfare in the Ancient times.* Woodstock, New York, London, 2003, p. 9.

Meyer, A.L. and M.V. Klicka. 1982. 'Operational rations, current and Future'. Department of Defense. Tech Report Natick TR–82/031 US Army Research Development Laboratory.

Personal communications. From Dr S. Rajasekhar. Division of Ethnobotany and Ethnopharmacology, Tropical Botanical Garden Research Institute, Thiruvananthapuram, Palode P.O. Kerala.

Pushpagandan P., S. Rajasekharan, P.K. Ratheesh Kumar, C.R. Jawahar, V. Velayudhan Nair, N. Lakshmi and L. Sarada Amma. 1988. 'Arogysppacha (*Trichopus zeylanicum* Gaertn). The Ginseng of Kani Tribes of Agasthyar Hills, Kerala, for evergreen health and vitality'. *Ancient Science of Life*, 7: 13–16.

Raloff, J. 2004. 'Coffee, Spices, Wine and the rest of You'. *Science News*, 165 (May 1): 282–284.

Roberts, Andrew. *Napoleon and Wellington*, Weidenfield Nicolson, London, 2001.

Sanjeev Kumar, V.A., Manish Gupta, S.N. Sabapathy, and A.S. Bawa. 2005. 'Self Heating Systems for ready to eat foods'. *Indian Food Industry* (Jan–Feb), 24(1):54–57.

Seabuckthorn: 'A Resource for Environment, Health and Energy' Seminar, March 12–13 2004, at INMAS, DRDO; Organizers, Directorate of Life Sciences, DRDO, New Delhi.

Sharma A.K., P. Pushpagandan, C.L. Chopra, S. Rajasekharan and L. Sarada Amma 1993. 'Adaptagenic activity of *Trichopus zeylanicum* Gaertn, the Ginseng of Kerala'. *Ancient Science of Life*, 8: 212–219.

Subramoniam, A., D.A. Evans., R. Valsaraj, S. Rajasekharan and P. Pushpagandan 1999. 'Inhibition of antigen induced degranulation of sensitized mast cells by *Trichopus zelyanicus* in mice and rats'. *J of Ethno pharmacology*, 68: 137–143.

Tilak, V.W. (Brig) & R. Bhadwar, (Lt Col), AFMS, India 1996. 'Ration Scales and Design considerations and the ground realities of meeting these requirements for the Armed Forces'. In 'Design and Supply of Foods for the Indian Armed Forces'. Services-Laboratory-Industry Interactive(SLI) Conference, December, 10–12, 1996. DFRL, Mysore. Proceedings, pp. 41–54.

Wang Mian-Ying, Brett J. West, C. Jarakae Jensen, Diane Nowicki, Su Chen, Afak Palu and Gary Anderson. 2002. '*Morinda citrifolia* (Noni): A literature review and recent advances' in 'Noni research· Acta Pharmacol Sin' 2002 Dec; 23 (12): 1127–1141.

Section – III

The Food Supply Chain

Authors's note

As per the directive of the Director General of Military Intelligence it is 'certified that the ***views*** expressed in this article (chapter) are made by the author in personal capacity and do not have any official endorsement'.

[The descriptions given, the diagrams prepared and the conclusions reached were based on the data and facts obtained directly through interaction with the appropriate authorities and observed personally during visits.]

12

The Indian Military Food Supply Chain System

> "Flour and fodder are the masters in war time. Neither armies nor their horses could function on empty stomachs".
>
> *Frederick II*

General Aspects

The Indian Armed Forces form a vast establishment comprised of a million plus personnel who are posted in units flung far and wide in the country in various commands and bases of the three Services. They are engaged in carrying out routine and critical operational assignments in the field. They are attached to peace units in administrative or training postings on transfers or are being sent for advance or specific training. They sail in ships and submarines for undisclosed periods of time and destinations.

New entrants – both direct recruit officers and officer cadets and the Other Ranks (ORs) are provided with basic military training as well as advanced education and training at various levels. They may be located in or close to urban areas and amenities or posted to regions which are not readily accessible by road, rail, or even air. The weather and climatic conditions and the terrains in some of the regions of military deployments are as formidable to bear as can be imagined. Some units are posted in islands like the Andamans, where there is neither agriculture nor a network of roads to convey goods and therefore everything must come from the main land by sea or air.

All personnel are entitled to free rations as per standard scale while in service. There are situations where the personnel cannot be provided with rations in kind, especially when they are far from their supply sources and when posted abroad. They are paid in cash on such occasions. In all other cases, when attached to peace and field units within the country, they prefer to receive rations in kind, such as grocery items, to be cooked and served (in messes) or carried as special operational food packs or in monthly grocery quotas for home cooking (family stations).

All the food must be procured from within the country, and as far as is possible from governmental agencies and some private suppliers. It is now possible to obtain the bulk of everyday foods from domestic markets because of the development and growth of agriculture, horticulture, and other food sectors like milk, sea food, poultry farming and food processing. This happened as a result of government policy and planning and due to post 1991 liberalisation imports of many food products. Except where fresh groceries are not practical, inclusion of packaged foods in rations occurs generally as substitute items or as essential operational food packs.

But who should be responsible for (a) procuring everything as per requirement and administrative sanction, (b) starting the purchase machinery, (c) verifying the bonafides of suppliers, (d) inspecting and assuring the quality and acceptability of the foods purchased, (e) transporting the consignments in the quantities intended to the rightful destinations, (f) holding the stock and periodic issue to units or individuals (g) seeing to it that everyday the proper amounts of rations are issued and (h) cooked and served? There is a very elaborate system in place for these purposes. This is the supply chain that will be discussed in this chapter.

The major players in the supply chain belong to the Quarter Master General (QMG) Branch of the Army Headquarters. The Directorate General of Supplies and Transport (DGST) is the principal office that is entrusted with the task to initiate, coordinate, manage and monitor the entire supply chain. The Army Service Corps (ASC) is the body that is staffed with personnel trained and experienced in logistics support. It has technically qualified personnel to carry out food inspection as part of the Food Inspection Organisation (FIO) and for food testing and analysis, there are the Composite Food Laboratories (CFL). The ASC is also the prime mover of stores and takes charge of the storage depots. Its role includes training of Pioneers and store keepers, and providing high caliber teaching and training of army cooks and stewards. The Navy also has a similar system for preparing personnel to take up duties in logistics and independently runs a training establishment for cooks and stewards. The Remount Veterinary Services (RVS) play an important role by providing mule trains for transporting baggage where no roads exist or where mechanised transport cannot proceed.

The story of the origin and emergence of the modern armed forces in India would not be complete without at least a brief foray into the historical origins of each of the principal players involved in the food supply chain and systems. And it would be quite educative to learn how the present form of the various organisations developed. The following descriptions and discussions therefore will be presented in four parts. Part One will address the historical origins in brief and the current functioning of the ASC, of the Supplies and Transport, the QA organisations, and the Catering and Logistics training establishments in the Army and the Navy. Part Two will address matters related to Animal Transport and the RVS. Part Three will follow the procedural path taken for purchase, procurement and transportation till the rations are delivered to the unit kitchens, field cook houses, and ship and submarine galleys. Part Four will describe where foods are prepared and served.

Every one of these institutions and services comes together and plays its assigned role in order to send and serve food to personnel. These various elements constitute the food supply chain and participate in the system of supplies as it exists in the Armed Forces today.

Supply Chain Part 1

The ASC and its Elements

The saga of the evolution of the Indian army (Gaylor, 1992, p. 248), including the unification of the States Forces with the Indian Army after the war and at the time of independence has been described briefly in Chapter 7. Every army required a support wing to take care of it in the garrisons and during troop movements, which included transport, provisioning of war materials like arms, weapons, ammunition, equipment, fuel and supply of foods for soldiers and for animals.

In British India, the Royal Indian Army Service Corps (RIASC) was responsible for transport and supply. But before such a term and nature of duties were designated, the responsibilities of supplies fell to the Army Commissariat department.

Commissariat in East India Company: Commissariat, the fore runner of the ASC traces its origins to Robert Clive's appointment as Commissary in 1748, though the year of its actual birth is taken to be 1760 when the supply and transport systems for the independent armies then extant in the Calcutta, Bombay and Madras Presidencies of the East India Company were unified to function under one authority. The Commissariat oversaw the procurement of animals and stores; supplies for them from contractors or through agents employed by the Company. Its functions also included arrangements for stocking supplies required for up to two months in the various forts and cantonments in the three presidencies and place the stores in charge of the garrison store keepers. Besides food stocks, they also kept items such as boots, quilts, sundry furniture, petty magazine stores and held even cavalry and artillery horses. Anything needed after the two month stocks were depleted, was procured by local purchase. All transportation was by means of bullocks – their generic term being cattle (Kulkarni, 2000, pp. 11–13).

To improve the organisational and practical aspects of the commissariat system and for effective and economical functioning, a more stable and permanent supplies and transport organisation was founded in 1810–11 as the Army Commissariat Department in each of the Presidencies. The system of procurements by contracts and through agents worked simultaneously. Staffed and run by civilians, the department had army officers only at a higher level, but there was no Commissariat officer as such. Officers deputed from the Artillery and Infantry were posted for a five year term. Under the British Warrant Officers and NCOs, Indian civilians were employed in various low capacities as animal handlers, cart drivers, nursing assistants, store keepers, horse grooms and clerks. While this was the peace time arrangement for supply and transport, in war time, more employees were taken in to handle the heightened demand. Temporary supply units were raised for the specific purpose of effecting supplies to the men engaged in war. Neither an ASC company to supply nor an Animal Transport (AT) existed then.

It made no economic sense whatsoever to the Board of Directors of the East India Company – a solely commercial organisation reigning over India – to maintain any standing units for supply or transport, seeing how grains, animals (cattle, horses, mules, camels and elephants) and other supplies could be found with ease anywhere. But was it really as easy as said, to gather all that was needed at the outbreak of war? Could the civilian supply source suffice? Apparently not, as it required the Governor General's intervention to obtain bullocks and elephants from Assam or Rangpur. The soldiers suffered too. The war with Bhutan (1864–65) showed how disastrous this line of thinking could be. Before that, however, in the Sepoy Mutiny of 1857–58, the Commissariat Department performed its duties under Lt. Thomas James in an exemplary manner, assisting the Garrison Commander during the second siege of Lucknow thereby saving the besieged British from starvation and death. Lt. James and the Bengal Commissariat acquitted themselves so well as to earn rich tributes all around. But the mutiny or the war of independence itself was a challenge and threat to the British and by Queen's Proclamation, India passed from being Company property to Crown property.

Royal Indian Army Service Corps (RIASC): The Royal Indian Army Service Corps (Crew, 1970) was made responsible for transport and supply. Transport was clearly animal centric. Draught animals were bullocks, camels, horses, ponies, mules and sometimes even elephants and yaks. Some time late in the First World War animals became the backbone of transport. The Indian regiments had usually managed on their own, fending for themselves and finding fodder for their animals. But in this war the Indian corps took up the overall responsibility of supplying food, fodder and fuel. The Commissariat Departments of the Presidencies had been merged several years ago along with the three transport departments. The combined services of transport and commissariat were now labelled Supply and Transport Corps in 1901. Having been established on the lines of the Army Service Corps in Britain, its name became, in 1935, the Indian Army Service Corps (IASC) with a 'Royal' prefix attached – RIASC. It established a training school in Chaklala, now in Pakistan. It seems that the RIASC was known as the Rice Corps during World War II and was expanded considerably. It rendered great service with its mule companies in France in 1939, taking part in the air supply columns in Burma and in the supply convoys to Russia.

After the Partition of India, the RIASC also fragmented. The term 'Royal' was dropped when India became a republic. It is now the Army Service Corps or ASC (Gaylor, 1992, p. 252).

The Critical Role of ASC – from Bareily to Bangalore: The Army Service Corps (RIASC Training Establishment) was first headquartered in Kakul, near the town of Abbotsville in Pakistan (now the home of the Pakistan Military Training Academy). After 1947, it was moved to Bareilly in India. Here training was imparted at three levels – to new entrants, to middle level officers (captains and majors) and to prospective battle commanders. The second tier cadre of JCOs and others receive basic military training and first technical training at the ASC Centre, South, Bangalore as well as vocational and trade oriented training. The ASC also deals with transport and runs the Army School of Mechanical Transport, which imparts training in transport supervision; these are also located at Bangalore. All these establishments were merged in May 1999 for efficiency and economy and now the training centers function simultaneously in the vast campuses of the ASC Centre and College, Bangalore. Training is provided to men who will be employed in various capacities in the Supply and Transport areas, which include how to harness and load an animal of the AT detachment using life size fiber glass replicas (Fig. 12.1), receive, stack and store bags of food materials (Fig. 12.2), as well as teaching even more skilled tasks like the testing of food materials received for quality and acceptability (Fig. 12.3 and Fig. 12.4). The Catering Training College is also located in this ASC Centre. The detailed history of the ASC may be found in a recent illustrated publication of the Army Headquarters (Kulkarni, 2000).

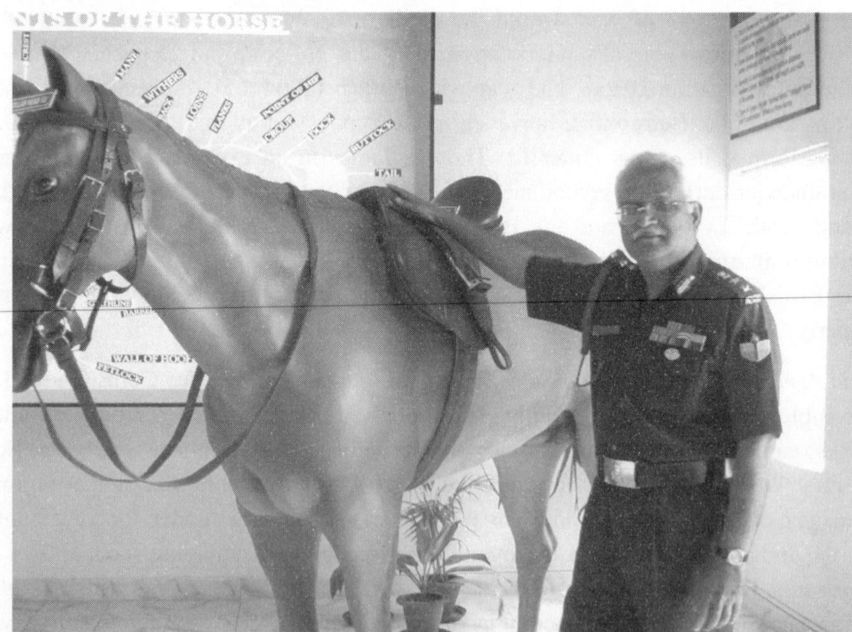

Fig. 12.1*:* Standing beside the model of a fiber glass mule in harness is the then Commandant, Junior Wing, Col. P.D. Kulkarni who gave the author a tour of the premises and provided much of the relevant information about the entire working of the ASC and S&T activities.

Source: The Museum of the ASC Centre and College, Bangalore

Fig. 12.2: Demonstration of Stacking of jute sacks in a pyramidal fashion as the picture shows and flat bed arrangement on standing metal racks are the two main stacking systems in the Demonstration unit, ASC Centre and College.

Fig. 12.3: Technical staff in a laboratory classroom learning to carry out food analysis at the ASC Centre, Bangalore.

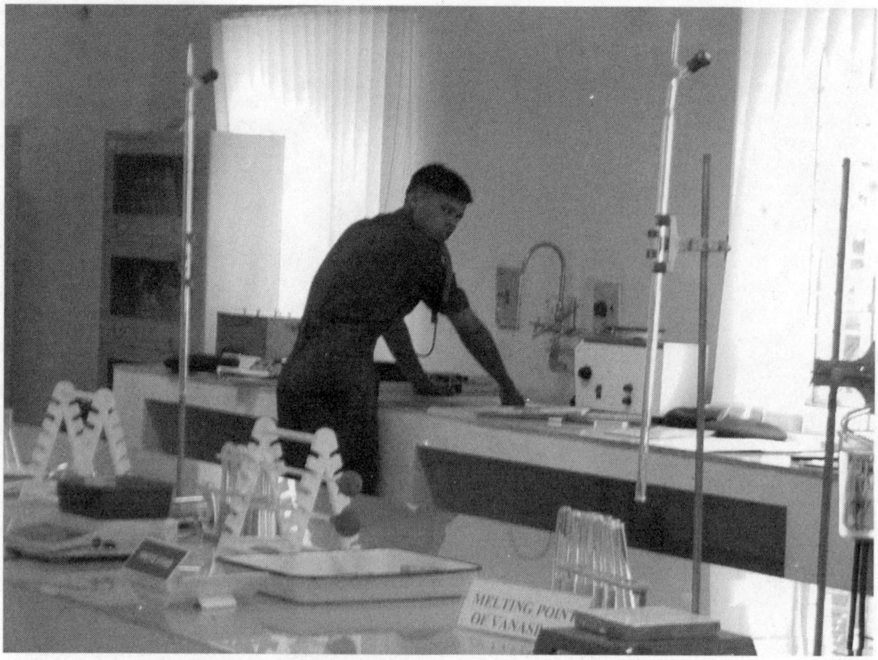

Fig. 12.4: Analytical lab in the ASC Training College, Bangalore

The Composite Food Laboratories and ST-7/8: In the 1920s, the limited variety of tinned food procured by the British India Army required inspection. Ghee or clarified butter was one of the major products and there was thus a ghee testing laboratory, at first in Kasauli and then later, in the 1940s, in Agra. '*Desi ghee*' as it was known was an item provided to Indian soldiers in World War II as their sole cooking medium. This testing laboratory was headed by an officer of the Medical Services from the Army Medical Corps (AMC). It continues to be headed by an army doctor of the rank of a Brigadier from the Preventive and Social Medicine speciality.

A need was felt in the following years for more laboratories. Six Composite Food laboratories, CFLs were established, one each in Delhi, Bombay, Calcutta, Madras, Lucknow and Jammu. There was one Appellate laboratory at the Army Headquarters known as ST-7 and ST-8 Laboratories and three Food Inspection Units to look after and monitor the wheat grinding operations (for *atta/suji/maida* etc.) in flour mills. The way this worked was that wheat purchased on Central contract basis from the Food Corporation of India, FCI, was milled under supervision of the Army. Adherence to specifications for acceptable quality wheat and milled products was necessary. The factories where tinned and other stuff was to be manufactured for Defence use and inspected by Technical Inspectors for the adequacy of infrastructure and conformity to hygiene standards (Discussions at ST-7/8, Delhi, 2005).

Presently there are three CFLs – in Delhi, Bombay and Jammu, with the areas of responsibility of all regions distributed among them.

Food Inspection Organisation, FIO: The Food Inspection Organisation specialist cadre was a separate entity until 1961 when it was merged with the ASC, though retaining specialist status (Kulkarni, 2000, p. 168). For better career prospects of the food inspection personnel, they were integrated fully into the mainstream ASC. Change of postings to ASC units after a stint in the Food Inspection Organisation was a far more welcome prospect than stagnation in the FIO. Staffing of this new set up was not a problem because newly commissioned officers (with a post graduate degree) were inducted. Officers who were science graduates were encouraged to obtain post graduate qualifications. An officer was also deputed to take up studies in Food Technology at post graduate level in an ongoing M.Sc. course under the Mysore University and conducted by CFTRI at Mysore. Technical assistants of the army and civilian Defence employees with science degrees were imparted laboratory training in food analysis at the ASC Centre, South, Bangalore. In course of time a short term Refresher Course and then a one year Post Graduate Diploma course, also under the Mysore University, was introduced in the Defence Food Research laboratory at Mysore.

Refresher Training at Mysore

A refresher Training Programme course in Food Science and Technology was conducted for several years in DFRL for the benefit of those senior officers who had spent considerable time in the Food Inspection Organisation and the ASC, and who held masters degrees, mostly in chemistry. A training programme at the postgraduate diploma level of the Mysore University was also specially designed and conducted at DFRL, Mysore, for the express purpose of training ASC officers in Food Analysis and Quality Assurance.

Officers with science backgrounds and particularly those experienced in Food Analysis and Food laws and the provisions in the Prevention of Food Adulteration Act (PFA, 1954) were posted to the various CFLs. The officers trained in these different ways served the purpose for a while. However, no one who takes any of these courses and acquires a University degree/PG Diploma can claim to assume the role and authority of a Public Analyst, a post under the Health Services of the Central Government. There is a separate examination to quality for that. Since the CFLs play a role in Food Inspection, Food Analysis and being responsible for pronouncing judgment on the quality and acceptability or otherwise of the food stuffs being ordered and procured, the head of a CFL is required to be like a Public Analyst in Army garb. On good authority, we are given to understand that since the PG–Diploma certificate of Mysore University from DFRL did not entitle the candidate for recognition as a Public Analyst (although it was very useful in teaching them analytical methods), deputation to this course ceased.

The course itself was a very well crafted and well rounded programme giving students a good grounding on theoretical aspects of food science and food technology and 'hands on' practical experience of food analysis in chemical, microbiological and physical methods as per the methods prescribed by the Indian Bureau of Standards, AOAC and Bacteriological Manual (USA). The knowledge accrued from such a course would have had immense influence on the way the ASC officers posted to CFLs discharged their responsibilities. Under any circumstances the Public Analysts' qualifying examinations conducted periodically under the Directorate General of Health Services, Ministry of Health has to be taken separately and there is no course of study for the subjects. Employees with years of experience and self study in the State Central Food Laboratories in the different states write and qualify for this recognition. Presumably the Army has made suitable arrangements. Certain ASC Officers from the CFLs are said to have qualified as Public Analysts by writing separate examinations after self study.

Where do these technical officers figure in the food purchase scenario? In the food procurement procedures the entire requirement for dry and tinned rations for one year is projected to the Army Purchase Organization (APO). The APO calls for tenders from registered suppliers. The contracts are concluded as per delivery schedules stated and agreed to. The factories and manufacturing units which are going to produce foods under Defence contracts are inspected for infrastructure, their fitness and capabilities and for the level of hygienic practices in manufacture etc. When the foods under contract obligation are ready, the officers of the FIO and CFLs deputed to carry out food inspection go back to the factory and draw samples and take them back to the laboratory for analysis. The entire stock is then cordoned off and kept secure in the factory until such time as its quality is determined for conformity with ASC standards.

Several kinds of tests are conducted on each product. There are specifications and standards of quality and acceptance which have been laid down by the ASC and all tests to ascertain quality are conducted according to official PFA approved methods. When the product is acceptable, the office of the DGST is notified, which in turn sends instructions to the factory to dispatch the material directly to the ASC depots, wherever they may be.

The CFL's role is crucial here because acceptance or rejection happens here. Rejection is a vexing issue in many ways: (a) the ASC depots do not get the required materials on time and the units will not receive their quotas, (b) the manufacturer who has invested considerable time, effort and money also stands to loose his investment and faces a financial crisis, (c) rejection of his material will not be accepted easily and there will be appeals. The firm will have to appeal within 14 days, (d) the food samples are then re-examined by the Appellate authority at the Appellate laboratory. The protocol for action thereafter is also quite streamlined. If the grounds on which the samples have been rejected initially are only minor infringements and are not abutting on safety and health aspects and are considered fit for consumption, then with a penalty of downward price revision, the product is declared acceptable. There could be, however, the same findings as found initially and of a nature that will compromise the consumers' safety and health, or if the product has grossly violated the standards, it is rejected. Finally, (e) it is not uncommon for the manufacturer to go to court again at this point. The CFL officers are kept busy one way or another.

When the goods are accepted, then too the CFLs are kept busy and involved. The ASC depots also send their samples from the stocks received to the CFLs in case of complaints. A visit to the Appellate laboratory, Delhi, which is known as ST-7/8, greets a visitor with an array of hundreds of samples of all sorts of dry and tinned rations in various stages of observation and analysis. The commanding officer explained that hundreds of samples pour in at regular intervals from depots complaining of stocks going bad before warranty, or wanting an 'extension of shelf life' decision on some of the tinned rations, or from suppliers laying claim to their legitimate settlement. There is limited staff to attend to all this.

To handle so much analytical work, the lab could certainly use more staff, particularly since the standard methods in common usage are really time consuming and tedious. The Appellate lab could also use a dose of modernisation to speed up things in microbiological and chemical quality assurance. Thirdly, the firms themselves should be made to bear the onus of having quality data generated as per standards laid down and have them submitted along with their invoices. It is how the military ration items in western countries are obtained from commercial sources.

Indian Catering Corps: What are rations without some one to do justice to them? The soldiers had always cooked their own food in the past; most were unskilled but a few were more knowledgeable. But a fighting soldier cannot devote time and effort to prepare his food at every meal time. It was the practice in the Crimean war for the listless soldiers to cook by rotation and the results, as may be imagined, varied from mixed to disastrous. Overall nutrition also suffered. Therefore, it was fitting that some effort was made to address this problem.

The Indian Catering Corps was created in May 1945 with the purpose of improving military cooking in general as well as cooking skills of individuals. Foreseeing the future possibilities of losing well trained cooks to civilian markets, a 15 year regular service was envisaged with no resource liability. However, this Service was short lived and was absorbed into the ASC in September 1948.

Recruitment and training of the catering staff in the Army – Gaya and Bangalore: The vast Army of India is composed of multiethnic and multi-regional troops and must be fed to the satisfaction of every member. For quantity, calorie and nutrient content, as has been discussed, the Service Ration Scales (SRS) meet the complete food requirements of hardworking men and women. As we have seen, many items in the ration scale are raw and grocery type materials which are used in preparing meals. Who is to do this preparation? The cooks of course and since an active fighting man cannot be taken away for the purpose of cooking, men are especially recruited for this purpose. Periodically, the call for recruitment is announced through national newspapers.

In the 1980s and 1990s, the ASC Centre, Gaya, had this singular task of recruiting. The hopeful candidates with at least tenth standard school education are eligible to apply. After entrance tests, the selected candidates are categorized as special cooks, mess cooks, and hospital cooks (special diets) and assigned to different regiments. Then all of them are trained in the ASC's Catering Establishment in Bangalore. A little change in the designation of the cooks seems to have taken place by the introduction of terms such as special chef and community chef, which act elevated the humdrum task of cooking into something more glamorous – that of a chef, and the best performing individual being named the Master chef. The trainees from different regiments and attached to the ASC's Catering establishment after the completion of training revert back to their own regiments. The regiments then post the freshly trained cooks to different units scattered far and wide.

Catering Training Centre: The training centre located at the ASC Centre South, Bangalore, is meant for the training of Army cooks. A walk through the Catering Company, No-4 Training Battalion's Cooks Training Centre accompanied by its Commandant is a revelation. Everything is spic and span. Every trainee is in his seat in the first of the classrooms, very attentively listening to the demonstrator who is giving instructions in Hindi and acquainting the young lads with the names of food ingredients – everything from rice, *atta*, different types of dals (lentils) (Fig.12.5) to the names of spices and vegetables and their pastes (Fig. 12.6) is taught and recorded and shown so that they may be able to identify the foodstuffs with their common names. In another class, kitchen appliances like stoves, burners, pots, pans, ladles etc. are displayed for familiarization. In yet another room, recipes are taught and discussed and the students diligently note down everything in their books so that in their practical class room they know how to use ingredients while preparing a food item (Fig. 12.7).

In Station '*langar* kitchens' and 'field cook houses' the food prepared for the men is typically of Indian regional cuisine but dominantly north Indian. Therefore, the *langar* cooks need only basic training in preparing the everyday fare. In their time off, they learn from the various food materials and ingredients displayed in the museum, where actual groceries filled in glass bottles are labeled and attractively displayed, as are the fibre glass look-alike fresh vegetables (Fig. 12. 8) and different meat cuts (Fig. 12.9).

Kitchen gadgets useful in food preparation (Fig. 12.10 a, b, c) including manually operated grinding and crushing implements and the different types of serving ware and eating ware (cutlery and

Fig. 12.5: The display of labeled items in the College Museum helps to identify basic grocery items used in everyday cooking.

Fig. 12.6: Students learn the intricate procedure of preparing a food item by assembling all the required materials – both dry spices (in their individual containers arranged in the round steel box) and the fresh stuff laid out ready for cooking.

Fig. 12.7: A recipe demonstration class in progress. ASC Centre and College, Bangalore

Fig. 12.8: Look-alike fibre glass replicas of common vegetables (for example brinjals) are displayed in the Cookery museum to help trainees identify them.

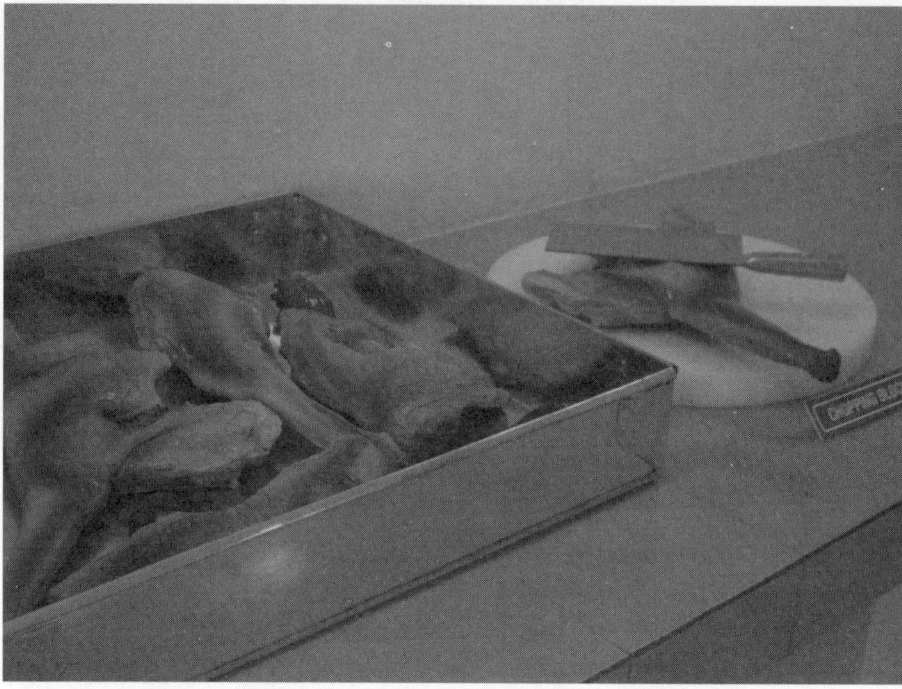

Fig. 12.9: Fibre glass replicas of meat cuts displayed in the College Museum.

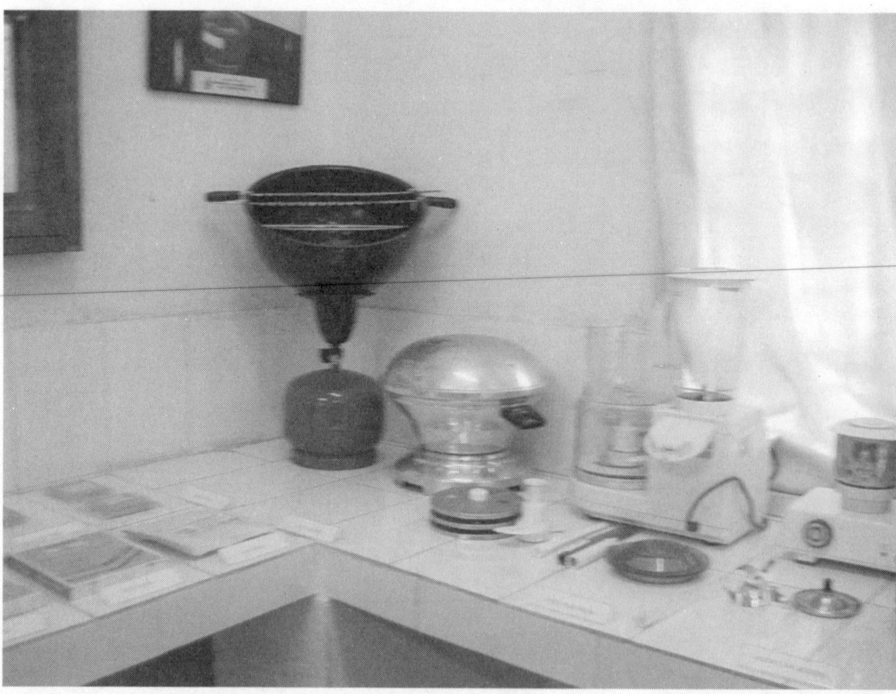

Fig. 12.10 (a)

Fig. 12.10 (b)

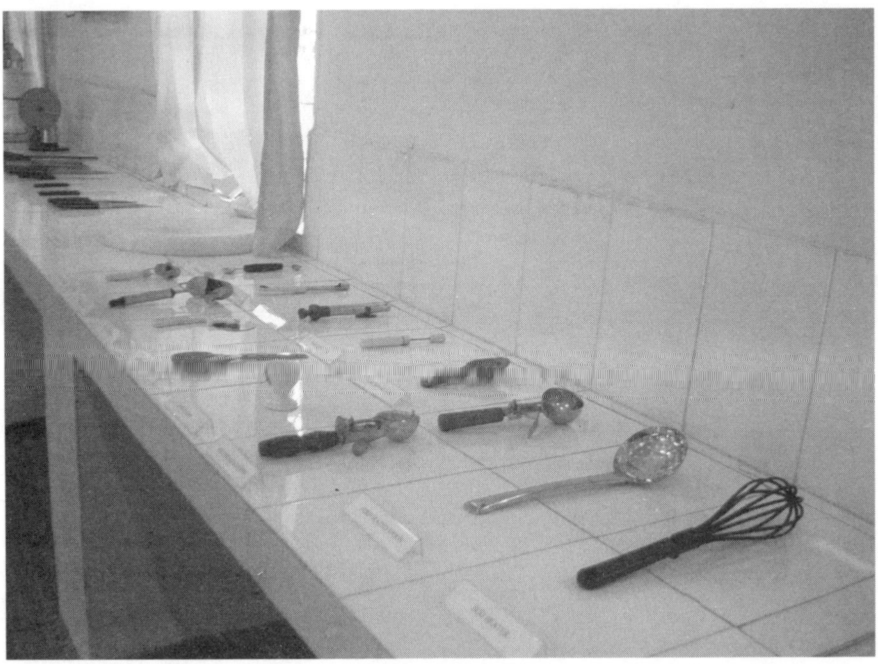

Fig. 12.10 (c)

Figs 12.10 (a to c): Sections in the College Museum display the various gadgets, implements and tools used in food preparation.

china) are present. All manner of cooking systems can be found – grill, *tandoor*, microwave oven, convection oven, gas burner and kerosene oil burner. The students are provided with basic principles of a hygienic kitchen and food practices and are instructed in the general importance of the nutrients obtained from the various food items so that they may best utilise the rations to cook with. They learn the difference between the different meat cuts, how to scale and fillet a fish, how to dress and ready a chicken for cooking and how to slice vegetables differently for different preparations.

The cooks for the officers' messes are required to train in a far advanced cuisine. The practical work hall is a place of subdued buzz where rows upon rows of youngsters clothed in aprons are seen to be busy, each with their own practical assignment of the day, which is preparing a menu under supervision and guidance. What the Training Commandant called a 'syndicate' – a group of four or five trainee cooks formed into one group for the day's practical class as shown in Fig. 12.11 and Fig. 12.12, work away at cutting, slicing, grinding spices, frying, sautéing, boiling, stirring and other chores of cooking to turn out vegetarian and non vegetarian, Chinese and Indian preparations. There are domestic gas burners for all standard forms of cooking and large cooking stoves and woks for Chinese cooking.

Modern kitchen appliances have been provided for everyday lessons in the ASC Centre during training as well as in the kitchens in all peace stations. Facilities for grinding spices (*masala* mixes) exist in the form of old fashioned grinding stone – a flat mortar and a rolling oval stone used like a pestle. Generally this is the appliance that is used in the field cook houses. Outdoor space to seat a large gathering of trainees has been provided and there are more cooking stations to accommodate another 100 or so trainees.

Fig. 12.11: Picture depicting a syndicate of four Army trainee cooks in a practical class preparing a meal for themselves (their own rations used) as per a set menu given by the instructor in ASC Centre and College.

Fig. 12.12: Picture shows a training class for Army cooks in progress at several cooking stations simultaneously in ASC Centre and College.

Food Service in Style: If cooking is an art, so is its elegant service. While the cooks and their assistants perform the task of food service for men in the ranks, for the officers, a re-creation of a club bar and of a fine restaurant, stands as an invitation. One walks into a scene of beautifully covered and set tables complete with artistically folded serviettes and elegantly laid tables all of which present an inviting atmosphere of cozy congeniality and fine dining. The crystal and glass flicker in their polished brightness in the glass cabinets above the bar and the display of cocktail making apparatus leaves one in no doubt that this is officers' space. And as befitting a superior club's atmosphere, the service is provided by stewards and waiters who have received thorough training in bar tending and table layout with the appropriate cutlery and china and food service. Taught to know about how to differentiate between the different glasses and crystal, their uses for various drinks, the service of breakfast or lunch or cocktails or dinner cannot be faulted and matches the western style dining arrangements. Since both the officers and the men who serve them in the messes possess a background of mostly traditional upbringing, the western table etiquette in dining and food service have to be learned or refined upon after joining the Armed Forces. It is part of cadet officers' training. Once acquired, these manners are put to use everywhere, in every service mess. In the field messes too there are separate dining quarters for the officers, though probably not as elaborate as in peace garrisons.

A prewar publication in Britain instructs British officers on India posting on the *do's* and *do not's* of life in the Army. These include dress rules and codes of conduct to be observed in the messes on a regular basis and when senior officers of the General Staff are being entertained. Much the same rules are followed even now.

Protocols and Elegant Service – a must, no matter where

Some instances that have stayed in memory from the time of this author's service in the Defence Food Research Laboratory are from a time when the official guest house facilities were minimal and frequently outside premises had to be rented to arrange official dinners for the visiting Army brass. When one Army General came on an official visit to the Laboratory, there was an official reception later for him and his lady wife. It was the custom to invite the city's very own elite to meet the visiting dignitaries. The drinks for the general were required to be presented on a silver tray, no less, and his lady was not to be given a bottle of soft drink to sip from but poured in a crystal tumbler and offered with a flourish. Where would a lab produce a decent looking crystal or glass tumbler and a smart tray much less a silver one? Even the rented premises did not possess these objects. A wooden tray and a large Borosil glass shallow tray/plate like dish (used for some high temperature experimental work) were found to add to the serving ware brought from home.

When one Navy Chief, after his official visit to the Laboratory, was considerably delayed in arriving for the evening reception organized in his honour, none of the other invitees–prominent public functionaries and dignitaries of the city were served to start the evening's happy hour. The scientists had awkward moments trying to explain why the party was not starting while awaiting the Chief Guest.

The guests have to arrive before the Chief Guest but cannot leave before him no matter what time it takes. One could not slip away because the VIP would go round and meet individuals before retiring for the day.

In gentle terms this author was informed that there are subtle differences between the way these things are done in the Navy and the Army. If the differences in food preparation, its service and style of eating between officers and men are quite distinct in the Army, further contrasts can be seen in style in the Navy, though the officers' cuisine is elitist and varied and includes some preparations from the western cuisine in all the three services. The US Navy officers enjoy dining in ward rooms staffed with stewards and waiters in the ships (Lynn, 1993) as compared to the modern US Army officers who eat the same foods and in much the same conditions as their soldiers.

INS *Hamla:* the Logistics and Catering Training Establishment of the Indian Navy

The Indian Navy is very well equipped for food service by its own trained staff working in well appointed galleys in the ships, and in shore establishments and reasonably so in the submarines. This is made possible by the Catering Training School situated in the Indian Navy Ship (INS) *Hamla.* It provides, among other services, training for cooks, chefs, stewards and bar tending as well as valeting duties and it is also where development of recipes is carried out. Essential training is imparted to cooks required for the 5-star quality catering in the Navy, Air Force, Army and even the President's Estate. A multi-cuisine specialty training base, the cooks are taught to prepare a wide selection of menus from both ethnic Indian as well as international cuisine to cater to all tastes and even visitors. For the officers, the steward service in the ward rooms is of 5-star quality, we are informed, also bar tending, table service, housekeeping and pantry duties. This last involves preparing coffee, sandwiches, salads as well as cocktails etc. For the men in the ranks, the cooks and their assistants themselves provide food service from separate kitchens and large dining halls.

INS *Hamla*, whose logo is depicted in Fig. 12.13, belying its prefix is not a ship (all navy establishments are named INS irrespective of where they are located) but a shore establishment of the Indian Navy, situated on a stretch of land abutting a beach in Marve, Malad West, Mumbai. It

Fig. 12.13: Logo of INS *Hamla*, Southern Command, Indian Navy

falls under Headquarters, Southern Command, Cochin, which is a Training Command. Commissioned originally as His Majesty's Indian Ship (HMIS) *Hamla* on 15 Jan, 1946 in Cochin, its role was to impart training in different types of naval operations. Then it became a training establishment for boys in 1954.

INS *Hamla* has two main and important roles in training: the first one in logistics and the second in imparting training to sailors in catering and cooking. Logistics, earlier called the Supply Secretariat was also located in Cochin. Although at first, logistics was not thought to require specialisation under the Supply Secretariat, it was later recognised to deserve its own space, with training in its various specialised branches. It was thus that in 1988 logistics training became a part of INS *Hamla,* which was being shifted from Cochin to its present location. It is staffed by the personnel of the logistics cadre.

Under this training command (TC) – the head of which is an officer of the rank of a commodore. Commodore H.S. Chopra from the logistics cadre took the initiative and authored a cofee table book of Navy Recipes. There are six branches: Management Studies (TC/MS), Professional Service (TC/PS), Computer Studies (TC/CS), Logistics Officer (LOGO), Principal Medical Officer (PMO) and the Senior Education Officer (SEDO) who is responsible for the general education and basic training of entry level cadets and all others.

Logistics: All naval cadet officers who have completed their three years of basic training and have graduated are posted to Cochin as sea cadets soon after induction. They are also required to spend four weeks in INS *Hamla* learning management and divisional duties. Thereafter they are allocated to different branches based on choice and merit. Those selected for the Logistics Branch undergo more intensive training through courses in the Logistics School. These logistics officers are deployed in the different navy units (ships, submarines and shore establishments) in charge of all supplies-materials, food and clothing.

Over a period of time, they are deputed to undertake longer and more advanced courses in management and other specialised areas working towards recognized post-graduate degrees (MBA) of Goa University and PG-Diploma of the Symbiosis Institute of Management Studies (SIMS) Pune. The Naval Institute of Computer Applications imparts training in basic and advanced computer studies for both the navy personnel and civilian employees of the Navy, computers having become very indispensable instruments for communication, data banking, record keeping, tracking and monitoring, other than its very high-tech use and applications.

All sailors selected for the Navy receive their orientation in INS *Chilka,* after which they go on attachment to ships. The entry level educational requirement being high school (10+2), the youth selected under different recruitment requirements are sent for professional courses depending on their performance, aptitude, preference and the navy's requirements.

In the Logistics School, they learn to be Writers (clerical work), and Stores Assistants (materials accounting including cash accounts and issuing). A class in progress is shown in Fig. 12.14. On a conducted tour of the training premises in INS *Hamla*, one caught glimpses of men and women in the brilliant white uniforms of the Indian Navy, attending various classes in logistics, management, computer studies (Fig. 12.15, Fig. 12.16 and Fig. 12.17).

The Catering Service: In the Catering school they are trained as cooks, chefs and stewards. In time, after gaining Service experience and a certain degree of seniority, they may be prepared towards Diploma of the National Council of Hotel Management (NCHM), Pusa, New Delhi. The training here begins with learning to identify and name the food materials, the old and new kind of kitchen appliances and gadgets, knives, Mess Trap (all things required in a kitchen), tableware-stemware, glass, china and cutlery, articles needed for mixing drinks, ice buckets, toaster racks, chafing dishes,

Fig. 12.14: A class in Logistics school, INS Hamla in progress for those deputed from the Army (2007).

Fig. 12.15: Officer Trainees in the Logistics class room.

Fig. 12.16: Fresh Naval officers undergoing mandatory training in INS *Hamla* along with the author (The EXO is seen on the extreme left).

Fig. 12.17: Women officers from the Nursing Service in Khaki uniforms (on extreme left and second from right) and women in blue (centre) from Navy's Computer Applications School with author.

tea pots and other such catering paraphernalia much the same way as it is done in the ASC Training Centre and College in Bangalore. They are taught the use of machines-grinders, juicers, mixers, steam boilers, cooking range, ovens etc. The Bar Room and Dining Hall models are replicas of the facilities found on ships. The steward training includes laying a table and arranging the crockery, cutlery and glass ware, serviettes etc. They become adept at laying a table for a high powered sit down dinner or a banquet for visiting dignitaries or arrange a buffet meal for any number of diners. The people are also taught to familiarise themselves with accounting procedures, including cash accounts.

In the INS *Hamla*, model galleys of a ship and a submarine are exhibited to familiarise the trainees with the confined space, equipment and gadgets in the cooking space of a galley (or the lack of these), the kind of storage cabinets, working counters and washing up areas they will eventually have to adapt to. Whether in shore establishments or on board the ships, food is cooked in the two classes of galleys, one meant for the sailors and the other for the officers.

In INS *Rajput* (a destroyer), the galley is large and looks like a compact modern modular kitchen, gleaming with stainless steel cabinets, worktops and water taps and wash basins, oven, wet grinder, deep fryer, scullery area with washbasin and platform for stacking. The mock training galley of INS *Delhi,* which is a different class of ship – a frigate in fact, is fitted with a long electrical cooking range and extra chimneys; it is equipped with labour saving appliances like a potato peeler, dough mixer, vegetable cutting machine, and also a floor model water boiler and for service there are hot cases and Baine-Maries as well as a food counter to serve the sailors. In contrast, a submarine's galley is very small. It has a small cooker-oven, a small grinder, washbasin, overhead cabinets, and a small working platform.

One never knows where a trainee will be posted on duty and therefore it is essential that he is familiar with the working space and conditions in both big and small vessels. There are dry stores which stock not only the basic ration items in large quantities but also a variety of exotic items, special condiments and flavorings, dessert toppings, salad oils and dressings. There are large size refrigerators to store fresh vegetables at the appropriate temperature and a small deep freeze to store fish and mutton.

Class Room Training: Young men in work room aprons and head caps, training to be cooks and stewards, are taught the basic elements of Indian, Continental and Chinese cooking, the specialised craft of baking a wide varieties of breads, buns and croissants and the artful decoration of celebratory cakes. The more sophisticated art of mixing and serving mocktails and cocktails, of producing 'the anytime snack' of sandwiches with various fillings, preparing tea and coffee trays, the etiquette of food service at the table for officers, the house keeping responsibilities of keeping the officers' quarters and officers' personal effects (valeting, like the orderlies perform in the army) are taught to those men who are training to be stewards. There is clearly a distinction in the level and kind of training given to the cooks who would cook for ORs and those who are destined to work in officers' messes and officer's galleys, or go back to the star hotels which deputed them for specialised training.

There are 12 training galleys in INS *Hamla*. In the training classes visited during the tour, lessons were in progress, preparing the special dishes selected for the day. After a brief instruction, the trainees gather the required pots and vessels (4-men utensil set), ingredients and begin work on two items. Every day, two dishes are prepared by one person. Marinating meat comes as a special instruction and each day, one or two trainees from each classroom are designated in the morning to begin the marinating process for chicken.

They can use any kitchen appliance that may be required and there are many modern gadgets to choose from which range from peelers, dicers, grinders, mixers, microwave and convection baking ovens, deep fryers and grills to high flame woks for Chinese cooking. In a separate hall there are appliances used in South Indian food preparations such as the wet stone grinder, *dosa* pans and *idli* steamers. The standard industrial cooking ovens in all the galleys are electrically operated; these are large and massive with four hot plates on top and a large baking oven underneath. Gas (LPG) is not used on board ships and submarines. Shore establishments may, however, use piped gas and gas stoves. These large ovens are of the same type which in an earlier era were wood or coal stoked, whether on board the ships or on land.

The practical classes (Fig. 12.18 and Fig. 12.19) are meant for the preparation of a full menu for lunch or dinner (Indian cuisine mostly, but also Chinese, Mexican, Thai) or a party cake or pastries or breads or the making of sandwiches or mixing cocktails (Fig. 12.20). Under the watchful eyes of the instructors, trainees prepare the food and present the end product for tasting and also eat it themselves for lunch. All the ingredients required to prepare such a wide range of foods are kept in stock.

The Navy is a Service which is more or less centralised in a few locations. The personnel come into greater contact with urban ways of life and are thus better informed about newer food fads and fashions; they are more aware of different types of processed products, cuisine and social customs and thus appear to be more cosmopolitan in their outlook. Their frequent travels to other ports in India and foreign countries exposes them to many more novel things than an average person in

Fig. 12.18: A cooking class in INS *Hamla*.

Fig. 12.19: A specialist class room where baking is taught; trainees have just turned out breads, buns, cakes and are observing a demonstration of frosting.

Fig. 12.20: Trainee stewards are taught the art and craft of making a variety of non-alcoholic and alcoholic cocktails.

other services is ever likely to experience. They also meet and observe other Navy's customs and ways of doing things. When they go on good will missions to other countries, they absorb the local flavours when they entertain and in turn, when they are entertained by the foreign navies.

They are used to the visits of dignitaries to their ships and shore establishments. The traditions followed in the Indian Navy are distinctly British in style and manners. Officers and sailors are segregated in many ways and not just by cadre and rank alone, a practice held onto diligently from the days of the Raj.

They receive visitors on board with ceremony. Their officers dine well and in style in their wardroom and entertain grandly when the occasion calls for it.

Their cooks must therefore be able to produce in the small galleys, besides the fixed menus, any kind of cuisine appropriate to the occasion and to the place of their visit and to suit the taste of the visiting foreign or Indian dignitary. All this entertainment is mostly managed with the variety of rations stored on board and supplemented with small extras purchased with their own contributory funds. Their chefs are thus equally adept at presenting a table of elaborate exotica for leisurely entertainment as well as the quickest of 'working meals' required during 'action stations'.

The Navy personnel eat well on shore and at sea, both sailors and officers (witness the weekly menus), subject only to the vagaries of the weather and rolling of the ship that might make elaborate cooking sometimes difficult, and not because of any other reason – material or otherwise.

Pakistan Army's Food Supply and Service Systems

The Pakistan Army Service Corps (PASC) carried the responsibility for supply and transportation. The pre-Independence training school at Chaklala, Rawalpindi conducted a catering school for training cooks and food service people much the same way as Bareilly did and Gaya and Bangalore

ASC Centre do for the Indian Army. The Navy also independently conducted a school for cooks at Pakistan Navy School, presumably on the lines of *INS Hamla* in the Indian Navy.

The Medical Directorate controlled and conducted the Military Food Laboratory at Lahore whose responsibility was food inspection of all the centrally purchased food items. An Armed Forces Institute of Nutrition is said to have been established after 1956, in Lahore for research and implementation of survey recommendations which were made after a nutrition survey of Pakistan Army had been conducted by a research team from the National Institutes of Health, USA (1959). At the time of the survey, the research team reported that the Pakistan food processing industry was embryonic as it was in India during the same period. There were 17 military dairies and milk pasteurizing plants, army run 'evaporated milk' plants, a ghee making plant, and tunnel dehydrators at different places for drying vegetables and meat required during war. Sugar and the edible oil industries functioned well. In the processing sector there were fruit and vegetable preservation units and there was too, a Pakistan Fruit and Vegetable Preserver's Association.

Training in food technology was given in the Punjab Agricultural College at Lyallpur where the experimental station was located, others being established at Tandojam in Sind, in Quetta in Baluchistan and in Peshawar in the North West Frontier Provinces. The Research and Development scene under Pakistan's CSIR was also unfolding in a manner similar to India's. A military Food and Nutrition Laboratory was engaged in studying transport and issue of atta, preservation of vitamins in cooking, soil-less farming, cold weather feeding of troops and pack rations.

Supply Chain Part 2

Remount Veterinary Service Corps and Animal Transport

Horses, camels and elephants have always been regarded as 'war' animals. From the description provided in the Kautilya *ArthaŚāstra* of the care, maintenance and training of these animals, it is clear that there was a long history before that period of employing animals for war work.

For transport of goods, supplies and equipment, the beasts of burden – bullock, ox, donkey, and mule were rounded up in great numbers to pull wagons and carts and carry head loads to support every army that ever marched, and all the camp followers as well. Elephants, camels, horse and bullocks were used in ambulance service in colonial India to carry and transport war wounded (Fig. 12.21 and Fig. 12.22). Paintings and sketches depicting animal ambulance services in British India in the middle 1800s are to be found in the National Archives of India Museum in New Delhi.

Animal transport – Military Train: Pack animals have been used throughout history to move supplies and wagon carts. Horses mostly, but mules, donkeys, bullocks and camels and even elephants have been pressed into carrying loads for civilian and military needs. The credit for organising food, forage and supplies for the marching columns of the East India Company's armies goes to Robert Clive, who was appointed in 1748 as the Commissary in the Presidency Army (Kulkarni, 2000, p. 11). It was due to his effort that oxen, camels and elephants were found for moving supplies and guns on primitive and non-existent roads and trails and across turbulent rivers.

The Commissariat Staff Corps had established a Military Train in 1856–59 which replaced the existing Land Transport Corps. It had three battalions; each had troops or sections with ambulance, wagons and pack horses. There was a Director General in charge of the Train. Each Troop section was a cohesively functioning unit consisting of one Sergeant Major, two sergeants, four corporals,

Fig. 12.21: A fine drawing of elephant ambulances in 1846. The bed like stretchers are balanced on the back and covered by screens and fine netting. The picture suggests that four persons could be carried at one time on one elephant.

Source: Reproduced with permission from National Archives, New Delhi

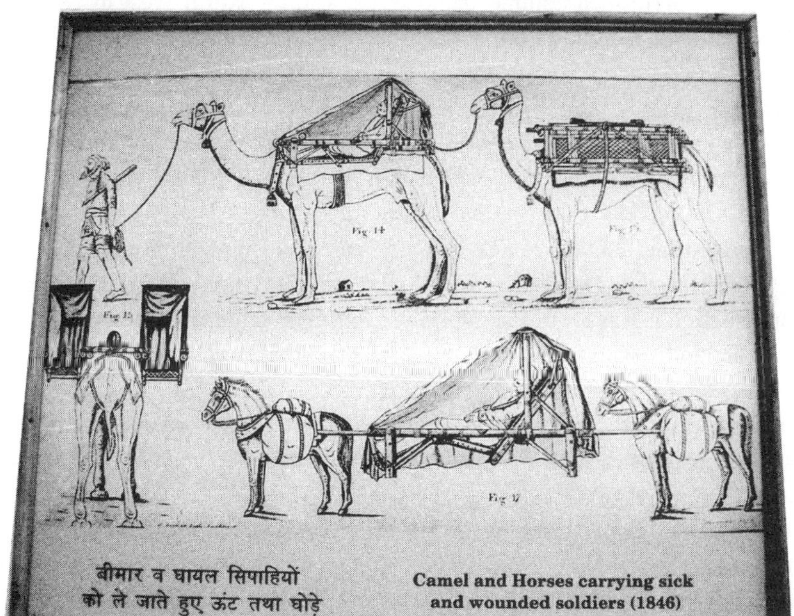

Fig. 12.22: Camel and horse drawn ambulance from 1846. While a camel could support one wounded soldier, a single horse is shown balancing a litter for two. Another type of ambulance was constructed where a reclining person would be carried on a device tethered to two horses one in the front and the other behind.

Source: Reproduced with permission from National Archives, New Delhi

one Transporter, one Farrier, one sergeant-wheeler, one smith and 56 privates. The retinue consisted of 41 horses, 5GS wagons (4-horsed), 1 corrugated iron wagon (also 4-horsed), 1 ambulance (2-horsed), 1 forge cart (2-horsed), 1 pack saddle, cacolet or litter. This Military Train stayed until the formation of the Amy Service Corps (Crew, 1970, pp. 48–50.).

So well organised was it that after the Sepoy mutiny in 1857, the Commissariat department was about the only part of the Indian Forces which was found to have performed in an exemplary fashion, needing no drastic changes after the governance of India passed into the hands of the Crown.

In regard to transport, which the army had to organise each time the British troops went to campaigns in Afghanistan (1838), in Iran (1856–57), in China (1860–61) (Kulkarni, 2000, p. 14), there was always the uncertainty of gathering adequate numbers of good, healthy animals capable of moving supplies when required. In the first Afghan war (1838), the camels that could be found were poorly cared for, carelessly maintained, and ill protected by the unarmed, untrained camel drivers. Many drivers died on trails and in combat or they deserted, leaving the poor underfed animals to die undefended. It was a highly unsatisfactory situation.

Camel Corps: To raise a camel transport, called the 'Scinde Camel Baggage Corps' (after Sindh), was the inspiration and experiment of Gen. Charles Napier, who planned to enlist, train, and arm the camel drivers and put them to work under supervision of regular army officers and NCOs. After a period of delay and because it was considered to be expensive, a unit was finally raised in 1845 which consisted of 1,800 men and 1,800 camels. The NCOs of the regular army in the rank of Jemmadars and Dafadars began to work in the camel Corps with the same status or position as in the fighting arms. It performed commendable services in the North West in 1848–49 during the Sikh wars and in the troop marches from Karachi to Multan and then to Peshawar. A reproduction of an illustration of the Scinde Camel Corps in the form of a water colour made by J.B. Bellasis can be found in Woodward's book (Woodward, 1978, p. 119). Charging into battle, it depicts a slim (for a camel) animal ridden by two men, the front one a camel driver in the typical uniform, cap and sword of the Army and another behind him who carries a gun with a bayonet as well as a sword.

It had been reported that 26,000 camels initially started in the animal transport train organised for the Second Afghan war in 1878–81. Matters were no better this time round. Due to very poor planning and organisation it was a disaster. No grass, fodder or grain was carried; none was available locally; the animals died of starvation and the cold and their drivers died the same way. In the rocky mountainous terrain, they could not be buried properly. The whole approach to visualising the animal transport seems to have been very insensitive and cruel. At an estimate, some 50,000 camels had perished a disaster of truly massive proportion not to mention the economic loss to the government.

After much debate and soul searching, a Transport branch was established in 1883, separate form the Commissariat department. It had 8,000 mules, 3,000 camels, 1,000 bullocks and 1,300 elephants. Some years later (1887), the two departments were merged to carryout the dual functions of supplies and transport or S and T, which is now a part of the present day Army Service Corps (Kulkarni, 2001, p. 16).

This brief foray into the past of animal transport (AT) will explain why the Indian Army needed animals. India at the time of British occupation was still a land of unchartered territories, of inadequate and poor roads, deep ravines and with steep rocky and narrow mountain trails. When the

Pathans of the Northwest kept intruding into British territory, the latter took an expeditionary force back into the Afridi-Pathan territory known as Tirah, a region where no white man was said ever to have ventured. The army was massive – 11,000 British soldiers, 20,000 Indian troops and camp followers, 8,000 horses, 18,383 mules and 1,440 ambulance mules plus a large number of camels, mountain ponies and carts, all in all some 55,000 animals. There were insurmountable difficulties of every description including what may be termed a systems failure.

The elephants had been employed by the Commissariat in the thousands. They were used in great numbers in the 1864 war in Bhutan, in the Abyssinian war (1867–8), in the Chitral campaign (1895) but slowly and by the end of the century, their numbers had diminished and in 1907 the elephant was 'retired' from the army. Now there are no elephants at all in the Indian Army, an animal which throughout the recorded history of India was an integral part of every Indian Army. Bullocks, camels, mules and donkeys continued to be in service for transport of supplies mostly as pack animals and also to draw supply carts (Kulkarni, 2001, pp. 17–20).

Silladar system: It was then thought expedient to maintain these animals beyond a small peace time reserve number. Several animals and drivers were taken to form the smaller Mule cadres, the larger Mule Corps, Camel cadres and Camel Corps and also Cart Corps. Silladar Camel Corps, first raised in 1889 lasted until World War II. Silladar was a system where each animal was owned by the man when he enlisted. The same man looked after his own and two other animals, the cost of outfitting the two animals (saddlery, harness etc.) being borne by the government but as a loan that was recoverable. A Silladar was in regular service for three months in a year and was paid Rs 9/- per month as salary. For the remaining nine months he was on a retainer fee of Rs 3/- per month, free to take the animals home and use them any which way. He was liable to report to duty on short notice. This system apparently ensured that the camels were looked after. The Government was not responsible for the loss of any animal by death or disappearance or any other way except in war time. In war time, a Silladar was given an elevated pay of Rs 18/- per month and the government also replaced an animal that was killed. It seems to have been a neat system of ensuring a steady supply of well cared for animals for war time service with minimum and hassle free maintenance responsibility on the part of the Government. The Silladar became a tradition, a vocation where children learnt to look after the animals in anticipation of and preparation for later service in the Corps. The Silladar Camel Corps saw action along with the Expeditionary Force sent to Somali land (Republic of Somalia) in 1903.

Mules: There was a Mule Corps since the turn of the twentieth century and the only means besides porters, of transporting goods in India around 1915. The Indian muleteer was paid Rs 9/- per month, way below that of a British muleteer whose pay was the same as that of a British soldier (Kulkarni, 2001, p. 259). The Royal Army Service Corps's AT was gradually phased out or disbanded but come 1939 and World War II, the British Army sought the urgent help of the AT of the Royal Indian ASC to support its Expeditionary Force in France.

In the annals of the British Indian Army Service Corps, the performance of the AT in World War II in Italy, in Syria (Kulkarni, 2000, pp. 66–69), Malaya, Hong Kong, the Arakans in Burma, the siege of Imphal (Kulkarni, 2001, p. 79) is proudly and gratefully acknowledged. It is a heart warming narration accompanied with action pictures of long columns of mules that does the ASC proud. The AT's role did not end with World War II. It has continued to render irreplaceable service in the mountainous terrains of the Indian borders from 1947 onwards. The Indian army also acknowledges the unwavering support received from the AT that marched with the battalion without which it would not have been possible to carry out the successful Zojila operations at a height of 10,000 ft in the Dras–Kargil Sector in 1948 (Kulkarni, 2000, p. 105). That is not to say that the Pack Transport groups, the AT and the Muleteers themselves enjoyed any great position. They were the first targets of any economy measures being considered. During the Army reorganisation in 1963 AT was also re-organised into administratively self contained and cohesive AT battalions. However, while saluting the 'AT boys', the hardest working category in the Indian Army, history has accorded recognition to the meritorious service of the mules themselves and awarded commendation in August 2000 from the Northern Command (Kulkarni, 2001, p. 260).

Equines: The cavalry was the dominant part of the armies in Europe, the United States of America, India and China.

The cavalry that had been an integral part of the armies in India through the ages until it gave way to mechanised battalions. The one cavalry regiment still in existence in India and in fact the only one of its kind in the world, is the President's Body Guard, which the Indian public sees on ceremonial occasions such as on Republic Day (January 26). There are camels used in the desert areas by the Border Security Forces for patrols in the sandy terrain. A camel contingent is also paraded on Republic day and plays a prominent role on the day of Beating the Retreat (January 29).

The mules, it appears, now form the backbone of the Army's Supply and Transport chain for the mountainous regions of our borders. The equines, which are the horses, mules and donkeys are important to the Indian Army in different ways as working animals, and as breeding stocks and are raised in the Army's stud farms. These farms are located in Babugarh near Meerut in UP, and in Hissar, Haryana. Two other farms located at Hempur and Saharanpur are training depots. Babugarh Stud Farm, which the author visited, is very modern and has excellent facilities and is staffed with veterinary doctors and surgeons in every specialty.

Canines: Although not a part of the transport and supply chain, canines are an important group of working animals in the Armed Forces. German Shepherds and Labradors are bred and the pups trained for definite jobs such as guard duty, detection of mines and bomb explosives, for search and rescue operations etc. Enough numbers are raised by the Remount Veterinary Service Corps to be self sufficient and if there are more pups/trained dogs available, they are then given to other organisations that employ dogs for specialised jobs. In the Army, dogs are not bred as pets. At the Central Military Veterinary Laboratory (CMVL), Meerut, an organisation under the RVS, the author observed the dogs under training. Raised from a mere five units in the mid 1980s there are some 85 specialised units in the Army at present, each unit has four squads with six dogs to a squad; 35 units are deployed in Jammu and Kashmir, 15 in the Northeast and an unknown number in the Western and Southern Army Commands. The Indian troops numbering 8,560 assigned to the UN peace keeping missions have taken three to four dog units on their overseas assignments.

The BSF, IAF, Director General of Civil Aviation, all State Police Departments, and the Indian Navy are the other users of trained sniffer dogs employed in various security and patrolling operations. Each of them maintains a certain number of dog units. Their care, maintenance and deployment are the responsibility of the dog units (personal communication from Col. D.P. Attrey, RVS).

According to a news item (*Deccan Herald*, January 10, 2007), the Indian Army has 12,000 dogs consisting of specialised breeds such as Labradors, German Shepherds and Belgian Shepherds in its Remount Veterinary Corps. These special breeds have been trained specially in anti-militancy operations, in sniffing out explosives and mines. The animals can even be airdropped to sniff out survivors of snow avalanches. In the past few years these dogs figured in more than 300 anti-militancy operations and 110 instances of explosives and mines detection. Recognised as being an invaluable element of the RVC and the army, the breeding kennels in Meerut have been awarded the 'Shaurya Chakra' and 29 special commendations from the Chief of the Army Staff.

Role and Importance of RVS: The Remount Veterinary Service (RVS)/Veterinary Corps (RVC) under the QMG's Branch is directly responsible for the breeding programme, for monitoring their health, for directing the nutrition and feeding programme of all animals and for their training. The veterinary officers of the RV Corps attached to the ASC are also given the responsibility of inspection and certification of meat animals and of fresh meat supplied to the Services.

Veterinary cover is provided by the RVS for all animals in the army, even when the work is controlled by the units themselves, such as horses in the Presidents Body Guard, in the Air Force Adventure cell, the Navy Adventure cells, the Riding School, polo clubs etc. The seed stocks of the horses are Arabian in origin. A life size monument at Baburgarh Stud farm venerates the first Arabian horse gifted to Prime Minister Jawaharlal Nehru. In 1979 a small number of animals of a pony breed known as Hafflinger (cross of Arabian stallion and Austrian mare from Haffling in the Tiral Mountains of Austria) were introduced (Kulkarni, 2000, p. 157) for trials in eastern and northern Commands to navigate treacherous mountain tracks. Subsequently, some 300 animals were imported but the results were disappointing to the Army as the animals were more delicate and not as surefooted on the narrow tracks as the mule. Mules and donkeys continue to be bred in the Babugarh stud farms. Babugarh is a wondrous place bristling with high specialty veterinary doctors of the RVS – surgeons, gynecologists and physicians and nutritionists equipped with modern testing laboratories. The facility has several clean and well laid out stalls holding animals of different ages. There are wide expansive grounds for training and exercises. This farm has also come into prominence as per media reports for its most recent achievement of IVF test tube production of a horse.

The Field Research Laboratory at Leh is engaged in breeding a mule using a mountain breed of horse (Fig. 12.23) envisaging that the offspring of the 'Zanskar' variety (Fig. 12.24) will be able to withstand the high altitude stress and be equally surefooted on the narrow tracks.

Milch animals: The British Cantonments had established Military Dairy Farms in different parts of the country; they were meant mainly to supply fresh milk and milk products to their own personnel and to provide extra milk rations to the troops. The maintenance and care of these milch animal herds also fall under the purview of RVS Officers.

In the RVS Headquarters, New Delhi, one estimate was provided of 22,000 to 24,000 military animals of which 18,000 to 20,000 are equines. These numbers may vary from 10,000 to 30,000 depending on the army's requirements. At any given time a large number of animals, except those on ceremonial duties or breeding stock, are deployed in different terrains (personal discussions with Col. S. Rajpal, RVS, 2005).

Animal Rations: The animals with jobs to do are taken care of and provided with adequate and nutritious rations (feed, fodder, grass) commensurate with the work they do. Their health, vigor and energy level will reflect in the load carrying capacity and performance. There are separate ration scales for every type of animal based on:

- Energy requirement,
- Function and
- Geographic/climatic conditions.

Fig. 12.23: Experimental animal stock for high altitude work for the breeding programme at FRL, Leh (September 2006).

Fig. 12.24: Zanskar mare: An experiment at FRL, Leh (September, 2006).

Understanding the digestive physiology, determining the nutrition requirements, recommending the nature and quantity of feed and fodder, and familiarity with the problems associated with feeding of each animal type fall within the purview of the military veterinary nutritionists, a highly qualified and trained group of officers within the RVC.

For Horses: Horses are now mainly used for ceremonial purposes, rides and sport and come from good breeding stock. They are classified as Ride A and Ride B type, based on the height. They are imparted good training and in the first four to five years of life, a horse is under the care of the RVC. This practice is very similar to what has been described in Kautilya *ArthaŚāstra.* A rapport between the animals and their trainers is thus established early in the training period. This familiarity helps in better performance.

Depending on the type of work performed, such as slow trotting, cantering, galloping or more strenuous effort, the energy (Kcal) required per hour per kilogram of body weight has been calculated. In the case of a horse, figures show that during ordinary working to galloping and show jumping, the energy requirements rise steeply from 0.5 kcal to 24 Kcal and for a horse under strenuous effort the figures are even higher and could be as much as 39 Kcal as per the Nutrition Research Council, 1973 (data from Col. Rajpal, RVS 2005).

The nature of work done by horses and mules is categorised as

- Maintenance work and
- Work production

Nutrition requirements of all ruminants, which include the equines (horse, mule, donkey, camel) are considered in terms of digestible crude protein (DCP) and total digestible nutrients (TDN) required by an individual animal for a particular type of work. Horses have been largely replaced by mules in all strenuous and load carrying requirements. The energy requirement from the feed are approximately equivalent to 0.75 of TDN per 100 lbs of body weight for horses weighing between 1,000 to 1,100 lbs.

It is recommended that horses be fed three or four times a day. This is necessitated by the fact that horses have a relatively small stomach and overeating at one time can produce colic or even a ruptured stomach. Frequency of feeding does not effect digestibility.

For Mules: Mules are meant for draft work. There are two types of work that they perform:

- Carry mountain artillery denoted as **MA**, comprising guns and ammunition. These are heavy loads, weighing far above what an animal can carry at one time. The artillery is therefore broken down into three parts – barrel, tripod and base plate. Each MA animal carries one item or piece based on how much it can carry; each piece weighs about 150 kg. For this purpose heavier animals are used and for carrying lighter loads, lighter animals are employed.
- Those that carry general service stores are denoted as **GS** and carry goods to units deployed in mountain areas, where the access roads are poor. The stores brought in as far as the roadhead by motor transport convoys are then loaded on mule backs. This load does not normally exceed 50 kg though the ideal load carry capacity is said to be abut 72.5 kg and sometimes loads greater than 50 kg have to be carried on flat terrain.

The GS mule carries weights up to 72 kg. Each animal carries tents, structures, bunkers, equipment and other supplies and its own ration feed, which is 5 kg per day. Even though mules are sturdy, sure footed and enduring, the climb up narrow mountain paths and trails is slow and arduous.

Further, higher altitudes provide progressively less oxygen, decreasing the animal's load carrying capacity. The animal can just about manage to carry 50 kg on these terrains. Therefore, due to the load factor, the animals are used for short distance hauls. Where animals cannot manage to go, men must carry the materials themselves, such as up almost vertical rocks and in the snow.

The supply line therefore includes mechanised transport which can go up to the roadhead, from where the supplies are loaded on to the animals and in the final stretches it is the hard backs of men.

The rations for the equines and canines and their stocking position are organized on the same lines as that for the men. A horse feed consists of gram, barley, bran and salt, all obtained separately and mixed with a mineral mixture, and with calcium and phosphate. The responsibility to formulate the feed rests with the '*godown* overseer', who concocts this feed mix in batches as per a standard formula for 200–300 animals at a time. It is then packed in amounts sufficient for 20 animals and sent onwards to units that have animals. Provision is also made for extra feed. A horse is entitled to 4–5 kg of this concentrate plus 8–9 kg of dry hay. Just as in the case of SRS, there are 'in lieu' items prescribed for animals. And when the weather conditions do not permit supplies to be sent by road, animal rations are flown in.

For Camels: Sources have confirmed that there is no camel breeding programme undertaken by the Army. Rajasthan's nomadic Banjara community who migrate from Rajasthan every summer in search of fodder and water for their animals are probably the only source of camels even though there is a government Camel Breeding and Research Station in Bikaner.

The roughage feed consists of mostly locally found leaves known as American babool and sun and air dried feeds and fodder consisting of about 90 per cent dry matter. Camels are classified according to the nature of work performed – hard and medium.

Camels are used exclusively by the Border Security Forces and presently there is only one camel battalion (about 750 animals deployed with the BSF for desert operations).

For Canines: Canine feeding is expressed in terms of kilocalories per day. Their prescribed entitlement ranges between 3,000 to 5,000 Kcal/day. Canines are the only animals that are authorized meat rations at the level of 600 g meat per day per animal.

The dog food consists of meat, *atta* or rice, fresh vegetables and dog biscuits. When last enquired, pelletised feed had not yet been introduced into the dog rations. There is a persistent requirement for calcium, vitamin B complex and at times mineral supplement. These are procured out of medical funds on an 'as is needed' basis.

Bricks/Bales: One battalion of Animal Transport consists of about 800 animals. All except the camels are deployed in the North, NE, and Eastern Sector and by the BSF on the western border. They add up to quite a large number. Having understood that each class of animal has its own recommended daily rations, one cannot but wonder at the massive quantities of feed and fodder that must be arranged in different parts of the country.

For this purpose compressed feed and fodder in the form of bricks and bales respectively have been designed and are being produced. Of predetermined size and weight, this compressed form of animal feed is compact, easy to pack and transport over long distances and is also amenable to air lifting.

Supply Chain Part 3

Procurement and Distribution

The concept of free rations to every serving uniformed personnel was introduced in the mid 1970s during the Prime Ministership of Mrs. Indra Gandhi. Until then, only a certain sum of monetary food allowance was authorised.

For the purpose of managing the procurement and issue of foodstuffs, all authorised ration items are grouped as:

- Perishables
- Dry Rations
- Tinned Rations
- Fuel – Coal, Kerosene oil, LPG
- Hygiene chemicals

The fresh perishable rations include fruits and vegetables, fresh/frozen meats, poultry meat and fish as well as fresh milk and eggs.

The dry rations comprise commodities such as flour, grains, milled items, pulses, spices, salt, sugar and other grocery items including oil in tins.

Tinned items are packaged, shelf stable foods such as sterilised milk in cartons and egg powder, butter, cheese, jams, various processed meats, fish, vegetables in brine, fruits in syrup, condensed milk, milk powder and many alternatives to the above.

The procurement procedures for each group of food are distinct and different, though they all have to go through administrative approvals and are subject to controls from the time of placing orders to the final distribution points in the supply chain.

Dry ration items are purchased through contracts placed by a central procurement agency while all fresh foods are obtained through 'local contracts' (based on briefing by DDGOL at Army HQ). Every item is either an 'entitlement' as per ration scale or '*in lieu*'. Oil, grains etc. are obtained through central procurement, directly from the Food Corporation of India (FCI). Orders are placed with various manufacturing firms for other ration items. Seeing how big the Armed Forces are, how geographically spread and what kind of terrains and climatic conditions and situations they normally operate in, it does not require a great amount of imagination to recognise that a very well structured and oiled machinery must exist that can coordinate the requisitions received from units from every corner of India, find suppliers for items, place the orders for the requisite quantities, and finalise their dispatch, organise the transportation and oversee the distribution and issuing of the stores.

The road, rail, sea and air supported transportation networks that exist in the country today facilitate the movement of men and materials to the remotest corners.

People who make decisions: The Army, which is the largest and therefore the dominant branch of the Armed Forces, is the main body whose various departments carry the overall responsibility of food procurement and distribution.

After a little probing it was found that there is neither a single all encompassing food policy nor a standard operating procedure, even though several policies of the past became amalgamated. The Army Headquarters (Fig 12.25) is divided into several branches each independent of the other but complementing each other for the smooth and structured functioning of the Army. The DGMO, DGMI and DGOL report directly to the VCOAS. In the next rung there is the Quarter Master General's Branch.

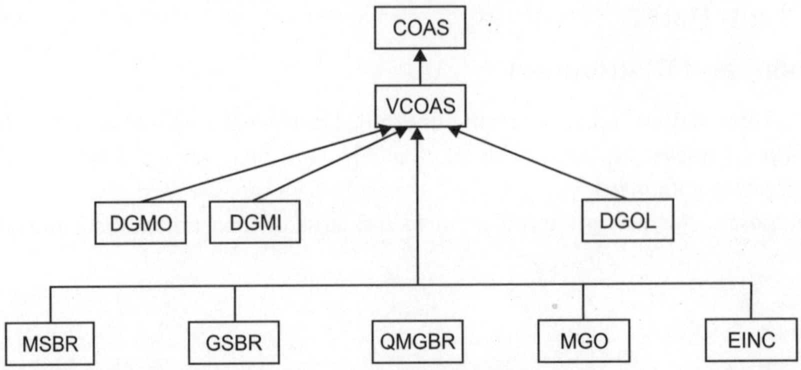

COAS: Chief of Army Staff; VCOAS: Vice Chief of Army Staff; DGMO: Director General of Military Operations; DGMI: Director General of Military Intelligence; DGOL: Director General Operational Logistics; MSBR: Personal staff Officers of COAS and other branches, management; GSBR: General Staff, Policy; QMGBR: Quarter Master General's Branch, MGO: Master General, Ordnance; EINC: Engineer in Charge

Fig. 12.25: Organization under Army Headquarters

Source: Courtesy, Col. A.N. Datta, Q1-B, DGST Br.

Office of the QMG: There is history attached to the office of the QMG. The office of the Quarter Master General of the land army in India was created in 1773 (QMG Correspondence, 1839–59). He had the rank of a Lieutenant Colonel, which was the highest rank that this office entitled the person to hold. The QMG at that time was said to be on the list of Lt. Colonels in His Majesty's Army although they were only captains in the Corps of Engineers. This particular office however conferred the rank of Lt. Colonel but not double pay for rank and position.

According to the original Home Department 1773 document, (filed under Public Branch Communiqué, Consultation, 6 Dec, 1888) it was declared by the General office (Orders of the Court of Directors, 6th Par, dt. 7 April, 1773) that the QMG's pay and *batta* were fixed at 20 shillings plus, which was the custom in England. From the poorly legible manuscript it is not clear how much the *batta* entitlement was. It was the Board's further opinion that the allowances granted to the QMG were adequate for 'at least whilst the country remains in tranquility and the army within the provinces' (On allowance of Officers 1883).

Today the QMG is of the rank of a Lieutenant General of the Indian Army and the pay and allowances are commensurate with the rank and service in the Army irrespective of peace or war situations. The Office of the QMG however has the same responsibilities now as in the past.

Before the current organisational structure of the QMG Br came into existence, there was one directorate for rations – that of DGST Military farms. The Additional DG, Operational Logistics (Food Policy) used to coordinate the logistics of several directorates; this task proved to be rather cumbersome. Today, there is a DG, Logistics – an independent policy-making branch, which determines the stocking policy regarding what needs to be stocked and for how long a period based on the strength of the forces (~1.3 million in authorised strength).

The QMG Secretariat carries under its umbrella nine directorates as well as the Deputy QMG (DQMG) who coordinates the function and activities of all the nine directorates. The Supplies and Transport (ST) directorate is principally involved with the procurement and transportation of all material goods, fuel etc. including foodstuffs. The Remount Veterinary Service (RVS) is exclusively in charge of all animals in the employ of the Indian Army; it provides mules for animal transport, essential for sending supplies to units in terrains not accessible by roads; the Military Farms (MF) keep and maintain the milch cattle (Fig. 12.26). The Canteen Stores Department (CSD) functions as a department store selling all manner of household items, appliances, and packaged food products and liquor. Vehicles like cars, motorcycles and scooters can also be purchased through the CSD. The goods here are available at considerably reduced prices. The Army Postal service (APO) operates through the DGST.

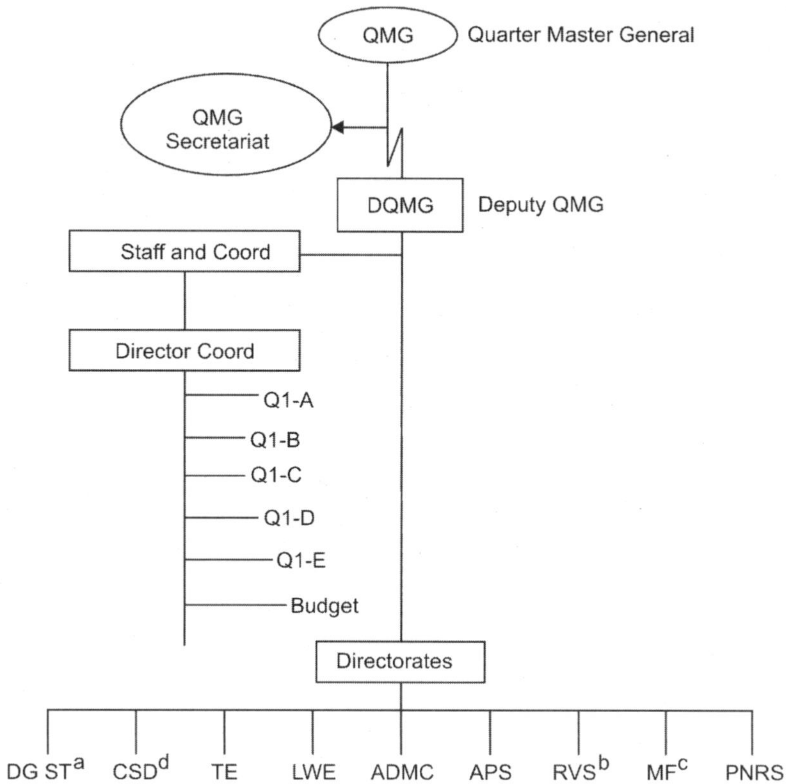

The principal participants in the supply chain are: a, b, and c.
[a]Director General, Supplies andTransport,
[b]Remount Veterinary Service,
[c]Military Dairy Farms
[d]Canteen Stores Department is a 'general store' from where goods may be purchased.

Fig. 12.26: Organizational chart in the Quartermaster General's (QMG) Branch

Source: Courtesy, Col. A.N. Datta, Q1-B, DGST Br.

Food Advisory Committee: From conversations and discussions with DDGOL, Q1-B and other senior officers in the QMG's Branch, it transpired that there was a body called the Food Advisory Committee constituted with the participation of the QMG – Quarter Master General, DMS – Directorate of Medical Services, DCV – the Directorate of Victualing and Clothing, Navy and a Representative of the Air Force. This committee meets regularly to discuss matters pertaining to the rations in respect of the following:

- Addition/replacement of items or deletion,
- Considering the nutritional value and calorie scales of foods and rations,

- Who might require more calories or when to allocate more.
- When to give pack rations i.e. timing, units being deployed, operational locale and length of operations and also matters like what substitute food items might be desirable/acceptable to provide variety and interest.

Stocking policy: The Deputy Director General Operational Logistics, DDGOL, is responsible for stocking, maintenance and replenishment of supplies, which includes transportation. A certain stock is necessary to effect issues regularly. Stock maintenance caters for:

- Any possible disruption in communication/transport such as road closed periods in J & K sector and other snow and mountain terrains, or non-availability of foods of any or a certain kind in regions like the Northeastern jungles.
- General staff reserves for operations where special troops are being deployed and who must be issued food rations to take along. These reserves also come in very handy to extend assistance to civilians and other nearby units that may find themselves in urgent need of maintenance rations.

Food procurement and supply in the Army – administrative and procedural steps: Every requisition, at all stages, is made based on the authorised ration scale and the strength of personnel attached to the unit. All three services obtain their rations after preparing estimates and submitting their requirements to the Quarter Master General Branch. Essentially this procedure involves nine steps.

Stage 1 – Ration Forecasting: The ration scales as per as SRS are authorised by 'Army Instructions' or 'Army Order', which is another term for the authority approving the rations and the Government's financial consent to go ahead with the said rations. Also included in the Government approval are the book debits for rations for the paramilitary forces, as well as the stocking policy as per the Operational Logistics Directives. The procedures are much the same in both the Army and the Navy and presumably in the Air Force. How the Navy decides on its stocking policy and the quantum of each type of rations would probably depend on vessel movement, personnel movement, internal and joint exercises and other naval operational considerations and likewise in the Air Force. The estimates from all the Services are received in the QMG Branch. The various steps–nine of them, in this process of forecasting and submitting requisitions to the QMG'S office in the supply chain are shown diagrammatically in Fig. 12.27.

Stage 2 – Central Purchase and Acceptance Procedures: Receiving the consolidated estimates in the QMG Branch is the final step in this stage of the procurement procedure. From here on, QMG's office prepares and submits the requirements to the Government for financial approval and instructions. Once this hurdle is crossed, the office of the Director General, Supplies and Transport, DGST, receives requisitions for the various ration items of dry, tinned and fresh rations and the quantity in which they are required and the key person to coordinate the efforts made in the procurement. Collating all incoming requests, DGST'S office in consultation with the QMG raises indents for dry rations and tinned goods in bulk, specifying the quantity and the location where a particular item is needed. This part of the supply chain is shown in Fig. 12.28. The major players in this part of the chain are the APO, CDPO, supplier groups, ASC's FIO and CFLs, ASC Mechanical and Animal transports, supply depots and air transports wherever necessary.

In the central procurement of dry/tinned rations the indents are sent to the Army Purchase Organization (APO), which is located in the Krishi Bhavan – the Ministry of Agriculture in New Delhi; it has a Service officer of the Central Defence Purchase (CDPO) in charge of purchases. The

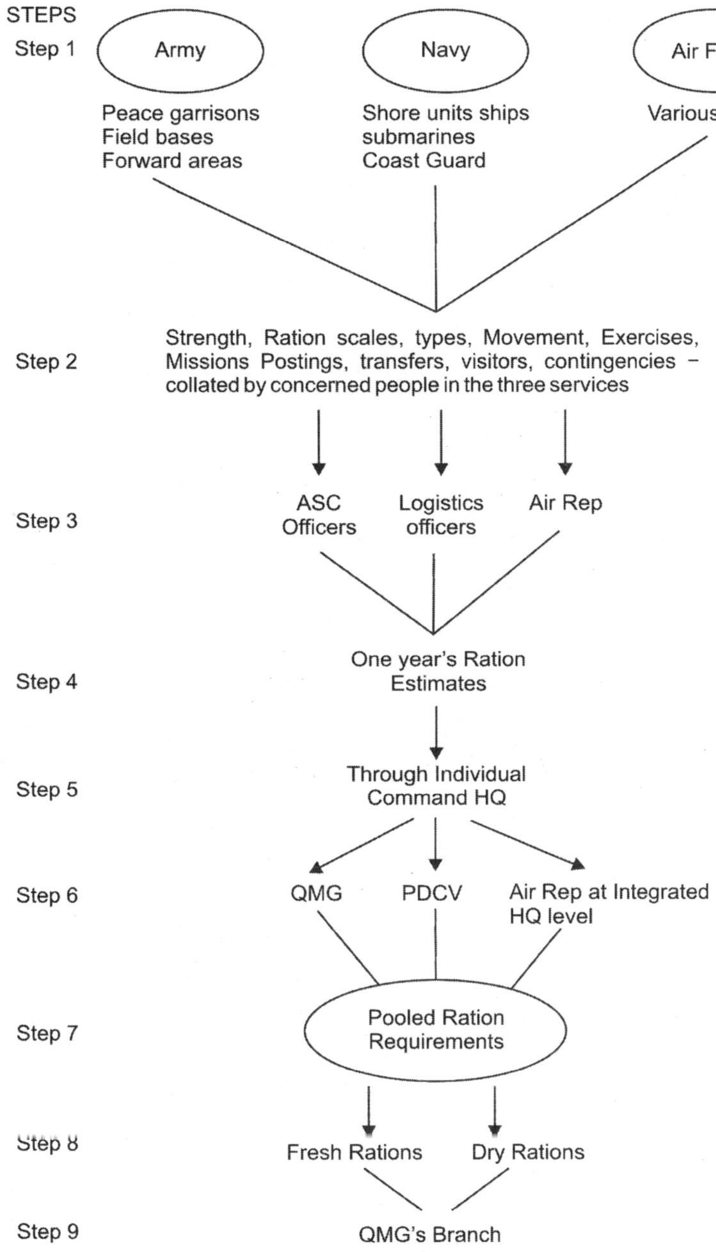

Fig. 12.27: Food Supply Chain Management, Stage 1: Forecasting of total ration requirements for one year

APO places contractual orders with various supplier groups (traders, stockists, manufacturers) of which it has an extended list. The Food Corporation of India (FCI) warehouses in different regions are included. They supply grains, wheat and rice. The Military Dairy Farms and the National Dairy Federation of India (NDFI) are contracted to supply milk and milk products. Along with the orders go the quality and packaging and portion size specifications for each item. These specifications have been laid down as per the ASC's technical standardization norms. There is a considerable amount

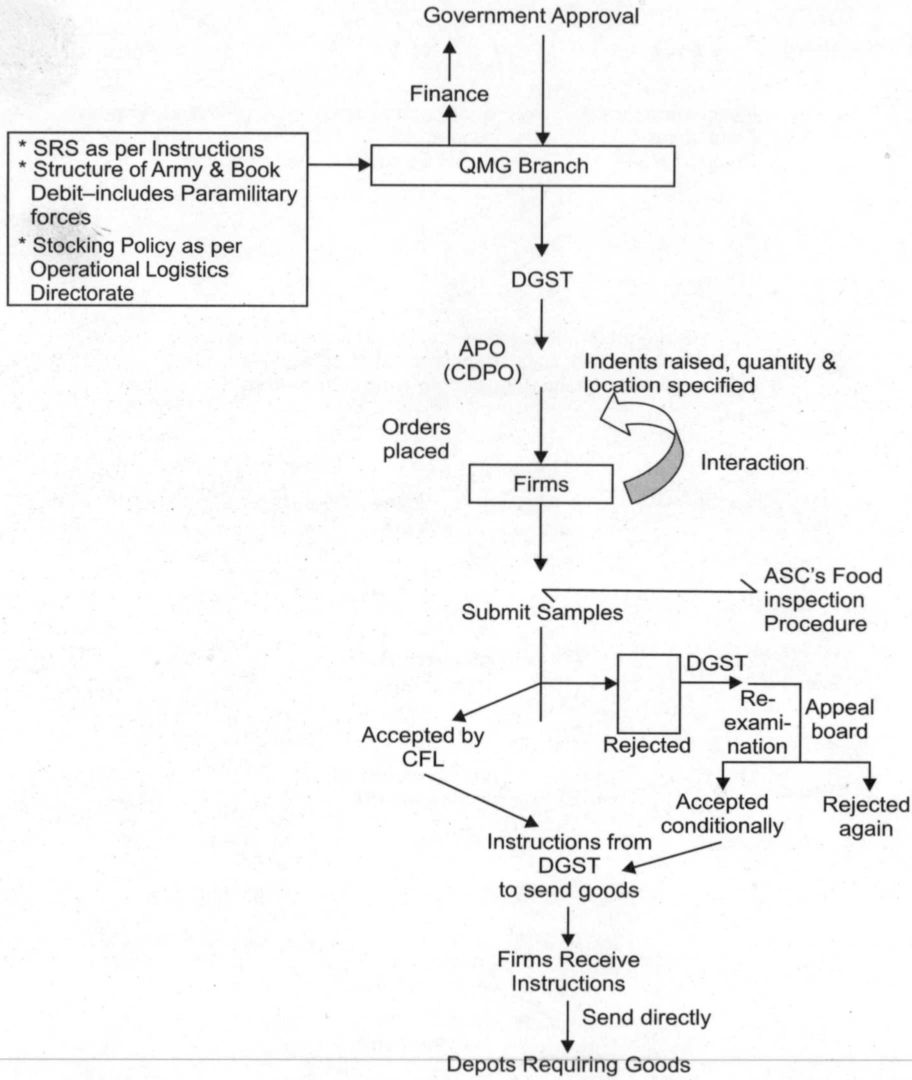

Fig. 12.28: Food Supply Chain and Management, Stage 2: Purchase and Procurement of Dry Rations
Source: Drawing based on discussions with Q1-B. Col. A.N. Datta

of interaction between the firms and the APO at this juncture. If the suppliers are in a position to offer or are ready to supply the goods sought, they are required to submit their product samples to the ASC's Food Inspection Team of Technical officers who are well versed in inspection procedures and quality assurance methods.

These teams are deputed to visit manufacturing units and warehouses and collect samples and take these back to laboratories. They are constantly on the move, traveling from one firm to another, carrying out their inspection jobs, assessing the manufacturing site premises and the process. At the CFLs, the foods are subjected to detailed physical, chemical, microbiological and organoleptic tests according to established methods of Quality Assurance and Food Analysis to determine their suitability and acceptability as per the existing product specifications. The DGST is informed of the results. If the verdict is in the affirmative, the DGST's office then issues instructions to the firms to dispatch the consignments directly to the ASC Supply Depots requiring them. In the event that a sample is found to be unacceptable and hence rejected by the CFLs, there is provision for the firms to go on appeal to the Appeal Board which also falls under the DGST. The samples are then resubmitted to the Appellate laboratory, the ST-7 and ST-8 where the foods are reexamined and re-evaluated.

Whenever the rejections are based on minor infringement or violations of specifications generally in the weight/portion packing, the products are ordered to be accepted conditionally; one of these conditions could be reduction in price. However, if the rejections result from gross defects and compromise safety, the food samples are rejected once again.

Stage 3 – Distribution from the Supply Depots: The further distribution of the stores, from the point of supply depots is shown in Fig. 12.29. How do the troops in the field units get their quota of rations? For this purpose there are ASC battalions which are field formations composite companies that are mobile. They are said to 'move in *bricks*' which comprise stores handlers and transport detachments. These 'mobile bricks' carry forth stores to different places.

Delivery to Unit Cook Houses: For practical purposes, the cookhouse is the destination of the foods received. The further travelogue is unfolded in one sector in J & K in an example explained by the Deputy Director General of Operational Logistics. All units which run a cook house are supposed to get their quota when the stores reach a supply depot. Units in and around Jammu such as those stationed in Nagota and Udhampur come up once a month, collect the allotted amount of rations (as per prior requisitions) and take them back by using composite platoons of the ASC. The bulk rations are broken up into smaller lots and are put in the custody of the Quarter Master of the units. The commanding officer of the battalion issues orders to the Quarter Master, Stores, to ration out the required quantity of food stuff sufficient for 10–15 days (or for 30 days for those companies located in remote areas). The Quarter Master, Company, collects rations for 7–15 days' requirement and deposits them in the Company's store house. A Non Commissioned Officer (NCO) is usually

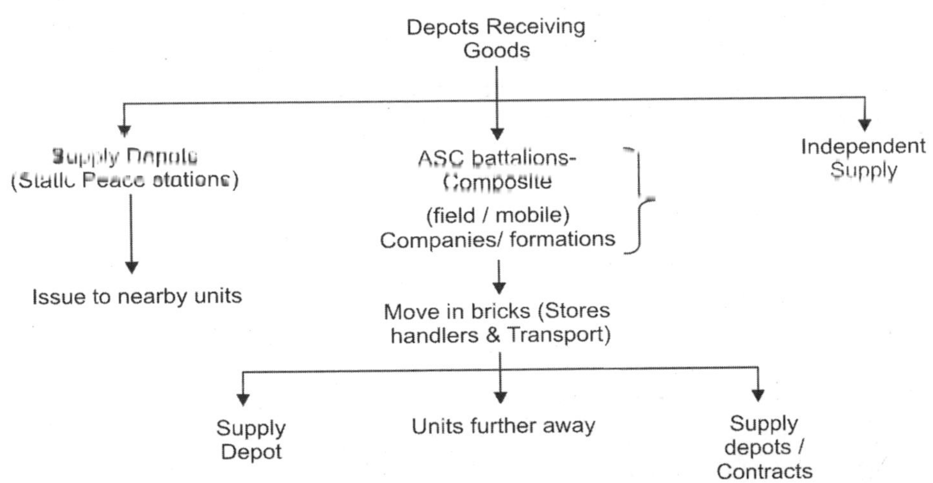

Fig. 12.29: Food Supply Chain and Management. Stage 3: Distribution. Movement in Bricks to various Depots after Procurement of Dry Rations

Source: Based on discussions with Q1-B, Col. A.N. Datta

in charge of the cookhouse, which is of course staffed with cooks and cooks' assistants. On a daily basis the NCO issues and distributes the raw materials to the cooks.

Air drops: From the point of dispatch by the central warehouses of the FCI and the firms, all goods are transported by road, though in earlier years, considerable goods movement occurred by rail too. In far off places where road transportation is not possible or is unsatisfactory, such as in sectors in Assam, Arunachal Pradesh and deep the northern snow clad mountain pickets, supplies are air dropped. These are then known as 'air maintained posts'. Such distant posts are continuously provisioned with not only food rations but also with other essentials like fuel needed for transport vehicles, for lighting cookhouse fires, to melt snow and to make a fire just to keep warm. The main cooking fuel in the forward areas is kerosene oil but in peace stations it is LPG and in certain installations, coal and firewood too. As mentioned previously under rations, there is an individual 'entitlement' quota for fuel too, as it is for food rations and everything else.

Tinned Foods: Tinned Foods are preferentially obtained from government run or Defence factories. Meat and milk products, tinned fish and jams, diced fruit and vegetables etc. are the principal tinned items.

Fresh and bulk foods: Fresh foods are perishable and are always obtained through local contracts placed on supply agents and contractors who trade in a variety of fresh food materials-meat, chicken, fish, eggs, fruits, vegetables, bread and milk. Although contracts are made on a regular or yearly basis, supplies are effected through out the year on the prior agreed price structure which is accepted after price bids are submitted and quotations evaluated for best advantage to the state.

Local contracts ensure that fresh foods are obtained from nearby places and quickly transported to the units positioned in the general vicinity and are accessible by roads, and at times only by air. In peace installations, the supply depots stock and issue perishables once, twice or three times a week. In field stations in the North and Northwest such as those in the mountains without access to motorable roads or in adverse weather, they are packed in large plastic crates and air dropped. In the north eastern snow bound areas as well as in the deep jungles, access is as difficult as in the northern sector. Often in the jungle areas even air supply is not possible and there is precious little to buy from local sources. It is there that tinned goods come in handy and it is not unknown that troops have had to subsist on such rations for long stretches.

The situation becomes even more problematic in the hot and humid climate. The dry rations held in bulk stock become infested and moldy and stale. Salt and sugar lump together due to absorption of moisture and everything that was edible is not so anymore or becomes disgustingly unappetizing and unappealing. It puts the troops in a most unhappy situation.

Summarised in Fig 12.30 is the process of obtaining both perishable and dry foods and their final destinations of an infantry battalion for example in Jammu and Kashmir area. The units place their indents to the quartermaster first. The requests move upwards to the supply depot. It also describes how the foods are issued to units, collected by the quartermaster of a unit, from where it is taken by quartermaster of a company where it would be stocked for a period of 7–15 days and quantities issued to the NCO in charge of the cookhouse who would ultimately issue rations for the day to the cook on a daily basis.

The entire supply chain from the time of making estimates, sending supplies to the supply depots and the manner in which these depots function to deliver the rations to the cook houses is a study in meticulous planning and execution.

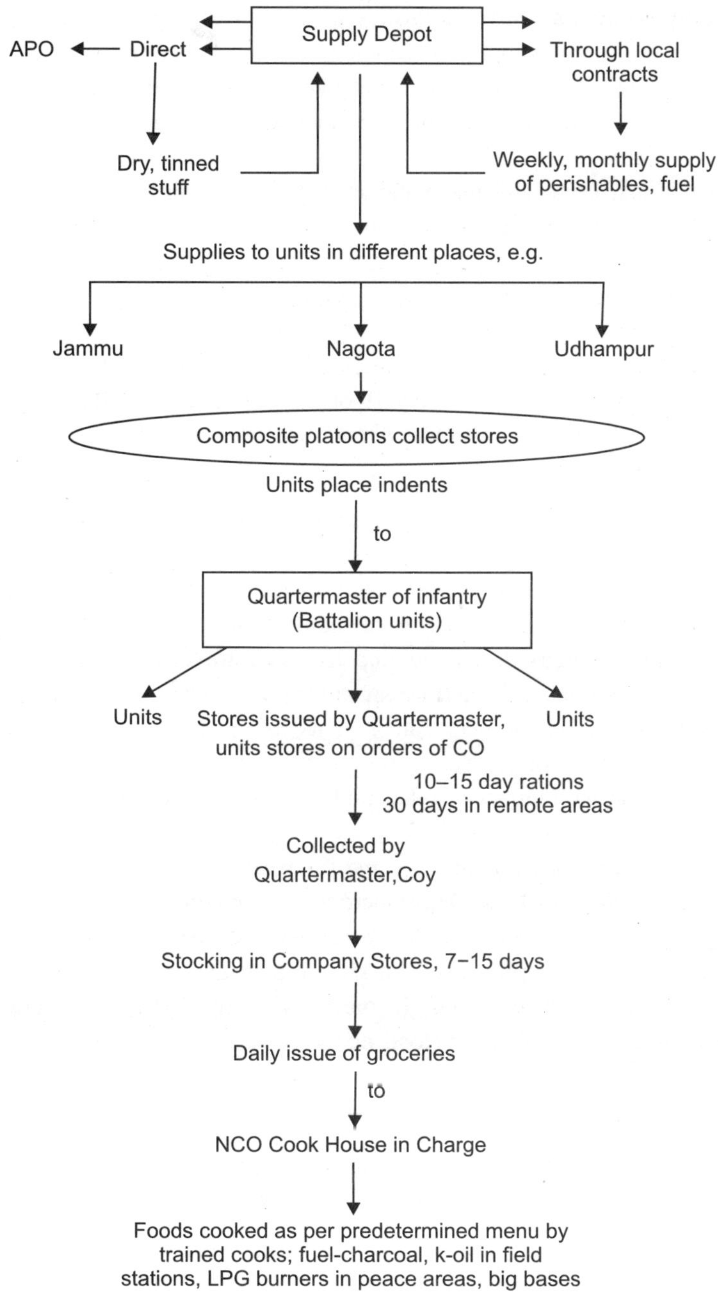

Fig. 12.30: How a supply Depot functions: for example a sector location in Jammu

Source: Based on discussions with DDGOL, Army HQ

Fuel: Fuel rations are as important as food rations. Coal, firewood, kerosene and LPG are all supplied as and where their particular use is convenient. Based on unit strength, location and terrain, climate and temperature and operational logistics, fuel entitlements are determined and stocks maintained.

Naval food supply logistics: Naval Logistics is the branch which plans, prepares estimates, procures, keeps in readiness and supplies all kinds of stores required by the navy, from equipment, spares, fuel, clothes, shoes, foods, mess trap and kitchen appliances to the most inconsequential looking items, stationary or toilet tissues, and important stuff like medicines and rescue and revival items.

A part of all this and especially the materials logistics pertaining to clothing and foods fall under the Directorate of Clothing and Victualing, PDCV. The latter is a uniquely navy term for feeding and foods (victuals) and clothing and essentials and not used in the Army context. There is a Principal Director of Clothing and Victualing operating from the Integrated Headquarters (Navy) whose responsibilities are similar to the Quarter Master General of the Army.

The food supply chain is just as well streamlined in the Navy as it is in the Army and the procedures are laid down in the Indian Navy Book of Reference (INBR). It is briefly described here because the way materials are collected, distributed, stocked and issued to units is somewhat different from that in the Army.

Ration estimates: Under the logistics officers of each unit, estimates of standard rations as in the entitled ration scales are prepared for officers and sailors as well as special provisions for submarine crew, for divers, marine commandos (MARCOs), air crews and rocket fuel handlers. Every ship has a known strength which varies from a small number of 75 to 100 (some as small as 40 in a submarine) to several hundreds in a large ship like a destroyer or an aircraft carrier. In shore establishments such as INS *Hamla,* the permanent staff may account for a maximum of 300 (officers and sailors included) but due to the very nature of its role in training, its numbers may swell to 700, depending on the number of courses in progress, the number of officers undergoing various courses in logistics and on the number of other ranks and sailors being trained in the logistics and catering schools.

In the Naval Bases where our fleets of ships and submarines are positioned and both in the bases and Headquarters of the Navy in New Delhi, there are innumerable personnel posted on duties of training, teaching, research and routine desk jobs as well as specialised tasks including material supplies. These are the shore compliments. The service personnel working in these establishments are also entitled to free authorized rations. In the navy's terminology, there are three groups of rations for the total inventory of about 40 food items:

- Basic rations: agricultural products such as rice, wheat, dals, flour, *suji*, sugar, salt, cooking oil/fat (vegetable) and spices.
- Necessary rations: all kinds of tinned items including the submarine and commando rations.
- Fresh rations: fresh vegetables, fruits, butter, milk, meat, fish, poultry meat (fresh or frozen), eggs and bread.

Yearly estimates and projections for rations are made by each of the three services. In the Indian Navy, every naval unit prepares its own ration estimates (including cooking fuel requirement) for one year based on entitlements, personnel strength, anticipated movement, visitors etc. This is forwarded to its Command Headquarters as shown in Fig. 12.29. It may be recalled that there are four Principal Commands in the Indian Navy as well as sub-commands. Each command's estimates for different type of ration items are then forwarded to the PDCV in New Delhi whose office compiles the total information. Similar forecast estimates are made in the Army and the Air Force, all of which provides a pretty accurate estimate of the total requirement of rations for one year. What changes in these estimates is the alternate items described in the ration scales (example fresh milk versus tinned or powdered milk, tetrapak UHT milk, malted milk products or cheese).

For agricultural items like dals and certain tinned provisions the navy is authorised to conclude local contracts through the Base Victualing Officer (BVO). In the matter of dals, the Navy is particular in keeping in stock some 15 varieties. This is mandatory, unlike in the Army where 'a dal is a dal' and only two to three varieties may be indicated. For items like sugar, oil, tinned or pouch packed rations; contracts are placed on government factories, Defence factories and other approved manufacturers under a rate contract system. The Indian Navy Canteen Services (INCS), which is independent of the Canteen Stores Department (CSD) of the tri-services, is an additional source to obtain a wide range of products at reasonable rates. Manufacturers of milk products like Amul and Mother Dairy supply a variety of their specialty products, such as milk, milk powder, butter and cheese. Under the contract system, the Base Victualing Officer, BVO, is authorised to place and conclude local contracts for condiments (yearly), for dals (six monthly) and for fresh items (yearly). The rate contracts are not always binding for tinned items which can also be obtained locally from CSD or the INCS.

Spices are obtained in bulk, mostly in the whole (unpowdered) form. Both the officers in charge and the cooks are wary of the possible adulteration of ground spices and spice mixes. During one interactive discussion with ships' cooks, it was given to understand that they preferred to use whole spices supplied individually, as it allowed them to be more innovative and individualistic in their work. But there is also considerable amount of interest in using the branded and quality assured packaged variety of spice mixes on board ships and submarines since these are certainly more convenient. Similarly the submarine galley staff was of one voice when they said that they would welcome substitution of the garlic bulbs and onions supplied in bulk to the vessels with the packaged form of onion, garlic and ginger pastes widely found in domestic markets. Handling these condiments in a submarine is a nuisance, the onion and garlic scales fly all over while hand peeling.

The CFLs inspect the Direct Indent (DI) supplies such as wheat, rice, sugar, white flour and *suji*. Wherever local contracts are operated by the BVO, for example for tea, spices, dals etc. and well known and approved brands are procured.

Fresh rations which are obtained through Direct Indent only. Fresh meat is obtained from municipal abattoirs (in Mumbai from Deonar Abattoir); other private firms supply frozen meat. Likewise, there are authorized fish mongers for supplying fresh fish. The poultry meat as broilers is purchased directly from such established and safety assured sources.

Base Victualing Yard and BVO. No matter from where the provisions are procured, the ration items must all reach the Base Victualing Yard (BV yard) which is the Navy counterpart of the Army's ASC supply depot (See Fig. 12.37). In a base area with significant navy presence such as in Mumbai, Cochin, Visakhapatnam, Jamnagar and Karwar, the BV yard receives all goods. There is no BV yard in Kolkata, therefore the units there are supplied by the Eastern Command, Visakhapatnam. The Andamans are under the Integrated Command of the tri-services and are provisioned separately. INS *India* is a shore establishment in New Delhi and looks after the officers posted in New Delhi. Where the navy presence is smaller, the units are provisioned by the nearest ASC depot. Otherwise the BV Yard at any base is independent of ASC except for bringing in certain goods and for supplying white flour and *suji*.

A Base Victualing yard has to be large, airy and spacious, functional and equipped with cold and frozen storage facilities; it has to be accessible and secure and as near the dock yard as can be.

Delivery to ships: There are daily delivery schedules for different ration items for the ships in the dock. Fresh milk and bread are delivered early in the morning, and vegetables, fruits, before the noon meal. Fish is provided only once a week on a Friday. Fresh meat issues are made three times a week and both fish and meat are delivered directly to the ships.

Dry rations like *atta*, rice, sugar etc. are usually supplied by the FCI in 50 kg bags. Such large bags cannot be handled in the ships and submarines for the simple reason that there are no cranes to lift and deliver nor any device to lower the bags through the hatches. Every bag has to be carried on men's backs and every bag and man has to move up and down the narrow and steep ladders through narrow openings and hatches leading to different deck levels. Also, as per International Labour Organization's (ILO) provisions, a man may carry no more than 30 kg on his back. A man can just about stand erect in a submarine. Navigating those innumerable narrow corridors and twists and turns in the stationary ship and the submarine, from the ward rooms to the pantries to the galleys.

So wherever labour and effort saving measures can be applied, they are at. The BV yard, rice is de-stoned, cleaned, ready for use and repacked in quantities of 25 kg. Likewise with wheat flour, which is specially ground in flour mills as required and then bagged. All other dry agricultural items are bagged in 25 kg or practicable sizes. Dressed mutton carcasses are cut to specified sizes to fit into cold storage shelves while whole fish can be kept frozen. There are large hooks suspended from ceiling rails in the freezer rooms on board a ship to hang several carcasses. Mutton is further cut into smaller chunks whenever required. Each consignment of vegetables to be issued to a ship's complement is likewise broken into lots of 10–15 kg a piece or a single bag of 5 kg for each vegetable. Potatoes and onions are put together in 10 kg and 6 kg weights respectively. Smaller sized bags are also more convenient to store inside the ships' cold stores and easy to access and use. The vegetables destined for a submarine are presumably cut up into smaller sizes wherever feasible and are bagged. There were cartons of processed food packs of some well advertised brands with whose range of products the Navy seems to be well satisfied. Pre-cooked dehydrated mixes in 500 g to 1 kg packs, and MRE rations are also held in the BV yard's stock rooms to be issued to ships and submarines as per their forecasts, indents and emergent situations. Cooking oils in the standard 'Ag Mark' tins are stacked on elevated platforms and on wooden racks. Spices, dals, and tinned rations are all kept in stock. Sugar is kept in rooms equipped with dehumidifiers to prevent the build up of atmospheric water vapour in the premises. This seems to be a sure way to keep the stocks dry.

The shore establishments are issued with dry and tinned rations on a monthly basis. Ships usually keep quantities sufficient for 30–45 days.

Fresh milk and bread are delivered to ships regularly and fresh vegetables are issued on alternate days to ships in the harbour. Three per cent of the monthly demand for fresh vegetables should be met with bitter gourd and one per cent in the form of 'green *masala*' (green chilies and fresh coriander and mint). In ships, the vegetables and fruits are also stored up to 30–45 days, for which purpose there are large chill storage rooms maintained at 12°C. Depending on their sailing schedules, and the strength and destination the ships can also stock supplies for 45 days to two and one half months. Smaller ships are deployed on short schedules (3–5 days) and therefore do not hold such large stocks. Submarines being smaller vessels have little storage capacity for the quantities required to go on long deployment. They do carry fresh vegetables and fruits, however, for they may sail without notice. Submarine personnel on deployment subsist, to a large extent on processed, ready to heat and eat foods. Meat is issued three times a week and fish once a week. The deep freezers in the shore establishments and ships run efficiently at −20°C to store these foods. If a ship plans to sail, its meat and fish quotas for the duration of the sail are delivered in the requisite quantities (the carcasses usually cut up into convenient portions) to be stored in the ship's freezer facilities.

Issue to shore units and ships: For the officers and sailors who are living with families at the base, the entitled rations are issued in kind (RIK) at the ration stands in the BV yard. Though there is provision to pay money in lieu of rations (MLR) to sailors @ Rs. 32.16/- per man per day and, cash in lieu of rations (CLR) to officers @ Rs. 32.35/- per day, they prefer to take RIK and not cash. Fresh rations are issued to them every ten days, three times a month on certain specified days of the week and at designated timings. Vegetables like potato and onions are pre-packed as per entitlement of one person for the duration while other fresh vegetables and fruits may be selected on the spot. Dry rations are issued for 30 days at a time. Officers may also buy any extras – dry, tinned and fresh at nominal rates from the stocks available. Frozen meat, chicken, fish, eggs or '*in lieu*' items such as milk, cheese or tinned fruit, jam in lieu of fresh fruits etc. are among the selectable entitlements. Bread is issued in the same manner. (This information was gathered after a tour of the yard and discussions with the Base Victualing Officer, Commander H. Dhulya, BV Yard, Mumbai).

All goods have to be manually loaded from the dockside, up the gangway and then into the ships through a narrow doorway (Fig. 12.31) and the open platform of submarines (Fig. 12.32), navigating up and down narrow staircases in the ships and down through a small hatch (Fig. 12.33) in the submarines.

Liquor comes under a separate entitlement for officers and men though not as part of daily rations. Sailors can get only rum (two pegs; one peg is 60 ml) but the officers can purchase three pegs/day of liquor (whiskey and other kinds) or beer within the monthly quota allowed for each individual. Officers may buy their drinks as required in the ward room. Those living with families may purchase their entitlements on a monthly basis from the CSD.

Fig. 12.31: On the deck of the submarine of INS Shankul, the author with the sub's officer waiting to go down through the hatch.

Fig. 12.32: On the decks of the Navy's destroyer INS Mumbai, the author with a ship's officer during the visit. Behind them to the far right is the narrow doorway through which one enters the ship. Once in, there are numerous narrow staircases, step ladder kind, leading to different levels.

Fig. 12.33: Going down the hatch in a submarine requires nimble feet and a tight grip. Every one and everything has to go down into the belly of the sub this way.

Storage, accounting, issue and food preparation are under the direct control of the ships logistics officer. The meat, fish and chicken are kept in the four freezers on board the ship. These freezers are maintained at −20°C to –25°C. The vegetables, bread and eggs are stored at 12°C. There is a separate storage room for oil tins. Only small quantities of foodstuffs are kept in the small refrigerator and in the overhead and below the counter locker space in the galleys. Articles of higher value (liquor, rum, extra cutlery) are stored in spaces under men's bunkers in the submarine (Fig. 12.34).

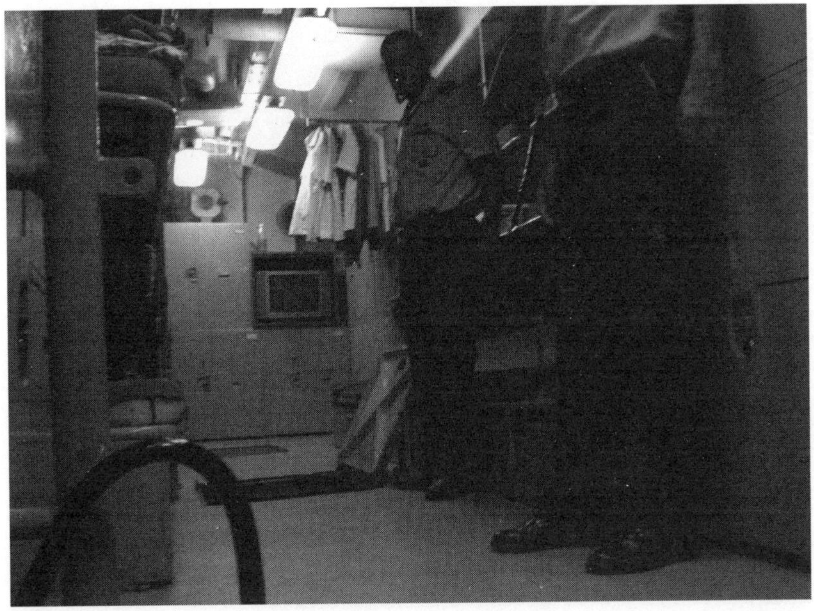

Fig. 12.34: Men's quarters in submarine INS Shankul. Bunks are similar to railway three tier coaches. The men also eat here, rest and sleep here. The open hatch on the floor is the storage section for liquor, fine crockery, cutlery etc. It leads to another tier below.

Space in ships is considerably bigger and there are actually large rooms with racks (Fig. 12.35) to keep the material organised. Stock inventories are posted regularly. In Fig. 12.36 one may find such a notice in the store room on board INS *Mumbai.*

Daily drawing of rations: The duty cook prepares a list of requirements for a day's menu and the vessel's strength on that day. The stores-in-charge issues foodstuffs three times during the day. Milk is issued early in the morning at 6.30 am for tea, along with bread to be served at breakfast. Mutton or chicken and such items are issued by 11.30 am and before noon all the materials are in the cook's hands. The chain of indent, procurement and ration delivery and their right of passage into the cook's hands onboard the ships, subs and shore establishments are diagrammatically explained in Fig. 12.37.

Food supplies in the Air Force: In each of the five operational Air Commands, situated in Delhi (Western), Gandhinagar (Southwestern), Shillong (Eastern), Allahabad (Central) and Trivandrum (Southern), there are, on an average, 20 bases.

In addition, there are two training commands – Air Training Command at Bangalore, the Aircraft Maintenance Command at Nagpur, and one Air Headquarters at Delhi. The Aircraft Systems Testing Establishments falls under the jurisdiction of the Air Headquarters. Air Force Station at Leh is the world's highest at more than 10,000 ft.

This wide geographical distribution of Air Force bases necessitates the same meticulous planning and organisation of food logistics as is prevalent in the Army and the Navy. Annual estimates of requirements of dry rations, tinned rations and fresh foods are forecast and the consolidated requests are sent up the chain of command in the Air Force and are passed through to the Quarter Master General. From here on the standard procurement and acceptance procedures come into force.

Fig. 12.35: The storage area in INS Mumbai is large as befits a big ship which also carries helicopters. Bagged commodities are held in the hold below decks.

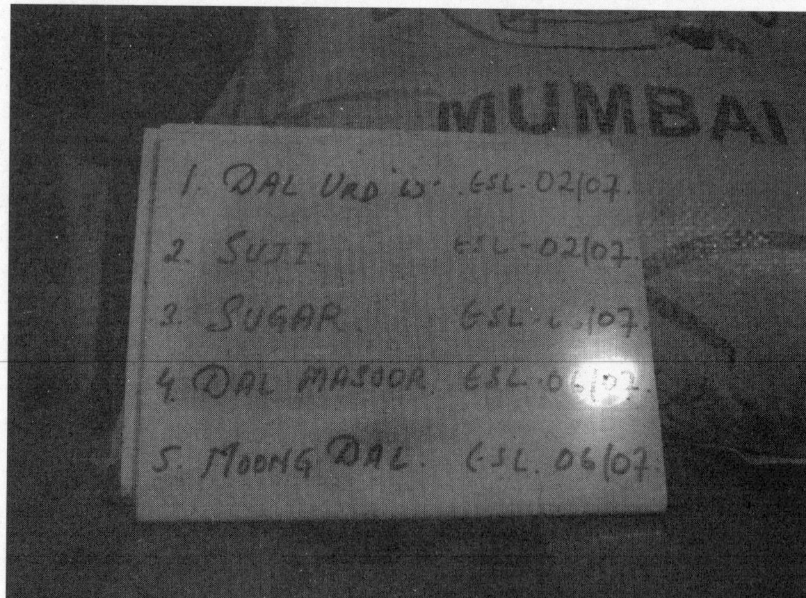

Fig. 12.36: Stock inventories are posted to help store keepers with daily issues

It would seem that the ASC supply depots nearest to Air Force installations in peace and field areas float local contracts for fresh foods and are entrusted with the disbursal and issue of rations to officers and to units. Where there is no ASC depot, the contracts concluded by Army authorities are operated by Air Force unit commanders. If the value of the contracts is less and if all the stuff

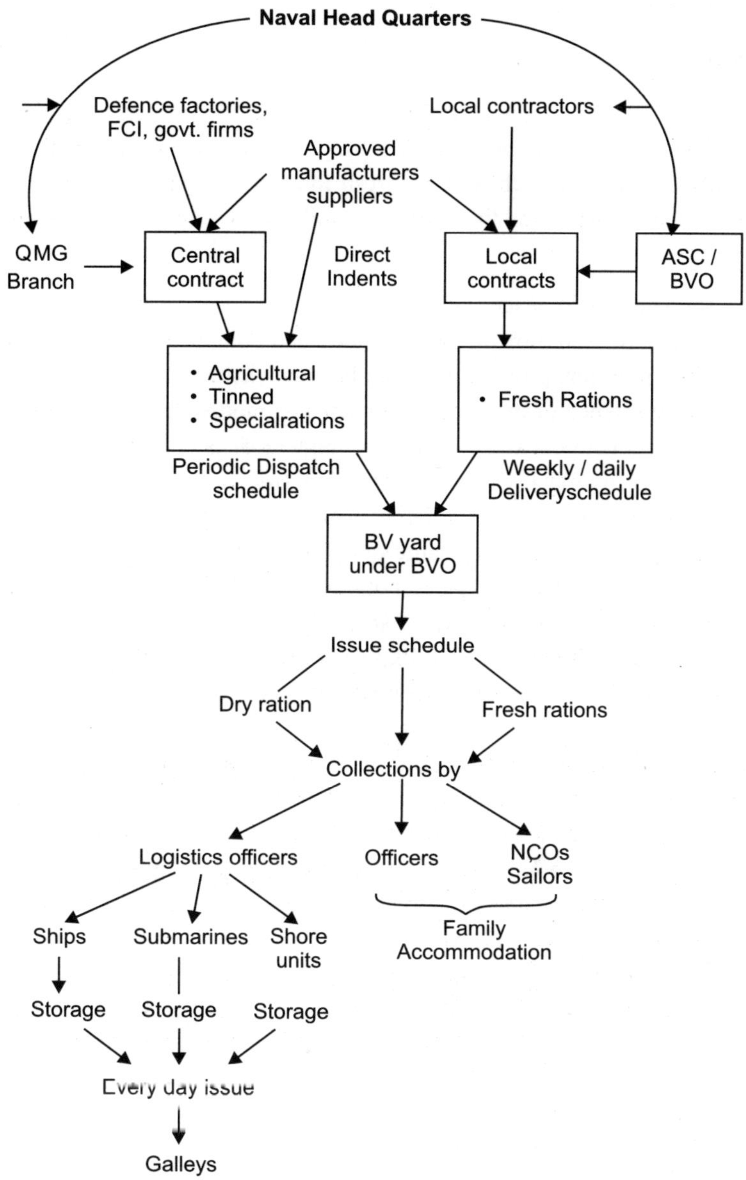

Fig. 12.37: Food Supply Chain Management: Ration procurement and distribution in Naval Units.
Source: Gathered from discussions with officers of the DGST Br, ASC and BV Yard.

is required at one place, a combined contract is concluded for Army and Air Force needs. The issue of rations to those entitled to free rations is carried out on a monthly basis for dry rations and once, twice or more frequently in a week for the fresh perishables. Officers and men eating in the unit messes and *langars* are not issued rations. Their quota of foodstuffs is surrendered (directed) to their respective units. This is also a standard practice (Discussions with Col P.D. Kulkarni, ASC Bangalore).

Supply Chain Part 4

Static Kitchens

In large military peace establishments or cantonments where the officers and men choose to live independently with families, the rations are drawn from the nearest supply depots, as per scale. The dry rations are collected once a month whereas fresh foods at designated times of issue in a week. Their respective kitchens provide for those officers and men living in cantonments and eating in the messes and *langars*.

Modern kitchens: The kitchens in peace stations and at the National Defence Academy, Khadakvasla and in INS *Hamla* etc. have some of the best planned and equipped facilities. Without a personal tour of NDA premises it is not possible to describe them in detail but informed sources in the Services vouch for the existence of excellent arrangements, modern equipment and kitchen gadgets and conveniences that facilitate cooking for a large number of people, meal after meal every day, four times a day and also for social occasions. The INS *Hamla* is equally well appointed.

Well equipped Army base kitchens have large steam double boilers/cookers connected to an in house steam generator capable of cooking large quantities of rice and dal.

Various types of cooking and frying pans, pots and vessels in different sizes are listed – the capacity of each being expressed in diameter. Except for the *chapatti* making '*tawa*' (griddle) and the deep-frying '*karahi*' (a multipurpose wok like vessel with two handles) and a few small sundry ladles made of cast iron, all other vessels are made of aluminum. If stainless steel pots are used in any of the kitchens, it would certainly be a welcome step in further modernisation. LPG was introduced into the defence services in a phased manner after an earnest proposal submitted by the ASC to the government. It was first launched in the Eastern Command in 1983 much to the great relief of the cook and his immediate environment (Kulkarni, 2000, p. 166). LPG is the main cooking fuel in large and small peace stations and wherever the civil gas supply system is in place. Gas burners mounted on stainless steel (SS) consoles are seen in the catering section of the Training Command in Bangalore. They look like work stations – one SS bench unit fitted with gas burner in the middle and a washbasin on one side. The trainee cooks work on domestic two-burner gas stoves placed on SS workbenches. Kerosene (known variously as kerosene oil, kero or oil) burners are the commonest form of cooking stoves and are generally used in all field stations. For this purpose a quantity of fuel – oil, steam coal, firewood or gas is an entitlement and forms a part of the individual's daily ration and is prominently listed in the SRS. There are situations where a specific form of fuel is more suitable and depending on the unit strength and its location, fuel of that type is provided. Other modern conveniences – electrical, electronic or mechanical gadgets are provided in the base kitchens, although these are not entitlements for a mess kitchen or a *langar* cook house nor are the much needed set of knives and therefore not of Government issue. The units purchase them out of their own funds, therefore grinders, mixers, choppers or food processors, different knives, microwave oven, convection hot oven, grills, outdoor gas heated '*tandoor*' oven etc. are found only in some Service kitchens.

Stationary kitchens: A static field cook house may be housed in a permanent structure at the base, in a semi permanent lean to under tarpaulins or in a partly subterranean construction as seen in Fig. 12.38.

Fig. 12.38: Replica of a subterranean field cook house, built for demonstration (ASC Centre, Bangalore).

The trainee cooks in the ASC's Catering establishment get a hang of such a work place from the demonstration cook house below ground. It has a sturdy roof, cooking platforms and adequate space for 2–3 people to work in. An assortment of cooking utensils of varying size and meant for different purposes, storage boxes made of cane works, oil burner in its own metal carry trunk, pressure cooker, milk can, frying woks and some ladles and spoons are issued in specific numbers for groups of men.

The Junior Commissioned Officers (JCOs) numbering 4–6 and attached to a unit have their own kitchens in field areas. For men in larger groups of 50 and 150, the scales of issue are naturally higher.

Each '*men set*' or MS items included are shown in Fig. 12.39, Fig. 12.40 and Fig. 12.41. The list of items is actually quite modest as can be seen from the description given below:

For one 150 MS (men set) the following items are issued:

'*degchis*' – large wide mouthed flat bottomed vessels, 4 large,
2 medium and
2 a little smaller, all with lids,
'*Parat*'– 2 small, one large, one medium,
karahi (deep frying wok) 1,
Pressure cooker 1 each of 22 L and 6 L capacity,
Kettle camp – 1
20L milk container 1
Tawa 1,
'*jharna*' 1
'*Katora*' 1
Tea kettle 1

Fig. 12.39: The array of kitchen utensils, a meat box or trunk (on the floor), and a kerosene tank (on the table) in the 150 men set.

Fig. 12.40: The cooking vessels in a men set: cooking stove, big wok or karahi, vessels of different sizes, flat saucepans, iron griddle (tawa), milk cans.

Fig. 12.41: Among the larger containers is the kettle, camp (foreground) with a lid which is an all purpose container to make tea, soups and dals. The oil cooker is large enough to take big vessels. Tea is served out of smaller kettles seen at the back.

There are a few odd spoons; ladles are perforated for frying and of the folding kind, and one oil cooker. For lighting purposes, there is one hurricane lamp. There are a few other helpful kitchen aids to grind spices (a flat stone mortar and pestle), a knife. For 150 men, these items are not really large considering that the cooks are expected to prepare the morning cups of tea to the night's dinner with just this number of utensils, in addition to preparing meal packets for short range patrols. The cook really has only one or at the most two individuals to help and no kitchen aids beyond the rudimentary. The meals comprise morning tea, breakfast, a tea break at mid morning (with snacks like *pakora* etc.), lunch, an afternoon tea, perhaps with snacks and then dinner. Numerous *chapatis* have to be rolled and baked and stacked, vegetables to peel and dice, spices to be ground on the old fashioned grinding stone and dal and rice to be cooked (which at higher altitudes do not cook well or quickly).

The cook has at his disposal an entire day's rations for the men, depending on that particular day's strength. As mentioned, units draw ration stocks for a month at a time and then send the appropriate quantities to the various companies where they are stored. A *langar* commander of the rank of an NCO is authorised to collect the rations from the stores and send it along to the cookhouse.

In field areas, the same cook house equipment is packed up during troop movement and taken along. For this purpose a woven cane basket covered on the outside with metal sheeting is provided. Succinctly put by a senior officer of the ASC during our interaction, the entire '*cook house scene is rustic'*. Only aluminum vessels are provided; their thin flat bottoms cause the inside of the vessel and the food to burn and char and blacken on the outside. The blackened pots and pans are difficult to scrub and clean. Such blackened vessels should not be used. But since stainless steel is heavy to cart, an alternative is called for.

Modernisation with mechanisation

Kitchen appliances: Understaffed and overworked, the cookhouse activities require a great amount of effort and time at every meal. These include (a) cleaning and chopping vegetables (b) grinding spices to prepare different mixes; (c) kneading atta (wheat flour) and rolling and cooking countless *chapatis* or *puris* and (d) cleaning up the used vessels, not forgetting that the food service is also undertaken by the cooks. Even when canned vegetables are used, the rest of the work described above continues. The single most arduous aspect of cooking and serving in any mess – officers or men's seems to be turning out hot '*chapatis*' or '*phulkas*' (puffed roties) at the rate of at least four per head. Clearly modernisation of cook houses in all the above aspects and in many more ways is called for.

It was given to understand that the process of modernisation has begun; after introducing gas and combination of gas and electricity for cooking in certain locations, a '*chapati*' making machine was designed and developed at the behest of ASC by food engineers in the Defence Food Research Laboratory, Mysore.

Chapati machine: The assembly line concept of *chapati* making incorporates a dough kneader run on electricity, from where the dough passes steadily into a device to make dough balls of the specified size; the balls are then fed into a presser or roller device where the balls emerge as flattened *chapatis*; from here they move forward on to a heating device, a flat metal plate heated by gas. The *chapatis* travel in slow motion, get heated on one side and are turned upside down and then puff on the second side. Depending on the dough capacity of the machine, any number of *chapattis* can be produced effortlessly by this process of mechanisation. It is said to be small enough to be portable and transportable in a vehicle, and can be operated on gas. However, its installation is limited to peace stations at present.

Gadgets only for some: It would indeed be another step towards modernisation if a kitchen appliance like a mixie/grinder for grinding the '*masala*' pastes were also to be provided to every field cook house, big or small. Right now, the peace station cookhouses manage to get some such appliances including *idli/dosa* dough grinders by courtesy of the unit's own efforts and funds. Since electricity in the field camps could be a limiting factor, the units which move with generators for lighting and communication purposes should be able to lend a little 'electricity time' to the cook house. But what is emphasised again and again during discussions is that food is not a priority when there is a war on and anything goes.

Spice of soldiers life: Most recipes from regional cuisine, and especially from the North, Northwest and East require hefty masses of wet ground spice mixes, sliced onions and freshly made ginger garlic paste. No compromise in this regard will satisfy the men. Using prepared powdered spices is one answer to this dilemma, but the units themselves (read cooks) are said to be emphatic in not wanting to use prepared ground spices in powdered form or even in paste form. The cooks and their clients feel strongly that flavours are lost and become stale on storage, that these powders could be adulterated, that the prepared spices are more expensive, that their cost allowance per ration will fetch them much smaller quantities than what are really needed for strong/adequate spicing and certainly far less than what may be procured if the units chose to buy spices of whatever type they needed within the allowance of 16g/man/day. There is a clamorous call to increase this allowance (justified perhaps) but there is none to ease a cook's life and make his work simpler by giving him a more modern spice grinding device than the grinding stone (Fig. 12.42)! It is an ancient form of grinding but was in use all over India and still is in the Northern parts.

Fig. 12.42: Grinding stone used in India from time immemorial. It is what is still the standard way to make spice and condiment pastes.

No cleaning and dicing aids: Cleaning and dicing of vegetables or chopping up meat is another task that is tedious and time consuming. Also, a large amount of water is necessary.

Some form of mechanical cutting appliances suitable for most vegetables would come in very handy. Potato peelers may already be in use in some big messes. But if the reality is to be faced and practical aspects viewed dispassionately, one could come to believe and accept that the cooks will not properly clean or wash nor peel and scrape. Everything is chopped as fast as possible by hand and fed into the cooking pot, sometimes with peels and all. Such is the way of things.

Providing selected, cleaned, peeled, precut vegetables is one way of addressing this issue. But considering the limitation on space for storage and work facilities and time to work in galleys and the nature of work in submarines, using precut vegetables and fruits in naval units is a clear option – as well as many other processed items.

Automatic dish washers: Cooks' assistant, called a '*masalchi*' (literally meaning the one who grinds the spices) is the dish washer. Considering the huge size of the vessels – *degchi, parat, karchi*, in the 150 MS or the slightly smaller variety for the 50 MS, no dishwasher presently available will be right, not that there is any provision for one on the cards.

As for eating utensils and spoons and tumblers/mugs/drinking canteens, the men keep their kit with them, bring them along at meal times and wash them off after a meal. The officers eat off china ware and use cutlery and glassware. Cleaning up after a meal for the officers is done by the mess serving staff and cookhouse staff. Atleast here, a dishwasher/sanitiser system to clean the large number of used eating ware could be thought of.

Refrigeration: Refrigerated storage systems exist in the galleys of larger units and in ships and submarines but no cool boxes are authorised for the kitchens in Army units to keep foods requiring chilled storage. Fresh supplies like milk are taken in daily; fresh meat is provided twice or thrice a week for which there are non-refrigerated meat boxes (metal trunks). Each unit collects its quota of fresh meat in these meat boxes. This is a relic from British times.

Therefore, fresh items are used up the same day. There are times during summer particularly, when the absence of a cool box is felt intensely. It is usual to prepare '*dahi*' (yoghurt) for lunch or *dahi* based preparations. Without refrigeration, '*dahi*', by its very nature, sours rapidly. The meat that is issued must be cooked immediately. Meat spoilage is a major concern in ambient temperatures and a cool box to keep the meat would have made great sense. Officers' mess may have refrigerators, ships and subs do have cold stores and deep freeze facilities, large and small ones respectively, but for men's kitchens in the units – in peace stations or field areas, no cool box is authorised. Under special dispensation, during troop movement by rail or during road works, a certain quantity of ice is an authorized ration item and one or two ice boxes per rail compartment are permitted for men and officers. In the deserts on our western border where the day temperatures can be scorching and thirsty, informed sources say that chilled '*lassi*' from the dairy and ice are delivered to the troops every day. And since there is no cool box for the jawans and border patrols, they bury the ice in the sand to make it last for a few more hours.

Mobile Kitchens

There exists a mobile kitchen on wheels where a two-ton truck has been modified internally to be fitted out as a kitchen, complete with separate storage racks for meat and vegetables and for vessels, a table top oil burner for cooking and a small sink at the end of the work bench. Neatly installed above this is a steam generator unit with its own water tank. The steam thus generated travels through a short pipe connected to steam kettles-double jacketed large cylindrical drums heated by steam in which rice, dal, vegetables etc. can be cooked for large numbers. There is limited storage space, but adequate for the essentials of cooking paraphernalia and there is adequate space for two people to work in. A retractable ladder at the open end provides access when the vehicle is stationary and is withdrawn when the vehicle is on the move (Fig. 12.43, Fig. 12.44 and Fig. 12.45).

But this is as far as it goes. This kitchen on wheels is a prototype, and we are informed that it goes along with convoys when the training battalion is deployed in the outskirts of Bangalore on exercise or on other training duties.

Prototype of a Mobile Kitchen

Years ago, the R & D engineers, (Ahmednagar) had also designed a prototype of 'kitchen on wheels', but it appears that this mobile kitchen never went further than the prototype. All we did see were photographs in one of the R & D meetings chaired by the QMG when a concept to design a kitchen for field feeding was proposed by food scientists (author included). All this is now relegated to the annals of the forgotten. The concept of such a mobile facility is attractive at least for introducing a few numbers in selected locations and units on a trial basis. There may be some unsurmountable administrative hurdles of which we know nothing. Then again, as with all or most matters concerning improvement in food service, there is an element of reserved approach particularly where it is not a matter of life and death.

Fig. 12.43: Kitchen on wheels – It is a two-ton truck fitted compactly with a water tank, waterline, electric steam generator, boilers, storage racks, counter space, wash up sink, and a stand up stove. The doors open at the back and the stairs are let down.

Fig. 12.44: Inside of the mobile kitchen are installed 100 L capacity cooker/steamers for meat, vegetables and dal/rice fitted on the left of the space. Steam is supplied from a small electrically operated steam generator.

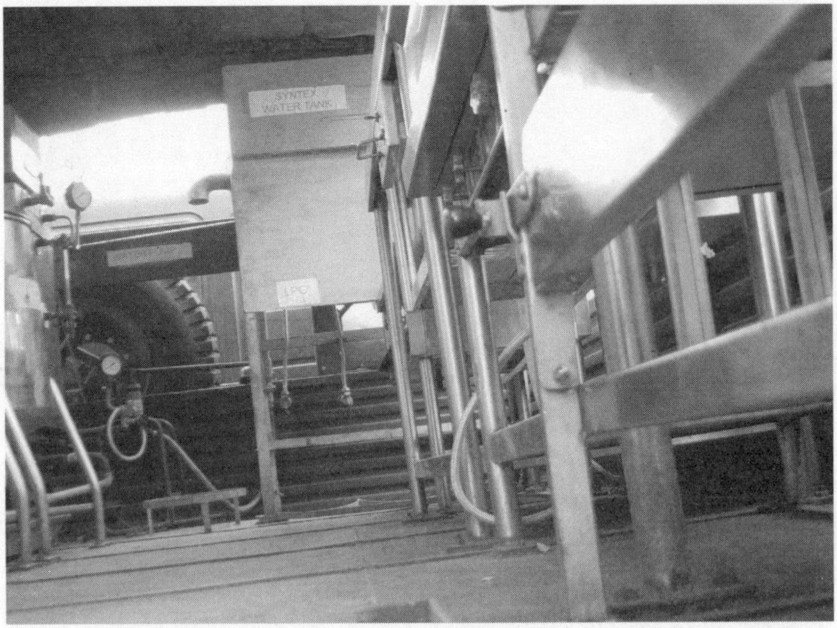

Fig. 12.45 : Inside of the mobile kitchen there is a water storage tank (facing), pipelines that feed into steam generator and working counter on the right.

However, every unit has the 'B' echelon to take care of food and service which is mobile and which will move with the main body of the unit or may be behind or ahead of the main column. Still a mobile kitchen tagged to the 'B' echelon would make it unnecessary to dig up ground to set up a cook house and avoid delays, time and effort spent on it to facilitate the undertaking of immediate cooking operations. While on the move, it is possible to work at non hazardous and manual kitchen tasks like peeling, cutting, grinding, kneading and keep things ready to start cooking the instant a halt is called.

In course of time it is hoped, that the advantages of using mobile kitchens for combat field feeding purposes and during troop movements will outweigh many traditional reservations which might still be harboured on modernisation of this nature.

Food Preparation and Service

Once the daily rations are in the hands of the cooks, preparations begin in the kitchens. The big bases and units have modern facilities while the smaller field units must manage with in field cook houses without gadgets. The meal plans are laid out in advance. The shore establishments and ships galleys are equipped with the standard set of cooking vessels, pots, kettles, cookers, pans etc. designated by men set as mentioned earlier.

Menus and meals: Earlier on, a rationale was given for determining Service Ration Scales based on the inclusion of a large number of dry rations, fresh foods and condiments. It was said that any number of dishes could be turned out to suit every regional and ethnic taste by the clever use of various foodstuffs and condiments, spices and sugar. Except when the field operational conditions are compelling enough to preclude cooking fresh foods, at all other times providing fresh hot meals which are appetizing, satisfying and morale boosting – to officers and men in all the three Services is a very important, if not the primary aim of food service as part of the food logistics in the Armed Forces. Not for the personnel of Indian Armed Forces will the processed meats, pastas, breads, sandwiches or chocolate would suffice. The standard Indian fare is preferred and that is what is turned out day in and day out except on special occasions though officers get a far greater variety (like Chinese, continental, Italian specialties) than the men in general.

Our staple food is *atta* and rice; there are substantial quantities of meat and vegetables, and dals, spices, condiments, milk and fruit etc. all of which are necessary to turn out dishes made in myriad different ways to produce a most awesome range of aromatic, fragrant foods. The Service cooks, chefs and master chefs are trained superbly to turn out multiple cuisine specialties, from the simplest field cooking to the best party fare equal to that obtained in any 5-star menus. The possibility of producing a variety of breakfast, lunch or dinner selections is illustrated amply from the menus planned on a weekly basis in a Navy mess. For the men of Other Ranks there is simple but wholesome and sumptuous food of the kind that is preferred by them as shown in Table 12.1.

And menus for the officers (Table 12.2) are a study in contrast.

Table 12.1: A typical menu for sailors

Breakfast	Bread, butter, jam, eggs, fresh sprouts or dal-fry, nutramul and variations from North Indian and South Indian cuisine (idli or dosa or puri or parantha or uttappam, upma and tea).
Lunch	Chicken/mutton/fish/egg, rice, vegetable curry, dal, a dessert or a fruit.
Dinner	Variations of lunch with bread or chapatti, dessert or a fruit.
Tuesday	Meatless day but everything else is included
Friday	Fish and of course everything else as usual

Table 12.2: Officers Meals in a Navy establishment (an old menu from INS India)

Breakfast Selections	
1. Masala poories, Aloo chole masala, cheese cube*	coffee
2. Bread, butter, jam, dal mix masala, nutramul**	coffee
3. Bread, masala Upma, dal masala, cheese cube	coffee
4. Uttapam, sambhar, chutney, cheese cube	coffee
5. Bread, butter, jam, dal masoor masala, cheese cube	coffee
6. Bhatura Punjabi, chole masala, cheese cube, achar	coffee
7. Bread, butter, jam, egg fry, potato chops, nutramul and cheese	coffee
Lunch Selections	Dessert/Coffee
1. Jeera rice, chicken curry, vegetable peas masala, Sindhi curry Curds potato chops	Shahi Tukda
2. Brista rice, Aloo palak, paneer masala, vegetable cheese masala, Dal masoor masala, Dahi piyaza, pickle	Jalebi
3. Mutton biryani, veg. Biryani Dahi Raita, Papad with coconut.	Gulab jamun
4. Brista rice, vegetable Kashmiri, shahi peas, palak paneer Dahi vada, dal arhar mix masala, papad.	Shahi kheer
5. Yellow rice, fish mustard curry, fish masala fry, veg. Masala, Palak peas masala, Potato bonda, Sambhar, curd, mixed pickle.	–
6. Cardamom rice, eggs fry masala, vegetable mix chilli fry, Veg. cutlet, Dal masoor masala, curd	Fruit Custard
7. Onion rice, chicken red masala, veg. Nawabi Vegetable-paneer cutlet, curd pakora curry.	Semiya payasam

Afternoon/Tea/snacks	
1. Onion pakora	Tea
2. Onion pakora	Tea
3. Fruit cake	Tea
4. Fruit cake	Tea
5. Namak para	Tea
6. Namak para	Tea
7. Namak para	Tea

Dinner Selections	
1. Butter Tandoori Roti/rice, eggs masala, Veg. Mix masala, Vegetable cutlet, Dal tadka,	Fresh fruit, coffee
2. Paratha/fried rice, vegetable kashmiri, chole mix masala, Dal fry masala, salad	Coffee
3. Bread/rice, vegetable sukha masala, dal mix masala	Fruit cake, coffee.
4. Tandoori roti/rice, chicken nawabi, cheese vegetable mix masala, Vegetable chops, dal masala	Coffee
5. Bread/Fruit pulav, vegetable palak paneer masala, Vegetable chops in masala, dal makhni	Fresh fruit, coffee.
6. Ghee Tandoori roti/rice, mutton do-piazza, vegetable do-piyaza, querket in gravy dal-chatpat masala	Coffee
7. Gujarat poories/rice, Aloo palak masala, eggs fry masala, vegetable chops dal masala	Tiranga kheer coffee

* and ** only for vegetarians

Variations to such menus are introduced from one week to another. There could be *palak puris, Ajwain puris, idlis, Punjabi halwa,* potato or mixed vegetable grilled chops, germinated dal (sprouts), boiled eggs, or grilled onion–tomato to replace one or the other or more items from previous week's breakfast menus. It should be noted that almost every menu has atleast one masala item (more spicy than normal) although all preparations require many spices.

Mutton or vegetable vindaloo, Ceylon curry, Madras curry, Bombay curry, Delhi curry, chicken Arabian, Asian Fried rice, sweet and sour sauce, chilli in vinegar, chicken kashmiri, mutton kheema, *urad* dal, egg, vegetable Croquet in gravy, vegetable Fugat, cutlet, vegetable Sakuti, mutton masala, are some of the more uncommon, regional cuisine or dishes.

Traditional milk based desserts and sweetmeats i.e., with fruit cakes, fruit custards, puddings and fresh fruit. After dinner, coffee seems to be an officer's prerogative, not for all other ranks, even as tea is invariably served at the traditional 'afternoon tea' time. They are provided with a more simple but substantiated fare common to middle class India. Also, coffee is not an item of issue for the sailors.

The meals prepared for the ORs in the army garrison kitchens are not as fancy as those meant for the officers, the food preferences of the former being more rustic and regional. The taste for the exotic and Western/Asian foods is much relished, and accepted, the appreciation of which was acquired by the officers in course of their preliminary officer training and military service. But that by no means is an indication that the men eat any less well than their officers.

Food on board ships and submarines: As per INBR NI/2/98, sailors are authorised fuel rations as cooking gas at 150 g per day per man in family accommodation; bachelor officers are entitled to 95 g per day in the ship's ward room. Food rations are standard items – dry, fresh, tinned, rice/*atta*/*maida* or biscuit, dal, oil, fruits, vegetables, potatoes, onions, eggs, mutton, milk, other processed items, sugar and spices.

Rations are issued at the time of sailing out in quantities sufficient for the period of sail. Most ships and submarines carry their own provisions for one month and an additional quantity for twenty five more days and take in more from other ships as needed. Submarines, by the nature of internal arrangements, limited galley, small storage space, basic minimal kitchen facilities and the nature of crew duties, receive more ready to cook/use items such as fruits in cut form, boneless meat or fish, ham or sausages and several instantised food products.

In the matter of provisioning/supplies, submarines are a priority, next in the order follows the ship's Field or the Aviation Crew. The submarines also are equipped with cold storage in the form of refrigerator and deep freeze.

Ships carry critical kitchen equipment, eating plates (own) and water for 60–70 men (Officers and ORs). During halts, stocks are replenished from stocking ports. Even when ships sail to foreign ports, sufficient tinned and dry rations are stocked for a period, and in addition another 25 days of stock is held. At foreign ports of call fresh fruits/vegetables may be purchased but this is rare and then only when the ships are away for 5–6 months. It is remarkable how self sufficient the modern ships can be and how well prepared with dry ration stocks the vessels are, not just to cover the period of sail but also to cover any eventuality or delays for a further unspecified period.

When a submarine calls at a foreign port, it is always attached with a Navy ship. The crew then eats in the ship. Feeding arrangements when two or more ships go together or when the fleet sails on exercises are not known.

Management and supervision of the galley: The meals are sumptuous in shore messes and ships as seen from menus presented. Meal planning is a weekly affair when breakfast, lunch and dinner menus are decided for each day. Thereafter, the day-to-day management is the responsibility of an Officer Of the Day, OOD, who not only supervises the hygiene and cleanliness aspects of cooking but also sees to it that food samples are taken from every meal until, in the words of an officer 'the food consumed is digested'. This is to ensure that should an untoward reaction occur in any one, and if food could be one of the reasons, samples are available for inspection and examination. This is indeed an admirable mechanism of food safety monitoring and assurance. To be able to identify any offending item or food prepared with certain ingredients would facilitate its isolation and deletion from menus or if required its destruction.

To feed so many people on a daily basis for long sailing periods calls for extremely elaborate and precise logistics planning and execution. Until the cooking methods and the cooks themselves imbibe and accept without reservation and prejudice elements of considerable modernisation beyond the modern kitchen gadgets, our kitchens are going to look like a minor war zone albeit with a wonderful chaos. The efficient cooks and their able assistants are multi-taskers and know exactly when to start cooking and when to begin the next chore like making chapattis (there is a machine to roll them out continuously, but baking is done manually) for the night meal on 'chapati day', when to take the kettle off the hob, when to go get the meat out of the freezer and begin marinating, when to stop it or to know when the 'dahi' has set. This kind of work is part of their training, which combined with the instinctive aptitude for the art and craft of cooking some of them possess more than the others, makes for superb cooks and great chefs capable of producing super special banquet fare in the same confines of a ship's galley.

Cooking in a Submarine galley: Everything required on a regular basis is kept jam packed in the tiny overhead storage cabinets (Fig. 12.46). There are larger storage areas for rations elsewhere. In the cramped galley space a pressure cooker standing on the floor and probably used for boiling rice is the main gadget (Fig. 12.47). This pressure cooker is used for a variety of cooking and frying is done in a small vessel (from the standard men set) as shown in Fig. 12.48.

The galley is located just around the CIC (Central Information Command) and a steady supply of coffee, tea or juice flows. Just rice and some vegetables can be boiled (in pressure cooker), eggs are cooked in a small vessel and tea or coffee can be made. Officers and sailors subsist on MRE rations. For a strength of about 40 people, dry and tinned rations, sugar, pulses and fruit juices are always stocked for 45 days at a time. Bread, eggs and most vegetables spoil faster than other items even in the cool rooms. When they are sailing for more than 15 days, only certain specific vegetables that can stay green and last the duration of the sail are used in these vessels. Other than the more durable root vegetables, only cabbage has been found to outlast any other 'green' vegetable. There are no deep fryers but frying can be done in a deep aluminum vessel. Frying is a rare event on board the submarine particularly when sailing, though *puris* and *pakoras* are favourites. It requires great ingenuity on the part of the cook to work and produce meal after meal in a submarine galley.

Frying events' are rare in the confined space primarily because it generates a lot of smoke and odours and is therefore resorted to only during periods of *shorting* which means coming up for fresh air for the purpose of battery recharging; shorting is done only late at night. Carbon dioxide build up in the close confines of a submarine is very closely monitored; its levels are kept well below

Fig. 12.46: Everything required on a regular basis is kept jam packed in the tiny overhead storage cabinets. There are larger storage areas for rations elsewhere.

Fig. 12.47: In the cramped galley space, a pressure cooker standing on the floor The multipurpose vessels (aluminum) are part of the standard issue men set.

Fig. 12.48: Galley space can barely accommodate two persons. The submarine galley crew specially set out to fry Alu Bondas in a small aluminum vessel for the officers and author during a mid morning tea break. The menu was the same that day in the ships and the submarines. A small tea kettle is on the boil at the back of the stove.

1 per cent and there are soda lime cartridges to absorb the gases. In a welcoming and hospitable gesture the officers had gone to a lot of trouble to arrange a special demonstration of frying in the tiny galley even though it is a rare event. The multipurpose vessels (aluminum) are part of the standard issue men set.

Submarine fare is dependent on processed foods to a large extent. Bulk packed dry mixes are helpful as are the packaged ready to warm *chapatis*, curries and other such preparations. There are numerous single portion packages (Fig. 12.49 and Fig. 12.50) to be opened for every meal for a complement of 40 men. Not many foods come in large portion packages. There is also a selection of survival foods on board the submarines (Fig. 12.51) which are taken from the Base Victualing Yard.

Despite the hardship, cramped space, and long hours when sailing, the officers are a cheerful lot and quite forthcoming when they learned the purpose of the author's visit and were very helpful (Fig. 12.52 and Fig. 12.53). Their only method of relaxing is to spend some time at the exercise centre to stretch the cramped muscles and to get in the daily physical work out in the confined space.

The officer's ward room is very cramped. They work and eat here as shown in Fig. 12.52. The young and highly trained officers in a submarine lead a very strenuous life and yet remain cheerful.

Water: Potable water in ships and submarines comes from municipal sources at the harbour jetty. The water storage capacity of a ship varies from about 300 tonnes in a destroyer to a much bigger one in an aircraft carrier with three times the personnel strength. There are de-salination plants in every vessel but the water thus produced is used for purposes other than for cooking and drinking.

Meals and meal timings: The Navy personnel eat bread for breakfast and for dinner. It is the one service where even the sailors get bread, essentially because *chapatis* are not made everyday. *Chapati* making is tedious and time consuming; each guy will eat no less than 3–4 *chapatis* and to make

Fig. 12.49: Processed food packs are popular in the Navy and a necessity in the submarines.

Fig. 12.50: There are certain dehydrated or ready to eat foods which are more popular than others and are kept in stock for submarines and for emergency and other essential purposes.

Fig. 12.51: Emergency/survival food packs are kept in readiness at the BVO to be issued as necessary. The picture shows Chikki slabs, mango bar, dry puffed Bengal gram, bottled water, cup of noodles and such items for submarine use.

Fig. 12.52: Officers' ward room in the submarine. The table space is only a little bigger than the small folding top provided in a AC railway coach.

Fig. 12.53: The cheerful faces of the young and highly trained and skilled officers in the submarine belie the fact that they lead very strenuous life on board.

some 1,200 to 1,600 *chapatis* (400 men) at every meal on a daily basis is not a small matter and for the same reason, no *chapatis* are served for lunch. Only rice and rice based preparations, together with meat/fish/vegetable curries and dals appear for lunch. *Chapati* making for the evening dinner begins at noon time and the finished *chapatis* are stacked, covered with a cloth and kept in a vessel till dinner time. *Chapatis* are provided four times a week during sailing to keep up the men's spirit and morale. This frequency may differ from ship to ship. Tuesdays are 'vegetarian' days. Fish is prepared only on Friday. This is so all across the Indian Navy. It seems to have happened because fresh fish is supplied only once a week on Fridays and it is best eaten fresh. Hence, there are fish curry and fish cutlets in the same meal in every ship and unit across the country for Friday lunch. Meats are cooked by afternoon for the night meal. Breakfast is bread; butter and jam and eggs or dal fry and tea. Lunch is rice, dal/*sambar*, vegetable and meat/chicken/fish preparation or variations with these ingredients and is ready by 11.30 am (those who have to report for watch duties beginning noon must eat). Dinner is served and eaten at 6.30 pm.

The cooks dish out the food from the same large vessels in which it was cooked and serve the sailors and other ranks across a service hatch opening into their dining hall; the men bring their own plate, spoon and mug. This hall is also the only place where they can assemble, relax and watch TV (Fig. 12.54).

The ships' stewards carry the food in serving bowls to the service pantry and serve the officers in style at the table in the ward room. The ship's ward room is a place for a sit down meal. There is a bar attached to it and a lounge for rest and relaxation. A ward room-lounge cum bar and dinning hall is meant for the officers only.

Fig. 12.54: Dining cum recreation hall for ORs in a ship. The food is served by the cooks through a wall hatch between the kitchen and the hall.

On the other hand, the submarine's ward room is a space that can barely accommodate a small table with benches on either side and is meant for the officers for dining and meeting. Again, due to the nature of duties and their work environment, there is little if any in the nature of sit down meals with the style of table settings and food service the Navy is accustomed to observe specially by its officers.

The men carry their food and eat anywhere they can temporarily park themselves in the submarine, generally in their bunking area.

There is no provision for the ships to buy stores directly in either Indian or foreign ports of call. If there should be a need for replenishment of any food, the naval unit at the port of call (within Indian waters) and the Indian Consulate (nearest to the foreign port) are advised before hand of the ship's requirements. Arranging for supplies is their responsibility and not of the ships.

Garbage disposal is eco-friendly to an extent. Kitchen and food wastes are pulverised in a garburator; used cans and food packs are collected in the bilges in the bowels of the ship and then thrown over board from the ships. But in the submarine there are two particular devices – one to compress and crush empty tin cans and another to compress a stack of empty plastic – polymer packages. These are stored in the allotted space till the submarine returns to its base and disposes of it in the harbour facility. Only human waste is treated in the sewage treatment facility as per maritime requirements and discharged into the sea.

Food service in ships and submarines continues on return to harbour. Ships returning from a sailing expedition will still have people who are posted there and who remain on board. Food is cooked for them. During peace time, people posted in family stations must go home for meals at the end of the working day on the ships. During sailing, every one eats on board. If the ship is in dry docks for repair and maintenance work, then the people are lodged and boarded in shore accommodations where they return to at the end of the working day. Their lunch is brought from the shore messes and served on board as the case may be. There is no cooking in such ships.

In the submarines in harbour, sailors do not remain on the vessel. They go to their shore accommodation and for meals. If they are sailing for short periods, cooking is done on board. When the submarine touches different naval ports, shore accommodation is provided for all as well as messing. As mentioned before, MRE rations are used only when they have been sailing for more than 15 days, after much of the fresh rations are gone, because the cold room capacity in a submarine is quite small.

Life in a submarine is hard and therefore, there is an additional allowance called hardship allowance of Rs. 7000/- per officer.

Coast guard: The Coast Guard follows the Navy's rules and regulations and is given the privileges of the services but is a civilian body of men and ships guarding and patrolling the coastal waters. The coast guard rations are similar to those in the Navy.

There are no more than 200 men in a large ship and generally much less. Their ships are also smaller. Their rations, supplies etc. follow the navy pattern and the navy deputes cooks to serve aboard the Coast guard ships.

Ships on Missions

INS *Tarangini* is one of the three training ships based in Cochin. The other ships are INS *Tir* and INS *Krishna,* which together form the first training squadron for cadets. '*Tarangini*' has undertaken round the world sailing trips from Cochin, with a complement of 12 officers, 25 cadets and sailors all together numbering 60 in the year 2001. The ship was outfitted with normal rations to last a while but mostly there were submarine type rations to last the duration of the sail. The provisioning and supplies were done by the Logistics officer and the BVO Cochin. The fresh rations as per the ration scale are provided in the pre-cut form and made up into convenient packets meant for each day and stored in the ships' cold rooms.

On missions: To unexpectedly have to rescue untold numbers of people from war zones, as happened in Beirut, Lebanon in 2006, the naval ships which happen to be in the vicinity find themselves not only engaged in actual rescue operations but also having to look after the welfare of the evacuees on board till they are conveyed to the selected destination. INS *Mumbai* had to provide for more than 2,000 people, with shelter, medical help, food and drink and resting place. The ships sailing out of harbour therefore carry quite large quantities of extra rations of all sorts for just such emergencies. Naval ships also rescued people from pirated merchant ships in Somali waters during 2008. Increasingly, Navy ships are having to rescue commercial ships and crew from hostage situations from pirate attacks in Somali waters.

Periodically, our forces participate in field, flying or naval exercises with the forces of other countries, for periods varying from one week to two months or more. There had been one naval exercise concluded in November 2006 and another in 2007. Described by the media as taking Naval diplomacy to a new height, the Indian Navy participated in a two-month exercise with the Navies of USA, Russia, China, Japan, Singapore, Philippines, Vietnam and New Zealand at different points of time and space (*Deccan Herald*, March 30, 2007, p.13). Four Indian battleships – the guided missile destroyers INS *Mysore*, INS *Rana,* one tanker (INS *Jyoti*) and a crew of 1,800 members sailing from Port Blair participated from March 24 in Naval war games with the US Pacific Command fleet, and Japan's Maritime Self Defence Force, off the Japanese island of Okinawa.

The naval cooks would be in readiness to produce not only every meal for the crew, but also the banquet style foods and table decorations, should there be such entertainments on board the ships, to entice the palates of the international visitors. That would mean stocking up not only their normal everyday rations items but many occidental, oriental and exotic foods and ingredients. It would also have meant carrying a great many packs of special rations, MRE rations and emergency rations which might be given in goodwill gestures to the foreign navies or at foreign ports, or which might be used by the battleship crews during certain war games when silence is called for or during action stations when the cooks also have to shutdown their kitchens quickly.

The ships usually carry dry rations for three months as a matter of routine when they sail in foreign waters where the exercises are taking place and if required there are ports like Singapore to take in fresh stores.

It is also a part of operational turn out to have one fuel tanker accompany the fleet of ships. One depot ship from the Indian Navy also sailed along with INS *Rana* and INS *Ranjit* in a six hour exercise with the Japanese Maritime Self Defence forces. There were receptions hosted for the visiting ships by the Chinese Navy. There would be reciprocal hospitality (*The Hindu*, 17 April, 2007), and knowing how our navy's supply readiness is organized, there would certainly have been banquets.

Landing parties: In an actual patrol of the territorial waters, if the war games and exercises include events of landing and simulated attack from a craft while approaching a shore or if it is required to go ashore for peace reasons or during an actual situation calling for a detachment of the fighting force to go ashore, 'landing parties' are sent to land and investigate, or attack from their landing craft. The landing parties are equipped, along with other essentials with one meal and one liter container (of galvanized iron covered with cork) full of water. These meals are of the 'ready to eat on-the-go' kind. The landing parties also carry jungle survival rations for any eventualities.

References

Corbishley, Gill. *Ration Book Recipes: Some Food Facts 1939–1954*. English Heritage, 1990.

Crew, Graeme. *The Royal Army Service Corps*. Leo Cooper Ltd., London, 1970.

Gaylor, John. *Sons of John Company – The Indian and Pakistan Armies 1903–1991*. Spellmount Ltd, Turnbridge Wells, Kent, 1992, pp. 248–252.

Guide and Instructions for Patrol Service Cooks. Issued under the authority of the Flag Officer, East Africa, December, 1943.

Kulkarni, P.D. VSM (Col) Chief Editor. 'Foot Prints and Milestones: A Story of the Army Service Corps'. By P.K.D. Kapoor, VSM, (Maj Gen) late., Directorate General of Supplies &Transport, Army Head Quarters, New Delhi, 2000, pp. 11–20, 60–79, 105–157, 260.

Lynn, John. *Feeding Mars–Logistics in Western Military*. Houghton Mifflin Co., 1993, (Readers companion, feeding armed Forces/Military logistics 100–web pages).

National Institutes of Health. 1959. 'A Nutrition Survey of the Armed Forces of Pakistan'. *The J. Nutr*. 68 (May–Aug), Supplement. 2, A series of seven papers by 20 researchers, Interdepartmental Committee on Nutrition for National Defence, National Institutes of Health, Bethesda.

On Allowances of officers, 1883 – Original Home Department Branch–Public Consultation, 6 Dec, Document No. 9, 1883. National Archives, New Delhi.

QMG Correspondence, 20 volumes 1839–1859 in 'Guide to Military Officers'. National Archives, New Delhi.

Woodward, Peggy. *Rise of the Raj*. Midas Books, Speldhurst, Kent, 1978.

Personal discussions and visits

The Deputy Director General Operational Logistics, QMGBr, Army Head Quarters.

Col. A.N. Datta, Q1-B in the QMG Branch, Army Head Quarters.

Brigadier Dr. Handa, Commandant, ST-7, Lucknow Road, Delhi. 2005.

Major General B.S. Panwar, ADG RVS, at the Remount Veterinary Service Corps (RVS) Head Quarters.

Col. S. Rajpal, (RVS), RVS Head Quarters, New Delhi.

Col. Dr D.P. Attrey, RVS (Retd), Animal Nutrition specialist and former Director, FRL, Leh, Later in DIPAS, Delhi.

Base Victualing Officer–Commander H. Dhulya, Base Victualing Yard, Mumbai.

Col. P.D. Kulkarni, Commander Junior Wing, ASC Centre and College, South, Bangalore.

Visit to ASC Centre arranged per courtesy DGST, Army HQ, New Delhi and discussions with Col P.D. Kulkarni, Commandant, Junior Wing, ASC Centre South, Bangalore.

Visits to INS *Hamla*–Southern Command, INS *Mumbai* and INS *Shankul* and BVYard in Mumbai, Western Command courtesy Principal Director Clothing and Victualing, Integrated Head Quarters, Navy and Logistics Command, Mumbai.

Section – IV

Science and Technology Component

13

Indian Food Industry and Food Science and Technology Inputs for the Defence Forces

The Rich Land and the Traditions of the Past

From writings and snippets of information scattered far and wide, one gets a picture of India in the pre–Christian era and Medieval times as being a country blessed with skills, crafts, material goods and a variety of spices and foods. Megasthanese, the Greek visitor in Mauryan times (320 BC) (McCrindle, 1972, 1974), Huen Tsang (AD 640), Fa-Hiaen from China in the first millennium and in the eleventh century, Al-Baruni Khwarizmi (born in AD 973) of Persian origin who came from the court of Sultan Mahmood of Gazni (in AD 1030) and wrote *Enquiry into India* in Arabic, titled '*Tarikh'ul Hind*' (Ahmed, 1988), Marco Polo passed through India during his travels between AD 1271 and AD 1294 from Venice to China and back and recorded his observations in the *History of the World* (Yamashita, 2001a and 2001b), Babur scrupulously maintained his journal the *Babur Nama* (Hiro, 2006), all testify to the wealth of the land. Before the British came, the Imperial Mughal court patronised the skills and crafts of the artisans and their goods were considered luxury items. There were region specific goods and produce and special food items available on trade routes. Almonds, spices, raisins and other dry fruits and high-grade salt were much in demand. Food grains, ghee, cooking oils, sugar etc., moved on river transport routes. Hereditary traders traveled all over India trading in salt, sugar, oilseeds and oil etc. Hand winnowing and hand pounding of rice and other grains, the preparation and extraction methods such as *Kolhu* for sugarcane crushing, *ghani* for oil seed extraction, *dhenki* a foot operated grinding stone and *chakki* for flour making driven by the muscle power of animals and humans (Achaya, 1994), hand churning of butter as seen in twelfth century temple carvings of Somnathpur near Mysore – all had been in use for a very long time.

To increase the keeping quality of foods, the traditional methods were salting, pickling, drying, and preserving sour tasting fruit with sugar (*murabba*) and sun drying (fish, grapes, sugared mango pulp and other fruit, seasonal vegetables).

With the British came their administration and the loss of India's wealth, but brought machines and then industrialisation. But India in the eighteenth century under the East India Company had no particular recourse to improving the living standard of the general masses and England herself had insufficient food for all; its agricultural practices were not advanced and it was only on the brink of industrialisation. The sole purpose to conquer and rule India was to benefit the home country. Their own army was not treated any better; the officers who hailed from rich or noble families and who had bought commissions in the army had their personal fortunes and means to live well. Farmers and convicts, soldiers and sailors all led a wretched life in rural England around the period 1696–1795. There was little fairness or justice shown towards the commoners and they fared no better as soldiers or sailors. The novelist Colleen McCullough's portrayal in her book *Morgan's Run* of the convicts' life aboard the ships brings alive the misery and dreadful fate of anyone unfortunate enough to have been a convict under transportation to Australia, or a Royal trooper or a crewman accompanying them (McCullough, 2001). If Britain had no measures to look after herself, there was no chance that India under the Company would benefit in any way. In *The Story of Civilization,* Will and Ariel Durante (1965) said, speaking of the England of Voltaire, that between 1696 and 1795, an improvement in agricultural methods was brought about by Charles Townsend, who introduced crop rotation and Jethro Tull, who invented a new plough to tackle and bury weeds and also invented a horse drawn mechanical seed feeder for planting in rows. The authors emphasised that these changes, though seemingly trivial helped enormously to increase farm yields without which more workers in more towns could not have been fed; these also created a more expectant and demanding urban population and thus helped the Industrial Revolution.

Food Industry in British Colonial Times

In the British Raj, India remained agriculture based in the manner of pre-Industrial Revolution England, therefore there was insufficient food. Industrial development did not yet yield anything substantial. Some of her own indigenous industries were lost, such as salt making and textiles, food grains were exported to neighboring countries and tea and coffee worldwide, and all the cotton/yarn was surrendered to England.

From 1757 onwards, after the Battle of Plassey, the British established their administration in Calcutta up until the time of India's Independence in 1947; much of the food industry continued to be traditional using methods and procedures known to the people for handling the harvest and food. A few newer techniques were possibly incorporated and product diversification was resorted to for a niche market but with no significant unit producing processed foods for the general population. A look at the 'processed' products in the agro sector in the time of East India Company discussed by Achaya (1994) will explain the state of processing (Table 13.1). These were the traditional food industries before controls began to be exercised.

Table 13.1: Traditional food industries in India at the beginning of the British period, 1757

	Starting material	*Processing*	*Products*
1.	Rice, paddy	Hand picking, manual methods	Flaked, puffed rice, parboiled, etc.
2.	Wheat	Grinding in chakkis	Flour, semolina
3.	Oil seed Several types	Crushing in ghanis	Oil, seed cake
4.	Sugar cane	Crushing for juice, boiling, some used directly as chewing cane	Jaggery, khandsari
5.	Salt from lake/ seawater; rock salt	Solar evaporation, mining	Salt, rock salt
6.	Farm milk	Collection/sale by village milkman, door to door sale, Preparations at homes or in small holdings	Fresh milk, Dahi, butter, butter milk, Ghee, preparation of concentrates and sweets
7.	Fruits/vegetables	None Door to door sale and in village markets, home cookery	Vegetable preserves as pickles, fermented and sun dried *badi* (for frying), fruit pulp dried as bars
8.	Palm tree sap	Traditional tapping like rubber latex	Arrack and toddy, palm jaggery
9.	Fish	Fishing in coastal areas and sun drying Freshwater fish	Dried fish, other traditional ways of utilization

Starting material	Processing	Products
10. Meat	Very small scale/individual slaughter of game/meat animals Maybe some traditional sun drying, pickling	Fresh and sun dried, leather and leather goods as by products, offal, adipose and other byproducts used by poor people
11. Spices and condiments	Traditional processing, flourishing domestic and foreign trade	Whole spices used in foods and extracts made for medicinal preparations
12. Leafs	Hand stitched	Leaf plates
13. Miscellaneous	Sun drying	Fruits/vegetables, pappad, *badi*, etc.

Salt, sugar, cereal processing, mechanised milling, organised dairy and animal products manufacture came into existence for the benefit of the British. Achaya (1994) has explained these developments succinctly.

Salt making, which was known since the Indus Valley civilization (2500–1500 BC), was an established industry and thrived well in the Bengal, Bombay and Madras Presidencies. It was one of the first indigenously made products targeted by Robert Clive. It was brought under British control for two centuries, earning revenues for the Empire by levying enormous taxes on the people in the name of free enterprise. Salt came to occupy a politically important and symbolic place in the history of India's independence movement (recall the famous Dandi march by Mahatma Gandhi and the Salt Satyagraha in defiance of British law). The only modernisation of the open bed solar evaporation for salt purification was the washing of the concentrated solution and treatment with lime (calcium oxide) and soda ash (sodium carbonate) followed by filtration and evaporation in open vessels; output rose from around one lac tonnes in 1757 to more than 22 lac tonnes from about 122 units, even as the British administration believed in 1898 that salt had no future in India. Compare that with what is available today in terms of the variety, purity, quality, brands, and levels of iodine fortification of salt.

Sugar (*shakkar*) and *Gur* manufacture, rice processing by traditional techniques has also been known in India for a long time. *Muri* or puffed rice, flaked rice, and wheat products like flour, *suji* produced in *chakkis* were the source of shelf stable foods. Mechanisation came in the form of roller mills and by 1947 there were 116 roller flourmills.

Biscuits (and bread) of different types have been the staple of soldiers. Its manufacture in India, however, began with two enterprising Bengalis called Mandal and Gupta, who first produced a traditional recipe, calling it '*Desi*' biscuits, in a *tandoor* (traditional oven) in Calcutta in 1887. Soon they were making the western style biscuits under the name 'Hindu' biscuits. During World War I the demand for biscuits rose dramatically and one Charles Holmes undertook to produce and supply biscuits to the Army. In 1925, the Britannia Biscuit Company (its new name) took shape and a factory was established in Bombay with the participation of yet another person from England. The Britannia Biscuit Company's archival material, 1983 (Achaya, 1994), would certainly yield a wealth of information in this regard. During the war years, thirteen factories manufactured 35,000 tons of a biscuit type known as '*shakkarpara*' for the Army. The Army had its own bakeries, and as with other foods in demand during World War II, bread was also in great demand and a few moderately sized bakeries came up in 1947. No one who has not experienced the bread boom in India slowly unfold from the mid 1950s to what it is today would believe that both rural and urban Indians would take to bread – a foreign food from outside of their tradition – with such gusto and enthusiasm.

Macaroni, vermicelli, rolled wheat flakes, sago globules (for invalids), *jowar, ragi* and barley derived malt, and malt syrup, starches and glucose were the other cereal products made in small quantities. Among the animal products, milk was the foremost to get attention. This had an early beginning in 1890; cream separators were introduced in Bombay around 1900. A.C. Stratton setup the Anand Creamery in Gujarat, which produced large tins (35 pound = 15.55 kg) of bulk creamery (cultured) butter for troops deployed in Iraq in World War I. It closed down and reopened and closed several times. It kept busy with conducting training courses and experimentation with the best way of using buffalo milk and for making condensed milk, skimmed milk, butter, ghee, and commercial casein and it examined the feasibility of transporting milk from Anand to Bombay. Military Dairy Farms operated essentially to provide thousands of pounds of fresh milk and butter for the British army. Cream cheese and evaporated milk were also being made for the army at Bangalore, Wellington and Karnal and a dairy school established in Lucknow made and sold dairy products as part of experimental training. The making of tons of ghee for Indian troops also benefited civilians. Produced in minor quantities were casein, *channa* (*paneer*) and western style cheese (though this was also imported for niche consumers). Later, powdered milk and ice cream were added to this list.

Most of the meat, fish and eggs produced were sold fresh. Processed meat like ham, bacon and sausages were imported to the tune of over 800 pounds in the early war years but this declined drastically as the war years lengthened. Export of meat in fresh form (beef, mutton, pork), which was held in cold storage on ships, to be consumed during voyage, consisted of the so-called 'exports'. It seems that the military procured large amounts of meat produced in military butcheries. Also, to supply meat for the troops particularly, there were seven meat processing (dehydration) factories set up by the government between 1943–45 in Naushera, Agra, Madras, Pune, Patna, Delhi and Anantapur and each factory had handled 120,000–490,000 animals during a two year period till the time all the units closed down in 1946. Meat strips brined in 10 per cent salt solution were dried in trays (8–10 hr) in forced draft counter current or re-circulating type driers. The meat was then packed in tins (3.3 lb each) and kept in a hot chamber for three hours. Some edible offal was also dried for consumption by British soldiers. Mention must be made of two leading manufacturers of meat products – Essex Farms, Delhi and the Central Dairy Farm, Aligarh. These firms were prominent suppliers of processed meat (canned) for the Armed Forces for many decades, and after independence, continued to be the major suppliers of processed meat.

Byproducts of animal slaughter and meat production like goat and buffalo skins, camel bristles, bone meal (fertiliser) and meat meal (both sterilised) were produced mostly in Madras, Bombay and Bengal.

Concept of War Time Foods

In the Sepoy Mutiny of 1857, the sepoys on the march carried roasted gram or puffed rice or both and perhaps *jaggery.* These were the dry snacks that the rural folk ate and were easily carried, tied in a cloth. A first person account by Sir George Otto Trevalyan (1992) of the Indian sepoys at the time of the Mutiny projects the life of a sepoy subedar of the Bengal Lancers as one occupying a position of complete trust of his British superior officers and commanders. The sepoys and subedars had access to plentiful food from their own resources in the village; their food was prepared and served and eaten in the religious tradition, being caste and class conscious and maintaining a distance from soldiers of lower rank.

Europe in the crisis of World War I ushered in an era of food rations for field use. It was necessary because men were enlisted in large numbers and shipped off, most of the fighting took place in the trenches and conditions were poor and food even more so. Records show that US troops in training were struck down with influenza during the pandemic of 1918 while still on their home shores and there were many fatalities. Those that left and fought in the trenches were given field rations in the form of hard biscuits and canned ham, very reminiscent of the food given to sailors and seafarers in Elizabethan times and to England's convicts under transportation. However, the twentieth century soldiers also got chocolate, coffee and sugar. The Indian soldiers relied on the time tested roasted gram (*chana*) and jaggery when their daily staples like rice, dal and other foods were not available.

India was the jewel in the British Crown and was drawn into another war, World War II by virtue of being a British subject, contributing to the war effort with men, materials, and food. The troops' hard rations were biscuits, canned ham and bacon as well as cigarettes. Allied army officers and ranks billeted in different accommodations, commandeered local food supplies and resources. The rations for the allied troops called 'K' rations were much the same as those in World War I. The Indian soldiers deployed in the eastern theatre also got the same type of rations as everyone else, including '*shakkarpara*' (deep fried biscuit made of flour and dipped in sugar syrup) and puffed rice.

A first person account of a World War II veteran, Hawaldar Abdul Bari, who joined the service as a lad and served in Mektella field in Burma during the war years (as told to this author in 2004 at one Ex-Service men's meet in Mysore) vouches for the fact that hot cooked food and fresh fruit were provided even in the field. Fresh fruits and vegetables and meat of both the *halal* and *jhatka* types were airlifted in C-4 Dakotas from Assam. There was a mobile bakery on trucks and *chapati* and dal were provided as hot meals. No Indian sweets were given but only what could be prepared in the camps. As a store keeper, Bari recalled that his duties included seeing to the packed rations which consisted of biscuits, chocolates (and cigarettes) and which were available for supplementing their meager fare. Their food allotments of that time compared with the 'K' rations are shown in Table 13.2. Abdul Bari also recalled that the quality of the canned foods like sardines, bacon, sausages, butter etc. had to be more carefully examined and checked (visually) before issue because there would often be bulging of the cans (signifying spoilage).

Table 13.2. Components of pack rations for the Army in World War II

USA/Allied forces	*Indian troops*
K rations	Tinned Ham Shakkarpara, Sattu powder, Puffed Rice, Puffed Bengal gram Biscuit, Coffee, Hard-boiled sweets, Chikki, Tea
Chocolate only for English soldiers	

Grow more Food for War Effort

A quite comprehensive and authoritative account of food administration in India and Japan in the World War II period between 1937–1947 was written within ten years of the war's end under a group of studies on food and agriculture in World War II. The project was carried out by the Food Research Institute of the Stanford University, California, by Sir Henry Knight (1954) of the Indian

Civil Service. Knight wrote that at the outbreak of hostilities the Government of India Act was replaced by Defence of India Act 1939. Passed by the Indian Legislature, it was a comprehensive regulatory measure to control everything, 'that can be used in the conduct of war effort and essential to the life of the community'. To provide for the men from the villages joining the army (whether enticed, cajoled, bedazzled or plain coerced) the argument was that the men had to be fed anyway, irrespective of their civil or military status. The difference was only that as soldiers, their grain rations were higher, thus making less grain available for others. In addition, there were the British and American troops. Apart from grains, the demand for meat, eggs, vegetables, milk, butter, ghee etc. increased substantially with the presence of British and American troops. These food stuffs, even in normal times, were in short supply. Could India as a base, support a large Allied military force to conduct large scale operations against the Japanese? It was doubtful.

The Indian Army totaled nearly two million men, though not all at once positioned in India; it was the largest volunteer army in history. And there were Allied troops gathering for the Far East offensives. Here the diet of the Indian troops differed from those of the Western Allied troops. The latter's demand for eggs, meat, fish and even vegetables far exceeded anything that the Indians ever used. Clearly, production had to be increased to meet the Army's demand for what are called the minor and subsidiary foodstuffs (minor in reference to grain) which could not be imported.

Due to the lure of price and also plagued by the difficulty of maintaining the cattle stock and feed shortage in off seasons, the village farmers began to slaughter young cattle, as well as milch cattle and farm cattle. Breeding stocks declined. Extraordinary measures were instituted. Protection of animal breeding stocks, milch cattle and working bullocks was ordered and a halt on slaughter of male cattle under three years of age, and milk yielding cows between 3–10 years of age and cows either pregnant or in milk. Eastern Command military units, military dairy farms and provincial agencies began to grow garden vegetables to supply the needs of the multifaceted allied force made up of British, Indian, American, Chinese and other troops. Goat breeding herds, imported pig breeds and duck farms all came under the purview of the Army's food supplies activities (Knight, 1954, pp. 230–233).

Civil Food Rationing

Civil food rationing came into effect with rice, wheat, flour, sugar, edible oil, cloth and such items being strictly placed under quotas; food grains had to be imported in substantial quantities, the domestic production having proven inadequate.

On an average, more than one million tons of grains were imported for five years up to 1941/1942 but it became increasingly difficult to maintain this level of imports due to increasing shortage of shipping. There were also exports of several foodstuffs including pulses and oil seeds of some 360,000 tons. The cereal grain imports gradually lessened between 1942–46.

Whether nutritional considerations were taken into account while determining the ration quota in India on lines similar to how they were determined in war time Britain is not apparent. However, a recommendation of the Food grains Policy Committee sent up to the Central Legislature in 1944 (*Memorandum*, 1945; Knight, 1954, p. 192) stated in its Basic Plan that rationing be introduced uniformly and not withstanding the claim by the Northern and North West provinces that they required larger portions of food grains (due to their larger physical size and stature) than the Southerners. Every adult's entitlement of food grains was fixed at 1 lb/per day, and of every child between the ages of 2 and 12 years to one half the normal adult ration, i.e. 0.5 lb. Thus, all across the country every adult was to get at least 7 lbs per week irrespective of any other reasoning. A rather interesting footnote to the history of wartime Indian civil rations is the observation by Knight (1954, p. 192), of the ancient Aryan adult's meal mentioned in Kautilya *ArthaŚāstra* (AS.8.112), where 1 *prastha* of rice (pure, un split) was the recommended grain portion, 1 *prastha* was equal to 1/100 of a bushel (see Chapter 8). Thankfully there is no evidence that the portions of grain, *supa* and ghee were reduced on gender and caste basis by the Government of India, unlike those stated in the *ArthaŚāstra*.

Strict rationing of food, clothing and petrol was introduced in the civil population in Europe and England too. Rationing was enforced all over India, particularly for wheat, sugar and other essential commodities.

Between World War I and the post World War II period covering 60 years in the twentieth century, the concept of foods for the armed forces became firmly established and acted upon.

Many discoveries and developments in various fields of science and technology and in particular parallel developments in biochemical and nutritional sciences and food science and technology, as well as the growth of agro-food processing industry in the western world have played major roles in designing rations containing foods of adequate quantity and nutritional content incorporating microbiological and chemical quality safety features, thereby replacing an otherwise seemingly arbitrary system of providing foods to the fighting forces. Scientific developments were slow to come in pre-independent India, both in the agricultural and food processing sectors.

Processed Food Industry in India – Pre-Independence

Foods for the Ruling Class

The range of processed foods in pre-Independence India was quite limited and these were principally used by the British people and the personnel of the Armed Forces. As pointed out above, the traditional food industries provided the bulk of foods to the people at large. The processed food industry, making non-traditional products, was confined to some seventeen food items in the early part of the century, of which some ten food items were produced specially for the British Indian Army personnel.

The modern type of foods included canned fruits and vegetables, dehydrated vegetables, canned and dehydrated meats, beverages – carbonated (soda) water and foreign type spirits, confectionary items like boiled sweets and chocolate, all of which were produced in factories

Dehydrated products – vegetables and meat were a high priority for the Army. Therefore, onion and potato dehydration factories were increased in number to 19 in different parts of the country; meat dehydration units were established in Poona, Patna, Madras, Agra and Delhi. A fruit canning factory opened in Narsapur. In total, there were 131 food processing factories to manufacture an assorted 13–14 items of processed foods for the Defence Forces with an annual output of 91,315 tons (Achaya, 1994, p. 234). By 1945, the production figures for what is quaintly termed 'Army biscuit', dehydrated goat meat and condiments powder were, respectively 34,238 tons, 8 tons and 25,050 tons. Condiments, then as now, were ration items for Indian soldiers, hence these were required in large quantities. Ghee, a most important dietary component for Indians and also their main source of dietary fat was in short supply. It was for these reasons that *Vanaspati* (a hydrogenated form of peanut oil) was popularized as vegetable ghee. In seventeen factories 117,245 tons of vegetable ghee was being manufactured in 1945, more than half of which was in Bombay (Knight, 1954, p. 235). Slow to be accepted and viewed with suspicion at first, Vanaspati soon caught on and another 27 factories were established for its manufacture. Readers from an earlier generation would recall such products as Dalda, Dhara and various brands of the white to light cream coloured finely grained mass of fat, solid at room temperature, and stable with a longer shelf life than either ghee or oil fat being touted as the only fat to replace '*Shuddha* Ghee' (Pure Ghee) in cooking, frying and bakery confectionary preparations. The Defence Forces adopted this product with such gusto that as 'oil hydro', it continued to form the principle and, until very recently, the only form in which the cooking fat ration was issued.

In such a scenario described both by Knight (1954) and Achaya (1994), where the Indian subcontinent slowly but steadily marched towards industrialisation, every step and initiative taken was driven by British needs. Beginning with the quest for salt, there was also an increasing demand for sugar, production of light beer and spirits for their own Defence Services and Europeans, establishment of military farms for manufacturing dairy products for their army, the increasing oil seed crushing to meet 'Home' requirements in England, growing of linseed only to meet foreign demand, starting and running of tea plantations in India as a result of a Chinese blockade making tea practically unavailable to the English upper classes after the 'opium wars', and processing and preserving fruits and relishes, chutneys and pickles and bottling them for the express purpose of satisfying the newly developed British palate for such Indian delicacies among British officers and families living in India and for those who returned to England after 'India Service'.

Any further development of these industries can be attributed to the recognition within India of their usefulness or desirability after the war years.

Food industries and prospects in India post Independence

A scientific symposium was organised in 1951 to address the various issues concerning food industry prospects in the country at CFTRI in Mysore by its Director V. Subramaniam. Among several papers read at this symposium, a survey of food industries in the immediate post independence period (Table 13.3) provides a very realistic view of this sector in terms of the type of industries that existed and their production output as described by Iyengar (1951). Two new industries were added on soon after independence, that of Baker's yeast and desiccated coconut. The Indian processed food scene during 1950–52 revealed that there were around 30 types of food industries comprising more than 5,000 large units with more than Rs. 150 crores invested as capital and more than 300,000 labour employed and which posted an annual turnover of Rs. 1,500 crores. Notwithstanding these figures, the food and population status presented a grim prospect. The state of our food industry may be gauged from an assessment of the population, the extent of cultivated land, food production and food imports between 1900 and 1950. In the assessment of food scientists and government functionaries, cultivation and food production did not appear to be adequate for the expected growth in population. For a 13 per cent increase in population there was a very gradual and very slow increase in the land area brought under cultivation and the food production registered only about 1.32 per cent increase in 50 years. Clearly a major food crisis stared India in the face immediately after independence. The population statistics predicted that by 1960, the figures would reach 400 million from the 361 million in 1950, while the food supply would increase only by 4 million tones. There were clearly things to be done and urgently, to address the food problem confronting the country. Initiatives had to be taken to gather scientific resources and to initiate hydroelectric cum irrigation projects (worth more than Rs. 430 crores). Also the wise men suggested that either import of food be undertaken or population growth be checked. Probably both were necessary.

Table 13.3: Processed food industries in India, 1947–51

Biscuits and Bakery Product[a]
Confectionary[b]
Vanaspati
Meat Canning[c]
Fish on Ice
Canned Fruits and Vegetables
Dairy-milk, ghee, butter
Sago globules
Cashew Nut processing
Margarine
Malt, and malt extracts
Aerated water
Breweries and distilleries
Infant foods
Baker's Yeast
Desiccated Coconut
Basic Cereal milling, Oil extraction, Sugar and Salt industries

[a]90 factories, [b]56 units, [c]39 units. These were the largest in number.
Source: Iyengar, 1951

The views of the Food and Agriculture Ministry and those of the technical experts of the time on the need and prospects of the food processing industry, makes one wonder at their conservatism and restricted vision, even while recognising the stark facts. The facts were that there were crop failures, chronic famines and lack of rice; any kind of alternate grains were also unaffordable. The loss of fruits and vegetables amounted to 25–50 per cent of the produce. Cold storage was thought to be more a fashionable fad than a practical way to preserve fresh produce and in any case, cold storage was unaffordable. Canning of fruits and vegetables, as practiced in other countries, though recognised to be the way to prevent losses through wastage, was not encouraged by the government of the day. Any budding industry at that time would have probably required some kind of subsidy or tax related support. Here lies a pointer to its quaint way of thinking: government officials reported that 'the food industry deserved no consideration either in subsidies or in taxation'. Further, they said that, because there were no fruits and vegetables nor even fish in sufficient quantities for canning, the meager quantities would not help in providing low cost foods. Instead, there would most likely be a scarcity in the market of these foodstuffs. No one thought of saving the 25 per cent loss occurring through spoilage and wastage.

Therefore, the government even refused to think of giving any subsidy to the fruit and vegetable growers. On the other hand, the government proceeded to import cereals from USA, Argentina and Australia and sold them at subsidised rates. Food industry, in their assessment, was a luxury industry and not an essential one.

The Armed forces' Food Supplies – The Early Years

The army saw action in Kashmir even as the rest of the country was still celebrating independence. There were thus operational requirements for foods for the fighting forces. And did we have anything suitable for such a need? Indeed we did not.

The domestic market provided the primary foods and their milled products, pulses, edible vegetable oils etc. for general consumers. Horticultural produce in the country was limited. Meat food was not an industry at all nor was fishing organised. Poultry industry as we see it today was yet to emerge. The processed food industry produced only a small number of food items, hardly sufficient to fulfill the immediate needs shown in Table 13.3. Iyengar's (1951) report showed that, the factories producing biscuits and bakery products made mostly fresh bread, cakes and pastries, 56 units of confectionery units produced boiled sweets and candies etc. and several units produced canned meat. Other foods such as fish on ice, canned fruits and vegetables, dairy products such as milk, ghee, butter, sago globules, cashew nuts, margarine, malt and malt extracts, aerated water, and some alcoholic drinks in breweries/distilleries were also produced. Industries for cereal milling, edible oil extraction, sugar and salt making also existed from the pre war years but the canning of fruits/vegetables and meat had been started for supply to the British army and canned butter was meant mostly for the troops fighting in Turkey during World War II. One can see from this meager list that beyond the basic cereals, pulses and oil and some canned stuff there was hardly anything suitable and appropriate for the military's operational requirements.

The foods that went into pack rations in post independent India were much the same as those in World War II (as in Table 13.2). There were many problems with what was supplied to Indian troops in action: these were tinned ham, *shakkar para* (disliked by the troops), *sattu* powder, puffed rice, puffed Bengal gram, hard boiled sweets, *chikki* (peanut bar) and tea. Biscuit factories such as the Britannia Biscuit Company and others closed down for lack of wheat. According to Banerjee (1951), who reviewed the state of Defence needs and existing food problems in 1947–51, chocolate production stopped because imports of cocoa powder stopped (imported chocolate was found to be superior in any case). Boiled sweets produced by Sathe and Co and others were being made with orange and lemon and other flavours but the troops found them to be sticky to the teeth and abrasive to the tongue. *Chikki* was of poor quality and so was the sugar. Tinned condensed milk, which was imported, would brown on storage. Milk powder was produced in small quantities and it developed browning and rancidity and was therefore unacceptable. The major quality problems associated with these processed foods are listed in Table 13.4.

Table 13.4: Problems encountered in certain food products manufactured for defence use in 1951–52

In Canned products	
Fruits and Vegetables	– hand soldering of cans, poor lacquers, low quality of sugar, salt; poor quality raw materials
No Fish canning at all	
Wheat Products	
Semolina, flour production stopped	– Closure of mills; only two units functioned
Atta	– Ground in *chakkis* and at home
Mixers for Calcium Fortification	– Imported
Dairy Products	
Milk Supply	– Very Limited
Ghee Production	– Affected, skim milk powder made and also imported for toning buffalo milk
Tinned condensed milk	– Imported from Holland, Australia, USA
Evaporated Milk	– Browning on storage, small drying plants needed
Imported tinned Butter	– Melted in summer heat

Chocolate, Cocoa Powder	
War time chocolate made in India	– Poor quality
US Origin chocolate bars with peanuts	– Melted
Cocoa powder	– Not made in India
Hard Boiled Sweets	– Sour and abrasive to tongue
Groundnut roasted, for candy	– Poor quality raw material, incomplete roasting, Chikki–nonuniform coating
Hydrogenated Oil	– Large purchases by Army, health concerns prevail
Soyabean Milk, for Nutrition Supplementation	– Soya not an important crop, no pilot plant for milk
Biscuits	– Scarcity of raw materials after war
Shakkarpara	– Recipe disliked
Urgently require ready to eat foods	– But items not identified
Somebody should make them	– But Who?

Source: Based on Banerjee, 1951

War time agriculture, particularly in UK and USA was intensified to become self sufficient in primary foods when naval blockades prevented goods dispatched from the colonies and friendly nations from reaching their destinations. In UK, land armies consisting largely of women folk were raised to work the fields and farms and operate the dairies. In USA, wartime agricultural efforts included raising pigs and urging the use of lard (pig fat) as a cooking medium for all sorts of cooking. In one issue, The National Geographic Magazine (2001) published a never before seen photograph of pigs carved out of lard and lined up in a choir singing their own praises. This lard sculpture was exhibited at the International Live Stock show in Chicago in 1942.

Military Food Needs in India Since 1947

After India's independence in 1947, determined development and growth of the food industry as a whole led to a slowly growing primary food and food processing sector to tackle the food shortages for the vast population and then to keep pace with the slowly awakening civilian consumers' needs. Many more food items entered the list of manufactured items. Food science and technology inputs in the ensuing 60 years have been tremendous, with the result that not just civilian needs or those agro-foods deemed to capture a share of the international trade market, but also the military food requirements and their nutritional status received attention. In a broad sense, whatever foods were available, they were of poor quality; there was limited variety and lacked features of convenience that would make those worthy of use in field situations. The importance of the development of nutritious convenience foods is significant in the light of what happened in 1961–62 when the Indian northeast woke up to the unexpected Chinese invasion and aggression in the eastern Himalayas, advancing from Tibet. The troops sent to deflect and control this situation fought under great odds – the hostile climate, high altitudes and the very rugged terrain, neither suitably clothed, nor properly armed. Among the many essentials they did not have or get, were suitable foods. Lack of convenience in food preparation was exemplified during this border war when the troops were issued flour to make their own *chapatis* in the field and found that the rice and pulses would take a very long time to cook.

Bhargava (1972), in the preface to his book, *Their Finest Hour,* says this 1962 debacle in NEFA was attributed to the Q.303 bolt–action rifle, no match to the Chinese automatic rifle. No matter, there was also the acute problem of the terrain which was snowy or rugged or both and a totally new experience and the altitude which caused immense hardship in logistics, the extreme cold against which the protective clothing they wore proved to be inadequate and there was the food (or rather there was not) which could not be easily carried or prepared or eaten under the prevailing conditions and which probably was not nourishing. The lesson driven home by this bitter experience was that we should never again be found in such a state of un-preparedness.

It was only then that serious note was taken of the acute problems of feeding troops in the field. The domestic market did not yet have foods considered to be suitable for this purpose and although initiatives had been taken for conducting research and development in food science and technology to meet and fulfill military needs and requirements, it was too early to come up with customised solutions.

What the Indian Armed Forces required was rice in a convenient form, to make it cook quickly and meat in a dehydrated form, plain or curried. They required canned vegetables of better quality and ready to eat *'chapati'* with long shelf life. The tinned butter that was supplied melted and de-emulsified in high ambient temperatures. They also needed operational field rations for 1 man, 5 men and 10 men, which could be conveniently carried in the *jawans*' backpacks and which possessed shelf life of six months to one year at ambient temperatures. However, such foods were not available commercially. The Compo pack up to the 1960s continued to be made up of roasted gram, puffed rice with *jaggery,* biscuits and tea, condensed milk and toffees/boiled sweets; the last two items were disliked and very unpopular.

An assessment of immediate future needs of the services as understood at the time may be summarised as shown in Table 13.5. The broad category of rations listed would have required many individual foods to make complete meals.

Table 13.5: Food requirements of the Armed Forces

Army	
Long life drinking water	
Compo pack Rations	– For patrols
Quick Cooking Foods	– For high altitude
Tank Crew Rations	– For armoured vehicles
Variety in Packed Rations	
Fresh Fruits and Vegetables	– For high altitude
Meat products, dehydrated	
Ethnic foods – chapatti, rice, dal	
Traditional food in place of chocolate – in Emergency Ration	
Navy	
Long life Bread, Submarine rations	
Action Messing Meal Ration	
Emergency Rations for high seas	
Air Force	
Emergency Flying Rations, Long lasting water	

Note: Though most requirements continue to be the same, other needs came up and even more sophistication has been added.

Uniqueness of Military Food Requirements

Each of the three wings i.e. the Army, the Navy and the Air Force has unique requirements associated with the specific nature of its work and the terrain and climatic conditions in which it operates. Over the years, the nature of operations involving the Armed Forces has undergone many changes and has widened vastly since they first saw action in Kashmir and then during the Chinese invasion. Because of the situations they find themselves in, their food requirements have become varied and more specialised and their expectations have also increased with each experience. Nutritional content, taste and acceptability apart, appropriate processing for convenience of handling and preparing, and long shelf life and selecting suitable and user friendly packaging for bulk, field and individual use as well as their transportability are the overriding features of foods for this group of consumers. Therefore one could rightly say that their foods are unique. The foods are selected based on several criteria to meet human needs, food safety standards, packaging criteria, logistic criteria. To be included in pack rations, they should be portion packed, shelf stable and convenient to prepare.

Troops in combat and on patrol duties require foods that can be easily transported or carried and quickly prepared or eaten hot or cold or dissolved before consumption. Neither grocery type rations used in base units nor the detachment level rations would serve the purpose, unless supported by 'B' echelons.

The foods for military situations come under names such as combat rations, emergency rations, survival rations etc. (the foods which keep the men going till found or till relief arrives). They are not full rations as one understands, but food packets only, each packet provides just enough energy calories (far less than normal) for each meal.

The Role of Food Science and Technology

The importance of this branch of investigative science, in itself a composite of several basic and applied areas in biology, chemistry, physics and engineering, lies in its application to the designing and developing of food products with many desirable features, in determining and selecting the most useful technology to preserve them from spoilage, staling and loss of essential nutrients, finding methods for making such products on a large scale for industrial application, making improvements with value additions, discovering novel and better uses for known ingredients and food substances, discovering newer substances for food and health applications, analysing and understanding the biochemical and chemical changes taking place in foods and their role in human nutrition, safety and well being. Investigating biological and chemical hazards resulting from consuming contaminated foods and food derived substances and searching for the best protective packaging to safeguard the food in all respects constitute important aspects of this subject.

Foods are defined by the processing methods applied to them. Any food may be processed if required but the intelligent choice of technology will require a sound knowledge base, trained professionals and good equipment and machinery. Some of the most popular technologies are those that have stood the test of time. New methods are emerging which are applicable to only certain foodstuffs. Foods are classified based on the technology applied. There are nine types that are more commonly applied. These are identified by Rehman as follows (1999, pp. 1–10):

1. Minimally processed – having quality of fresh foods without conventional food preservation techniques such as freezing, canning, dehydration. Yet they are convenient to prepare, serve and

consume. The main steps are sanitising, trimming, shelling, cutting, slicing, dicing, packaging and storage at low temperatures to prolong life.

2. Preserved foods – Products that change little during manufacture where the main preservation methods do not alter the individuality of foods, such as the canned, frozen and dehydrated variety.
3. Manufactured foods – Products prepared completely based on mixing and processing of individual ingredients which have been made by one or more basic preservation methods. Examples are sausages, cured meats, jams, marmalades, wines.
4. Formulated foods – Products made completely based on mixing and processing of individual ingredients to result in a shelf stable end product. These are breads, biscuits, cakes, ice cream.
5. Primary derivatives or pure products – These are components derived from raw products through purification, e.g. starches from corn, potato, tapioca; sugar from sugar cane and beets; fats and oils from crushing seeds.
6. Secondary derivatives – Products derived from applying further steps on basic components, e.g., hydrogenated fat from oils.
7. Synthetic foods – Products made through microbial or chemical synthesis, e.g., Vitamins and other nutrients.
8. Functional foods – Products having a positive impact on an individual's health, physical well being, slowing and ameliorating aging and mental health problems.
9. Medical foods – Foods that can prevent and treat diseases.

Purpose of Processing and Selection of Technologies

Every substance harbours micro-organisms of different kinds, both good and bad, like the spoilage type, infectious kind, toxigenic kind, fermentative type, putrefying kind. But every kind requires water as medium to grow and exhibit its physiological activity. To preserve food beyond its natural shelf life of 1–2 days or more, depending on the substance, various processing methods are employed.

These methods of processing all aim to inhibit microbial growth, and microbial activity and thus prevent spoilage and/or prevent recontamination (Gould, 1989).

These methods include low temperatures, lowering of available water content known as water activity, adding acidic components and or preservatives, fermentation, surface coating, removing gas content or lowering oxygen and making up new gas mixtures. In dehydration, water is removed (lowering of water activity) by various methods.

More drastic methods necessary to inactivate, kill or destroy microorganisms are application of steam at high temperatures (sterilisation as in canning and retort process), short exposures to high heat as is done for sterilised milk, pasteurisation to kill pathogens as for fresh dairy foods, and to arrest spoilage organisms in fruit juices, even wine; blanching in hot water briefly before dehydration by different methods, usually done for vegetables, cooking thoroughly as in everyday food preparation, deep fat frying and exposure to gamma radiation (up to 10 KGray) known as radurisation (radiation pasteurisation) and radappertisation (sterilisation).

Packaging is resorted to for preventing recontamination as well as for hygienic processing, hygienic storage and aseptic processing (Gould, 1989, 1995) such as for the preservation of fruit juices in *tetrapak* cartons. Newer methods have been attempted in recent years which involve high pressure applications coupled with pulsed electric fields, claimed to be eminently suitable for fruit juices (principally to enhance the flavour component), Ohmic heating and Hurdle method. When more than two or three methods are used in small doses and in a synergistic fashion, the technique has been termed Hurdle processing, first intiated by Lothar Leistner, a German meat scientist (Leistner, Rodel and Krispien, 1981; Leistner and Hechelmann, 1993). The idea is that if some microbes escape one inhibitory method and still survive in partial numbers, they would be killed or injured and inhibited, unable to grow and multiply due to the next hurdle in their way and the next subsequent one and so on. Eventually, all the hurdles acting either synergistically or in sequence will inhibit every single microbial cell or their numbers, rendering them incapable of causing spoilage even if a few of them do survive.

Combination technologies like the Hurdle can also be attempted by combining freezing, dehydration and addition of preservatives alongside moisture reduction, gas packing, modified atmosphere storage, low temperature storage and high pressures etc. A recent conference on emerging technologies (DFRL, 2007) has discussed these methods and the products that are possible.

In recent years several products have appeared in the market offering wider choices to the consumers and there are also many variations of the same type of food.

The present day domestic manufacturing is in a position to produce and supply on a large scale many types of primary, secondary and tertiary processed convenience products of good quality. The bulk of the army's purchases are made from these sources.

The different operations the army found itself engaged in since 1947 and the difficulties the troops encountered and still do in operational areas in difficult terrains and climates were causes enough to make the Government of India take the matter up in all seriousness and in good earnest to do something and do it soon.

Actually this 'something' was the initiation of the attempt to supply substantial quantities of pre-cooked dehydrated rice, what is now called the "PD rice" for short in the Indian military food jargon. The process involves cooking rice by steam and then subjecting it to dehydration in hot air cabinets. The dried rice with a moisture content of about 8 per cent keeps well and cooks much faster than raw rice. The pilot scale facilities to carry out this processing were already installed in the Central Food Technological Research Institute, Mysore (CFTRI), and the personnel to do the processing were drawn from the newly established Defence Food Research Laboratory, DFRL (established December 1961 under the Defence R&D Organization, Ministry of Defence, Government of India) also in Mysore.

Food science and technology did step in at a time when other solutions could not be found immediately and therefore clearly came to be recognised as being most essential not only for the development of the Indian food processing industry in general but also specifically for understanding and attending to the myriad food related problems of the armed forces as they surfaced.

Developments in Food Science and Technology for the Defence Forces

The 1960s Scenario

Research began but the fruits of that were to come sometime later. Post 1962, one of the first undertakings was to investigate the dehydration of a variety of vegetables (Bhat *et al.*, 1974). Fresh fruits and vegetables are highly perishable and have very limited shelf life. Although these are supplied to the troops in peace areas the need for processed forms arises in emergency or combat feeding and in high altitude cold regions. Dehydration had been the method of preservation from early times. Sun drying is still used in many parts of the world. Dehydration had been brought indoors to obtain high quality dehydrated products processed under controlled conditions says P.S. Raju, Head of the Division of Fruit and Vegetable Technology at DFRL.

Work on the preservation and extension of the shelf life of *chapati* (Kameshwar Rao, Malathi and Vijayaraghavan, 1966) went on for quite some time, the various physico-chemical and microbiological problems related to texture, starch staling, spoilage characteristics, stabilisation and acceptability. Only in the 1970s was a product standardised (Arya, Vidyasagar and Parihar, 1977) and its microbiological spoilage profiles studied (Vijaya Rao, Leela and Sankaran, 1979).

Bread was given an extended shelf life by designing a fungistatic wrapper (Ghosh *et al.*, 1977).

Work also began on the preservation of fresh meat, although 'meat on hoof' (transporting live animals for meat purposes) was the standard and accepted form. Until then the Indian concept of fresh meat was to cook it at the earliest opportunity after slaughter. It continues to be so to a very large extent, to buy fresh meat from small individual butchers' stalls. More organised fresh meat production takes place by butchering in municipal slaughterhouses under the authority of the city veterinary health officer. The Armed Forces have their own and separate slaughterhouses under the direct authority and supervision of Army Service Corps (ASC) and the veterinary officers of the Remount Veterinary Service (RVS) posted to ASC depots in different regions. While this method ensures supply of fresh meat to units located near the depots, transporting meat to far away places to units in the field is always full of uncertainties viz. spoilage due to long exposure (of more than six hours) at high ambient temperatures, delayed transportation, impassable terrain, bad weather conditions and especially the absence of any refrigeration at either end and during transportation. So the study of meat and meat food preservation and the attendant microbiological problems assumed an all-important facet of Defence R&D at the time (Vijaya Rao, Bhagirathi and Sharma, 1983; Vijaya Rao and Bhagirathi, 1985) and as a matter of fact, it still is. Meanwhile, curried spiced meat and meat in brine in cans were being made by commercial manufacturers which provided the bulk of processed meat rations. The Indian canning industry has fulfilled a great need in this respect. Armed Forces are the single largest consumers of canned foods in the country and some meat products are processed exclusively for the services. The laboratory also conducted several studies on canning of conventional foods, which the canning industry had not been doing. War time processing of meats and vegetables were the only products in this category. That is when studies were carried out on canning of Indian type of foods − curries, *pulavs*, desserts etc. (Mathur *et al.*, 1973). The concept of thermally stabilizing pouch packed foods in retorts, the pioneering studies of Lampi and colleagues (1977), was intriguing enough to begin work in this area. The forerunner to the final technology outcome as we see today in India was the work of Ghosh and colleagues at DFRL (Ghosh, *et al.*, 1980). They conducted pilot scale studies to establish many of the process parameters which came to be very useful in developing the retort pouch technology for meat, fish, vegetable and rice based foods.

The 1960s R&D also concentrated on developing ready to eat survival foods in the form of compressed bars of known calorific density, nutrient composition and adequate shelf life to replace the only other such item being used i.e. the milk chocolate bar. These survival bars were cereal based. Around this time too, the first generation 5–man and 10–man Compo packs were designed, with an assemblage of assorted items providing three meals/day per man. The foods still had to be prepared at each meal, but were an improvement over the *shakkarpara* sweets, roasted gram or rice or flour rations.

The 1970s Scenario

In the 70s, research focused on several technologies simultaneously in order to expand the scope of food technology application to develop newer food items. The first was to begin dehydration of meat by freeze dehydration. Dehydration of meat and vegetables was already known in India from the wartime production in the 1940s. There were, however, some problems associated with softening and cooking of the dehydrated stuff due to a phenomenon called 'case hardening'. It is well known that imperfect control of the dehydration process for fruits and vegetables may seriously impair the quality of the products by causing undesirable changes in shape or structure, cracks, case hardening, denaturation of proteins, browning reactions, oxidation of unstable components or microbiological spoilage due to physical, chemical or biological manifestations. Alternative methods were being examined: one was known as freeze dehydration. Beginning with a small experimental facility in Delhi's Defence Science Laboratory, the technology of freeze drying rose to be regarded as a 'god send' to dry fresh meat so that it re-hydrated and cooked rapidly. It was light in weight and could be packed in cans to withstand any type of transportation hazards. Soon, a very large freeze-drying facility was created in Tundla near Agra, equipping it with two very large freeze-drying plants imported from Holland. The facility had its own slaughterhouse and packing machines and large quantities of dried meat began to be supplied to some of the army units posted in different operational places. It is quite another matter that meat in this form was not welcome to the troops. After some time, not only were the Tundla operations shut down and disbanded, the plant and machinery sold but the experimental facility from the Defence Science Laboratory also shifted to DFRL.

Other technologies that came to be regarded as very useful were the application of high temperature short time dehydration or HTST. Many types of vegetables in diced form could be successfully dried by this method (Jayaraman *et al.*, 1982). Many whole and split pulses and peas were prepared by this method by the same team of investigators, especially to make quick cooking dals for high altitude rations.

In addition to this technique, attempts to preserve fruits and vegetables in moist form utilised the concept of intermediate moisture (IM) where the water content in the fresh food is reduced and replaced with sugar and salt by a process of osmosis. Jayaraman *et al* (1976) reported development of shelf stable IM fruit slices from guava, pineapple, mango, banana (Ramanuja and Jayaraman, 1980) as well as jack fruit, sapota and apple (Jayaraman, 1988) and also from carrot (Jayaraman and Das Gupta, 1978). These products have many advantages like ready to eat, moist mouth feel texture, stable at ambient temperature, reduced weight and bulk and enhanced per unit nutrient (Personal communication from P.S. Raju).

One of the early attempts to make convenience fruit based products was to use ripe mango. It was prepared in the form of a fruit bar by the method of vacuum shelf drying (Jayaraman *et al.*, 1976). It brought quality and standardization to a traditional confectionary normally made by open sun drying. For dehydrating milk and milk products such as milk shakes, *dahi* (yogurt), buttermilk and whole liquid egg, spray drying technique was applied. A more acceptable formulated product called omelette mix came out of this early effort of making spray dried egg powder but continued to be studied until much later (Satyanarayana Rao *et al.*, 1995)

The quest for 'compo rations' continued, as well as the search for flexible and rigid packaging materials.

In the civil sector the food, processing scenario was changing too. Summarised, it went in the following manner.

Changes and developments in the processed food industry 1950–70: In the existing industries like cereals and cereal products, modern milling methods were introduced. 'Green Revolution' happened with the diligent efforts of agricultural scientists led by M.S. Swaminathan at the Indian Agricultural Research Institute, New Delhi. We were growing more food.

The dairy industry expanded and was modernized and there was the 'White Revolution'. We witnessed 'Operation Flood', empowering rural milk farmers through cooperatives and equitable distribution of standardised milk to urban areas, thanks to the foresight and vision of Dr. V. Kurien and his exemplary work at Anand, Gujarat.

More attention was paid to the fruit and vegetable sector too. Edible oil production took off on a large scale and there were many manufacturers of 'Vanaspati', the hydrogenated vegetable oil.

Biscuit production, principally by the Britannia Biscuit Co. and Sathe's Biscuits, as well as bread making industries, expanded moderately. White bread, sweet buns and bakery made biscuits of different kinds became acceptable as alternate snacks to the traditional Indian snack foods. Some of the latter also began to be made on home and cottage scale and sold door-to-door and retailed through bakeries. Both baked foods and some of the traditional snacks belong to the finger foods category and both are ready to eat and shelf stable.

Among the soft drinks, Coca Cola made its appearance in the mid 60s in metropolitan towns. Aerated, ready to drink bottled soft drinks, fruit flavoured, mostly orange and lemon, were produced by some manufacturers. These became a welcome addition to the only other alternatives which were the concentrated squashes and cordials.

In the health and energy beverages and food sector, the much touted and dependable Ovaltine gave way to two or three other malted products; Horlicks continued to hold sway in this market segment.

No particular progress occurred in diversification of the confectionary industry; varieties of milk toffees and boiled sweets with more flavours and fillings (manufactured by firms such as Daurala, Ravalgaon, Sathe's), some éclair type tasty bits and the much-in-demand chocolate bar by the Bourneville Cadbury Company.

A very significant development occurred in the plantation products sector like tea and coffee. The estates came under Indian management, and Indian consumers could now look forward to buying some standardised brands of tea – orthodox and blends as well as the 'instant' variety. The traditional South Indian filter coffee powder made of coffee-chicory mix remained in the hands of small retailers, mostly confined to South Indian markets. These mixes made with freshly roasted beans and arbitrarily mixed with chicory powder varied from one retailer to another as well as showing batch-to-batch variations from the same source.

Sugar and salt came in just one variety, sold loose in small quantities or in bulk. Their quality differed vastly from batch to batch. Sugar at controlled prices was available only through the public distribution system on a family quota basis with a ration card. Anything extra had to be purchased in the open market at high prices. Packaged sugar cubes – refined, white and crystalline, for table purposes was not an item for general consumption or affordability. It was used mostly by high end hotels and restaurants.

It can thus be said that what did happen in the food industry during these 20 years was modernisation of the existing industries, a certain degree of expansion, a small amount of diversification, a little export and Indian management of plantation estates. What was also initiated during this time was the introduction of powdered milk, the baby food formula having been already introduced in the 1960s, multipurpose food mix and the use of defatted ground nut and soy protein in powder and beverage form. A novel feature of the time was the beginning of advertisement of food products.

What did not happen: More significant was what did not happen. Newer technologies were not adapted for better processing (except in milling), for better yields or for preservation and conservation. There was a general lack of awareness regarding the importance of quality and safety, of the necessity for standards and specifications. And those who were aware felt nothing much could be done about it as the right type of raw material required for production of consistently good quality products could not be obtained. Consumer awareness of everything concerning foods, whether processed or not, was minimal and of course no attempt was made by anyone to provide any type of nutrition or safety related information to them. There was no law for labeling. It was a suppliers market all the way through.

Developments in the 1980s

Product development and technology application are facets of the same quest for suitable foods for the Armed Forces. The 1980s saw a surge in R&D in this field. There were developments and advances in food science and technology in general and scientific efforts resulted in a wide variety of food products. Solar dehydration, retort pouch technology, canning of a variety of foods, not just meat and fruits and vegetables, many types of labour and time saving dehydrated foods known as 'instant mixes' with multiple ingredients and a shelf life that enabled their storage, instantiation of pulses and cereals and certain vegetables by high temperature short time pneumatic dehydration for quick cooking at high altitudes improved dehydration of vegetables, more items for compo packs, different types of survival bars as well as expanding the packaging research to various polymers and aluminum cans and their safety and suitability.

Studies were undertaken on gamma irradiation of spices for disinfection and disinfestation and on water for longer storability without staling. Potable water as part of the survival rations posed particular problems of staling even in the canned form (for the Navy) and therefore the attention of scientists was engaged to find better methods of preserving it. Spices and condiments are entitlements in the basic rations. The spice production techniques in practice in our country were the inherent cause of spoilage by insect infestation and fungal attack. The indigenous farm centered handling and drying techniques also led to a very heavy contamination with soil and faecal micro flora of both spoilage and hazardous nature and practical and safe decontamination methods were needed. Hence gamma irradiation, at the time allowed only for preventing sprouting in onions and potatoes, seemed a possible solution for spices. Experiments conducted by scientists of DFRL in association with BARC (Bhabha Atomic Research Centre) at Mumbai proved that within certain permissible limits of irradiation, spices could be successfully decontaminated. Since then the Government of India has permitted the gamma irradiation of spices for the purpose of microbial decontamination. Now wheat and milled wheat products are also allowed to be irradiated for preservation.

A wide variety of cereal foods based on Indian cuisine were developed and produced by the application of various technologies – freeze drying, hot air drying, canning and retort pouch. Microbiological concerns of the individual ingredient and of the final products were addressed in studies to establish microbial profiles and permissible limits for safety and hygiene of many basic ingredients used in formulating products.

Foods for special missions and operations: The early 80s was a period filled with mission oriented programmes undertaken by the armed forces and oceanographic explorations and other civil expeditions, all requiring some component of their rations to be of the special type. Shelf stable and palatable processed foods of the convenience type with defined nutrient content and a high degree of microbiological safety and packaged for durability and protection were not yet available in the domestic market.

All at once, the Indian Armed Forces needed foods for high altitude operations in the Siachen sector. Their personnel were also participating in mountaineering expeditions, including an Everest expedition, Naval sailing expeditions and even the Indo-Soviet Joint Manned Space Mission. There were Government of India sponsored exploratory and scientific expeditions to Antarctica, lasting several months. Expertise from and involvement of food scientists was in urgent demand. A very wide range of convenience foods emerged out of the R&D activity – giving a choice of ethnic foods designed to deliver calories and nutrients in a most palatable, ready to eat/quick to prepare form, quality and safety assured as per standards, with weatherproof and sturdy packaging and long shelf life. These food items were included in different menus and rations for different missions and many of them continue to be part of special rations and Compo-packs. Dehydration and retort processing methods were used very effectively to make products. It was also the time when freeze dehydration, which had earned a bad name for the unwelcome meat it had been used to make in the late 1960s, was revived.

Freeze drying, hitherto applied only for meat and then for drying two kinds of fruit juice powders with poor shelf life, came in most useful in producing a wide variety of instantly rehydratable products: pineapple, mango, red grape as powders, soup powders (mushroom, vegetable), fruit bits (mango, banana), desserts, breakfast cereals, rice preparations, meat, chicken (large pieces) and *paneer* based foods, all of which were used at one time or another in special operations food packs. Many of them had been originally developed as Space foods and some of them were included in the Air Force's Joint Indo-Soviet Manned Space Mission (Sharma *et al.,* 1984). A larger variety were developed and made ready for the Insat-1C ISRO-NASA Pay Load Specialist Mission in the Space Shuttle (Vijaya Rao et al., 1986a, 1986b). Meat foods were required to be specially examined in view of the past history of rejection on many counts; large boneless pieces were successfully freeze dried and preserved for a long time as a result of sustained quality control measures (Radhakrishna *et al.,* 1988). Later came a further range of products such as *dahi* cultures, fish curry, shrimp, sapota (chiku), avocado, capsicum, carrot, aromatic herbs used in food preparation, as well as the application of combination methods using both freeze drying and hot air drying. Typically, many of these efforts did not get written up as a research paper but were reported in scientific presentations and remain either lost in national symposia proceedings or in Project Technical Reports. Several such reports of completed projects which belong in the archives but are termed confidential, shelved somewhere, and are not available for research and reference.

Emphasis on Quality Assurance of processed foods: This was also the period in the early to mid 80s when the emerging principles of preventive safety, which later became known as Hazard Analysis Critical Control Points (HACCP) concept were first applied in pilot scale production of mission foods in the laboratory. The concept itself was new to begin with, having originated in the 70s with the Pillsbury Company of USA for making high quality and microbiologically safe foods for Space use. The Defence scientists were quick to adopt a version of this system as a linear integrated product safety (LIPS) protocol in all pilot scale productions at the laboratory level. The overall emphasis also came to lie on microbiological quality assurance methods, systems and kits for all types of products and for foods and particularly for fresh and processed meats (Vijaya Rao and Bhagirathi, 1985; Vijaya Rao, Bhagirathi and Sharma, 1989) and for formulated dehydrated as well as other products (Vijaya Rao and Srihari, 1993; Vijaya Rao, 1994). It was necessary to design and produce foods to conform to nutritional, chemical and microbiological criteria.

The ASC has its own specifications for contractual purposes when purchasing from the open market. For the foods developed in the laboratory, new data were generated by experimentation and by market survey of existing products and ingredients to help make new specifications and quality standards. Awareness of training needs in quality assurance and food safety became a major focus of the scientists in reference to the foods meant for the Armed Forces because at this time too, technologies were being transferred to entrepreneurs and the manufacturing industry, and they needed guidelines and specifications to enter the Army's food procurement register. To help recognise and test for quality and safety, ASC technical staff officers were given refresher and advanced level courses in food analysis and quality assurance.

Some of the parallel developments in the domestic processed food market which happened as a result of technology infusion from foreign sources and due to the own initiatives of the established Indian and multinational companies were important in making available a wider variety of products, both fully processed and semi processed, for the Indian consumers. Not only did a few products based on popular and regional recipes appear, but there were newer packaging materials which helped to make the packaged foods appear a little more attractive, more shelf stable and user friendly and therefore more acceptable. These foodstuffs could be used as substitute items in the basic rations and some of them could also be included as special ration items. Since they were readily available in the market, obtaining them in the necessary large quantities was not a problem either.

Food packaging has seen a steady growth. The industry went from jute and paper sacks (for bulk dry rations), glass bottles for beverages and jams and jellies, wax paper and glassine for baked foods, cans for wet foods, oils and fats, plastic backed jute bags (for sugar) and bag in the box for oils to sachets and tetrapak cartons for milk (pasteurized and UHT – ultra high temperature processed respectively) and juices and every manner of plastic and aluminum foil made pouches for all types of products. There were many hiccups before all this could be achieved. Many polymers are manufactured in India but the thermal resistant polymer used in retort processing of foods is still imported.

A revolution of a sort also happened when small quantities were sachet packed. Begun as an experimental marketing venture for shampoos, strip packing of small amounts for single use (1g to 5 g or more) has outperformed every other type of portion pack. Its customer friendly size gives the impression of affordability. And there is no doubt whatsoever that small portion packs of jams, butter, pickles, ketchup, beetle nut, sugar, salt, pepper, coffee, tea etc. which are leak proof and easy to store find great application in the hospitality and catering industry. It is also very convenient to assemble military operational rations using some of these pre packed items. Before the advent of the strip packing concept and machinery, the tea, sugar, pickles etc. to be included in the Compo Rations were prepared laboriously in the laboratory at Mysore.

Food Developments in the 90s and After

Having acquired and demonstrated the ability to design/fabricate/produce processed or preserved foods as per nutritional quality, safety and operational requirements, the scientists diverted their attention to other requirements. One such task was to find ways and means of providing fresh fruits and vegetables (particularly salad type) to the Siachen sector. In the absence of refrigerated transportation, near non-existence of the concept or practice of quality grading of fresh produce both by suppliers (the contractors) or the buyers (the ASC), fixation of low prices for bulk procurement (contractors therefore supplied any available stock, fresh or otherwise) and the use of fragile bamboo baskets to transport the fruits and vegetables in trucks and aircraft, a whole new set of investigations were carried out to tackle the matter of sending fresh material without damage, spoilage and wastage. The use of 'keep fresh' chemicals (to slow plant respiration and delay fruit ripening) was a strategy that paid dividends. The concept was based on employing oxygen scrubbers and methane absorbers. New multiple-use containers of sturdy plastic were introduced for packing fruits and vegetables. Quality and colour grading methods were tested. Modified atmosphere packaging or MAP of fresh fruits and products under decreased oxygen and increased carbon dioxide levels (Chauhan, 2006) and minimal processing was used to stabilise pre-cut vegetables packed in polymer pouches and stored either at room temperature (for short life) and under refrigerated (for longer life) aimed for Naval use (Raju *et al.,* 2002).

A variety of concentrated fruit juices for low temperature storage were produced. High calorie sweetened puddings in the dehydrated mix form went on trials for high altitude use.

Aluminum cans were designed for food use and tested extensively in a joint study with a firm making small containers for pesticides. A larger pilot scale retort, which is a sterilizing chamber (capacity 250 kg/load) was designed by scientists in the laboratory and fabricated with the help of a private engineering firm, to process foods in flexible pouches. The technology could now be used for commercial exploitation and several bold entrepreneurs launched retort processed foods in a big way, especially for the export market. The aluminum can technology was most successfully adopted for the canning of tender coconut water.

There were other practical problems that still evaded the right solutions. Fruits and vegetables supplied in any form continued to freeze in the subzero temperatures prevalent at very high altitudes. What was to be done to prevent this? Using anti-freeze systems was one approach (Vibhakara, Singh and Dasgupta, 2003). Fruit bits treated to be freeze resistant were acceptable but vegetables treated in the same manner were not. Fruit juices processed aseptically in tetra packs froze into solid blocks and their thawing consumed a large amount of precious fuel.

Meat and meat products continue to signify protein rich 'proper' diet for the hard working *jawans*, but there was no meat based product – either curry or as rice *pulav* type in a dry form to be used in rations (there were canned meat chunks and *kheema* (mince) in brine and curried form made commercially). Dehydrated form of curried meat mince and meat *pulav* – both quick cooking and shelf stable, possessing high microbiological safety were developed by a combination system of using freezing followed by freeze dehydration and finishing by hot air dehydration or vice-versa and tested for troops' acceptance in field trials. These two products usually prepared in pilot scale quantities in the laboratory were much in demand for all manner of army expeditions. One 'whole meal supplement' concept produced nutrient dense dry soup mixes and compressed bars containing a well-researched combination of instantised cereals, dry fruits, protein source and natural sweeteners. Both were handy as quick meals or snacks for any operational situations, having qualified in the field under actual user conditions. These were the forerunners of the current crop of nutribars that are being imported.

Most of these products did not get to see the light of day beyond pilot scale manufacture and the investigations and the performance of new products were reported in many scientific symposia and annual conferences but the details lie buried in some technical reports of the laboratory, unavailable for reference. Even as the food industry, with or without help from Indian R&D, went ahead to establish its market with home produced and imported food products, Defence related food science and technology efforts in India were exclusively directed towards fulfilling the needs of the Indian Armed Forces and led to productive outcomes in small and big ways. These fall into several areas:

- Products and processes,
- quality and safety standards and quality systems,
- analytical and quality assurance techniques,
- training of army officers, industry personnel and student groups in the subject of food analysis and quality assurance,
- producing foods on pilot scale in the research laboratories on all those occasions when foods were required on a priority basis and when there were no commercial sources and
- effecting technology transfers to commercial enterprises.

The application of appropriate processes and giving suitable packaging for fresh and processed foods both for extension of life, human safety and overall protection from spoilage and damage and trouble shooting at anytime with reference to food associated problems are the key components in a successful bid to use food science and technology for the Armed Forces. In all these efforts what has been glaringly lacking is marketing or PR efforts outside the Services.

The Kargil war gave impetus to the retort process technology and launched it in a big way into the Indian domestic market. The Army needed large quantities of operational foods and it was using Compo packs containing dehydrated instant mixes. By the act of convincing the Army brass to take the 'Meals Ready to Eat' packs and persuading the only manufacturer at that time with an installed retort of a certain capacity for pouch processed foods to make the necessary quantity for the troops, it was possible not only to introduce retort processed foods in a big way but also interest others to enter this field. All the products and processes must ultimately find use in the civil market.

Though there were increasing number of products from 1960 onwards on the market shelf as a quick glance at Table 13.6 would show, the Armed Forces could not possibly use them because of their unique needs.

Table 13.6: Food products on the market shelf and their utility for the Defense forces: the 1960–90 scenario

	Civilian Market	*For Defense*
Variety	*Limited*	*Do not meet the needs*
Packaging	To be attractive, interesting, Attention grabber	Not sufficiently attractive – not primary need, label information important
Preparation	Home kitchens	In field, no facilities
Nutrition, Composition	No specific emphasis but wholesome family meals	Very important
Safety/Quality	No particular recognition	Very important
Take off	Reasonably predictable, based on market research	Never specified, unpredictable
Storage	Purchase as needed	Large stocks kept in depots affected by
Shelf Life	Adequate for 3 months	climate, pests, long shelf life desirable
Transportation and Cartoning	Chilled or at *RT, by Road, Rail, cold stores at destination	Road Rail, Air, Special Cartons, No cold store
Availability	No problem if not available	At short notice – critical
Cost considerations	Primary, determines take off levels	Not primary, but important enough

* Room Temperature

A summary of technology outcomes, from Defence R&D in terms of processes employed and the type of products developed till the year 2000 and thereabouts, for the Armed Forces is presented in Table 13.7. A slew of technologies for dehydration such as hot air dehydration (HAD), high temperature short time drying (HTST), spray drying, freeze drying (FD), vacuum shelf drying, combined methods, in-pack processing of wet foods, intermediate moisture technology (IM), anti Freeze IM products, compression methods for food bars, canning and retort pouch technologies, hurdle methods, reverse osmosis for juice concentration, anti freeze systems, stress reducing and appetite enhancing products, high vitamin and antioxidant rich beverages, desserts and confectionary foods, development of aluminum cans, standardising polymer pouch material for retorting, combination of freezing and freeze dehydration, modified atmosphere packaging (MAP), minimal processing and numerous approaches to quality and safety assurance by way of analytical methods, test kits etc. were the result of this activity.

Overall Processing Technology Status, 1970–2000: Between 1970 and 1985, India possessed and used technologies for baking, canning, hot air dehydration including spray drying, traditional snack making and plastic packaging in its nascent stage. Dairy products technologies were more evident. From the early to mid 80s onwards, up to the close of the century, more sophisticated technologies began to be utilised. These were IQF (individual quick freezing) particularly for shrimp, aseptic processing for fruit juices and pulps, extrusion and flaking as well as extrusion cooking for cereal products and freeze-drying for green pepper and some small amounts of vegetable bits. Flavour enhancement and making dry formulations using ingredients made by different techniques also received a certain amount of attention. Chocolate, coffee and tea processing became more widely used. Meat processing and meat products technology were recognised to be important for better utilisation of available resources. 'Tetra Pack' technology – heat processing of fluids like fruit juices and milk caught on. But the most significant introduction was the awareness of quality and safety and the systems to achieve them in production. Most large scale and some medium scale industries in the private sector were in a position to claim that their products conformed to their own pre established quality norms because they had installed ISO 9000 systems.

Table 13.7: Result of Technology inputs between years 1962–2000 plus from DFRL: Processes, Food Products and Techniques

Hot Air Drying (HAD) Rice, Veg Pulav mix, Khichdi mix, Meet kheema, peas curry, dal curry, Meat pulav, several types of vegetable dices, *Bisibele bhath* mix and any number of traditional foods, Halwa and upma mixes – for types of rations	**Combined Technologies for Instant Mixes,** Suji Halwa Mix, Upma Mix, Vermicelli kheer Mix, Vermicelli Upma Mix, Nutrient soup Mix, Carrot Halwa mix, orange drink mix, flavoured milk mix, Mango milk shake mix, dahi mix, Karhi mix – new products for possible ration use	**Hurdle Technology – for longer shelf life** Vegetables, Fresh Meat chunks Precut Fresh fruit and fruit pulp in packs, fresh cut salad vegetables, fresh fruit juice sweetened, pickled vegetables – for ration packs
HTST Whole chana and other legumes, vegetables, Dal curry – all quick cooking, vegetable pieces for assembling other mixes – for HA[a]	**Preserved, in-pack treated** Chapatti, Phulka, Puri, Bread, fried snacks, High protein Nutritive biscuits – for rations	**Intermediate Moisture Technology – pouch packs** Tropical fruit slices, cut vegetables – for ration substitutes

Contd.

Spray drying Omlette mix, scrambled egg, Avial mix, buttermilk, yogurt, milk shakes–special supplies Vacuum Shelf dried – Fruit bars–Mango-rations	**Compression Technology** Cereal bars, Soft bars Energy bars, Meal Replacement Nutri – Bars, milk powder, emergency/ survival bars – special rations	**Reverse Osmosis** Fruit juice concentrates pomegranate juice – enabling technology
Freeze drying Fruit juices, soups, breakfast cereals, meat and chicken chunks and pulavs paneer curry, peas pulav, Veg. Curry, instant puddings, coffee–special rations	**Confectionary** Groundnut chikki, Almond chikki, some traditional sweets – for Compopacks	**Freeze resistance methods and Frozen IM products –** Fruit slices, fruit drinks for HA[a]
Canning (MS cans) Veg. Pulav, Meat/chicken pulav potato peas curry, Halwa, fruit cake, Kheer. Coconutwater–General use **Retort Process – thermal resistant** polymer packs, Thermally processed pouch filled rice, meat, vegetable preparations, desserts, curries–enabling technology and for MRE rations **Aluminum cans –** – can development – coconut water – Different foods, Enabling technology	**Combination of HAD with freezing/ freeze drying** For quick cooking rice, meat kheema and pulav, yellow vegetable slices and greens – for general application and for special rations **Modified Atmosphere packaging and minimal processing at RT and refrigeration** Fruits, vegetables, meats For general application Utilization of less common cereals and millets – snacks, – breakfast cereals – In meal bars – general use	**Appetite enhancing** products- chewables, suckables, munchies **Stress reducing herbal products (from DIPAS) High vitamin and antioxidant rich fruit drinks and teas (from FRL, Leh)** – all for HA [a] **Oxygen/Methane Scrubbers –** to keep fruits fresh and give longer storage life – for army and navy store houses, general application
Physical quality grading by non invasive methods – QA[b] Fruit and vegetables	**Chemical Quality – QA[b]** – shelf stability – Rapid tests, – Kits	**Microbiological Quality – QA[b]** – Profiles – Rapid tests, Kits – Product standards

[a]High Altitude; [b]Quality Assurance requirements

Range of Products: The range and variety of products put on the market shelf widened and expanded as a result of technology development and technology infusion due to the R&D efforts of government research laboratories and universities within the country and to a small extent by individual companies. The concept of super markets, department stores and exclusive food stores, first successful in metropolitan cities gradually spread to other cities and towns. One only had to walk around these places to see the shelves leaden with products never before seen by consumers in India.

To mention only a few, salt was one of the more significant sectors to benefit from the new knowledge, technology and concern for public health. Several varieties of cooking and table salts were introduced: coarse and a little wet or free flowing and finely crystalline, standard or sparkling white, iodized or not for bulk and retail sale. Iodination of salt became mandatory as a preventive measure for goiter and hypothyroidism.

A whole vista of convenience foods appeared, dry 'ready to cook' mixes like *Gulab Jamun* mix, *Upma* mix, *Dhokla* and *Idli* mix (Fig. 13.1) as well as *Payasam* (*kheer*) and *Vada* mixes and many more. 'Heat and eat' type retort pouch processed rice meals for vegetarians (Fig. 13.2), and a whole range of meat, chicken and rice preparations joined this line up. Chilled, and frozen snacks and entrees (Fig. 13.3) as well as many types of takeaway foods began to be manufactured. Semi processed extruded food intermediates like vermicelli, varieties of pasta and extrusion cooked instant noodles became major hits with the young and adults alike. Extruded snacks as finger foods, either in the ready form or to fry at home were popular.

Fig. 13.1: Jamun dry mix to Upma dry mix – a sweet and a savoury can be said to be two landmark products with wide appeal. They now come in attractive Standi-pack units.

Fig. 13.2: Retort pouch technology meets everyone's needs by making it possible to process moist foods. Flavoured rice in several varieties is available. Many meat based pulavs and curries are also being processed.

Fig. 13.3: Frozen foods of a variety never seen before in the consumer market in India include many snack items for refrying or quick heating.

Breakfast cereal foods made from flaked/shredded/extruded wheat, rice and corn, rolled oats and muesli etc. were fortified with dry fruits, bran, nutrients, dehydrated fruits etc. targeted and reached out to the upwardly mobile, health conscious young professionals and busy corporate personnel.

For those who preferred traditional foods, except for *Vada* and *Upma* mixes there was nothing else. A recent entrant to this range of traditional breakfast foods are *Idli* and *Dosa* fermented batters for chill storage in ready to use form. The small cottage industry segment produces such items for local retailing in cities in the South.

Many varieties of instant formulas began to be produced. Weaning foods in the so called delectable tastes and flavours, presented in attractive packs and containers and with a lot of health related information on the labels did their best to wean milk fed babies away from traditional weaning baby meals. Even these traditional home recipes were made on cottage scale and sold in urban markets.

The dairy industry outdid all others by coming out with a variety of cheeses, cheese spreads, butter, ghee, cream, liquid milk brands, yogurts and milk powder (whole and skimmed), evaporated and condensed milk and dairy whiteners. Ice creams bearing foreign brand names and having exotic tastes and flavours made by big companies vied and jostled with national and local brands. There are other instances too, like breads and 2–minute noodles which seem to have become institutions by themselves and as popular as the very traditional 'always there' items.

Among the fruit products there are not only the jams and sweetened juices but also bottled concentrates/crushes far beyond the orange and lemon varieties. Synthetic and nature like fruit flavoured juice powders and fruit flavoured milk shake powders, both in ready to dissolve form or ready to prepare at home form became huge successes because of aggressive marketing aimed at children and later because people did not seem to mind preparing it at home even though sugar or milk came from their kitchens.

There was a boom in the vegetable oil sector not only because of the wider choices available to the consumers, many claims of 'good for heart' PUFA content (poly unsaturated fatty acids) and superiority but also in the way the edible oils could now be bought i.e., in elegant and attractive, sturdy but light weight packaging (Fig. 13.4). Bag-in-the-box type of cartons were popular for a time. *Vanaspati* – the hydrogenated vegetable fat of different brands competed desperately for a market share against refined, deodorised, decolourised oils and oil blends with and with out PUFA claims. PUFA oils and the ensuing health benefits were widely advertised to impress upon the thoroughly confused consumers.

Fig. 13.4: Packaged oils in sachets and gallon jars. The health claims for each one as well as the expected shelf life are shown in the printed nutrient labels on the package itself.

Confectionary products such as chewing/bubble gums, toffees, boiled sweets, caramel and chocolate-coated sweet drops etc. were seen in many varieties and were affordable to the young consumers. While milk chocolate varieties produced by some dairy food groups and multinational companies had more visible market presence than before, their pricing made them more a special occasion item for the average consumer and thus created only marginal impact.

The traditional and regional sweetmeats came out in a big way and in many different forms but with little induction of modernised technology. They remained little more than a home/catering scale production and were confined to individual or franchise shops. Homemade chocolates and bakery style festive cakes and pastries which used to be sold only in small shops in hill stations and big metropolises attempted to capture a larger market segment. However, the quality of all such home style products varied tremendously and their safety aspects were not even recognised fully. Many of the milk based popular sweets have a short shelf life; *Khoa* – a concentrated form of milk used in several types of confectionary became a source of microbial hazard and food poisoning. Now there are big players in the market. The famous KC Das and Company of Kolkata, whose traditional Bengali sweets became a by-word for the best sweets, was the first to can their famous '*Rasogullas*' (cottage cheese balls cooked in syrup) in order to extend its shelf life. Chocolates or even traditional sweets never before sold in festive gift packs were pioneered by the Nestle Company and Haldiram and Co.

Traditional fried and snack foods appeared as portion packs in plain and printed attractive packs. Potato chips were made on home/cottage scale in the normal way but then the big manufacturing concerns made their presence felt with sophisticated machinery, quality control and gas packing for longer life. While the majority of consumers went for the lower priced home-style products, there were enough takers in the metropolises and tourist places for the packaged brand name and more expensive items to be successful as lifestyle foods.

Around the mid 1990s, another phenomenon was witnessed. Along with the processed, cooked or finished foods of the kind mentioned above, primary foodstuffs received the much deserved attention by way of value addition. Until now, these items were found in the corner grocery stores and sold in retail. The big companies first paid attention to such products. The grocery items like rice, *suji/rava* (semolina), *atta*, wheat, and pulses, whole spices etc. were cleaned, de-stoned and neatly packed in retail packs or bulk sacks. A step beyond this was to fortify wheat flour with vitamins and other nutrients and multinational companies like Pilsbury and Hindustan Lever started this. Other manufacturers joined in with their brands. Suddenly one did not have to, if one did not want to, buy wheat grains, de-stone and clean them before sending it for milling. Today the wheat milling industry supplies whole wheat flour plain, or fortified with vitamins or with other whole grain meals (Fig. 13.5).

Spices – whole, ground, individual or in mixtures as well as oleoresins produced by several manufacturers under their own brandname were added to the convenience products range. Of greater innovation were the spice pastes – semi solid, thick and moist concoctions in flexi packs

Fig. 13.5: The trend swings back to 'finish at home' flour mixes announcing health benefits. The latest among the fortified flours is one which is a multi grain type introduced in the year 2007.

and bottles to reduce the tedium of home preparation of many complicated ethnic foods. To add flavour, colour and brightness and increase consumer appeal to many products, a whole range of mostly synthetic substances was being used.

Fruit juices, aerated soft drinks, processed drinking water, Indian made foreign liquor, Indian brand beers as well as liquid milk and branded tea and coffee producers wooed the consumers with claims and counterclaims in advertisements for preferential market segments.

One of the greatest surprise entries into the 90s market was the wonder of bottled water. In those days too, those who carried drinking water did so only during rail and road travel or in school bags for kids' use. Anyone else carrying water for drinking was considered nothing short of eccentric. The scene has changed now, to put it mildly. Practically no one is seen without a bottle of water outside home and everyone expects to be provided with safe and hygienic drinking water at all times. Indeed, bottled water is flaunted and has become a part of table decoration along with flowers arranged for dignitaries in any public meeting. The boom in this industry due to intense reaching out tactics of manufacturers is matched equally by the soft drinks industry. In fact, there is a veritable war on. From zero presence in 1970, the Indian mineral/bottled/drinking water market was worth more than Rs 600 crores in 2002. Media reports said that the Nestle Co. had acquired 70 brands of water and operated in 130 countries including 'Pure Life', 'Perrier' and 'San Pellegrino' brands. The Coca Cola Co. started with a brand 'Himjal' in India. Between 1999–2002 many more brand names for bottled drinking water have become visible and today there are countless pure water suppliers, manufacturers, bottlers and distributors among private firms, both in the large (Indian holdings and MNC) and small-scale sector.

There are now infinite number of brands in the domestic market, some regionally popular and others nationally. The packaging size varies between one use 250 ml bottles and tumblers (airlines use this), 500 ml, 1 L, 5 L even 25 L, some of which come with their own dispensers. From time to time, concerns have been voiced about the quality and safety of one brand or the other with regard to microbial levels/faecal organisms, presence of organic matter and debris and more recently about unacceptable levels of various pesticides.

In the aerated soft drinks area, the scene appeared to be totally cornered by two firms: Coca Cola Company and Pepsi India, who are marketing from soda to soft drinks under many brand names. Even so, as regards the consumption rate in India, it is low, around five bottles/head/year according to newspaper reports in 2002 compared to 150 bottles/man/year consumed in a country like Philippines. Not withstanding the aggressive marketing of these products, the low consumption rate reflects our population size, and the sections that cannot afford to buy them and the conservative nature of Indian consumers in general towards aerated soft drinks. Despite this, there are any number of manufacturers of aerated soft drinks in the domestic market at the present time and notwithstanding the fact and the knowledge that these synthetic soft drinks provide empty calories and, therefore, are not nutritious, there is a dedicated clientele for each type. A lifestyle statement is being made when one buys, offers and accepts such a product. It is also considered safer to drink a bottled beverage like this in the absence of clean water although there is no dearth of water in the bottled form.

Tea, a major product of India until now, has been viewed as a hot drink made with milk called '*chai*'. In the West, hot lemon tea and iced tea are both popular as refreshing beverages. Green tea as a health drink is gaining ground everyday. Though there are several brand name packaged teas in leaf, powder and dust form available in India, none of the beverage variations have been popularised and presented as alternative tea drinks. There are no high profile advertisements but media reports say that the big MNCs are all poised to enter this field soon with instantised preparations. The Tatas have launched a *chai-unchai* outlet to popularise tea in several forms. Packaged teas with herbs, fruit flavours, with spices and 'masala', in different portion packs and as tea bags have hit the market in the last three years or so. Tea in the leaf, granular and dust form, in pure form and as blends, sells in millions of kilos in India and registers its presence in the international markets. Of late though, herbal teas with various health claims are to be found

Packaged coffee – beans, powder, pure or blended with chicory, instant or filter type, bottled *latte* etc. – is an industry which is worth several crores of rupees and many brands have emerged. The freshly prepared brew which was traditionally available in South Indian hotels and restaurants is also a product that interests both the smaller entrepreneurs and the MNCs for expansion.

Fruit juices have established themselves as another briskly growing sector since the 90s. The now widely available aseptically processed whole fruit juices – single or mixed fruit type, fruit and vegetable juice mixes and packed in cartons – tetra packs in 200 ml and 1 L amounts are preferred over bottled squashes, nectars and fruit concentrates and fruit crystals of yesteryears. Prominent brand names like Tropicana, Onjus, Real, Active and many more vie with the aerated drink selections of Coca Cola, Sprite, Orange drinks, Pepsi etc. Some claim that no extra sugar has been added and some are silent about it. All in all these are highly sweetened drinks and carry a hefty price tag compared to the aerated drinks. There is a consumer section devoted to this product too.

Technological Inputs and Outcome from Year 2000 till Today

Forays into the application of modified atmosphere packaging or MAP, 'active packaging', 'smart packaging' as well as finding self-heating/self-cooling packaging systems are being made at the laboratory level for fruits and vegetables.

The Ready-to-eat foods, some of which are cut fruits and vegetables, some in the IM form and some in the frozen form, do not find a large market. The dehydrated variety is more in the nature of ready mixes and according to some reports (Bawa, 2007) manufacturing units have been established in the Middle East and UK. These products are much in demand in USA and Canada where large segments of the Indian Diaspora reside.

The trend of dehydrated fruit bits mixed with nuts called Trail Mixes, so very popular in North America, have not yet caught on with Indian consumers simply because no one seems to be importing this product and the indigenous food industry appears not to realise the potential of such a healthy alternative to fried snacks. Apple, peach, pear, different berries, raisins, banana, almonds, walnuts, peanuts, soya etc. are the principle constituents of such trail mixes.

Irradiation of foods though permitted and practiced in some 35 countries, is confined to two commercial processing units, one near Mumbai and another in Nasik. Bawa stated that more units are likely to be set up soon by entrepreneurs. The Government has approved the irradiation treatment of more than 14 items in India for the purpose of extending storage life. These include potato, onions, semolina, and spices like turmeric, chili, black pepper and coffee beans.

In the preceding two decades, some technologies that came to be commercialised are now in the main stream of processing 'ration' items for the troops, thus lifting the constraints and limitations on the quantity that could be generated by pilot scale manufacture in the research laboratory. Prominent among these technologies is hot air dehydration to prepare instant food mixes and retort pouch processing by which many food items can be made for Meals Ready to Eat (MRE) type of operational packs. The bulk of the MREs are made by this process which is actually steam sterilization of food seated in a polymeric pouch, to achieve destruction of microorganisms. This is carried out in a 'retort'. Aluminum can technology was originally investigated for canning fresh coconut water and adopted for canning of fish. Between one successful transfer of technology to another there were many processes that never took off but stayed at the laboratory or pilot scale level. Most products however continued to find use in supplies affected from the laboratory for various emergencies and special military needs. There were others that never saw the light of day as commercial products.

Commercial ventures based on imported technology, equipment, and packaging materials floundered. Those who came up with some food formulations on their own caught the market's interest for a while but soon disappeared for being unable to find a proper market niche or for other reasons.

Even as retort foods – vegetarian and meat based, became widely acceptable and definitely by the Armed Forces (mostly vegetarian items), another innovation that would help the soldiers to quickly heat the foods *in situ* was designed in the form of a self heating package. Constructed with polymeric materials and using chemicals to generate exothermic reactions, it was intended to be used by soldiers on the go and particularly in the lonely picket posts high up in the Siachen (Sanjeev Kumar *et al.,* 2005).

At this point it is worthwhile taking a rapid look at how the food industry has grown in the last 2–3 decades. The figures available for the year 2003 published in the Directory of Food Processing Industry and Trade (2003) tell their own tale.

The food industries in India as of 2003 include flour mills (820 units), fruit and vegetable units 5,198 units (processing only 2 per cent of the produce), many varieties of spices amounting to 25–30 per cent of world production and processed for value addition worth Rs. 3,500 crores (US $900 million), 22 million tons of oil seeds of many varieties; fish processing in 418 units meat processing (171 units) converting less than 1 per cent of the 4.5 million tonnes of meat produced from the largest live stock population in the world (470 million: 50 per cent buffalo and 15 per cent cattle); the largest milk production in the world, more than 81 million tonnes in year 2001 but only about 15 per cent of which is produced in the organised sector; broiler and egg production, primarily in the unorganised sector, initially registered a very fast growth but appears to have slowed down with the demands from Europe, Japan and other countries falling sharply after the mid 1990s.

The size of the semi processed and ready to eat packaged food industry is valued at Rs. 4,000 crores or US $ 1 billion, which is said to be growing at 20 per cent. The so-called consumer food industries comprising ready to cook types based on pasta and cocoa, bakery products, biscuits and soft drinks are among the largest. The annual production of bread, biscuits, pastries buns, rusks and such snack items mostly produced in the unorganised sector is estimated to be more than 30 lakh tonnes, bread and biscuits alone amounting to 15 lakh and 11 lakh tonnes, only 35 per cent of which emanates from organised industries. Pasta has made a place for itself in the domestic consumer market, and being semi processed, it can be finished at home in a myriad ways. These include noodles, vermicelli, macaroni and spaghetti.

Chocolates, that pre war army ration which was beset with quality problems, today is a flourishing industry; there are 20 units in the manufacture of different cocoa based products in numerous varieties, shapes, sizes and flavours, drinking chocolate, cocoa butter substitutes, cocoa based malted milk foods claiming the health food label, all amounting to 34,000 tonnes.

The runaway success of soft drinks, the third largest packaged food type in India is evident from its production figures, 66,000 million bottles in 2003 and growing assuredly, produced in 100 plants all over the country and sold out of 7 million outlets. It has an export market to the tune of

Rs 700 crores per annum. The 100 per cent juice in tetra pack cartons made by several manufacturers also gave the Indian consumers a fruit product which they considered to be fresh and without preservatives. In 2002, this market was said to be growing at 15–20 per cent. In 2008 it was reported that Tetrapak invested more than 88 million Euros to build a sate of the art packaging plant as per information posted on the web (www.tetrapak.com; www.thehindu businessline.com/Hindu Business news). Not to be outdone is the bottled water segment, India being the tenth largest consumer of this product in the world. In 2002, it was estimated to have had a turnover of more than 10 billion and even though it occupies only 5 per cent of the beverage market in India, branded water is the fastest growing one.

In the alcoholic drinks and beer making sector, growth is as impressive as in the other areas. There were, in 2003, 56 beer manufacturing units under license with an installed capacity of 1,216 lakh doz. per annum. From non molasses sources, output of alcoholic drinks is comparatively small. Wines, which until very recently were unaffordable to the Indian consumer because of high cost of imported varieties is being made in the country's vineyards. Increasing in popularity among the affluent middleclass, the wine industry is said to have produced some 1 million bottles of good quality.

The export figures for the processed foods falling under fruits and vegetables, animal products, rice, walnuts, marine products, alcoholic beverages, milled products, ground nuts and guar gum crossed Rs.14,000 crores.

Figures for many other sectors have shown similar upward trend and it would not be out of line to assume that in the ten years ensuing the 2003 estimates, the food processing industry has grown several fold.

Decade of developments: This decade of developments in the food area had many firsts:

- Contract farming by MNCs to assure the availability of the right type raw material – in quality and quantity: tomatoes for the manufacture of sauces and ketchup and gherkins for pickled gherkins for export.
- Air-cooling of freshly harvested grape, mangoes, apples even strawberries etc. to box them for longer shelf life.
- Modified atmosphere packaging for sorted and graded fruits and vegetables.
- IQF method, which until now was used for freezing shrimp for the export market was applied to freezing fresh, cleaned and sorted green peas and certain cut vegetables by the processing unit of the National Dairy Development Board.
- Gamma irradiation for microbial safety, preventing infestation and extending quality and shelf life of spices and wheat was permitted.
- Although the retort pouch technology had been in use for making limited number of MRE (meals ready to eat) for the Indian Armed Forces and studies on it had been initiated in the 1970s (Ghosh *et al.,* 1977, Ghosh *et al.,* 1980), it was commercially launched only in the late 1990s for making a limited variety of foods for the armed forces and then emboldened by its acceptance in the domestic market it expanded for export purposes.
- The concept of HACCP or Hazard Analysis Critical Control Points programme for clean and safe production of foods was diligently propagated by Government, food scientists and other experts to bring awareness about safe manufacturing. There are accredited certifying agencies for this purpose and the broiler chicken and shrimp industries have the HACCP system in place.
- And with much effort, product labeling laws made it mandatory to provide nutritional and shelf life information on every packaged foodstuff.

Processed Foods in the Rations

Technically speaking, all foodstuffs, barring fresh fruits and salad vegetables, which are eaten as they are without cooking, are subjected to some form of processing. Even surface cleaning and sanitizing, peeling, cutting, dicing of fruits and vegetables for direct consumption or for further treatment could be termed 'processing'. At the farm level, sun drying and winnowing of grain is 'processing' as is hand pounding to de-husk and stone grinding to make flour.

Milled products also include crushed or broken grains and semolina or *suji* from wheat, rice and other grains, millets and pulses. Though they are all low moisture (12 per cent or less), shelf stable forms, in common parlance they are raw ingredients which cannot be consumed as such and thus have to be converted in a kitchen into appropriate and palatable forms of food for consumption. Some of them like semolina and flour can also be used to prepare yet another form of shelf stable extruded and dried intermediate known as vermicelli, a form of Indian fine pasta. This has to be cooked further. At a higher level of processing there are refined starches extracted from corn and rice which are used in food preparation.

Sun drying of whole spices – black pepper, red chili, cumin, coriander, mustard, cloves etc. has been a long standing practice and the only form of processing these items ever received until just two decades ago. By the 1990s however, there came into the domestic market a whole plethora of carefully harvested spices, cleaned and dried under controlled conditions. Sometimes these are irradiated (Cobalt–60 source), packed whole or in ground form as individual spices or in mixtures. Lately, there are spice-condiment pastes which come bottled or in flexi packs to provide a vide choice of culinary condiments. Hot air dehydrated condiments also provide an alternative to the fresh ones.

There are many tinned/pouch packed moist or dehydrated food items made of meat, fish, poultry egg, fruits and vegetables, milk origin, some of which find their way into Service rations principally as substitutes in lieu of some basic ration items. There is also a small range of pouch packed meal items meant for use in special circumstances.

Processed foods as substitutes: The current list of processed foods which figure among the substitute foods authorised in the ration scales, allows for a reasonably wide selection to be made from among those found in the domestic market. The selection of food products is based primarily on (a) the necessity for including items from each food group, (b) locating a good manufacturing base and continuous supply within the country for the processed items, (c) amenability of the suppliers to follow the existing system of requisitioning, central purchase and stocking policy prevalent in the Armed Forces, (d) sold in appropriate packing, and assurance of their shelf stability and safety, and (e) comparative cost considerations for replacing the main ration items with the processed ones.

Currently the largest number of processed items procured by the Defence sector is in the tinned form. Every item is listed as tinned or *td* in short. These are:

Meat tinned : Meat is usually mutton (from sheep or goat). Tinned meat, rather canned meats, come as chunks steeped in brine, or in curried from, meat mince, also curried. Other types are pork meat, luncheon meat, sausages and bacon. Venison (deer meat) is also listed as an acceptable substitute for the Navy.

Fish tinned : It is mostly sardines packed in oil, though there may be tuna and mackerel too.

Vegetables tinned : Potatoes in brine appear to be the main vegetable in this category, although at certain times okra and any other vegetables may also be obtained. There are not many varieties of canned vegetables because of general unpopularity. The few that are produced are mostly made for the Defence sector.

Fruit tinned : A limited variety of diced fruit singly or as mixes can be found; these are papaya, guava, mango, peaches, pears etc. in syrup; fruit pulps-usually mango and mango nectar, pineapple and orange juice etc. are produced domestically. Since the advent of the new processing technology (aseptic process) a range of fruit juices in cartons (brick packs/tetra packs) have become available. Other fruit products are single or mixed fruit jams, jellies and citrus marmalades.

Milk and milk products tinned : 'Milk-tinned' as it is quaintly put in the official language of procurement, is only tinned in the condensed form called 'condensed milk, sweetened', as well as 'evaporated milk, unsweetened'. The Ultra High Temperature (UHT) treated milk has come as a boon to the Services in sectors where fresh milk is not supplied and milk is required to be stored. Milk powder, whole, was once an important ration item.

Tinned butter and processed cheese are two other milk products. Interestingly, there is no listing for '*ghee*'– clarified butter, which was once the cooking medium in the civilian sector and the Indian Armed Forces.

There are a number of shelf stable processed foods. These are refined oil standardized; dehydrated vegetables (onions, garlic and herbs, potato), whole milk powder and skim milk powder, Nutramul, egg powder, drinking chocolate, soluble coffee, groundnut, dry fruits (raisins, currants) and nuts, biscuits, chocolates, corn flakes, oats and oatmeal, tomato ketchup, pickles in oil, vinegar, corn flour and corn starch, custard powder, texturised soya chunks (TVP, texturised vegetable protein), ice cream powder mix, gelatin (sheet or powder), *papad* and ground pepper. Semolina, *dalia*, vermicelli, noodles and pasta, Bengal gram flour (besan) and white flour also figure as substitutes or rather alternates in lieu of small quantities of cereals or pulses.

Foods Specially Made for the Services

Nowhere else but for Defence use, are the specially produced long life *chapati* tinned, or *parantha* tinned (lately in flexi packs), precooked dehydrated dals (pulses), freeze dried juice powders (only from DFRL) and other items required from time to time are produced. Any item required by the Armed Forces and which is not made by the domestic industry ends up as an urgent request to DFRL.

Siachen rations: To deliver the daily energy and nutrient needs through foods acceptable to ethnic tastes and involving minimum preparation or cooking time, minimum facilities and low expenditure of fuel, combat type ration packs are required. At the time of the start of the Siachen hostilities, aside from the standard but limited variety of tinned stuff, there were no special foods suitable for high altitude and certainly none which could be procured from commercial sources. The troops could not possibly subsist on tinned rations alone. Several processed foods developed by Defence food scientists were tested. These foods were mainly of the dehydrated variety. Having been associated early on with the food support effort for Operation *Meghdoot,* as the Siachen operations were known, it is remembered as a period of frenetic R&D activity and one of great urgency. The dehydrated foods already under development for Compo rations appeared to be suitable as convenience foods for this operation. However, a major hurdle was to manufacture these products in sufficiently large quantities. Coincidentally, a small-scale industrialist in Mysore offered to produce the necessary quantities under the guidance and technical assistance of the scientists. It was one of the very first instances where laboratory-industry collaboration rose to the occasion and successfully produced large quantities of dehydrated plain rice, *khicdi,* vegetable *pulav* and spiced dal curry. Many of the products were also prepared in the pilot scale facility of the research laboratory.

No one said that it was the perfect answer but everyone knew that there were no other options or products in the domestic market at that time. The upside was that these products were familiar foods, spicy and salted in the way Indian meals are prepared. They provided bulk, had the right mix of major nutrients, appeased hunger and gave some degree of satisfaction, at least until the taste buds became jaded and appetites were lost. They were also conveniently packed in portion sizes in plastic polymeric pouches, possessed a long shelf life and did not spoil and required minimum cooking time. In their sturdy inner and outer packaging they were not fragile and could be air dropped without damage.

The downside was that being dried foods they required water for rehydration, which could be obtained only by melting ice. It was always a major task to chip away at the ice outside bunkers. Tremendous amounts of fuel was required to melt the ice, then to rehydrate the dried foods, to thaw and heat other canned foods, to prepare a hot beverage like tea and to keep warm. The used food packages became garbage and a nuisance but were required to be kept from flying in the wind and polluting the surroundings as well as causing the outpost to be detected.

This generation may not know that the numerous varieties of processed foods in pouches and soft drinks in brick packs/cartons and a great many convenience variety of soup powders, snacks and sweets now found abundantly in the domestic market shelves were yet to appear at the time when the Siachen conflict flared. There were only bottled fruit concentrates and squashes and canned fruit juice, and cut fruit in syrup and vegetables in brine and meat in tin cans. Cadbury's chocolate bars, certain brands of toffees and boiled sweets, a few brands of biscuits, milk powder and (and especially ordered egg powder) were all that were available.

The men must eat but evinced little interest in the food and had little appetite and even lesser inclination to eat. To tempt them to eat and take in the necessary number of calories, many food items were specially authorised and supplied. These included dried fruits and nuts, chocolates and even Indian sweetmeats. Journalists who reported about the ongoing conflict during 1992 were informed that innovative ways were found by the jawans to transform an uninteresting meal into a novel dish such as hot Maggie noodles wrapped in an omelet. But in 1984, these noodle packs had only just appeared in the Indian market and very likely had not yet been introduced into the Service rations as a substitute for other cereals. Eggs are not authorized rations for the jawans except *in lieu* of meat and milk, but of course in Siachen, eggs would have been a special issue item. But they froze!

There were minimal facilities in the bunkers to indulge in any energetic cooking activity even if one was so inclined, although the situation was much better in the base camp. Meal times were not pleasurable, and meal preparation was not easy; the chocolate bars became as hard and inedible as rock, every canned food item (the moist and those with liquid content) was frozen solid, the canned milk powder always turned rancid and became unpalatable.

Throughout the 1980s and much of the 1990s, it was impressed upon those concerned with operations and supplies and with food and nutrition that the supply of fresh vegetables like onions, tomatoes, carrots, radishes and green chilies, amongst many other vegetables, was a priority in the Siachen sector and that ways must be found to deliver them in the most convenient and ready to eat manner. A flurry of investigations ensued and several packaging options were examined. It must be said here that though the research scientists did come up with some solutions for this and other similar requirements, clever packaging and products, the bottleneck was always the production of any item, food or packaging, in large enough quantities, there being no manufacturer ready to produce the wholly military use items. It must also be said here that the Army was not ready to accept any product(s) developed by the laboratory which were considered suitable for high altitude preparation; their specifications were inconsistent and kept changing each time, their expectations were rather unclear and there was always something extra that needed to be incorporated. All this led to delays, field trials with uncertain outcome, and further delays.

Twenty-six years after the Siachen conflict began, and though the guns fell silent in 2003 after a unilateral ceasefire, the presence of the Indian Army on the Saltoro range is very real. During this period the Army has learnt how to deal with the high altitude, the awful weather and temperature conditions; it has a greater understanding of the physical and physiological stresses and is better equipped to provide medical aid; it is better trained, better armed, better equipped and has become more experienced in every way to continue this battle. The Army is also better fed than ever before. Instead of the dehydrated mixes of the 1980s the troops are now issued retort pouch foods as part of Meals Ready to Eat. This advancement has come about as a direct result of the researches carried out by defense scientists and transfer of technology to industry. The domestic market today produces many shelf stable food products, vegetable and meat, fish, poultry based snacks, fruit products, health beverages, cereals, confectionary items, biscuits and the like in user-friendly portion packs. While all these products may be used in the civilian consumer market, for Defence use, their inclusion as part of substitute rations or special rations is determined by their calorie content and nutrient profile, shelf life and safety features and the existence of a supply chain in the important sectors of operations to deliver the consignment in a manner essential to the quality of the food. The other considerations would be the foods' operational suitability, transportability, and cost.

It must be remembered that everything which contains moisture or water freezes to solid rock at the temperatures prevailing in Siachen. All fresh and dry rations are transported in fiber reinforced plastic crates in quantities sufficient for four to six men. In the bunkers, anyone who has even the least claim to culinary interest or capability, let alone expertise, is promptly elected to be the camp cook. Some of them even know how to roll out *chapatis*. Since the troops dislike egg powder they are provided with whole fresh eggs, which freeze. The cook has to first boil them to defrost before doing anything further. Any fruits provided to them likewise are required to be boiled to soften. The favourite drink of the Siachen jawan is said to be a concoction made from mixed fruit jam stirred up in hot water. Hot sweet foods like *kheer* etc. are relished.

What the men do not like could make a long list: milk powder, all sorts of fried snacks, oily foods, and even some sweetmeats. Canned meat and vegetables and especially potatoes are also disliked. There is a strong belief among those deployed at high altitudes that the canned foods such as curried meats (spicy) are the cause of frequent gastric disturbances and extreme flatulence. But surprisingly, the pouch foods like *pulav*, *dal makhni* and such items (all spicy foods) produced in the UK and sampled by the troops and officers on peacekeeping missions abroad apparently never caused any such gastric trouble. This is indeed mysterious because all these foods undergo the same high temperature steam sterilisation. The only difference could have been in the level of spicing and of course that they were deployed at normal sea levels and not altitudes.

MRE: In the past six years, Meals Ready to Eat (MRE) in retort pouches and meal packets assembled as compo packs have come to occupy a major part of the supply of operational rations, first on field trial basis and then upon full acceptance. Before they could be manufactured, dozens of different foods had been especially developed and produced within the Defence Food Research Laboratory. After technology transfer only one manufacturer under the banner MTR Industries of Bangalore had been making retort pouch foods for Defence use. Pouch foods are being produced by others now as well.

Since the advent of modern fruit processing methods, many types of fruit beverages in liquid and dried (crystals) form have made inroads into the bottled squash and juice market as well as doing away with freeze dried juice powders.

Bread is an alternative for *atta*/rice; a portion of either can be exchanged for bread in the Army and Air Force officers' rations and for everyone in the Navy. The troops sometimes are given 'Biscuits Service' when the latter are in stock and must be utilised before their shelf life expires. What particular type of biscuits these are has not been clarified. For some reason, long life bread has not been seen as an important ration item except in the Navy and aside from developing preservative wrappers for freshly baked bread, no other attempt has been made to induce longer shelf life. Small loaves of soft breads probably are more amenable to some form of 'keep fresh' treatment, even irradiation but it has not been done.

Cold chain requiring foodstuffs: There really was no cold chain to speak of in the Services and, therefore, procurement of foods requiring chilling or freezing, except in handling fresh meat, was never contemplated as an option. In large freezer rooms, boxed meat cuts are stored at airbases such as Chandimandir, from where they are transported by air in unrefrigerated condition and delivered or airdropped at higher altitudes in the Northern sector. Since there is provision for chill or frozen storage in the Navy ships, frozen meat, chicken/fowl, fish etc. are stored on board. Presently, a very large variety of frozen heat-and-eat pouch packed foods – mostly meat and chicken based as well as *chapatis* and *paranthas* have come into the domestic market. The Navy is the most likely Service to need them.

In the last few years, due to the availability of refrigerated transportation, Army trucks are able to transport frozen dressed chicken and other flesh foods to outlying supply depots and posts.

Summer in India can be cruel. Getting ice in summer months is an indescribable joy to the troops, especially for those deployed in the Western desert areas. Large ice boxes carried in trucks are used to transport the ice in great quantities over long distances every day.

Chilled fresh milk is another refrigerated item which travels long distances to be delivered. Only when the fresh milk is not available is the processed milk – in the powder and condensed form, issued. It has been told to the author that chilled buttermilk *lassi* is also now being supplied by the Rajasthan Dairy industry to the border outposts in the Western desert.

Fresh eggs do not actually require refrigerated transportation but definitely benefit by it. There was no mention of the need for sending vegetable supplies by refrigerated transports to any of the units. But other chilled food types could definitely be included if indicated as ration items.

Bottled water: There was a time not too long ago when water was canned for inclusion in Navy Survival Ration packs. Flexi-packs and PET bottles came along with an entirely new culture of 'bottling' safe mineral/drinkable water. The service ration scales do not *per se* list bottled water as an entitlement. Under certain situations, it is authorized to the ranks in armoured units and those on road work duties. Bottled water definitely falls under 'processed' commodity. It is however a component of certain pack-rations and emergency rations.

Research on newer products for better nutrition and health, termed probiotics and phytochemicals is ongoing. Probiotics is the name for a group of desirable bacteria colonizing the intestinal tract that help to maintain the gut barrier and prevent colonization of pathogenic organisms. Probiotics have been found to enhance immune function and decrease the incidence and severity of diarrhea. The specific organisms are the lactic acid bacteria, *Lactobacillus acidophilus*, *L casei*, *Enterococcus faecium and Bifidobacterium* species (Gibney, Macdonald and Roche, 2003, p. 304). Certain dairy products containing probiotics are now available though it might be pointed out that the traditional fermented milk foods such as buttermilk and *dahi* are made by lactic fermentation and even some of the other traditional foods and beverages are rich in probiotics. Non medicinal therapeutic virtues of various botanicals and low calorie sweeteners seem to occupy centre stage as evidenced by many small and big investigations (Jacob *et al.*, 2008; Guptha, Daisy and Brinda, 2008). These are not yet popular in the domestic market under this nomenclature, possibly because many such substances are prescribed for therapy under traditional Indian medical practice. Phytochemicals, as the very name suggests, are substances found in plants and participate in a number of physiological functions in the mammalian systems. They are present in a variety of fruits, vegetables, greens, beans, legumes, cereals etc. They are classified as phenolic phytochemicals (flavonoids), other phenolics (tannins, stilbene, lignans), carotenoids, phytosterols, sulphur containing compounds etc. They have been found to exert beneficial effects on cardio vascular disease, cancer and immune related functions. The knowledge about the compounds and their specific role is incomplete. Chemicals from black tea, green tea, lemon, lime, mandarin, orange and soya diets, anthocyanins (purple, red pigments in fruits and vegetables), lycopenes of tomato and carotenoids from carrots and other green and orange coloured vegetables and aromatic herbs and tubers like ginger and turmeric, phytosterols from brassicas, oats, natural vegetable oils, all cereals and their products, and glucose inolates from brussels sprouts, mustard greens, radish etc. have been recognized and have become subjects of intensive research in nutritional sciences (Gibney *et al.*, 2003, p. 307). Again it may be said that many of these substances, called nutraceuticals, form a part of traditional diets. New terminologies, assigning specific functions to these compounds and finding their precise beneficial roles have come from concentrated research in recent times.

Foods for Niche Markets

Many products have been produced for special purposes.

- Special purpose foods such as sports drinks, endurance/performance enhancing foods and beverages.
- Energy food bars with better nutrient profiles. A 50 g bar delivering 200 Kcals may contain pumpkin seeds, sesame, flax, sunflower seeds, raisins, dates, other nuts, vegetable oil, mixed grain cereals, vitamins and minerals, binding agents, emulsifiers, sweeteners or sugars (www.wonderenergybar.com). They are quite tasty and filling, one can miss the next meal without

feeling hunger pangs after eating one bar. There is also no dearth of muscle building foods, beverages and food bars aimed at sports persons and athletes and those who need high density foods with high nutritive component.

- Adventure foods
- Products which will help the service sector industry like the railways, airlines, tourism, pilgrimage organizers, and hotel and catering businesses.
- Fortified breads (with multigrain seeds, flour and protein isolates) and traditional foods, special ingredients and supplements for health, home and hospitality industry.
- Health boosting substances and botanical preparations using traditional indigenous knowledge and copycat items popular in western countries. These include a variety of plant products such as alicin, capsaicin, lycopene, isoflavones, many minerals like calcium, zinc, choline and shpingolipids of animal origin. Flooding the Indian market, imported products containing extracts of spices like cinnamon, cardamom, nutmeg, infusions using leafs from plants such as *Brahmi*, *Shankapushpa* and *Ashvagandha*, soy protein isolate, flax seeds, edible fiber and any number of antioxidants minerals and vitamins have found a niche market.
- Low calorie/diet foods and substitutes, sweeteners and fat substitutes with nature like tastes and mouth feel to use in Indian preparations. Use of fructo-oligosaccharides (non-digestible) as sweeteners in diabetic preparations is one of the options.
- Foods and substances for special missions for both army and civilian use.
- Foods and packages for disaster relief operations, special uses such as refugee aid and world food aid programmes, and foods capable of meeting the requirements of target groups in the national nutritional programmes.
- Improved packaging for antimicrobial action incorporating nanosilver particles (George *et al.*, 2008)

Though intensive research is being conducted, there is no specific recommendation for any of the critical areas such as stress relief, radio protection, energising and long sustenance foods, clinical nutritional foods and menus, nutrients and foods for brain function, and safety enhanced items for use by the immune-compromised, GM foods for engineered traits in the nature of firm tomatoes, golden rice and protein rich potato or tailored nutritional substances for individual needs depending on the genomic make up which falls into the area of nutrigenomics.

Governmental Support to the Defence Science and Technology Component

The Defence budgetary allocations have steadily risen every year. In the 2009 budget, an amount of Rs. 1,41,600 crore was provided to the Ministry of Defence, a significant increase of 34 per cent over that in 2008. A substantial amount of this increase is meant towards the increased salary and pension of Defence personnel (after the sixth Pay Commission's recommendation) and for hardware procurement. The Army gets the lion's share of the funds (41 per cent), the Navy gets Rs. 8,322 crore plus another Rs. 300 crore for other things, and the Air force Rs.14, 318 crore. The hardware budget is hiked from Rs. 41,000 crore in 2008 to Rs. 54,824 crore in 2009. There is, however, no specific mention of how much of the remainder would be given for the Science and Technology component in the Defence Research and Development Organization, Ministry of Defence. This organisation received Rs. 5,454 crore (out of a total defence budget of Rs. 89,000 crore) in the year 2006–07. This level of funding is meant exclusively for the development of technologies, systems and products from agriculture to aerospace and everything in between. The salaries of scientists (7,000) and technical personnel (12,000) of the DRDO are paid out of another 18 per cent of the DRDO funds (Ramachandran, 2007). There are nine Life Sciences laboratories in the DRDO and their combined total budget is a mere 2 per cent of that of the DRDO. The allocation to the sciences and particularly to life sciences and food sciences is not likely to be any different from before. It would be relief enough if it were not cut further. Clearly the emphasis is laid on building a world class Armed Force by equipping them with the latest machines, communication devices, weapons, crafts, clothing and training. Food is apparently a mundane thing and therefore not given the same level of importance. Some lessons in un-preparedness went home after the Chinese debacle but not others. One only needs to look at how the concepts of designing rations for modern armies and war, the variety, range and quality of combat foods, and field food services are being improved upon constantly in other countries notably USA, Australia, Canada and UK (described in Chapter 11) to admit that Food Science and Technology has a definitive place in the scheme of things along with weapons and supersonic aircraft.

In the Defence Food Research Laboratory, at Mysore, which is one among the Life Sciences Group, the total current human resource strength is around 200, 40 to 43 scientists of the DRDS in a pyramidal structure with cadres of scientist-B (at the entry level) at the base ascending to one scientist G (Director). The Defence Research Development Technical Service personnel and support staff comprise the rest. The total strength has never been more than 230 or so.

The Services have Expectations – Some Pointers

The work continues on the designing and development of newer foods and systems for the use of the Armed Forces. Meanwhile there are some insights gleaned from discussions with senior Army and Navy officers during the research phase of this book.

(a) *Variety:* They face the specific problems of finding the appropriate foodstuffs or packed products at the right time and in the right place. They would much appreciate a greater choice and variety, at least in their Compo rations.

(b) *Bread*: an item that officers in all the three services are entitled to is not an authorised item for the jawans in the Army but it is so for the sailors. One believes it is the same in the Air Force as in the Army. *Chapati* making in the Army and Air Force kitchens and shore based naval units is not as tedious as it is in the ships and submarines, who therefore keep stocks of bread. The shelf life of bread is poor, 2–3 days at room temperature and about 15 days in a cool room, but by then, it becomes dry, they may keep a few weeks at frozen temperatures. In earlier times, bread used to be baked in big ships but now there are *chapati* making machines installed.

(c) *Vegetables*: The ships and submarines on long sail quickly use up the fresh and more delicate vegetables in the first ten days, keeping the tougher and root vegetables for later consumption. To increase the storage capacity of the vessels and to decrease the time and tedium involved in peeling, paring, cutting and dicing of vegetables, precut–vegetables may be thought of.

(d) *Ready to prepare foods for submarines:* The pre-cooked, dehydrated variety of *upma*, rice, *pulav, biryani*, ready to eat *parantha, halwa* and curries, instant *rasam* etc. are a great boon to the submariners.

(e) *Large portion packs:* Every food packet comes as one–portion of about 200 g. When some 40 men have to be served a complete meal in a submarine, there are many individual packs to be opened, heated and served. The small single portion packs of pre-cooked dehydrated rice or *pulav* or even retort pouch foods are not practical for the submarine's daily food service. Larger packs of the meal items would be advantageous.

(f) *Tray meals – preserved, ready to eat*: Another technological variation of retort pouch foods is 'tray rations'. For a standard Indian type of meal consisting of rice, and/or *chapatis*, dal, vegetables or curry and variations thereof, arranged in compartmented plates or trays would make abundant sense. High density plastic trays of any desired size and depth can be designed to have two or more compartments for heat processing of foods with similar moisture content. In DFRL the packaging experts have already done this as part of a project involving development of Space shuttle foods and delivery systems. A twin cup tray prototype was designed, produced and tested for overall performances.

(g) *Limited menus*: While there is ample scope for drawing up different menus for each day of the week and for choosing any number of ways to prepare vegetables, eggs, meat or fish, and turn the cereals and milk into an equally wide array of preparations, limited only (if at all) by the cook's skills (there are some 5–7 cooks in a ship at a time and their combined skills can be awesome), it is the tinned rations and even more, the MREs which are limited in variety.

(h) *Simpler foods*: A question that was posed was, 'why can't there be simpler foods?' In a processed form, a *'thali'* (a plate) meal of not more than three items would be very welcome according to some Navy officers who appeared to be more progressive in their outlook.

(j) *Remove misconceptions about processed foods*: In the Navy, as in the Army, during interactive discussions it was found that people held ambivalent views about processed foods. Even as they welcomed the availability of newer products, they distrusted the technology of processed foods and mistrust the manufacturers and disbelieve the scientists.

(k) *Development of markets closer to forward areas*: Making the barren hills in high altitudes like Ladakh grow plant varieties had been a dream in India. Now it has been achieved to an extent by the DRDO's agricultural scientists and by determined efforts from the Field Research Laboratory (FRL) in Leh. The growth of fruits and vegetables in Leh area looks to be a success story. The Laboratory developed 'protected cultivation' for vegetables in the form of solar green house technology, and introduced many cultivars of apples, propagation tips for apricot etc. It has developed growing techniques for alfalfa fodder, for flowers, wild plants and especially the propagation techniques for Seabuckthorn fruit (*FRL*, 2007). Other laboratories, notably DEBEL in Bangalore, designed incubators that could be used in poultry hatcheries in the rarefied and cold atmosphere. Today, as per the FRL's technical brochures, the broiler industry is flourishing. In the Eastern belt, again the Field Laboratory at Tejpur, Assam, made efforts to develop agriculture and horticulture. Such efforts were intended to benefit both the army units deployed there and the local populace.

It is possible to address many of the supply problems related to fresh produce, but not without the help and co-operation of state civil agencies. The push to horticulture being given by the Government at the Centre and in several states has resulted in a remarkable growth in this sector.

Genetically Modified Foods

Genetically modified organisms (GMOs) can be defined as organisms (and micro-organisms) in which the genetic material has been altered in a way that does not occur naturally by mating or natural recombination. Known widely as genetic engineering, genetic manipulation or recombinant DNA technology, it allows selected individual genes to be transferred from one organism into another, also between non-related species, by means other than crossing. When the GMO is a crop plant, it is referred to as a GM or transgenic crop. The first generation of GM crops was created for two main reasons – to increase the yield of a crop and to improve food quality.

Any improvement in yields, insect resistance, herbicide resistance, drought resistance, salty soil resistance and such characteristics for increased agricultural yields, increasing protein content, implanting vitamin 'A' genes where they normally do not reside, introducing mechanisms to delay ripening of fruits to allow better marketability and storage are some of the methods that find universal application. The important approaches are, introduction of tolerance to herbicides, particularly in Soya bean (Padgette *et al.,* 1995), and insect resistance as in Bt cotton (Cheng, Sardaana, Kaplan and Altosaar, 1998). Trait stacking or insertion of genes is used to enhance the yield potential, improve the nutritional characteristics, improve stress tolerance, and even modify the ripening characteristics of the harvested product (Smith *et al.,* 1990). Identifying and locating genes for the creation of a GM crop for the required trait is currently the most limiting step. Enhancement of Vitamin A in rice (Ye et *al.,* 2000), delaying ripening in fruit using antisense technology, tolerance to abiotic stress like salt tolerance, (Gisbert *et al.*, 2000), decaffeination of coffee, increasing nutritive value of potato with higher protein content enhanced by cloning the seed alumin gene AmA1 from *Amaranthus hypochondriacus* (Chakraborty; Chakraborty and Datta, 2000). According to the Department of Biotechnology, Government of India, there are several food plants other than potato, such as *brinjal*, cauliflower, cabbage, chickpea, groundnut, maize, pigeon pea, sorghum, rice, tomato transgenic plants which are under development at various institutions in the country. GM has already generated considerable heat and debate in the country.

Genetic Modification Regulatory Mechanism in India

According to the provisions of the Food and Safety Standards Act 2006 (www.mofpi.nic.in), no person shall manufacture, process, export, import or sell genetically modified articles for food except in accordance with the regulations made under this act. This act is yet to be enforced. As per the new trade policy announced by the Government of India, the import of GMOs/LMOs (living modified organisms) for the purpose of (a) R & D; (b) Food; (c) Feed; (d) Processing in Bulk and (e) For environment release, will be governed by the provisions of the Environment Protection Act, 1986 and Rules, 1989. The import of any food, food, raw or processed or any ingredient of food, food additives or any food product that contains GM material and is being used either for industrial production, environmental release, or field application will be allowed only with the approval of the Genetic Engineering Approval Committee (GEAC). Institutes/Companies who wish to import Genetically Modified material for R & D purposes will submit their proposal to the Review Committee for Genetic Modification (RCGM) under the Department of Bio-technology. In case the Companies/Institutes use these Genetically Modified material for commercial purposes, approval of GEAC is also required. At the time of import all consignments containing products which have been subjected to Genetic Modification will carry a declaration stating that the product is Genetically Modified. In case a consignment does not carry such a declaration and is later found to contain Genetically Modified material, the importer is liable to penal action under the Foreign Trade Development and Regulation Act, 1992.

Under these circumstances, it becomes very clear that developing a food substance for the exclusive benefit of the Armed Forces is not an option; much less is the likelyhood of importing any GM labeled product for this purpose. Whatever is being done in this field is for general application and as and when something suitable is found, tested, accepted and allowed as per regulatory laws, it will become available to all consumers including the military, through the normal food chain.

New Technologies

Several new food processing technologies have been tested in recent years; prominent among these being Ohmic heating, high pressure application, magnetic pulse fields and such, but none of them have found wide application or as consistently as other time tested technologies. Even the hype about edible packaging, employing plant and animal based substances, though promising, has not yet come to the forefront. Like organic farming, which is recognised as the solution to a healthy way of life in this chemical laden farming atmosphere, it is not in a position to cater to millions, and these new technologies are restricted in their uses.

On the other hand biotechnological manipulations not bordering on crop plants directly but in enhancing the production of useful substances by plant tissue cultures and fermentation are more readily accepted.

Gene replacement methods in medical therapeutics have been a hot field of investigation and provide hope for the incurable conditions (Gibney, 2003, p. 25), but could open up new approaches in treating nutritional diseases.

Nutrition related genetic studies have bordered on population studies to map the occurrence of modern lifestyle diseases like cardiovascular syndrome, high cholesterol, high blood pressure, diabetics, obesity and the like. But now the field of Nutrinomics – nutrition and individual genomics (Gross, 2007) has opened up. Scientists are studying genetic polymorphism in relation to diet and its responses to explain why some people will or will not respond to dietary recommendations. The responses are very complex and depend on genetics and environment. Though gene expression *per se* is understood, it is not clear how the foods eaten will affect gene expression but they are believed to do so. If these aspects are explained it is likely that in future, by establishing the presence of a gene that might be responsible for obesity or diabetes in an individual, a tailor made diet for that individual may be designed to address the specific health problem. It may well tell us if vigorous exercise, jogging, running or dieting etc. will help in weight control or if a particular diet say Atkins or South Beach diet, a Mediterranean diet or other model diets will be beneficial at all.

It looks more feasible and achievable to map the individual's genes and design a specific diet. Scientist Craig Ventner who published his own entire genome on the internet recently has stated that he was able to detect genes in his genome which predisposed him to certain medical conditions and therefore he was already instituting lifestyle changes and modifying his food and nutrition in light of these revelations. It then rests on the individual's informed choice and preference to follow diet recommendation. Since DNA fingerprinting has been accepted as one of the means of establishing or confirming paternity and an individual's identity in forensics, identifying specific gene(s) in individual patients–individual genomics (Gross, 2007) for the purpose of designing a diet tailored to a specific need cannot become objectionable and is likely to take off in a big way if the cost of such testing could be brought within reach.

Cultured meat: After food fermentations, food engineering, plant tissue culture, biotechnological transformations, DNA technology, cloning operations, GM foods with desirable features and nutrinomics, it is now the turn of the concept of meat tissue engineering. Reviewing this topic, Pathak, Bukahari, Bhatt and Sharma (2008) of the Sher-e-Kashmir University of Agricultural Sciences and Technology in Jammu, pointed out that embryonic myoblasts or satellite cells had been isolated from the skeletal muscle of porcine and bovine origin more than 10–20 years ago. It is believed that using a single myogenic cell from an animal or co-culture with fat cells in a medium mimicking the animal's digestive system environment in a bioreactor: physical, mechanical and biochemical requirements and nutritional components, it may be possible to generate cells which could be processed into edible meat. The main advantages are that the meat thus produced will no longer need huge animal farms and their maintenance and slaughtering of large number of animal herds; it will mean that their feed and fodder requirements will no longer be of concern, thus reducing costs enormously in the upkeep of animals until slaughter; the *in vitro* ratio of saturated to unsaturated and poly unsaturated fats can be modified and controlled as per current nutritional concepts; external microbial contamination and meat associated food infections and disease outbreaks can be totally eliminated or drastically reduced. Making innovative products out of meat tissue and then processing them for long storage would engage the efforts of all kinds of food specialists. The challenges lie in how to build in the protein content; fat distribution and meat texture which impart the typical taste and mouth feel of meat. The advent of such meat is far off but the technology will eventually develop to put such a meat on the market shelf.

It has caught the imagination of at least one group of individuals other than scientists and that is the People for Ethical Treatment of Animals or PETA. It has announced on the net a contest with a reward of $ 1 million to any one who will develop a commercially viable *in vitro* chicken meat product without using any animal derived product except for the initial starter cells. They hope to sell chicken nuggets produced in this fashion by June 30, 2012 (www.google.com/fake meat).

References

Achaya, K.T. *The food industries in British India*. Oxford University Press, 1994.

Banerjee, B. 'Food Industries & Requirements of the Defence Forces'. In Symposium on 'Population, & Development of Food Industries in India'. Proceedings, pp. 197–203. Dec 1951, CFTRI, Mysore.

Bawa, A. S. 2007. 'Historical developments in food science and technology – Indian perspective'. *J. Food Sci. Technol*, 44(6): 553–564.

Bhargava, G.S. *Their Finest Hour*. Vikas Publishing House Pvt Ltd., Delhi, 1972.

Bhat, B.P., Bhagirathi, D., Mathur, U.K., Bhatia, B.S. and Nath, H. 1974. 'Development of quick cooking dehydrated curried vegetables using fried potatoes, peas, cabbage and French beans'. *J Food Sci & Technol*, 11(2), 60–63.

Smith, C.J.S., C.F. Watson Chakraborty, S., N. Chakraborty, A. Datta. 2000. 'Increased nutritive value of transgenic potato by expressing a nonallergenic seed albumin gene from *Amaranthus hypochondriacus*'. *Proc. Natl. Acad. Sci. USA,* 97 (7): 3724–3729.

Chauhan, O.P., P.S. Raju, R. Shylaja, D.K. Dasgupta, and A.S. Bawa. 2006a. 'Synergistic effects of modified atmosphere and minimal processing on the keeping quality of pre-cut papaya (*Carica papaya* L.)'. *Journal of Horticultural Science and Biotechnology*, 81(5): 903–909.

Cheng, X., R. Sardana, H. Kaplan and I. Altosaar. (1998) 'Agrobacterium transformed rice plants expressing synthetic cry1Ab and cry1Ac genes are highly toxic to striped stem borer and yellow stem borer'. *Proc. Natl. Acad. Sci. USA*, 95: 2767–2772.

Department of Food, India. Memorandum on the Food Situation in India. Submitted to Central Legislature 1945.

Directory of Food Processing Industry & Trade, Ministry of Food Processing Industries, Government of India, 2003, pp. A–3 to A–5.

Durante, Will and Ariel. *The Story of Our Civilization. Part IV. Age of Voltaire*. Simon & Schuster, New York, 1965.

Flash Back Food: Hogs Wild. *National Geographic Magazine*, 2002 May, 201(5). Inside Back Cover.

FRL at a glance. DRDO. Booklet, Leh, Ladakh, 2007.

George, Johnsy, M. Easwaramurthy, S.N. Sabapathy, & A.S. Bawa. 'Development and evaluation of nanosilver incorporated antimicrobial packaging material'. Abstract no. FP–03. Symposium on Health Foods. ICFOST 2007. Souvenir. Kharagpur, Dec 30, 2007–Jan 2, 2008.

Ghosh, K.G., K.G. Krishnappa, A.N. Srivatsa, K.C. Eapen & P.K. Vijayaraghavan. 1980. 'Pilot plant production of thermo stabilized ready to eat pouch foods'. *Res.Indus*. 25:140–144.

Ghosh, K.G., Srivatsa, A.N., Nirmala, N. & Sharma, T.R. 1977. 'Development and application of fungistatic wrappers in food preservation II, Wrappers made by coating process'. *J.Food Sci.Technol,* 19:21–269.

Gibney, Michael J., I.A. Macdonald, and H.M. Roche. *Nutrition and Metabolism.* Blackwell Sciences Publication, Oxford, UK, 2003.

Gisbert, C., A.M. Rus, C. Bolarin, J.M. Lopez-Coronado, I. Arrilaga, C. Montesinos, M. Caro, R. Serrano and V. Moreno 2000. 'The yeast *HAL1* gene improves salt tolerance of transgenic tomato'. *Plant Physiol.* 123: 393–402.

Gould, G.W. 'Over view: New Methods of Food Preservation'. Blackie and Academic and Professional. Glasgow, 1995.

Gould, G.W. *Mechanism of Action of Food Preservation Procedures*. Elsevier Applied Sciences. London, 1989, Introduction.

Gowda, Lalitha. 2008. 'Brief on the current position and status of GM Foods in India'. Personal communication.

Gross, L. 2007. A New Human Genome Paves the Way for Individual Genomics. Plos Biology, 5(10), e266, doi;10.1371/journal.pbio.0050266.

Guptha, Rani, Daisy and Brindha R. Probiotic. 'functional foods – Non medicinal treatments of gastrointestinal diseases'. Abstract no. FN 14. Symposium on Health Foods. ICFOST 2007. Souvenir, Kharagpur, Dec 30, 2007 Jan 2, 2008.

International Symposia on Emerging and Novel Food Processing Technologies. December 19–20, 2007. Joint Organisers: DFRL and Shastri Indo – Canada Institute, Calgary Canada Defence Food Research Laboratory, Mysore.

Iyengar, N.V.R. Survey of Food Industries. In Symposium on 'Food Population & Development of Food Industries in India'. Proceedings, pp. 160−175, Dec, 1951, CFTRI, Mysore.

Jacob, Mabel Merian, Platel, Kalpana, Srinivasan, K. and Prapulla S.G. 'Evaluation of fructo oligosaccharides as sweetener for diabetics'. Abstract no. FN-10, Symposium on Health Foods. ICFOST 2007 Souvenir, Kharagpur, Dec 30, 2007–Jan 2, 2008.

Jayaraman, K.S., Gopinathan, V.K., Pitchamuthu, P. and Vijayaraghavan, P.K. 1982. 'The preparation of quick cooking dehydrated vegetables by high temperature short time pneumatic drying'. *J Food Sci & Technol.* 17(6), 669–678.

Jayaraman, K.S. and Das Gupta, D.K. 1978. 'Development of storage stability of intermediate moisture carrot'. *J Food Sci*, 43, 1980.

Jayaraman, K.S., M.N. Ramanuja, M.K. Venugopal, R.K. Leela, and B.S. Bhatia, 1975. 'Studies on intermediate moisture pineapple'. *J. Food Sci Technol*, 12(3): 17–21.

Jayaraman, K.S., Ramanuja, M.N., Govardhan, T., Bhatia, B.S and Nath, H. 1976. 'Technological aspects of use of ripe mangoes in the preparation of some convenience foods for Defence Services', *Indian Food Packer*, 30 (5), 76.

Jayaraman, K.S. 1988. 'Development of intermediate moisture tropical fruit and vegetable products – technological problems and prospects in food preservation by moisture control'. CC SEOW Ed. London. *Elsevier Applied Science*, 175–198.

Kameshwar Rao, G., M.A. Malathi and P.K. Vijayaraghavan. 1966. 'Preservation and packaging of Indian food II.: Storage studies on preserved chapatis'. *Food Technology*, 10(12): 208–216.

Knight, Sir Henry (ICS). *Food Administration in India 1939 – 1947*. Stanford University Press, Stanford, C.A. 1954, Food Research Institute's Publication, pp. 5–235.

Lampi, Rauno A. 1977. 'Flexible packaging for thermo processed foods'. *Advances in Food Research*, 23:306–426.

Leistner, L. and Hechelmann, H. 1993. 'Food preservation by hurdle technology', In Food Preservation Conference Proceedings. US Army Natick Research Development and Engg Centre, Naticks, USA.

Leistner, L., Rodel, W., and Krispien, K. 1981. 'Microbiology of meat and meat products in high and intermediate moisture ranges in water activity influences on food quality', Rockland, L.B. and Stewart, G.F. Ed., New York Academic Press, 855–916.

Mathur, V.K., C.H. Siddiah, B.S. Bhatia & P.K. Vijayaraghavan, 1973. 'Canning of conventional Indian meals for Defence requirements'. *Indian Food Packer*, 27(2):46–51.

McCullough, Colleen. *Morgan's Run*. Bantam Books, 2001.

Ministry of Commerce and Industry, Department of commerce Notification No. 2 (RE-2006)/2004-2009 New Delhi, Dated 7th April, 2006.

News round up. *Indian Food Industry*, 2005, 24(4): 22–23.

News round up. *Indian Food Industry*, 2005, 24(4): 22–25.

Padgette, S.R., K.H. Kolacz, X. Delannay, D.B. Re, B.J. Lavellee, C.N Tinius, W.K. Rhodes, Y.I. Otero, G.F. Bary, D.A. Eichholtz, V.M. Peschke, D.L. Nida, N.B. Taylor and G.M. Kishore. 1995. 'Development, Identification and Characterization of Glyphosate – Tolerant Soybean Line'. *Crop Science*, 35:1451–1461.

Pathak, V., S.A.A. Bukhari, Z.F. Bhat and Nagendra Sharma. 2008.'Prospects of in vitro meat'. *Indian Food Industry*. 27(6): 33–35.

Qayamuddin Ahmed.(ed) *'India' by Al-Baruni*. National Book Trust of India. 2nd edition, 1988.

Radhakrishna, K.R., D. Vijaya Rao, K. Jayathilakan, Joyce D'Souza, & T.R. Sharma, 1988. 'Studies on freeze drying of rehydratable poultry products as large pieces'. *Indian Food Packer*, 42:41–45.

Raju, P.S., N. Ashok, Mallesha and D.K. Dasgupta. 2002. 'Physiological and quality changes during minimal processing and storage of shredded cabbage'. *Indian Food Packer*, 4, 51–58.

Raju, P.S. 2008. A Brief on Processed Technologies developed in Fruits and Vegetables at Defence Food Research Laboratory at Mysore. Personal communication.

Ramachandran, R. 2007. *The Hindu*, February 2.

Ramanuja, M.N. and Jayaraman K.S. 1980. 'Studies on the preparation and storage stability of intermediate moisture banana'. *J Food Sci & Technol*. 17 (4), 183.

Rehman, M. Shafiur. *Hand book of Food Preservation*. Marcel Dekker Inc. New York, Basel, 1999, pp. 1–10.

Sanjeev Kumar, VA, Gupta, M. Sabapathy, S.N. and Bawa, A.S. 2005. 'Self heating system for ready to eat foods'. *Indian Food Industry*, 24(1) 54–57.

Satyanarayanarao, T.S., M.N. Ramanuja, N. Ashok, H.S. Vibhakara 1995. 'Storage properties of whole egg powder incorporated biscuit'. *J Food Sci & Technol*. 32 (6), 470–476.

Sharma, T.R., Jayaraman, K.S., Vijaya Rao, D. & Srivatsa, A.N. 1984. 'Food for Space'. Project Pavan (Indian Air force). Indo- Soviet Space Mission April 1984. Technical Report DFRL, Mysore.

Smith, C.J.S., C.F. Watson, C.R. Bird, W. Schuch, and D. Gierson. 1990. 'Expression of a truncated tomato polygalacturonase gene inhibits expression of the endogenous gene in transgenic plants'. *Mol. Gen. Genet*. 224: 477–481.

Srivatsa, A.N. 2008. A brief on Retort Process Technology. Personal communication.

Vibhakara, H.S., Singh, S.K, Das Gupta D.K. 2003. 'Effect of humectants on quality of frozen intermediate moisture products from apple and pineapple and their pulps'. *Indian Food Packer*. 2003 (3), 48–55.

Vijaya Rao, D., B. Bhagirathi and T.R. Sharma. 1989 '*Carcinoscorpius* amoebocyte lysate assay for the rapid determination of microbial status and quality of meat'. *J.Food Sci Technol*, 26: 181–186.

Vijaya Rao, D. and B. Bhagirathi 1985. 'Microbial changes in mutton due to repeated freezing and thawing'. *J. Food Sci. Technol*, 22:422–427.

Vijaya Rao, D. and K.A. Srihari, 1993. 'Microbiological studies on the production of dehydrated convenience foods. A case study on multi component assembled product Avial mix'. *J. Food Sci. Technol*. 30: 403–407.

Vijaya Rao, D., R.K. Leela and R. Sankaran. 1979. 'Microbiological studies on in-pack processed chapatis'. *J. Food Sci. Technol*. 16:166–168.

Vijaya Rao, D. 1994. 'Microbiology of Indian Foods – Problems and some solutions'. In National Conference, Nutrition Society of India. National Institute of Nutrition. November 1994, Hyderabad.

Vijaya Rao, D. Space Microbiology-Food related studies. In 'Microbes for Better Living' International Conference MICON-94, Association of Microbiologists of India, DFRL and Ministry of Food Processing. 9-12 Dec 1994 Mysore. Proceedings 1995; Editors R Sankaran and K. Manja. DFRL. pp. 425–440.

Vijaya Rao, D., B. Bhagirathi, B. and T.R. Sharma, 1983. 'Fluctuations in the quantitative predominance of bacterial groups in fresh and stored mutton'. *J.Food Sci.Technol,* 20:277–281.

Vijaya Rao, D., T.S. Vasundhara, K.R. Radhakrishna & T.R. Sharma. 1986a. 'Food for Space' STS/INSAT 1C- Pay Load Specialist Mission. Technical Report-1: Storage Studies. DFRL, Mysore.

Vijaya Rao, D., T.S. Vasundhara, K.R. Radhakrishna & T.R. Sharma 1986b. Food For Space STS/INSAT Pay Load Specialist Mission. Technical Report 2. Simulation Meals & Organoleptic Tests. DFRL, Mysore.

Yamashita, Michael, Marco Polo I. Venice to China. *National Geographic Magazine*, May 2001*a*.

Yamashita, Michael. Marco Polo II. In China. *National Geographic Magazine*, June 2001*b*.

Ye, X., S Al-Babili, A. Kloti., J. Zhang, P. Lucca, P. Beyer and I. Potrykus. 2000. 'Engineering the provitamin A (β-carotene) biosynthetic pathway into carotenoid free rice endosperm'. *Science*. 287: 303–305.

Section – V

Wars and Food Supply Logistics

14

Logistics and Food Supplies in Wars – Past and Present

> 'The success of military operations depends upon supplies; there is no difficulty in fighting and in finding the means of beating your enemy either with or without loss; but to gain your objects, you must feed.'
>
> *Wellington in India*, 1804

Logistics – Meaning, Definitions, General Aspects

The word logistics as explained by Baron Antoine Henri Jomini (Jomini, 1838, p. 252) is derived from the title '*major general*' or *merchal des logis*, an officer in eighteenth century France whose duty it was to lodge and camp the troops, to give directions to the marches of columns and to locate them on the ground. In an earlier period, logistics was limited only to details of marches and camps.

In the Prussian army, the term Quartermaster was given to the person in charge of encampments and troop quarters (logis). These functionaries became equivalent of chiefs of staff to the commanders of the day (Sarin, 2000, p. 678).

Logistics belongs to an area of non-combatant activity and is the practical art of moving armies. The archaic meaning of logistics is the science of computation. In Greek, *logistikos* means 'skilled in calculating'; it is still used in mathematics as 'logic' or 'logarithmic'– but seems unrelated to modern military application except in estimating requirements and planning in advance.

The objective of any and all logistics effort is to create support for combat forces. Functional and technical efficiency should not dominate what are called the 'command perspectives', although in the majority of instances, a functionally effective system will help increase combat effectiveness. Special training is to be provided by way of simulated war exercises in logistic readiness (Eccles, 1959, p. 175).

Living off the land, though very simplistic in nature and hard on the populace, provided the generals of ancient armies the advantage of moving troops quickly without having to make elaborate arrangements. Then the concept of carrying stuff along for a few days until more organised camp facilities could be created was born. The magazine system of the Romans required good roads, animal and water transports, and supply depots to replenish food stocks. The rolling magazines of the sixteenth century likewise kept moving their positions as the army advanced. The movement of the army's fighter arm could often be hampered by the long supply lines. The dependence of the former on the latter has been increasingly evident in modern warfare, even though transportation, communication and food systems have progressed remarkably.

Tail and teeth are two components of an army and without either one being sufficiently prepared the outcome of a war could be uncertain, if not disastrous. The supply wing or the **tail** provides the combatant arm, known as the **teeth**, with everything to fight the war and both have to be planned in detail for logistics to be successful. Logistics, an extremely important aspect of military strategy and planning is not the easiest of things to satisfactorily achieve at the best of times and in war with its myriad twists, locations and unexpected or unanticipated obstacles, the best laid plans go awry and the most well prepared army could face acute shortages. Two examples of hiccups in logistics could be cited in the Spanish Armada, the launch of which was delayed due to time spent on replenishing with fresh foods that spoiled during preparatory stages and hence ran into foul weather, and Napoleon's winter campaign in Russia, whose plan for a short campaign in summer extended into the severe winter and ran short of food with no replenishments available in the countryside. Waging wars spread across several continents poses major logistic problems, as in the two world wars, involving some awesome logistics supply and transportation of men, vehicles and materials of war, fuel, food, clothing and medicines and medical aid. Sometimes the tail was much too long and unwieldy. Animals, rail, road and seaway were all necessary for transportation. The supply lines became easy targets for enemy attack on ground, on sea and by air. Protecting the storage dumps become one of the prime necessities of the side being attacked.

The teeth to tail ratios i.e. the ratio of the fighting arms to support lines have shown different figures over time. Gone of course are the huge ponderous armies which prevailed in Europe and India. On good authority, what used to be a 50:50 ratio at one time progressively became 60:40 and then 65:35. New endeavours are now directed towards further reducing this level of dependence on the logistics support line within the Armed Forces. To reduce the tail, the major drive is towards outsourcing. This could apply to repairs, recovery, accommodation, mechanical maintenance, cleaning, provisioning and even introducing cooking gadgets to reduce the numbers involved.

The Logistics System

A logistics system supplies all necessities of the defence forces in peace time and in war. In the advent of military operations, two elements – the combat and logistic actions affect each other (Hooper, 1972, p. 259). These two are combined to achieve an optimum level of operational readiness. Logistics is vitally important in determining strategy (Wilson, 1952, p. 3). The Encyclopedia Americana describes logistics as consisting of three elements – Supply, Movement and Services (The Encyclopedia Americana: 17, p. 688).

Supply: Supplies should come, most preferably, from within the country. For that to happen, the country should possess natural resources or be in a position to produce or manufacture all its requirements – every single item of supplies and equipment. For this purpose, its economy should be strong and stable and its industrial base sound and solid. Investment in technological research for the development and improvement of all elements of the logistics system requires huge amounts of money, an indigenous industrial base and technical expertise as found in the west. Countries like India and China are aiming to catch up with the west and are probably close in certain aspects.

Movement, supply mechanisms and LOC: Movement involves transporting men and materials to wherever the deployment is and wherever the action will be.

A line of communication or LOC, denotes the link between the source of supply and the place of consumption. Roads and coastal and inland waterways were the ancient Egyptian and Roman lines of communication. The British Empire and other colonial empires grew out of strong navies and merchant shipping. In the occupied territories, a system of roadways and railways was placed to interlink the country. In World Wars I and II, huge troop transport ships and fleets moved men and supplies. After World War II, moving troops and supplies by ships and air transports came to be the mainstay of LOC and in the second half of the twentieth century, all rapid landing of troops and support systems and supplies to distant battle zones were effected by military aircrafts. The Berlin airlift of 1948 was one of the biggest air supply operational efforts. The British had to send more than 2 million tons of food and fuel into starved Western Berlin when the Soviet military government of East Germany closed all road routes.

In India, rail and road links are well established and extensive, and the bulk of the movement of goods takes place by these means. Where the rail head ends, the road convoys take over and where movement by roads is not possible, as in steep mountainous terrains, animal transport is resorted to. There are some border posts which are exclusively air serviced by the IAF. Civilian aircrafts are also commandeered for military operations.

Management of services: The third arm of logistics – the management and administration of all major undertakings takes on the responsibility of not only *finding* everything – food, clothing, civilian manpower, and maintaining them and the equipment, support facilities and hospital facilities but also their actual *supply* and *delivery*. Operations Research and automatic data processing are used in managing military resources as well as the mountains of paperwork that become inevitable in man–material management. Innovative and new ways to deliver supplies in normal times and in combat zones are constantly under research and development.

Before the age of mechanisation, there were chariots for the braves, war animals to fight and pack animals for the baggage train; there were bows and arrows and spears and lances and battering rams; then came hand guns and heavy cannons borne on animal drawn carts; the men of the cavalry but mostly of the infantry undertook long and tedious marches through every kind of weather and terrain, carrying the very basic foods of their time. The soldiers could carry only so much on their person. Sending forward units to establish depots at strategic locations along the route to replenish stores was the brainchild of Alexander the Great. The Roman magazine system, from which the concept of modern supply depots stemmed, is amply illustrated by the Napoleonic meticulousness in war planning which was elaborate and included arrangements for replenishment along the route of march.

Logistics of food supplies: A study of certain wars in Europe and North America, till the beginning of twentieth century, throws light on the importance with which the food supply was regarded, ensuring the continuance of a war till a decisive end had been reached and the extraordinary measures taken to ensure a steady supply to the troops in the war theatre. If the governments of the various warring factions had the responsibility of providing food and equipment to the fighting forces it was no less their responsibility to arrange for the needs of civilians caught in the general scarcity of food and everyday things. The plans for growing more food and food rationing for civilians, without affecting the health of the people, as witnessed in Britain at the advent of World War II is a study in food policy and planning and war preparedness. Britain's rationing was extended to India and every Indian during that period experienced war time food scarcity and severe rationing. An anatomy of the British administrative planning that went into the logistics for the Army in the Second World War has been provided by Wilson of the war office (Wilson, 1952).

The United States of America has the world's largest and most complex logistic system. When last checked, there were some four million items in its military catalogue list of procurement. It provides costly military aid to certain countries and to strategic partners; its Navy and Air Force lend logistic support; both the US Air Force and the Naval air wing have developed the 'in flight' or mid air refueling techniques, enhancing their reach without interruption or delay. It has been involved in all the major wars of the twentieth and twenty-first century, though none of them were fought on its own soil. Its civilians did suffer privations but not on the scale that other countries had to.

Any foreign military commitments call for a strong domestic economic-industrial base. Britain ruled the seas for centuries with one of the strongest Navies of any country with imperial ambitions and is said not to have been able to maintain the logistics system necessary for foreign military commitments, though it supported the United States as an ally. But then, most of the former European colonial powers presently depend upon the US Armed Forces' excellent logistic capabilities.

The former Soviet Union had large natural resources and a strong military–industrial base. To wield communistic influence it exercised control over the eastern European countries through continuous garrisoning, using men and arms, roadways and supplies. Within its own borders, the line of communications used railroads, rivers and canals. From the end of World War II, when the Soviet Union established its stake and control of East Germany, it launched several military operations – invasion of Hungary in 1956, invasion of Czechoslovakia in 1968, clashes with China on its borders in 1969, and creation of the Cuban missile crisis in 1962. Its merchant and naval fleets were strengthened. Experts observe that the logistics systems of China are not on the same level as of some other countries (The Encyclopedia Americana: 17, pp. 688–690). Despite belonging to a 'nuclear' and even 'Space' category of nations, it seems that the internal LOC is weak and depends on railways and waterways. Neither are their merchant and naval ships adequate, nor do they possess adequate transport aircraft.

When Sino-Indian hostilities broke out in 1962, its forces would not have had to undertake a mass invasion. Tibet captured, the Chinese forces assembled quietly, probably requiring minimal logistic support. And since the Chinese diet consists mostly of fresh unprocessed foods low in animal fats and sugar; mostly rice, wheat, vegetables, bean curd and small quantity of eggs, fish, meats and nuts and a Chinese division requires only some 200 tons of supplies a day, (The Encyclopedia Americana: 5, p. 495; The Encyclopedia Americana: 17, p. 690) it would not have been very difficult.

The Israeli logistics capabilities are built on its strategy of aggressive military defence. The whole country becomes a battle zone. The small peace time army expands some ten fold and carries out lightning attacks on borders. Movement of troops is effected by air and trucks (The Encyclopedia Americana: 17, p. 690). World Wars I and II had multiple theatres of operations and stretched over four years. Apart from bearing weapons and missiles the logistics issues predominated in all planning. Naval fleets, air transports, road convoys and railways, all became necessary links in the logistic chain. The Vietnam War lasted even longer than World War II, from 1965 until a total cease fire and withdrawal in 1972, but was concentrated in a jungle terrain with hardly more than primitive approaches and trails. All supplies were dispatched by naval fleets to the nearest ports – thereafter, all outposts were air supplied and maintained. In the sudden eruption of war in the Falklands in 1982, Britain sent men, materials and missiles by air. Operation 'Desert Storm' carried out by US troops in the Iraq war of 1991 is a classic example of short, swift and concentrated action on distant soil using friendly ports (Saudi Arabia) as the landing base.

Logistics in the Ancient Past

The original intent of logistics pertained to moving the troops and settling them in camps. It meant planning, preparations and assembling all the war materials, sufficient food stocks for a period, finding surface and water transport, establishing posts for replenishment, as well as sea ports. Roads were poorly laid or non-existent; the terrain was very difficult, the availability of water, fodder, and food grains was uncertain and the climate was equally a challenge to moving large numbers of men and material.

Marching to battle in ancient times was an immense exercise because of the poor infrastructure, large numbers and long distances involved. Food and fodder did not always concern the generals and commanders. It was more important to move the army towards the expedition's objective of the moment.

Historians specialising in each period of history have written volumes providing exhaustive details about ancient and medieval wars. There have been some notable events, from the famous Trojan war of antiquity, Herodotus' first record of war in history (1470 BC), the insatiable expeditions of the Greeks, particularly of Alexander the Great (340 BC–326 BC), the Roman Republican wars (till AD 600), the Crusades of the Dark ages (AD 1100), wars in the Venetian empire (AD 1200–1300), to the 100 years war between France and England around AD 1346. Every European nation of today has its own blood splattered history. In the thirteenth century, a mighty war resulted when a Russian prince warrior of Kiev marched against Chengiz Khan with a band of 80,000 warriors. He was met by the Mongol's army of more than 240,000. Chengiz Khan and his fleet footed cavalry spread terror and dread everywhere they went, trampling, scorching and butchering the countryside.

The Period till Alexander

The Assyrians were known to have been mighty warriors of their time, during 3000 BC–1300 BC, and marched some 100,000 men to the peripheries of their borders across Mesopotamia. There were archers, cavalry and spearmen. Herodotus' first record of war (1470 BC), in ancient Egypt, involved a 20,000 strong army of Thutmosis that moved against the king of Kadesh into what is now central Palestine, and the Battle of Megiddo (1469 BC), the first recorded battle in history, ensued (Perret, 1992, p. 235). Megiddo was a fortified city close to the plains of Esdraelon (Israel) and the war erupted when the kings of Megiddo and Kadesh rebelled against the authority of Egypt vested in the Pharaoh Thutmosis III. They were crushed and their city plundered (Spaulding and Hoffman, 1994, p. 11).

Persians, around the time of 500 BC, were veterans of all-terrain warfare, possessed a loyal cavalry and lancers, even though theirs was a multinational force. The Greeks and particularly of Alexander the Great (340 BC–326 BC), revealed an unquenchable thirst for adventure. His war fleets did not take food or water on long voyages, they were accompanied by a flotilla of supply vessels and transports. Like Ptolemy, Alexander used the method of ramming and boarding enemy vessels. His invasion into Persia accomplished, the soldiers made an excellent job of living off the land.

Ancient China witnessed incessant wars but all these were fought within its own territory and between warring tribes and warlords. The army was a rapacious and cruel group of unskilled peasants who looted and scorched the countryside through which they proceeded. It was a splintered conglomerate of numerous territories ruled by warlords till the time of the Chin dynasty which ruled for 2,000 years.

The Indo-European Aryans in the Ṛg Vedic times from 2000 BC upto around 600 BC did not seem to have troops on a large scale (Dupuy and Dupuy, 1993, p. 365); there were numerous small states which were engaged in more localised struggles. They did not have to, nor did they plan to, march long distances across distant borders.

The Roman Republic

The Roman Republic of 400 BC had the best armed, heavy and light infantry. Ptolemy, who engaged his army in the Punic wars (264 BC–146 BC between Rome and the Carthageans), it is said, possessed 500 war vessels, 150,000 seamen and marines and individual fleets of no less then 350 ships. Each of the ships carried 300 rowers and seamen and 100 marines. They used grappling devices or Corvus and boarding bridges to engage other ships or to land. The Roman armies and supply system were so finetuned to travel that they are said to have had no parallels and the Roman soldier of the time was the most disciplined and welltrained of all, but furnished his own arms and equipment.

The Roman legions marched truly long distances. History tells us of Sempronius' march in the first Punic war. His men marched from the extreme south of Italy, to the north, for a continuous four weeks, each day covering no less than sixteen miles (Shaw, 1936, p. 46). The Roman soldier was especially trained for carrying great weight. The men had to carry everything that may be needed – not only arms and equipment such as spears, spikes and swords, rampart stake, their own protective shields and helmet but kitchen stuff, instruments and tools for erecting fortifications and food and provisions for many days as well. The Roman empire was so vast, and its army so huge, that just to keep it all within 'civilization' the Roman military had to travel nearly 3,700 miles from where the legions were posted in Jerusalem to guard the wall of Antoine in Scotland. The heavy burdens that a soldier was made to carry earned him the name *impeditus* in the time of Marius (first century BC), as well as another derisive one called *mulus Marianus*.

Julius Caesar made his soldiers carry a load much heavier than the modern day soldier. Each carried seventeen days' rations. A transport that accompanied the legion carried another 30 days food supply. This entire heavy load did not deter or hinder them, however, because when necessary they would just as quickly divest themselves of all baggage and the column would convert itself into battle order (Shaw, 1936, p. 47). It was also perfectly authorized to disperse the moving column of the army to find its own food and forage (Dupuy and Dupuy, 1993).

The Roman soldier was reared and trained for special hardy values such as frugality and was discouraged, rather forbidden, from carrying any but the barest of necessities authorised in war. It was not for nothing that Cicero called the Roman army '*exercitus*' – the one who knows the road and the complete meaning of exercise and the strain of the route march, staggering under a load that was truly enormous. This level of self containment allowed for great mobility, but naturally also led to the plundering and looting of the countryside. The soldiers took what they wished. Mobility on the route being important, the main supplies were collected and sent onwards to a supply magazine.

In Feudal Europe

After the decline of the Roman Empire, Europe was plunged into a barbaric and primitive way of life and the entire infrastructure that once made the Romans supreme, collapsed (McKinley, Howland and Dann, 1994). Lacking any means of livelihood, it was to farming they turned, growing everything a community would want, there being no semblance of proper governance. In medieval Europe, the feudal system prevailed and was responsible for raising the necessary force strength with every able bodied man of any trade in the fiefdom and leading it into battle only on the promise of war loot. The soldiers were left to their own devices enroute. Those able bodied young men who did not readily join, or hesitated to do so, were treated mercilessly. Their houses, barns, fields or pubs were burned down, their women molested and children and older men impaled on lances and the men themselves thrashed and tortured until they agreed to march with their lord.

The latter was himself committed to provide military services to his superiors and thus to the prince and king. In their major crusades between AD 1096 and AD 1204, during the long marches and brief cross over the seas, the soldiers fended entirely for themselves, subsisted on what they brought from home and then looted and razed every town and land they passed through. Antioch, Jerusalem, Anatolia, the whole eastern Mediterranean and Constantinople were all plundered and subjugated. They did not however reach the holy land (Mckinley *et al.*, 1994, p. 64).

Thus dawned the feudal age, where the landlords ruled on land that was originally or theoretically gifted by the king. The feudal lords had absolute say and the last word over the life and death of their vassals, who also had to take up arms at their lords' command and march to war. Kings had only a nominal role in the scheme of things except owning all land under them. Feudal rule controlled the populace while the King was far away and was only concerned with getting more than his due share of the revenue from land. This landlord was known as the suzerain. It was customary for a suzerain to let out most of the land under him to one, two or even three minor personages who were called vassals. It was allowed for each vassal in turn to let a bit of his land received as fief to a third rung of persons to whom he became the suzerain in turn. This land letting was profitable to the suzerain, for he demanded, expected and extracted certain services including military services. For his own family's needs and his personal military retainers and servants (both landless), the suzerain did hold on to some land. At each rung of the fiefdom the lower vassal would perform and provide the same duties and services to his suzerain. The ladder of feudal order is depicted in Fig. 14.1. By this method, military obligations were passed on to others and the history of Europe is replete with feudal wars fought by the suzerains among themselves when one vassal refused to provide service to his suzerain. The greater lords had to be careful and vigilant to check and arrest this 'sub infeudation' too far down, lest they lost all control of their lands (Easton, 1955).

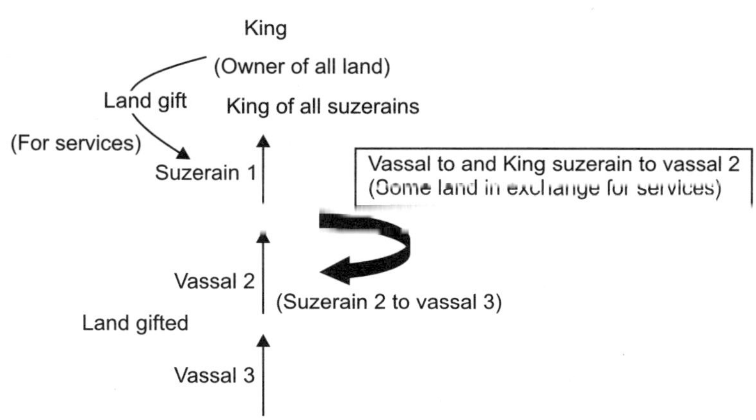

Fig. 14.1: Sub infeudation – the ladder of feudal order

Europe Emerging from Medieval Times

In the sixteenth century, Europe had few roads and these were pretty poorly laid and maintained. Massive armies moved ragtag in such conditions. There are similarities between the mass and composition of the moving army in Europe of that period and the king's armies marching to battle in India. Both had a large combatant force of foot soldiers and mounted cavalry (in India elephants too besides the cavalry) and an even larger segment of the non-combatant camp followers. Machiavelli had reflected on the difficulties of supplying food to the soldiers as per their expectations and had felt that the old Roman system of giving them flour and other essentials to make their own food was better.

In the seventeenth century, there were no specifically planned and established lines of communication. The commanders moved their armies because it was imperative to find fresh food supplies for their survival; they proceeded in any direction they thought expedient and without having to maintain contact with base. But they also followed the course of rivers. Examples of such a strategic approach with no logistics are found in the career history of king Gustavus Adolphus of Sweden when he landed at Peenemunde in 1630 with 10,000 men. He proceeded with no particular plan or direction, besieged a town or a fortress on the way, placed a garrison there in charge and gained a supply base. There were so many points to man that he needed more troops, and more food supplies to feed them and was now compelled to raid, plunder, rob and destroy the neighbours in order for the men to survive (VanCreveld, 1977, pp. 13–14).

The Magazine System revisited: The problem of maintaining big armies in Europe at that time, embroiled in what is known as the 'thirty years war' continued and the situation was saved from totally degenerating into the chaos of the middle ages by the devise of the magazine system by two Frenchmen, the father and the son team of Le Tellier and Louvois. The magazine system was known to the armies of the Roman Republic. Therefore it was really a rejuvenation of the ancient Greek and Roman systems, where supply depots or magazines in strategic places used to be established on the planned route. Their marches were phenomenal, covered long distances, large territories and huge numbers of troops. But since then the armies had become smaller, the area of operations more restricted and hence the need for magazines was not felt.

Estimation of food stocks in the magazines: A properly established magazine from the earliest times was meant to hold fifteen days of stores for emergency needs (or for 30 days in Roman times) and there were meant to be several such store houses on the way. Regular convoys under escort brought up supplies from base – loaded on animal drawn wagons and carts on contract or obtained from local peasants. After studying in detail the various factors that were important in supplying the armies, the Frenchmen created two types of magazine systems. One system was meant to maintain garrisons in frontier fortresses, always ready for a protracted siege. Enough supplies to feed men for six months, and their horses for two months, were to be stockpiled for each fortress garrison. The stocks were not meant for daily use. The second system was designed to feed the field armies on campaigns beyond France's borders. A chain of magazines were established on allied territories for this purpose.

In a meticulous way, the stocking was estimated by Louvois based on the number of men multiplied by the number of probable days of campaign (usually six months). The price for each item of purchase (from contractors) and the cost of transport, storage and distribution yielded the total cost. Contracts were then drawn up. Since all purchases were made on credit taken from the state, there were problems of delayed payment to the suppliers. The supplies were to be hauled by requisitioned wagons and barges. Agent collectors were sent from France into allied territories to fill the magazines at the designated places. Except the artillery, France provided little food supplies. Everything else was obtained from outside her borders (Van Creveld, 1977, pp. 17–22).

Free and daily bread: Soldiers in Europe, emerging from the dark ages and going to war, appeared to have benefited from arrangements of some kind for providing food rations. It is at this time in history that the principle of providing free ration to soldiers came into practice. Two pounds of bread per day (or equal quantity of hard biscuit) was every soldier's daily free entitlement. This could be supplemented, when possible, with meat and beans, which were sometimes given free and at other times at half or one-fourth the market price. There was however, no proper control on the daily intake, which led to wastage or barter for wine.

Louvois had built a very large army of 120,000 men to invade Holland in 1672, perhaps the largest ever since ancient times. He sought and received allied help in Cologne for establishing magazines. A typical army in the 1670s would very likely be 60,000 strong and would have some 40,000 horses (cavalry, artillery and baggage). The daily food requirements for such an army, by one estimate (Van Creveld, 1977, p. 2), were some 120,000 lbs of bread and maybe another 60,000 lbs of other foods and beverages. And the horse rations at 20 lbs per animal would weigh 800,000 lbs. This colossal amount of food and feed, 920,000 lbs per day, had to come from the stored stocks in magazines or moved in convoys but mostly from local procurement.

Feeding the Wars in the Eighteenth and Nineteenth Centuries

Wars in this period were fought more to settle personal grievances than at any other time in history. How opposing neighbours settled scores is described by Van Creveld (1977, p. 27). One simply marched into another's territory and the army lived off the land and stayed there for as long as it took to make the opponent give in, very much in the fashion of a bully. A magazine was established for temporary use in a cleverly chosen location. If the intention was to annex the city, then it was preserved; otherwise it was razed. Supplies were commandeered (and money demanded) by force or persuasion, from the inhabitants by sending raiding parties. On pain of execution or the threat of burning the magistrate's house, it was no wonder that Maurice de Saxe said 'supplies will not be lacking!' The enemy simply ate all there was to eat. Most eighteenth century campaigns were characterised by ravaging enemy territories to feed the moving armies. That is, until Napoleon came along.

Napoleon was said to have been a brilliant tactician who planned his campaigns well. He moved with large armies whose requirement for grain, meat and bread for the men and feed and fodder for the horses, was arranged in different places enroute by requisitioning local replenishment. As a means of self containment they carried along a quantity of food to last a few days

In nineteenth century Europe, the foot soldier's load was big – the British soldier in the Peninsular war for example, hefted between 50 and 70 lbs. In 1854's Crimean war, an individual load of a Frenchman amounted to some 68 lbs and at times even 75 lbs while his British counterpart carried 64 lbs. The Prussian soldiers in battle with Austria and France in 1856 and 1870 respectively carried 56 lbs (Shaw, 1936, p. 51).

Napoleonic methods: Though the origin of the organization of the lines of communications goes back to the Roman Republic, its modern version can be traced to Napoleon, but whose concepts were misread and introduced by the Clausewitz doctrines and the system approved by the King of Prussia in 1867. The massed army of men would move in the front according to their pre-planned schedules and predetermined routes. The supplies would follow behind them in an uninterrupted stream. The staging system of supply called the *etappen* would drag behind a chain of magazines and bases, each of which was formed along the way when the distances were too great for the supply or flying columns to traverse and efficiently serve the moving mass. When the length of the rolling magazine became too long in the rear, the troops' supplies failed. In a war in 1866, the Prussians innovated and established a continuous replenishment from the rear.

The system that operated – one for food and forage and another for communication is explained in the following way (Shaw, 1936, pp. 79–80). Each corps of the army was complete in itself and had 31,000 combatants. The accompanying transport was minimal – one wagon each for ammunition, hospital, treasury and officers' baggage, but none for provisions. The soldiers themselves were expected to carry iron rations sufficient for three days, the rest coming from five supply columns that followed each Corps. Each column was made up of 32 wagons, carrying three day's rations for men and forage for the animals, presumably 10 or 11 wagons carrying one day's ration between them. Once the day 1 rations were gone, the wagons returned to the rear for replenishment and loaded up day 4's rations. As each set of wagons delivered the provisions, it joined the rear and replenished. Thus, 160 wagons kept up a steady supply of food and forage for the moving army. A somewhat similar mechanism but with 9 columns of 33 wagons each operated for supplying ammunition by replenishment from parks or dumps. The bulk of the war materials were sent by train, from where the stuff moved in several hundred wagons keeping a two day distance from the main moving army. Shaw emphasises that priority was given to the food supplies of soldiers, to sustain them and make them fit to fight. Since the soldiers depended on the daily supplying columns for food, they carried only three days' iron rations to cover any emergencies.

Expeditions, Wars and their Food Supplies

Historians describe the different campaigns of wars or other expeditions in some considerable detail but the food supplies aspect is only marginally touched, if at all. Long naval and land expeditions, circumnavigating many continents were undertaken to gain trade opportunities, for discovering new sea routes and lands and for exploratory purposes by countries possessing strong navies. To elucidate these features certain sea expeditions and wars taking place from the sixteenth to twenty-first century have been selected.

Sea and Naval Expeditions

Sea travel became the accepted means of such adventures from those of Alexander (Easton, 1955, p. 271) to Marco Polo and Christopher Columbus; Great Britain under Henry V, Spain under King Phillip, and France under Louis XIV had well endowed and superbly crafted sea going vessels. These nations and the Dutch became the early explorers from Europe. The Navy was necessary to reach a destination and go to war or for trade. During the Dark Ages, King Harold Haradra of the Vikings (around AD 1012), along with William of Normandy (William the Conqueror), invaded Saxon England to wrest the crown from Prince Harold the Saxon, who had been nominated to be the next king after the death of Edward the Confessor. Marco Polo's travel in the thirteenth century took him across the world to China and was recorded for posterity in '*A History of the World*'. The voyage of Columbus with a fleet of ships at the behest of Queen Isabella of Spain to discover a shorter and quicker route to the East ended not in the discovery of the eastern lands but in a near disaster due to the very hazardous nature and length of sailing in uncharted seas, from exhaustion, lack of food, rebellion of the sick seamen, long distances between land falls, sea piracy and the extreme situation of a mutiny. Luckily for him, his last land fall was what later turned out to be the shores of the New World. Although all such sea going vessels set out equipped and well provided with enough stocks of food and water, no amount could possibly last the entire length of a voyage of thousands of miles.

From the earliest times, European sea farers sought treasures, fine silk, spices, gems, gold, metal and other materials from the East. The Dutch established trading posts in Southeast Asia and monopolised the spice trade. The French landed among other South Asian regions and occupied Indonesia and a bit of southern India. The Portuguese came for spices and other goods and occupied Goa. The British, not to be left behind and to wrest the monopoly of the spice trade from the Dutch, took a foot hold in India during Mughal times.

Also, on one count or another, England and France, and England and Spain, were at war with each other and used the might of their navies to engage in frequent combat. The British naval force was developed by Henry V, in 1416 (Pimlott, 1993, p. 179) and the supremacy of England began its long reign when her fleet defeated the Spanish Armada in 1588 in a confrontation arising from religious differences. The cost of the wars, by 1685, was very high and the burden naturally fell on the largest of the land holders, who paid high taxes even as the merchants reaped huge profits (Strayer *et. al.*, 1971, p. 307). Tipu Sultan, among the Indian rulers, appears to have been the only one to have understood the importance of having a navy for trade with other countries, notably France and Turkey, as well as bringing all trading of spices, sandal and silk production under state monopoly.

The Spanish Armada: Spain's naval force was probably the first invasion force after the dark ages. The Armada was called the most fortunate fleet (*La felicissima armada*) and was believed to be Urca Invincible or *La Invincible* (Easton, 1955, p. 394). The Duke of Parma, with an invasion force of 30,000, and the Duke of Medina Sidonia commanding an escort fleet of 130 ships (galleons, galley ships that could be rowed with oars, frigates that were used for scouting and big unwieldy 'Urcas' to carry supplies) heavily armed with 2,400 guns and several thousand rounds of ammunition set sail.

The English fleet commanded by Lord Howard and his deputy, Sir Francis Drake, prepared to face the approaching armada. Their fighting man–strength of 47,000 lay in wait along the South coast and the lower Thames – 105 ships of England were pitted against 125 of Spain.

The food situation: One month's supply of provisions and water had been loaded and made ready for the armada's departure in October 1587 and not in sails until May 1588 due to unavoidable delays in departure. The food spoiled and it was seven months before they could set sail. There was a further delay of 30 days due to time spent gathering fresh food and water. Their food consisted of bread or biscuit, meat, wine, olive oil; olives were the usual fare of people in those times. The soldiers' rations in the sixteenth century Spanish army were 740 g biscuit, 95 g meat and 24 g bacon or fish or cheese and 1.14 L of wine per day (Erdkamp, 1998, p. 43 and Appendix). The meat, fish and biscuits were packed into casks. The olive oil and wine, as was the practice, were sealed in stone amphorae of 20–30 L capacity.

In two weeks of sea combat, swift maneuvering and sure gun fire on the part of the English gave them the upper hand. The plan of the two Spanish commanders to rendezvous had not materialised and Medina Sidonia was desperate for reinforcements. The English ships also began to run out of provisions and needed urgent replenishments. They were at an advantage because the fleet was within easy reach of their coast.

The Spanish armada, forced to turn back via the North Sea, faced unseasonable storms of the Northwest coast of England and lost many ships. The fortunate and invincible armada, launched with a bang and belligerence, returned with a whimper, spent and unsuccessful, having lost about half their ships. Wind and weather defeated them as surely as gun fire and close combat would have, had they made a landing on the English coast. The English fleet came out of the campaign without loosing a single ship (Mysteries, 1991 p. 394).

The voyage of HMS Endeavour: A sea voyage of discovery and exploration, the purpose being scientific study of the South Seas as desired by the Royal Society, London, was undertaken by His Majesty's Bark '*Endeavour*', under the command of Captain James Cook, during 1768–71. Captain Cook's sea voyage is a landmark expedition in carrying out scientific observations and in the meticulous way he planned for the long voyage and the forethought given to providing the victuals necessary to keep a group of ocean bound people alive, healthy and functioning. There were lessons for the Navy. The world's navies would forever be grateful to Cook for his contribution to nutritional and medical management of Vitamin C deficiency that inevitably affected the seamen sailing for long periods and subsisting on salted meat and weevil ridden hard biscuits. And for that reason it deserves a place amidst accounts of food provisioning and supply logistics.

Cook maintained a meticulous journal of the long sea voyage and from his chronicles there is much to learn about how the voyages were planned and about the goods the ship took on board for a total complement of 85 men. This number included the seamen, the Royal marines, civilian passengers, which included a young Fellow of the Royal Society, Joseph Banks, whose interest was Botany, a Swede named Daniel Carl Solander, also an able botanist, Dr Munkhouse, who was a surgeon, Mr Green, the astronomer, and one cook. On board the ship there were tons of food stores and supplies, several sheep for meat for the personal use of the civilians and the captain (and their personal servants) and perhaps a few senior ship's men. Cook's original log books, journals, notes and observations in Cook's Journal are preserved in the archives of the Hakluyt Society, Cambridge, UK (Beaglehole, 1968). Captain Cook's account of the voyages highlight the long and arduous sailing which took the ship from England to Polynesia and the South Seas, Falklands islands, via Brazil, Madagascar, India, Tahiti, Batavia and the Tasman Bay. In the three voyages he undertook the preparations for such lengthy and arduous trips, each time required numerous notes and letters to and from the Navy Board of the Admiralty. Most frequently the letters were addressed to the Victualing Board.

The men who sailed in the '*Endeavour*' were Navy men – young, below age 30, men who though not specially distinguished in any way, were willing to work very hard; they were capable, alert, cheerful, indefatigable, fearless and loyal.

Provisioning of the '*Endeavour*': 1768 May–June: James Cook, a lieutenant when the first voyage was undertaken, carried on a lively correspondence with the Victualing Board in the matter of provisioning. The Navy Board of that period had become aware of 'scurvy' and knew the preventive measures to be taken to keep it at bay. Cook noted in his journal that on June 15, by Order of the Admiralty, the following quantities of foods (Table 14.1) for a 12 month period for 70 men on Foreign Service were to be delivered to his ship *Endeavour* by the Victualing Board (from Cook's Journal; Beaglehole, 1968, p. 613).

The beer allowance was meant for one month and brandy (spirits) in lieu of the remaining quantity. There were, however, specific requests from Cook to the Victualing Board to be supplied with wine and water in casks, a supply of arrack, more salt, lesser quantity of currants, no almonds and increased quantities of sage and spices.

Table 14.1: The list of provisions requisitioned by Cook to be delivered to his ship Endeavour

Bread in bags	21,226 Pounds
Beer in Puncheons	1,200 gallons
Spirits	160 gallons
Beef	4,000 Pieces
Flour in lieu of ditto*	(meaning *beef) in half barrels 1,400 pounds
Suet	800 Pounds
Raisins	2,500 Pounds
Peas in Butts	187 Bushels
Oat meal	10 Bushels
Wheat	120 Bushels
Oil	120 gallons
Sugar	1,500 Pounds
Vinegar	500 Pounds
Sauerkraut	7,860 Pounds
Malt in Hogsheads	40 Bushels
Salt	20 Bushels
Pork	6,000 Pieces
Mustard seed	160 Pounds

He found the malted grain to be the best medicine to combat ill health and scurvy – even more than orange and lemon juice. Cook's observations and notes on scurvy are quite detailed in nature and form a part of his Journal that runs to some 753 pages titled 'His Majesty's Bark Endeavour, River Thames'.

At different places, the ship purchased wine, water, fresh beef, onions, extra fruits and vegetables, all sorts of fish, hog meat, and poultry but as all these were fresh foods, none of them would keep for any length of time at sea except the jerked beef (salted, cured and dried), sugar, molasses, yams, cassava (manioc) and pumpkin etc. Bread and flour were scarce in all these places, so the men made do with yams and other such starchy vegetables.

Regarding the general health and maintenance of the ship's complement, the salt beef and pork rations had been reduced. The men were in the habit of mixing up the beef fat with flour, a practice that was strictly banned by Cook. There were other dietary changes made from the moment of leaving England. Butter and cheese issues were restricted, and raisins were provided with flour instead of pickled suet.

Water purification: While water filled in casks was loaded in sufficient quantity, it would not keep beyond a period and would foul very easily. The Admiralty note authorizing provisioning also ordered a machine for sweetening foul water. There is no further description of the equipment.

The final word: Apart from its botanical discoveries, astronomical observations and finding new lands, the voyage was characterised by various dietary precautions for health management. Additions and modifications, proper ration management, innovative use of unpalatable foods, timely purchase of local produce, even so far as trying outlandish foods offered in strange new lands such as dog meat, installing a water purifying system on board were Cook's innovations. In an unequivocal acknowledgement of the role of sauerkraut made to the Navy's Victualing Board, Cook reiterated that, 'it is the surgeon's, officers' and my opinion… that sauerkraut had a great share in… preserving people from scorbutic Taint… and that… it will always be found extremely beneficial to seamen… obliged to live long upon a salt diet.' On sauerkraut's keepability, Cook further reported that 'it has the further quality not to loose any part of its efficacy by keeping… used the last of it long after two years on board and it was then as good as at the first'.

The Napoleonic Wars

The Austrian campaign: Before Napoleon Bonaparte, the French army was an assembly of men who were part of the French Revolution. They were ill clad and most had no shoes. They carried any manner of weapons they could find. When he assumed leadership, Napoleon found the French army to be a pathetic sight; practically 'naked and ill fed'. Napoleon had grand designs of conquering Europe. The administrative machinery of the Ministry of War Organization was inadequate to feed, dress, equip and provide transportation for the army beyond the borders of France. The responsibility of these tasks in the field fell on the *intendent general*, who exercised his authority only in the limited zone of operations. Further supplies could not be sent since there was no communication link between the ministry and the field generals until Napoleon's time. He thrust the responsibility on an '*ad hoc*' basis upon the field commanders, they believed that it was downgrading their status or was in the nature of a punishment to perform such tasks.

The huge numbers mobilised: Soon after he crowned himself Emperor of the French, he made plans for expansion and would not rest till Austria was his; there remained Russia but he would come to that in a while. Italy, Spain and German provinces were already a part of the French Republic and under negotiated treaties of peace, and as allies, they were all bound to provide support, troops and hospitality to his army. In August 1805, Napoleon decided to go to war against Austria. His ministry was faced, at short notice, with the task of having to put together a transport and supply apparatus for 170,000 French troops marching from the camps in Boulogne to the Rhine – the deployment zone. And there were 80,000 new recruits to be organised and deployed as well. A French historical novel titled '*Desiree*' (Selinko, 1954), set in Napoleonic times provides a gripping account of Napoleon's life and times from Desiree's point of view, who as a teenager was to have married him but was jilted for Josephine and after a passage of time ended up marrying General Bernadotte (later to become one of the eighteen Marshals of France, governor of Hanover, and still later, the adopted Crown prince of Sweden). It also narrates Napoleon's preparations for marching into Austria when Bernadotte was the Governor of Hanover and Commander-in-Chief of the French troops. Organising supplies on such a large scale, especially since Napoleon wished that his troops be well fed *enroute* and in the camp, called for an efficient handling of the situation. His Chief of Staff, Bertheir, within a matter of two days, laid down and communicated the sequence of formations and the precise quantities of provisions that a regiment should draw from each individual place along their route of march. Napoleon's two Corps Commanders, Marshal Marmont and Marshal Bernadotte, came from Holland and Hanover respectively to concentrate the forces at Gottingen and then Wurzburg. Marmont had been advised to live off the territory in friendly Holland and Bernadotte was instructed to carry seven or eight day's supply of biscuits and avoid burdening the neutral Hesse-Kassal (Van Creveld, 1977, pp. 44–45). '*An army marches on its stomach*' is an adage attributed to Napoleon and he did everything possible by way of advance planning to arrange for carts, food, feed and fodder for his army of men and animals.

Rations and quantities: He ordered his commanders in France to have ready, 500,000 biscuit rations at Strasbourg and another 200,000 at Mainz, in 25 days, and a million biscuit rations from Bavaria; the 700,000 rations to provide for 116,000 men for six day's, which along with four days of bread (as reserve and eaten only in emergency) had to last till Bavaria. Another four day's supply awaited them in Ulm. Similar elaborate preparations were made for 55,000 men of the Corps in the northern sector for nine days' rations in addition to the four days bread they all carried. Napoleon thus planned that his Grand Army could subsist fully for two weeks without requisitioning at all (Van Creveld, 1977, p. 49). The transport requirement amounted to some 4,550 wagons, artillery alone needing no less than 2,500 horse. Van Creveld (1977, p. 50) describes the various problems faced by the Commanders, their complaints and inter Corps competition to corner the maximum available resources, problems of advancing with so much artillery, baggage, men and stores which ultimately resulted in each Corps having only some four days bread and biscuit rations instead of the original 35 days planned for.

Quartering and sourcing food: The '*Ordonnateurs*', the people on the staff of the Corps and specially charged by the Corps Commanders to look after the Corps' supplies as per the broad directives of the Imperial Headquarters, did a tremendous job and only one Corps was told to live off the land, find accommodation and forage on their own and to exist without irritating each other (Van Creveld, 1977, p. 52)

It was the practice to lodge men and their mounts with civilian inhabitants. The unwilling hosts had to provide the rations fixed for each man plus the wood required for cooking. The ration scale at the time was 1½ lb bread, ½ lb meat, 1 ounce rice (or 2 ounces dried fruit) per day. The officers, on the other hand, had no fixed ration scale, but were to be fed decently in accordance with their rank, but were charged not to make excessive demands on their hosts. If the corps were placed too close together the *ordonnateurs* commandeered provisions from the near by areas on the strength of receipts which would be later honoured by the French Treasury. The demand to provide provisions to the troops was made in advance.

Napoleon did not allow his army to plunder at will and instructed his men to treat the people of the territories they passed through, or in which they were quartered, as if they would treat the French people themselves – with respect and as their own. The procurers – the *ordonnateurs,* were successful in requisitioning enormous quantities of food stuff along their passage through every town and hamlet. In examining the Napoleonic war supply mechanism we learn that the continental wars did not require lengthy troop marches of several months or years (such as the ones Alexander had undertaken), the distances traveled were not long and allies in territories through which the army had to pass were used effectively to deliver the requisitioned supplies. To move men in vast numbers, an able general like Napoleon would have seen the necessity of establishing depots, magazines and store houses along the way, keeping open the lines of communication to keep supplies reaching the men at all times. By all accounts he did admirably well in this aspect. Finding all the transport animals and the number of wagons to carry the war materials – ammunition, artillery, rations – was a Herculean task in the early nineteenth century. However, Napoleon's march to Moscow next is a saga of how things could go horribly wrong inspite of the best planning.

The Russian Campaign: 'The first quality of a solider is fortitude in enduring fatigue and hardship. Bravery but the second', and 'poverty, hardship, misery are the school of good soldiers'. These were the words of Napoleon on the quality of a solider (Thompson, 2002, p. 12). Nowhere were such qualities put to test as in the disastrous winter campaign in Russia. His aim was to take Moscow and then St Petersburg. Napoleon himself is said to have equaled Alexander the Great and Genghis Khan in intellect and in the relationship of the intellect to military skills and virtues (Dupuy, 1987, p. 9). All the advance planning notwithstanding, Napoleon's Russian campaign was fraught with unprecedented hurdles and difficulties that decimated his army of 400,000. When he embarked upon the campaign it was hot, but soon the army walked into the bitter Russian winter. This caused him to withdraw from Moscow in ignominy. Nigel Nicolson researched and reconstructed the events in a succinct way (Nicolson, 1985). Napoleon had wanted to make a quick campaign – a mere six weeks by his reckoning, and arrangements for supplies should have been made for at least a two month period. As it turned out, the battalions marched out with rations for just twenty days. He depended too much on the resources of the country the army moved through. The local resources were inadequate to sustain his huge army. Napoleon had never before marched with an army as large as this. It was nearly double the size of the enemy. His 'Grand Army' was spread over a war front of 250 miles and had to traverse on inadequate roads. The main army was accompanied by another army of bakers, tailors, masons, shoemakers, gunsmiths, camp followers and historians. Luxuries were not to be foregone, even in the field; the senior officers carried every paraphernalia felt to be essential for personal comfort and for maintaining the style of living which they were used to. This included carpets, plates and other 'essentials' and servants riding in carriages and wagons that followed the trails. Not to be outdone, the troops too emulated their officers to a great extent. Every division of the troops was trailed by its supply train. There were numerous draught oxen captured in Poland and Prussia and there were more than 200,000 horses in the supply column. Where was all the feed for them to come from? The oxen were eventually killed and eaten. But each horse required some nine kg of fodder per day as well as oats and meals and mere grazing in the fields would not be adequate. There were more than 100,000 cavalry and artillery horses. The horses were allowed to graze and for want of anything else, they fed on unripe rye in the fields and died in the thousands. The 20 days of ration supplies did not last even this period, there was no bread for the troops; the grinding mill to grind corn and the field ovens to bake bread could not keep up with the demand; they also broke down and finally fell silent. Slaughter of the cattle accompanying the battalions was resorted to for their daily food. The starving troops began to be struck down by various ailments – dysentery, diarrhea, diphtheria and typhus. In the near absence of any medical help, thousands fell sick and some 60,000 men died even before a shot had been fired. Napoleon had planned for and had anticipated a quick campaign, in and out before winter set in and return to Paris long before his absence could be felt. Before reaching Vilna, men and horses were falling, incessant storms soaked them through and thunder deafened them. The roads became mud traps for the guns and wagons. Their sheer weight made them sink into the mud and therefore had to be abandoned. The water wells became polluted.

While all this terrible suffering befell Napoleon's army, there was no such suffering for the Russian army. Tsar Alexander's three armies had the total strength of 208,000; the first Army itself having 127,000 in 6 Corps. No dead horses were seen on the road, no stragglers, no stores and wagons left behind; neither cannon nor sick men found abandoned. Was their commissariat then very much more efficient? Perhaps not; they had recourse to main depots, which were more easily accessible. They too felt the acute shortages of food, fodder, and water. The villages had been razed to the ground. The French soldiers searching for potatoes in the field to assuage their hunger were mercilessly shot by the peasants.

When at last Napoleon marched into Moscow in that terrible weather and took his first look at the Kremlin, waiting to be received in grand style by the vanquished, nothing happened and no one came. There was no one and nothing substantial left. To make matters worse the Russian's 'scorched Earth' policy reduced everything in the countryside to ashes. The soldiers who, for too long had been prodded on with promises of food and rest, took the city by storm and plundered what they could find and ignored the stern orders from Napoleon to desist. The return to Paris was, if anything, even more tortuous for what remained of the Grand Army.

The Crimean War

The Crimean war is better known to readers for the name of Florence Nightingale and the role played by her than either the reason for war (which was to take control of the Black Sea and the Dardanelles by Russia) or for the strength and strategies of the opposing armies – Russians on one side and French and British on the other. Continental wars were no novelty. Throughout the seventeenth and eighteenth centuries, a state of war prevailed within Europe. And thanks to Napoleon, the armies extended themselves far beyond the borders of their own countries and kept both the British and the Russian forces engaged. In the mid 1850s, British forces were spread thin in India and elsewhere in their dominions. The need to recruit more troops and deploy them quickly into war theatres was the over-riding concern of the Crown. There was no thought or awareness about the necessity of looking after the soldiers in any way different from what had been the practice in the past. Captain Cook's meticulous observations on the health of the men on long voyages and how he prevented and reduced the incidence of death and disease with proper control of diets did not seem to have made any impression or impact on the powers that be, nor did it make any significant difference to the soldiers in the field, though it might have gotten the attention of the Admiralty.

Dispatches from the warfront in Crimea brought news of the ghastly conditions prevailing there and of the pitiful medical facilities and the frightful fatalities. There would have been many more war casualties but for Florence Nightingale, that angel in disguise who ministered ceaselessly to the health and wellbeing of the soldiers – the sick, the wounded and the invalided – in the military hospital. There was no doubt that Florence Nightingale's ceaseless effort in nursing helped enormously in reducing the number of outright fatalities, but even so, Crimean war casualties would have continued because of the equally aggravating circumstances due to the awful food that came to be the fate of the soldiers. And as awful and as thoroughly undernourishing as it was, this sorry state of affairs would have continued but for one other person whom the history books appear to have forgotten. That individual was Alexis Soyer, an Englishman in London and a member of the Reforms Club.

In 1854, Britain dispatched a collection of ill assorted and ill prepared regiments to the east, to face the mighty Russian Army. The senior commanders were strangers to each other and to their men and had not trained with the latter since they assumed charge of their brigades only after reaching the battle area. Their force commander Lord Raglan included, were all old, way beyond 60 years of age; they were eclipsed by the Duke of Wellington, none of them ever having seen action beyond Whitehall's offices! That men were tragically dying in the merciless cold and pitiful camp and hospital conditions was known only because officers wrote letters home. War time reporting by journalistic deputation was non-existent. However, there was one who braved the situation to go to the battlefront and send dispatches to the newspaper '*Times*'. And that is how the public in England knew of the tragedy unfolding in the Crimea (Barthrop and Ray, 1995, p. ix).

The Crimean Army had no logistic backing whatsoever for its cavalry, guns, infantry and sappers. Medical help was primitive; there was no ambulance service and what there was, was manned by drunks and pensioners. Transportation of the wounded was effected by carrying on a man's back or horse back to the ship by which they were to be evacuated to Constantinople. If they did not die on the way, packed as they were like sardines, they surely succumbed to the utterly dreadful conditions existing in the base hospitals where everything was unhygienic, insufficient and hopeless (Barthrop and Ray, 1995, p. viii).

Not that the soldiers, at least those that were still alive and fighting, were any better off. The Crimean winter caused the land to be bare of everything, windswept, snow covered; the men wore tattered uniforms, sheltered in leaking tents, covered themselves with one thin blanket and slept on stony ground. They had to gather twigs to make a fire and cook their meal consisting only of salt beef and biscuit. If they even longed for a hot beverage, all they had was raw, green coffee beans; to make coffee out of these one had to light a fire, roast the beans, grind or crush them somehow and then brew the coffee. How could they even gather kindling for so much cooking fire?

The reports of the great war correspondent W.H. Russel from the scene of battle enthused Florence Nightingale and Alexis Soyer (see Annexure 5) to go to Scutari to render help in their own particular ways.

Soldiers' food allowance and everyday cooking: The English soldier's allowance was one pound of meat (salted) and one pound of bread per day. Plus some coffee, salt, sugar and water; each man carried his own rations and cooked his own meal. The French troops on the other hand, received smaller meat rations but bigger bread portions. They formed messes of twelve people, with one man elected each day to be the cook. The cook was thus able to take his time and cook the food properly and thoroughly, particularly the salted meat, which always required more time to soak and hours to soften, time which the soldiers never had. The French troops carried 'Canteen Kettles' known as 'marmites' which Soyer thought were far superior to, and much larger than, the British ones, and which were made of better metal. In the camp, while some said that one soldier cooked for 16 men with two canteens, Soyer found 5–6 men cooking for a company and there were ten kitchens to a regiment of ten companies (Barthrop and Ray, 1995, pp. 140–141). No vegetables ever formed a part of the rations and lime juice, considered at that time to be a necessity, remained unissued at one time for weeks due to official slackness, lack of planning and confusion; scurvy among the soldiers was common. His other observations in the hospital kitchens included the way the meat was handled and made ready for cooking, the short change in the quantity of meat issued, the conditions of the corroded/tarnished copper boilers, the very poor quality of poultry meat, the pathetic store house with sorry looking vegetables, preserved meats, soups, sweetmeats and mostly the way the cooks prepared the patients' food. With his detailed investigations and observations on the cooking practices and the demonstrations he held of new wholesome recipes, and with the active cooperation of the generals and the officers of the regiments Soyer visited, he came out with innovations that had far reaching effects on the turn of events in the Crimean war. Soyer brought in so many innovations that it changed the way armies equipped themselves in the future. These included *Soyer's stove,* made with a combination of two devices, which was now very fuel efficient, a *Scutari teapot* provided with a removable filter, a *baking cum stew pan*, new recipes for camp cooking and recipe book for specific use by army cooks. One might surmise that though initially very poorly prepared for this war, the British very soon realised the importance of a 'good feed' for speedy recovery as well as sustained nourishment of soldiers as 'good care' when it was pointed out to them by an ordinary citizen with expertise and good intensions willing to help and show the way. There is no better way to salute Alexis Soyer and his '*Culinary Campaign*' in the Crimean war than to recall, recount and remember his contributions.

The Boer War

The Anglo-Boer war in South Africa fought between 1889 and 1902 was a clash of wills between the Afrikaner *volk* (to stay independent) and Britain's grand imperial ambitions. Boers declared independence and sent an army under the leadership of Kruger to the Natal Province even as Transvaal Republic, Natal Province and Orange Free State were preparing to form a Federation within the British Empire. After preliminary confrontations and engagements between Boer and British troops, Kruger did consent to accept the provisional peace offer made by British Prime Minister Gladstone in Queen Victoria's reign. But where a region holds the promise of untold wealth to come – from the diamond mines in the Kimberleys and gold on the Rand discovered in 1886 in the Matabele land in Transvaal, the peace could not last long. Cecil Rhodes, who gained monopoly of the Kimberleys and wished to exploit the land, created a potentially explosive situation which in the British mind warranted the show of an army to prevent war.

Britain gathered her scattered forces (from Britain, Malta, Egypt, Crete and Mauritius), all together numbering 10,662 men and sent them to Durban, South Africa. Transport was to be provided for them locally upon their arrival. This, including the locally raised troops, brought the British army strength to 27,500. The 64-year-old Sir George White, Quarter Master General at the War office, took command of the army.

Although the empire's regular army strength was considerable – 227,159, half of whom were infantry and some 20,000 cavalry, half this strength was positioned in UK and the great majority were posted in India, while the rest were scattered. It was decided to use only the white troops. Because of this reason, great numbers of the Indian Army consisting largely of native troops were not used in this war (Carver, 2000, p. 13). The British officers of the Indian Army however, joined individually and served to command locally raised units and to serve on staff. Though plans for military mobilisation and preparations were begun in 1889, what seemed to have escaped the attention of the planners was the absence of a plan for obtaining provisions, particularly horses, believing that the latter could be easily procured from local sources. It fell to the Admiralty to ship the cavalry and infantry divisions. Also, there was less than expected response to the call for enlisting and even lesser number found fit and qualified to join.

Against this force, the Boers' strength was estimated to be 50,000 men, in the ages of 16 to 60 years, grouped into four Burgher Commands according to their ages and formed into groups as small as 300 or as big as 3,000. With rebels from the Natal and Cape Cod colonies, and men from Foreign Corps composed of assorted Irish, Dutch, German, Scandinavian, Italian, French, American and Russian men, the Boers numbered 87,365 in all (Carver, 2000, p. 14). The artillery, fortress guns, field guns and mountain guns, obsolete and small in number had still to be manned in different locations.

Rations, foods and supplies: Descriptions of the situation in regard to food and supplies can be found in the diaries, war missives and reports of British civilians, soldiers and their officers in Lord Carver's accounts (Carver, 2000). From these we obtain a sense of what the soldiers' and civilians food rations were during the time of the Boer war.

The soldier's rations were at first – bully and biscuit, presumably at 5 pounds per day, which was all that was allowed. Conditions in the field were even worse. The rations were then reduced to one and half pounds per day – literally a starvation allowance on which the soldiers were expected to march and fight. It was no wonder then that in the debilitated state, thousands of soldiers suffered from enteric fever and dysentery on their way to Bloemfontein.

The British supplies depended on the railways. The major logistic problems of this war were supplying the army and moving it over vast distances. Most of the effort of the army, it has been said, went into keeping the food supplies coming in, getting sufficient forage for the animals and guarding the railway lines and animal drawn wagon convoys on rough tracks.

Supply of bread was a major problem due to the large and clumsy field ovens, which could not be carried along. The alternative was the biscuit, which was not a favourite among the men. Matters had been far better managed during the Afghan war where fresh oven baked bread for the troops was provided when the army marched from Kabul to Kandahar. To overcome the problem with water supply in the barren and dry countryside. The system of '*bhisties*' prevalent in India and was imported. A *bhisti* was an employee who supplied establishments with water in a skin bag or a '*puckal*', which is a canvas bag slung over the back.

Tending to the huge number of transport animals and cavalry horses was no small matter. In one incident narrated by an NCO in his letter home (Carver, 2000, p. 99) there were 200 wagons drawn by 3,000 oxen across Waterval drift which stalled on the steep and muddy slopes. The animals needed to rest and graze too but the threat of an attack by the enemy was ever present; they had eyes on the wagon trains of supplies too and ambushed the train and scattered the animals. Roberts ordered his men to abandon a third of the wagons for lack of animals and proceed on the march. The men knew the consequences of losing the wagons carting food and forage: depletion of their ration allowance. And it did happen, and they were put on quarter rations. According to the narration, the men would have rather risked a few lives than leave the loaded wagons behind.

The supply situation dominated the thoughts and actions of the commanders. We also find in the exploits and actions of Baden-Powell (he of the Scouts fame in later years) charged with protecting a small town of white population and three native places, his concerns about procuring food for the people who exchanged their sugar quota for flour. No milk was found for the public and then when available, only with doctor's permission for the sick, the elderly and children. His first act was to enforce rationing.

The soldiers lived on siege rations – 16 ounces (one pound) of bread, a little piece of fresh meat and a spoonful of tea and sugar per man per day. Obtaining flour was a rare event but now and then soldiers managed it and attempted to make their own bread. There was very strict rationing for civilians. Baden-Powel now compulsorily acquired the grain stocks of the natives, rationed it and then made the natives buy it back! But when this did not mend the food situation, he introduced forcible reduction of the natives' rations, thinking to drive them away into Kenya where food stocks were supposed to be accumulating but not many natives could be thus driven away.

Emergency and innovative food preparations using hither-to unacceptable grain and meat began to appear under the directions of Baden-Powel: eating forage oats, horse meat scraped off the skeleton thin animals using the carcass for preparing some sort of soup with salt peter and spices and sausage. The horses' own entrails and intestines could be used to stuff the sausage meat. Cut in water supply and lights by nine in the evening would affect the rural folk more. Every one made do with dry bread, black tea and coffee, without sugar or milk. To obtain even the meager rations that were allowed – one half pound of meat per adult per day was a struggle in itself. Supplies ran out so quickly that many went back disappointed after hours of standing in long lines.

In the end, what did the Boer war achieve? Not much, it has been said. The vision of a rich British dominated white South Africa remained unfulfilled, partly because no wave of Anglo-Saxon immigrants came and partly because by 1906, a previous treaty for internal self-government was honoured and the Afrikaners held political power. This war proved to be very expensive and cost many lives for no purpose or gain.

At an estimate, out of some 52,000 war casualties, 20,721 perished in the war: 7,582 killed in action but more than 13,139 died due to disease, according Lord Carver. A high death toll of 7000 to 12,000 accounted for losses on the Afrikaner side. It was also mentioned that some 18,000 to 20,000 died in concentration camps.

Scholars have said that the lessons learnt in the Anglo-Boer war decisively influenced Britain in the art and craft of war preparedness, which stood its Imperial army in good stead in the First World War.

American Revolutionary War, 1773–78

America was a huge territory and in the eighteenth century, it was a colony of immigrants numbering less than three million of which one-sixth were slaves from the African continent and was principally an agricultural country. In the North, New England raised plenty of animal and crop food and fruits. The middle country was known as the wheat belt; there were enough surpluses to export both wheat flour and livestock. The Southern States practiced diversified agriculture and had little to spare (Higginbotham, 1971, p. 304). European and other foreign goods and cargos came from and via the West Indies and American tobacco was exported. American leaders had wanted to ensure self sufficiency and home manufacturing. The creation of salt works was one such need; having an iron industry was another.

A law enacted in the British Parliament, known as the Tea Act in 1773, granted a virtual monopoly to the East India Company to sell its tea for much lower prices than the smuggled Dutch tea being marketed (Rankin, 1964, p. 19–20). All the tea came from China but was marketed by different trading companies. For the free thinking and enterprising American colonists, this monopoly granted to one company was not acceptable. Resentment grew and one day on 16 December 1773, the people of Boston, a flourishing town and a big trading port, dumped 342 tea chests of the Company into the sea. This act of defiance, termed 'rebellion', came to be famously known as the Boston Tea Party.

Since such a rebellion in Massachusetts could not be tolerated, the British government proceeded with punitive measures to teach the rebels a lesson and nip the rebellion in the bud; but this did not happen. Therefore, the flourishing city of Boston was to be destroyed, the Boston port closed, the government of Massachusetts taken away from the citizens and the King's army deployed on the streets of Boston. An uneasy peace prevailed. Every official measure would only further increase the people's determination to oppose. One version of the account of the American Revolution, given in 1850 by a Chinese government official, recounted by Rankin (1964, p. 13–15), was that a duty on tea used to be levied when it was sold but England levied another tax over this, which the buyer had to pay. And this the American people would not accept.

The manner, in which the English in England perceived the colonized, particularly the New Englanders, appeared to characterise their general attitude towards their colonial subjects. The New Englanders were described as a 'set of sly, artful, hypocritical rascals, cruel and cowardly' by Lord Percy, writing to the Secretary of War (Rankin, 1964 p. 20). While ruling a colonial state, they despised the locals, looked down upon them and treated them with contempt.

A large force was deemed to be necessary to terrify the Americans and break up their assemblies. All through the autumn of 1774 and winter of 1775, there was fighting; the Americans were watching the British soldiers' movements and the soldiers were trying to discover the meeting places of the rebels. These initial stages were remembered clearly in the memoirs of a Boston silversmith, Paul Revere, recounted by Rankin (Rankin, 1964, p. 21–29).

The Army: There was no standing American army as such. Britain's land forces in early 1775 exceeded 48,000, of which 32,294 were infantry, 6,869 cavalry and 2,484 artillery (Higginbotham, 1971, p. 122–123); the force strength was quite insufficient. The red coated British soldier of the time has been described as an ignorant country boy, lured by gin into volunteering; more often than not he could be a convict left with only two choices – enlist or go to prison or worse be deported to a penal colony. And when he naturally chose to enlist, then it was service in the army for life. And because of this and the fact that no one really cared for their well being, enlistments were not sufficient to raise the numbers required. More incentives were offered to deserters, the promise of short duration service of only three years in a bid to complete recruitment by the end of 1775.

The officer class was the gentry and there were well to do aristocrats who could buy their commission into the King's army (£2,600 for a Majorcy and more than £5,000 for a Lieutenant Colonelcy). The generals were members of the Parliament even while serving in the American colonial service. They are said to have lacked the professionalism desirous in field officers.

The navy had a limited mobilisation; 'judicious economic measures applied in naval affairs' caused the decline of the fleet – in ships' numbers, in repairs and maintenance, and in the crews available (Higginbotham, 1971, pp. 128–129).

Food, rations and supplies: Food was plentiful – pork, beef, bread, rice, corn meal, other fresh farm and garden produce, till the autumn of 1776, it was grown locally and came from New England for the patriotic forces operating near Boston. As the war between the king's troops and the local patriotic forces progressed, there was loss of everything, so much so that the Congress encouraged the soldiers to grow potatoes, turnips etc. This was not very successful. In July, a Resolution of Independence was adopted by the Congress and on 4 July, it declared Independence. As the campaigns continued, food became scarcer during 1777–78; men endured hunger and starvation amidst plenty. Their meager rations consisted of 3 oz. of meat (one ounce = 28.35 g) and 3 pounds of bread for one entire week and there were times when there was no food at all of any kind for two days.

The problem was also said to be transportation, due to poor roads which became even worse in rain and snow; lack of animals, and finding food stocks. The farmers had little surplus and sold what they could for depreciated currency. For the strength of 15,000 soldiers, according to General Washington's estimate, 100,000 barrels of flour and 2 million pounds of meat were needed. The Quartermaster and his teams had to hire horses, oxen and wagons, which had to be sent over riverboats and the rural folk were unwilling to part with their animals and were distrustful of the hire teams. For lack of forage some 15,000 horses starved to death. The setbacks suffered at Valley Forge were attributed to shortage of wagon teams to bring pork from New Jersey and flour from the wharves of Susquehanna (Higginbotham, 1971, p. 304). There was not one main depot where the entire needs of the army could be assembled; there were supply depots around the main army camp and on the proposed route of march during advance or retreat. Acute shortages of food could be really debilitating to the soldier in combat and this is what caused General Washington to retreat rather suddenly through New Jersey in December 1776. And although by this time it had been known that the English Captain James Cook had had a successful voyage on his ship *Endeavour* without allowing scurvy to take toll of the health of his sailors and soldiers, the British Navy itself did nothing about it or did not seem to realise the grave necessity for fresh fruit, vegetables or even lemon in the diet. The British soldiers in America felt the brunt of this lack of fresh fruit and vegetables. Salt was needed to preserve meat and fish. It used to be imported from the British West Indies before 1775. Now the prices shot up; there was hoarding and salt became scarce. Both the civilians and the army felt its acute shortage. Without salt, meat could not be stored in the army depots. The cattle were therefore fed on hay and corn and were driven to slaughter where the meat was needed (Higginbotham, 1971, p. 305). But finally this war was won by the American colonists, bringing to end the British rule in America. Canada remained under the Crown, which attracted Americans for its large landmass and thin population to enter into a futile war with it in 1812 that came to be known as the forgotten war. Service of supply in this war have been amply dealt with by various authors (McKee, 1927, Risch, 1962). Except to run up huge bills to sustain the war and in recruiting soldiers by giving away large tracts of land and high pay as incentives for enrolling, it seemed to have achieved little (Hickey, 1989; Mahon, 1972).

American Civil War, 1861–65

The American Civil War came about due to an accumulated set of problems and differences between the North and South. The immigrant populations of the Northern States had benefited from the cultivation of cotton and food crops – corn and wheat, practicing animal husbandry and employing modern inventions and equipments in farming. President Abraham Lincoln would bring certain reforms against which the Southern States rebelled. The reforms pertained to abolishing slave labour that worked on cotton plantations which southern wealth and lifestyle were founded upon. Abolishing black slave labour inherent and essential to the Southern way of life would mean drastic changes in their economy and the way their social life was perceived. The Southern States, therefore, seceded from the Union, no longer willing to accept the new ways and wishing to be independent (Craven, 1969, pp. 5, 23,). In rebellion, they formed a Confederacy of States separate from the Federal Union. In 1861 Lincoln sent troops to curb the rebellion.

Army strength, supply and transport mechanisms: From the descriptions of the day-to-day life of the civil war period, we learn that in early 1861, the US Army and Navy were small and scattered over the country (Denney, 1992, p. 9). There were less than 16,000 officers and men combined, most of them posted in the west for the protection of the settlers against the marauding native tribes and the rest scattered across the country. The senior officer in the service was 75 years old and had never commanded any army of more than a few thousand men and he now refused to lead the Confederate army choosing to stay with the Union. At the beginning of the conflict, there were only 1,108 officers of all grades and ranks, of which 387 resigned to join the Confederacy, while 162 officers of the 'Slave State' elected to stay with the Union. More men were enlisted during the course of the war but material supplies were becoming progressively scarcer, food availability had decreased and the transport mechanisms, both road and rail, were inadequate for the two armies. Long wagon trains – some 25 miles long, traveling on road, had to pass through wilderness and moved painfully slowly. Troops had to be moved to battle and supply bases at strategic forward locations had to be established. Rail lines were used for this purpose but this service line came at a high cost. The Northern rail tracks were 22,000 miles long while the Southern States had only about 8,500 miles of track. In every way, the North was better equipped to move men and materials while the South was hampered and handicapped due to fewer miles of tracks, fewer locomotives, less resources, greater problems of repair and maintenance, challenges of communication – mail and telegraph and poorly developed steam river-boat traffic.

It has been said (Denny, 1992, pp. 13–14) that teaching and training field sanitation to the troops became a major problem – particularly to the men from the Western and Southern States who came mostly from the farming communities and their (including officer's) ideas of personal hygiene and use of toilets were different from the people in the Regular Army. Enforcement of good sanitation on General Sherman's insistence, regular inspection of the troops, their messes and of the water sources, helped stay the sickness rate to low levels but mortality rate due to typhoid and other intestinal infections was seventeen per cent. Diseases were rampant in both armies. Sick rates increased from one year to the next but improved field sanitation instituted by the Sanitary Commission brought this rate down. This is also the first time in the descriptions of wars of the past that one comes across a mention of the importance of field sanitation in combat areas. The French military observers were so impressed by these arrangements in 1861–62 that they took the drawings and instructions for implementation in their own land.

Food logistics: Food logistics were not an easy matter either. Few officers had any experience in waging a long campaign, though no one would have envisaged at that time a campaign lasting any great length of time. How to feed the thousands of men and animals every day became a major concern to the Army as the war progressed. This was a war within a country; the fighting stretched between the North and South, the army of the hitherto one country split into two, each competing for the same materials, supplies, animals and foods. The supplies did not have to come from outside their country, the men had only to be mobilised by rail and road within the country, and everyone ate the same kind of food, the sources of which were dwindling. The South suffered more from lack of food than did the North.

The Fable of the Soup Stone

A children's tale – the Soup Stone tells the story of a soldier in America on his way home from war (possibly during the Civil war), and his charming and clever way of finding food in a village when traveling long distance.

Night was falling and the young soldier was tired and needed shelter and food. He came to a farmhouse and asked the owner for a little food and shelter. Times were hard, the harvest was poor and the people had little to spare so of course the farmer could offer none.

The soldier, unfazed, then asked for a large pot of water and was given it by the farmer's wife. The solider said he would show them a favourite family recipe and took out a stone from his pocket. He turned it three times and then dropped it into the pot of water, put the pot on the fire and began stirring the water. He murmured aloud that if a little salt could be added it would make the brew more flavoursome. Obligingly, the farmer's wife put a fistful of salt into the water. The stone soup was being stirred all the time. The soldier wondered aloud if perhaps a carrot could be found. The farmer, his wife, and the soldier went into the garden and pulled a few carrots. These were washed, peeled and chopped and added to the water. The soldier continued to engage the farmer and his family in conversation with his reminiscences, and mentioned in passing that a few potatoes would really thicken this soup. The farmer's wife went to the cellar, got a few and in the process some salted beef as well. She returned with her finds, all of which went into the soup pot. It truly promised to be a grand soup when done and with a bit of onion and a bit of cabbage added, there was no doubt it would be a soup for a celebration and a festive time. Struck by the truth of it the farmer asked his son to run to the neighbour and see if a few onions and some cabbage could be found. The farmer's son returned with onions and cabbage. These vegetables were added to the pot and the soup – it smelled heavenly. They were ready to sit down and eat the soup.

The farmer's wife, to celebrate the event and the grand meal waiting, set a fine table with a pot of flowers for cheer. From somewhere a loaf of bread and a jar of cider appeared on the table. They all sat around the fire, ate bowls of the hot bubbling wonderful soup and they all agreed that they had never eaten a better meal or a tastier one. After some more hearty, after-dinner conversation, the soldier was very kindly shown a place in the barn to spend the night. He spent a very restful night in a warm place and with a full belly. When the next morning he got ready to go, he said, in gratitude of all that the farmers' family had done for him, he wished to present the soup stone to the farmer's wife and added that the 'stone would never fail her'. It was accepted with great appreciation. The soldier went happily on his way and there in the middle of the road he found another soup stone (Van Rynbach, 1988).

A compendium of the civil war was prepared by Fredrick H. Dyer, who based the compilations on official records (Dyer, 1994). The official records exist in more than 120 volumes, encompassing all aspects of the war. There were numerous problems with the quality of foods and finding sufficient food stocks, sanitation and finding transportation animals. These will be found in Annexure 6.

Wars in the Twentieth Century

World War I

In the twentieth century there were two major wars, both came to be known as world wars, World War I, 1914–18 and World War II, 1939–45. Early in the century, the European continent was viewed as the centre of the world because it dominated diplomacy, trade, social development and political thought, said Pimlott (1986, p. 6). The countries aligned against each other in the First World War were Germany and Austria-Hungary, called the Central powers on one side and France, Russia and Great Britain, known as the Allies, on the other. They were the wealthiest, the most educated, the most technologically advanced and the most industrialised countries at that time.

The cascade of events leading to war began on 28 June, 1914 (Dowswell, 2004, p. 7) with the assassination of the Archduke Ferdinand of the Austro-Hungarian Hapsburg Empire, the feeling being the Austrians' discrimination and neglect of the Germans (Gilbert, 1994, p. 110). A Bosnian-Serb national in the empire's outpost, called Sarajevo, was blamed for the assassination (Gilbert, 1994, Introduction). Serbia had to pay for this dastardly act (Groom, 1976, p. 25) and therefore, Austria-Hungary served an ultimatum to Serbia and immediately afterwards declared war. Since Serbia was under Russian protection, Russia mobilised its army. This made Germany feel threatened on its eastern borders and therefore Germany declared war on Russia. But first it wanted to deal with France on its western borders therefore it also declared war on France. Both the German and French armies were mobilised. In the midst, Belgium, which was a neutral country was invaded by Germany in its march into France. Great Britain was an ally of France and declared war on Germany on 4 August, 1914 and imposed a naval blockade.

This war, which at first was believed even by the German emperor Kaiser, to last no longer than three months, went on for four long years and drew into its fold all the continents barring the Arctic and the Antarctic. The Ottoman empire and Bulgaria sided with the Central powers, while much later, Italy, Romania, Japan and China and the United States of America (incensed by the sinking of the stream ship *Lusitania* in 1915 and a German naval blockade in 1917) entered the war in support of the Allies (Dowswell, 2004, p. 7). The colonies of France, Germany and Britain were drawn in too.

Troop mobilisation: According to Keegan (1999, p. 27), all European armies had military plans but had very little to do with any 'national security policy'. The Kaiser, when made aware of a ten year old Schlieffen plan – a 'policy war document' (Hatt, 2001, p. 62) must have seen merit in it and resurrected it at this time. The war was fought on two fronts. Within the first fortnight of August 1914, the German peace time army strength of around 800,000 swelled six times by the mobilisation of recruits. More than 1.85 million men, fully equipped, were dispatched to the front with Belgium and France and were ready to fight (Keegan, 1993, p. 307). Even the Russians were able to mobilise their First and Second Armies speedily, in Poland.

Within a month of the outbreak of hostilities, European railway organisation was in perfect shape to undertake war time movements of troops from garrisons to battle fields. Several divisions of the French infantry, the very huge armies of Germany, Austria and Russia, together with several million horses were mobilised.

There were no tanks in World War 1 until 1916. Men were unable to move in the fire zone without getting mowed down. The movement of ammunition between the railhead and the guns in position was the job of the horses. And the horses had to be fed, thus it seems that horse fodder was one of the single largest items of cargo unloaded at ports in France and destined for the British, fighting in the western front (Keegan, 1993, p. 308). Likewise, the German army also employed some 1.4 million horses during 1914–18. Most of these animals must have perished.

European army strength and logistics: At the start of the war, the major powers had navies for protecting their coastal waters and patrolling and maintaining their sea trade routes. Germany and Britain particularly depended on maritime foreign trade for much of their raw materials and food. France could get by if the short sea route to North Africa were open and available but neither Russia nor Austria-Hungary needed external sources to feed their own people and equip their armies, in the beginning. The prospect of starvation loomed large if the sea routes were blockaded for long. As the war progressed, German U-boats (submarines) attacked British shipping; tremendous losses resulted every month by such attacks and one ship out of every four did not make it back; the losses kept increasing every year and by 1917, 3.7 million tons of shipping had been lost. The ships had to be organised into convoys under naval escort to move from Gibraltar to Britain (Pimlott, 1986, p. 38–41).

The armed camps of the European Armies in 1914 teamed with millions of troops – 4.5 million from Germany, 4 million from France, 1 million from Great Britain, 0.11 million from Belgium, 3 million from Austria-Hungary, 6 million from Russia, and 0.2 million each from Serbia and the Ottoman empire (Pimlott, 1986, p. 8). To equip all the men with guns, shells, rifles, machine guns, bombs, not to say clothing, boots and food, each country's affairs and economy were converted to function on a war footing.

The British armed forces sought volunteers as per their recruiting policy. In 1914, many had been killed in the first months. Reinforcements would come from the British colonies of the empire – Australia, Canada, New Zealand, South Africa, India and other small colonies, but for immediate purposes, the civil population was inspired by Lord Kitchener to enlist in the service of their country. Conscription was also resorted to in 1916 in Britain and in 1917 in the US. The shortage of man power was met by employing women in large numbers in every industry and manufacturing sector. The well-established social order of women minding the hearth and home and men earning bread and butter outside was changing and the war changed the world.

There were major offensives and battles of this Great War, writ large with disasters of monumental proportion. The casualties suffered by the Allies in the initial 19 months during 1916 and 1917 were about 1.75 million. Many more perished as the war progressed, as told in a memoir entitled the '*Poor Bloody Infantry*' (Groom, 1976, p. 170). A colossal destruction of men, materials, land and economy in every country, near and far, was the outcome.

As the Allied orders for food, ammunitions and other war related supplies ate up the British and French capital investments in USA, they began to borrow money from the latter by the middle of 1915 and it became a creditor nation. Even as the prices of everything – cotton, petroleum, copper and nitrate rose, great demands were made on the factories for arms and food processing. Mining activities rose and the transportation industry surged. The Americans, according to Robert Zieger (2000, p. 96) benefited so much by this war trade ($6 billions in 1916 as against $2 billion in 1913).

The trench war: The First World War was notable and unique in several respects for the first air maneuver and for its trench system, especially on the Western Front. The First World War was largely fought in the trenches by the French, British and German armies. It has been said that as soon as a maneuver was over, both the German and the British sides 'dug in', not just figuratively but literally. The 'digging in' began by the end of 1914 on the Western front. The trenches were deep and long troughs in the ground which extended from the Swiss border to the channel coast, though not always connected. A trench was in the shape of a deep blunt 'V', lined and walled with wooden planks on one steep side, a drainage sump in the bottom and ingeniously crafted on the other side of the 'V' to have niches called 'fire step' and another at a higher level for keeping ammunition. On the ground level, the open mouth of the 'V' was protected by sandbag parapets. In course of the war an elaborate trench system evolved, complete with communications, support lines, dugouts and machine gun posts. After a few months of usage and deadlock, and during continuous rains in winter, the trenches turned into waterlogged, dreadful holes. Standing in sometimes knee deep or waist deep water for a long time caused trench foot and cold injury in the soldiers (Pimlott, 1986, pp. 52–53).

Everything required by the troops was stored in the underground trenches that snaked all over the territory and were like a maze or a network where the dug out, firing lines, and the machine gun positions were in the first line of attack immediately behind barbed wire fences; the communication trenches and mortar trench were in the channels connecting the first line with the second support line and then the third support line and so on.

Incarcerated below ground, life in the trenches was a nightmare (Remarque, 1929). One unit manned the frontline for about one week or longer as required, come winter or continuous rain. Then it was relieved by another unit. There was no regular patrolling as one would do on the ground, except to go up surreptitiously at night near the enemy trenches without alerting them and for listening into hushed conversations for intelligence gathering or for repairing the barbed wire. In rains, their diet was monotonous, canned food – no hot meals. The men suffered from a variety of diseases from cold injury, colds, influenza, infestation with lice and runover constantly by huge field rats which fed on the corpses. Everyone on both sides of the Western Front suffered.

A newly arriving soldier would enter the reserve trenches at the back of the network, move up through the support trenches and then to the front line trench. The three somewhat parallel lines were joined by communication trenches. The trenches were deep and soldiers could walk fully erect without being seen above ground. The fire step facing the enemy allowed the man to stand on it and take aim. One may imagine trenches to be like sunken battlements in underground fortress, laid in parallel and all connected by little passage ways and small courtyards and alcoves!

The Germans had plans to maintain their position for a long period of time and had taken special care with their trenches, with electric lights and running water and therefore had the best constructed trenches of all, their very deep dugouts also offering protection from any British or French shelling (Hansen, 2001, p. 24). The British and the French regarded the trenches as purely temporary structures (expecting to push the enemy back) and therefore their trenches had little beyond the basics. Also, they believed in their soldiers roughing it out and not become soft with comforts. The soldiers were expected to also rest and sleep in the open trenches under a waterproof sheet or when located in the rear support lines. They had no helmets until mid 1916 and discipline was very strict and punishment swift and excessively harsh; some sound even barbaric and often capital for offenses such as disobedience of orders, cowardice, desertion and mutiny etc.

Always in the position of firing, the men spent time between getting bored and getting shot at and killed. There was however no shooting at mealtimes, starting with breakfast! There were also days when there was no shooting and several weeks at a time went by without any enemy action. At such times, life was humdrum for the soldiers, with routine work: digging trenches, cutting firewood, mending equipment, writing letters, delivering their garments or just relaxing and sleeping when the occasion and the lull permitted. There were clandestine night patrols above ground besides sentry duty conducted with periscopes. When firing commenced or continued, those who were wounded or killed just fell back into the trenches.

The underground squalor due to insufficient water, waste and generally unhygienic conditions of the toilets, rain, rats and the all pervading lice, made life hell for the men on the front lines. In contrast, facilities and conditions were better in the rear reserve trenches and the quarters for officers were especially good. Well behind lines, in the reserve lines, the colonel of the battalion HQ lived in a most comfortable dugout. In an autobiography of Robert Granes (engineer) it has been mentioned that the facilities included papered walls, with pictures hanging on them, table with an ornamental lamp and plenty of polished silver and whiskey and easy chairs, spring mattresses on beds, and a gramophone (Hatt, 2001, pp. 15–21). The soldiers in all the armies suffered equally.

Food and cooking in the trenches: Canned food (pork, beef or beans) and hard biscuits were the usual bill of fare in the Allied front lines. Hot meals made in kitchens in the rear trenches were the prerogatives of those in the support trenches, rarely sent up to the front lines if the enemy was shelling (Pimlott, 1986, p. 53; Hansen, 2001, p. 31). There were large cylindrical wood burning stoves, vessels and pails and work tables (Hatt, 2001, p. 21). There were underground kitchens in the Western Front and judging by the descriptions provided, they were equally terrible and minimally equipped. The German trenches, as has been mentioned before, were better built and designed sturdily with elaborate underground channels which were deep enough for walking straight. It took the Germans months to build these along the Hindenburg line. However, in Arras, the Allied troops utilised an existing old cave system under the city, and by joining them and making entrances, they had perfectly protected underground walkways from the center of Arras to the German front. It was well lit, furnished to house the Brigade Headquarters communication lines and a cookhouse as well (Hatt, 2001, pp. 42–43).

French soldiers were paid and fed often and amply (Keegan, 1999, pp. 316–318); they also received cash allowances paid directly to the dependents of those wounded and killed. Hundreds of thousands of men in trenches had been killed between 1914 and 1916. The German general Erich von Falkenhayen decided to fight the war by taking French lives rather than French territory at Verdun. Between February and December, 350,000 French and 300,000 Germans had been killed or wounded with no territory won or lost (Dowswell, 2004, pp. 89).

France could feed the troops and people on food produced within the country, but increasingly there were fewer people to tend or till the land. Britain was able to continue food imports until mid 1917 when the German U-boats began destroying the Allies commercial shipping. German food trade suffered because of the Allied naval blockades. Availability of fish and eggs, sugar, butter and vegetables declined greatly. 'Turnip winter' of 1916–17 was the sobriquet earned because the tasteless turnip was the only vegetable available.

The French soldiers now found that they had to put up with harsher conditions than the British (Dowswell, 2004, p. 94). Desire for peace grew out of acute hardship, denial of leave, food and treatment plus civilian discontent, all of which culminated in the French infantry's mutiny in 1917. It was believed that the army had been subverted by civilian antiwar agitators. By the time the mutiny ended (after 6 weeks), there were 3,427 court-martials and 554 soldiers given death sentence (48 actually shot) (Keegan, 1999, p. 331).

The summer of 1918 was the bloodiest and the hardest of all. Germans were losing faith in their leaders, felt discontent with the imperial government and angry with the flourishing black market, which left only potatoes and turnips for everybody except the rich (Hatt, 2001, p. 54–55). In an unofficial Christmas Day Trench Truce on the Western Front, 1914, all shelling ceased. On Christmas Eve, the German and British soldiers sang carols, called greetings and even ventured out of trenches into no man's land to meet (Hatt, 2001, p. 17). A German officer, Lt. Johannes Niemann, when told by his orderly that both the Scottish and German soldiers had come out, himself observed through binoculars that they were exchanging cigarettes, schnapps and chocolate. Much later, a real football match was played! Such was the spirit of Christmas in that time, in peace or war.

The soldier's kit. The personal kit of an officer in 1914 weighed in at a total 42 lb 14oz. His Service dress, boots, underclothing, cap, braces and identity discs together weighed 12 lb 6½ oz. The rations and water weighed 6 lb 2½ oz. His gun and ammunition were worn on the person, bandolier fashion for mounted duty. Other items in the kit comprised the field service pocket book, cap, comforter carried in great pocket, compass, wire cutters, field dressing in the skirt of the jacket, binoculars or telescope (2 lb), great coat (7 lb), clasp knife, handkerchief, map and matches (Bull, 1998). Apart from these, the valises containing perhaps more clothing and personal items were supposed to be carried in transport.

Serving officers in all the armies engaged in the western and the eastern fronts received comfort gifts sent from home. In the trenches, the British officers regularly subscribed to special food hampers from Harrods of London. Officers of the Austrian-Hungarian army requested some comfort items and personal items like socks, scarves, underwear, cigarettes and such things (Gilbert, 1994, p. 180).

India in World War I: India was a subject nation of the British Empire. The war efforts of the British Government were directed towards mobilising resources from her colonies, economic support and man power and buying bonds. Physically fit young men were needed desperately for the armies required to fight the war in different places. The unceasing efforts of the Lt. Governor of the Punjab, Michael O. Dyer led to vigorous campaigns, flattering praise in public durbars, challenging the courage, loyalty and physical prowess of the Punjabi soldier, all of which led to massive enlistment from schools, colleges and the peasantry. Punjabis (their numbers were the largest – 350,004) and other communities, the second largest number 142,000 coming from Uttar Pradesh, swelled the ranks from 1914–18 (Bakshi, 1988, p. 2) because of liberal rewards and financial incentives (Rs. 500 to 1000 per entitled man) being offered.

In East Africa: The Indian army had two branches: a combatant branch and a non-combatant branch and there were glaring deficiencies (Pradhan, 1991). Pradhan is very critical of the state of Army organisation and the state of readiness of the soldiers of the Indian Army sent to war. He faults them on many counts: inadequate training, unaware of techniques of warfare, ignorant of climate and geography, deficient in modern weaponry (as compared with European armies), less than sanctioned numbers of Sappers and miners, no electrical and mechanical services, understaffed and highly inadequate Signal services which affected communications. The concept of grouping men into companies did not prevail.

By the account in the Government of India's compilation on the Army and its evolution (Pradhan, 1972), the Supply and Transport branch consisted all of 3,858 men. Pradhan's recounting of the army supply depots revealed that in 1914, the British troops were generally positioned near a big supply depot which came under the charge of S & T officers, and there were smaller depots further away to provision detachments when they moved. Apparently food and clothing were stocked in nine different depots at headquarters of divisions. There was a stores officer posted at Cawnpore whose responsibility was to procure clothing, shoes, and other leather articles locally. The Station's Divisional Commander procured other necessities.

South Africa was a nightmare. Supply and Transport did not undertake the responsibility to organise or procure and provide food and rations except in certain locations, nor to arrange to feed the injured or the wounded. The Silladar animals got no feed and fodder from the S & T and there seemed to be no solutions to the supply problem. The two railway lines were no help at all and in the rains the bush grew so fast that roads became not only unpassable but untraceable. Neither animals nor mechanical transport could really progress. The German troops had engaged porters to carry their rations and arms and ammunition. Their families also traveled with them, a reason for the men not to lack decent cooked food and not to feel homesick (Pradhan, 1991, pp. 150–152).

When they went to war in East Africa, some further glaring deficiencies surfaced. Just before embarkation, many more units than the original two of Force B were given machine guns with no time or training practice. How could they possibly use these weapons effectively? The men who made up the units came from different parts of the country, creating non homogeneity, being so very important in any group activity. Nor were there officers who could knit them together because they also were strangers to the men and often saw them just before departure. Most of the troops had no operational experience nor had any familiarity with the armies and weapons provided.

The conditions on the battleground were no less daunting for such an inadequately prepared fighting force. The main military operations took place at an average height of 3,000 ft, with the sea on one side. High humidity, and widely varying temperatures fluctuating between night time temperatures of below freezing to day temperature of boiling heat. The wide bushy land and streams, water tracts, unseasonal and long stretches of rain causing slush and swamps and small floods, made troop movement near impossible and bogged them down with endless waiting for improved conditions. The few existing roads were equally impassable and the two railway lines always presented a convenient target for the German army. And this caused a very grave supply problem.

The British depended on draught animals and the railways, both of which presented immense problems. The animals became feeble and tired and perished in huge numbers: in a two week period in 1916, alone 10,000 horses, 10,000 mules, 11,000 oxen and 2,500 donkeys died. The railways were always vulnerable and were frequently cut. Shortage of supplies and the exhausting conditions often allowed the enemy to melt away into the dense bush. The Germans had porter transport, employing bands of native tribes to carry their baggage and supplies. Even so, casualties were high on both sides and there was poor medical help at hand. But soon, a new supply transport vehicle came into operation in late 1917 – to send supplies from Germany. This was the zeppelin L59 plane that landed on sea. As a flying machine, it was a huge oval tub like structure, with enormous haulage and storage capacity. It flew 3,600 miles over the sea through enemy territory, carrying 11 tons of ammunition, 3 tons of medical stores, 30 machine guns, mail and radio parts etc. The attempted delivery of the goods in German East Africa failed – basically due to a recall signal sent via radio to divert the aircraft while the zeppelin was approaching Khartoum (Macksey, 1989, pp. 78–79). The campaigns were kept supplied by motor transport running from the railhead onto roads specially constructed for the purpose over 450 mile, and in 6 months. It was not the 3-ton lorries but light vehicles – thousands of them, which kept bringing supplies. The wear and tear not with standing (for which repair workshops were established), thousands of black natives were trained as drivers (Macksey, 1989, pp. 78–79).

Disease and pests and the climate took their toll; more than 7,000 died of disease as against some 3,443 battle casualties. And some 28,000 oxen perished in a short time. The peak strength of the Indians in the British armies was 2,150,000 (Gilbert, 1994, p. 112). Despite defective organisation, preparedness and provisions, the service of the Indian troops was much commended. Several gallantry medals were earned by the Indians and Gurkhas for their distinguished services

In the offensive at Pyrenees Salient, the Indian troops were led by British officers in hand to hand fighting in the trenches and performed in an exemplary manner, despite the heavily falling snow in November and the ferocious German rifles and machine gun fire (Gilbert, 1994, p. 112).

The direct costs of World War I, in a reliable estimate, were said to have been approximately $186,333,637,000 and the indirect costs were $151,646,942,560. For the first three years, the cost was an average $123 million a day, rising to a staggering $225 million per day in 1918! The British Dominions and colonies contributed a great share, India contributing $601,279,000 towards war finances after Canada ($1,665,576,000) and Australia ($1,423,208,000) (The Encyclopedia Americana: 29: 361).

World War II

Barely twenty years after the end of World War I, another war erupted in 1939 and lasted till 1945, encompassing the whole of Europe, Africa, the Middle East, Russia, Asia and the Pacific region. It pitted several armies against each other in a war that was unprecedented, in strength, equipment and strike capabilities. It was a war that involved Germany, Italy and Japan forming an axis against

Britain, other European countries, Russia, British Dominions and the United States of America. In this war, more than 50 million people were killed or wounded in action, in concentration and death camps, and remains in the memory for a great majority of that generation as the fall of Dunkirk, bombing of Pearl Harbour, Battle for Iwojima, Normandy landings on D-Day, and such other significant landmark events but especially the genocide in Nazi Germany where six million people of the Jewish faith were exterminated in concentration camps and when two cities in Japan, Hiroshima and Nagasaki were atom–bombed nearly out of existence.

There was a long build up prior to the outbreak of war. Germany, after World War I, defeated and humiliated, its national pride and selfworth at an all time low had also lost considerable territory in the Treaty of Versailles, 1919–21. Adolph Hitler's ascendancy into political power coincided with this demoralised state of the German people. Hitler's dangerous autocracy and increasing belligerence strove to lift the morale of the people and he declared in 1937 that Germany needed *lebensraum* or Living Space to accommodate its increasing population, to maintain their living standards and to provide sufficient food supplies. Financially struggling, its trade and commerce becoming limited in scope and the rising fear of dependency on foreign nations for its food, Hitler divined that the solution lay in occupying agriculturally useful space in regions of Eastern Europe which did not have population burdens (Liddlehart, 1970, pp. 6–7).

A series of aggressive actions followed, such as the move to reoccupy the demilitarised zone of the Rhineland in 1936, the demand for the return of Sudetenland from Czechoslovakia, his march into Austria in 1938, his plans to send troops to help General Franco in the Spanish civil war (though in this he was dissuaded by his generals). Britain and France, in their appeasement policy, remained silent and complaisant. He therefore foresaw no conflict and anticipated no war with Britain. And as Britain and the United States of America had their rearmament programmes going well and as Germany was undergoing economic problems, a general lull descended.

But the tide was turning ever so slowly. Hitler wanted Danzig and quite a lot of Poland as well as Czechoslovakia. The British cabinet of Prime Minister Neville Chamberlain reversed its stated position of appeasement and pledged support to Poland against threat from Germany to ensure peace in Europe (Liddlehart, 1970, p. 3). Danzig, on the Baltic coast, a port city now known as Gdansk in modern Poland, was a contentious issue between Germany and Poland since after the end of World War I it was given to Poland as part of post-war settlement. A conflict between the two countries regarding the future of Danzig is ascribed as the reason why open warfare erupted on 1 Sept, 1939 (Overy and Wheatcroft, 1989, p. 1). Hitler wanted Danzig back and also a free route to East Prussia through the Polish Corridor.

British Expeditionary Force: Two days after Hitler's march across the Polish frontier, Britain and France, unsuccessful in their attempts to make him withdraw, declared war on Germany. A British Expeditionary Force consisting of 150,000 men, 25,000 vehicles and guns and 140,000 tons of stores, crossed the English Channel and disembarked in several French ports. To move such masses and quantities further inland, both the French railways and civilian labour assisted. The entire operation from 9 Sept to 4 Oct 1939, lasting 24 days, went without a hitch (Wilson, 1952, p. 3). The main base was too far and open to air attacks and the LOC too stretched, the British Army in Belgium was cut off from base ports and encircled by the Germans within sight of the sea and waiting for the Navy to help them. The evacuation of the B.E.F by the Royal Navy from Dunkirk in May 1940, called 'Operation Dynamo', though said to be successful, chalked up a slaughter of men on a huge scale – some 130,000 casualties and 112,000 killed (mostly French), (Wilson, 1952, p. 4) was a major disaster.

While the Americans and the British could maintain re-supply to troops through mechanised transport, mostly trucks, the Germans, as well as the Russians had to take recourse to the service of enormous numbers of horses, lacking other means of transport – which in any case required fuel. Shortage of fuel occurred because of heavy engineering manufacturing – tanks, aircrafts, U-boats. Horses were therefore necessary and 2.75 million horses were inducted by the Germans (Keegan, 1993, p. 308).

World War II logistics: Following Dunkirk and the fall of France, a historian observed that the extent of British military un-preparedness became manifest: the bulk of the equipment had been lost in France, there were no reserves and production was insufficient to replace the lost equipment material and to arm the new armies (Wilson, 1952, p. 5). This war was also fought on various fronts, beginning in Europe, against Germany and the Axis, ending with the bombing of Japan. There would be battles in different theatres of war – East Africa, Benghazi, Egypt, Greece, the Middle East, and the entire Far East and Japan. US Pacific confrontation started after hostilities began with the Japanese airstrike on Pearl Harbor. Offensive and counter offensives taking place practically simultaneously in places removed by long distances, the Allied Forces had to have tremendous logistics plans to support the war on all fronts. In Europe, the coast had become heavily fortified and defended by the Germans after Dunkirk.

Five years after the first British Expeditionary Force landed in France, the Allied Expeditionary Force, in June 1944, under the command of Gen. Dwight Eisenhower of the United States Army, put together a massive force for landings at Normandy. It was planned initially for 1 May 1944 (Wilson, 1952, p. 59) under the codename 'Operation Overlord'. Again, as in the beginning of the war, in the first 24 days of this operation 476,000 men, 88,000 vehicles and guns and 449,000 tons of stores of British and Canadian elements crossed the channel to land on the beaches. The figures for the American Army would have been equally large and very likely much larger (Wilson, 1952, p. 3). In assembling such an Expeditionary Force, more than 2,300,000 soldiers were moved by special trains within Britain. Special freight trains carried more than 600,000 extra tons of materials that could not be carried by the coastal sea trade. The actual landing day in the coast of France-designated 'D' Day, was decided for first week of June, determined by the tide and moon (Wilson, 1952, p. 51), as the weather in the Normandy coast was known for being most unpredictable.

Food supplies for 'Operation Overlord': The provisioning for food supplies for this operation and the constant maintenance of supplies in the period immediately preceding landings and afterwards was done by issue of packed rations (Wilson, 1952, p. 57). Normandy rations have been discussed elsewhere in this book. The food for consumption the day after landing included 24 hour rations packed in water proof covers. Compo-packs, about 3.5 million and self heating soup and cocoa, 3 million tins, were issued for consumption during the channel crossing and during the first few days after landing. For about five weeks after the landing, troops were provided with free issues of packs containing cigarette, soap, toothpaste, razor blade and letter cards. Normal canteen supplies could only be established after this time. Some statistics for the readiness and arrangements for before and after the invasion are quite illuminating.

There were many monumental tasks for D-Day and after. Accommodation was provided for 1,350,000 Americans and 70,000 hospital beds were established; 20 million square feet of covered and 33 million sq ft of open depot storage and workshop accommodation were made ready; 20,000 tons (60 million gallons) of petrol were filled into 4 gallon containers in army depots before 'D' day; 2 million vehicles' spare parts, 150,000 miles of signal cable were gathered; 750,000 sets of clean underclothing was assembled and 3,500,000 vomit bags were also very thoughtfully included (for those who might be sea sick or just sick!).

In the 14 days following D-day, 730,000 men, 127,000 vehicles and 489,000 tons of stores were landed. By comparison, from 4 June to 31 Dec 1944, 450,000 tons of food was shipped for the British troops (Wilson, 1952 p. 59).

Reserve supplies: The supplies had to keep coming for maintenance, replacements and further buildup. For this purpose huge quantities of reserves would have had to be stockpiled. The build up of reserves was based on the formula of 'D'+3 days (2 day's reserves for the troops already landed), D+41 days (14 days reserves for troops ashore), from D+42 to D+90 (half day's reserve), reaching a figure for D+90 of 21 day's plus 7 days food for working margin, and after D+90, 21 day's maintenance entered with each 'divisional slice' (Wilson, 1952, p. 90).

The war was being fought on several fronts, but the two major theatres were in Europe and the Pacific. The Burma campaign was another challenge all together. The Southwest Monsoon that lasts five months brings torrents of rain, about 200 inches per day, obliterating every vestige of road, bridge, and low land, difficult to overcome by itself without the added aggravation caused by malaria. In 1943–44, the tenuous single LOC link between India and Burma was the Bengal-Assam Railway, also frequently washed out in the rains and the flood prone Brahmaputra River, to cross which there were limited river craft. Therefore, supplies for the allied troops were airdropped, from the base fields in Assam. An octogenarian war veteran residing in Mysore remembered that while serving in Burma, their units were supplied fresh vegetables and fruits as often as could be managed and that they cooked fresh *chapatis* or rice and dals and vegetables every day in the field.

The Japanese were already in central Burma, which was malaria free, and their communication lines were open, and their supplies for forward troops came via interior roads and railways emanating from Mandalay. They were also sitting amidst the rice fields of the Irrawady basin (Wilson, 1952, p. 78–79). The Japanese soldier was said to be tough, frugal, jungle trained and subsisted mainly on rice! So it was not a great hardship for him. When 100,000 troops rapidly surrounded Imphal and Kohima – then part of Assam (which was air supplied) and cut the Allied communications, the Japanese took minimal supplies along and planned to capture the vast British stores. For all their tactics and bravery in the filed, Imphal and Kohima could not be captured and thus the stocks and stores so essential for Japanese subsistence remained out of reach for them. Starvation and disease caused high battle casualties (Wilson, 1952, p. 82). The Japanese were formidable and caused demoralisation in the British troops which were also exhausted after practically one whole year (February to December 1943) of unsuccessful counter offensives (Messenger, 1995, pp. 243–244).

The campaigns in Burma brought to the fore one aspect of soldier training-deficiency in coping with the jungle and hilly terrains. After the Arakan debacle and the Chindits' expedition, jungle warfare schools were established in India to train men and officers in the art and craft of jungle operations and survival.

Germany's logistics: The German supply system in Europe was mostly linked to the rail and road system of movement. Basically the supplies were gathered in home depots and parks, all of which were then forwarded to the railhead. At destination, different Army supply columns took over their further handling. Some columns took the rations, food and clothing etc. to an Army dump and Army parks and collection points and other columns carried equipment. From here the division supply columns carried the goods to the division distribution and collection points. The individual battalions or companies were supplied by the battalion supply columns. There were also Army railheads through which the railway lines traveled to Army bases, parks and depots. These received goods directly from home depots, parks and even factories via the various collecting and forwarding stations. The road flow for conveying further the goods brought by rail to the Army railhead, traced its way through army dumps, parks and points, to the corps dumps, the division dumps, the regimental points and the battalion points to finally reach the company points. Road transport also delivered supplies to the troops directly, going straight from the Army dumps. At every station the road transports both picked up supplies meant for troops or for delivery to the next station (Macksey, 1989).

Desert supplies: In the deserts of the Middle East, during the Arab revolt at the time of World War I, camels were used in the guerilla war against the Turks to bring in supplies. In the western desert however, during World War II it was a different scenario. There were no animals but all supplies had to traverse the desert. Supplies had to be first transported by ships. Protection of the sea lane and the landing ports became a major preoccupation. The roads and desert tracks were always under attack. Ships were lost at sea, leading to shortages of fuel, which limited road operations. Both the Italians and the Germans suffered due to tremendous shortages.

Whether it was the British in Benghazi or Rommel in Toburk, each side would gain a logistic advantage at one time and then lose it at another time without any conclusive results (Macksey, 1989, p. 112). Rommel dismissed any supply problems that cropped up, saying it was the responsibility of his Quartermaster.

A feature of the desert war was that both the German and the British troops succumbed in their morale and suffered health setbacks due to the unpalatable and nutritionally deficient rations which were often scrounged from enemy sources.

Korean War and Logistics of Food Supplies

The war in Korea, (1950–53) according to Brigadier General John S. Brown, Chief of Military History, USA (McGrath, 2000), was the first major armed clash between free world and communist forces. In retrospect, there is much to learn from this war in which the US and UN forces were engaged against communist Korea. There are lessons that can be learned on military preparedness, global strategy and combined operations in military alliance among others.

The United States had put in place a very effective supply system of goods and foods originating mainly from its own shores. Consequently, the US troops in the Korean War were far better fed and provisioned than in World War II, an outstanding feature being the large amount of fresh foods that was available to them-shipped from San Francisco. In a 6 month period in 1950–51, overseas supply figures indicated that 19,600 cattle (to obtain boneless beef), 71,000 hogs (for ham) were estimated to be required. Poultry and turkey yields (from 794,670 and 65,950 respectively) and vegetables derived from 835 acres of potatoes, 114 acres of cabbage and 8 acres of carrots were shipped. In a single month, canned foods were produced from 51 acres of apples, 79 acres of peaches, 41 acres of pears, 104 acres of tomatoes and 487 acres of corn (Huston, 1989, pp. 193–194).

In the beginning of the Korean war, getting sufficient quantity of operational rations and processed items was a problem. To remind the readers again, 'A' rations used perishables to prepare hot meals in kitchens and 'B' rations had more canned and dehydrated items. Consequently, more than half the items used were fresh foods and the troops got to eat two hot meals a day (a luxury in any war and particularly on the front lines). It is easy to get used to good things. Even when the supply of processed food improved, the soldiers would not agree to revert to cold rations. Fresh meats were used most often, compared to canned meats. Tons of steak, whole eggs (in shell), potatoes, salad greens, fruits, were sent north from Pusan. Though most of the supplies originated from the US, there were large quantities obtained from Japanese hydroponic gardens that produced onions, lettuce, radishes. Daily airlifts of more than 15,000 lbs were sent to the front lines. The daily shipments increased to 65,000 lbs within a short time and included tomatoes, cucumbers and eggplants.

Handling of fresh foods: The procurement and shipment of fresh supplies from the US was attended to by the Quartermaster market center system. Through its efforts in World War II, it had become quite experienced in devising means of dealing with spoilage of both fresh and frozen foods.

A 'reefer vessel' system (refrigeration) was utilised for shipping the perishables. These vessels left San Francisco every 10 days and after reaching Korean ports, transferred the goods to floating cold storage barges, then to refrigerated railway wagons of the Korean National Railway and finally to the 'reefer vans' at forward supply points. This last transport not only distributed the food to 'division break down' points but also served as a temporary store house. There were several misses and hiccups no doubt (some wagons left behind, pilferage) but all in all, it proved to be a remarkably satisfactory system (Huston, 1989, p. 194).

Supply of non-perishables: The US food industry was producing and supplying, even in World War II, a variety of products such as dehydrated milk, potatoes, eggs, milk, prunes etc. Among the added features in the Korean war was recombined ice cream. The plants had been established in the Far East in 1949. Now the 'B' rations could be improved a little but still much of the stuff that went into the making of these were hard to find. The items had to be drawn from reserve stocks held for certain eventualities. Cans of Mexican beef and gravy −10 million pounds of it were purchased, as well as huge quantities of fruit juices to drink in lieu of the very poor drinking water in Korea.

The 'K' ration of World War II, with limited choice, was replaced by 'C' rations in which a wide variety of meat selections were introduced. The 'C' ration itself went through several versions during the war period. Now cooked beef was unwanted spam! The five-in one rations meant for detachments and crews in tanks etc. required mess gear to cook and heat and was refused by the Eighth Army early in 1951 because the crews in forward units did not take their mess gear and could not heat the cold food. C-rations were unpalatable and unacceptable to men even in one lunch time meal despite being provided hot meals for breakfast and supper. Consequently, the rations were wasted (Huston, 1989, pp. 195–196). The production and supply position of Individual Assault Food Packets, which had been geared up to meet large scale and continuous requirements for operational rations during World War II, fell as there was really no demand for such items in peacetime and hence there was no agency supplying ready rations. Defense contracts were placed on food manufacturers for supplying canned beans, fruit, beef and 75 other items. Then another defense contract had to be made with another group to assemble the items into rations. Canners were required to hold in stock a certain quantity of the season's manufacture for the exclusive use of the Armed Forces. The Chicago Quartermaster Procurement Agency then carried on assembly operations.

In September 1950, the assembled rations were coming out in large numbers at a daily rate of 20,000 rations. By June 1951, more than 51 million C rations, 8 million 5-in-1 rations and 4.5 million individual assault ration packs had been produced. At various times during 1950–52, the Quartermaster Base Depot at Pusan and the army units positioned in Korea and Japan, put together in 19 to 70 days, several tons of supplies and several days of reserves for C and B rations. And even if the shipments were delayed, the Base supply point held a buffer stock of adequate numbers of rations and assault packs at an estimated daily requirement of 278,000 B rations, 33,000 C rations and 4,700 assault packs. Thus the Eighth Army had always plenty to eat, never went hungry and after an initial period of stabilisation, there was plenty of good food (Huston, 1989, p. 196).

In the Far Eastern Command, the Japan Central Exchange supplied a great variety of other articles needed to support the combat troops. Though all such items fell under the 'miscellaneous' class, these nevertheless had to be factored in while calculating the tonnage, for transportation, space and storage. On sale to the men were different types of candy, tobacco, beverages, snack and other foods besides rations, toiletries, dry seeds, tableware, automotive parts, souvenirs and such, through 'post exchange' in depots in Japan. Other facilities, such as a meat processing plant, bakeries and exchange stores were functioning in Tokyo and Yokohama. Under the Central Exchange's supervision, branches and sub-branches conducted brisk business in snack bars, refreshment and eating stalls, beer halls, garages, even bottling plants, bowling alleys and more than a thousand outlets providing personal services (Huston, 1989, p. 210). After the first year of the Korean war, the sales of all these goods, worth about $110 million, by the Japan Central exchange, earned a hefty war time profit of 10–15 per cent.

Logistic problems: There were logistic failures in this war as happens in every war at some point. Supplies sent by sea between 1950–52 were not always smoothly transferred and distributed; items required for combat support did not reach the needy, mainly because too many ships brought in huge quantities which, when unloaded, were piled up in the seaports in mountains of unidentifiable items and thus could not be issued to those forces that needed them. They blocked and took up available space and because of that, even the clearly identifiable items in the ships waiting to unload could not be brought ashore (Eccles, 1959, pp. 175–176).

Supplies were also sent by small cargo boats to navigate the tidal basin of Inchon to transfer to ships anchored in the stream which sailed around the peninsula towards the east coast of North Korea (Eccles, 1959, p. 225). Marine and infantry divisions moved forward via amphibious landing. Emergency deliveries of supplies, evacuation of casualties to Japan, movement of troops to Japan and back (sent for recreational and rest purposes) were affected by airplanes, though it was the costliest means of transportation. Transport planes capable of carrying heavy loads and to operate in small airfields were not yet available for operations in Korea. To supply distant or isolated units, airdrops using conventional aircraft and helicopters were the only means. While hovering over and around the drop zone, men from the quartermaster unit riding in the plane literally kicked the bundles of supply out of the side doors. There were of course instances when the bundles did not land in and around the designated zone and the kicker, if not properly practiced, also got ejected (Huston, 1989, pp. 236–237). The airdropped supplies were picked by manual carrier labourers recruited with the assistance of the United Nations Civil Assistance in Korea and later by the Korean Army (Huston, 1989, p. 258).

Vietnam War

Vietnam war does not evoke the same kind of sentiments in the veterans and the public as did World War II. Those who fought, mostly young conscripts just turned 18, died in the thousands; of those who lived through the unmitigated circumstances, a few completing their tours of duty won field gallantry awards. Some infamous names have been associated with brutality inflicted on civilians but many turned to drugs or became wheelers and dealers; those who survived but were captured were subjected to unspeakable forms of torture and many have not been traced till today. It aroused a public outcry and opposition and youth in thousands, especially in the universities, participated in protest marches. They were considered very unpatriotic. Many were conscientious objectors. They received very hostile treatment from that section of the public which supported the war. There were deserters who had to flee the country to avoid being arrested and court-martialed. There was no winner – only a ceasefire. Those who lived to return never received a hero's welcome. There was no victory celebration. There was only sullen, angry silence. Vietnam is thought by many to be a national shame.

From 1962 on, when communists were threatening invasion of Laos from the Thailand border, in a rapid response, US marines (1,800 of them) were landed via amphibious ships. By the same means, in 1965 ground forces were sent to Danang and Chu lai for many amphibious actions along Vietnam's coast (Hooper, 1972, p. 42). In the US, there was no national mobilisation or call up of reserves, no special war budgeting, believing that the war would end in the same fiscal year. The North Vietnamese and the Viet Cong (VC) military effort had a political objective.

Vietnam, it has been said, was a war without fronts, fought at once, everywhere. Vietnam did not exist on any English language map in the 1940s. It was the French who brought the country together with Laos and Cambodia under French Indochina (Warren, 1990, p. 17). Vietnam was a jungle, a poor agrarian country and an easy target for communist aggression that had progressed through the 1950s. From 1966 on, the United States went to war in an effort to prevent and crush the communist influence of North Vietnam. For the Americans, it was a truly far off place – some 9,000 miles away and when the troops landed, everything had to be provided for them from scratch. The logistics for this war were an immense task but with the experience of past wars, the troops landed and dug themselves in fortified structures.

In the war zone itself, Special Forces erected camps on the lines of ancient fortresses. A central square of buildings was approachable by a road for vehicular traffic surrounded with water. Another outer perimeter wall around this separated this moat like waterbody from the outer compound wall. Between this outer wall and the outer perimeter wall there could be roads, waterbody and two–man foxholes (Warren, 1990, p. 83). The men lived in rat holes underground to escape Vietcong attacks.

Crushingly poor, and no match for the high technology supported United States, the North Vietnamese army and the Vietcong soldiers struck with superb jungle tactics. They resorted to camouflage, ambush, and using an assortment of body traps like the 'Pungi Stakes' (dipped in poison and placed in pits) and 'bouncing Betty', which were mines designed to blow up at crotch level, and frontal assault to isolate American bases. They ate their frugal rice meals obtained from the local people.

Logistics support: According to Lt. Gen. Victor H. ('Brute') Krulak, Commanding General, Fleet Marine Force, Pacific Fleet, the war in Vietnam was a logistic war (Hooper, 1972. p. 4). Support emanated from 27 major base camps established within the United States – self contained, hugely staffed, efficiently administered but functioning away from the fire and danger and death raging in the jungles, with everything that a technologically sophisticated war machine could provide in the way of airplanes, helicopters and communications (Warren, 1990, pp. 82–83).

The North Vietnamese had their own logistic problems, their war materials and supplies came from China. Some goods came by rail, but the great bulk came in from the USSR and Red China in ships docking in the river port of Haiphong. In the first three years of the Vietnam War the US never authorised blockading and mining the approaches but concentrated more on blocking the inland movement of goods through jungles in the 'Ho Chin Minh Trail'.

Recounting the role of the seventh US Naval Fleet, Hooper states that in 1965, it began air and surface patrols to check infiltration. Airstrike planes from aircraft carriers carried out many bombing sorties, until air bases could be constructed. The services and logistic support for the units of the fleet and the personnel would have included everything under the sun needed to maintain the machines as well as the men – health of their body, mind and spirit and their entertainment too. The Viet Cong employed *sampans* (narrow river boats) which glided quietly through the narrow inland canals taking goods from one point to another and probably ensured that throughout the 1,100 mile coast line, the VC had well stocked supply bases (Hooper, 1972, pp. 5, 43).

From different places in Vietnam, repairs were affected by repair ships and tenders, mobile units. Ammunition came from special ships meant for such combat support; fuel was delivered by fleet oilers, fast combat support ships and by Naval Supply Depots. Provisions came via provision ships, combat stores ships and fast combat support ships. Freight, consumables, mail, movies, all had either fast combat ships or 'under way' replenishment ships (Hooper, 1972, p. 45). Underway replenishment meant transfer accomplished at sea.

Some statistics provided by Hooper as 'guesstimates' for the quantity of supplies sent for the US troops in 1967, (based on World War II known campaign figures) show that there were 15,000 short tons of ammunition fuel, 450,000 short tons of aviation fuel, 2,699 tons of provisions and mail amounting to some 3,400,000 pounds. The figures are double and in some cases even treble of that supplied in World War II. Also, whereas in the former there were 100 items being supplied by sea, in the Vietnam War these items rose to 21,215. All provisions emanated from US ports, typically San Francisco; the goods were carried in store ships of different carrying capacities which sailed every 35 days and then later every 28 days. The critical items carried were chilled items. Later, fresh provisions such as vegetables and fruit were obtained from Taipei's (Hooper, 1972, pp. 47–54). The Marines landed with their own 30 day supply. One officer and seven men went north of Saigon and began construction of storage facilities. 33,000 sq feet of covered storage was built in the Danang area in 1965 (Hooper, 1972, pp. 94–95).

Vietnam was 6,900 nautical miles from San Francisco and 12,400 miles from New York (via the Panama Canal). C-141 jet propelled crafts, flying at high speeds, assisted in supply deliveries to Vietnam, each carrying 21 tons on average. But for the bulk of the supplies, it was the ocean going ships, some of the large ships being able to load 300,000 tons at a time. Wet cargo, such as fuel, went by sea and dry cargo such as ammunition, greatly in demand, went by air. As regards personnel, half the numbers in 1965 were transported by sea. Jet airfields were constructed by 1967 and facilitated movement of personnel up to 80 percent by air.

There was a full range of medical services in place for the 8,000 Americans sent to Vietnam in 1962 as illustrated in a pictorial presentation on the Vietnam war titled 'Dust Off'. There was an innovative air ambulance service brought from Fort Meade, Maryland. Many evacuation missions were carried out. A 2½–ton truck converted into a mobile kitchen was given by the stores officer to support one unit but there were no cooks. Finding the whole situation untenable, they brought along with them a six months' supply of C-rations.

A stupendous amount of logistic support was created in far away Vietnam by the United States to support a war that called for conscripts within their country and from their Allies – the Australians. The protracted war in the jungles with the wily and slippery Viet Cong (VC) and the jungle pests was not the kind of war the US soldiers had ever known. The US troops battled against the guerilla type ambushes of the VC in the thick jungles. The US resorted to spraying Agent Orange on vast tracts. The ignoble Mailai incident, when it became known, shocked and scandalised the world for the indiscriminate napalm bombing of civilians. The picture of the near naked child in flames running on the street seared the hearts of millions. It is another matter that the captain in charge of the operations was later held guilty and court-martialed.

There were antiwar protests throughout the length and breadth of America and especially in the small towns, colleges and universities from where the Vietnam conscripts came.

When the US withdrawal began after the fall of Saigon, there was a stampede during evacuation of first, the Americans, then of the several Vietnamese family members of the US soldiers. The last ship out of Saigon and the cramming of the last few civilians on board the ship as well as the desperate and pathetic scramble to climb aboard is also a picture that will remain indelibly in the minds and hearts of all who saw it. It will forever be a reminder of how, in a protracted war, even a nation like the US with its superior military, naval and air strength and with its kind of logistics support, had to bow down to the jungle tactics of the Viet Cong who only had their primitive support system but were a determined people driven by ideological compulsions.

The casualties on both sides kept growing and antiwar demonstrations in the US began to be raised by the young people from 1966. According to an American historian, Henry Steele Commanger (Warren, 1990, pp. 126–127) the Americans could not be a power.

The cost of this war was astronomically high in human and material loss. Of the 3 million men and women who served, 57,690 were killed, more than 303,000 wounded and some 500,000 to 700,000 suffered from post traumatic stress disorder (Warren, 1990, p. 175). The number of Viet Cong and North Vietnamese armed forces killed was 600,000 men, unknown number of communists and Vietnamese people dead; South Vietnam had 224,000 killed. Everything in their country was disrupted. After 1975, an estimated 100,000 South Vietnam civilians were sent into Hitler style concentration camps by North Vietnam. Agent Orange, a defoliant used extensively by the Americans in Vietnam gave rise to, among other ill effects of war, skin rashes, birth defects in children and cancer etc. About one million Vietnamese had to flee their country as refugees.

There were many war heroes, many were decorated and won medals for their valor and bravery in different campaigns. Many died in action or went missing. The Vietnam War Memorial in Washington, D.C., a polished black granite edifice is actually a wall on which the names of all those killed are inscribed.

In 1986, when the US intervened in Central America, there were public protests. Charles Litkey, who was awarded the Congressional medal of Honour in November 1968 for valour in Vietnam, renounced it in July 1986 in protest, and saw the US action in Central America as yet another Vietnam (Williams, 1976, p. 283).

Wars in West Asia

Gulf war, 1990–91: Technology reigned supreme, in deploying superbly trained forces, or equipping them with sophisticated communications, weapons, arsenal, transportation, medical aid or supply logistics, food rations and food services.

The Iraq war of 1991 was precipitated by the sudden invasion of Kuwait on Aug 2, 1990 by Saddam Hussein, the leader of the dominant Ba'ath party and the military dictator President of Iraq and hostilities in the Persian Gulf region broke out on Jan 17, 1991 between the US allied coalition forces and Iraq. The Iraqi army of 100,000 was poised on its borders, negotiations were in progress on 31 July with the OPEC (Oil Producing and Exporting Countries) (Pearce, 1992, p. 15). Iraq accused Kuwait of stealing its oil and invaded Kuwait with the deployment of sea, air and land forces (Pearce, 1992, p. 6). Iraq had a huge Armed Force, quantity rather than quality. Only the USA, compared to other quantitatively large armies of China, Syria, Egypt, North Korea, Cuba and Russia, possessed the highly advanced and technologically outfitted Armed Forces. The allied coalition forces eventually numbered nearly 750,000 (Darwish and Alexander, 1991, pp. 100–108).

The first example of a modern war fought with modern weapons and which was sustained by modern subsistence and service systems of a superior armed force was this Gulf war. It was won by superb air power and highly talented, trained and equipped pilots and aircraft personnel as well as due to superb support of every description. It was, according to the Americans, an Air-Land Battle 'hyper blitzkrieg' – a recipe for mobile comprehensive warfare (Dunnigan and Bay, 1992, p. 264). There were altogether 400 hours of ground war, starting early February. The preparation for this war spanned three to four months. To assemble troops, equipment and supplies thousands of miles away in the desert required no ordinary level of preparedness.

In describing the organization, equipment and the state of the Iraqi Army, it has been said that since the 1980s it was 'an army with a country attached' (Dunnigan and Bay, 1992, p. 74). Its Army had eight Corps, the Republican Guard Corps having eight divisions, all together more than 65 divisions (51 of infantry) bolstered up with Special Forces brigades and artillery, supply, maintenance and support units. There were several bomber aircrafts and 500,000 men in the air force while the navy had 5,000 men. The total pre war strength was about 1 million, with an impressive arsenal of different range missiles like the Scud, Al Hussein, Al Abbas and Laith type as well as thousands of tanks, armoured personnel carriers, infantry fighting vehicles, towed artillery (thousands of pieces of many different calibers), several hundred self propelled guns and multiple rocket launchers obtained from USA, Russia, Brazil and other sources (Dunnigan and Bay, 1992, pp. 84–86). Iraq's programme of developing '*Aslihatul Dammar Ashammel*' or weapons of mass destruction goes further back to 1974 when Saddam was the Vice President, Chemical Weapons. Despite this impressive array of battle forces, and being more familiar with trench style fighting with Iran, Iraq had no experience in mobile warfare, lacked the ability to effectively man and operate communications equipment and lacked trucks for mobility.

American heavy equipment – armoured vehicles (6,000) and trucks (30,000) were sent by sea. Their ground army's tail (support) was short, not enough personnel for support and maintenance. Almost half a million US troops were sent to Saudi Arabia by 1990 end. The local expatriate Americans housed almost 40,000 troops in their own homes for five months, giving them home comforts and a semblance of normal life. A comparison is drawn with Vietnam where it took four years to send 536,000 troops, while such a huge force (660,000), was sent to the Gulf within six months. Most of the British troops (who were in Germany) traveled by air to Al Jubayl with a stopover in Cyprus while some troops and all the equipment were sent two weeks in advance by merchant ships sailing from German ports (Pearce, 1992, p. 26). But, everything had to be transported by trucks and other ground vehicles. There were headaches, hold ups and administrative mixups.

Gulf war logistics: There is little that can be gleaned about Iraq's supply logistics. There was a good road network, there was also a wide highway from the Persian Gulf to Baghdad and under the APD programme (Arab Projects and Development programme, a Palestinian non-profit organisation was helping Arab countries in a variety of developmental activities) railways had been developed in several Arab countries. Iraq's war with Iran was just behind the borders where troops and supplies could be moved with relative ease and speed. Iran on the other hand, in the previous decade's war had to move its supplies over mountain ranges which hindered mobility and the supply chain (Dunnigan and Bay, 1992, pp. 88–89). Iraq fought a World War I style trench war and did not experience any great difficulty in sustaining its troops and maintaining supply lines.

Kuwait, surrounded by desert, was another matter. In desert operations, water becomes a crucial component of survival and hence a weapon. For an assured drinking water supply, a desalination plant is a must, which then becomes vulnerable to aerial attacks. In war games, the planners and strategists of the US defence agencies, in July 1990, had simulated combat situations with Iraqi forces while examining their own plans, and had decided that both sides would have to function under limited logistic capabilities. But in actual review, it was found that the Allied forces would very likely be far better placed having some 450 logistics points (for supply). Allies had their logistics base in Saudi Arabia and were in a position to supply any military operation. Iraqi policy of invasion of Kuwait, officially, was looting. Everything was to be plundered and pillaged and sent back to Iraq and the rest of it to be destroyed and the Kuwaitis driven out. And that is almost what happened in the five months of Iraqi occupation (Dunnigan and Bay, 1992, pp. 390–392). Kuwaiti forces being small in comparison to the Iraqi force had little capability to either fight or resist the invader.

The American forces had been receiving training to operate in combat situations involving air, sea and desert wars. They were well honed in desert warfare by way of training imparted to the armoured and mechanized units in the North American desert. And not just the desert, their training included using equipment and operating under the awfully dusty, sandy, dry and very hot conditions. This was not an army that took on Kuwaiti defence on an '*ad hoc*' basis (Dunnigan and Bay, 1992, p. 306). At this exact point in time, the United States possessed an Armed Force that was all dressed up and ready to go; an opportunity had to present itself. Kuwait, say Dunnigan and Bay, gave the United States Armed Forces, a perfect battlefield – no jungles and urban targets like in Vietnam, no mountain terrains as in Korea, but a vast expanse of desert ideal for air war and high tech weapons. But a desert also means there is no cover, no vegetation of any sort and no water, and food spoils very quickly in such high ambient temperatures.

There were three operations by the western alliance code named:

(a) Operation *Desert Shield* – defending Saudi Arabian territory – a defensive position.
(b) Operation *Desert Storm* – a counter offensive to enforce UN sanctions in Iraq and liberate Kuwait
(b) Operation *Granby* – a name for the British Operations in the Gulf.

The Kuwaitis and Arab coalition called the conflict *Harb Tahir al-Kuwaiti,* and the Iraqi name for this war was *Um Maorak* or the 'Mother of All Battles'.

Quantities of supplies: There were 400,000 tonnes of freight sent from UK and Europe, 15,000 vehicles (both armoured and unarmoured) and 80,000 tons of ammunition. Till 28 February, 10,000 tonnes of food, clothing (upper and under), bibles, sunglasses, desert shawls, combat boots, camouflage nets, poles, rolls of chemical agent resistant material in hundreds and thousands as well as 330,000 tonnes of general stores were deployed. Calculated for the Force Daily Supply Rate it worked out to 1,200 tonnes of ammunition, 600 tonnes of petrol/oil/lubricants, 50 tonnes of rations and 700,000 litres of water (Pearce, 1992, p. 26).

According to one source, in Operation Desert Shield/Storm combined, some 4.79 million prepackaged ration meals, 2,687.5 tonnes of bulk food and 200,717 gallons of water were used. Whether these figures represented the quantities used by the American troops alone or by the entire allied coalition troops is not mentioned (www.defenselink.mil/news/Aug2000). However, according to the US Quartermaster Professional Bulletin released in 1991, the chief of Army Field Feeding, Peter Motrynczuk, informed that several million ration meals (160 million, inclusive of A, B, T and MRE rations) were sent to the Gulf (Motrynczuk, 1991).

Field facilities: A Force Maintenance Area (FMA) was engaged, setting up different sites to accommodate 13,000 people and 5,000 vehicles of the British troops arriving in the Gulf. Baldrick Lines, a tented city, housed FMA's logistic units. When the main divisions arrived, several camps had come up. A training and fitness center was also soon established and a 600 bed field hospital as well. Baldrick Lines would receive the incoming supplies, food, fresh fruit etc. Soon in one camp, christened 'Blackadder', a completely containerised kitchen was established. It was designed by FMA's catering officer, Major Cliff Noons, and was constructed in Bahrain and shipped to Blackadder. Rare photographs of desert camp life show a British soldier taking a shower outside a tent from water stored in two large capacity water cans (may be 5 gallon cans) and delivered through a long tube to which a shower head had been affixed. Another clever improvisation for hygiene was 'Desert Rose'– the RAF version – an upright plastic funnel cup attached to metal (or perhaps rigid plastic) tube which was fixed into the ground. These closet devices for men were demarcated and very quaintly labeled 'officers', 'executives' (Pearce, 1992, pp. 32–45).

Water supply: Desert operations, no matter how high tech or sophisticated, require men to endure the heat, the dust and the dryness. Dehydration could become the biggest killer and the next singularly hazardous condition could arise due to drinking or using contaminated water spreading disease and laying the men low. Iraqi troops had carried desalination plants. The Desert Shield and Storm personnel had access to 1 liter bags of water to go into cargo pockets of their combat dress. There was bottled water, water in cans and tankers.

Water purification units based on the reverse osmosis (RO) principle, probably located in Al Jubayl provided the main body of fresh water which was carried in water tankers. In terms of volumes and quantity (after ammunition and fuel), water is the third most difficult commodity to transport. At the time of this war, there were no field tests and water testing kits for biological testing of water. By 1996 however, there appear to have been RO based water purification units of different capacities such as 150 gallon per hour (for water with more than 1,000 ppm TDS, Total Dissolved Solids), and 75 gallon per hour and 125 gallon per hour units called light weight water purification units especially meant for small units and medical detachments (www.gulflink.osd.mil/timeline).

Feeding policy: The US soldiers were generally fed on a 'feeding standard' which provided per day per man two hot meals and one Meal Ready to Eat (MRE). They also ate two A-Rations in seven days. This was more to get them used to eating MREs. Packaged food, never popular at the best of times are the only way the men can get subsistence during difficult operations and eating MRE once every day is a good strategy to make them aware of the quality and quantity of food and the method of its preparation and eating. The US Army Quartermaster Center's revised feeding policy stated that the field commanders should provide the soldiers with three quality meals per day. For this purpose there is a 'family of rations' [www.qmfound.com/army_family_of_rations.htm pp. 1–3].

It was this revised feeding policy that came into being during the Gulf war. The basic individual ration was the MRE group ration, which included unitised T-Rations (tray rations), B-Rations and A-Rations, the latter consisted of foods prepared from fresh perishable and refrigerated items. To produce meals, cooks, kitchens, cooking and refrigeration facilities and class I support are required wherever they may be served. A-Rations comprised about 35 per cent of the daily rations consumed in the operations (460,000 meals per day). B-rations were useful during the Gulf operations and came to be preferred and comprised 39 million meals or 22 per cent of the total rations shipped for use in Desert Shield/Storm.

An earlier version of B-rations was T-rations, simple and completely packed and also made of a mix of fully cooked and semi-perishable foods. Included are fully cooked tray pack entrees (the main western meal comprising meat food), vegetables, desserts and starches (rice, potato, pasta, bread, crackers and such). A recent development was pouch bread-shelf stable, and very like natural bread. Packed as 12 individual servings in one bag, 8 bags in one box. The tray pack container is an innovative all purpose devise and serves as a packing, for heating food '*in situ*' and serving. There are ten breakfast and ten lunch/dinner menu selections. Supplemented with milk, bread, dry cereals, fresh fruits, salad material and condiments, T-rations provide sumptuous and nutritionally complete meals.

As the number of menu choices suggest, there is quite a variety: egg omelets, ham, pork sausages and beef preparations for breakfast, and chicken, hamburgers, turkey etc. for lunch/dinner. T-rations come in what the Quartermaster Professional Bulletin calls a module (probably meaning man-packs) in a container with a specified number of meals (the original 36 revised to 18); 12 of these modules or 216 meals are made up into one pallet. It is a convenient way of organising hundreds of meals into units, and for providing variable menus without repetition with the advantage of least effort put in to serve the meals. In the Gulf operations, more than 20 million T-rations were shipped and 9,800 such rations were served daily.

Nearly 45 million MREs were shipped to the Joint Operations Area. Three to five days of basic load was given to the units which were thereafter supported in the theatre of operations with class 1 ration needs.

According to the Quartermaster Professional Bulletin released in the autumn of 1991, the new improved MREs for Operations Desert Shield/Storm were said to have had an increased size entrée, two breakfast entrées (ham and egg omelet and corned beef hash, name brand candies, Tabasco pepper sauce, Taster's Choice Coffee, beverage powder, fresh fruit, fruit juice and wet towelettes.

A high heat resistant chocolate bar, the Hershey Desert Bar was specially developed and produced for use in high temperature climates so the chocolate would not melt and run (www.qmfound.com/army_family_of_rations.htm). The fat component would be of a high melting point type. This chocolate bar, much written about in the media reporting the war in progress, became quite popular and will therefore continue to be included in some of the 12 MRE menus.

A sum up of the Desert Shield/Storm rations would thus show that the shipped rations came in various quantities as A-Rations (35 per cent), B-Rations (22 per cent), T-Rations (11 per cent) and the rest MREs. There was also a bulk shipment of Flameless Ration Heaters, which never got to the users properly. The heater should have been a part of the meal pack for effective use. This situation is said to have since been remedied.

War in Afghanistan – 2001: In terrorist attack on the World Trade Center in New York city on 11 September 2001, more than 2000 innocent civilians died. Based on the intelligence gathered by the United States through several means and on the investigations conducted by US agencies, the perpetrators of the heinous attack were identified and its originators traced to Al–Qaeda. The United States took counter measures and declared war on Al–Qaeda and its elusive but very powerful leader Osama bin Laden. Al–Qaeda were being assisted and supported by the Taliban in the mountain caves of Afghanistan. Effectively the war was on Afghanistan.

The invasion started on 7 October, 2001, in a military operation named 'Operation Enduring Freedom' jointly launched by the United States, NATO forces and assisted by the Northern Alliance of Afghanistan. The NATO coalition partners – alphabetically listed, were Australia, Bahrain, Canada, Croatia, Denmark, France, Germany, Italy, Japan, Lithuania, Netherlands, Norway, Pakistan, Poland, Portugal, Romania, Spain, Sweden and UK, some of whom were there from the beginning and some joined later. They contributed variously with troops, Special Forces, machines, vehicles, equipment, aircrafts, ships, submarines. The Northern Alliance provided majority of the Afghan forces. The US and British forces began aerial bombardment with strike aircrafts and missile launches from ships and submarines of Kabul, Kandahar and Jalalabad, targeting the electricity supplies, the home of the Taliban Leader Mullah Omar and Al–Qaeda training camps respectively. There were ground forces in the form of Special Forces, Marines, and Commandos who were superbly trained, equipped and mobile. These men could locate the Taliban's positions and communicate the information for air support.

The opposing combatants were the Taliban, the tribals, Pashtuns and foreign fighters of Al–Qaeda who fought with small arms, rockets and grenades. The Taliban forces, tribal in origin and training, even when possessing some fire power and communication devices were no match. By November 12, the Taliban fled from Kabul and the next day the Northern Alliance moved in and with the CIA Special Forces planned more bombings and strikes to cut Taliban supply lines near Mazar-i-Sharif.

The bombings in Afghanistan in these early months were carried out on the mountain caves of Tora-Bora and aerial strikes on Konduz. When the Taliban fled to Pakistan after the amnesty sought by Mullah Omar was rejected, Kandahar was taken by the Afghan tribals and the US marines established a base at the airport. There was another US Base established by the Air Force at Bagram, North of Kabul.

In March 2002, the battle of Shah-i-Kot, southeast of Gardez, took place when the Taliban regrouped and mounted guerilla type attacks. These people had only small arms, rocket propelled grenades and mortars but were ensconced safely in caves at altitudes of 10,000 ft (3,000 m) and in hillside bunkers.

Soldiers of the ground forces: To let the readers get a sense of how the US and coalition soldiers were equipped to fight at high altitudes, above 8,000 ft (2,440 m), on rocky terrain and in sub-zero temperatures, a brief description from a photograph published in *Time* Magazine in 18 Mar, 2002 of a soldier's attire is provided here.

From top to toe, he was a fierce, independent, well protected one man assault force. His helmet of Kevlar carried a luminescent tape so that US aircraft could identify an allied soldier on the ground. He wore night vision goggles, radio intercom headset and carried a shoulder strapped antenna. There was a second radio set to communicate with aircraft. His main arsenal was a M4 carbine with grenade launcher and laser designator and two pouches of ammunition holding six magazines each with 30 rounds, all of these slung over his shoulder. From the shoulder also hung a bandage pouch, gas mask pouch and a second side arm. On his feet, he wore insulated leather boots, the knees protected by kneepads. He wore a bullet proof Kevlar vest under uniform blouse, carried binoculars, knife and a map as well as plastic tie strips to handcuff prisoners. His back pack contained a water bag, MRE packs, extra ammunition, first aid kit, a sleeping bag as well as winter clothing.

With all this going for them, reports said that in 'Operation Anaconda' – the battle of Shah-i-Kot was the bloodiest of them all and more Americans died in it than at any time in this war. Until this battle, the brunt of the fighting was taken by the Afghan forces who must have died in hundred and thousands, not to speak of the countless civilian casualties and innumerable citizens who became war refugees.

A new regime has taken over; there is a President and a Government in place and reconstruction of Afghanistan goes on. Numbers of coalition forces continue to be deployed in Afghanistan as of now although some countries ended their participation and some other countries joined in. The stale mate with the Taliban continued, deeply entrenched as they are in their mountain hideouts which all the fire and ground and air power of the combined US-NATO forces failed to penetrate. With a new regime in place in the US, its forces have launched a fresh major Afghan assault in 'Operation Khanjar' or 'Strike of the Sword', which is to storm deep into Taliban territory in a river valley. This operation is intended to seize practically the entire Helmand river valley, the heartland of the Taliban insurgency and the world's biggest poppy production zone (Deccan Herald, 3 July, 2009). Poppy of course is the source of major revenue which has been feeding the war and insurgency by the Taliban.

War in Iraq, 2003: Before the 2001 Afghanistan war had progressed much more than 18 months, war clouds gathered over Iraq on the issue of President Saddam Hussein and his hidden cache of weapons of mass destruction. Even as a new regime took charge in Afghanistan and before the world could begin to grasp and digest the immeasurable harm done to the Afghan land, people and economy in search of the Taliban and Al–Qaeda, a second punishing war against terrorism was launched, beginning March 2003 on Iraq. This Gulf war, codenamed 'Operation Iraqi Freedom' has been fought with hi-tech resources at the disposal of the United States, UK and coalition partners.

The Iraqi Army, Air Force and Navy (www.cdi.org) had become considerably reduced from the time of Operation Desert Storm in 1991. Where before it had an army strength of 955,000 in 47 divisions and other smaller units, it was now only about 350,000 strong, had 24 divisions, and possessed 2,300 tanks and 1,000 artillery pieces. One Iraqi division could not possibly face one US division because of shortages of spares, difficulties in maintenance and lack of technically skilled personnel to use the tanks and artillery it had. The Air Force likewise was decimated and in 2003 it reportedly had some 130 attack aircraft, 180 fighters together with support aircraft, none of which were new. The Navy was small and weak and consisted of one operational missile boat, five non operational in-shore patrol craft and not much else. The crack Republican Guard, numbering 60,000–80,000 and special Republican Guard upto 26,000 in war time, were considered to be very effective land forces in the Gulf region.

The might, the arsenal, the technology and preparedness of the US and coalition troops were such that within a very short time, Saddam was deposed and captured and the country run by US troops. Troops stationed to administer and maintain status quo until a responsible government take over found themselves entrenched in Iraq. Civilian sectarian strife, increasing factional discontent, animosity towards the US and its military's handling or even its continued presence and support to the few political names that might form a government in the region did not allow an acceptable government to form or for the US troops to withdraw. The US found itself in a bind over this issue at home and internationally.

In the war in Afghanistan and Iraq, it is apparent that there were two types of combatants: on one side were the fighting forces drawn from different countries, cultures and even certain differing ethnic origins but mostly of Anglo-European extraction, who had been transported to fight on a land, terrain and region unfamiliar to them, while on the other side were a people of somewhat similar middle eastern commonality and background who were fighting on their own land. The Afghans, both in the Northern Alliance and in the Taliban, locals in every sense, needed little to subsist; they possessed little by way of worldly goods and they could move stealthily and launch guerilla attacks and their frugal nature of living required little logistic planning and tail end support to deliver foods and other essentials.

Food and rations for the local forces: Since no supply lines have been mentioned in any of the literature consulted, it is assumed that both the Northern Alliance's tribals and the Talibani guerillas lived off the land. And with the continuous bombing and strafing of civilian encampments and a virtual halting of all trade related movement, no food commodities could enter Afghanistan and what little stocks there were would have been soon exhausted. The tribals would have also ambushed any supply convoys of the opposition which were being brought in from supply bases in Pakistan and Kuwait. For civilians, the only recourse lay in receiving UN Food Aid in refugee camps. Even these agencies and their personnel have been targeted. BBC News reports datelined 24 Sept, 2001, have said that the Taliban seized some 1,400 tonnes of food from the UN World Food Programme (www.news.bbc.co.uk).

Lacking any information on the military rations of the Iraqi armed forces or of the Afghan fighters, one can at least learn a little about the type of food eaten by them, which will reveal the nature of supplies of both dry and fresh foods that would be required to support their war effort. As for the US and NATO forces deployed in these combat zones foods and food service systems are among the best and an elaborate supply mechanism is continuing to deliver.

Afghani and Iraqi foods, both flavoursome, bear some similarity to North Indian and Mughal Cuisine. Some of the names of the dishes are almost the same as those in Indian cuisine (See Annexure 7). Rice, wheat flour, lamb, beef, chicken, at least some vegetables, milk, sugar, spices, dry fruit and cooking fat are used in these preparations.

In the military garrisons in Iraq, there would have been kitchens for cooking and proper food service, though nothing is known about the Iraqi ration scales or the calorie or nutrition profile of their meals. After the fall of the Iraqi regime and fifteen months of street fighting, the remnants of the Iraqi forces were reduced to eating rice with red sauce made of unknown ingredients. Lunch in the military camps comprised of a giant steel pot of rice mixed with red sauce, cooked on a small fire. The soldiers ate this three times a day. Spartan as it is, the quality of the food and not its quantity would be worrisome. Poor food is reported to be effecting the soldiers' health and fitness. According to a story of July 17, 2006, filed by Ben Gilbert from Baghdad, due to corruption, wastage, fraud and theft in civilian contracts, the latest purchase of foodstuff was so substandard (bags of rice, some flat bread, and rotten pulverised tomatoes) that half the soldiers in a 150 man unit quit after eating the same rotten food for one year at a stretch (www.marketplace.publicradio.org.).

Reporting about the distressing state of food availability in Iraq, 24 months after the start of war, a press service information (Jim Garamone, *American Press Service*, 25 April, 2005) revealed that the Iraqi forces were given US combat rations because the foods under Food Aid given to the country were 'little more than crumbs'. It was air dropped from heights of 40,000 feet, the colour of the packets (yellow) were the same as cluster bombs, and the dropped food packs burst on impact or got spoiled.

The humanitarian aid supplying the daily ration packs consisted of US military rations for Iraqis with three meals per pack, containing two main dishes like barley stew, rice and vegetables with sauce, red beans and rice. Each pack also contains packets of crackers, peanut butter, cookies and strawberry jam. None of these are perishable but all of them may not be liked. Having fewer calories (2,200 kcal/day) than the US military rations (nearly 4,000 Kcal/day) but with 10 per cent protein, these ration packs were being provided to the Iraqi forces (now battling insurgents and militants in civil war) and to those people with military connections.

Non-perishable, with a three year shelf life at 80°F (<30°C), the ration packets, each costing $4.35, do not appear to be particularly culturally appropriate. The everyday Iraqi food is quite different from the Western cuisine type foods in the combat rations. If they did not like or get this food, the alternative would be much worse. There is no comparison however, of this situation with the rations and food services for the US marines and soldiers of Strike force and Expeditionary units deployed for 'Operation Enduring Freedom'.

Rations and field food service for US and coalition troops: The US Defence Logistics Information site (www.olive-drab.com) lists 24 MRE Menus, each containing five to seven food items, five types of accessory packets labelled A, B, C, D, and E, each with 14 items, a spoon and one flameless heater. The accessory packet provides tea (instant with sweetener and lemon flavour), coffee, sugar, creamer, salt, chewing gum, matches, toilet tissue, hand cleaner, apple cider, red pepper, seasoning blend (salt free), candy (vanilla/caramel) and chocolate.

Although, to the Iraqis, it might have meant as sumptuous a meal as can be managed in a combat zone, reports say that the US troops found fault with the field food service and the quality of the foods. Due attention is being paid to bring about several improvements. It is not ascertained if the NATO troops sent by the participating countries were provided with their own kind of combat foods or whether they shared the US MREs and ate 'A' rations when feasible. The British and the Canadian 24 hour Operational Ration Packs, Meals-Combat Individual, and the British 5-man and 10-man Operational Ration Packs are comparable to the US MRE combat ration meals, at least in general concept and content and variety.

For field procurement, a well established Defence Procurement system is in place; every single item carries a code number in the master list of all the stores including food required for the forces. Every item is ordered from commercial sources by code number, in multiples as required. The characteristics and quality parameters, portion size, the appropriate or recommended packaging and other details are embodied in the code. Before the US bases were established in Kabul and Kandahar, the ground forces subsisted on what they could carry in their backpacks. Once the bases were set up, one imagines that the kitchens opened up and hot meals began to be served.

The aerial bombings were carried out by the aircrafts based on carriers and the battle ships launched missiles. The food for the crews and the troops on the vessels would be served out of the ships' galleys.

Wars on Indian Soil – From Sepoy Mutiny to Kargil

Sepoy Mutiny of 1857

The Sepoy mutiny of 1857 was not the first though it became the most notable and started in the 19th Bengal Infantry at Berhampore. There was one in 1764 in the 1st Regiment of Bengal and another in 1806 in Vellore, a Kutch rebellion is 1816, a Sepoy mutiny in the 47th Regiment at

Barrackpore and then again in 1844 (www.wiki.fibis.org/index.php?title=19th...of Bengal...Infantarly). Reasons for those revolts varied (Wolpert, 1993, p. 233) but generally originated from unpopular measures taken by the East India Company. The method of suppression adopted by the British was brutal; unarmed sepoys were blown away by cannons or fired upon by artillery and their leaders hanged. Several hundred died. No expression of discontent was allowed in any form. Mutiny was crushed every time, setting a merciless example, but the sepoys mutinied again in 1857. The reasons were found in the feelings of utter humiliation the sepoys began to experience. Hostility towards the British built up even as both the sepoys and officers were on reasonably good terms with each other. Further, the English looked down upon the locals with contempt and obvious discrimination even as they made full use of their inherent capabilities and of course played upon their religious prejudices and general poverty.

Added to these weighty grievances of previous years, the trigger to this simmering rage was the introduction of the breech loading Lee Enfield rifle (which used cartridges) replacing the old musket known as Brown Bess (Edwards, 1963, p. 9). The cartridges were smeared with animal fat and lard to increase the efficiency of the Enfield's fire power. Wolpert comments (1993, p. 232) that 'though the British showed great ingenuity in its manufacture, it was incredibly stupid on their part to smear the cartridges with animal fat'. The composition of this 'animal fat' was five parts tallow, five parts stearine and one part wax. Rumours about the pig and cow fat being used were denied by the officers as being untrue. The sepoys were even told that if they wished, any oil/lubricant used for their food preparation could be used on the cartridges. It was also apparently told to them that it was no longer necessary to bite the new cartridges which could be readily torn open with their fingers (Pennington, 2003, pp. 112–132). But the sepoys remained unconvinced. When they still refused to load the rifles, humiliation and expulsion followed. Their uniforms, worn with pride in their role as sepoys of the Raj, were stripped of insignias. Hatred for the Raj spread throughout the northern belt from Calcutta to Meerut, sweeping Delhi, Lucknow and Cawnpore (Kanpur) (Trevalyan, 1992; Lawrence, 1994, p. 226). Mangal Pandey (whose name is now synonymous with the mutineers and heroes who fought British imperialism for India's independence), apparently in a drunken frenzy, incited his regiment to rise up against the Raj. He shot and wounded a British officer, the Adjutant of the regiment. For this act, Pandey was court-martialled and sentenced to death and hanged in the presence of the regiment and his regiment was disbanded ignominiously. Two days later, the 3rd Indian Light Cavalry regiment, which was in Meerut practicing rifle drills refused orders (Pennington, 2003). One fateful day, 85 sepoys who refused to load rifles were arrested, chained and put in prison. The pot boiled over the next day, 10 May, 1857. The mutiny alighted in Barrackpore near Calcutta. Sepoys in Meerut rose up in rebellion and massacred the English residents of the town and marched to Delhi 30 miles away (Metcalf and Metcalf, 2002, p. 100) to seek the poet emperor Bahadurshah, who was the last remnant of a once glorious Mughal empire.

When the mutiny erupted, there were 40,000 Europeans in the Company and Royal Army to 300,000 Indian troops spread across regiments from Barrackpore to Meerut. The period 1854–57 was also the time of the Crimean war, necessitating the deployment of troops to the front. Britain was gathering her forces and withdrew British contingents from India, leaving 4 regiments of cavalry, and 22 battalions of infantry and no artillery or engineer units. The Commander-in-Chief and his staff were vacationing in Simla.

March to Delhi: When the native troops marched from station to station, streams of small carts accompanied, each cart carrying one or two young and pretty ladies in veils, one or two old women and a large number of children – underfed, thin and nearly naked and with protruding stomachs. In

Delhi, they were welcomed by Indian soldiers and though the British blew up the powder magazines, the sepoys liberated the palace and its occupants. Bahadur Shah, old and immersed in his poetry and paintings, unable to lead the sepoys or sustain the surge rising in his favour, proved a futile leader and emperor. The sepoys now went on a rampage, plundered the city, looting and stealing and butchering, and spent themselves away in pleasures of momentary conquest (Wolpert, 1993, p. 98), in a state of drunken celebration, prematurely as it turned out. In the process, several thousand innocents were killed – both Europeans and Indians.

There are any number of anecdotal and narrative versions of this rising (Sir John Kayr, 1878; Sir Evelyn Wood, 1908; Sherer, 1910; Majumdar, 1963; Edwards, 1963; Metcalf and Metcalf, 2002; Wolpert, 1993; Lawrence, 1994). Personal touches come from the memoirs of Sitaram Pandey, Subedar (Lunt, 1873) and of Sir Otto Trevalyan (1992).

Some believed there was a conspiracy. As a sign of conspiracy, authors have pointed out that there were *chapatis* and lotuses somehow involved, though this is not mentioned in any official records. These two items were apparently widely circulated, passed on from one village to another, throughout northern India, the Bombay Presidency and went as far down south as Hyderabad. Some believed thought that the government was forcing conversion into Christianity. Superstition became associated with this circulation of chapatis; the original design and purpose – as obscure as they were, having been entirely lost somewhere along the way (Majumdar, 1963, p. 378). British historians have held that there was a conspiracy in which Moulavi Ahmadulla of Faizabad, Nana Sahib and even the Rani of Jhansi figured (Majumdar, 1963, pp. 337–338).

However, Sir John Lawrence, according to Majumdar (1963, p. 379), concluded after examining that there was no basis to support the theory of an organised conspiracy. So the mutiny was attributed to the spontaneous act of a section of disenchanted sepoys in the absence of strong leadership. Trevalyan (1992, p. 21) commented that 'the insolence and greed of the soldiers, their impertinence and impatience of discipline and their lust for power were the effective causes of the out break', although the proximate cause was the insult to their religion. An Indian Official of the Raj, and loyal to it, with 20 years of service, Sayyed Ahmed Khan, in the aftermath of the rebellion and its suppression, wrote in an Urdu essay (later translated into English) that the cause of rebellion lay in 'the British ICS Officers' pride and arrogance that led them to consider the natives of India as undeserving of the name of human beings' (Metcalf and Metcalf, 2002, p. 99). Further, he insisted that the revolt was not a mere mutiny on the part of disgruntled soldiers but an expression of their multiple grievances such as the British contempt for Indians and the racial distancing.

The mutiny was quelled and Delhi recaptured by 20 Sept; Bahadur Shah surrendered to the military and in quick succession both Lucknow and Cawnpore were taken (India Today, 2000).

The campaigns to put down the widespread mutiny engaged the British all through 1857–58. The outcome of the mutiny was that the East India Company, a trading organisation, would no more be allowed to rule India. By an Act of Parliament, signed by Queen Victoria in August 1858 and by a proclamation, the governance of India passed into the hands of the British Crown. General amnesty was declared and extended till 1 Jan, 1859. Meanwhile, the aging Bahadur Shah, King of Delhi and the last Mughal Emperor, after a summary trial during January–February 1858 was exiled to Lower Burma. Lord Canning, the first Viceroy of the Queen, declared that the mutiny had ended and the rebellion put down (Edwards, 1963, p. 196).

In contemporary Indian history, this uprising is referred to as the First War of Independence and its 150 years was celebrated in 2007. As can be expected, reporting about the logistics aspects is non-existent. The distances were not long, the garrisons were well equipped and it required only that the officers take command and gather English troops and find animals to cart their immediate supplies.

The Border Wars since Independence

There have been five wars on Indian soil since independence, and an ongoing military engagement since 1984. The Indian combat calendar given by Cardozo (2003) reads as follows (Table 14.2):

Table 14.2: Border wars in India since Independence

S. No.	*War*	*Year*	*Duration*
1.	Jammu and Kashmir war, ceasefire on 1 Jan, 1949	1947–48	14 months
2.	The Sino-Indian war	1962	30 days
3.	The Indo-Pakistan war	1965	15 days
4.	The Bangladesh Liberation war	1971	13 days
5.	The Siachen	1984–till date	26 years
6.	The Kargil war	May–July 1999	65 days

Source: Cardozo, 2003 and media reports

According to Messenger (2003), till 2001, there have been only two official histories released by India and none at all by Pakistan. These two reports published by the government cannot be found. These publications report the operations in Jammu and Kashmir (Prasad and Dharmpal, 1987), and the Indo-Pakistan war of 1965 (Chakravarty and Prasad, 1992). The official report on the 1962 Chinese invasion of India, though ready, for some undisclosed reason has not yet been released. The Bangladesh Liberation war has been written about by different people with focus on different perspectives: by Bhargava (1972), Ramachandran (2001), Sukhwant Singh (1980) and others. The 1999 Kargil conflict was written about by several authors – Amarinder Singh (2001), Gen. Bammi (2002), Jasjit Singh (1999) and others and the immediate post war assessment was made by the Kargil Review Committee in 1999. The latter's findings were published in the form of a Report in 1999–2000 (Subramanyam, 1999). Accounts written by veteran officers and generals provide some indepth information on specific aspects of each war. Cardozo's '*Paramvir*' however, addresses the various wars from before independence with the heartwarming angle of individual bravery and gallantry. There are no official versions. The following account would certainly have been more exact had such material been available. Only very brief sketches of these events are given here because the last word is not out and it is difficult to pinpoint important moments.

Many writers surmised that the two newly independent countries – India and Pakistan followed two different ideologies while restructuring their armies. While India took its cue from the nationalist, secular minded leaders and the existing army structure on British lines, the Pakistan Army reoriented and aligned itself to identify more with the subcontinent's Islamic and Mughal rulers of the past and clearly chose to be Islamic and geared itself to defend its people from a supposed threat from Hindu factions in the Punjab and Hindu dominated part of the rest of the country. East Pakistan was carved out of East Bengal, which had a dominant Muslim population.

Indo-Pakistan War, 1947

At the time of partition, land and border areas, wealth in the treasury perhaps and the Indian Army, were all shared based on some formula and the princely states fell in line to become part of the divided country. Maharaja Hari Singh, the ruler of Kashmir was a Hindu with a Muslim dominated population. Just before independence was declared, and having dithered until then, he decided to accede to India but it is said, he failed to complete the act of accession and for this reason Kashmir became a contentious and disputed subject between India and Pakistan over border delineation in the western part and has remained so.

Conflict erupted barely two months after independence. The Battle for the Valley, the first of the conflict, began in October 1947 over a perceived threat which arose when the Muslim subjects were said to have rebelled against the Maharaja and were aided spontaneously by tribals from adjoining areas. Panic stricken, the Maharaja appealed to the Indian Government for help and quickly executed the documents of accession. The Indian troops were airlifted to Srinagar and the airport was secured; they fought the Pathans and prevented the fall of Srinagar. True to the ancient fashion, the invaders got busy looting and pillaging. As there was no solution to be found, Prime Minister Nehru took the issue to the United Nations on the advice of Lord Mountbatten.

Jammu and Kashmir was fragmented and divided between the two warring countries. This division as temporary as it was, continues to exist. The upshot of 14 months war was that Indian troops have been posted in Jammu and Kashmir ever since and there appears to be no easy solution to resolving the Kashmir issue and hence the status quo continues, despite demands for demilitarisation by Pakistan. In 1957, Kashmir was claimed by India despite Pakistan's protests and UN disapproval (Parkinson, 1977, p. 81).

India–China War, 1962

On the eastern front, India and communist China signed a non-aggression treaty in April 1954, even as Tibet was being annexed by China. The slogan singing euphoria of 'Hindi-Chini Bhai-Bhai' did not last long. Border clashes between Chinese troops in Tibet and the Indian army slowly escalated from 1959 to 1960 even as meetings at government level were being conducted (Report of Govt Officials, February 1961). The Chinese were quietly, surreptitiously and methodically arming and deploying troops about which the Indian Army seemed to have been oblivious. There are many theories, many speculations and some explanations about the nature and quantum of intelligence failure. On 20 October, 1962, the frontier troops were taken by surprise and were attacked by China, both in the eastern borders and in Jammu's northeast region (Lall, 1988). In Ladakh, the mountainous borders are barely some 30 km away. The beautifully blue but highly salty Pangong-Tso lake separates India and China in this sector. The hills in the backdrop lie in Chinese territory, seen from the shore in Ladakh.

A battle of considerable proportions took place at Tsenjang across Namkhachu in the NEFA region. This was found to have been a tactical move in the main battle plan of the Chinese. They wanted to establish a foothold first and capture Tawang. October was a vulnerable time for the Indians because of the impending winter and with plans to strengthen the posts in the coming summer. The Chinese routed the Indians, ran in as far as Bomdila and onto the plains of the Brahmaputra valley. Outnumbered, outgunned, utterly unprepared for mountain warfare, possessing obsolete guns, without proper equipment, clothes or food, it was a debacle of no mean order for the Indian army. There are many views and opinions expressed on the outcome and the debacle (Kaul, 1967) which came to be labeled the 'Himalayan Blunder' (Dalvi, 1967). There came, however, a Chinese declared unilateral ceasefire as suddenly as the conflict had started, on 21 November, 1962; the 30 days of unprovoked invasion by China netted it a new border line covering mountain passes and

several thousand square miles in Indian territory. John Lall (1988) says that some scholars believe the Indians brought the war on themselves by showing a willingness to negotiate but not budging an inch from rigidly held positions, while China believed that the boundary treaties negotiated with neighbouring Nepal, Burma and Pakistan were reasonable. On the other hand, India had given refuge to the Tibetans, who could be potential dissidents, and no other country had a link to a vital territory of theirs and no one else had wanted China to restrain from using force in Tibet.

Arunachal Pradesh, one of the Seven Sister States in the northeast, and Sikkim, are now bones of contention, China claiming parts as its own while India has no doubts regarding her rightful ownership. Brisk development plans are afoot to improve infrastructure there. China has already built mountain roads on the other side of the Himalayas and introduced a rail line to Natu La in Tibet at 14,000 feet, to facilitate trade and travel, but definitely an infrastructural development of considerable logistic importance for China. India is doing likewise and putting in access roads to facilitate commercial activity. Chinese air and ground border incursions are reported periodically.

Driving up to Natu La from Gangtok, Sikkim, is a slow road journey because of narrow roads, landslides and incessant military and civil traffic and work in progress. The area is utterly arid, and rocky and full of rubble from landslides and construction work. A fortified wall can be seen running on the top of the mountain stretch separating India from Tibet. Both sides have built garrisons and have deployed military regiments; one can see the Tibetan side from atop the Indian garrison at Natu La (Fig. 14.2). At the peak, a memorial to soldiers was erected by the Army in 2002. Constantly under observation from the Chinese, the soldiers on this tarred road, walk to other areas (Fig. 14.3). They are located in the garrison but dotted on the mountain tops on lonely vigil are soldiers who live in rocky bunkers. They have to be air supplied. Approaching Natu La, one is struck by the lonely plume of smoke from a cooking fire, visible from a long distance (Fig. 14.4).

Fig. 14.2: Overlooking the Tibetan side of Natu La in 2008.

Fig. 14.3: The military personnel deployed on Natu La walking the road below are always under observation by the Chinese post as the red sign board behind the men warns.

Fig. 14.4: Smoke arising from a lonely mountain top bunker

India-Pakistan War, 1965

Fighting broke out between India and Pakistan again in April 1965 in the region of Rann of Kutch. Indian troops were halted after UN intervention in August. Pakistan did likewise on 1 September. Gen Parvez Musharraf, the former President of Pakistan, mentions in his book that the Indian side attacked on 6 Sept, strafing a passenger train and killing many civilians and that the war lasted 17 days (Musharraf, 2006). Kashmir itself was a stand off, neither side gaining much advantage of any decisive nature from the hostilities with tank battles and air strikes, All that happened was that the supply lines were disrupted. The United Nations demanded a ceasefire from both countries and on 27 September it was agreed to; the two opponents retreated to a line held on 5 August (Parkinson, 1977, pp. 81–82).

Bangladesh Liberation War, 1971

The war referred to in India as the Bangladesh Liberation war was precipitated in 1971 in Eastern Pakistan due to internal unrest arising out of repressive measures meted out to the Bengali people by the government based in West Pakistan (Parkinson, 1977, p. 82). The aspirations of the Bengalis were not being addressed and it was unthinkable to the government functioning in West Pakistan that any local leader should get an upper hand. When Sheikh Mujibur Rehman emerged as the political leader of East Pakistan and declared, as a sign of independence, that the area would become the State of Bangladesh in March 7,1971, (www.bangabhaban.gov.bd/mujibur.html) the government of Pakistan could not possibly countenance such a move and sent in its troops to establish control and be in readiness to subdue any uprising. Thousands of refugees began streaming into India. India's intervention on behalf of the Bengali movement came by way of sending its troops on 4 December, although by late October itself the Indian troops had crossed to lend assistance to the local guerillas called the 'Mukti Bahini'. In terms of preparedness, this war was said to be well prepared, according to a veteran of this war and the officers in Operational Logistics. India's ground, naval and air strengths had been most effectively deployed. Reading the thumbnail sketches of individual heroisms and gallantries of this war (Bhargava, 1972, p. 7), one gets only a hazy picture of the total war scene. The aircraft carrier INS *Vikrant* had been moved under closely guarded maneuvers and secrecy from Bombay to somewhere in the Bay of Bengal before emergency was declared in Pakistan on 25 November by General Yahya Khan. On 4 December, Sea Hawk jet planes, Alouette helicopters and turboprop anti-submarine craft took off from the Vikrant's decks and attacked naval installations in Chittagong and Cox's Bazar (Bhargava, 1972, pp. 116–117).

The airstrikes were so successful that the Pakistani forces were unable to use the sea and inland waterways. By 13 December, there were reports that groups of Pakistanis were trying to escape into Burma by the overland route of Cox's Bazar (Bhargava, 1972, p. 120).

About the same time, fighting had broken out in the west with a Pakistani air attack on 3 December, immediately followed by a ground offensive at points in Jammu and Kashmir. India countered with offensives advancing in Rajasthan and towards the Sind desert (Parkinson, 1977, p. 82). The Indian air attacks were directed towards crippling Pakistani air power and incapacitating the oil refinery. The Pakistani air defense system was not on alert and they lost two Sabre-jets sitting on the ground as well as some fuel tanks but swiftly retaliated. The oil refinery near Rawalpindi and an air base at Chaklala were protected by a screen of guns. Flying in pairs, and employing clever feints, the Indian air pilots tried to strike from an unexpected direction but were foiled by the

enemy. Unsuccessful once, a second attempt was made a few days later – first the refinery and then the airbase were shot up, setting fire to whatever fuel tanks were remaining and also destroying a heavy transport helicopter. The Indian fliers returned unscathed (Bhargava, 1972, p. 137). It was a debacle for Pakistani forces. On 16 December, after 13 days of conflict Lt. Gen Niazi, the former Commander, Eastern Command, signed the instrument of capitulation and surrender. For this unforgivable act, his pension was taken away. In his memoirs, he said that he wrote many letters to the then President of Pakistan, Sardar Farooq Ahmed Leghari and once again in 1995, asking for the restoration of his pension and reinstatement of the honour of the Commander of East Pakistan but got no reply (Niazi, 1998). He felt totally betrayed. He observed that a military burial was given to a fallen Pakistani soldier, Dafadar Sarawar of a tank regiment who blazed his way into the Indian position to destroy a tank but was himself cut down. The Indian troops reversed arms and gave him a fitting burial. No one seemed to have done that since World War II (Niazi, 1998 pp. 290–303). He also mentions that he had only 45,000 men from West Pakistan and during the days when open war went on, four of his heroes were given military burial by the Indians.

Siachen

The name Siachen is synonymous in the minds of the Indian army, the people and the government with freezing temperatures beyond human endurance and a kind of demarcation in tacit agreement since 1949, an agreement which was breached and the region engulfed by Pakistan using cartographic means. In the 1949 Karachi agreement, the line of control (LOC) or ceasefire line, rested at map coordinates NJ 9842 latitude 98° East and longitude 42° North and the 1972 Simla agreement found no occasion or reason to alter this. Siachen has some very challenging peaks of the Karakoram range – Sia Kangri, Teram Kangri, Saltoro Kangri, the Rimo group and Mamostang Kangri when at first in international maps and then in Pakistan's maps, Siachen began to be shown as part of Pakistani territory along with some 10,000 square kilometers of Indian territory, there was a reckoning between the two countries. India launched a military operation codenamed 'Operation Meghdoot' to pre-empt any Pakistani intrusion along the Saltoro range and take control of Siachen. This was in April of 1984 (Raghavan, 2002).

Spread over 110 kilometers, with temperatures dipping incredibly low due to heavy winter snows, swept by blizzards, this 'third Pole' is one of the most desolate places in the world and its highest battlefield too. 26 years later, the Siachen tenure for army personnel deployed there – who carry out vigil and patrol duties for periods up to a maximum of three months – is still the most uncertain and dreaded posting ever. As much as they are trained to endure physical hardships and engage in combat of all kinds, this incarceration in Siachen, guarding the borders and stopping Pakistani intruders, exposes them to incalculable physiological and psychological stress. Yet, many endure these conditions and equally many succumb. In fact, more fatalities have occurred due to the extreme weather conditions than there have been in actual battle with Pakistan in all these years. And from all reports the situation is no better on the Pakistani side.

Kargil War, 1999

The Kargil war came after the opening up of the border at Wagah crossing and beginning of bus travel to Lahore during the reign of the NDA Government.

President Parvez Musharraf, who at the time was Army Chief of Pakistan and Gen. V.P. Malik, the Chief of the Indian Army at the time, have given accounts of this conflict from their points of view (Malik, 2006 as well as the Kargil Report, 1999). According to Gen. Musharraf (Musharraf, 2006, pp. 87–88) Kargil was not a one-off operation, but the latest in a series of moves and counter moves at a tactical level at the LOC by both countries. There were border crossing infringements since 1998. Pakistan had noticed large gaps between Pakistani defence positions in the Dras and Kargil sectors which made it possible for the Indian army to cross over easily. He also said that India had been creeping forward. The Pakistani army believed that during summer and autumn, a general Indian offensive was in the offing. Therefore, they planned a defensive maneuver. A plan to block the gaps in a 15 to 45 km stretch took shape to deny access across the LOC. Secrecy was essential at this point. The Rawalpindi Corps, using limited forces, embarked on the planned maneuver, keeping the Northern Light Infantry, composed of locals, in the second line. They were to occupy the forward positions with strict instructions not to cross the watershed along the LOC. The Indians, Pakistani forces knew, were totally oblivious to their gathering strength. The first confrontation, according to Gen. Musharraf, occurred on 7 May, 1999.

Kargil never should have happened. The lessons from the 1962 Chinese debacle were either forgotten or worse, never learnt. An intelligence failure alone it was not. Failure to believe, heed and act upon several warnings, first from the Leh station of the Intelligence Bureau that, after the May 1998 Pokharan nuclear test, there was increased infiltration and heightened Pakistani military activity along the LOC, then second, in July, that M-11 missiles and new mines had been deployed, third, RAW reports that a mortar regiment, Northern Light Infantry and Baluch Regiment were brought in and were being imparted commando training, and finally, the military's own intelligence apparatus' findings that not only many terrorists but also great amounts of ammunition supplies had been brought in via vehicles and pack animal transport, as well as several other small and scattered reports from field officers asking for reinforcements, were causes that allowed the war to happen, according to an analysis carried out by Praveen Swamy (The Hindu, 5 May, 2006).

The first to ring the alarm was a shepherd who was grazing his sheep in these ranges and noticed the incursions and reported it to the nearest army post. Collectively, India's intelligence services are said to have provided numerous warnings on hostile Pakistani action 11 months before fighting broke out. Requests – verbal and written, from field officers asking for more troops, were sidelined, even ignored, and the threat of any impending action or war was seen as a bogey. If only the concerns of the officers were taken more seriously and troops positioned on point 5165, *Pariyon ka Talab* and on point 4660 (the figures denote height in metres) or Tiger Hill, and perhaps an Indian pre-emptive action taken in response, the fighting may not have broken out in May 1999. But the political climate in the country at the time was delicately poised, under a semi-expectant, semi-euphoric state of mind. With expectations from seeing great peace strides being taken in cementing friendship between the two countries under Prime Minister Bajpai at the helm of affairs, the XV Corps and 3 Infantry Division completely failed to upgrade Indian defences along the line of control.

War Preparations and Food Logistics

Ration Planning

The food chain takes low priority in India; allocations towards food is limited compared to allocations for arms and ammunition.

To sustain a war effort, an important exercise is to decide how much food reserves should be in stock. In discussions with ASC officers it was said that, since at high altitudes weather conditions are very unpredictable, advance planning is done based on past information. A perusal of weather data for ten years throws light on when the conditions could be conducive for movement of goods and men and when the roads might be closed due to heavy snowfall and other natural obstructions. Therefore, using such collected information, a reserve ration stock for three to six months is held at command level. In Sikkim, Ladakh and Siachen, there exists an acceptable level of stocking beyond which any overstocking is not practical and proves prohibitively expensive.

These reserves are broken down to 7 day or 14 day or one month rations for Army posts located at different distances. The posts nearest the command post will be issued rations, maybe for 7 days, and those furthest away would get rations for longer periods or as deemed necessary. The men must trek up and down to fetch and carry their rations from one post to another. If this should fail, air supply is the only way to link these isolated posts.

Presently, there is in place an established and standard system of serving foods to the troops on the move whether of an operational or non operational nature. Upon examination, it is reminiscent of the magazine system of olden times in Europe. Being prepared with rations for *n* number of days before connecting with a base camp with kitchens and hot foods is also reminiscent of World War II logistics before 'D' day.

Troop Mobilisation

In border areas and at higher altitudes, for the past several decades, there has been a continuous requirement for the Army's presence. ASC's supply depots have been established at the most convenient and essential points to carry on the task of supply of stores and other materials to the regiments scattered in far flung areas. These units are kept on constant alert and are considered to be in the zone of conflict with a possibility of a more serious situation developing. Those officers and units on operational deployment are entitled to field scale rations applicable to specially designated areas.

The troops in various units, regiments or divisions are also 'mobilised' on strategic deployment where a war like situation is unfolding or is deemed to have arisen. They travel by road, their columns moving briskly in transports as 'Echelons' or by troop trains to the nearest rail head, from where they travel further by road. Troop movement by ships has been rare in the current Indian context although our Navy's ships are positioned as required.

Naval fleets were ready and poised to go into action during the Bangladesh Liberation war in 1971. The ships were out of ports and in proximity to the theatre of operations, too far for the harbour parties to deliver food. In these times the ships' galleys come into their own, preparing the meals separately for the officers and other ranks. More recently The Navy and the Coast Guard have been vigilant on waters abutting Sri Lanka and the Arabian Sea coastline.

In the forward areas on land borders, access by roads is difficult due to the nature of the terrain or due to bad weather conditions, and troops also travel in transport aircraft of the Indian Air Force to cover stretches otherwise inaccessible.

Troops who have struck camp must be provided with their daily food, until such time as they reach a base camp where cookhouses can be established or where they already exist. No matter where they are or may go, their rations go with them or follow. The descriptions given below adhere to the Army Service Corps terminology.

Rations during Troop Movement

The ASC manages the entire distribution and issue of stores and all other material to peace stations and participates equally proficiently in reaching foodstuffs and war materials to the theatre of operations in war time.

Four-day rations: In the ASC terminology, rations and supplies are designated 'A' day, B, C and 'D' day rations, signifying the quantum to be issued during mobilisation.

- 'A' day means today's rations, where every man gets his personal ration, should he and his unit march out at 0500 hrs and is in the first line of transport. If they should march at noon, the 'A' day rations will comprise the unconsumed portion of food meant for the day, and if they start at 1800 hrs they will carry 'B' day rations in advance.
- 'B' day rations mean food for tomorrow. If the units move out at daybreak, the 'B' day rations are loaded in the second line and are ready to march or are waiting for a refill. During march at noon, 'B' day rations go in second line transport. At 1800 hrs or after the march, the 'C' day rations are made ready to be delivered or loaded in second line transport.
- 'C' day rations are generally at the supply rail or at road head enroute and are meant for the day after tomorrow.
- 'D' day means for three days later.

The troops are provided with normal peace ration scales that have to be taken along during mobilisation towards the warzone where making immediate arrangements for cooking may take a while.

'The normal period covered by the issue of a ration will be midnight to midnight and will include breakfast, mid-day meal and the evening meal, in that sequence' says an official note concerning wartime rations, and their supplies are effected through the ASC (Personal Communication, from Col. Kulkarut of ASC; ASC Manuals; and General Sharma). Since the field Service Ration Scales are a little different from the peace scales, it may not be possible to provide the former until after a few days after the mobilisation has begun. To compensate for this, a messing allowance in cash is also authorised for this period or until the field ration scales become available. Priority is given to troops with columns, over those in cantonments, in the matter of allocating field scales, if there should be insufficient stocks.

The significant point is that everyone – officers, ORs, non-combatants and even the temporary personnel or civilians serving in the area of operations and who are entitled to rations under their specific terms of reference, will become eligible for free rations upon entering the theatre of operations.

For this transition to take place, there is a clear system of financial sanction and grant of rations. One must appreciate the fact that in a warzone, requirements are different, facilities are limited, frequency of supplies may be interrupted and fatigue and bad weather conditions make physical, mental and psychological demands on the troops. Provision must be made for greater quantities of fuel, such as more fuel oil – kerosene, soft coke, steam coal and firewood, which are required not just for cooking purposes but also for lighting lamps and running burners for warmth.

Organisational Aspects and Grouping for Movement

The organisational planning pertaining to feeding the troops on the move is meticulous. A brief insight into the organisation of food service during troop movement was provided by veterans.[1]

Grouping in 'Echelons': The units are grouped into three 'Echelons' designated as:

'F' or fighting echelon,

'A' or operational support echelon, and

'B' echelon for logistics and feeding elements.

It appears that when a move is starting, the Integrated Administrative Elements, essentially the Quartermaster Staff, are on wheels. These 'elements' include the sub-unit level or Company (Coy) level men like Company Quartermaster and NCO in charge of the Mess and Mess personnel, '*Langar* Commander', cooks etc.

All the equipment required for cooking in the field are carted along, such as utensils, oil cookers, field storage containers, and on occasions the 'kitchen on wheels', which is an Army truck (2 tonner) that has been modified as a 'kitchen'. The self contained field kitchens or '*langars*' fall under the organisational sections of field units or subunits. This also includes officers' messes for the feeding of Headquarters officers and attached 'elements'. All the above are part of the 'B' echelon of the unit under the Quartermaster, which may operate brigade wise or unit wise or as independent Coys or subunits. Not to forget the re-supply chain; it connects up with the 'commodity' points or 'supply points' manned and set up by the ASC and which are also mobile; they leapfrog from one place to another as often as required as per logistics planning and Operational and Administrative orders.

'B' echelons – the feeding echelons play a crucial role due to their unique position with rear linkages for re-supply, middle role in organising cookhouses and cooking, and with forward linkages for distribution of hot and/or packed meals to troops. The food is distributed through 'collection points' set up by the ASC, where collection parties of platoons or subunits are sent to receive. The latter return to their own grouping and hand out the food.

Food Supply and Service

Depending on the situation and the mode of transportation, three types of meal supplies are planned.

- When the troops are moved by ships, it is possible to organise continuous cooking and feeding in designated galleys. When movement occurs in trains with no kitchen cars, covered wagons supply cooked hot food or meal packets at designated halts along the route.
- At other times, when non-operational moves are taking place in the field, harbour parties and *langar* parties ('B' echelons) may move ahead and leapfrog, carrying hot meals, and be ready to serve food on arrival of the main body.
- During advance to combat or on operational moves, the 'B' Echelons trail the main body, and depending on the daily orders, the food is also distributed at designated delivery/distribution points in forward posts, at sunset and predawn. Here, the 'B' echelon stays put while the main body moves.

In combat, whenever possible, hot food is served. Reserves and emergency rations are always on hand. The rations are collected from the ASC supply points established between logistic nodes and forward points. Cooking is done under unit arrangements in 'B' echelons. Distribution occurs at designated Food Points, at designated times. Packed/tinned/precooked and emergency rations are used as reserves and operational contingencies when hot meals are not feasible.

Soldier's backpack in battle order: In battle situation, soldiers carry along the essential and immediate requirements. Their backpacks contain the following items during defensive and offensive fighting:

a. Rations	24 hr survival rations, unconsumed portion of that day's ration (MRE or freshly made *Puri/Sabji* (curry))
b. Water	1 L in HDP bottle
c. Ammunition	
d. Equipment	
e. Blanket	
f. Mosquito net	
g. Fighting equipment	

Total weight: 18–22 kg

Feeding Wars in Different and Difficult Terrains

The Indian Army feels justified in saying that never has any operation after 1947 failed due to lack of feeding. In 1947, the Indian Army was spread out too much, due to fear. The troops were generally barrack bound. Some 150 men stayed in one place and ate in the mess. In battle, they became scattered and could not get back for lunch. Therefore, the food was carried in buckets and taken to pickets. At that time, no equipment was authorised for a company of men spread out in different pickets. They depended largely on the traditional *Gudh-Chana* (puffed Bengal gram and jaggery). Their platoon was authorised vessels but all the foodstuffs came in large packing sizes of 100 kg airdropped by the Food Corporation of India (FCI); these had to be repacked into smaller lots.

In August 1948, General Cariappa learned that the garrison at Leh needed supplies desperately. Two mule columns were detailed to convey the supplies from Manali to Leh. A column named 1 Arjun had 218 Gurkha Rifles less 2 Coys and carried 800 rifles. The second column, codenamed '*Chapati* column', carried 30 days supplies. Thousands of mules and porters were engaged to form those two columns. Gathering so many animals, finding and detailing the numerous porters, proved to be tremendous administrative work. It took the columns, trekking their way through snow covered mountains, three weeks to reach Leh. The land routes to Zojila were needed to enable stocking of supplies for the winter when for six months the mountain passes would be totally blocked by snow (Sinha, 1992, pp. 122–123).

In 1962, during the Sino-Indian border conflict, there was no infrastructure in the northeast, the area was totally undeveloped and no roads had been constructed by the Army, nor did it have proper vehicles due to lack of maintenance. There was no civilian infrastructure either and the Army had to rely greatly on the animals and porters for moving supplies. There were no storage place, no accommodation for the troops and no bunkers. Trenches had to be dug. No local resources were available to fall back on or to make local purchases of foodstuffs. Thus, to maintain a force in the mountains and the snow, the carriage of foods, their storage and preservation became major problems. The foods, poor in quality, were of the very basic kind and there was just enough in the country due to poor agriculture and India was getting a lot of wheat under the PL480 scheme from the United States of America. The fuel used was coal – very voluminous, bulky and messy, along with the traditional *chulha*. In the unit cookhouses, rice and dal took a long time to cook and once cooked there was no provision to reheat the food and if eating was delayed, everyone ate cold food. And yet they survived, everyone got to eat, if only *shakkarpara* and everyone was clothed; how well is beside the point. It is a fact that there were no adequate snow wear and warm woolens or blankets; women of the country knitted mufflers, scarves, sweaters, socks etc. for the men.

In short, the Army stood at a serious disadvantage for its lack of specialised equipment, clothing, even appropriate food to support mountain war in the extreme cold.

Caught unprepared, due to the belief that China would never resort to armed hostilities on the border (Lall, 1988, p. 273), Indian troops found themselves joining their first sizable battle on 10 October, 1962. The Indian post at Senjang, across Namkachu, northeast of Tawang, in Kameng Frontier Division of NEFA was surrounded (Lall, p. 272). At 4,000 meters, this sudden development necessitated moving troops, 7th Brigade, Eastern Command, under Brig. J.P. Dalvi, within 48 hours, to the north of Namkachu. The Chinese attacked in strength on 8 and 10 October and the defending 9 Punjab and 2 Rajput fought till their ammunition ran out.

They had just 50 rounds each and were sent off to battle in olive greens, with a single blanket to protect them from the biting dry cold (Lall, p. 278). Within a short span of time, High Altitude Pulmonary Oedema (HAPO) struck all ranks and the Corps Commander, Gen. Kaul as well. Lall concludes that India committed a series of horrendous mistakes and Gen. Kaul's own account of the events of this conflict is also very illuminating and tells how drastically matters went wrong (Kaul, 1967). China appeared to gather forces near Ladakh, which diverted the attention of the Indian forces, while massing troops and war materials on the eastern borders.

There were no combat foods that could sustain the men in the extreme cold, no food that would cook quickly at that altitude, no ready to eat items that would save time and effort. There were no warm clothes to give them a semblance of protection from frostbite. A daily dose of rum was supposed to infuse the required warmth! The conditions of the troops was so pitiful that even a public outpouring of solidarity and sympathy shown in the form of donations of gold, and cash etc. to help the war effort, as well as knitted socks, scarves, sweaters for the troops, or the hurried production of pre-cooked dehydrated rice by the Mysore based research laboratory, did not help matters much.

War logistics in dry hot and cold deserts could be yet another challenge. The western Indian deserts in the Rann of Kutch and Rajasthan border with Pakistan, are daunting and hostile.

The Rann of Kutch is a salt wasteland lashed by winds and submerged during rains. The Border Security Force is deployed in these regions to patrol and keep vigil. Typical of a desert, while day temperatures could be as hot as 45°C or higher, the nights are bitterly cold. The BSF *jawans* patrol on camels. These animals are the sole means of transport. Water, food and all other supplies to the desert posts can be conveyed by conventional means only up to a point. Beyond this, the men have to live in isolation in the remoteness of the desert, often 'incommunicado' for weeks on end, waiting for supply deliveries. Food, according to a news report in July 2000, is unsatisfactory; there is no water supply for weeks and the men have to trudge at least 50 km to call home to speak with their families. Whatever communication facilities might exist, are reserved for official use.

In 1983–84, at the start of 'Operation Meghdoot' in Siachen, maintaining posts at altitudes of 16,000 ft and above in the wild and inhospitable weather said to be 'no place for human beings' (*Raghavan*, 2002, pp. 112–114) became a matter of grave concern. It was the terrain and weather that were so much more dangerous than the enemy action at that altitude.

Points on the Sol Toro range are so precipitous that there is hardly any space to erect more than Pill boxes and gun mountings. How would fresh bulk rations (if and when these did reach) be taken there and used to prepare foods?

At the elevation of 21,000 ft the temperatures are at least −55° Celsius in winter and −20°C summer, the deep crevasse temperatures touching −165°C. There are pincer-sharp and strong iron like ledges jutting out. The inclination of a climb angles at 65° to 70°. Tethered for safety, climbing is a Herculean task and one can hardly move a few meters at a time.

For up to 8000 ft no acclimatisation is necessary, though to function at 10,000 ft a period for acclimatisation is necessary. Hypoxic conditions increase substantially at 18,000 ft and very few can withstand heights of 21,000 ft. Everyone destined for Siachen posting is first sent to the Siachen battle school, the period of training lasting over 21 days. This is essential to learn the skills and crafts of mountain maneuvering, rock and rope climbing, to hold flying fox position – that is to climb the rocks in the upside-down position, to climb the steep inclines carrying their full load of 18 kg, and learn to mark the trails with piles of stones.

Supply system: Small helicopters, known as the Cheetah, are the only lifelines carrying food and medical supplies, fuel and ammunition in Siachen. They also act as ferries for evacuating the wounded. Meant to fly only up to elevations of 18,000 ft, the Indian Air Force pilots of the Air Observation Posts (AOP) have been known to take these Cheetahs to 25,000 – 26,000 ft during reconnaissance flights to mark targets.

One helicopter sortie to the air maintained camps is estimated to cost around Rs. 50,000/-. Equally expensive is the cost of evacuation of the sick and wounded and it depends entirely on weather conditions. There are other constraints too: the load carrying or delivering capacity of the helicopter diminishes with altitude due to high winds and rarefied atmosphere. At times, the *jawans* in the camp can get only two jerrycans of kerosene at a time. Thus, conveying 40 litres of fuel to a Siachen post, one of the highest priorities, at a working cost of Rs. 1250/- per liter, is one of the most expensive airlifts.

Half links: There are men in bunkers, deployed in positions at even higher positions who cannot receive air drops. For collection and delivery of supplies, the camp above is linked to a camp below. The man from the upper camp climbs down halfway and a man from the lower camp climbs up halfway. Here the delivery of supplies is effected and any other exchanges, including the sick and wounded being evacuated. Then both parties trudge back to their own respective camps.

Considering that a man can carry only 2 or 3 kg of weight of food at such heights, one can imagine the extreme hardships that have to be borne and the number of trips up and down. Added to these difficulties are the hobble effect, the HAPO and HACO which can be debilitating and life-threatening.

The Indian Army, permitted in September 2007, in the name of adventure sport tourism, a group of selected cadets from military academy, led by an officer and accompanied by a woman reporter and a camera person, to trek up to 'Kumar' post at 16,000 ft. Although this sector falls under the Indian Army's jurisdiction, there were strident voices and a protest note from Pakistan.

Though there is a tacit ceasefire, Siachen remains a disputed territory. The Government will not stand down or demilitarise the zone, nor will it be able to take a complacent view of any real or perceived move to alter the *status quo*.

In the 1999 Kargil war, the pressing need was for reinforcement but the troops never lacked food and feeding. In the mountains, it is said, a superiority of strength in the ratio of 9:1 is required to capture a post. In Kargil, the Indian Army did induct nine times more troops and therefore, the food stocks must have been insufficient at some point. In comparison, we are given to understand, in the words of World War II veteran officer Col. Par Chaudhary of 'Outram Rifles', that a superiority ratio of 3:1 was adequate in World War II.

The motorable roads towards Kargil travel only to a certain distance (Fig. 14.5). After motorable roads end everything had to be carried up the steep tracks on mules and then by the men.

In Kargil, food and water were said to have been the major limiting factors in planning operations, according to Baweja (2000, p. 88), who knew it as an insider. Whatever happened to all the Compo packs and MREs? It is believed by people who are in the know that it was in this war that the pouch processed (retorted) foods which go to make the MREs developed by DFRL and manufactured in a limited way by an entrepreneur, really came into their own. The increased administrative work of moving ammunition up the heights also became burdensome. The logistics of food supplies in the Kargil war, from Baweja's point of view, were quite different from what some others have expressed. Often, there was no food for more than 24 hrs at a time during the battle for Tololing. The food had to come from the base to the road head, from where it was delivered to the fire base where the troops had to be sustained for more than 72 hrs.

Therefore, it was decided to establish a cookhouse halfway to the fire base. Who would spare time to cook? Halfway up was not a really safe position to work in.

From the base camps only animal pack trains could carry supplies up the steep and almost precarious mountain paths. Finally where even the animals could climb no more, the men must climb the steep rock faces and carry supplies on their backs. The men could carry either a food pack weighting 2 kg or 100 bullets. A net blog recounts how on Tololing the food carriers (porters)

Fig. 14.5: The motorable winding roads of the desolate landscape from Leh and the higher reaches This road leads to Changla Pass at 17,800 feet, towards the Chinese border. Leh-Kargil way, through Khardungla Pass is much the same when it is open.

who on some occasions brought cooked food from the base would climb all night to deliver sacks of puris and potato curry packed in plastic shell casings!

Diaries of Pakistani soldiers came into the possession of the Indian Government and reveal the extent of hunger that beset them. The Pakistan Government's refusal to resupply arms, ammunition and food left them high and dry, cold, hungry and sick. They ate grass and snow while frostbite numbed their limbs and ripped their skin.

We lost 600 Indian soldiers who went down fighting in the treacherous mountains.

Endnote

1. Personal discussion with Gen. Y.N. Sharma (Retd.) PVSM AVSM SM, of the 2nd Battalion of Grenadiers and General officer in Command, Central Command and a veteran of 1971 war, (in Hyderabad) and by Maj. Gen. (Retd.) S.G. Vombatkere of the EMS (in Mysore) and Col. P.D. Kulkarni, Commandant Junior Wing, ASC Centre, Bangalore.

References

Amarinder Singh. *A Ridge Too Far: War in the Kargil Heights.* Motibagh Palace, Patiala 2001.

Bakshi, S.R. *Nationalism and British Raj*. Atlantic Publishers and Distributors, New Delhi, 1988, pp. 2–4.

Bammi,Y.M. Lt. Gen.(Retd). *Kargil 1999: The Impregnable Conquered.* Gorkha Publishers, Noida, 2002.

Barthrop, Michael and Ray, Elizabeth (Ed). *A Culinary Campaign by Alexis Soyer*. Southover Press, London, 1995, pp. viii–xi, 104, 140–1, 207, 249, 324–331.

Baweja, Harinder. *A Soldier's Diary: Kargil. The Inside Story*. Books Today, an Imprint of India Today Group. New Delhi, 2000.

Beaglehole, J.C. 1968 (Editor). *The Journal of Captain James Cook On the voyages of Discovery. 'The Voyage of the Endeavour 1768–1771'*. First published 1955, reprint 1968 & corrigendum) Cambridge, Published for Hakluyt Society at the University press, pp. cci–ccii, 94, 613–4.

Bhargava, G.S. *Their Finest Hour:Saga of India's December Victory*. Vikas Publishing House Pvt. Ltd., Delhi, 1972, pp. 7, 116–117, 120, 137.

Bull, Stephen. *Brassey's History of Uniforms – World War One, British Army*. Series Editor Tim Newark. Brassey's, London, Washington, 1998.

Cardozo, Ian (Maj.Gen. Retd). *Paramvir: Our Heroes in Battle.* Lotus Collection Roli Books, 2003.

Chakravarthy, B.C. and S.N. Prasad (Editors). *History of the Indo–Pak War 1965*, New Delhi, History Division, Ministry of Defence, Government of India, 1992 (released 2000).

Collier, James Lincoln and Christopher Collier. *With Every Drop of Blood (a novel of the civil war).* Bantam Double Day Dell, New York, 1992, 1994.

Craven, Avery. *Reconstruction: The Ending of the Civil War*. Holt, Rinehart and Winston Inc., New York, 1969, pp. 5, 23, section 12.

Dalvi, J.R. *Himalayan Blunder. Sino Indian War of 1962*. Thacker and Co. Bombay, 1967.

Darwish, Adel and Alexander, Gregory. *Unholy Babylon: the Secret History of Saddam's War*. Victor Gollancz Ltd, in Great Britain, 1991, pp. 100–108.

Deccan Herald, May 7, 2006.

Denney, Robert E. *The Civil War Years. A Day by Day Chronicle of the Life of a Nation*. Sterling Publishing Co. Inc., New York, 1992, pp. 9, 13–14.

Dikshitar, V. Ramachandra. *War in Ancient India*. Macmillan & Co. Ltd., Madras, 1944.

Dowswell, Paul. *True Stories of the First World War*. Usborne publishing Ltd., London, 2004, pp. 7, 50–69, 89–94.

Dunnigan, James F. and Austin Bay. *From Shield to Storm: High Tech Weapons, Military Strategy and Coalition Warfare in the Persian Gulf.* William Morrow and Co. Inc., New York, 1992, pp. 3–400.

Dupuy, R.E. & Dupuy, T.H. *The Harper Encyclopedia of Military History from 3500 BC to the Present.* Harper Collins Publishers, New York, 1993, p. 365.

Dupuy, T.H. *Understanding War: History and Theory of Combat*. Paragon Publishers, New York, 1987, p. 9.

Durante, Will and Durante, Ariel. *The Story of Our Civilization*. Simon and Schuster, New York, 1965.

Dust Off. *The Illustrated History of Vietnam War*. Bantam Books, New York.

Dyer, Frederick H.A. *Compendium of the War of Rebellion: Wars of 1861–65*. Barefoot Publishing Company, 1994.

Easton, Stewart C. *Heritage of the Past*. Rinehart and Co. Inc., New York 1955, pp. 271 & 394.

Eccles, Henry E. *Logistics in National Defence*. The Stackpole Company, formerly Military Service Publishing Co., Harrisburg, Penn,1959, pp. 175–176, 225.

Edwards, Michael. *Battles of the Indian Mutiny*. B.T. Batsford Ltd, London, 1963, pp. 9, 134, 196.

Encyclopedia Americana, Vol 5, International edition, Grolier Incorporated, Danbury, Connecticut, 2001. p. 495.

Encyclopedia Americana, Vol. 17. International edition, Grolier Incorporated, Danbury, Connecticut, 2001. pp. 688–690.

Encyclopedia Americana. Cost of War. Grolier Incorporated, Danbury, Connecticut, 2001, Volume 29: 216–361.

Erdkamp, Paul. *Hunger and the Sword. Warfare and Food Supply in the Roman Republican wars 264–320 BC*. J.C. Gieben Publishers, Amsterdam 1998, p. 43, Appendix.

Gilbert, Martin. *The First World War-A Complete History*. Henry Holt & Co Inc, New York, 1994, pp. Introduction, 110–112, 180.

Great Mysteries of the Past. *Readers Digest*. Editor: Gardner Associates. The Readers Digest Association, Canada, 1991, p. 394.

Groom, W.H.A. *Poor Bloody Infantry-A Memoir of the First World War,* William Kimber and Co ltd, London, 1976, pp. 25, 170.

'Guide and Instructions for Patrol Service Cooks'. Issued under the authority of the Flag Officer Commanding, East Africa. December, 1943.

Hansen, Ole Steen. *The War in the Trenches Raintree*, Steck-vaughn publishers Austin, New York, 2001, pp. 24, 31.

Hatt, Christine. *Documenting History: World War I, 1914–1918*. Franklin Watts, A Division of Scholastic Inc. New York, Toronto, London, New Delhi. First American edition–2001, pp. 15, 17, 21, 42–43, 54–55.

Hickey, Donald R. *The War of 1812: A Forgotten Conflict*. University of Illinois press, Urbana, Chicago, 1989, pp. 5–7, 76–77.

Higginbotham, Don. *The American War of Independence: Military Attitudes, Policies and Practices 1763 – 1789*. The Macmillan Company, New York, 1971, pp. 122–129, 304–305.

Hooper, Edwin Bickford (Vice Admiral). *Mobility, Support, Endurance – A Story of Naval War 1965–1968*. Naval History Division, Department of the Navy, Washington D.C, 1972, pp. 4–5, 42–47, 94–95, 259.

Huston, James A. *Guns and Butter, Powder and Rice: US Army Logistics in Korean War*. Selinsgrove, Susquehanna University Press, London, Toronto, 1989, p. 193–196, 210, 236–237, 258.

India Today, May 1992.

India Today. 'Come Home to History–Past 1000 years'. The Millennium Series. Volume 2. New Delhi, June 2000.

Jasjit Singh, *Kargil* 1999. The Institute for Defence Studies. Knowledge World, Delhi 1999.

Jomini, Baron Antoine Henri de. *The Art of War*. Greenhill Books, London, 1996, p. 252.

Kaul, B.M. *Untold Story*. Allied Publishers. New Delhi, 1967.

Kaye, Sir John. History of the Indian Mutiny, 1857–58, Commentary for the close of 2nd Volume of Sir John Kayr's History of the Sepoy War, Col. G.B. Malleson, Vol I, London, William H. Allen, 1878.

Keegan, John. *A History of Warfare*. Key Porter Books Ltd., Canada, 1993, pp. 304–332.

Keegan, John. *The First World War*. Alfred A. Knopff, New York, 1999, pp. 27, 316–318, 331.

Kimmich, C.M. *The Free City: Dazing and German Foreign policy 1919–1934*, New Haven, 1968.

Lall, John. *Aksaichin and Sino Indian Conflict*. Allied Publishers Pvt Ltd., 1988, pp. 273–278

Lawrence, James. *The Rise and Fall of the British Empire*. St. Martins Press, New York, 1994, p. 226.

Liddel-Hart, B.H. *History of the Second World War*. Cassel & Co Ltd. 1970, London, pp. 3–7.

Lord Carver (Field Marshal). *The Boer War*. The National Army Museum Book. Sidgwick and Jackson, Pan Books, 2000, pp. 13–14, 98–99.

Lunt, James (ed). *From Sepoy to Subedar: The life and adventures of Subedar Sitaram Pandey: A native officer of the Bengal Army*. Translated and first published by Lt. Col. Norgate, Bengal Staff Corps at Lahore, 1873 (1st English Ed). Vikas Publications, Delhi, Bombay, Bangalore, 1970.

Macksey, Kenneth. *For want of a Nail: the Impact on War of Logistics and Communications*. Brassey's, UK-Maxwell Pergamon Publishing Co. London, Oxford, 1989, pp. 78–79,112.

Mahon, John K. *The War of 1812*. University of Florida press, Gainesville, 1972, p. 78.

Majumdar, R.C. *The Sepoy Mutiny and the Revolt of 1857*. Firma K.L. Mukhopadhyay, Calcutta, 1963, pp. 337–338, 363, 378–379.

Malik, V.P. General (Retd). *Kargil: From Surprise to Victory*. Harper Collins Publishers India, 2006.

McCutcheon, Marc. *The Writer's Guide to Everyday Life in the 1800s*. Writer's Digest Books, imprint of F & W Publications, Cincinnati. Ohio, First Ed. 1993, pp. 138–139, 234–235

McGrath, John J., 'The Korean War-Restoring Balance 25 Jan–8 July 1951', Washington, Centre for Military History, 2000.

McKee, Marguerite M. 'Service of Supply in the War of 1812'. Quartermaster Review 6, (Mar–Apl) 1927, pp. 44–55.

Mckinley, E. Albert, Arthur C. Howland and Matthew L Dann. *World History. Vol 1*. Atlantic Monthly publishers and distributors. New Delhi, 1994, p. 64.

Messenger, Charles (Ed). *Military History*. Fitzroy Dearborn Publishers, London, 2003.

Messenger, Charles. *Century of Warfare. The Book of the Major BBC TV Series*, Harper Collins, 1995, pp. 243–247.

Metcalf, Barbara and Metcalf, Thomas R. *A Concise History of India*. Cambridge University Press, Cambridge, UK, 2002, p. 99.

Mitchell, Margaret. *Gone with the Wind*. Harper Collins, 1935.

Motrynczuk, Peter, Chief of Army Field Feeding Systems Branch, Army Center of Excellence, US Army Quartermaster School, Fort Lee, Virginia. 1991/www.qmfound.com.

Musharraf, Parvez. General (Retd.). *In the Line of Fire: A Memoir*. Free Press, New York, 2006, pp. 45, 87–88.

Niazi, A.A.K., (Lt Gen, Retd). *The Betrayal Of East Pakistan*. Manohat Publishers and Distributors, New Delhi, 1998, pp. 290–303.

Nicolson, Nigel. *Napoleon–1812*. Harper and Row Publishers, New York, 1985.

Overy, Richard and Wheatcraft, Andrew. *The Road To War*. Macmillan Ltd., London, 1989, p. 1.

Parkinson, Roger. *Encyclopedia of Modern War*. Routledge and Keegan Paul, London, Henley, 1977, pp. 7, 81–82, 116–120.

Pearce, Nigel. *The Shield and the Sabre: The Desert Rats in the Gulf.* London, HMSO. 1992, p. 6–46.

Pennington, William, Capt. MC, RA (Retd). *Pick up your Parrots and Monkeys: The life of a Boy soldier in India*, Cassel, London, 2003, pp. 112–113, 132.

Perret, Bryan. *The Battle Book. Crucial Conflicts in History from 1469 BC to the Present.* Arms and Armour, London, 1992, pp. 203–5, 235

Pimlott, John. Series Editor. *Conflict in the 20th Century Vol 1: The First World War*. Franklin Watts, New York, London, Toronto, 1986, pp. 6–53.

Pimlott, John. *The Guinness History of the British Army*. Guinness Publishing Ltd. 1993, p. 179.

Pradhan, S.D. *Indian Army in East Africa, 1914–1918*. National Book Organization, 1991, pp. 7, 150–152.

Pradhan, S.D. 'Organisation of the Indian Army on the Eve of the Out break of World War 1'. *The Journal of the United Services Institute of India*. Jan-Mar 1972. Delhi.

Prasad, S.N. and Dharmpal. *Operations in Jammu and Kashmir*, New Delhi, Controller of Publications, Government of India, 1987.

Praveen Swamy Interview of Gen. Deepak Kapoor, *The Hindu,* May 6, 2006.

Raghavan, V.R. (Lt.Gen.Retd). *Siachen. Conflict Without End.* Viking by Penguin Books India, New Delhi, 2002, pp. 112–114.

Ramachandran, D.P. *Legion of the Brave*, East West Books, Madras Pvt Ltd., Chennai, 2001.

Rankin, Hugh F. *The American Revolution.* G.P. Putnam and Sons, New York, 1964, pp. 13–15, 20–29.

Remarque, Eric Maria. *All Quiet on the Western Front* (Im Western Nichts Nerves) Im Propyloan–verlag, Berlin, 1929. (Original in German).

Report of the Officials of the Governments of India and the People's Republic of China on the Boundary Question. Ministry of External Affairs, Government of India, February 1961.

Risch, Erna. *Service of Supply in the War of 1812: A History of the Corps, 1775–1939*. Washington, 1962, pp. 81–180.

Sarin, Pramod (Brig). *Military Logistics: The Third Dimension*. Manas Publications, New Delhi, 2000, p. 678.

Scott, 1888. Letter of Brig. W.M. Steel to Gen. Twigfall, Fort Smith, April 15, 1863. Vol. 22: 819–820.

Scott, 1888. Letter of H.Q. Hay's Brigade to Hon. John Perkins Jr. Richmond, Jan 9, 1863. Vol. 21: 1097.

Scott, Robert N. (Lt Col) 3rd US Artillery, Secretary of War. *The War of the Rebellion. A Compilation of the Official Records of the Union and Confederate Armies*. Washington, Government Printing Press, 1888. Series 1, Volumes XIX, XXI, XXII, Correspondence. Letter of General R.E. Lee to Secretary of War, Vol. 21: 1016, Nov. 17, 1862.

Scott, 1888. Vol. 21: 1080–1091.

Scott, 1888. Letter of General R.E. Lee to Gen. S. Cooper, HQ Army of Northern Virginia. Nov. 18, 1862. Vol. 21: 1018.

Scott, 1888. Letter of John B. Floyd, Maj. Gen. Commanding, Virginia State Line to Col. J.T. Anderson, Chairman Military Committee, Jan 21, 1863, Vol. 21: 1104.

Scott, 1888. Letter of R.G.H. Kean to the Commissary General's Office; Nov. 20, 1862. Vol. 21: 1017.

Scott, 1888. Letter of Gen. R.E. Lee to James A. Seddon, Secretary of War, Jan 20, 1863. Vol. 21: 1100.

Selinko, Anne Marie. '*Desiree*'. Translators-Arnold Bender and E.W. Dicks. First Published 1953, W Heinemann. Phoenix Paperbacks, London, 2006.

Shama Sastry, R. *The Arthasastra of Chanakya*. English translation Books V-XV British India Press, Bombay, 1910, Book 10. chapters 2, 4; Book 5, chapter 5, Book 13, chapter 4.

Shaw, G.C. (Brevet Lieut. Col). *Supply in Modern War*. Faber and Faber Ltd. London, 1936, pp. 46–7, 51, 79–80.

Sherer, J.W. (C.S.I.). *Daily Life during the Indian Mutiny: Personal Experience of 1857*. Legend Publications, Allahabad, India, 1910, Reprinted 1974.

Sinha, S.K. (Lt Gen Retd). *A Soldier Recalls*. Lancer International, New Delhi, London, 1992, pp. 122–123.

Spaulding, Oliver Lyman and Nickerson Hoffman. *Ancient and Medieval Warfare*. Constable and Co. ltd., London, 1994, p. 11.

Strayer, J.R., Hans Gatzke, W. Harvison, E. Harris and E.L. Dunbaugh. *Western Civilization since 1500*. Harcourt Brace Jovanovich Inc., New York, 1961, 1971, p. 307.

Subramanyam K. *From Surprise to Reckoning*. Report of the Kargil Review Committee, New Delhi, Sage Publications, New Delhi, 1999.

Singh Sukhwant (Maj. Gen.). *Liberation of Bangladesh*. Lancer Publishers Spantech and Lancer, New Delhi, London, 1980.

The Encyclopedia Americana. International Edition, Grolier Inc. Danbury. Conn. 2001. Vol. 17: 690–1.

The Encyclopedia Americana. International Edition, Grolier Inc. Danbury. Conn. 2001. Vol. 5: 495.

The Organization of Logistic Support Systems. Proceedings of a Conference, Luxemburg, under NATO Scientific Affairs Committee Bureau, The English University Press Ltd. 1972, p. 26 and 17 MB.

The Second World War: Quartering Army. The War Office, 1949, London HMSO, pp. 2, 64, 80–81.

Thompson, Julian. Editor. Modern Warfare. 'The Imperial Museum Book of Modern Warfare: British and Common Wealth Forces at War 1945–2000'. Sidgwick and Jackson, and Imperial War Museum. London, 2002.

Time Magazine. March 18, 2002. Assault on Shah-i-Kot.

Todd, Jack. *Desertion (In the time of Vietnam)*. Houghton Mifflin Company, Boston and New York. 2001.

Trevalyan, Sir George Otto. *Bart. Cawnpore*. Indus Publishers, New Delhi, 1992. An Imprint of Harper Collins Publishers India Pvt. Ltd. First published 1865, New Delhi [also published by Macmillan and Co. Ltd., London, 1907], pp. 4–6, 21–22.

Van Rynbach, Iris. '*The Soup Stone*' Retold and illustrated. Green willow Books, New York, 1988.

VanCreveld, Martin. *Supplying War: Logistics from Wallenstein to Patton.* Cambridge University Press, Cambridge, London, 1977, pp. 2–27, 44–60.

Warren, James A. *Portrait of a Tragedy: Americans in the Vietnam War*. Lothrop, Lee and Shepard Books, New York, 1990, pp. 17, 82–83, 126–127, 175–197.

Williams, Reese (Ed). *Unwinding the Vietnam War. From War into Peace*. For Washington Project for the Arts, 1976, p. 283.

Wilson, H.W. *The Second World War 1939–1945. Army Administrative Planning*. The War Office, London, 1952. p. 3–5, 51–59, 78–90.

Wolpert, Stanley. *A New History of India.* 4th Edition, Oxford University Press, New York, Oxford, 1993, pp. 98, 232–233.

Wood, Sir Evelyn, *Revolt in Hindustan*. Methuen & Co. London, 1908.

Yamashita, Michael. 'Marco Polo – The History of the World'. A pictorial depiction. *National Geographic Magazine.* May–June 2001.

Zieger, Robert H. *Americas Great War*. Rowman and Littlefield Publishers Inc, Lanham, New York, Oxford, 2001, p. 96.

Personal communication:

In conversation with Col. Par Chaudhary (Retd), World War 2 Veteran, of Outram Rifles. Hyderabad, 2005.

In conversation with a Captain just returned from Siachen tour of duty and posted to Training Command, ASC Centre and College, Bangalore. 2005.

In the End

There is no end to the wars in this segment of the 'anthropocene epoch', the age of the humans, a term coined recently by geologists for the period that began with agriculture.

Our own recorded history bears witness to this phenomenon. And because of what and who we are, wars will not end. Armies will continue to be raised, trained, nurtured and deployed. Old conflicts are carried into the new century. We are not too far off the mark from the 'Hundred years war' in Europe's history. Conflicts which began more than 65 years ago are still festering; ideological, economic and border issues that might have been settled continue with more belligerence or ferocity than ever creating the tense situation in the Indian subcontinent. We need all our protection forces to guard against every kind of anticipated and unexpected hostile situation. Therefore, there is no question of not having well-trained and well-equipped security forces as well as standing armies.

In the finance budget of 2010–2011, a sum of Rs 14,7344 crores (US$31 billion) has been allocated towards defence, much of which would go towards the proposed modernization of the Forces. The science compoment represented by the DRDO in the previous budget got seven percent (Rs 9,809 crores) of the allocation to run its 51 laboratories, where 5,000 scientists and 25,000 technical and other personnel are employed (www.idsacomments/budgertryfor India's Defence 2010).

There has been 11.8 percent increase in defence allocation in the just announced 2011–12 budget to Rs 16,4415 crores. The major chunk of this allocation will go towards acquisition of hardware for modernisation such as combat aircrafts, heavy lift helicopters and artillery guns. The DRDO's share amounts to Rs 5,600 crores (*The Hindu*, March 1, 2011). A lot has been delivered and a lot more is expected from these laboratories. The more recent developments are personal wear products to combat cold weather and food for survival in pill form. There are many spin off benefits from Defence Research for general use.

A new war doctrine called the 'Cold Start' is being mentioned since 2004. It is said that the doctrine has emerged due to the necessity of making the Indian Army ready to fight in a NBC environment and to act offensively but short of using nuclear weapons (www.southasiaanalysis.org/papers23/paper2293/html). The neighbouring countries are well aware of these development (www.asiantribune.com/news/2010/01/10/cold-start-indian-threat-pakistan-china).

With the new war doctrine, says Harsh Pant (*Deccan Herald* Feb 5, 2010), is an attempt to acquire the ability to fight limited wars under the nuclear umbrella. It is speculated that the logistics of troop movement by air and ground forces will be accomplished very rapidly, within 72 hours, which is plausible because of the proximity to the border areas. It all boils down to a higher state of planning and preparedness. The doctrine is still in its developmental stage. With the new war doctrine, the food and its supply logistics may also change from that of the past.

In this era of electronic, cyber and satellite guided wars, the highly trained skilled officers and technicians who are going to operate their machines with the help of computers will now be classified as the arm chair or sedentary workers. Would they still need the 4000 calories plus per day of food designed for hard working men? Theirs will be a more mentally stimulating task requiring high levels of focus, hand-eye coordination and quick thinking. And until robots take over, they shall need a different kind of sustenance – brain foods to perform these very focused tasks.

The global nuclear diplomacy has been active in the past year between the 'have' nations. The quest by India to be a nuclear power, a story told so lucidly by Raj Chengappa (2000) continues even though it is one of the 'have it' nations. In this context being prepared for any possible radiation exposure makes abundant sense. Though there are protective clothes and systems for this purpose, there is no antidote or a food that might be given to mitigate the effects of intended or accidental exposure.

The need for food will continue with or without wars. Futuristic projections though not quite in the context of new war doctrine have been discussed by scientists (DFRL/2010). We can only wish that human intellect and talent and national resources will be directed towards human development, where small militias will take the responsibility of maintaining law and order, and there will no longer be any need for the massive standing armies. But that is a wish unlikely to be fulfilled.

References

Chengappa, Raj. *Weapons of Peace: The secret story of India's quest to be a nuclear Power.* Harper-Collins Publishers India, New Delhi, 2000.

Futuristic Food Requirements of the Armed Forces – Stakeholders' Meet. Defence Food Research Laboratory (DRDO), Mysore, 11–12 March, 2010.

Annexures

Annexure 1

Vedās and *Sāstras*

The monosyllabic '*Ohm*' of Brahma embodied all knowledge, which was entrusted in it's entirety to the sage Vyāsa (meaning editor, compiler, according to Minor, 1982) and charged to arrange the Vedas. Vedas are '*Śruti*' literature believed to have been revealed or discovered when the ancient sages placed themselves in touch with reality (Rice, 1988). As such, the Vedas belong to the history of the world and to the history of India, and are from a time with no records. It is believed that Vishnu took the form of Vyāsa. Again, it is repeatedly told that the Vedas are eternal, beginning less and not made of man. At every Dwapara age, Vishnu took the form of Vyasa for the benefit of mankind, divided and then sub-divided the Vedas so that mankind, with its limited prowess and energy, could understand them. The form in which Vishnu divided the Vedas is named Veda-Vyāsa (Dutt, 1894, pp. 171–173; Vishnu. 3.1). Vyāsa charged four of his disciples who were proficient in these works to undertake the task. They were Paila, Vaisampāyana, Jaimini and Sumanta. Each of these disciples went on to write one Veda. Their disciples in turn and there were many – divided and subdivided and wrote many additional texts and in many forms and versions. Vyāsa also took Suta or Suka, named Lomaharshana, as his disciple in writing Itihasa and the Purānās. The original tree of the Vedas gave out many branches; many more trees were added. It thus became a forest of trees of knowledge. The various subdivisions are depicted in Fig. A-1.1.

Annexure 2

The Ancient Concept of Time

There are legends and beliefs attached to precisely when these literatures appeared. For this reason one needs to understand how time was measured. Time was reckoned by the ancients in the form of *yuga*, *kalpa*, and *manawantara*.

There are four Yugas or epochs marking the passage of time which are: *Krita*, *Treta*, *Dwapara* and *Kali*. These four yugas moved in cycles and followed one after another. The actual time elapsed between each Yuga covered a monumental span of years, as shown in Table A-2.1. Since divinity was the uppermost characteristic, time was also stated in terms where human measure would reflect the eternity of divinity – in this instance Brahma. In Table A-2.2, the concept of *Kalpa* is expressed, as well as the relationship between one human year and one of lord's years. One human year is called one *Samvatasara*, a term in common usage in southern India for the year spanning 365 days. One divine year comprises 360 lunar *Samvatsaras*. One *MahāYuga* thus equals 12,000 divine years or some 4.32 million years and one *MahāYuga* is only a day (or a night) in the life of Brahma. His full life period is said to cover 100 years. The *Krita Yuga*, which in human understanding spanned nearly 1 ¾ million years, was but a short time for the gods – 4,800 years only. Interestingly, *Kali*

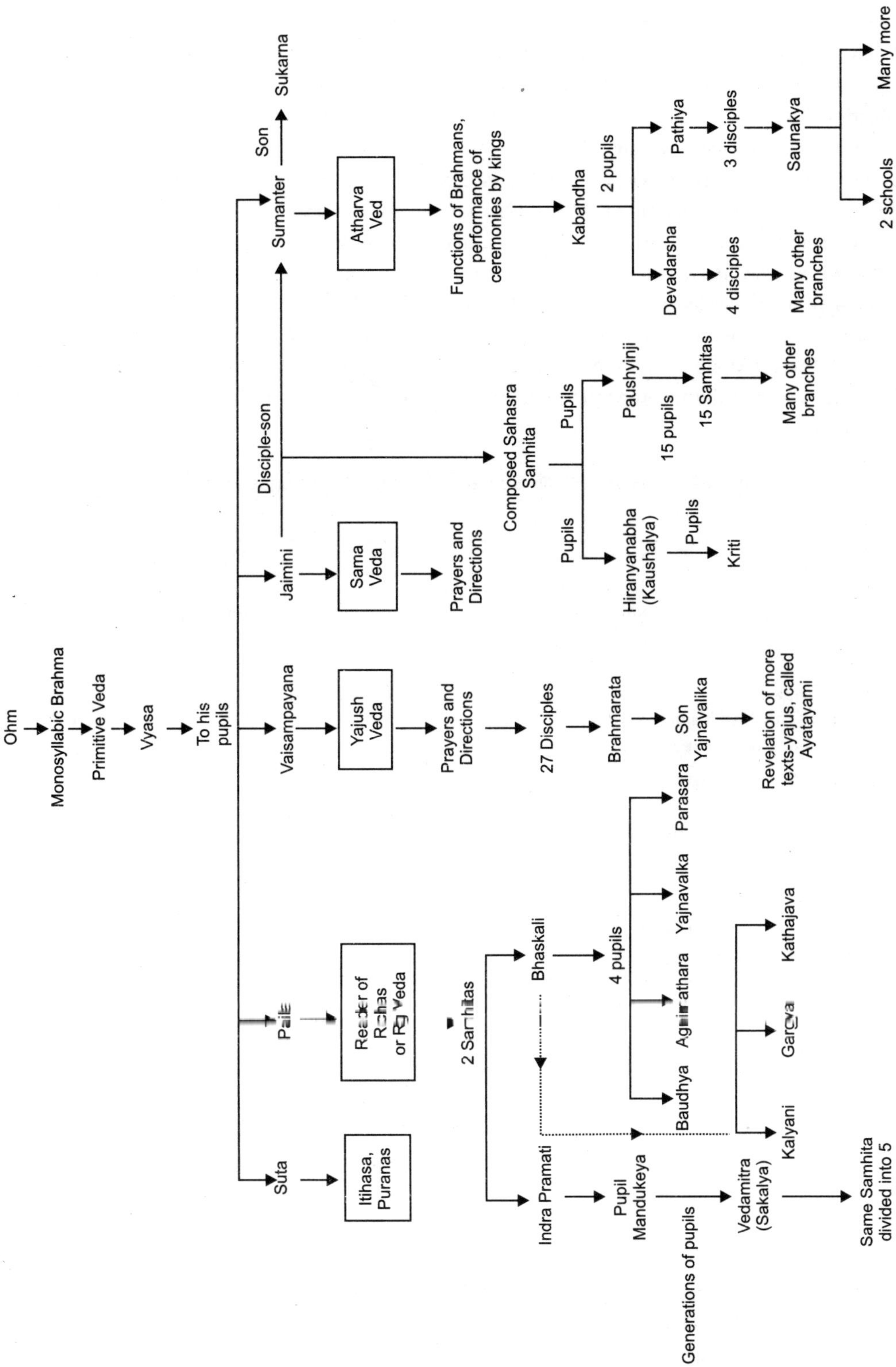

Fig. A-1.1: Trees of Forest of Knowledge (Vishnupuranam)

Yuga, which is believed to last 432,000 years is said to have set in from the year 3102 BC and we have a long way to go and many millennia to pass before another Yuga will show. These are mind boggling numbers but really not that long when we take into account the millions of years it has taken for the biosphere to reach this stage and for the human species to evolve in the present form and who knows what shape we shall all be in the future.

It is also said that in every *Krita* age there is a presiding *Manu* or the law giver who becomes the legislator. During this period of *Manu,* also known by the term *manawantara* (Table A-2.3), *Manu* as well as the seven *rishis*, kings of gods, and sons of *Manu,* rule over the Earth. From the description of *manawantaras*, each of which has even more staggering number of years in it – 337 million human years, we learn that the first *Manu* was *Swayambhuva* (Brahma himself).

The seven *rishis* were *Vashistha*, *Kasyapa*, *Atri*, *Jamadāgni, Gautama*, *Viswamitra* and *Bharadwaja.* The celestials were *Adityas, Vasu*s and *Rudras* and their king was *Purandhara* (Vishnu 3.1). It is believed that the incomparable energy of Vishnu rules over all the *manawantaras* in the shape of divinity.

Table A-2.1: Ancient Hindu Concept of the Cycle of Yugas in years

Yuga	*Human Years*	*Divine years*
Krita Yuga	1,728,000 years	4,800 years of Gods
Treta Yuga	1,296,000 years	3,600 years of Gods
Dwāpara yuga	864,000 years	2,400 years of Gods
Kali Yuga	432,000 years	1,200 years of Gods
* 1 Mahā Yuga	4,320,000 years	12,000 years of Gods
* Present Kali Yuga =	The fourth or the last quarter of 28th Mahā yuga	
• 5,018 years of this Kali Yuga have expired		
• Kali yuga begins from year 3102 BC		

Source: Krishnamachariar, 1937; Dutt, 1894: Vishnupurānam

Table A-2.2: Ancient Hindu Concept of the Cycle of Yugas in years

• 1 human year	=	1 Samvatasara
• 360 lunar Samvatsaras	=	1 Divine year
• 12,000 divine years (with 4 yugas or 4,320,000 human years)	=	1 Maha yuga
• 1000 Maha yugas (1000 × 4,320,000 years)	=	1 day of Brahma, 1 Kalpa
• 1000 Maha yugas (1000 × 4320,000 years)	=	1 Night of Brahma
• 35 such days and nights	=	1 month of Brahma
• 12 such months	=	1 year of Brahma
• 100 years	=	full period of Brahma's Life
• Brahma's age	=	Two halves known as Pararddhas – Purva and Uttara or Prathama and Dvitiya Pararddhas
• Prathama Pararddha now expired	=	In the beginning of this, Brahma Kalpa or present cosmos was born. At the end Padma Kalpa happened where Lokapadma arose from Hari's navel.
• First Kalpa of Dvitiya Pararddha	=	The present or Varaha Kalpa, the incarnation of Varaha or Boar
• Now, we are in the First Day of the 51st year of Brahmadeva called Sveta –Varaha-Kalpa	=	18,001st Kalpa of Brahma

Source: Krishnamachariar, 1937; Dutt, 1894: Vishnupurānam

- In *Krita Yuga*, Vishnu was born as the great ascetic Kapila who imparted wisdom.
- In *Treta Yuga* he was born as the Lord Paramount to repress the wicked and protect the three worlds.
- In *Dwāpara Yuga* he was born as Vyāsa to give us the four Vedas and its various divisions and branches
- At the end of the fourth or *Kali Yuga* he shall be born as Kalki and shall take mankind to the path of piety.

At the end of every four Yugas, the Vedas are believed to disappear. The sage Parāsara states in Vishnupurānam that there have been 28 Vyāsas and each divided the Vedas into four in the previous Dwāpara age. In the next Dwāpara, Drauni – son of Drona will be the Vyāsa, when after his (Parāsara's) son, who is the actual Vyāsa, will cease to be (Vishnu 3.1: 171–173).

Table A-2.3: Concept of Time in Manwantaras

- Each Manu reigns for 71 ¾ Mahāyugas
- 14 Manus reign during the Day of Brahma
- Each Manwantara = 857,142 6/7 Divine years = 337,142,657 ½ human or lunar years
- With every day and night, age of Brahma declines
- Six Manwantaras have expired
- The present Manwantara is the 7th of Varaha Kalpa

Sources: Rice, 1988: Amarkosha 1, Kāla Varga 130–134, 143–151

Annexure 3

Ancient Terms for Weights and Measures

Kangle (1972) has explained the terminologies used in the ArthaŚāstra (AS) for weights and measures. According to this, 200 *palas* of masabeans, used in weighing gold, where 10 beans make 1 *masaka* of gold, (AS 2. 19, 11–17) are equal to one *drona* (AS 2.19.29) for revenue purposes. Table A-3.1 depicts the various measures described in a series of verses in terms of *palas* advocated for trade and payments and also the relationship in the weights of *drona, khari, vaha* etc. (AS. 2.19.3, verses 29–36).

Table A-3.1: Measures employed in revenue and trade

200 palas of masabeans = 1 drona for revenue measure	
187 ½ palas for trade	
175 palas to make payments	
162 ½ palas for measuring out to the palace	(Verse 29)
Adhaka, prastha, kuduba are smaller measures; each ¼ of the preceding measure	(Verse 30)
16 dronas = 1 khari	
20 dronas = 1 kumbha	
10 kumbhas = 1 vaha	(Verse 31–33)

Source: Arthaśāstra 2.19.3, verses 29–36

The grain measures of *adhaka*, *prastha*, *kuduba*, *drona*, *khari* and *kumbha* are measures to be made of dry hardwood, one fourth (¼) measure of which is included as top heap. It seems that liquids, wine, flowers, husk and even charcoal and lime (calcium oxide or calcium carbonate) were measured in these devices (AS 2.19.34).

As per Amarakosha (Rice, 1988) 1 *drona* of milk is equivalent to 3 and ¾ quarts (3 ¾) which works out to 3.5 litres. One *drona* is also equal to 4 *adhakas* and there are several other terminologies for volume measures equaling 1 *drona* (Table A-3.2). *Drona* is also a vessel or a bucket or a trough, according to Monier-Williams (1899, p. 502). We have seen that it is a grain measure too, sometimes recorded as being equal to 4 *adhakas* and may measure between 1 *maund* 14 *seers* and 2 *maunds*, according to Sircar (1966, p. 101). The larger measures for grains as shown in Table A-3.3 are constructs and calculations using the terms in *ArthaŚāstra.*

Table A-3.2: Conversion tables – liquid measure

Volume measures
1 drona = 4 adhakas
Or = 16 pushkalas
Or = 128 kuncis
Or = 1024 mushtis
Or = 200 palas
Or = 1/20 kumbha

Source: ArthaŚāstra, Amarakoha, p. 144

Table A-3.3: Conversion tables – larger measures for grains and other articles at different times in history

*Terms in ArthaŚāstra**	*Amarakosha***	*Calculated values using Standard tables, US*
1 adhaka* 1.814 Kg	7 lbs 11oz avoir dp.	3.515 kg
1 drona	4 adhaka= 30lb 12 oz	14.06 kg
1 khari	5 dronas = 153 lb 12 oz	70.30 kg
1 vaha	20 kharis = 30,75lbs	1406.00 kg
Smaller measures		
1 adhaka 1.814 Kg	4 prastha = 7lb 11oz	3.515 kg
1 prastha	¼ adhaka = 4 kuduva	0.8788 kg (~881g)
1 kuduva	¼ prastha = 2 prasrta	0.2197 kg (~220g)
1 prasrta		0.1098 kg (22g)
1 prasrta	2 palas	0.054925 kg (~ 54 g)
1 pala	½ prasrta or prarta	0.0274 kg (28 g)
1 palardha	½ pala	0.0137 kg (~ 13 g)

* ArthaŚāstra – Kangle's commentary provides a value of about 4 lbs. or 1.814 kg for one adhaka. Every value based on this is doubled or halved.
** Rice, 1988: Amarakosha, Kanda 2. Vaishya Varga, pp. 674–684.

Adhaka is a measure of capacity, often regarded as 264 handfuls or ¼ of a *drona* also may be equal to 16–20 seers by some accounts, according to the Epigraphical Glossary (Sircar, 1966, p.101). The '*seer*' was a term much in use until the 1950s; a seer was measured in a tall wooden or metal cylindrical container. To say that 1 *adhaka* equalled 16–20 seers seems much. One *adhaka* is said to be equivalent to between 3–4 lbs (assume avoir dp.) according to Kangle's commentary on its use (1972, p. 208). But as per Amarakosha (2. vaishya varga, pp. 674–684), one *adhaka* weighed 7 lbs 11oz avoirdp. which is almost twice as much as what Kangle's estimation ran. However, since *adhaka* seems to have been a common middling weight, i.e. a starting term for both larger measures as well as smaller ones and since everywhere grain measures were indicated in terms of *adhaka* and of course *drona*, *pala* etc, one must have some idea of how much these weighed in kilos and grams to understand whether the grain rations given to men in general (and soldiers) were adequate for a meal by today's standards. The weights using the value of 1 *adhaka* = 4 lbs, have been depicted in Table 2.6 of Chapter 2 as shown by Kangle's commentary on *Arthasastra*. Table A-3.3 here is a construction based on one *adhaka* = 7 lb and one (1) oz as given by Rice in *Amarakosha*.

One would also find another discrepancy between the measures shown for 1 *khari* (16 *dronas*) in *ArthaŚāstra* (Table A-3.1) and the one given in Amarakosha which is 5 *dronas* (Table A-3.3) Naturally, the estimates of subsequent weights would vary depending on which particular equivalent was used. A large weight known as *Bhara* was thought to be a weight equal to 2,000 *palas* and one *bharaka* known as one load (Sircar's glossary).

One researcher reported that 1 *pala* was said to be equal to 35 g (as per Table 2.4 it amounts to 28 g) and 1 *kumbha* was equal to 250 g (Achaya, 1998, pp. 14–15). Since even firewood was measured or weighed in *palas*, it seems rather absurd to accept that it would have been measured out in multiples of 35g. There must be synonyms where *pala* is also a large measure for certain objects. This is perfectly plausible (as will be seen with manufactured weights) when we find that the names of smaller weights of silver, gold etc. seem to be similar even though their denominations change.

When metal and other weights came into usage, at first the silver, gold and copper weights could only be related to the known weights of berries and seeds, particularly masa beans, gunja berries, mustard seeds and rattis as these probably were the most prevalent currency in trading (Table A-3.4). The metals had to be mined and extracted and this enterprise was state controlled.

Table A-3.4: Weights used by goldsmiths

Copper weights
80 rattis = 1 karshnapana = 8.72 g
(*Abrus precatorius*) orange red, with a black dot = 1 ratti seed* = 0.109 g as reported by some authors

Silver weights
2 rattis = 1 masha = 0.218g (then 1 ratti = 0.109 g)**
16 mashas = 1 dharana or purana = 3.488 g
10 dharanas = 1 shatamana = 34.88 g

Gold weights
5 rattis = 1 masha = 0.545 g
16 mashas = 1 suvarna = 8.72 g
4 suvarnas = 1 pala or nishka = 34.88 g
10 palas = 1 dharana = 348.8 g

*1 ratti seed = 0.109g as reported by some authors
** With 1 ratti equal to 1.825 grains or 0.119 g as found by Sircar (p. 275), all other calculations will change.
Source: Sircar 1966; Achaya, 1998

Throughout history, coins recovered from archaeological excavations indicate that they were one definitive way to mark an era of the reign of a king (which every monarch resorted to) and provided irrefutable evidence of the ascendancy of a monarch to the throne and for commemorating his rule.

Manufactured weights: These were made of iron or stone obtained from Magadha and Maikala hills (Madhya Pradesh). The making of weights and measures was both a science of precision and an art and it was mandatory that these be stamped and certified by government officials. Once the usage of balances came into practice, their weight, height and length were specified (AS 2.19.11–17). Various markings on the balance were made (scored) for different weights: markings to indicate weight from 1 *karsa* to 1 *pala*, then another marking up to 10 *palas*, then 12, 15, 20 *palas*. The next increments by 10 *palas* successively provided markings up to 100 *palas*. *Parimani*, a larger balance made with double the quantity of metal used for *samvrtta* and a longer beam was used for weights beyond 100 and scored for 20, 50 and (two) hundred *palas*. The weights also occurred as *bhara* equal to 20 *tola* weights.

A *pala* also contains 10 *dharanas* (AS. 2.19.19) and 100 of these *palas* were used in revenue measures. Quaintly, when used for different purposes or class of people, the description proceeds to say 'less by 5 *palas* are measures for trade, payment and for measuring out to the palace'.

Meat, metals, salt and even gems were weighed in these balances made of variable beam lengths (AS 2.19.24).

As for individual weights (AS 2.19.22–23), half *masaka*, 1 *masaka*, 2,4,8 *masakas*, 1 *suvarna*, 2,4,8 *suvarnas* as well as 10, 20, 30, 40 and 100 *suvarnas* were the standard weights for precious metals. These were naturally equated with a definite number of beans, berries and grains (Table A-3.5).

Table A-3.5: Denomination of weights for silver and gold in standardized format as per ArthaŚāstra

- 10 Masabeans or 5 gunjabeans = 1 masaka of gold
- 16 of these (beans) = 4 karsas
- 1 pala = 4 karsas
- 81 white mustard seeds = 1 masaka of silver
- 16 of these or 20 simbabeans = 1 dharana
- 20 rice grains = 1 dharana of diamond
- ½ masaka, 1 masaka, 2, 4, 8 masakas
- 1 suvarna, 2, 4, 8 suvarnas
- 10, 20, 30, 40, 100 suvarnas

Source: ArthaŚāstra: 2, 19.

All we really need to convert one ancient term for any measure into grams or grains is to find at least one name and one weight matching that term which is accepted by general consensus by different authors. But it has proven to be a difficult proposition so far to find such a common agreement.

Adyamashaka or ½ *mashaka* was the smallest goldsmith's weight, equal to 5 seeds of *Abrus precatorius* or *gulaganji* (orange red pea, some times with a black dot) or *ratti*. One *ratti* or *raktika* or gunja is said to weigh around 1.825 grains or 0.119 grams or 119 mg as per the Epigraphical Glossary (Sircar, 1966, p. 275). This author's experiments with dried *Abrus* seeds gathered in April 2007 and weighed in a chemical balance showed the weights to be in the range of 217 to 308 mg with an average weight of 236.87 mg (SD +/- 36.69501). Sixteen *adyamashakas* made 1 *karsha* which was shown as being approximately equal to ½ oz (*Amarakosha*); since 1 oz. avoirdp is equal to 28.349 g by standard conversion, the 16 *adyamashakas* should equal 14.17g.

The Glossary goes on to say that 1 *palam* equals 4 *karsha*; and a weight of gold equal to 16 *mashas* would weigh 75 grains or 4.86 g. In Table A-3.6 are depicted the different copper, silver and gold weights according to three different author sources:

Table A-3.6: Weigh for copper, silver and gold

	Denomination	*Weight*	*Source*
A	1 Adyamashaka	5 ratti seeds (Abrus)	Rice: Amarakosa, 1988
	16 adyamashakas	1 karsha	2.671–6 77
	4 karsha	1 palam	
	16 karshas of gold	75 grains	
	1 palam of gold	2 oz	
	100 palam of gold	1 tula of gold	
B	1 karsa (Karsha)	80 rattis (may be 120 also)	Sircar's Epigraphical Glossary 1966
	Or 1 karsapana	80 rattis	
	1 silver karsapana	32 rattis	
	1 gold karsapana	80 or 100 rattis	
	1 copper karsapana	80 or 100 rattis	
C	1 silver karsha	16 masha = 80 rattis	Monier-Williams1899: Sanskrit-
	1 karsha	¼ pala = 1/400 of Tula = 175 grains troy	English-Dictionary

From these descriptions we find that specific weights were assigned to the various terms:

a. 16 *mashas* = 75 grains or 4.86 g,
b. 1 *karsha* = 280 grains troy = 18.144 g.
c. It is also found that though 16 *mashas* and 16 *adyamashakas* were both equal to one *karsha*, they varied in weights i.e. 11.4 g and 18.1 g respectively.
d. However, 4 *karshas* equaled 1 palam in both these cases. Achaya's (1998) sources reveal yet another set of table of weights of copper, silver and gold.

From section B of Table A-3.6, it can be ascertained that 80 *rattis* equaled 1 *karshnapana* which was equal to 8.72 g. The terms *ratti*, *masha*, *pala* occur here too.

In a commentary on the subject of weights and measures described in ArthaŚāstra, Kangle has commented (Kangle, 1972, p. 134) that since a *masaka* is the name of a weight equal to 1/16 *suvarnas*, (which is also referred to as *masa*), as well as of a copper coin equivalent to 1/16 of a *pana* (AS. 2.12.24), there is ample scope for confusion. Kangle has quoted another source for the weight of a gunjaberry, which is 1.8 grains (or more accurately 1.8295), rounded off to 2 grains; this converts to 0.12 grams or 120 mg (2 grains multiplied by a factor 0.0648). One *karsa* is 80 times that (160 grains), which equals 10.368 gram, this is nearly the same as a modern *tola*. A similar conversion of terms can also be found in Sircar's Glossary. Confusion also arises since a *karsa* or a *suvarna* is the weight of a *pana* as well as the coin *masaka*. Thus, there are 2 unconnected *masakas*: one is a coin (gold) and one is a weight, (*karsa* was the name of a weight in ancient Iran, so in India it was an imported term).

To confuse matters further, if 1 *pala* was said to be equal to 10 *dharanas*, which seems to be the same as 1 *pala* of 4 *karsas*, then 88 mustard seeds were equal to 2 *gunjas*. If it were so, a silver *masaka* would be 2/5th of a gold *masaka*. A *dharana* was a silver coin weighing 24 *rattis* or a half of a *galyanaka* according to Lilavati's treatise. It was also a silver coin of 32 *rattis* as per Manu and a gold coin of 320 *rattis* according to Sircar (1966).

Price of articles: In respect of currency or what passed for it, we first saw copper, silver and gold metals served the purpose, which however weighed against gunjaberries, masabeans, mustard, rice and ratti seeds etc. Presumably, these were the most acceptable form of payment at that time. We have some idea from description in ArthaŚāstra about the prevailing market prices for each measure of a tradable article.

The price of one *drona* (of which commodity is not specified) was one and a quarter (1¼) *pana*, that of one *adhaka* was three fourth (3/4) of a *pana*. Six *masakas* fetched one *prastha* while 1 *masaka* got you one *kuduba* (AS 2.19.36).

In the sixteenth century, after Babur conquered Ibrahim Lodi and took control of Hindustan, he recorded many terminologies for measurements. Significantly, many terms then prevalent continued to be in use till long after British rule ended and it is not uncommon to even now find rural folks using the same terms. As shown in Table A-3.7, *rati, masha* (8 *ratis*), *tola* (12 *mashas*), *ser* or *seer* (14 *tolas*) and *maund* (80 British pounds) were used in various contexts. The term *taank* applied to pearls and other jewels whereas *rati* was applied to weigh diamonds and other precious gems. The Kohinoor Diamond is said to have weighed 320 *ratis*. *Tola* was a common weight for gold and for certain fine substances like spices, chemicals, medicines etc. while *ser* was used in measuring liquids, grains and pulses. A *maund* was a large measure for grains, wood, iron and such other materials.

Table A-3.7: Weight measurements in India recorded in Babur Nama

1 rati	=	8 grains of rice (Babur, p. 279) or 64 mustard seeds or 512 poppy seeds
8 ratis	=	1 masha (Babur, p. 274)
4 mashas	=	1 taank* or 32 ratis
5 mashas or 40 ratis	=	1 mishqals**
12 mashas	=	1 tola or 96 ratis
14 tolas	=	1 ser (2 British pounds)
40 sers (or seers)	=	1 maund or manban or man (80 british pounds)
12 manbans	=	1 mani
100 manis	=	1 minasa

* Pearls and jewels were weighed by the taank

** The Kohinoor diamond weighed 8 mishqals or 320 ratis. Achaya (p. 15) has stated that 32 ratis was the weight of the earliest silver coin and one pala was 320 ratis, equal to 34.88 g.

Sources: Hiro, 2006; Achaya, 1998

Even as Sircar (1966) described certain terms in use, probably in Bengal, in southern India too similar terms were being used until the late 1950s. These represent both small and large weight measures. The names *rati* or *ratti* or *gunja* berry or *guriginja* appear to be synonymous with each other; 32 *ratis* was equal to 1 *varaha*; 16 *varahas* to 1 *palam*, 8 *palams* to1 *ser*, 5 *sers* to 1 *veesa* (40 *palams*), 8 *veesas* or 40 *sers* to 1 *manugu* (or 1 *maund* in Babur's time) and 20 *manugus* to 1 *baarauva* (*bhara* or a load) according to an 'out of print' Telugu publication 'Hindu Desam-Tulamanam' from Madras (discovered in a family archive) which was used in the Telugu speaking regions for teaching school children and was very likely produced in all the southern languages for use in the entire Madras Presidency. The very name suggests that the terms were in usage all over the country

Measurement of space: In our present preoccupation about measures, one feature of special interest is how the ancients measured space (as well as time). Length, breadth, height, distance etc. mattered in the calculations to make roads, build forts, erect walls, move armies and supplies and also for travel over distances by land and sea, gauge the time taken to travel and arrive after covering a distance, plan for and execute long marches, lay siege to forts and ensure transport and availability of adequate war and natural supplies to sustain the huge armies. Length, breadth and girth defined the size and quality of horses, camels and elephants in the country. Measures were required to build balances to weigh other things. For carpentry and other works as well as to measure rope, cloth, poles etc.

Again the comparison of size began with some thing as natural as a nit or louse! A compilation of various measures abstracted from *Arthaśāstra*. (AS. 2.20.2–25) is presented in Table A-3.8.

Table A-3.8: Measures of space described in the ArthaŚāstra

Small measures	
8 atoms	= 1 rathacakraviprus (chariot wheel particle)
8 rathacakraviprus	= 1 liksa (nit)
8 nits	= 1 yuka (louse)
8 yuka	= 1 yavamadhya (barley middle)
8 yavamadhya	= 1 angula (finger, the maximum width of the middle finger's middle part of a middling man)
4 angulas	= dhanurgraha
8 angulas	= 1 dhanurmusti
12 angulas	= 1 vitasi (span)
14 angulas	= 1 sama/1 sala/1 pariraya/1 pada or foot
2 spans of hand	= 1 aratni (cubit) or 1 hasta of prajapati

Source: ArthaŚāstra. 2.20.2–25

Angula was a term frequently encountered in everyday measurements in Kautilya's time, but some present day readers may be familiar with this term used in colloquial language by elders in the family. A span of hand, a hand length and the foot are natural measures from body parts, easily remembered and used. The term *hasta* has different measures too.

One *hasta* and a *dhanurgraha* made a *hasta* for the purpose of weights and measures. One *hasta* and a *dhanurmusti* were equal to 1 *kisku* or a *kamsa* (these may be tools). A measure of 42 *angulas* was used by carpenters to make a sawing *kisku*. Specifically, this measure of 42 *angulas* was used in measurements concerning the camp, the fort and royal property. Fifty-four *angulas* made a *hasta* for forest produce, and a rope woven from plant fibers and other such articles were measured by yet another *hasta* of 84 *angulas*. This was also known as *vyama.* Two spans equaled 1 *aratni*, 4 *aratnis* equaled 1 *danda*, a *dhanus*, a *nalika* and a *paurusa* used for household purposes. One hundred and eight *angulas* was a unit of measure for city walls. Horses and elephants were graded with these measurements. In Tables A-3.9 and A-3.10 are given the larger measures for length and distance up to 1 *yojana*. Sircar (1966, p. 386) provides a figure of about 9 miles or 14.4 km for 1 *yojana*. But according to Achaya (1998, p. 195), 1 *yojana* was equal to 5.2 kilometers (which is nearly one third of the former figure).

Table A-3.9: Larger measures of space and distance

4 aratnis or 6 kamsas	= 1 danda (to measure lengths of rope, gifts to Brahmins and guests, clothing perhaps?)
10 dandas	= 1 rajju
2 rajjus	= 1 paridcsa
2 dandas	= 1 bahu
1000 dhanuses	= 1 goruta
4 gorutas	= 1 yojana (distance)

Source: Sircar, 1966, Glossary

Measure for speed: The speed of chariot horses and riding horses was defined by the number of *yojanas* they may be able to cover in a day. A good chariot horse should be able to travel 6, 9, or 12 *yojanas* while 5, 7.5 and 10 *yojanas* could be covered on the road by riding horses and pack horses (AS. 2.30.39).

Table A-3.10: Measures of length

1 angula (finger breadth)	= 8 Yavas
24 angulas	= 1 hasta (span of a hand)
4 hastas	= 1 danda (pole or a rod)
1000 dandas	= 1 krosha (later called kos)
4 kroshas	= 1 Yojana (either 5.2 km or 14.4 km.

Source: ArthaŚāstra 2.30.39

Annexure 4

Troops on March

According to Kautilya, freshly arrived and long travelled armies (not tired), may fight after taking position but without mingling with any other new army. The tired army may go into battle after it is refreshed from bathing, eating and sleeping but not the reduced army whose leaders have been killed.

Troops whose supply of grains was cut off or whose supply of men and stores was cut off, or that which lost grain may fight after providing them with grain brought from another quarter. It may also be provided with moveable or immoveable foodstuffs, meaning animal and vegetable foods. That army to which men and provisions cannot be supplied may not fight.

It appears that men carried some grain with them when they marched or had access to stores from which to replenish grain and other food and that from near battle areas and encampments, both meat and vegetable foods could be made available to the troops under certain circumstances.

Campaign Food Stocks and Growing Food

The kings and generals knew and understood food provisioning as an important aspect of war. It was important to protect citizens from hunger and want during extended hostilities, to be prepared for a long siege and to plan strategies for arrangements for food during marches and encampment. Expeditions were long, sometimes spanning many years, during which time the camped troops must be self-sufficient. A full fledged township was established, together with combatant and non-combatant elements and life went on as usual except when there were skirmishes or pitched battles.

The prosperity of a country or a territory has always attracted invaders. It happened to the pre-Vedic Indus people, which eventually wiped out their civilization. A land adorned with crops, rich in mines and minerals, plenty of commodities for trade, climate conducive to breeding cattle, copiously watered, abounding in woods, swarming with elephants and inhabited by virtuous, diligent and pious people signified prosperity, said Kāmandaka (Kā.iv: 51–52). In *Vishnupurānam* (Dutt, 1894), during a conversation with Maitreya, Parāsara emphasised that the city dwellers under the monarch having provided themselves with shelter from cold by building artificial forts, inner cities or by locating rocks and trees and water sources, must proceed to grow various useful (economically) food giving plants (Vishnu. 1: III). He emphasised that the king must ensure the planting of seventeen kinds of plants for food and fourteen types of plants for religious rituals and sacrificial ceremonies as well as fruit bearing trees and thorn bearing trees in forest lands (Śukra 4.4: 95–102). The king should have the forts well stocked with war materials, contingencies, as well as grains, troops, arms and treasures. The fortresses themselves were to be surrounded by *parikha* (moat of water) and *parigha* (protected by bricks, sand and mud) (Śukra 4.6: 23–24). Thoughtful stocking of stores was imperative and a pre-requisite (AS, 4), and a waterwell for every ten houses was the norm. Grains, oil, sugar, salt, medicinal articles, dry and fresh vegetables and dried meat stock piled in plenty. For the cattle and other animals, meadow grass and hay were gathered. A truly varied mix of articles, matches, skins, charcoal, animal tendons, poison, horns, bamboo came form the forests. Fibrous garments, strong timber, weapons and armour and stones, all of these to last for years together without feeling any want. Both citizens and the troops were looked after in this way. Periodic exercise to discard the old stock and replace it with new and fresh stock acknowledged the fact that they knew fully the effect of longtime storage on all articles of use – food, wood, grass and other stores.

Commissariat's Role

Both in the epic times as well as in the Mauryan period, cutting off of supplies to opponents in a long siege was an accepted method of strategy, pointed out Dikshitar (1944) and every monarch intending to go to war or confronted with the imminence of an impending war, first made sure of the strength of his own fortifications and stocking of essential stores to outlast any siege to his own fort. Megasthanese observed that a resourceful commissariat, in circumstances of a besieged state, became very important. The commissariat worked closely with the superintendent of bullock trains and carts and also was also responsible for seeing to the dispensation of food and war materials to the army on the move; this division also controlled the huge retinue of servants, drummers, grooms, mechanics, physicians, astrologers and other (Dikshitar, 1944). According to Thapliyal (2002), while the store houses in military camps were well stocked with weapons, food, water, fodder, honey and butter, general army needs were met by tailors, weavers, builders, weapons repairers, washer men and such people accompanying the marches.

The most ideal time for an attack was when the food stock of the enemy was exhausted and the new crop not yet harvested (AS. 10.2.18–19). Chanakya observed that while on the march, the strength of an army could be calculated by observing its supplies of food, fodder and bed spreads and thus their quantity should be concealed from the enemy.

Before the march begun, it was the ruler's responsibility to consider the supply needs and to see that estimates were prepared for the quantity of food, fodder and other materials required, based on the distance to be covered, time taken for travel and camping, the strength of the army, the villages and forests on the route likely to yield food and fodder. Estimates for all these were based on the measurements (AS 10.2.1–3) then in use.

There were other sources and other means to provision the army. Many items could be gathered from the forests through which the army traveled; they could carry a lot of stuff along from the home country and expect, demand or petition allies to contribute towards the war effort such items as may be required (AS.10.2.5–7). Food could also be captured; therefore the king was advised to set out to conquer that part of the enemy territory which had plenty of corn (corn could mean barley, rice or other millets in use during that period) (Kā.15, 4) While in the early period, the rulers never planned or allowed the destruction of standing crops, the military treatises make no bones about advocating total destruction of grain. This deprived the enemy of food and added strength to the attackers. A king cognizant of enemy movements should enter such territories where there was no likelihood of facing difficulty on the route for supply of food and support from allies.

It was advocated that the route of march in summer should meander through woods abundant in water. The king should also march his army slowly, so as not to cause fatigue, and to choose a route where there was plenty of food and water. Otherwise, there was all likelihood of losing men (Kā. 7, 13). Kāmandaka noted that while the loss of men and munitions was destructive, loss of money and food was a drain on the land and resources (Kā. 7, 23). Whether during marching or encampment, troops must be kept cheerful and well fed. The success of a king on an expedition lay in maintaining the morale of the troops and in preventing the destruction of camp pavilions, clothing, drinking water, foodgrains and in receiving the continued support of allies; destruction of such essential life supporting elements was said to be the death of kings (Kā. xvi, 32, 39).

Thapliyal (2002, p. 75), commenting on supply systems, quoted lines from the Vedas which said that the Vedic Aryans had devised means to maintain armies in the battlefield, to keep them well fed, with regular daily rations. These supplies could have come from the state store houses. To prevent this from happening, they took measures for 'voluntary' contributions from the people or commandeered their stocks. Goods were also assembled through raids and forays of the soldiers on active duty.

Thus, every time a king planned an expedition or proceeded through a territory and went to war, it was the people of his own land, or that of the allied country or that of the enemy territory who paid the price. Not for nothing was the king referred to as the 'devourer of people' in the Ṛg and Atharva Vedas (Thapliyal, 2002 quoting RV.1.64.4, AV.4.22.7).

The Soldiers' Responsibilities

On the general deployment, character and conduct expected of the troops in the king's employ, *Śukranīti* is explicit (Śukra 4: 7). It seemed a sound policy to maintain a respectful distance both physically and socially between military men and lay people and to disallow any credit transactions between them. The former directive still holds true as modern armies are housed in cantonments, and they move in their own social circles created by their lifestyles, rank and camaraderie. To give a sense of cohesiveness and continuity, the troops were required to be stationed at any given place for at least one year. It is much the same even now, barring adverse climatic conditions and terrain which dictate more frequent change of personnel for the sake of their health and fitness.

That no man may go unaware of military regulations and duties, it was a policy of the generals to communicate, every eighth day, with the troops. Obedience and discipline as well as a sense of honour and duty were drilled into every man (as is the practice even today) during basic troop training and every individual was directed to forsake violence, rivalry, procrastination, indifference to injuries of the king, and refrain from conversations or forming friendship with enemies and never to point a finger at their commanders (Śukra 4.7: 763–774).

It was considered so important for the troops to be separated from civilians that the former were forbidden to enter any village without express permission, for any reason and definitely never for any personal needs, arms or for seeking food.

The troops were to be made responsible not only for their personal arms and uniforms but also for their own provisions. This very likely meant that they brought their own provisions into the garrisons and battle. For this latter purpose, food and water had to be carried by the troops themselves, along with their arms and uniforms.

In order to maintain independence and total self sufficiency, Śukrāchārya instructed that every soldier must carry not only his own provisions but also one vessel measuring one *prastha* and another larger vessel in which food for many might be cooked (*Śukra* 4.7:775–776.). There would be other sources for the replenishment of food provisions, not the least being capture of the enemy's food stores, naturally taking measures beforehand to deprive them of grain, even in the form of standing crop. Some of these strategies appear to go directly against the oft repeated observation of scholars speaking on ancient agricultural practices that the farmer-husbandman was to be left alone to carry on his job of farming and that his crops and his land were never to be harmed in any ongoing conflict or war. Men of his class were regarded as public beneficiaries (Dikshitar, 1944; AS.13.4). Kāmandaka, commenting especially on military expeditions, warned the king to beware the evil tides when his corn was standing in the field, when he spoke of proper season for expeditions, neither too hot not too cold, nor rainy nor dry and when all the earth was covered with corn (Kā. 15, 36). A standing crop was both a boon and a danger in the season for wars.

Annexure 5

Alexis Soyer and his Contributions to Better Camp Cooking

Alexis Soyer

It seems that both the middle classes in Victorian England and the well to do people were accustomed to eating gargantuan meals and very possibly suffered from indigestion. They spent large amounts of money on food. Something had to be done about this situation and people in different walks of life attempted to bring some sanity to this excessive spending and unhealthy eating. There were cookery books, particularly from one Isabelle Mary Beaton, whose writings on household management, published in the 1850s made an impact on the eating habits of people. To match wits and knowledge with Mrs Beaton in the cookery area was one Alexis Soyer, a very well known chef of the Reform Club in London. He wrote three very interesting cookery books – one for high society (*The Gastronomic Regenerator*), one for the middle classes (*The Modern House wife*) which became very popular indeed, and a third one titled '*A Shilling Cookery for the People'* for the rest. This last came about as a result of a long tour of investigation into the eating habits of the poor throughout the British Isles (Bentley, 1968). Victorian era Londoners come across as being lethargic, their gastronomic habits very poor in their utter disregard for cookery and recipe books with ingenious and economic ways of cooking; they even drew water from the Thames which was polluted with sewage. They were suspicious of foreign food and cooking, except for a small minority. So many things confused the English housewife. To think that it was this tribe that was ruling India and showing utter contempt for the natives seems incredible. What Soyer instructed the general English public in his books at that time was what we have become aware of in the late twentieth century through several media articles and scientific studies and seminars in regard to home economy and how to select and buy nutritious food cheaply and how to prepare some tasty and wholesome meals. Therefore he considered himself eminently suitable and knowledgeable to study the battlefield and camp and war food situation on the Crimean front.

Soyer begged permission to go to Scutari at his own expense, and to assess the camp and cooking facilities available to the army of the East and improve them where possible and suggest some changes in Military hospitals. Armed with letters of introduction and help from the Duchess of

Sutherland, Duke of Cambridge and the others, he requested to be allowed to proceed to the camps for which military help was requested. And thus it was that Soyer descended in Scutari.

His investigations, suggestions and inventions created little enthusiasm in the British Camp. But supported enthusiastically and whole heartedly by Florence Nightingale, who wielded great influence with the generals and officers, Soyer changed almost every aspect of mess cooking and established a permanent improvement in the way the troops were fed throughout the army (Soyer, 1857). Some of the landmark achievements were innovative, practical and led to better nutrition of the soldiers and ultimately helped win them the war.

Innovations in the Kitchens

Soyer's stove: Soyer designed a field stove, known as 'Soyer's Stove' which remained in the service o. the British Army for a very long time from its first appearance in 1855. This stove was a combination of two devices 'of a steam boiler with a removable container on top' (Barthrop and Ray, 1995, p. xi). He determined that the stove would consume some 12–15 lbs of fuel and at the rate of 20 stoves for a regiment the total fuel requirement would be 300 lbs per 1,000 men. Pointing out the economy of the stove, he showed that this was almost one tenth of what 1,000 men would be normally allotted (3500 lbs) at the rate of 3.5 lbs per man per day. The stove had multipurpose utility – from preparations of salt beef, pork, and Irish stew to tea/coffee and cocoa drinks. The stove could also be fitted with an apparatus for baking, roasting and steaming. Four hundred small field stoves were ordered for immediate use of the whole army in the Crimea. The stoves have proved incredibly valuable and apparently they were in use in the Gulf War of 1991, only now fired by bottled gas or petrol instead of coal or wood (Barthrop and Ray, 1995, p. xii).

Scutari teapot: He designed a vessel known as Scutari tea pot, with a removable metal cylindrical filter for the tea. Less tea could be now used and in a very clean way, avoiding the practice of tying tea leaves in a cloth and dumping it into the same boiler which had previously been used for boiling soup!

Baking/stew pan: Soyer's baking/stewing pan was a marvel which could be hung over a fire or placed on a hob and which could be also used for steaming or boiling; it had a padlock for the lid which was opened only when the contents were cooked.

'We are so tired of the preserved meats' was an often heard refrain from Lord Raglan, the Force Commander of the British Army, and from senior officers in the field. What was the cause of this? There were many, as Soyer discovered. Firstly, the meat used was not of prime quality, secondly it was not properly preserved; thirdly the entrails of the animals might have been included in the tins (meaning the tin cans used for processing and preserving meat). It was not uncommon to preserve salted meat in cans for long periods, even a couple of years and while there should have been really no reason to find meat offensive smelling, putrefying and discoloured, these things happened. Soyer opined that insufficient cooking and perhaps inadequate exhausting of atmospheric air (air removal) both contributed to the putrefaction (Barthrop and Ray, 1995, p. 207). Considering what we now know of canning defects and the causes thereof, Soyer's uncannily astute and intuitive observations were right on the mark.

A great part of Soyer's contributions pertain to showing how to use the salted meat to make edible, acceptable and even tasty meals.

Soyer's Food Craft for Camp Application

There were many improvements in cooking methods, from the way he showed how the tough salted meat, when cut up in smaller pieces, soaked faster and cooked better to pointing out by his own cooking and demonstration that cooks should do the seasoning while cooking rather than leaving it to the soldiers. He devised many recipes, generally using much the same ration items and introducing inexpensive ingredients to extend the quantities, to make them nutritious and taste better. To his credit is the development of new and innovative camp foods like:

(a) Bread biscuit – a bread baked in the form of a very large biscuit which was shelf stable and could be softened by dunking it in tea, coffee or soup and found to be invaluable for campaigns and at sea (Barthrop and Ray, 1995, p. 140).

(b) Almost instant soup made out of ground baked peas meal, a table spoon of which could be softened with a pint of boiling hot water poured over it!

(c) Formulating a vegetable mixture for drying and for issue to the troops to replace the existing single vegetable produced by a firm in Paris. He suggested a mixed vegetable combination for drying in the proportion of carrots 20 lbs : turnips 20 lbs : parsnips 10 lbs : onions 15 lbs : cabbage 20 lbs : celery 5 lbs : leeks 10 lbs with 1lb of aromatic seasoning of thyme, winter savory, bay leaf, pepper and cloves; all were to be pulverized and mixed with vegetables.

(d) A meat recipe which the soldiers could easily prepare using 2 lbs of salt beef and 2 lbs of pork cut to about a quarter pound (~120 g) pieces plus cold water to be put in the pan and set on the fire. When the water was lukewarm, the meat was taken out and washed thoroughly. This washed meat was now cooked in 3 pints of water along with a quarter pound of sliced onions, 2 oz of sugar, a tea spoon full of pepper and 2 oz of rice – all this to be stewed gently for 2 hrs.

(e) Suggesting that brown bread be baked in the ships' huge floating bakeries.

(f) Using the skimmed off animal fat obtained by simmering the meat properly in water in his stew pot and dispensing with the very rancid butter which was what the soldiers got for cooking and for spreading on bread.

Soyer not only developed such nutritious tasty and easy to prepare camp food recipes but he also kept scrupulous record of the quantities used, yields obtained and noted down the full recipe so that any soldier cook who could read would be able to follow the directions for cooking.

Soyer's camp recipe book: His numerous recipes catered to large numbers (Barthrop and Ray, 1995, pp. 324–331). There were Soyer's simplified recipe to cook salt meat for 50 men, Soyer's Army Soup for 50 men (Barthrop and Ray, 1995, p. 249), Soyer's culinary emblem of peace – a monster dish of sea food, vegetables, mixed pickles, eggs, salad oil, seasoning, herbs etc., Soyer's food for 100 men using 2 stoves, stew for 50 men, a recipe to cook for a regiment of a 1,000 men, Turkish pilaf for 100 men, tea for 80 men, coffee for a mess of 10 soldiers, coffee Turkish fashion, Cocoa for 80 men and a series of small recipes, some 20 or so, for a squad outpost or picket of men, which may be increased in proportion of companies. These consisted of soups of various kinds, for cooking in the frying pan, suet dumplings and such items.

Compiled into one book, this fund of innovation, creativity and commonsense comprising army recipes was called '*Soyer's Field and Barrack Cookery for the Army*'.

These recipes, claimed Soyer, while applicable for barracks and in camp, could also be used on the march by using Soyer's New Field Stove. The recipes were equally useful to the Navy.

After Soyer's death, the War office published instructions to '*Military Hospital Cooks*' incorporating his recipes and methods. There is a naval recipe book issued by the War office in 1943 during World War II with instructions for ships' cooks on how to prepare various items for groups of men. A quick glance at the contents of this manual of recipes suggests a flavour of Soyer in the elaborate way many issues are dealt with.

Michael Barthrop, one of the editors of the 1995 reprint of Soyer's original record '*Culinary Campaign*', commented that the Crimean Army survived to marcn and fight again and win the war 'mostly because the troops regained their strength through better feeding arrangements instituted by Alexis Soyer' (Barthrop and Ray, 1995, preface, p. x).

Annexure 6

The Civil War Years – Army's need for more Food and Horses

Equipping the Army

In the beginning, the States took the responsibility for outfitting the regiments – with proper uniforms, undergarments, blankets, eating utensils and weapons. The cost of providing all this was borne by the Federal government. Not only were the uniforms etc. shoddy, but the food too became a major problem. Rather than a common company kitchen for 100 men, men grouped themselves into small informal messes and from among those who could at least boil water; one was selected by lottery to cook the pooled resources. The results, as we may imagine, were disastrous – both taste and health wise – inedible because of the quality of materials and cooking and unhealthy because the solders fried everything in bacon fat – rice, beans, beef, soaked hard tack and anything else that could be added.

And yet, the Union armies were said to have been the best clothed, the best equipped, the best fed and the best disciplined the Earth had ever seen (Craven, 1969, p. 23).

Foods, Rations and their Quality

America during the civil war years had already been using canned foods; canned meats were available since the 1820s, even though the variety was quite limited. Dehydrated vegetables were also packed in cans. Tomato ketchup – a favourite condiment in the American diet and ice cream, two inalienable foods that most people associate with the American way of eating are also of a similar vintage. There were street vendors of ice cream in New York City by 1828 and hand cranked ice cream churns for home use had been invented by 1846 and ketchup was made in homes but was sold in bottles from 1876 onwards.

The civil war rations for the troops on both sides – Union and Confederate, appear spartan; beef, beans, flour and potatoes were the main items, plus condiments, coffee and sugar when supplies were possible. Often there was no food and they went underfed and even unfed. The civil war soldier is said to have faced more misery and more kinds of misery than did the American soldiers in World War I or World War II.

Various terms for foods used in the American military rations are unfamiliar to many readers. Tinned beef was '*embalmed*', a nick name by which the meat given to the Union soldiers became known. It was sold to the army by the Chicago Meat Packers and was also called '*salt horse*'. This army issue beef was so highly saturated with salt that it had to be soaked for hours to wash away a part of it so that it could be eaten. The salt preservative gave the meat a shelf life of two years. The name 'salt horse' came to be used by the soldiers because horse shoes and mule shoes were often found in the barrels with meat but never Ox shoes! Whether this name made an oblique reference to the possibility of horse or mule meat and not ox meat (beef) having been used for salting cannot be ascertained. It was labeled and sold as beef. It was yellow green with rust, having been out of the brine and when boiled, gave off an offensive stench. Meat also came in the form of salt pork for the troops on both sides of the war (McCutcheon, 1993, pp. 138–235). Hard tack was a Union staple, hard baked bread made from flour, salt and water; measuring 3 x 3 x ½ inch, it was hard, stale and infested with worms and weevils. To eat this they had to be crumbled and soaked in coffee. It was so bad and hard that the men called it variously – teeth dullers, worm castles and sheet iron. Camp gossip said that these crackers had been around in storage since the Mexican war! The soft corn bread was a Confederate delicacy and their staple.

Fresh vegetables were scarce and very expensive and therefore seldom issued (Denney, 1992, pp. 13–14). Late in 1862, the Union rations occasionally consisted of dried compressed mixed vegetables in cake like form. Suspected to be of highly questionable quality, these tasteless vegetables were nick named 'desecrated vegetables', and labled 'not fit for hogs.' But they stored well and thousands of tons of this product were issued to Union troops across the combat territories. There were soups and stews made by using some of these items. 'Lob course', a Union army name was a soup made of salt pork, hard tack and anything else available. 'Cush' was a Confederate preparation made as a stew of beef or bacon, corn bread and water, with most of the water boiled away. It was also known as 'Slosh'. Bully soup was a hot cereal prepared with cornmeal, mashed hard tack boiled in water, wine and ginger and served to Union troops. This was also known as 'Panada'.

Coffee originally came as raw green beans which the soldiers had to first roast in camp kettles. Later the Union soldiers were given a paste of instant coffee mixed with cream and sugar. Coffee was usually in shortage for the Confederate soldiers (McCutcheon, 1993, pp. 234).

Scouring for more horses and food: Cavalry horses were in short supply too. A letter originating from R.E. Lee in 1862 and sent by one Hon. George W. Randolph, HQ Army of Northern Virginia to the Secretary of war in Richmond, reveals how much anxiety the subject of horses and subsistence was causing the army (Scott, 1888, 2: 1016 – *Operation in Northern Virginia*). The fact that horses had been arranged to be purchased and brought from Texas for the cavalry seemed to partly satisfy the army field commanders, not that these were readily forthcoming. Every measure had been taken to economise so that future wants could be met in some way. Food shortages led to men from the ranks beginning to struggle due to hunger. There was insufficient food already and after consultations with the Chief Commissary of the Army, a small increase in ration quantity was contemplated – the increase for flour. It became 1 1/8 lbs and for beef it was 1¼ lbs. The letter explained that flour was ground from the wheat available and the quantity of meat was collected as "meat on hoof". No other components of the rations, except salt, could be obtained, nor were there any extra bread or vegetables for purchase. The entire ration consisted of only the bread and the meat. Scouts were sent out to scour the countryside to locate sources from where extra supplies could be obtained. In 1862, in a letter written to General A. Cooper, R.G.H. Kean, Chief, Bureau, War (Scott, 1888, 21:1017) wrote that the purchase of 1,000 horses from Texas had been authorized, and that Counties of Madison and nearby areas were being examined to ascertain what food could be found. In County Greene, the triumphant location of 43,470 bushels of wheat (1 bushel = 35.238 litres), and 207,100 pounds of pork, in Madison County 6,937 bushels of wheat, and 33,400 pounds of pork and in Culpeper County 17,450 bushels of wheat and 50,000 pounds of pork were reported as well as the welcome news that similar quantities of corn and hay could also be found, provided the occupation of these areas by the enemy could be prevented (letter of Nov. 18, 1862). By 1863, nearly 4,000 more force strength had been raised to penetrate the enemy occupied territory. The dire necessity of finding at least 100 pack mules was frustrating the Major-General commanding the Virginia State line (Scott, 1888, 21:1104), who said that he had raised more forces but was entirely out of stock of axes, picks, tents, cooking utensils and necessary clothing to protect the men from frostbite.

Poor health due to poor nutrition: It needs no great imagination to visualise the dire state of health of the soldiers. Medical reports sent to the Army's Surgeon General in January 1863 enumerated the list of causalities which occurred in November 1862, and included the ominous news that there were 60 cases of variola (small pox) and variloid among the men returning from the general hospitals in Richmond (there was no system of quarantine) and that an epidemic could be imminent without proper mode of 'bivouacking'. Soldiers just camped in open air. Scurvy was likely to break out in the whole army because of lack of sufficient amount of vegetables in their diet. Their entire ration comprised only of unsmoked bacon with an occasional quantity of beef thrown in and flour, all being of inferior quality and issued in small quantities. The Army doctor was asking for potatoes and vinegar as being absolutely essential for the maintenance of the health of the troops. He particularly wished to impress upon the subsistence department by drawing attention to the fact that the 'campaign may be a disastrous one simply for the want of antiscorbutics'. The condition of the Army of Northern Virginia was otherwise fine and only needed proper food for efficiency.

Letters from various places were streaming in, each bemoaning the lack of some important item of clothing or food or supplies. James Crenshaw's letter to Col Northrop, Commissary General CS Army, Richmond, brings out the fact that by January 1863 there were serious shortages of both wheat and of wagons to cart it. Although there was wheat available in Rappahannock and Madison up to 300,000 or 400,000 bushels, wagons had to be found for its transportation. The General was to be approached to come up with a plan or a system of procurement of wheat supplies. Some months ago, 1,000 barrels of wheat flour had been ordered which had still not been delivered. Likewise the horses had to be fed (Scott, 1888, 21: 1080–1091). In another instance, out of 1,500 new recruits reporting for duty, more than 400 had no shoes or proper clothing and were thus ineffective even in drill routine (no shoes) and in the bitter cold (no under clothes, no shirts, no coats, maybe only one blanket) how could they possibly even keep up with the marching column (Scott, 1888, 21:1097). When sugar had been introduced into the rations, General Robert E. Lee wrote to the Secretary of War on January 20, 1863 (Scott, 1888, 21:1100), informing him that to procure more bacon or other meat, they were planning to exchange the sugar with the salt meat stocks held (and retained) by the citizens. Sugar was more expensive than bacon and thus the citizens might be more willing to agree to the exchange offer – of 1 pound of sugar (cost $1.25 per pound) for 2 pounds of bacon (35 cents per pound). He pointed out that by offering sugar in small quantities, many thousands of pounds of bacon could be obtained in one county alone.

The biggest killer in this war was disease; 110,000 Northern and 94,000 Confederate soldiers were mortally wounded in battle but 388,580 men died from diarrhea, typhoid, typhus, malaria and pneumonia; diarrhea being the single biggest anxiety, even more than gunfire (Craven, 1969, Section 12).

Annexure 7

A Taste of Afghani and Iraqi Foods

Afghani food (www.afghan-web.com) has been described under four categories: Appetizers which include: *bolanee* or *boulanee* made from small potatoes and meat as in Indian *samosa* (fried snacks filled with potato curry), *sambasa*, Zardak-wa-Kishmish and Sambosa; main meal items like *Qubuli Palaw* (made with lamb, rice, carrots and raisins and possibly spices), *bonjaan-chalow*, *kofta-wa-chalow*, *Mantu, Murg Kabab*, *Murg sherwa,* beef kebob. Some of these names will be familiar to Indians. Familiar too are some of the desserts such as *firnee* (custard), *Shir–Yak* (may be a *kheer*), *Bakleva* (a very fine nut and dry fruits filled pastry), berry shake and *Khatai* (*Kulcha*). Afghani bread is *naan* (like pita bread) or flat bread. Some miscellaneous items such as *dogh*, meat sauce, yogurt sauce, salad dressing, *Korma chalow* are also among the side dishes or accompaniments to the main meal. In good times and for celebrating, huge meals called *Dastarkhani* were prepared which included several types of dishes (www.marga.org/food/afghanistan).

Iraqi food is also described as being spicy and flavoursome. The cuisine utilises rice, barley, flour, lamb meat, beef, beans, yoghurt, vegetables, lentils, sesame, dry fruits, nuts, olive oil, and spices. There are mixed preparations using a variety of ingredients; there are sauces, soups, pastries and such. The names of the various preparations may sound unfamiliar, such as '*barmia*' (a one dish meal of lamb meat, garlic, tomato sauce served with rice or pita bread) and *labna* (yoghurt cheese with flavourings made from hung yoghurt, the mass is rolled into small balls and covered in olive oil), rich soups (made from grains, lentils, beans) and spicy casseroles made with meat and vegetables called '*Tepsi Baytinija*', foods like *tahini* (sesame paste eaten with pita bread, *Shabbat* chicken, *Kiko* (flat lamb pies) potato beef *Kebba* (Kebobs), date nut cakes, filled pastries etc. (www.recipebazaar.com). Much the same kind of dry and fresh foodstuff used in Indian cuisine and which comprise Indian military rations are required for preparing these Iraqi foods.

References

Achaya, K.T. *Indian Food–A historical Companion*. Oxford University Press, Hyderabad, 1998, pp. 14–15, 195.

Anon. Hindu Desam-Tulamanam (Telugu). Pedda Bala Siksha. (School text in the old Madras State).

Barthrop, Michael and Ray, Elizabeth (Ed). *A Culinary Campaign by Alexis Soyer*. Southover Press, London, 1995, pp. viii–xi, 104, 140–1, 207, 249, 324–331.

Bentley, Nicolas. *The Victorian Scene – A picture book of the period 1837–1901*. Range Weiden Field and Nicolson, London, 1968.

Craven, Avery. Reconstruction. *The Ending of the Civil War*. Holt, Rinehart and Winston Inc., New York, 1969, pp. 5, 23, section 12.

Denney, Robert E. *The Civil War years: A Day by Day Chronicle of the Life of a Nation*. Sterling Publishing Co. Inc., New York, 1992, pp. 9, 13–14.

Dikshitar, V. Ramachandra. *War in Ancient India*. Macmillan & Co. Ltd. Madras, 1944.

Dutt, Manmath Nath. *Vishnupurānam* or *Dharmasāstra*. Elysum Press, H.C. Das, Calcutta, 1894, pp. 171–186 and Part 3 Sections 1, 3, 6 and Part 4 Sections 3 and 5.

Ganapati Sastri. T. (Ed). *Kāmandakīya Nītisāra*. Commentator Śankarārya (English translatior-Anon). (Original Sanskrit version by Rajeshwar Sastri: 1886). Trivandrum Sanskrit Series number 14. Trivandrum 1912.

Hiro, Dilip (ed) Babur Nama: *Journal of Emperor Babur*. Penguin Classics, Penguin Books India Ltd, New Delhi, 2006. Babur, pp. 274, 279.

Kangle, R.P. *The Kautilya Arthasastra*. Second Edition. Bombay University, Motilal Banarasi Das, 1972, Book 2, Chapter 19, verses 11–36; Chapter 20, verses 2–25; Chapter 30, verse 39; also pp. 130–208.

Krishnamachariar, M. *History of Classical Sanskrit Literature*. Tirumalai Tirupati Devasthanam Press, Madras, 1937.

McCutcheon, Marc. *The Writer's Guide to Everyday Life in the 1800s*. Writer's Digest Books, imprint of F & W Publications, Cincinnati. Ohio, First Ed. 1993, pp. 138–139, 234–235.

Minor, Robert N. *Bhagavad-Gita*. Heritage Publishers, 1982.

Monier-Wiliams, Sir M. *Sanskrit-English Dictionary*, Clarendon Press Oxford, 1899, p. 502.

Rice, Lewis. *Amarakosha of Amara Simha*. Fourth Edition, Asian Educational Services, New Delhi, 1988.

Sarkar, Benoy Kumar. *The Śukranīti – The Sacred Book of the Hindus*. English Commentary & English Translation by Gustav Oppert. 1882 The Panini Office, Bhuvaneswari Asram, Allahabad, 1914. Sukra: Chapater 4, Section 3, verses 55–59, 71–111, 150–200 and 851–856.

Scott, Robert N. (Lt Col) 3rd US Artillery, Secretary of War. The War of the Rebellion. A Compilation of the Official Records of the Union and Confederate Armies. Washington, Government Printing Press, 1888. Series 1, Volumes 19, 20, 21. Correspondence. (a) Letter of General R.E. Lee to Secretary of War, (b) Vol. 21: 1016, Nov. 17, 1862.; (c) Letter of General R.E. Lee to Gen. S. Cooper, HQ Army of Northern Virginia. Nov. 18, 1862. Vol. 21: 1018.; (d) Letter of John B. Floyd, Maj. Gen. Commanding Virginia State Line to Col. J.T. Anderson, Chairman Military Committee Jan 21, 1863 Vol. 21:1104; (e) Letter of R.G.H Kean to the Commissary General's Office; Nov. 20, 1862. Vol. 21: 1017; (f) Letter of Gen. R.E. Lee to James A. Seddon, Secretary of War, Jan 20, 1863. Vol. 21 :1100.; (g) Letter Vol. 21:1080–1091; (h) Letter of H.Q. Hay's Brigade to Hon. John Perkins Jr. Richmond, Jan 9, 1863. Vol. 21:1097; (i) Letter of Brig. W.M. Steel to Gen. Twigfall, Fort Smith, April 15, 1863. Vol. 22: 819–820.

Shamasastry, R. *The ArthasŚāstra of Chānakya* (English Translation). Books V–XV. British India press, Bombay, 1910.

Sircar, D.C. *Indian Epigraphical Glossary*. Motilal Banarsi Das, Delhi, 1966, pp. 100–386.

Soyer, Alexis. *Culinary Campaign*. Routledge & Co. London, 1857.

Thapliyal, U.P. *Military Organisation in Ancient India*. Section I: In Volume X, Part 3: *Historical perspective of Warfare in India – Some Morale and Materiel Determinations*. S.N. Prasad (Ed). *History of Science, Philosophy and Culture in Indian Civilization*. Series. General Editor – D.P. Chattopadhyaya. Published by Bhuvan Chandel, Distributors Motilal Benarsi Das, New Delhi. 2002b, pp. 68–103.

Index